Olaf Kaltmeier, Antoine Acker, León Enrique Ávila Romero, Regina Horta Duarte (eds.)
Biodiversity – Handbook of the Anthropocene in Latin America II

**The Anthropocene as Multiple Crisis:
Perspectives from Latin America**

Editorial

The aim of the six-volume Handbook **The Anthropocene as Multiple Crisis: Perspectives from Latin America** is, first, to think about the Anthropocene from a particular region of the Global South. Thus, this Handbook offers a platform to discuss the multiple "anthropocenic" socio-environmental crises from a specifically Latin American point of view, without losing sight of their global and planetary dimensions. The second objective is to systematize, from the perspective of Latin American social sciences and humanities, the multifaceted environmental crises that reached and crossed the planetary boundaries of the earth-systems and led to the new geological time of the Anthropocene. In doing so, we generate an empirical basis for the genealogy of the Anthropocene in an unprecedented global region with key regional and historical differentiations.

The series is edited by Olaf Kaltmeier, Eleonora Rohland, Gerardo Cham and Susana Herrera Lima.

Olaf Kaltmeier is a professor of Iberoamerican history at Universität Bielefeld. Since its foundation in 2008, he has been the director of CALAS – Maria Sibylla Merian Center for Advanced Latin American Studies in the Humanities and Social Sciences. He is founding director and member of the Executive Board for the Center for InterAmerican Studies (CIAS) at Universität Bielefeld and director of the collaborative research project "Turning Land into Capital".

Antoine Acker is an environmental historian and professor at Université de Genève, with a particular interest in international connections and the place of Latin America in the history of the Anthropocene. He directs the AnthropoSouth: Latin American Oil Revolutions in the Development Century project, and co-directs Lost Cities, a collaborative project funded by the Gerda Henkel Foundation.

León Enrique Ávila Romero is a full-time professor-researcher in Sustainable Development at the Intercultural University of Chiapas (UNICH). He is the leader of the consolidated academic body "Heritage, territory, and development in the southern border of Mexico", a member of the SNI-CONACyT level I, and an honorary member of the SEI Cocytech.

Regina Horta Duarte has been a full professor at Universidade Federal de Minas Gerais in Brazil since 1988, and is currently a permanent professor of its Graduate Program in History. Her research focuses on the Brazilian Republic, history and nature, the history of biology, and animal history. She coordinates the Center of Animal History (CEA-UFMG).

Olaf Kaltmeier, Antoine Acker, León Enrique Ávila Romero,
Regina Horta Duarte (eds.)

Biodiversity –
Handbook of the Anthropocene in Latin America II

[transcript]

The project, on which this book is based, has been funded by the German Federal Ministry of Education and Research (Bundesministerium für Bildung und Forschung, BMBF). The responsibility for the content of this publication lies with the author.

Bibliographic information published by the Deutsche Nationalbibliothek
The Deutsche Nationalbibliothek lists this publication in the Deutsche Nationalbibliografie; detailed bibliographic data are available in the Internet at https://dnb.dnb.de/

This work is licensed under the Creative Commons Attribution-ShareAlike 4.0 (BY-SA) which means that the text may be remixed, build upon and be distributed, provided credit is given to the author and that copies or adaptations of the work are released under the same or similar license.

Creative Commons license terms for re-use do not apply to any content (such as graphs, figures, photos, excerpts, etc.) not original to the Open Access publication and further permission may be required from the rights holder. The obligation to research and clear permission lies solely with the party re-using the material.

First published in 2024 by Bielefeld University Press, Bielefeld
© Olaf Kaltmeier, Antoine Acker, León Enrique Ávila Romero, Regina Horta Duarte (eds.)
An Imprint of transcript Verlag

Cover layout: Leon Che Ernst Pöhler, Bielefeld
Cover illustration: Fernando Efrén Sandoval
Copy-editing: Olaf Kaltmeier, Luisa Raquel Ellermeier, Eric Rummelhoff, and Omar Sierra Cháves
Proofread: Luisa Raquel Ellermeier, Eric Rummelhoff, and Omar Sierra Cháves
Formatting: Eric Rummelhoff
Printed by: Elanders Waiblingen GmbH, Waiblingen
https://doi.org/10.14361/9783839470121
Print-ISBN: 978-3-8376-7012-7
PDF-ISBN: 978-3-8394-7012-1

Contents

Acknowledgements 9

Academic Advisory Board 11

General Introduction

The Anthropocene as Multiple Crisis
Latin American Perspectives on Biodiversity
*Olaf Kaltmeier, Eleonora Rohland, Gerardo Cham, Susana Herrera Lima, Antoine Acker,
León Enrique Ávila Romero, Juan Arturo Camacho Becerra, Virginia García Acosta,
Anthony Goebel McDermott, Ricardo Gutiérrez, Regina Horta Duarte, Cecilia Ibarra, María
Fernanda López Sandoval, Sofía Mendoza Bohne, José Augusto Pádua, Elissa Rashkin,
Heidi V. Scott, Javier Taks, Helge Wendt, Adrián Gustavo Zarrilli* 15

Colonial Period

Introduction: Biodiversity and the Anthropocene in Colonial Latin America
Regina Horta Duarte, Antoine Acker, León Enrique Ávila Romero and Olaf Kaltmeier 49

Biodiversity in the Southern Cone in the Colonial Period
Colonial Heritage Spoken in More-than-Human Words
Ana Lucia Camphora and Miriam Adelman 57

Biodiversity in the Andes in the Colonial Period
Livestock and Biodiversity after the Spanish Conquest
Aliocha Maldavsky and Marina Zuloaga Rada 77

Biodiversity in the Amazon in the Colonial Period
Neil Safier 103

Biodiversity in Mesoamerica in the Colonial Period
Christopher Valesey and Martha Few 123

Biodiversity in the Caribbean in the Colonial Period
Human–Animal Relations
Rodrigo C. Bulamah 139

From the Mid-Nineteenth Century to 1950

Introduction: Biodiversity and the Anthropocene in Latin America from the Mid-Nineteenth Century to 1950
Olaf Kaltmeier, Antoine Acker, León Enrique Ávila Romero and Regina Horta Duarte 159

Biodiversity in the Southern Cone from the Mid-Nineteenth Century to 1950
Second Conquest and First Acceleration in the Genealogy of the Anthropocene
Olaf Kaltmeier and Eduardo Relly 167

Biodiversity in the Andes from the Mid-Nineteenth Century to 1950
Tropical Andes in the Key of the Anthropocene
Tyanif Rico Rodríguez and Olaf Kaltmeier 195

Biodiversity in the Amazon from the Mid-Nineteenth Century to 1950
Science in the History of Amazon Megadiversity
Magali Romero Sá, Dominichi Miranda de Sá and Lorelai Kury.............................219

Biodiversity in Mesoamerica from the Mid-Nineteenth Century to 1950
Dialectics between the Capitalinian and Communian Ages
Alberto Betancourt Posada 243

Biodiversity in the Caribbean from the Mid-Nineteenth Century to 1950
Reinaldo Funes Monzote 261

From 1950 to the Present

Introduction: Biodiversity and the Anthropocene in Latin America from 1950 to the Present
Antoine Acker, Léon Enrique Ávila Romero, Regina Horta Duarte and Olaf Kaltmeier 281

Biodiversity in the Southern Cone from 1950 to the Present
John Soluri 293

Biodiversity in the Andes from 1950 to the Present
The Tropical Andes and the Sixth Mass Extinction Event
Kenneth R. Young 315

Biodiversity in the Amazon from 1950 to the Present
Towards a Great Biocultural Simplification
Felipe Vander Velden 335

Biodiversity in Mesoamerica from 1950 to the Present
Alternatives and Conflicts
Yolanda Cristina Massieu Trigo 363

Biodiversity in the Caribbean from 1950 to the Present
Ryan S. Mohammed and Lanya Fanovich 385

Appendix

Biographical Notes 413

Acknowledgements

This Handbook series on *The Anthropocene as Multiple Crisis: Latin-American Perspectives* is the outcome of the Laboratory of Knowledge on multiple ecological crisis of the Maria Sibylla Merian Center for Advanced Latin American Studies, CALAS.

As editors of the series, we would like to pay tribute to the hard work and patience of our authors, who were fundamental to the existence of this publication project consisting of six thematic volumes on the Anthropocene from Latin American perspectives. Such a monumental work on the Anthropocene – covering diverse historical epochs and all regions of Latin America and the Caribbean – is only possible with the support of the international academic community. More than sixty-nine reviewers from seventeen countries contributed their expertise and sharp criticism, motivating the improvement of each chapter. All these reviewers constitute our Academic Advisory Board. Furthermore, all chapters were collectively reviewed in editorial conferences by the editors of the other volumes of this series.

Under the direction of Olaf Kaltmeier, we set up an editorial office at Bielefeld University. The general coordination of this editorial office was in the hands of Luisa Raquel Ellermeier. Luisa, Omar Sierra Cháves, and Eric Rummelhoff organized the editorial process and proofread, translated, and revised all chapters. Omar was the main coordinator of the volume on Biodiversity. Rafael García was responsible for formatting the texts. Ann-Kathrin Volmer and Nadine Pollvogt organized the editorial conferences in the CALAS headquarters in Guadalajara, Buenos Aires, Quito, and San José de Costa Rica. They all did an outstanding job in making this Handbook a reality.

Special thanks go to our publisher, Bielefeld University Press (BiUP), who supported this project with great enthusiasm right from the start. Sabrina Diab-Helmer clarified all organizational aspects of publishing, and Vera Breitner and Gero Wierichs handled the editorial details, attending to all our extra requests. Bielefeld University has generously supported the open-access publication.

The series also stands out with its aesthetic design. Fernando Efrén Sandoval has created a work of art for each of the volumes. Using these pieces, Leon Che Ernst Pöhler from BiUP has designed memorable book covers.

The publication of this series would be impossible without the financial support of the German Federal Ministry of Education and Research (BMBF). We would especially like to thank Michael Sondermann from the BMBF and Ursula Bach from DLR for their trustful cooperation.

The Editors

Academic Advisory Board

Julio Aguilar, Harvard University, US—Susana Aldana, Pontificia Universidad Católica del Perú, PE—Patricia Alvers-Melo, Universidade Federal do Amazonas, BR—Nelson Arrellano, Universidad Academia de Humanismo Cristiano, CL—Aleida Azamar, Universidad Autónoma Metropolitana, MX—Reto Bertoni, Universidad de la República, UY—Johannes Bohle, Universität Bielefeld, DE—Rike Bolte, Universidad del Norte, CO—Martin Breuer, Stiftung Preußischer Kulturbesitz, DE—Joseph Büker, Universität Bielefeld, DE—Diogo Cabral, Trinity College, IE—Santiago Cabrera, Universidad Andina Simón Bolívar, EC—Natalia Calderón, Universidad Veracruzana, MX—Nathalia Capellini, Université de Genève, CH—Gabriel Carini, Universidad Nacional de Rio Cuarto, AR—Micheline Cariño Olvera, Universidad Autónoma de Baja California Sur, MX—Rafael Chambouleyron, Universidade Federal do Pará, BR—Joel Correia, Colorado State University, US—Nicolas Cuvi, Facultad Latinoamericana de Ciencias Sociales, EC—Irène Favier, Universidad Grenoble-Alpes, FR—Sabrina Fernandes, Alameda Institute—Júnia Ferreira Furtado, Universidad Federal de Minas Gerais, BR—Wolfgang Fuhrmann, Universität Leipzig, DE—Nelson Camilo Forero Medina, Universität Bielefeld, DE—Carolyn Fornoff, Cornell University, US—Wolfgang Gabbert, Universität Hannover, DE—Gabriel Garnero, Universidad Nacional de Córdoba, AR —Margarita Gascón, Consejo Nacional de Investigaciones Científicas y Tecnológicas, AR—Oliver Gliech, Freie Universität Berlin, DE—Carlos Goméz Florentin, Universidad Nacional de Asunción, PY—Sarah Hines, University of Oklahoma, US—Jochen Kemner, Universität Kassel, DE—Wesley Oliveira Kettle, Universidade Federal do Pará, BR—Casey Lurtz, John Hopkins University, US—Filomeno Marchena, University of Curaçao, CW—Stuart George McCook, University of Guelph, CA—Diana Alejandra Mendez Rojas, Universidad Nacional Autónoma de México, MX—Marina Miraglia, Universidad Nacional de General Sarmiento, AR—Dominichi Miranda de Sá, Casa de Oswaldo Cruz, BR—Thomas Mougey, Centre Alexandre-Koyré, FR—Andrea Montero, Universidad de Costa Rica, CR—Iris Montero, Brown University, US—Samira Peruchi Moretto, University of California Los Angeles, US—Chloe Nicolas-Artero, Politecnico di Milano, IT—Aceneth Perafán Cabrera, Universidad del Valle, CO—Fernando Resende, Universidade Federal Fluminense, BR—Danilo Rios, Universidad de la República,

UY—Octavio Rosas-Landa Ramos, Universidad Nacional Autónoma de México, MX—Julia Roth, Universität Bielefeld, DE—María Luz Ruffini, Universidad Nacional de Villa María, AR—Maria Grace Salamanca, Université de Lyon, FR—Juana Salas, Universidad Autónoma de Zacatecas, MX—Carlos Sanhueza, Universidad de Chile, CL—Juan Martín Sánchez, Universidad de Sevilla, ES—Estela Schindel, European University Viadrina Frankfurt, DE—Frederik Schulze, Universität Münster, DE—Pablo Ernesto Suárez, Universidad Nacional de Rosario, AR—Renzo Taddei, Universidade Federal de São Paulo, BR—Melina Tobias, Universidad de Buenos Aires, AR—Alejandro Tortolero Villaseñor, Universidad Autónoma Metropolitana, MX—Ronny José Viales Hurtado, Universidad de Costa Rica, CR—José Antonio Villarreal, Universität Bielefeld, DE—Ann-Kathrin Volmer, Universität Bielefeld, DE—Emily Wakild, Boise State University, US— Rosa H. Yáñez Rosales, Universidad de Guadalajara, MX—Michael Zeuske, Universität Bonn, DE

General Introduction

Source: Fernando Efrén Sandoval (2021).

The Anthropocene as Multiple Crisis
Latin American Perspectives on Biodiversity[1]

Olaf Kaltmeier, Eleonora Rohland, Gerardo Cham, Susana Herrera Lima, Antoine Acker, León Enrique Ávila Romero, Juan Arturo Camacho Becerra, Virginia García Acosta, Anthony Goebel McDermott, Ricardo Gutiérrez, Regina Horta Duarte, Cecilia Ibarra, María Fernanda López Sandoval, Sofía Mendoza Bohne, José Augusto Pádua, Elissa Rashkin, Heidi V. Scott, Javier Taks, Helge Wendt, Adrián Gustavo Zarrilli

The Anthropocene is probably one of the most disruptive concepts in contemporary science. It has the intellectual power to question ideas previously thought to be obvious, such as the modern-Western separation between nature and culture, because Earth's history no longer follows only natural laws but is shaped by the history of human societies. Conversely, these histories can no longer be understood without the inescapable consideration of planetary systems and their boundaries. Beyond its impact on academia, the emergence of the Anthropocene concept is a historical-political event, as it marks the global need not only to rethink but also to fundamentally remake the relationship between humanity and nature.

The concept of the Anthropocene has gained strength in the global public arena over the past twenty years and has been hotly discussed by the social sciences and the humanities for the past decade. The word was coined in 2000 by the Dutch atmospheric chemist Paul Crutzen and the U.S. American biologist Eugen Stoermer at a conference in Cuernavaca, Mexico. Both scientists observed the profound changes that human beings had caused to the environment. Based on this, they attempted to express the global reach of the great anthropogenic changes with the new term. Thus, the Anthropocene emerges as a new geological era in which humans introduce unprecedented amounts of CO_2 into the atmosphere through the massive use of fossil fuels. In addition, another major anthropocenic problem has been the large-scale extraction of non-renewable resources. Other processes by which human beings have come to change all spheres of the planet include plastic pollution, nuclear

---

1   This introduction aims to provide the reader with an overview of the conceptual and organizational principles of this six-volume handbook on the Anthropocene in Latin America. To improve readability, we have dispensed with the usual academic references. In each article, the reader will find a detailed and individualized bibliography.

waste, ocean acidification, the extinction of species, the fossil energy regime, the depletion of water sources, and the massive use of agrochemicals and pesticides. All of this constitutes the multiple crisis of the Anthropocene.

Given the above, it is clear that the Anthropocene is more than just a new fashionable term to refer to climate change as it has been widely, yet incorrectly, understood through the media. Nor is it simply a new concept useful for comprehensively addressing known environmental problems, although these issues obviously play an important role in its understanding. The novelty of the perspective that led to the coining of the term "Anthropocene" is fostered by the technological and informational possibilities of Earth system sciences to collect and process data like never before since the 1990s. In this way, it was possible to make visible the alterations, or rather the anthropogenic damage, in all the systems of the planet.

This is not the place to present all facets of the reflections on the concept of the Anthropocene carried out in the social sciences and the humanities. For our purposes, it is sufficient to refer to debates that offer novel perspectives to understand the historical singularities of Latin America in the Anthropocene. In this regard, discussions have recently resumed and continued about the Anthropocene and its derivatives such as the Capitalocene, Plantationocene, Chtulocene, Necrocene, etc.

In this context, the Latin American debate is particularly useful when it comes to relating multiple environmental crises to various sociocultural crises related to capitalism, coloniality, and racism. Here, approaches to environmental justice, the ecology of the poor, Latin American environmental history, nineteenth and twentieth century Latin American critical thought, and the approaches developed by Indigenous, Afro-descendant, peasant, and/or feminist movements and communities become relevant. An example of this from the Andean region is the concept of *Buen Vivir* (Good Living), *sumak kawsay*, based on the idea of the need for a turning point, *pachakutic*, according to which the poor governance and immoral leadership of global neoliberal capitalism with its colonial foundations must be substantially overcome.

Planetary thinking in the Anthropocene can and should be approached differently depending on the places of enunciation embedded in different constellations of power. In this regard, our concern is to broaden the debate, which so far has been largely carried out predominantly in the Global North by the natural and Earth sciences, to include a perspective from Latin America rooted in critical humanities and social sciences.

The aim of this six-volume handbook, *The Anthropocene as Multiple Crisis: Perspectives from Latin America*, published by the Maria Sibylla Merian Center for Advanced Latin American Studies (CALAS), is, first of all, to think about the Anthropocene from a particular region of the Global South. In this way, this handbook offers a platform for discussing the multiple "anthropocenic" socioenvironmental crises and their possible solutions from a specifically Latin American point of view, without losing sight of their global and planetary dimension. The second objective is to systematize, from the perspective of Latin American social sciences and humanities, the multifaceted environmental crises that have met and crossed the planetary boundaries of Earth systems and led to the new geological time of the Anthropocene. With this, we have produced an unprecedented empirical basis for the Anthropocene's complex genealogy in a specific region of the world – in this case, Latin America – with key regional and historical differentiations.

Thus, our perspective combines the already mentioned planetary dimension with a perspective that takes into account the local and regional specificity of ecosystems and socioenvironmental relationships in Latin America. The humanities and social sciences pose different questions in relation to the new geohistorical temporal layer of the Anthropocene. This task is by no means trivial. Rather, it is a multifaceted search process in which the initial assumptions of the definition of the Anthropocene in the Earth sciences are questioned, corrected, completed, and expanded. This starts with historical classification. The question of whether there is an epoch called the Anthropocene, and also of when it begins, was initially addressed by the Anthropocene Working Group (AWG) of the International Commission on Stratigraphy and was weighed according to geological considerations.

Based on the geological and socioecological evidence, 1950 has been proposed to be the year of the "Great Acceleration" despite the first defenders of the Anthropocene having proposed previous historical periods, such as the Industrial Revolution or the invention of the steam engine by James Watt in 1769. Reference may be made here to the smoking chimneys of Manchester factories. But precisely this origin narrative, based on the historical experience of the West, is criticized from a Latin American perspective. Manchester's industrial dynamics relied on the supply of cotton for textile production or sugar as a source of calories for the labor force. Both resources were produced in new plantation systems on the Atlantic coasts of America based on the introduction of neobiota and the labor of enslaved people forcibly brought from Africa. Equally worth mentioning is the mega-mining that emerged during the European colonization of Latin America, symbolically expressed in the system of Potosí, the silver mining center in present-day Bolivia. The silver mined there laid the foundations for the capitalist development and subsequent industrialization of Western Europe. Thus, mega-mining and plantation economies do not constitute mere gradual changes in human use of the environment, but rather mark a fundamental and planetary rupture in the social metabolism, that is, in the management, use, and exploitation of natural resources.

Recognizing the deepest historical roots of the Industrial Revolution leads us to reconstruct a genealogy of the Anthropocene in which it cannot be separated from coloniality, the rise of the capitalist world system, and racial capitalism. Thus, 1492, the year of European contact with the Caribbean and the Americas, is a turning point in world history and represents a fundamental rupture for the Indigenous peoples and cultures of America. Along with the conscious and unconscious introduction of new plant and animal species, European pathogens arrived in America, together with the colonial violence against Indigenous peoples, a massive number of fatalities, and the consequent cultural ruptures. Ninety percent of the Indigenous population died as a result of the conquest, either through direct violence, the destruction of their living conditions, or the introduction of new germs. It was one of the greatest genocides in history, wiping out 10 percent of the world's population. The abandonment of a large part of the agricultural area and the subsequent spontaneous reforestation caused a drop in global temperature at the beginning of the seventeenth century, coinciding with the beginning of the Little Ice Age – responsible for extreme atmospheric events on the planet.

In biological terms, the Columbian Exchange was so fundamental that biologists set 1492 as the milestone for the categorization of neophytic plants, distinguishing them from the native plants established in a given biome. With the Columbian Exchange of species, a homogenization of flora and fauna took place between the American continent, Africa, and Eurasia.

The criticism of European/Western capitalism as a driver of the Anthropocene goes hand in hand with a radical critique of European/Western modernity and the recognition that the Anthropocene puts an abrupt end to the European teleological notions of development, progress, and civilization. We stress the criticism of the leveling effect of the Anthropocene concept in the way that it has been coined by the natural sciences, insofar as it implies that the human species is responsible for the great transformations of the environment to which the concept refers. The danger of this approach is to ignore not only the sociohistorical differences between the Global North and the Global South but also the differences between different ethnic and "racial" groups (even if we acknowledge the fact that there are no biological races), as well as those between social classes within the respective regions of the world, especially in terms of consumption patterns or even cosmological representations.

Not all human societies have a predatory approach to the non-human environment, nor do all humans have the same ecological footprint. Perceiving human beings as a single species that destroys ecological environments ignores asymmetric power relationships and how they influence interactions and practices between human beings and the environment. Some voices from the humanities, however, are beginning to question the absolute rejection of the species category. They advocate the cultivation of a dual perspective that addresses not only the asymmetries of power that fracture human experiences and histories but also the geobiological history of the planet, where the human species constitutes a minority life form, despite having undoubtedly become a geological force with a profound impact on the entire planet.

In this sense, the notion of the Anthropocene requires us to question precisely the gap between the scientific idea of a single planetary system, the universe, and the multiverse of forms of existence and life on Earth. Despite recognizing and stressing the need for planetary thinking, this handbook highlights the current disconnect between global quantifications of systemic limits and the political and social realities historically constructed in the territory. This is where the handbook revisits the concept of planetary boundaries, approaching it from the social sciences and the humanities. In other words, while Earth system sciences conceive of the planetary from a satellite's point of view, we will get closer to the ground without completely losing our planetary perspective. We will reduce the spatial scale to the regional and local while also adding temporal depth, which we will then attempt to reconnect with the planetary perspective. This approach is necessary if we want to investigate the impact that different regions had on the acceleration or slowdown of the planetary rise of the Anthropocene during different historical conjunctures. It is also relevant for keeping the focus on the extremely unequal socioenvironmental dynamics of the Latin American Anthropocene, where European/white settlers "naturalized" Indigenous and Afro-descendant peoples as exploitable resources.

On the other hand, the Anthropocene's genealogy is invariably constituted as a history of conflicts and crises, having developed in Latin America from the beginning of the Conquest to the present day in a very violent way. However, those who were subject to such violence should by no means be understood only as passive victims. In this particular region, there have always been creative social responses to overcome multiple socioecological crises. From our perspective, these approaches are an integral part of a genealogy that cannot be conceptualized solely as a linear history of decline.

Through these debates between the editors of the handbook, we identified the most important thematic axes for understanding the Anthropocene's genealogy. We enter into a critical dialogue around the general approaches of a planetary Anthropocene, expressed, for example, in the debate on planetary boundaries and the historical and contemporary experiences and reflections proposed by the social sciences and Latin American environmental humanities. Faced with the continuous conjunctures of colonization from the Conquest to current extractive practices, the importance of deforestation, and the dynamics of the technosphere's advance, especially in urban zones, we identify **land use** as a paradigmatic theme for understanding the Anthropocene from Latin America. For this reason, we dedicate the first volume of the series to this topic. Within this theme, we are interested, firstly, in aspects of environmental change associated with different forms of land use, such as planting, ranching, livestock, or the large-scale clearcutting of forests for infrastructure projects. In addition, we are especially interested in the interconnection with extremely unequal and sometimes violent social processes and crises that originate from these aggressive land uses.

Biodiversity is another central aspect of the Anthropocene discussion. Latin America and the Caribbean are home to 40 percent of the world's biological diversity and seven of the world's twenty-five biodiversity hotspots, including six of the seventeen megadiverse countries and the second-largest reef system on the planet. This region also has Indigenous forms of management, as well as a long history of preservation that is threatened by dynamics of commodification and dispossession. For this reason, a volume is dedicated precisely to biodiversity.

A research project on the Anthropocene, such as the one we present here, must necessarily pose questions related to **climate change** without reducing it exclusively to the global variation of the Earth's climate due to natural causes. The Anthropocene has caused unprecedented changes in this regard in Latin America, often linked to social conflicts and demands for environmental justice. On the other hand, the issue of **water** is inevitably related to climate change and raises important questions on issues such as human consumption and pollution. This vital resource has generated numerous socioenvironmental conflicts during the Anthropocene. Therefore, two volumes in this series are dedicated to climate change and water, respectively.

Due to its importance since the beginning of the conquest, we dedicate a volume to **mining and energy,** which addresses mining extractivism from the silver of Potosí to the lithium of the Altiplanos' salt flats. Mining is inextricably intertwined with the energy sector and its various regimes. Both are linked to specific social processes and structures, in particular, the extreme exploitation of labor leading to slavery, as well as the displacement of Indigenous populations in favor of the use of fossil, or even renewable, energy. These tensions and contradictions comprise the focus of our volume on the subject.

In the discourse on the Anthropocene in the humanities and social sciences, the visual and artistic representation of the concept has occupied a special place, as the question of what images we use to narrate the Anthropocene emerged quite early on. For this reason, we are dedicating a special volume to the **visual representations** of the Anthropocene's genealogy.

In a complex project such as this handbook series of the Anthropocene from Latin America, it seems appropriate to provide guidelines to facilitate reading for all kinds of audiences. The handbook is neither a simple edited volume nor a compendium. Rather, it is organized according to a conceptual matrix in order to understand and address the Anthropocene's genealogy from Latin America. Therefore, all volumes have the same basic structure. Each is structured by a temporal axis divided into three historical periods: the colonial era, the middle of the nineteenth century to 1950, and 1950 to the present day. In turn, each of these respective periods is preceded by a general historical introduction to the topic. This allows for a contextualization from a broad Latin American perspective, making it easier for the reader to navigate the general debates. After this contextual introduction, the main entries follow. These entries synthetically discuss the Anthropocene's genealogy with respect to the volume's theme in large regions of Latin America. From the south to the north of the Latin American continent, the reader will find for each of the three historical periods five descriptive and analytical chapters of about 10,000 words, including a coherent bibliography, on the Southern Cone, the Andes, the Amazon, Mesoamerica, and the Caribbean. To depict the structure of the handbook's matrix in more detail, we first present a concise characterization of the three relevant periods, placing special emphasis on the phases of intensification and acceleration of anthropocenic dynamics. Secondly, we present the regions of Latin America and the Caribbean that will help us to analyze anthropocenic dynamics beyond the methodological nationalism that still predominates in the social sciences. And thirdly, we explore the different elements and variables that are covered in this volume on biodiversity.

Periods of the Anthropocene's Genealogy in Latin America

Since its proposal in 2000 by Paul Crutzen and Eugene Stoermer, the Anthropocene has now begun the process of being ratified as a new geological epoch in Earth's history. Although the Anthropocene Working Group, a subgroup of the International Commission on Stratigraphy, is interdisciplinary, the argument for the ratification and acceptance of a new epoch is purely geological. In other words, for the Commission to recognize the Anthropocene, it needs, first and foremost, stratigraphic evidence of such planetary human influence on all natural systems. That is to say, it looks for a marker, the so-called "golden spike," in the natural record of soil and rock layers, as well as the atmosphere. Evidence from Earth system science and human history points to a post-World War II marker in the 1950s. In 2023, the Anthropocene Working Group (AWG) proposed Lake Crawford, in Canada, as the Golden Spike, given that the radioactive fallout from the atomic bomb tests of the 1950s and other anthropogenic changes in the environment are especially marked here. Although this proposal has not been accepted by the Geologists of the Subcommission on Quaternary Stratigraphy in 2024, it coincides with the beginning of a phase that members of the AWG and associated researchers have dubbed "The Great Acceleration." This time reference, from 1950 to the present, is included as the last of three axes that we have identified as relevant to a specifically Latin American perspective on the genealogy of the Anthropocene. However, we argue that to understand the process that led to the geological definition of the Anthropocene, it is necessary to grasp dynamics and processes prior to the 1950s.

From a Latin American perspective, we propose tracing the Anthropocene's genealogy to the European Conquest of the American continent starting in 1492 with the Columbian Exchange, the plantation system, and mega-mining. Thus, the colonial era in Latin America is understood as the phase of intensification of important features in the genealogy of the planetary Anthropocene. A second phase begins with the end of the colonial empire and the processes of independence in America. In addition to profound political changes, this phase encompasses an accelerating moment for the historical construction of the Anthropocene, especially from the 1860s to the world economic crisis of 1929. Finally, we include in a *sui generis* manner the Anthropocene phase from 1950 to the present day. Within this phase, it is possible to detect an intensification of anthropocenic factors in Latin America, especially since the 1960s with the Green Revolution and oil exploitation, as well as the eighties with neoliberal policies that accelerated extractive economies and mass consumption.

Colonial Period

1492, the year of European contact with the Caribbean and the Americas, marks a turning point in world history. For the Indigenous peoples and cultures of America, it represents a fundamental rupture and even the end of their worlds. From the perspective of the European conquerors, the so-called "New World" emerges, altering the existing medieval vision of the world. For the first time, the imagination of a global "single world" arises. At the same time, the conquest and colonization of the Americas become the starting point for the formation of a capitalist world system.

In this way, 1492 marks a milestone in environmental history. An intercontinental exchange of biota begins that fundamentally changes both the "Old" and the "New World." Plants from America, such as potatoes, tomatoes, or corn, leave their mark on European cultures and become national foods. At the same time, cane sugar makes its way into Europe and provides the energy reserves for the subsequent Industrial Revolution. The Americas today are hard to imagine without the biota introduced by European colonizers, from bananas, citrus fruits, and coffee to chickens, cows, pigs, sheep, and horses.

In 1492, a large-scale socioenvironmental transformation began, from landscapes characterized by Indigenous land use to Europeanized ones. From this abrupt alteration arises the accumulation of extractive capital. It is important to recognize that, clearly, the Caribbean and American environment was not only extensively modified by Europeans, but also by the numerous and diverse Indigenous populations that inhabited both continents, as well as the Caribbean archipelago for millennia before. Our argument for 1492 as a turning point is one of scale and intensification. In other words, with the arrival of European contact, specific practices of exploitation and extractivism that were unprecedented on the continent became widespread. In fact, the introduction of new species favored the conquest of Indigenous populations, as well as the domination of vast rural areas of the American territory.

One of the anthropocenic processes of the colonial phase was the massive reforestation that occurred after the genocides of Indigenous populations as a result of pathogens and European violence. The natural scientists who have modeled this process argue that the disuse of cleared agricultural space led to a large-scale regrowth of forest cover – a massive carbon sink – which, in turn, tangibly cooled the climate around 1610. This theory is known as the Orbis Spike Hypothesis and has also been suggested as the beginning of the Anthropocene. This is a highly controversial topic in climate science, given that this period is also associated with the beginning of the Little Ice Age, but it raises important questions about the relationship between human societies and the Earth system. In any case, the continuity of the colonial process reversed this environmental dynamic, producing extensive deforestation.

On the other hand, the colonial era left as a legacy the development of the plantation system that some academics have called the Plantationocene. In the plantations, systematic techniques of overexploitation of nature were developed, connected also to the excessive exploitation of subaltern labor, that is, Indigenous and African slavery. Human muscle strength (African or Indigenous) was violently exploited as energy to power these plantation machines, thus connecting to the energy history of the Anthropocene's formation and to the process of building European modernity from the margins. The plantation system became an epicenter of confluence between early capitalism and racism, becoming part of the Anthropocene's genealogy. Starting in the last years of the eighteenth century, this process of colonial occupation was decisive in abolishing the natural limits of the solar energy economy in the imaginary of modern capitalism, opening the way for the unrestrained and unlimited expansion of extractive frontiers. This made overexploitation of the land a fundamental characteristic not only of the Americas and Europe but of the global capitalist system.

From the Mid-Nineteenth Century to 1950

During the nineteenth century, the industrial model developed in the European eighteenth century was consolidated. Although the Latin American countries that were becoming independent sought their own ways to carry out social, political, and economic transformations, such transformations were part of global and international struggles of an accelerated imperialism and nationalism. Political and economic changes brought about social transformations in the forms of production, the management of natural resources, and the dimensions of exploitation, accelerating towards the end of the nineteenth century. Although the break with the colonial model was gradual, the oligarchies acquired greater power through the Latin American independence processes, dividing and distributing capital together with the territories of production and the complicity of the landowners.

Nationalism, represented in forms of development, also fragmented territories and the uses of natural resources. New geographical and naturalistic explorations and a new conquest of the environment marked the beginning of the nineteenth century. This century is also considered the era of the second globalization, entailing the consolidation of unequal ecological exchange. There is talk of a second Columbian

Exchange related to a global metabolic fracture. Based on this logic, exchange networks were consolidated. This involved not only the exchange of raw materials for industrialized goods, but also the trade of difficult or impossible to replace goods – such as energy, soil nutrients, and biodiversity – for rapidly replenished goods, such as industrial products.

The period between the 1860s and the world economic crisis of 1929 served as a phase of economic liberalization and modernization associated with a new integration of the region into world capitalist structures and a strong reinforcement of extractive economic sectors. Within the framework of the handbook, it can be understood as a phase of intensification and acceleration of the Anthropocene, comparable only to the metabolic rift of the Conquest. With the exception of a few regions, the predominant agricultural model was the exploitation of vast *haciendas* and plantations. In addition, this period is characterized by a process of internal colonization and land grabbing in peripheral regions, referred to by some historians as the Second Conquest. The extraction of raw materials such as rubber, henequen, and mate gave rise to new estates (*latifundios*), export-oriented elites, the establishment of feudalized forms of labor exploitation, and the rapid destruction of natural landscapes.

State formation played a crucial role in the structure of the nineteenth century, marking the definition of new forms of land use and outlining enclave economies in various regions of Latin America. This process was strengthened by new technologies such as steam, electricity, and the subsequent modern means of transport derived from these technological innovations. In the economic transformation of independent Latin American countries, foreign capital investment played a key role, both in the exploitation of agricultural land and in mining. Foreign companies from the United States, Great Britain, France, and Germany accelerated economic and political transformations, directly impacting land exploitation.

With regard to land tenure, the transformation of properties contributed to the displacement of Indigenous communities and the cooptation of others who had been exploited under conditions of semi-slavery in the hacienda system. This phenomenon was observed in different regions of Mexico, the Andes, and the *estancias* (ranches) of the Southern Cone. In Caribbean countries, independence came late and led to new dictatorships at the beginning of the twentieth century. Demographic growth went out of control in some regions, leading to a separation and even segregation between the rural and urban worlds. The motto of "Progress and Order" regulated business and daily life in the nineteenth century. This included hygiene and control measures conducive to new forms of segregation and inequality, which in turn had negative impacts, both on Indigenous communities and on increasingly urbanized populations. It should be noted that at the end of the nineteenth century, the first responses emerged to mitigate anthropocenic effects. Conservationism was consolidated with the creation of natural protected areas in several countries. The biotic flow began to be controlled – albeit under a reductionist conception of conservation spaces – either as untouchable and unaltered areas, intended as pristine or as reservoirs of exploitable resources in the future.

From 1950 to the Present

The period from the mid-twentieth century to the present is known, from an anthropocenic perspective, as the Great Acceleration. It is a period marked by the accelerated consumption of natural resources, raising serious questions about the viability of the Earth system. This phenomenon is the result of important transformations in the world economic system, including the exponential growth of gross domestic product (GDP), population growth, increasing urbanization, energy production and consumption, and the use of fossil-based fertilizers, among other variables.

All of these large-scale socioeconomic transformations have drastic effects on the components of the planetary system beyond the expected natural variations. In the context of Latin America, these changes are reflected in the modification of the phosphorus and nitrogen cycle, which has resulted in the eutrophication of rivers and soil degradation due to industrial agriculture. In addition, an alteration has been observed in the carbon cycle with the loss of sinks due to deforestation and a dangerous increase in carbon dioxide and methane emissions from agricultural sources. Also, changes have been registered in the hydrological cycle with more frequent extreme events of droughts and floods and greater impacts due to the vulnerability of productive systems and urban habitats. Furthermore, there has been an increasing demand for water reservoirs for irrigation and hydroelectricity. Another relevant impact is the simplification of ecosystems and agroecosystems, which has led to a generalized loss of biodiversity.

Since the mid-twentieth century, Latin American governments and elites have assumed changing roles in driving their nations' development models and schemes. In the first stage, coinciding with developmental theory, production and consumption were oriented towards the "catch up," the theory of rapidly reaching the progress and well-being of Euro-Atlantic societies. During this period, local elites and governments adopted a planning approach to the future, with a programmed increase in the scale and pace of production. The import substitution model was implemented, allowing some countries in the region to satisfy the domestic market and to industrialize moderately: Brazil, Argentina, and Mexico being the most prominent. The Economic Commission for Latin America (ECLAC) was created in 1948, and the dependency theory was developed, which allowed the region's situation of marginalization to be explained from a structuralist perspective.

Towards the end of the 1990s, with the wave of neoliberal policies across Latin America, the role of the state was consolidated as a facilitator and intermediary for private transnational capital. Under this scheme of welfare political control, companies were able to freely access natural resources and territories through mechanisms such as public-private partnerships. In parallel, selective integration into the world market based on the exploitation of natural resources encouraged agroindustry and extractivism, such as mining, agroforestry, or fishing. With the new millennium, progressive or neodevelopmental governments spread throughout the region. Although they assumed greater roles of state control and planning, these governments facilitated the arrival of global capital mainly oriented to the production and export of raw materials associated with the commodity boom, aimed at increasing the public budget allocated to social policies. Despite their differences, all these models have had in common the primary target of economic growth as the governing axis of the economy, as well as public policies aimed at strengthening the economic bases of the Great Acceleration.

In this period of acceleration, an increase in the rate of extraction of natural resources for the world market has been seen, giving rise to what are known as old and new extractivisms that include the mining, agriculture, forestry, fishing, and urban sectors. In addition, there has been a new Green Revolution characterized by the use of monocultures based on transgenics, the massive use of harmful agrochemicals, and intensive water consumption. Large areas of the region have also been deforested for the expansion of the agricultural frontier, leading to a further significant loss of biodiversity.

Another crucial aspect of the Great Acceleration has been the need to increase the production and diversification of energy sources. In Latin America, there has been an early use of hydroelectric energy, creating profound environmental impacts, both in the flow of rivers and in the production of greenhouse gases that have contributed to global warming. Widespread rural and urban electrification processes have been favored. However, hydrocarbon extraction has also played an important role. New frontiers of oil exploitation, whether offshore (the Brazilian coast and the Gulf of Mexico) or in the Amazon rainforest (particularly in Peru and Ecuador), have helped to increase the supply of fossil fuels in the global market and to delay the international energy transition. In fact, the accelerated integration into global markets has led to the advancement of production frontiers towards non-anthropized areas, causing significant impacts on natural ecosystems and local communities. In addition, there has been a growing presence of financial capital and fictitious economies, characterized by cycles of financial crisis. During this period, internal, regional, and international migration has taken on a new dimension in terms of quantity and quality. In particular, regional migration has intensified due to greater obstacles blocking movement to the countries of the North, although there are still migratory flows to those regions. On the other hand, water management has been oriented towards intensive extraction, both in the industrial and agricultural spheres, generating significant pollution of the region's main hydrographic basins.

Anthropogenic climate change and natural climate variability are also prominent phenomena during the Great Acceleration. The Latin American region is one of the largest terrestrial carbon sinks, in part due to the existence of biomes with less anthropogenic transformation, such as the Amazon, the Mayan Jungle, and Patagonia. Greenhouse gas emissions, however, have not been kept below the sinks. Meanwhile, the increase in the scale of agroindustrial and urban enterprises has produced a continuous increase in waste generation and pollution. During the Great Acceleration, an increase in economic and social inequality has been observed in Latin America, which has meant that different social groups have different levels of destructive capacity. A significant change has been the relative loss of the states' monopoly on the use of force, leading to the emergence of organized crime groups that are involved in the processes of production and environmental predation, controlling territories in both rural and urban areas. At the same time, Latin America has witnessed the rise of resistance movements and proposals for local alternatives, especially around feminism and environmentalism.

Technological changes and transformations in communications have been profound and extensive during this period. Satellization and fiber optics have revolutionized communication media, allowing for a diversity of messages and greater appropriation of the media by subalternized movements and organizations. Nevertheless, there has also been a concentration in the distribution of cultural messages, posing challenges in terms of the democratization of information and culture.

In conclusion, the Great Acceleration has been a period of intense socioeconomic and environmental changes in Latin America. The accelerated consumption of natural resources, development models oriented to economic growth, extractivism, water management, anthropogenic climate change, inequality, and migration are some of the key aspects that define this stage. Latin America faces significant challenges in achieving a sustainable development that guarantees the preservation of its natural resources and the well-being of future generations.

Anthropocene Regions in Latin America

Regarding space, the handbook combines the perspective of planetary boundaries with a regional approach that takes into account the local and regional specificity of climates, ecosystems, and socioenvironmental relationships. The operationalization of this regional approach for the handbook project poses a complicated task. In macro-regional terms, the handbook is limited to what today corresponds to Latin America, including South America, Central America, Mexico, and the Caribbean. However, given the wide variety of climates and ecosystems in this vast region, we have proposed to define smaller and, at times, even larger areas. To this end, we do not want to rely solely on the geopolitical units of nation-states – important entities for the political regulation of the environment. Often, such territorial divisions ignore natural boundaries, while, at the same time, climate extremes tend to disregard human-created national borders. Finally, from a heuristic standpoint, we chose to define five areas that we consider suit what we would like to show in the six handbooks and that, according to our approach, are characterized by a certain ecological and cultural coherence without national borders. From south to north, these regions are as follows: the Southern Cone, the Andes, the Amazon, Mesoamerica, and the Caribbean.

Southern Cone

The Southern Cone can be defined in a combined manner. In biophysical terms, its hydrographic network, which corresponds to the Rio de la Plata Basin, stands out. In geopolitical terms, it is defined by historical processes that determine flows of people and material wealth. While still taken into account, these flows transcend the national borders of neighboring states. From a political-administrative point of view, the definition of the Southern Cone has varied. In the colonial past, the delimitation of the viceroyalty of the Rio de La Plata and the Jesuit-Guarani territory outlined a region. The Southern Cone would encompass Uruguay, Argentina, Chile, Paraguay, southern Brazil, and even the southeastern tip of Bolivia, forming a region with common structures in a heterogeneous scenario. More recently, the Southern Cone acquired geopolitical meaning in the seventies, as well as a commercial and customs significance with the creation of Mercosur in the nineties.

In the colonial period, the region was an important corridor that linked the silver mines of Potosí to the Atlantic. Much of the territory of the Southern Cone had not yet been conquered and controlled by the Spanish Crown but was kept in the hands of various Indigenous peoples. The southern part of the region, especially, was controlled by the Mapuche, whom the Spanish Crown could not conquer. During the colonial period, the relationship between Indigenous peoples – particularly the Guaraní in south-eastern Bolivia, southern Brazil, northern Argentina, and Paraguay – was fundamental for inter-ethnic relations and landscape transformations, especially due to the Jesuit presence until their expulsion at the end of the eighteenth century.

This geopolitical situation changed dramatically in the second half of the nineteenth century. We can speak in the Southern Cone of a Second Conquest, which found its highest expression in the bilateral Chilean-Argentine military campaign against the Mapuche in the 1860s.

Figure 1: Anthropocene Regions in Latin America

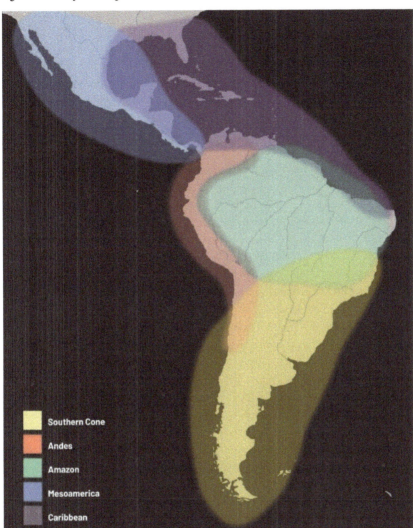

Source: Own Elaboration.

Parallel to this violent grabbing of Indigenous territories, a massive process of European immigration took place. In the middle of the nineteenth century, the Southern Cone states received a large number of settlers of European origin. In fact, the Brazilian Southeast, especially the megalopolis and the interior of São Paulo and even Rio de Janeiro, can be integrated into the Southern Cone due to its similar characteristics in terms of economic structures and the important role played by

European migrations in its overall human composition. Colonial and neocolonial ambitions to create "Neo-Europes" are reflected in many city names, urban landscapes, dietary habits, and agricultural practices in the Brazilian Southeast. From a European perspective, mass immigration was a biopolitical solution for the rural population, impoverished and made redundant by industrialization.

The environmental characteristics of the Southern Cone region vary widely due to its extensive territory and geographical diversity. The region is home to a great diversity of ecosystems, including subtropical rainforests, temperate forests, steppes, grasslands, wetlands, deserts, and glaciers. On this backdrop of complexity, heterogeneity, and abundance of natural resources, there are some structuring features of the territory that provide it with identity. A very important one is the presence of its three main rivers: Paraná (4,352 km), Paraguay (2,459 km), and Uruguay (1,600 km), which make up the Río de la Plata basin. These rivers are among the largest in the world, while the Rio de la Plata estuary is the widest in the world.

The La Plata Basin, the central part of the Southern Cone, integrates a large part of the territory of Brazil, Argentina, and Uruguay, as well as all the territory of Paraguay. In this vast territorial expanse, various biomes or ecoregions converge, each with very distinctive characteristics. Some have already undergone severe transformation or degradation, while others are on the path to degradation: the Paranaense Forest, the Pantanal, the Chaco, the Iberá Wetlands, the Pampas Grassland, the Delta, etc. All these are unique ecosystems globally and hold significant ecological value. One of the largest wetland systems in the world is also in its territory, including the recharge and discharge areas of the Guaraní aquifer.

Historically, the colonization of the interior took place mainly through the Paraná, Paraguay, and Uruguay rivers. These also form the transportation routes that today connect the region to the world market. Large quantities of soybeans, cereals, meat, and iron ore are shipped here.

But it is not only the La Plata Basin that gives the Southern Cone its identity. In turn, a second integrating pillar of the region is the presence of the Andes, as an axis that structures a specific space and a fundamental part of the territory. Chile to the west and the Andean regions of Argentina and Bolivia to the east create a socioenvironmental-cultural framework of notable specificities. In the case of the Southern Cone, the southern Andes, with their two sub-regions, are key. First, the arid Andes – from the north of the Chilean-Argentine border (Cerro Tres Cruces) to the Pino Hachado Pass in northern Patagonia – stand out for their aridity and their great heights, such as Mount Aconcagua (6,960 m MSL). The Atacama Desert is an ecosystem characterized by its extreme drought, with precipitation not exceeding 18 mm per year. It is a subregion with intense geopolitical and socioenvironmental conflicts in which, as a result of productive activities, considerable changes have been observed in the natural environment, related to mining activities, such as large-scale copper and lithium mining. These metals have become emblematic of the new mining impetus in the triangle of deposits formed by Chile, Bolivia, and Argentina. In this region, there are also a series of socioenvironmental problems, which can be interpreted as the result of human-induced alterations to the natural environment that have affected the population. The second sub-region is the Patagonian Andes, extending south of the Pino Hachado Pass with the Patagonian Andean Forest. In southern Argentina and Chile. we find Patagonia, which extends from the Colorado River in Argentina to the Strait of Magellan in Chile, covering approximately 1,043,076 km² in total. The strait, as a natural inter-oceanic passage, saw great commercial activity until the inauguration of the Panama Canal at the beginning of the twentieth century. Another view of this region is from the fragmented and insular coastal edge connected to Antarctica, with a population attentive to maintaining sovereignty flags.

Faced with the vastness of resources, the notion of dispute has been present in the various territories of the Southern Cone, from Gran Chaco to Patagonia and the Southern Andes, the land where colonists exercised sovereignty by eradicating the aborigines. The genocide of the original peoples was accompanied by the destruction of the ecosystems in which they lived. Further west, in Chilean territory, another dispute: the resistance of the Mapuche people to the advance of the Chilean army from the north and the colonists from the south. This conflict remained active for much of the nineteenth century and does not seem to be fully resolved. Conflicts over Indigenous territories are still active and are exacerbated by interest in mining areas, the southern sea for salmon farming, or the rivers for hydroelectricity, among other resources.

The Southern Cone has been blessed with an enormous variety of flora and fauna and extensive ecosystems. However, rapid population growth, industrial expansion, mining, agriculture, forestry, and large-scale hydraulic engineering projects have caused great territorial deterioration and strong socioenvironmental conflicts throughout history. This history is indicative not only of the abundance of natural resources and the natural productivity, goods, and services provided by these ecosystems but also of the tensions, imbalances, and conflicts that their exploitation has caused throughout their historical development. In conclusion, the Southern Cone presents itself as a region rich in biogeographic and cultural diversity, marked also by significant environmental and socioeconomic challenges. The sustainable management of its natural resources, the preservation of its unique ecosystems, and equity in the access and use of these resources are key elements for a future development that guarantees the prosperity of the region and the well-being of its inhabitants. A deep understanding of the region's environmental and social history is essential to address current challenges and build a more sustainable future for the Southern Cone.

Andes

The Andes region encompasses the countries crossed by the Andes Mountains, located in the tropical zone of South America, between 11° North and 27° South latitudes. In administrative terms, it includes the south of Venezuela, Colombia, Ecuador, Peru, and Bolivia, as well as the tropical parts of the Argentine and Chilean extreme north. From a natural point of view, the region has common elements in relief, altitude, and climatic behavior, but with significant variations. While the northern areas of the Andes experience two rainy and two dry seasons, the central Andes are characterized by only one rainy and one dry season.

The Andes Mountains are divided into two main mountain ranges: the Cordillera Negra in the west and the Cordillera Blanca in the east. These are connected by transverse mountain ranges and their valleys, as well as by the elevated lands of the páramo in the north and those of the Altiplano, a wide plateau that reaches its largest extent in Bolivia. The great elevational variation of the Andean region, which ranges from sea level to heights of more than six thousand meters, creates several altitudinal floors with different ecological characteristics. The climatic influence of the El Niño-phenomenon and the Humboldt marine current, which circulate along the Pacific coast, also translates into climatic diversity along the latitudinal gradient. These features range from very humid ecoregions on the North Pacific coast, such as the Colombian Chocó, to desert ecoregions on the Peruvian coast.

The Andes are home to several ecoregions that are internationally recognized as biodiversity hotspots. In fact, the region constitutes a complex mosaic of more than 130 ecosystems, including páramos, punas, and Andean valleys, with high levels of biodiversity. The tropical Andes are a leading region in endemism worldwide, with an estimated rate of more than 50 percent in plant species and more than 70 percent in fish and amphibians. Thus, it is the region with the greatest diversity of amphibians in the world, with around 980 species, 670 of those endemic.

When we refer to the Andes, we mean three diverse geographic zones that comprise the Pacific coast, the Andes, and the Amazonian foothills. The region's diverse ecologies have been used and shaped by humans for more than 14,000 years. The formation of complex human societies based on agriculture dates back approximately one thousand years before the Inca expansion in the fifteenth century. On the coast, the construction of monumental structures and urban centers in several valleys of the central and northern coast of Peru, such as the Supe Valley, cannot be comprehended without taking into account the maritime resources provided by the Humboldt Current, especially the rich fishery. The key characteristics of Andean societies, such as the specialization of social roles, the emergence of formal belief systems, the increase in food production, and technologies for systematic data recording, are evident more than a thousand years before the Incas began their imperial expansion in the fifteenth century.

Over the millennia, Andean societies in the mountain range have employed diverse strategies and technologies to survive and thrive in a challenging physical environment. These strategies include the construction of irrigation systems and terraces, innovations that enabled the spatial and seasonal expansion of agriculture. They also facilitated the proliferation of species suitable for agriculture, such as corn and potato varieties, as well as the domestication of camelids. In addition, Andean societies promoted demographic expansion, especially in the mountain range. These technologies were complemented by the emergence of dispersed settlement patterns, allowing communities to take advantage of a wide range of ecological zones at different altitudes, with their diverse available resources. Although these strategies fostered the self-sufficiency of many communities, the Incan imperial expansion introduced a policy of integration evidenced in the construction of an extensive road network, as well as in the relocation of ethnic groups, and the storage and distribution of food, textiles, and other goods.

From the imperial scale to the level of the *ayllus* – the basic social units in Andean communities – existing physical infrastructure and organizational practices formed the initial basis of colonial society after the invasion of the Spanish conquerors. However, the prolonged turbulence of the conquest, aggravated by epidemics and depopulation processes, caused the deterioration of road, irrigation, and cultivation systems in many areas of the Andean territories.

On the other hand, the viceregal policy of introducing large-scale mining manifested itself dramatically in silver mining in Potosí, an industry that emerged as the epicenter of large continuous movements of forced and free Indigenous workers, as well as goods. This restructured communities in the surrounding provinces and, among other environmental effects, led to deforestation. The appearance of mega-mining during the colonial regime marked an acceleration point in the Anthropocene, with its collateral effects of excessive land and water use, deforestation, and pollution.

Mainly in the northern Andes and the eastern foothills, the colonial exploitation of gold deposits, which often relied on enslaved Afro-descendant workers, accompanied silver mining. Whereas the extraction of precious metals was crucial during the colonial era, the second half of this period witnessed economic diversification in many parts of the Andes. Although the wars of independence in the nineteenth century brought about political and social changes, the exploitation of primary resources remained the main economic base of the new Andean republics. In Bolivia and Peru, the decline of mining during the wars was followed by a process of recovery and transformation, driven by foreign investment, industrialization in the Global North, and the introduction of machinery powered by steam and electricity in many mining sites. Overall, trends toward intensification and expansion of mining operations have continued into the twenty-first century in response to growing global demand for a variety of metallic and non-metallic minerals.

In all the countries of the region, the rise of the oil industry, especially during the last five decades, represents a parallel intensification process in the extraction of subsoil resources. The mining, oil, and gas industries, dominated in many cases by transnational corporations, have been responsible both for severe ecological degradation in many areas of operation and for the production of socioenvironmental conflicts. At the same time, agricultural industrialization has had diverse impacts on the Andean region since the second half of the nineteenth century. These include cacao plantations in Ecuador, coffee plantations in Colombia, cotton and sugarcane plantations in Peru, and the unrestrained exploitation of seabird guano off the Peruvian coast, followed later by nitrates, to promote the development of intensive agricultural systems in the North, especially in Great Britain and the United States. This transfer of resources marks a profound metabolic rupture in Andean ecosystems.

The agrarian reforms of the 1960s and 1970s mainly caused a modernization of the agrarian structure, including the introduction of the agrochemical packages of the Green Revolution. With the implementation of neoliberal policies that began in the 1980s, the orientation towards exports intensified, giving rise to new agroindustries, such as the expansion of African oil palm, especially in Colombia and Ecuador. This was alongside the more traditional monocultures of coffee and bananas, which have produced a great deal of deforestation.

In the coastal valleys of Peru, the industrial-scale cultivation of a variety of agricultural products for external markets contributes to the worsening of the water deficit faced by many communities. Local or regional conflicts over water and other vital resources are intertwined with the impact of anthropogenic climate change at the trans-Andean level, driving, among other things, the retreat of Andean glaciers.

Despite a long history of colonialism and its profound legacies, many Indigenous and Afro-descendant communities have succeeded in defending and rebuilding high degrees of cultural and territorial autonomy. Nowadays, especially in Ecuador, Bolivia, and southern Colombia, Indigenous movements constitute a considerable political force, sometimes manifesting as resistance to extractive projects or as new forms of care for the natural environment. These forms of care are also expressed in the concept of *Buen Vivir*.

Although all the countries of the Andean region defined themselves as multicultural or even plurinational in the 1990s and countries such as Ecuador and Bolivia incorporated rights of nature into their constitutions, extractivism deepened. Today, the various socioenvironmental conflicts in the Anthropocene era are at the center of fundamental debates about the future of the Andean region. These conflicts are also manifested on a global scale, as seen in the Bolivian-Chilean-Argentine highlands, which is becoming a new pole of rare earth metals extraction, especially lithium, to support the Green Deal and the CO_2-neutral industries and transportation of the Global North.

Amazon

The Amazon is a region defined by its belonging or proximity to the Amazon River basin, which crosses nine nation-states: Brazil, Colombia, Peru, Bolivia, Ecuador, Venezuela, and the three Guianas. Each of these nations has different trajectories in their relationship with the forest, both quantitatively and qualitatively. In Brazil, the Amazon is connected to the Cerrado and the Northeast through a history of migration since the end of the nineteenth century, linked to activities such as rubber extraction, mining, livestock farming, and logging. The Amazon has also been a supposed ecological paradise to which the victims of drought and the inequalities of the plantation system were encouraged to flee and settle. In the north, the Amazon River system is connected to the Orinoco, the third largest river in Latin America. Across the Atlantic, the Orinoco River system was an important entry point for extractive economic activities in the Amazon, such as the exploitation of rubber, the felling of native trees, livestock farming, and mining. Being a difficult-to-access area for the European colonizer, the otherness of Amazonian nature has been the source of numerous myths and cultural representations that have served to justify its exploitation or conservation, given that it is the largest rainforest reserve on the planet with a great diversity of biomes.

Although the concept of the Amazon has served to exemplify the notion of nature in its most "pristine" state, it is actually a historically constructed concept. At the beginning of colonization, it was not spoken of as a totality. Rather, it was established sociohistorically in the mid-nineteenth century, as until then, the Amazon only referred to the river and the river system associated with it. European knowledge of the area was gradually recorded in the cartography of the sixteenth and seventeenth centuries, showing imaginaries built on the idea of an exotic and exuberant Eden, as threatening as it was paradisiacal.

Despite the predominant image of a "virgin" jungle, the Amazon region is cultural. It has been transformed by humans for around 10,000 years. Indigenous and certain mestizo populations are important actors, even though forest biodiversity is the result of millions of years of evolutionary processes prior to human presence. During the colonial period, among European and Creole travelers and settlers, the predominant idea was that of a "green hell," the scene of the great drama of man against a wild and unhealthy nature full of dangers arising from its flora, fauna, climate, and human groups, associated above all with the idea of the cannibal. Over the centuries, various projects coexisted or alternated such as the conquest of the jungle, its exploitation, or its occupation, later moving to a conservation discourse framed by the idea of the region as a global natural heritage beyond the protection managed by specific political entities.

In the countries of the Amazon, this region has generally not been a geopolitical center, but rather a territory in a certain limbo, considered to be a reserve for the future. The predominance of national structures as determinants of public policies, whether of colonization, exploitation, or conservation, does not take into account the fact that non-human forms of life and many human populations do not always live according to the assumptions of Western structures. Animals, plants, and rivers experience and renew their existence through cycles and movements that do not consider borders. However, the actions that each nation does or does not implement in the jungle may determine whether the life of these beings on its borders is viable. Both official policies and the demands of social movements are becoming important in the continuous construction of a territory in which the Anthropocene – apparently less visible here than in more urbanized places – is constantly maintained as a structuring principle. This is evidenced by the numerous interventions carried out in the Amazon since the first half of the twentieth century. From that point on, an increasingly extractive economy with varying intensities broke out. In addition to the extraction of natural resources, the expansion of nation-states entailed the occupation of land for agriculture and livestock, as well as the development of large infrastructure projects. By the 1970s, there was already flagrant harassment of the jungle, marked by the invasion of the territory. There were slight variations in the implementation of the occupation projects according to the historical processes of each country.

In many Amazonian areas, the second half of the century was also characterized by the incursion of religious missions, first Catholic and then Protestant, whose presence had strong impacts on the organization of the native peoples, both in the management of resources and in their relations with the environment. In the twenty-first century, the growing political role of evangelical churches and their representatives has been supportive of right-wing factions with little willingness to stop environmental devastation. Instead, they have come into open conflict with environmental and land defense movements. The case of Brazil during the administration of Jair Bolsonaro, when the destruction of the Amazon rainforest increased alarmingly, exemplifies this alignment of forces and the threat it poses to the region. Given the key role of the Amazon in global ecology, the ease with which governments, ultimately transitory, are able to trigger environmental crises that impact their countries and the entire planet is worrying.

In contrast to this bleak landscape, several projects emerge that amalgamate multi- and transdisciplinary perspectives with the purpose of recovering or generating ways of inhabiting the Amazon in a sustainable manner. Although the region has become a testing ground for a new Green Economy, the weight of extractive capitalism, represented by mining and oil exploitation, among others, remains overwhelming. In addition, harmful practices such as clear-cutting, livestock farming, and other archaic predatory economic forms persist.

It is worth noting, however, a change in approach that considers biodiversity not only in terms of biological diversity and physical environment, such as waters and soils, but also in relation to sociodiversity. The latter is perceived as an element that must necessarily be integrated into conservation actions. In this context, non-dualistic thinking acquires relevance when reflecting on the Anthropocene, stressing the need to not separate nature and culture. Instead of erecting visions based on the ancient myth of a "virgin" jungle in which the human being is simply a hindrance – an idea that has been used more to displace Indigenous and peasant communities than to curb large-scale exploitation –, one must consider that the challenge lies in building conditions favorable to ecological balance. Indigenous and traditional worldviews, revitalized by current generations, offer ways to rethink the relationship between the human and natural worlds.

Mesoamerica

We propose to include the Central American Isthmus and Mexico in a new notion that we call Greater Mesoamerica. The conceptualization of Mesoamerica, presented by Paul Kirchhoff in 1960 and originally published in 1943, has been very useful because of its specificity, making it possible to distinguish a given area in geographical and cultural terms. Mesoamerica has solved problems associated with unclear concepts, such as Middle-America, used in the handbooks of the 1960s, whose translation into Spanish was never clear. In addition, it geologically identifies Mexico as part of North America, while also being part of Latin America. However, Kirchhoff's definition omits northern Mexico and part of southern Central America, leading us to propose a more inclusive notion.

In this volume, we will consider Greater Mesoamerica the geographical and socioenvironmental space that encompasses the entire Mexican territory, the five Central American nations that formed the Captaincy General of Guatemala (Guatemala, Honduras, El Salvador, Nicaragua, and Costa Rica), as well as the present-day Belize and Panama. Greater Mesoamerica, as we conceive it here, does not intend to analytically homogenize the biocultural diversity that characterizes this region; rather, we start from the premise that, despite this diversity, historical processes have taken place that present parallels in the field of socioenvironmental relations, differentiating it from other Latin American territories.

In ecological and socioenvironmental terms, the subregions of Mexico and the Central American Isthmus have peculiarities and interrelationships that we must highlight. Mexico is a megadiverse country thanks to its geographical position, connecting North America with Central America, and its strategic location between two oceans: the Pacific and the Atlantic. This allows for the conjunction of nearctic and neotropic vegetation in that territory. Mexico ranks first in terms of reptile diversity in the world. Half of the country is desert, and more than 50 percent of its national surface has a rugged topography with hills and mountains. Most of the territory experiences severe droughts, and the availability of water is mainly in the south-southeast.

This is clearly a geographical Vavilov center, defined as the place of origin of domesticated plant species of great economic importance. Led by corn, the dietary basis of the region, these species include chili, tomato, pumpkin, cacao, amaranth, and others that form part of the world's food heritage. Mexico has more than twenty biocultural regions, where language and culture are combined with natural biological species, generating broad and diverse knowledge systems. Mexican cuisine, in recognition of this biocultural richness, has been declared an Intangible Cultural Heritage by UNESCO. However, this wealth is under threat and requires urgent protection measures.

Central America stands out as the only region in the world with both an intercontinental and an interoceanic position. This isthmus links North America with South America, separating the Pacific Ocean from the Caribbean Sea. It extends from Tehuantepec in southern Mexico to the Atrato Valley in northeastern Colombia. Formed 3 to 4 million years ago in the Pliocene, the isthmus has been a bridge for North-South movement for about 10 to 12 thousand years. Its unique location gives it a variety of contrasting landscapes, including mountain ranges, intermountain valleys (altiplano), hillsides, and coasts. The region is characterized by its climatic diversity. Tropical and subtropical climates predominate, but microclimates abound.

There is a great contrast between the mountainous areas – composed of hills, mountains, volcanoes, and plateaus – and the slopes. This climatic diversity is reflected in the region's natural richness. Its diverse life zones host forests that range from the very humid, humid, and rainy to the dry. The isthmic condition of Central America explains the presence of flora and fauna from North and South America. Until Nicaragua, the vegetation is nearctic, and from the south of Costa Rica, the vegetation becomes neotropic. The combination of species in these regions explains the vast biodiversity of this subregion.

Greater Mesoamerica clearly covers a period that precedes the beginning of the genealogy of the Anthropocene, which, from this project's perspective, stems largely from the European invasion. However, we will limit the period of study in these handbooks starting with the considered territories' conquest, that is, the colonial period, based on the logic of the intensification of exploitation processes. Therefore, the concept of Mesoamerica present in the contributions of these handbooks must be understood from a broad geographical, cultural, and socioenvironmental sense, as stated above. It is, then, an operational concept that does not ignore the diffuse and subtle nature of inter- and intraregional divisions, nor does it ignore the socially constructed nature of any spatial delimitation, especially – although not exclusively – when it comes to socioenvironmental relations.

Caribbean

The Caribbean, whose core was delineated by different groups of various-sized islands, is characterized by the territorial interaction between these insular and maritime spaces, as well as the surrounding coastal areas in the Gulf of Mexico. This is known as the Circum-Caribbean, and we include it in our conception of what we call the Greater Caribbean, which also includes the Atlantic coast of northern Latin America with Colombia, Venezuela, and the Guianas. It was the first region "discovered" by Christopher Columbus. The island of Hispaniola (currently the Dominican Republic and Haiti), in particular, became the geopolitical epicenter of the Spanish and other European powers. It was called "the gateway to the Americas," at least until the mainland (*Tierra Firme*) – with more promise – was discovered and began to be conquered.

From the perspective of the Anthropocene's genealogy, the Caribbean is a particularly vulnerable region in relation to climate change in historical times, i.e., the colonial imaginaries of "primitive climate engineering," and also to anthropogenic climate change since the Great Acceleration. First, the Caribbean archipelago has been especially exposed to weather extremes such as hurricanes, droughts, and extreme rainfall, as well as to geological extremes such as volcanic eruptions. Second, these small island ecosystems were extremely sensitive to disturbances, such as large-scale deforestation undertaken by colonizers to create sugar plantations.

The Caribbean is a point of confluence between various geographical areas of the American continent, located in the middle part of the continent in much of the Atlantic Ocean. This has allowed large territories of the Caribbean to become gateways, both by sea and by land, for the migrations of people from European countries and the American continent itself. In addition, the Caribbean was the first region in the Americas to experience migrations of flora and fauna, especially with the arrival of Spanish inhabitants who introduced new livestock species and various agricultural products. The anthropogenic change caused by the European arrival was, to a large extent, related to the introduction of pathogens, causing the massive death of Indigenous populations and the abandonment of land cultivation in different Caribbean regions.

It is no accident that, until today, the Caribbean is recognized globally as a large tropical and mountainous area contrasted with coastal activities. It brings together vast territories with a wealth of terrestrial and maritime biodiversity that, for centuries, have been a meeting point for migrants from Europe, America, Asia, and Africa. The migratory diasporas to and from the Caribbean had such intense periods that we can say the region has provided conditions for complex and conflicting *mestizaje*.

After European colonization and the beginning of the transatlantic slave trade, the extractive plantation industries, which exploited the labor of large numbers of enslaved Africans, gave rise to highly stratified and socially vulnerable societies in this geographically fragile environment of small islands. From this perspective, there are numerous analogies and a shared history of forced migration, racial stratification, and systematic ecological exploitation as in the Brazilian Northeast. Both regions, of roughly the same demographic size, are fundamental nexuses of the Afro-Atlantic world and constitute spaces of ecological circulation that are paradigmatic for the colonial plantation system, in addition to its enduring legacy in the creation of the Anthropocene. The northernmost part of Northeastern Brazil, that is, states such as Ceará and Rio Grande do Norte, are sometimes included in classifications of the Caribbean.

During the colonial period, the Caribbean was one of the most important markets for people exploited by the international slave trade, financed by European economic powers. To a large extent, current migrations from the Caribbean are due to very complex processes of the anthropocenic degradation of territories and popular settlements, as well as to the violent penetration of criminal groups that have forced large sectors of the civilian population to take refuge in neighboring countries or seek migratory routes to the United States.

Since the conquest, violence and political instability shape the Caribbean region. At the end of the eighteenth century, Haiti was the epicenter of the first major revolt of people freeing themselves from the yoke of slavery in America. Since then, the conditions of slavery and labor exploitation have been intolerable for large sectors of the civilian population. However, at the same time, the Caribbean has been a space of great transformation and anthropocenic resilience, despite extractivist policies focused on land use changes, the exploitation of aquifers, the introduction of non-endemic fauna and flora, the extraction of oil, clandestine logging of forests, and the extraction of minerals. Countries such as Cuba, Haiti, Barbados, and the Bahamas are just a few examples of nations that have experienced dramatic transformations with great effects on their inhabitants due to the extractive policies implemented from colonial periods until today.

In anthropocenic terms, Indigenous and Afro-descendant communities have been especially affected due to the occupation of their ancestral territories and the implementation of industrial-scale monocultures. Paradigmatic examples of this are bananas, cacao, and coffee, products with great global demand that are grown using labor under precarious conditions, often equivalent to slavery. Another manifestation of anthropocenic devastation in the Caribbean is sugarcane, which has resulted in extensive deforestation to grow tubers imported from the Philippines, depleting water reserves due to intensive water use.

In addition, the mining of precious metals such as gold and silver has been a significant factor of anthropocenic devastation. Land use and the pollution of rivers with toxic substances, such as mercury and cyanide, have seriously affected the natural environment. Copper mining since the nineteenth century and nickel mining in the twentieth century have had a global impact and have wreaked havoc on diverse ecosystems. These activities have also profoundly transformed the region's cultural forms and traditions.

In short, the Anthropocene has had a significant impact on the Caribbean region, especially from the nineteenth century to the present, due to abusive and uncontrolled extractive policies in populations that have suffered a long history of systematic impunity, corruption, government abuses, discrimination, and endemic racism. In addition, the phenomenon of mass tourism in the twentieth century has affected the natural resources and biodiversity of jungles, mountains, and beaches through the international sale of land and property to European and North American foreigners. Finally, we wish to emphasize that, given the historical legacy of colonialism, slavery, and continued economic dependence on European powers – even after political independence – together with anthropogenic climate change, these small island states remain vulnerable. However, creative regional solutions are emerging to address the climate crisis, especially in the form of specifically and innovatively structured disaster insurance programs.

Biodiversity

Defining and assessing biodiversity – a term that has almost become a cliché – is a complex challenge for many reasons. First, because we study biological diversity at the same time that it is precipitously collapsing in front of us. Moreover, it is not simply a matter of quantifying the presence of species of flora or fauna in a given space and time. Biodiversity also entails phylogenetic variation (i.e., whether species belong to the same genus or to several genera), the balance between populations of each species, and genetic diversity between individuals of the same population. All this is relevant: diversity does not depend only on the absolute number of species, but on the medium and long-term sustainability of populations, their continuity, and – remembering that life is never static, but a constant change without predetermined directions – on their capacity for adaptation, speciation, and resilience in the natural processes of selection. Crucial factors such as biomass levels and nutrient retention in the soil depend on this diversity, as well.

Biological diversity includes a universe of relationships, coexistence, and processes in which human beings have been unequivocally involved since we appeared on the face of the planet. In assessing trends in the rate of diversity loss in the coming decades, a group of scholars must project different scenarios according to different socio-cultural choices that depend on civil societies, government agencies, international organizations, Indigenous peoples, Afro-descendant, and peasant communities, as well as scientists. The loss will be greater or lesser depending on the ability to implement options that effectively control global warming, fossil fuel consumption, and land use. Given that so much change depends on urgent and radical approaches to social justice, inclusion, and political transformations, our argument is that biodiversity is and will be, first and foremost, biocultural, and it cannot be otherwise. In Latin American history, the massive simplification of the environment –especially the transformation of different ecosystems into monocultures, cattle grazing areas, and human urbanizations – has gone hand in hand with the imposition of ecological and engineering knowledge based on modern-Western cosmological principles, which attribute a utilitarian and economic sense to non-human species. In many cases, the marginalization of Indigenous, peasant, and Afro-American cultural models that privilege cooperation among species constitutes a major threat to biodiversity.

In the same vein, it is also important to contextualize the conceptual history of the term biodiversity. The precise concept has a short history dating back to 1986, when U.S. natural scientists and policymakers applied it at the National Forum on Bio-Diversity. However, this invention was closely linked to the neo-imperial conquest of the Caribbean and Mesoamerican tropics by the United States since the late nineteenth century. But even without using this term, the abundance and difference of the flora and fauna of the Americas was a recurring theme in the imagination of European conquerors and travelers, although in the seventeenth and eighteenth centuries, visions of the degradation of such flora and fauna also predominated.

Latin America's biodiversity has been a fundamental factor in the invention and colonization of the Americas. Until recently, the region's flora, fauna, and biomes were considered laboratories of diverse processes and dynamics related to globalization, from the "Columbian Exchange" to biopiracy and even the implementation of new forms of agroforestry, such as commercial plantation systems or, finally, the cultivation of transgenic soybeans. These different examples connect Latin American biocultural experiences with the Earth system's different cycles and acceleration that have occurred in the last five hundred years, making the region's biodiversity a crucial topic of study for understanding the Anthropocene. In this sense, the debates surrounding the use, appropriation, commodification, and conceptualization of Latin America's biodiversity are vital to understanding the genealogy of the recent Anthropocene period from a longer-term perspective beginning in 1492. This volume of the Handbook of the Anthropocene in Latin America aims to enrich recent debates on the Anthropocene with critical perspectives from the social sciences and humanities. Thus, we start from the hypothesis of understanding biodiversity not only in biological terms and as something apart from society but also as a biocultural diversity present in the social world and diverse cultures. This perspective of an entangled environment implies an attempt to reduce the intensity of social conflicts, reduce the abuses of power structures, and curb the appropriation of the biosphere. In fact, cultural encounters and crossbreeding, especially in contexts of resistance, have contributed locally to restore and enrich Latin American biodiversity. Such is the case, for example, of the Brazilian Quilombos – often resulting from an alliance between runaway ensalved Africans, Indigenous people, and poorer whites – who cultivated and cared for a rich mix of native, African, and European species as an alternative to the plantation model's oversimplified colonial norms from which they fled. Within this conceptual framework, we are particularly interested in six areas of research on biocultural diversity, which we will explain below. It is worth mentioning that these fields are not strictly separate but overlap and articulate through multiple pathways and channels.

First, we will explore the issue of knowledge production about biocultural diversity, which we can understand as the co-evolution between biological diversity and cultural diversity, and the resulting process of adaptation between them. We consider the existence of different worldviews to relate "the natural" to "the cultural." The modern Western vision of a separation between the two is part of an artificially compartmentalized world in which other ways of thinking and approaching reality are excluded, preventing us from observing the complexity of today's world. Therefore, modern and Western knowledge is only one of many ways for the production and creation of knowledge. From debates with different schools of thought, the emergence of other epistemologies becomes possible, which we can call biocultural, in which emerge dialogues on wisdom, hybridization, and points of conflict between Western, Indigenous, Afro-descendant, and popular understandings. Latin America has a unique position in world history in this regard, illustrated by the continuous encounters and clashes between different cosmologies that accompanied colonization and European heritage. The prevalence and existence of a biocultural memory – which has survived more than 530 years of colonization and cultural homogenization processes promoted by nation-states – is proof of the strength of the Latin American peoples' contribution to humanity's heritage.

Secondly, and related to the previous point, we break down the field of biocultural diversity imaginaries. Our intention is to identify collective symbols and tropes such as referring to the rainforest as the "lungs of the world," to the "savage" or "barbarian" as opposed to "civilization," and to the tropics as paradise or the tropics as hell. The myth of an Edenic nature coexists with the myth of nature's degradation, and the same happens with human beings and their affective relationships – oscillating between fear and idealization.

Third, we turn our attention to understanding the interactions between animals, humans, and non-humans. We allude both to the smallest organisms, such as bacteria, and to the processes of domestication and other practices involving animals confronted with humans or human spaces, such as habitation, housing, and migration. In this sense, we aim to demonstrate the agency of different species in the formation of relationships between animals, humans, and non-humans.

The fourth field focuses on the fundamental aspect of humanity's alteration of the Latin American biosphere, or more precisely Western-colonial humanity. We begin our exploration from the beginning of the "Columbian Exchange" and the accelerated circulation of neobiota, through greenhouses and selective breeding to genetic modification.

Fifth, we explore sociocultural transformations, interventions, and regulations of biosphere diversity. For example, we raise questions about legal regulations, from colonial timber laws and the establishment of protected areas to the designation of nature reserves. We also include cultural norms, as well as civil regulations on hunting, fishing, and extracting timber and other forest resources.

Sixth, and complementing the previous point, we also investigate the biocultural diversity of the technosphere. Within this continent characterized by urbanization, we explore the dynamics of organisms in the urban and industrialized environments of the technosphere. We also understand industrialized livestock, agriculture, forestry, and fish farming systems as integral expressions of the technosphere, exploring them in terms of their impacts on the reduction of biocultural diversity and their contribution to the sixth extinction in the Anthropocene era.

In short, this volume offers a biocultural approach to the diversity of life, exploring imaginaries around it over time, considering interactions between humans and other-than-humans, and focusing on events of biological invasions, sociocultural transformations with diverse regulations and legal norms, and the fatal impacts of the dynamics imposed by the technosphere. We wish to offer content and analysis that is not only innovative and original but, above all, full of transformative potential in the context of the challenges faced by Latin America in the Anthropocene.

Final Words

We proudly present this volume as part of a series of handbooks that have carried out the pioneering task of approaching the Anthropocene from a specific regional perspective. Its realization has been made possible thanks to the dedicated work of a team of twenty editors and more than seventy authors of diverse disciplines from various regions of Latin America, the United States, and Europe.

For two and a half years, we have met at editorial conferences and workshops at CALAS headquarters in Guadalajara, Buenos Aires, Quito, and San José de Costa Rica, as well as at various virtual editorial conferences. These meetings have led to lively and, at times, controversial debates. Now, we present to you the product of this fruitful international and interdisciplinary collaboration.

We have made a significant contribution by approaching the planetary scale of the Anthropocene from a regional perspective. We have shown what the Anthropocene can mean in its socioenvironmental and sociotechnical dimensions, as well as in a long-term perspective. Assuming a perspective from Latin America involves turning to existing debates and problems related to multiple socioenvironmental conflicts, which require critical perspectives from the social sciences and the humanities. With our work, we hope to have promoted the debate on the Anthropocene from critical Latin American perspectives and to have provided inspiration for perspectives on confronting the multiple crises in the Anthropocene. Last but not least, we hope to serve as an example for other regional perspectives on the planetary in relation to the Anthropocene, especially from the Global South.

Translated by Eric Rummelhoff and revised by Luisa Raquel Ellermeier.

Colonial Period

Source: Fernando Efrén Sandoval (2021)

Introduction: Biodiversity and the Anthropocene in Colonial Latin America

Regina Horta Duarte, Antoine Acker, León Enrique Ávila Romero and Olaf Kaltmeier

Bartolomé de Las Casas was fascinated by a plant. Its bouquets had "the workmanship of a bird's feather," sprouting on slender stems. As his fingers ran over its delicate blade, it shrank, closing in on itself. But the same effect was not produced when a stick or other inanimate object was used. The plant only reacted to human touch, "as if it were a sensitive, living thing." About a century later, the Jesuit Simão de Vasconcelos, in an account of "the things of Brazil," also described the uniqueness of this "living herb," capable of sensitivity, which produced rare effects at the lightest touch, as well as curling up during the night and returning to show off its pomp at dawn. The amazement felt by these and other Europeans for the New World also accompanied the idea that everything there was waiting for them, a paradise created for the glory of the Christian kingdoms to be conquered. Animals and plants seemed imbued with revealing mysteries of divine reason, like hieroglyphs of a higher, metaphysical world. Just like the sensitive plant (*Mimosa pudica* is a plant of the Fabaceae family, native to the tropical regions of the Caribbean and Central and South America.), everything there would be waiting for the touch of the conquerors, who would set that world in motion and give it true meaning. This way of thinking gave rise to the name given to the meeting: Discovery – as if it had been destined for them by divine design (Las Casas 1875: chap. CVIII; Vasconcelos 1865: 131; Buarque de Holanda 1994: 223–224).

The "discovery" of a "New World" constituted the "most astonishing encounter in our history," in which the scrutiny of the places – their people and other beings, their mountains and rivers, their soils and landscapes – did not derive from the curiosity and desire to know the other in order to learn from their differences, rather it was an undertaking motivated by the longing for precious metals, power, and souls (Todorov 1987: 28). The amazement produced by nature was explicit in each story: as well as the sensitive plant, these men were impressed by hummingbirds, sloths, tamanduas, passion fruit, pineapple, cacao, in short, a myriad of beings that made up a stunning diversity. Simultaneously, they reduced nature to a repository of indicative signs, the intelligibility and interpretation of which necessarily led to the expression of God's supreme truths (Buarque de Holanda 1994: 107). Conditioned by

Western culture and by an episteme based on similarity, they lived in a world that curled in on itself: "the Earth repeated the sky, the faces were reflected in the stars, and the grass hid in its stems the secrets that served man" (Foucault 1997: 26), like the sensitive grass observed by Las Casas.

In naming the "New World," the conquistadors were following the Christian tradition that since original sin, the world known up to then was in continuous degradation. But behold, they arrived in a place resembling Paradise: a nature teeming with life, with its unchanging green, a perennial spring, and men sustained by fruits supposedly born without sowing in landscapes of exuberant and promising abundance (Buarque de Holanda 1994: 207). It was up to them, therefore, to occupy the space that had been designated for them, to enjoy the paradise – reserved for so long and finally given to them by divine design – everything there in abundance. Doubts about the humanity of the Indigenous people were dispelled by the papal bull *Sublimis Deus* in 1537, which encouraged controlling the bodies through submission to work and the souls through catechesis. As for everything else, it was left to the Christian conqueror to simply dispose of at will, for everything would be waiting for him: rather than an encounter or a discovery, the arrival of the Europeans was more like an invasion followed by a long plunder (Cunha 1992).

The idea arose that all that land and its beings were static in a mythical time, in large part, from the reluctance of Europeans to see and understand what existed there, that is, landscapes full of culture and history. It is a fact that there were isolated accounts such as those of Francisco de Orellana, who described many cities on the banks of the Amazon River in his voyage between 1541–1542. He was discredited as a fabulist, but today his accounts have been recovered by some researchers who have identified the vestiges of complex urbanization from 2,500 years ago. In Amazonian areas that today belong to Ecuador, for example, there were settlements, highways, and roads; drained fields; and embankments, in a model of "green urbanism" that mixed residential and agricultural areas, with modifications in the morphology of the territory and the manipulation of vegetation cover (Rostain et al. 2024). Archaeological research estimates human occupation of the jungle at 12,000 years. In these and other regions of the New World, their original inhabitants manipulated the soil and cultivated plant and animal species, creating environments of rich cultural and agrobiological diversity (Balée 2013; Levis et al. 2017; Neves et al. 2021; Peripato et al. 2023).

In Mesoamerica, Mayan and Aztec urban occupations knew express longevity and practiced sustainable models of urban agriculture with species diversification (Isendahl and Smith 2013). The Atlantic rainforest region, from the north to the south present-day Brazil, underwent substantial variations in its extension and characteristics during the Holocene period. The Indigenous populations' successive movements and waves derived from a wide and varied mosaic of cultures; languages; and agricultural, gathering, and hunting practices, an inseparable part of the history of the rainforest (Araújo 2016: 116).

In the Andean Cordillera, pre-Inca and Inca human populations and camelids were co-constituted in the relational context of a multi-species history. Llamas were bred for millennia, used for food, wool, cargo, and religious rituals, and selected for their morphological, reproductive, and behavioral characteristics. The Spaniards ruthlessly slaughtered them for consumption or used them for work in the mines, where their life was short and full of suffering. The arrival of sheep and cows brought microorganisms that contaminated them. Finally, the account of a soldier to a Spanish doctor bezoars in llama intestinal tracts, triggered a hecatomb as an avid search began for these stones considered medicinal and given away as precious (O'Gorman and Gainor 2020; Wakild 2021; Stephenson 2023).

The paradisiacal abundance of the New World proclaimed by the conquistadors was thus the result of the becoming (because they were continuously in dynamic transformation) of people, plants, animals, soils, and rivers over many millennia. Curiously, in the middle of the eighteenth century, the image of the Americas would swing to another extreme. In the theory launched by the Count of Buffon, deepened by Cornelius DePauw, and which would have a great impact on European thought, the idea of a pristine and immaculate nature shifted to that of a continent marked by weakness. According to this theory, a hostile and impoverished nature existed there, full of humid and noxious vapors, inhabited by submissive and passive savages, full of insects and other harmful animals. Plains, mountains, jungles, and rivers harbored decadent, weak, and senescent life forms, with no future but to be replaced by the vitality of the humans, plants, and animals of the Old World. These, in turn, were to be surrounded by cautionary provisions to prevent their affectation by tropics (Gerbi 1996: 19–76).

Whether in the vision of a paradise or a decadent continent, of vitality or impotence, of abundance or decay, the most diverse inhabitants of the Americas – human and non-human – were denied both past and future. The present showed itself to be implacable, Christian and European. In addition to the genocide of native populations, in which microorganisms played a decisive role, colonization was carried out with the avid destruction of vegetation and animal life. As the plantation system spread, it changed landscapes and ways of life among species. As Donna Haraway has stated, for over 500 years, the plantation has been simplifying the number of actors, establishing conditions for the proliferation of some and the disappearance of others, in radical ruptures that lead to the "substitution of peoples, crops, microbes, and life forms; forced labor; and, crucially, the disordering of times of generation across species, including human beings" (Haraway, Tsing, and Mitman 2019: 6).

Timber extraction drove shipbuilding in a world of transoceanic empires; tropical rainforests gave way to sugar mills in the Caribbean islands and in the North Atlantic of Brazil. These mills, in turn, demanded wood for their facilities and firewood for the ovens, which often produced conflicts between private and official interests, leading to the emergence of legislation regulating the cutting of wood (Funes 2008: 80–141; Miller 2000: 43). However, it is essential to note that plant and animal beings were not presented as mere passive recipients of colonizing actions nor was the forest just a stage: rather, they asserted themselves as active agents in the networks of interests, calculations, and diverse projects (Cabral 2016).

In addition to exotic plants, ships docked on the shores with animals that, in turn, conquered the territory. Their fertilizing droppings disseminated the seeds of plants "as foreign to America as they were to themselves, forever altering the soil and flora" (Crosby 1993: 145). Horses, chickens, pigs, oxen, goats, cats, dogs, and rats arrived with a frightening capacity for reproduction and dispersion, competing for territory and food, as well as being vehicles for microorganisms unknown to the local fauna. Undoubtedly, the changes affected both sides of the Atlantic: colorful birds and primates, among others, crossed the ocean to the delight and amazement of the inhabitants of the Old World. Plants cultivated for millennia by Indigenous people, such as corn, cacao, chili, tomato, potato, and tobacco, would forever change European tastes.

Like tastes, knowledge was transformed in the Old World, and despite their self-centeredness, the colonizers were very attentive to everything they could extract from the experience and knowledge of the Indigenous people, even if they scrutinized everything through the lens of their own values, expectations, and understandings. The accounts of Jesuits and Dominicans were the free translation of this listening, guided by the Christian vision of creation, like those of Las Casas, Gaspar de Carvajal, Alonso de Rojas, Cristóbal de Acuña, and so many others. The itineraries of this knowledge transfer in connected histories had complex dynamics, making it necessary to examine – through anthropological and historical critique – how Indigenous people thought about knowledge in their own terms (Safier 2010).

From the mid-eighteenth century, natural history began to be systematically instrumentalized as essential knowledge for the power of empires, and the founding of botanical gardens was part of these efforts: the first appearing in Kingstown in 1765 (St. Vincent and the Grenadines), followed by others: La Gabrielle in Cayenne (1788), the Royal Botanical Garden of the Viceroyal Palace of New Spain (1788), and the Horto Botânico Belém do Grão Pará in Belém, Brazil (1796). Expeditions of naturalists gathered collections, produced detailed accounts and illustrations and fed museums, in a systematic inventory guided by the desire to classify and organize plants, animals, minerals, peoples, and geographies. This is the case of Alexandre Rodrigues Ferreira in the Amazon under the command of the Portuguese Crown between 1783 and 1792, as well as that of Martín de Sessé and José Mariano Mociño in the Royal Botanical Expedition to New Spain between 1787 and 1803 (Ferreira 2007; Mariano Mocino and Sessé 2010). If Carl Linnaeus claimed that he felt as if he were prying into God's secret cabinet and its secrets through his "system of nature," his many disciples around the world were surveying the immeasurable collection of natural objects, like Adam in paradise naming the created beings for his own enjoyment and usufruct (Pratt 1999: 67).

Between 1492 and the end of the eighteenth century, regions of the vast territory of the Americas underwent colonization processes at different densities that affected them in a non-linear and not always continuous manner. Considering 1492 as a milestone for analyzing biodiversity in the Anthropocene in Latin America and the Caribbean does not imply taking an "end of the world view" or determining the beginning of a unified, progressive, and inexorable movement of destruction. It is not a question of looking to the colonial world for the origin of the mass extinction of species and cultures that we face, as if we were destined for it from the beginning. Genealogy allows a divergent approach to the investigation of origin: it explores the plurality of histories, their discontinuities, their deviations, their resilience. It highlights the multiple faces of America, the complexity of its biocultures, ways of living, and relationships among the various beings. It offers a story of confrontations, struggles, and agency, not a fatalistic and paralyzing narrative of death and submission (Foucault 1979: 15–38). From this approach numerous protagonists emerge in addition to the human invaders (although these do not constitute a homogeneous mass either): jungles, Indigenous people, llamas, rivers, mountains, soils, herbs like that sensitive one mentioned before, tubers such as cassava, enslaved people, imported animals that became wild or involved in unexpected relationships, in short, so many entities intertwined in varied practices, movements, and cosmovisions.

Concepts and actions that seem obvious have to be evaluated in their historical complexity. This is the case, for example, with domestication. Contrary to the Edenic accounts in which the Indigenous people would live like Adam before the fall, consuming what nature offered them, many researchers point to the domestication of plants and animals. However, many Amerindian peoples never thought of themselves as domesticators. In their vision, they and the most varied beings of the forest – including spirits – have always been interconnected in a process of mutual cultivation, in which each being exists in the relationships it builds with other beings. They never conceived nor longed for the submission of the entire jungle to themselves. From this discontinuity between the meanings of domestication, anthropologist Manuela Cunha reiterates a "recipe for a good life in a forest full of life" that includes sharing rights with other beings of the Earth and the awareness that humans are among the many parties involved (Cunha 2019).

In the following chapters, the reader will find analyses that break with the tragic stories of the continuous and relentless destruction of cultural biodiversity from the beginning of colonization to the present day. Historical research evidences a myriad of lost events, forgotten narratives, dissident practices, creative existences, and trajectories of human and non-human beings that insisted on becoming in the interstices of colonizing violence, often constructing unusual alliances and new biocultural configurations in creative lines of flight (Deleuze and Guatarri 1987: 298). All of this offers invigorating news that the past harbored numerous possibilities, worldviews, and relationships. Mapping them is a decisive step in identifying promising dissonances in our own present, listening carefully to "ideas for postponing the end of the world" (Krenak 2019).

Translated by Eric Rummelhoff and revised by Omar Chávez Sierra.

References

Araújo, Astolfo. 2016. "Dez mil anos de convivência: a arqueologia da Mata Atlântica." In *Metamorfoses Florestais*, ed. Diogo de Carvalho Cabral and Ana Goulart Bustamante, 106–123. Curitiba: Prismas.

Balée, Willliam. 2013. *Cultural Forests of the Amazon.* Tuscaloosa: University of Alabama Press.

Buarque de Holanda, Sérgio. 1994. *Caminhos e Fronteiras.* São Paulo: Companhia das Letras.

Cabral, Diogo. 2014. *Na presença da floresta.* Rio de Janeiro: Garamond.

Crosby, Alfred. 1993. *Imperialismo Ecológico.* São Paulo: Companhia das Letras. Orig. pub. 1986.

Cunha, Manuela C. da. 1992. *História dos índios no Brasil.* São Paulo: Companhia das Letras.

———. 2019. "Antidomestication in the Amazon." *HAU: Journal of Ethnographic Theory* 9, no. 1: 126–136.

Deleuze, Gilles, and Felix Guatarri. 1987. *A Thousand Plateaus.* Vol. 2. Minneapolis: University of Minnesota Press.

Ferreira, Alexandre Rodrigues. 2007. *Viagem filosófica.* Manaus: Valer.

Foucault, Michel. 1979. *Microfísica do poder.* Rio de Janeiro: Graal. Orig. pub. 1971.

———. 1997. *Las palabras y las cosas.* Buenos Aires: Siglo XXI.

Funes Monzote, Reinaldo. 2008. *De los bosques a los cañaverales.* Havanna: Editorial de Ciencias Sociales.

Gerbi, Antonello. 1996. *O Novo Mundo: história de uma polêmica (1750–1900).* São Paulo: Companhia das Letras. Orig. pub. 1955.

Haraway, Donna, Anna Tsing, and Greg Mitman. 2019. "Reflections on the Plantationocene." *Edge Effects.* https://edgeeffects.net/haraway-tsing-plantationocene/.

Isendahl, Crishtian, and Michael Smith. 2013. "Sustainable agrarian urbanism: the low-density cities of the Mayas and Aztecs." *Cities* 31: 132–143.

Krenak, Ailton. 2019. *Ideias para adiar o fim do mundo.* São Paulo: Companha das Letras.

Las Casas, Bartolomé de. 1875. *Historia de las Indias*. Vol. 3. Madrid: Imprenta de Miguel Ginesta. Orig. pub. 1561.

Levis, Carolina, Bernardo M. Flores, Priscila A. Moreira, et al. 2018. "How People Domesticated Amazonian Forest." *Frontiers in Ecology and Evolution* 5, no. 171:1–21.

Mariano Mocino, José, and Martin de Sessé. 2019. *La Real Expedición Botánica a Nueva España*. Vol. 14. Mexico City: Siglo XXI/UNAM.

Miller, Shawn. 2000. *Fruitless Trees*. Redwood: Stanford University Press.

Neves, Eduardo Goés, Laura Furquim, Carolina Levis, et al. 2021. "Peoples of the Amazon before European colonization." In *Amazon Assessment Report 2021*, ed. Carlos Nobre, Andrea C. Encalada, Elizabeth Anderson, et al., 8.1-8.40. New York: United Nations Sustainable Development Solutions Network.

O'Gorman, Emily, and Gaynor, Andrea. 2020. "More than-human histories." *Environmental History* 25, no. 4: 711–735.

Peripato, Vinicius, Carolina Levis, Guido A. Moreira, et al. 2023. "More than 10,000 pre-Columbian Earthworks are Still Hidden Throughout Amazonia." *Science* 382, no. 6666: 103–109.

Pratt, Mary Louise. 1999. *Os olhos do Império*. São Paulo: Edusc.

Rostain, Stephan, Antoine Dorison, Geoffroy de Saulieu, et al. 2024. "Two Thousand Years of Garden Urbanism in the Upper Amazon." *Science* 393, no. 6679: 183–189.

Safier, Neil. 2010. "Global Knowledge on the Move: Itineraries, Amerindian Narratives, and Deep Histories of Science." *ISIS* 101, no. 1: 133–145.

Stephenson, Marcia. 2023. *Llamas Beyond the Andes*. Austin: University of Texas Press.

Todorov, Tzvetan. 1987. *The Conquest of America*. New York: Harper.

Vasconcelos, Padre Simão de. 1865. *Crônica da Companhia de Jesus do Estado do Brasil e do que obraram seus filhos nesta parte do Novo Mundo*. Lisbon: A. J. Fernandes Lopez. Orig. pub. 1663.

Wakild, Emily. 2021. "Learning from the llama." *História, Ciências, Saúde – Manguinhos* 28: 1–21.

Biodiversity in the Southern Cone in the Colonial Period
Colonial Heritage Spoken in More-than-Human Words

Ana Lucia Camphora and Miriam Adelman

The distinct biomes of the Latin America Southern Cone are an interconnected plurality of coexisting worlds. They exist as tangible and intangible realities, which, since historian Alfred Crosby's (1993) pioneering work on the simultaneously human and environmental causality of history, we can see through the lenses of a new paradigm. The adoption of a postcolonial approach allows one to consider the decisive influence of animals and plants – both native and exotic species – on the triumphs and failures of European colonialism (Esparza 2021). The condition and protagonism of non-human animals throughout history thus return to the stage that blindly excluded them during the centuries in which the epistemological and institutional contours of anthropocentric thought had them thoroughly eclipsed (Urquijo 2022).

In understanding the notions of animality as an intrinsic element of colonialism, this chapter commits to another way of thinking about the world while recognizing the predicaments that the Humanities face in confronting that which had, since their origins, been largely invisible or unthinkable (Dutra e Silva and Fernandes 2022). Contrasting worldviews constructed within contexts of colonial plunder illuminate the intersubjective realities that had their presence erased from the historical record. This takes us beyond the naturalistic narratives that deeply mask asymmetrical relationships and contributes to new approaches to non-human animals' emotional lives, cognitive capacities, and even politics, as Meijer and Bovenkerk (2021) argue.

This chapter proposes a nuanced colonial historiography, aiming to enrich ongoing debates on the colonial roots of the Anthropocene through critical reflections on how non-human animals have influenced narratives on Southern Cone territorialities. The recognition of new historical sensitivities widens our understanding as listeners, breaking through the silencing of other messages, those coming from the whinnying, neighing, chirping, barking, and singing out of other voices, or of other "vital choreographies" (Cabral and Vital 2022), ones that are not merely auditive. By bringing to centerstage parts of a world so equivocally yet markedly relegated to the periphery, we move beyond the anthropocentric view that places humankind at the center of the grand order of natural processes, in which "other" living beings appear by chance, as mere commodity or productive forces, muted by the modern perspective that stubbornly attributes passivity to nature (Kelly 2018).

The emergence of narratives produced in conviviality with other animal species breaks with the anthropocentric argument that the domain of textual language is limited to interactions between humans (yet not *all* humans). Only through human mediation, mainly through writing, does one access the presence and meaning of other animals' participation in historical processes, as 'multispecies co-authorship' (Cabral and Vital 2022). This "rediscovery" unfolds through holistic forms of thought that seek to reintegrate the fragmented view of nature produced by scientific paradigms of modernity (Dutra e Silva and Fernandes 2022). As we strive to overcome yet another of the great modern humanist illusions shaped through the binary oppositions of civilization/barbarism and nature/culture, we look at such categorical distinctions as an expression of colonial dynamics in more-than-human societies (Cederholm et al. 2014).

Colonialism flourished in the drawing of boundaries between human and natural worlds that inaugurated early Western perceptions of Latin American biodiversity. This view was rendered familiar to European sensibilities over a vast and historical campaign of cultural colonization, economic subjugation, and religious conversion (Caraccioli 2021). From the sixteenth century onwards, the introduction of large European domesticated mammals – mainly equids and cattle – into New World territories is a widely recognized phenomenon that became a cornerstone of colonial development. These exotic species were thus one of the most incisive strategies of control over colonial spaces and systematic influence on native people's ways of life (Palermo 1986; Turner 1990; Crosby 1993; Anderson 2004; Camphora 2021). Furthermore, these processes' persistent, long-term impact affected the presence (and death) of human and non-human life forms at a crossroads where natures, cultures, and temporalities became tragically entangled (Carey 2009).

From historical records on practices and situations that reveal how human and animal lives were both intertwined and yet held at a discursive distance, possibilities arise for a better understanding of the roots of Anthropocene in the harnessing of non-human energies. Such use constitutes one of the pillars of an entire historical period, given the massive conversion of other animals into global capital and the deep environmental implications this has had. In the present text, we revisit some of the circumstances that have forged such encounters, examining the various forms of human and non-human relations in which cattle and horses loom large. Understanding their influence on the biodiversity of the Southern Cone can provide new and needed perspectives on the region.

Early Connections with "Others" in Colonial Spaces

This chapter argues that the hegemonic concepts of nature and its entities were forged in the interregnum between colonialism and Western science. At this point, we want to highlight the etymological origins of the term "frontier," referring to that which lies ahead "on the margins of the inhabited world" (Poyer 2021: 444). In place of the ancient meaning of a boundary that arises to distinguish the "we" from the "others" (Comissoli 2021), "frontier" refers to the point of encounter with a place expected to expand further; thus, it connotes movement and mobility, a "moving beyond" or "into."

The objective significance of colonial territories as a living laboratory in which the natural sciences flourished has ushered in a new order in which many of the constraints that regulated medieval exchanges are overcome. On the Latin American continent, the *Historia general de las Indias*, written by the Spanish soldier, historian, and botanist Gonzalo Fernandes de Ouviedo and published in 1526, was the first report to describe the natural landscape of the Caribbean. The year 1588 marks the appearance of the Spanish priest Father José Acosta's *Historia Natural e Moral de Las Indias*, a scientific treatise of the New World that crystallizes the conflictive beliefs of Church cosmology and the progress of European science (Ford 1998). In a synthesis of the encounter between Europe and the Americas, the Jesuit rhetorician explored New World phenomena, merging empirical and experimental principles with the Catholic faith. Latin American biodiversity was thus incorporated into a natural and moral framework at the intersection of philosophy and theology (Valle 2013; Caraccioli 2021).

The Church was strategically positioned at the center of this intrinsic relationship between colonialism and modern natural sciences, bent on a mission in which knowledge became a veritable tool for the expansion of empire. The Jesuit colonial project was based on specialized activities, and systematic observation of meteorological patterns, geographic surveys, social differences, and changes in the natural landscape. They received large donations of land and gifts of cash and valuables to be invested in rural endeavors that also benefited from significant fiscal advantages. They were even referred to as pioneers and "scientific farmers" due to their role in the introduction and cultivation of alfalfa, forage, grapes, and sugar cane (Clarence-Smith 2020).

The realms of science and faith were not separate fields of inquiry for missionaries living in close contact with different tribal villages. Missionaries gained access to a complex and vast field of traditional knowledge and practices rooted in native understandings of local realities. Between the seventeenth and nineteenth centuries, thirty Jesuit Missions settlements were established in the Southern Cone, mainly in Argentina, Brazil, and Paraguay, on lands originally occupied by Guarani Indigenous peoples. Called *reducciones*, these settlements constituted a spatial, religious, economic, social, and cultural system to sustain ranching, yerba mate plantations, and networks of trails and waterways extending across the Uruguay River and its tributaries (UNESCO n.d.). It was from the appropriation of native customs, knowledge, and practices that many typical Southern Cone industries arose, such as mining and native species extractivism. The "mule economy" (Clarence-Smith 2020) that we will examine below was a strategic market that flourished on Southern Cone missions.

Colonialism was essentially dependent on Amerindian original knowledge of the rich biodiversity of the South American continent. Yet for a long time, historical silence regarding the countless sources of native knowledge awarded science alone the power to speak about nature (Barbosa 2017). Furthermore, Southern Cone landscapes were not the main stage of the first natural resource inventories of the continent. According to Herrera et al. (2014), surveys of the native vegetation of the Argentine pampas did not begin until the eighteenth century. Inventories of the French botanist, Auguste Saint Hilaire (1779–1853), the German botanist, Julius Léopold Eduard Avé-Lallemant (1803–1867), the Swedish botanist, Carl Axel Magnus Lindman (1856–1928), and the Argentine botanist, Federico Bernardo Vervoorst (1923–2008) established systematized information on the biodiversity of the region.

When, in the early decades of the nineteenth century, the English naturalist Charles Darwin (1809–1882) rendered a clear portrait of the different Southern Cone ecosystems, he was also able to identify the accumulated environmental impacts of the colonial period. Between 1816 and 1822, Auguste de Saint-Hilaire traversed the southern and south-eastern regions of Brazil, the Rio da Plata, and the Argentine Missions province, part of Uruguay and eastern Paraguay. He gathered between six and seven thousand plant species and described many botanical species that had been previously unknown to Western science. His scientific work was mainly concentrated on the Brazilian Atlantic Forest and the medicinal uses of numerous native plants (Lamim-Guedes 2018).

The Eurocentric order – in which the natural sciences became a major tool of Western culture – acted as the central underlying logic of ever-increasing needs for new sources of wealth that could ensure capital accumulation on the part of existing empires (Leite 2015; Herrera 2021). Scientific knowledge of nature was thus wed to interest in national development, maximizing utilities and wealth from the exploitation of natural resources. It also shaped discursive repertoires on the many subaltern "others" and their roles. By the 1820s, all the Southern Cone countries had acquired formal independence, and the concept of nature had become a pillar for building national identities. A progress-oriented Eurocentric logic undergirded the patriarchal, speciesist, and colonialist logic that drove capitalism forward through national projects of development fueled by power, capital, and nature (Carvalho 2021).

Intruders, yet Colonial Partners

The introduction of exotic species, aiming at their acclimation, turned nature into a purely instrumental entity. The long-term environmental and social consequences of such engineering would eventually become a veritable "Pandora's box" (Sennett 2009). There is ample evidence of how intractable and intense the environmental damage promoted by a single exotic species can be. In 1820, in a region close to Montevideo, Uruguay, the French botanist, Auguste de Saint-Hilaire (2002: 189) wrote that "European plants become tyrants here, taking over vast expanses and expelling the indigenous species."

In 1833, near Guardia del Monte, Argentina, Charles Darwin (1913) identified two European plants, fennel (*Foeniculum vulgare*), and cardoon (*Cynara cardunculus*). The latter proliferated on both sides of the Andean Cordillera, across the continent, and could also be found in wilderness locations in Chile. There alone, a region of several hundred square miles was described as "covered by one mass of these prickly plants [...] impenetrable by man or beast" (Darwin 1913: 125).

The introduction of horses, cattle, and mules responded to increasing demands for transportation, mining, and agriculture. It also reflected the demographic collapse of most Amerindian territories after the conquest. In the Southern Cone, the introduction of mules was a decisive contribution to overcoming the limitations of the llama (*Lama guanicoe*), the camelid species native to South America, domesticated by Indigenous peoples of the Andes for use as beasts of burden. By the 1640s, mules became the Jesuits' chief source of income. By the mid-eighteenth century, there were about 25,000 mules that each year traveled the route between Córdoba and the region of Salta, located to the east of the Andes, laboring at an altitude of 1,200 m. The high death rates in the mining zones, coupled with their sterility, drove the market for mules. A dozen or more Jesuit colleges – such as the colleges of Córdoba, Santa Fe, Buenos Aires, Asunción, and Tucumán – owned and managed ranches in the province. Livestock raising was concentrated in a cluster of eleven estancias stretched out across what is today north-western Uruguay. Chilean colleges and missions were involved in the mule economy, but on a smaller scale (Clarence-Smith 2020).

By the end of the colonial period, there may have been 2 million mules in Latin America, the highest ratio in the world: one for every five to ten inhabitants. How can the impact of the intensive use of horses and cattle on the American continent be summarized? These invasive species became close partners to the diverse groups of human beings, transforming economies, cultures, landscapes, as well as the ways of life of native peoples, Europeans, and the animals themselves (Palermo 1986; Crosby 1993; Anderson 2004; Vander Velden 2015; Clarence-Smith 2020; Jones et al. 2019; Adelman and Camphora 2020; Camphora 2021). Large herds of cattle and horses made their way across the plains and prairies of the Southern Cone in all directions, running from storms, wildcats, or foxes. The dissemination of tangible and intangible elements intrinsically associated with the continuous processes of conquest and occupation depended on their service and toil.

Horses: the Novel Deities

Horses "returned" to the American continent in 1495 with the arrival of Christopher Columbus, after their ancestors had disappeared, some eight to ten thousand years earlier (Turner 1990). As of the 1530s, they were brought to the American continent spreading out as a military asset in the brutal and centuries-long campaigns that perpetrated genocidal violence against the native cultures of the Americas (Gabbert 2012). Horses' propagation across the continent was highly determined by the deployment of military troops, sent initially to mining regions and to sites of greatest resistance to European occupation. In Brazil, one of the first accounts of the use of horses against native peoples refers to an episode that took place in May 1555, in the province of Bahia. Six horsemen and seventy-foot soldiers invaded a Tupinambá village that they saw as a threat to cattle and colonial settlements. The final toll of several days of conflict included the loss of many horses and several Amerindian villages, which were burned and razed to the ground (Calmon 1958). In April 1781, the native leader Tupac Amaru II was drawn by four horses and quartered by henchmen in the city of Cuzco, Peru (Gabbert 2012).

In 1541, the Spaniard Pedro de Mendoza introduced the first horses to what today is the city of Buenos Aires, but he himself left the region in the face of intense native resistance to the European explorers (Palermo 1986). The animals that were left behind, especially those that reached the rich pasturelands of the Pampas, were certainly successful in their struggle to survive. In many regions of the New World, horses adapted well and began to reproduce rampantly. Hunted like wild animals, they were considered a "plague," consuming forage that had been destined for cattle grazing. A campaign of successive extermination of feral horses was begun (Crosby 1993). Travelling over the borderlands of Brazil, Argentina, and Uruguay, Saint-Hilaire (2002) described more than one encounter of cavalry troops with herds of wild horses that mingled with them, circling around their own mounts, and getting in their way. On another occasion, a wild donkey was stabbed to death. Yet from these wild herds, considered harmful destroyers of pasturelands or guilty of luring domestic horses into the wild, horses to be trained for work and riding were also rounded up.

Human, environmental, and military conditions motivated native peoples' encounters with horses. As early as the sixteenth century, some Amerindians benefited from the unprecedented ease of traversing vast areas that horses gave them. Within the universe of relationships that made up the subsistence dynamics of the original populations and other native species of the Southern Cone, the appearance of equids was one of the most brutal changes affecting native cultures. Native peoples who were unaware of domestic animal husbandry systems were already using horses as mounts and food. Techniques for capturing (and taming) these large and powerful animals were initially unknown to them. Hence, rather than reproducing the Iberian equestrian culture, they invented their own (Palermo 1986).

Figure 1: A South American Chief of the Charrúa on his Horse

Source: Jean-Baptiste Debret (1800).

Horses also became a powerful weapon of war that would improve their advantages in the conflicts to come (Turner 1990). Thus, whether explicitly or not, equestrian activities served to transmit European values and customs, encouraging changes in the worldview and subjectivities of native peoples as well as other members of a culturally mixed and highly unequal colonial society. The economic and cultural transformations promoted by horses (and by cattle) were more intense for groups that had greater access to colonial commercial systems (Palermo 1986). Changes were glaring, from the use of *boladeiras*, snares, stirrups, changes in combat strategies and weapons, eating habits – through a diet based on mare meat – to ways of life altered by the mobility that horses provided, and new spiritual beliefs. In the valley of the Rio Negro, Argentina, Charles Darwin (1993) came across a famous tree which was reverenced by the native peoples as the altar of Walleechu. There, horses were slaughtered as a sacrificial offering, an act believed to ensure both human prosperity and the rugged resilience of mounted equines.

The horse, as an entity that became a part of native cosmology, was thus woven into the nature-culture that defined the identity and sense of belonging of the Rankul people, an ethnic group recognized on the basis of environmental specificities (*rankül* and *che* mean people from the canes and from the *carrizales*, typical vegetation of certain regions of the Argentine Pampa). These interactions were woven into representations that flaunted biodiversity. For example, in winter solstice ceremonies, in June, in the southern hemisphere, the dance of the Inhandú (*Rhea americana*) imitated the movements of this bird, a symbol of Rankul communion and unity. In another ceremony, that of the black bull (*Curru Toro Magüen*), the symbolic connection with an exotic species expressed a connection to nature. The bull was associated with the fertility of the land and bodies, and also invoked a request for rain in periods of drought (Giacomasso and Curtoni 2017). Thus, the biocultural significance of equines and cattle merged with other immemorial native icons.

Movement over large areas of ground was spurred by the desire to round up animals from semi-wild herds of cattle and horses. As noted by Palermo (1986), while this greater mobility did not necessarily signify sedentary peoples' conversion to nomadism, it certainly increased the processes of transculturation by facilitating interethnic contacts. For the Tehuelche, the horse facilitated migrations that had previously been carried out on foot, whereas the presence of foals in certain regions even served to motivate new migrations. In addition to a diet based on mare meat, the trade in leather and animals became their main economic staple, as well as cattle raising. The mediating role that is attributed to the horse in first peoples' interactions with other native beings and species is undeniable. In 1870, the Argentine writer and traveler Lucio Victorio Mansilla (2003) recorded his journey through Rankul territory. In the Pampa, horses had become absolutely essential; with a good horse to ride, there was never a lack of animals to catch or hunt. Roasted mare's meat was common, as well as the similar roasting of the flesh of other native species, such as guanaco, gamma, ñandú, and Montez cat.

By the mid-nineteenth century, the so-called "gaucho war" technique had emerged, consisting of a military tactic that was adopted by the rebels, based on the use of light cavalry. Securing a supply of horses – through confiscation, capture, or purchase – became a vital asset of warfare. Horses were the true "agents of war" of the Brazilian Farroupilha Revolution (Menegat 2021). In a seminal study of culture and male identity in the Pampas, Leal emphasizes persistent patterns of human-horse relations that are simultaneously utilitarian, symbolic, and emotional, noting, "The horse is part of the gaucho's perception of his own body, and an extension of it. The symbol of the classical centaur, mythical half-man, half-horse, is appropriated in an original meaning: strength, savage passion, invincibility, and liberty." (1989: 265–266)

According to Saint-Hilaire (2002), the inhabitants of the villages outside the city of Montevideo never went anywhere on foot, always using horses. Yet despite the evident importance of the horse for first peoples, there are no reports that they engaged in breeding. At least until the second half of the nineteenth century, neither settlers nor natives developed systems for raising horses or cattle, beyond the occasional corrals built to handle cattle and sheep in the Pampas and Patagonia (Palermo 1986). According to Darwin (1913), people had large numbers of horses which they subjected to thoughtless handling, marked by the lack of even minimal care. Deprived of maize in the dry seasons, animals became thin and weak.

Brutality and violence were taken for granted, as often happens today, as an expression of the traditional practices of extensive livestock raising and equestrian culture. Darwin described the crude gaucho method of taming horses, beginning with a lasso thrown to catch hold of the two front legs of the young wild horse. Next, a tough bitless bridle was fixed to the animal's lower jaw, and a narrow thong threaded through the eye holes and several times around both jaw and tongue. Thus "the horse, from dread and astonishment at thus being bound round the waist, throws himself over and over again on the ground, and, till beaten, is unwilling to rise" (1913:160). The same procedure was repeated two or three times until the horse had been tamed.

Mares had a different fate since riding them was considered ridiculous. Soldiers' and gauchos' habits of eating mare's meat were well-documented. Mares were used only for breeding and threshing wheat or were slaughtered exclusively for their hides or for tallow to be used in making soap (Saint-Hilaire 2002). The mare was also traditionally considered the gaucho's best "sexual partner" (Leal 1989).

Cattle as Environmental Vocation

Cattle multiplied into immense herds occupying the extensive fields of the Southern Cone, considered amongst the best grazing land in the world. There were more than 100 million hectares of sub-humid pasturelands in the Rio de la Plata basin. On the western slopes of the Pampas lay the Uruguayan *campos* and an extensive region of Brazilian pasturelands that stretched into the interior of Paraguay. A mosaic of more than five hundred species of grasses distributed in the different plant formations within this natural continuum consolidated this economic landscape with the best possible conditions for the multiplication of herds. The latter was such a good match for these surroundings that their massive presence has not usually been considered a factor that impacts biodiversity (Parera, Paullier, and Weyland 2014; Cesco 2015).

The unquestioned usefulness of these pastures for extensive livestock ranching led to the definition of the Brazilian pasturelands as potentially integrated into environmental conservation. Nonetheless, the scope and continuity of the impact it had on ecosystems led to ineluctable transformations of the flora and fauna of the region. In the 1830s, Charles Darwin (1913) noted that the native vegetation of the region was undergoing continuous modification: some native species – such as the guanaco, deer, and ñandú – were vanishing, while the carrion vulture increased in numbers, due to the exponential increase of carcasses. There are records of extensive herds of cattle and horses succumbing to long periods of drought, stuck in the mud as they strove to find water, or consuming salt water due to lack of access to freshwater sources. Brailovski (2009) notes that the introduction of large herbivores generated a rapid enrichment of soils, attracting Indigenous peoples and, with them, the use of fire. There was a vague initial perception of the scope of the environmental changes caused by the spread of livestock in the Southern Cone throughout the colonial period.

Based on the review of literature survey carried out by the authors mentioned above, around a hundred species of terrestrial mammals were identified in the region: *Ozotoceros bezoarticus, Lycalopex gymnocercus, Chrysocyon brachyurus, Galictis whose, Chaetophractus villosus, Dasypus hybridus, Lagostomus maximus, Cavia aperea,* and *Ctenomys spp.* There was also *Chlamyphorus truncatus,* an armadillo whose underground habits are so strict that its eye sockets have atrophied. Currently, there are between 450 and 550 species of birds registered, of which sixty are considered strictly dependent on the vegetation found there. Among the emblematic species of the Southern Cone pasturelands, the *Rhea americana, Nothura maculosa, Chauna torquata, Vanellus chilensis, Furnarius rufus,* and *Cistothorus platensis* stand out. Several of the species identified were later classified as endangered, while others, such as *Anodorrhynchus glaucus* and *Numenius borealis,* have gone extinct.

By the end of the eighteenth century, the market for beef and mutton in Buenos Aires was one of the largest that had ever been seen. Meat-salting plants processed the carcasses of large animals and hence facilitated the city's meat supply. Hide export was dependent on international trade variations, influenced by tax measures, transportation, and military conditions – war or peace – in the Atlantic. Regarding places with economies based almost exclusively on animal husbandry, both Darwin, and Saint-Hilaire agreed that in regions where the socio-economy was centered on salted meat, horse and mare hides, and tallow, the abundance of horses and cattle fostered a culture of waste and neglect, rather than reverence for the animals as assets or sources of wealth. Saint-Hilaire (2002) observed that the joy that preceded the moment in which men killed and quartered cattle sometimes went far beyond the desire to satisfy hunger.

Grotesque sacrificial activities were a part of different stages of the development of regional economies. The *"arreada"* or *"vacaria"* of Southern Brazil was an emblematic ritual that lasted several days. The risks were so great that rather than using enslaved labor, members of the "undesirable" population were sent out to do the job. These men employed methods for the slaughter of the cattle that were described as cruel, irregular, and "exquisitely savage", in which they mingle with the cattle:

> the one in the middle takes a long stick garnished with a very sharp half-moon at the end, with which he knocks down all the cattle, or the number that is needed; he then goes back along the same path, and with a pike spears each one, penetrating its entrails, causing its death, and then the others jump off their mounts to remove the hide. (Azara 1904: 117; quoted in Freitas 1993: 443)

The meatiest parts were sent to the salting area, where they were spread over the *charqueadas* on long poles suspended four meters above the ground so that the meat would dry in the wind and sun. The shredded carcasses were then sent to cauldrons, where their tallow was extracted. The fat extracted from the bone marrow and brains were used to make candles, and the bones served as fuel for the ovens (Debret 1940: 243–244; cited in Cavalcante 2000: 74). In Argentina, bone fences were erected with hundreds of thousands of steer skulls, in as many as nine layers. They were laid on top of each other like stones, with the horns protruding: "some walls were older and longer, topped with green grass, vines and wildflowers growing from the holes in the skulls, looking picturesque but also somewhat sinister" (Crosby 1993: 161).

Colonial Ontologies of the Anthropocene: Some Current Considerations

The development of production techniques within both the crafts-based and industrial systems sought answers to the call to "conquer new lands" (Sennett 2009: 22). Such endeavors arose from a dialogue between practices and ideas which would eventually lead to a "Pandora's box" dimension of environmental crisis, as we now know. Perhaps the most paradigmatic case of devastation related to the power of invasive species to impact native ecosystems can be found in the introduction of the North American beaver (*Castor canadensis*) to Tierra del Fuego Island, in 1946. Its environmental and economic impacts have been monumental (Anderson et al. 2009).

There is also the historic human interaction with horses and cattle which we have discussed above, infused with taken-for-granted forms of violence. This colonial heritage, marked by aggression and control over bodies, was largely incorporated into traditional equestrian cultures of Latin America. Equines' naturalized condition thus became that of living beings to be sacrificed within a system of power that was played out in the carnivorous sacrifice of an anthropocentric and phallocentric model. Examining Derrida's (2009) concept of the "carnophallogocentric," Llored (2016: 65) sees in this "past and present" form of sacrifice a fundamental way of drawing boundaries between the human and the animal.

Anthropocentric intentions and actions that subjugate living animals to male sovereignty thus reveal the innermost signs of human law. From this vantage point, it is animal sacrifice, more than any other social institution, that enables us to understand this sovereign power in its real and symbolic expressions. It allows us to apprehend the form of sovereignty that lies at the core of Western policies, originating in the modern State, and which only makes sense through the separation of "man" from animal (and the feminine): non-political entities to be sacrificed on the altar of modern politics. There is a robust set of discourses that authorize this death, assuming a dual function in carnivorous societies.

Hence, Southern Cone territories, once they were established as meat-supplying colonies, became a locus *par excellence* of the capitalist transatlantic machine. Methods changed when the Industrial Revolution brought the regional culture of reckless expenditure of cattle to an abrupt halt. Southern Cone livestock then became a strategic asset, renewing economic links with Europe, and the end of a series of wars was followed by the recovery of the cattle herds in the La Plata region. In Pelotas, Rio Grande do Sul, canned meat gelatine was produced from the residue of cattle shin bones boiled in a large candle and soap factory (Bell 2000). At the end of the nineteenth century, a new imperialist cycle, propelled by the cattle industry, reconnected certain regions of the Southern Cone to Europe and England, in particular.

As an emblem of this complicated colonial past, the Palacio Rosado, the official seat of the Argentine government, takes its name from the mixture of cow blood and lime used in painting its walls (Aboglio 2017). It thus encodes a symbolism that marks the architecture of South American power, resting heavily on the legacy of previous centuries. In a grotesque tale by Argentine writer Esteban Echeverria, "The Slaughter House" (Flores 1942), a veritable reproduction of Argentine society as a whole is staged on that "muddy, blood-drenched floor":

> Nearby two Negro women were dragging along the entrails of an animal. A mulatto woman carrying a heap of entrails slipped in a pool of blood and fell lengthwise under her coveted booty. Farther on, huddled together in a long line, four hundred Negro women unwound heaps of intestines in their laps, picking off one by one those bits of fat which the butcher's avaricious knife had overlooked. Other

women emptied stomachs and bladders and after drying them used them for depositing the offal. (Flores 1942: 395–396)

In 1864, the first transnational meatpacking plant was built on the Uruguayan bank of the Uruguay River. Defined as "a colossus" (Lewowicz 2016: 25), the corned beef meat factory Société Fray Bentos constituted the first experience of major world capitalism in Latin America. From 1881 to 1890, 1,549,000 heads of cattle were slaughtered at Fray Bentos. Between 1872 and 1908, the volumes of meat and wool produced per hectare in Uruguay more than doubled (Barrios 2020). By the end of the 1860s, the Fray Bentos slaughterhouse consumed around six thousand metric tons of coal per year, also dumping around twenty thousand metric tons of animal waste into the Uruguay River.

By the early twentieth century, with the spread of the refrigerated meat industry, the Fray Bentos plant became marginal. By 1913, Uruguayan incomes were only 10 percent lower than France's and about three times higher than the Latin American mean; the Argentine experience was similar (Barrios 2020). By 1914, more than 40 percent of Britain's meat supplies were imported, mostly from the southern hemisphere, indicating that this significant economic relationship sustained a veritable "informal empire." The Fray Bentos plant finally closed in 1979, and in 2015, the site gained UNESCO recognition as the Fray Bentos Landscape, Cultural, and Industrial Site (Lewowicz 2016).

A bizarre counterpart to the above recognition is the fragility of biocultural significance of the Andean Condor, a native species that has even been considered a national icon of Chilean unity (Jacques-Coper, Cubillos, and Ibarra 2019). Yet this bird is gradually disappearing from the current worldview of the Aymara people. Although some Chileans may advocate the need to preserve the culture in order to conserve the species, or vice versa, there has been little clarity about what is to be transmitted. The desire to preserve the culture is clouded by uncertainties regarding which cultural domains and practices would be transmitted through the condor's conservation. The decline of the condor population is attributed primarily to variation in the ungulate population (main carrion source) and possibly to climate change. The migratory process that has led to the depopulation of the Andes foothills and the growing influence of Pentecostalism beliefs are also factors that are cited as affecting the integrity of a tradition.

Other examples of a persistent legacy are worth mentioning. The "blood farms" run by the multinational pharmaceutical company Syntex in Argentina and Uruguay are a cogent demonstration of the persistence of the contemporary system of biopower erected on the pillars of colonialism. Today, in both countries, around 10,000 mares are kept for the extraction of equine gonadotropic hormone (ECG), marketed by the animal production industry to stimulate and synchronize heat in sows, sheep, goats, and cattle. More than 10 liters of blood are extracted from each mare during each pregnancy through procedures that are repeated once or twice a week over a period that goes up to twelve weeks. For greater efficiency in the production of ECG, mares are submitted to induced abortions at around the hundredth day of gestation to be newly impregnated. An estimated 20,000 abortions are induced annually (Animal Welfare Foundation 2018).

In their symbolic dimensions, the "blood farms" illustrate the precarious inheritance of colonialism. These "blood farms," intrinsically dependent on a non-human female body, are modeled after the gaucho ranch, where mares are handled by employees who can be identified by their gaucho attire. Clothing, geographic location, and ethnic origin take us back to the traditional culture of men dedicated to rural activity and skilled in horse riding. Handling is mediated by blows and whips. Blows to the vagina and on the head are the expression of the workers' anger and frustration in the face of the resistance of unmanageable animals subjected to stress and fear. In a perverse circle of virulent mistreatment, pregnant mares, terrified and stressed, are paralyzed with fear, resistance, and misunderstanding. In this situation, men's anger and violence rise, and they become harsher in their already extreme punishments and subjugation strategies (Camphora and Castro n/d unpublished manuscript). It is also a gendered system in which expressions and institutions that are associated with the feminine are disqualified, represented as less civilized, more emotional, and instinctive, and therefore as "deserving" of their subordinate condition (Felski 1995).

The resilience of these contemporary practices upholds the global markets of the Anthropocene, through institutional lacunae that sustain asymmetries between Latin American governments and European regulatory systems. It is no coincidence that Argentina and Uruguay are the main exporters of horse meat to the European Union in a market characterized by inadequate identification, lack of traceability, and animal welfare concerns (Ghislain and Martin 2020). Extending questions of justice towards non-human forms of life implies that "we no longer think of 'extinction' without using the category 'life'" (Chakrabarty 2016: 110).

Thus, an environmental history of the Anthropocene endows us with the tools we need to begin to rethink the biodiversity of the Southern Cone from a more inclusive and decolonial perspective. Overseas "exchanges" have been fundamentally asymmetrical and can be more aptly defined as ways of appropriating, exploiting, and often exterminating the natures and first peoples of colonized territories (Kersten 2013; Teletchea 2017). We must now recognize and challenge this persistent legacy, one that is reproduced and re-enacted at diverse cultural and institutional levels within different loci of social, economic, and political relations.

References

Aboglio, Ana M. 2017. "Caballos y políticas de la animalidad. Reflexiones acerca de una etnografía contemporánea." *Revista Latinoamericana de Estudios Críticos Animales* 4, no. 2: 225–252.

Adelman, Miriam, and Ana L. Camphora. 2020. "*Crioulos e crioulistas*: Southern Brazilian equestrian culture in a changing world". In *Horse Breeds and Human Society: Purity, Identity and the Making of the Modern Horse*, ed. Kristen Guest and Monica Mattfeld, 104–120. London: Routledge.

Anderson, Virginia. 2004. *Creatures of Empire: how domestic animals transformed the early America*. Oxford: Oxford University Press.

Anderson, Christopher B., Guillermo M. Pastur, Maria V. Lencinas, et al. 2009. "Do introduced North American beavers *Castor canadensis* engineer differently in southern South America? An overview with implications for restoration." *Mammal Review* 39, no. 1: 33–52.

Animal Welfare Foundation e.V. 2018. *Production of PMSG in Argentina & Uruguay*. Report. Freiburg. https://www.animal-welfare-foundation.org/service/dossiers/production-of-pmsg-in-south-america.

Barbosa, Roberto G. 2017. "Traços de uma contra-história da ciência para uma educação científica crítica: imperialismo e colonialismo." *Ensino & Pesquisa* 15, no. 4: 220–236.

Barrios, Emiliano T. 2020. "Resources, environment, and rural development in Uruguay, 1779–1913." PhD diss., King's College/University of Cambridge.

Bell, Stephen. 2000. "Social networks and innovation in the South American meat industry during the pre-refrigeration era: Southern Brazil and Uruguay in comparison." *Scripta Nova – Revista Electrónica de Geografía y Ciencias Sociales* 69, no. 84.

Brailovski, Antonio. 2009. *Memória Verde*. 8th ed. Buenos Aires: Debolsillo.

Cabral, Diogo de C., and André V. Vital. 2022. "Las fuentes escritas a luz de la noción de coautoría humano-animal." In *Historia ambiental de América Latina Enfoques, procedimientos y cotidianidades*, ed. Pedro S. Urquijo, Adi E. Lazos, and Karine Lefebvre, 275–293. Morelia: UNAM/Centro de Investigaciones en Geografía Ambiental.

Calmon, Pedro. 1958. *História da Casa da Torre*. Rio de Janeiro: José Olympio.

Camphora, Ana L. 2021. *Animals and society in Brazil from the sixteenth to nineteenth centuries*. Cambridgeshire: White Horse Press.

Camphora, Ana L., and David Castro. n/d. "Fazendas de sangue: não olhe para baixo." Unpublished paper.

Caraccioli, Mauro José. 2021. "José de Acosta and the ends of empire." In *Writing the New World: The Politics of Natural History in the Early Spanish Empire*, Mauro José Caraccioli, 103–125. Gainesville: University Press of Florida.

Carey, Mark. 2009. "Latin American Environmental History: Current Trends, Interdisciplinary Insights, and Future Directions." *Environmental History* 14, no. 2: 221–252.

Carvalho, Priscila T. 2021. "A modernidade colonial e o constructo especista-racista." *Revista Latinoamericana de Estudios Críticos Animales* 9, no. 2: 122–135.

Cavalcante, Nelson. 2000. "Os animais do Reino." In *Animais do descobrimento: raças domésticas da história do Brasil*, ed. Nelson Cavalcante and Arthur da Silva Mariante, 28–41. Brasília: EMBRAPA.

Cederholm, Erika A., Amelie Björck, Kristina Jennbert, et al., ed. 2014. *Exploring the Animal Turn Human-Animal Relations in Science, Society and Culture*. Lund: Pufendorfinstitutet.

Cesco, Suzana. 2015. "Meio Ambiente e Fronteira: a exploração dos recursos naturais na fronteira Brasil-Argentina-Uruguai." Paper presented at XXVIII Simpósio Nacional de História – Lugares dos Historiadores: Velhos e Novos Desafios. Florianópolis, SC, June 27–31.

Chakrabarty, Dipesh. 2016. "Whose Anthropocene? Revisiting Dipesh Chakrabarty's 'Four Theses'." *RCC Perspectives* 2: 101–114.

Clarence-Smith, William G. 2020. "Jesuits and mules in colonial Latin America: innovators or managers?." In *Cultural Worlds of the Jesuits in Colonial Latin America*, ed. Linda A. Newson, 209–228. London: University of London Press/Institute of Latin American Studies.

Comissoli, Adriano. 2021. "Reflexões em torno de fronteiras e alteridades voltadas à investigação em história." In *Fronteiras na História: atores sociais e historicidade na construção do Brasil Meridional (séculos XVIII-XX)*, ed. Ânderson M. Schmitt and Murillo Dias Winter, 11–36. Chapecó: Editora UFFS.

Crosby, Alfred W. 1993. *Imperialismo ecológico: A expansão biológica da Europa: 900–1900*. São Paulo: Companhia das Letras.

Darwin, Charles. 1913. *A naturalist's voyage round the world*. London: John Murray, Albermale Street.

Debret, Jean-Baptiste. 1800[?]. *Tamoio Warrior* [painting]. Wikimedia Commons. https://commons.wikimedia.org/wiki/File:Debret2.jpg.

Derrida, Jacques. 2009. *The beast & the sovereign*. Chicago: University of Chicago Press.

Dutra e Silva, Sandro, and Valdir Fernandes. 2022. "Historia y racionalidad ambiental en el lado sombrío de la modernidad." In *Historia ambiental de América Latina Enfoques, procedimientos y cotidianidades*, ed. Pedro S. Urquijo, Adi E. Lazos, and Karine Lefebvre, 61–77. Morelia: UNAM/Centro de Investigaciones en Geografía Ambiental.

Esparza, Joseph. 2021. "A Natural Arch: Ecological Imperialism and the 'Crosby Effect' in American Environmental Historiography." *History in the Making* 14: 235–264.

Felski, Rita. 1995. *The Gender of Modernity*. Cambridge: Harvard University Press.

Flores, Angel. 1942. "El Matadero, Esteban Echeverria." *New Mexico Quarterly* 12, no. 4: 389–405.

Ford, Thayne R. 1998. "Stranger in a Foreign Land: Jose de Acosta's Scientific Realizations in Sixteenth-Century Peru." *The Sixteenth Century Journal* 29, no. 1: 19–33.

Freitas, Décio. 1993. "O capitalismo pastoril." *Ensaios FEE* 14, no. 2: 438–465.

Gabbert, Wolfgang. 2012. "The longue durée of Colonial Violence in Latin America." *Historical Social Research / Historische Sozialforschung* 37, no. 3: 254–275.

Ghislain, Stephanie, and Iwona Mertin. 2020. "From stable to fork: EU Horse Meat Imports." Report, Eurogroup for Animals. Ed. Hugh Barton-Smith. Brussels.

Giacomasso, María V., and Rafael P. Curtoni 2017. "Patrimonio y paisaje cultural rankülche. La relación pasado-presente en la construcción de 'Pueblo Ranquel'." *Intersecciones en Antropología* 18: 233–244.

Herrera, Guillermo C. 2021. "Nature in the Midst of Crisis and Development in Latin America: An interview with Guilliermo Herrera Castro by Sandro Dutra e Silva and Claudio de Majo." *Global Environment* 14: 406–421.

Herrera, Lorena, Carlos Nabinger, Federico Weyland, et al. 2014. "Caracterización de los Pastizales del Cono Sur, servicios ecosistémicos y problemática actual de conservación." In *Índice de Contribución a la Conservación de Pastizales Naturales del Cono Sur. Una herramienta para incentivar a los productores rurales*, ed. Aníbal Parera, Inés Paullier, and Federico Weyland, 21–39. Montevideo: Aves Uruguay.

Jacques-Coper, Andrés, Guillermo Cubillos, and José Tomás Ibarra. 2019. "The Andean Condor as bird, authority, and devil: an empirical assessment of the biocultural keystone species concept in the high Andes of Chile." *Ecology and Society* 24, no. 2.

Jones, Emily Lena, William Taylor, Juan Bautista Belardi, et al. 2019. "Caballos y humanos en el Nuevo Mundo: investigaciones arqueológicas en América del Norte y perspectivas para Argentina." *Anales de Arqueología y Etnologia* 74, no. 2: 247–268.

Kelly, Jason M. 2018. "Anthropocenes: A Fractured Picture." In *Rivers of the Anthropocene*, ed. Jason M. Kelly, Philip Scarpino, Helen Berry, et al., 1–18. Berkeley: University of California Press.

Kersten, Jens. 2013. "The Enjoyment of Complexity: A New Political Anthropology for the Anthropocene?." *RCC Perspectives, Anthropocene: Envisioning the Future of the Age of Humans* 3: 39–56.

Lamim-Guedes, Valdir. 2018. "Species of the Brazilian flora and its uses in the 19th century in 'plantas usuais dos Brasileiros' by Auguste de Saint-Hilaire." *Fronteiras: Journal of Social, Technological and Environmental Science* 7, no. 1: 202–228.

Leal, Ondina. 1989. "The Gauchos: male culture and identity in the Pampas." PhD diss., University of California at Berkeley.

Leite, Bruno M. 2015. "Os animais brasileiros na cultura europeia da época moderna de Thevet a Redi." In *Representações da fauna no Brasil – séculos XVI-XX*, ed. Lorelay Kury, 40–82. Rio de Janeiro: Andrea Jakobsson Estúdios.

Lewowicz, Lucia. 2016. *Lemco: Un colosso de la industria cárnica en Fray Bentos, Uruguay.* Montevideo: INAC.

Llored, Patrick. 2016. "O outro feminismo (a inventar) de Derrida: as implicações éticas e políticas do carnofalogocentrismo." *Revista Trágica: estudos de filosofia da imanência* 9, no. 2: 61–76.

Mansilla, Lucio V. 2003. *Una excursión a los indios Ranqueles.* Biblioteca Virtual Universal.

Menegat, Carla. 2021. "Dos cruzamentos e das fronteiras: projetos individuais e trajetória nacional – relações Brasil-Uriguai no século XIX." In *Fronteiras na História: atores sociais e historicidade na construção do Brasil Meridional (séculos XVIII-XX)*, ed. Ânderson M. Schmitt and Murillo Dias Winter, 191–211. Chapecó: Editora UFFS.

Meijer, Eva, and Bernice Bovenkerk. 2021. "Taking animal perspectives into account in animal ethics." In *Animals in our Midst: the Challenges of Co-existing with Animals in the Anthropocene*, ed. Bernice Bovenkerk and Jozef Keulartz, 49–64. Cham: Springer.

Parera, Anibal, Ínes Paullier, and Federico Weyland. 2014. *Índice de Contribución a la Conservación de Pastizales Naturales del Cono Sur. Una herramienta para incentivar a los productores rurales.* Montevideo: Aves Uruguay.

Palermo, Miguel A. 1986. "Reflexiones sobre el llamado 'complejo ecuestre' en la Argentina" *Runa* 16: 157–178.

Poyer, Viviane. 2021. "Fronteiras do contestado: imigração e política internacional em meio a uma guerra no Brasil Meridional." In *Fronteiras na História: atores sociais e historicidade na construção do Brasil Meridional (séculos XVIII-XX)*, ed. Ânderson M. Schmitt and Murillo Dias Winter, 442–464. Chapecó: Editora UFFS.

Saint-Hilaire, Auguste de. 2002. *Viagem ao Rio Grande do Sul.* Trad. Adroaldo Mesquita da Costa. Brasília: Senado Federal.

Sennett, Richard. 2009. *O Artífice.* Rio de Janeiro: Record.

Teletchea, Fabrice. 2017. "Wildlife conservation: is domestication a solution?." In *Global Exposition of Wildlife Management*, ed. Lameed Gbolagade Akeem. London: IntechOpen.

Turner, Frederick. 1990. *O espírito ocidental contra a natureza.* Rio de Janeiro: Campus.

UNESCO. n.d. "Jesuit Missions of the Guaranis: San Ignacio Mini, Santa Ana, Nuestra Señora de Loreto and Santa Maria Mayor (Argentina), Ruins of Sao Miguel das Missoes (Brazil)." https://whc.unesco.org/en/list/275/documents/.

Urquijo, Pedro S. 2022. "Consideraciones para una aproximación a la historia ambiental." *Historia ambiental de América Latina Enfoques, procedimientos y cotidianidades*, ed. Pedro S. Urquijo, Adi E. Lazos, and Karine Lefebvre, 22–41. Morelia: UNAM/Centro de Investigaciones en Geografía Ambiental.

Valle, Ivonne del. 2013. "From José de Acosta to the Enlightenment: Barbarians, Climate Change, and (Colonial) Technology as the End of History." *The Eighteenth Century* 54, no. 4: 435–459.

Vander Velden, Felipe. 2015. "Os animais domésticos europeus na América Portuguesa." In *Representações da fauna no Brasil – séculos XVI–XX*, ed. Lorelay Kury, 12–81. Rio de Janeiro: Andrea Jakobsson Estúdios.

Biodiversity in the Andes in the Colonial Period
Livestock and Biodiversity after the Spanish Conquest

Aliocha Maldavsky and Marina Zuloaga Rada

The European invasion of America in the late fifteenth century and the conquest of large territories of the continent led to the introduction of Eurasian and African animals and plants, generating changes in the American biota and environment whose effects on *stricto sensu* biodiversity have not been precisely identified. According to the field in which the concept is used, there are several definitions of biodiversity (Núñez, González Gaudiano, and Barahona 2003). It is "the property of living systems to be different, that is to say different from each other. It is not an entity, a resource, but a property or characteristic of nature" (Solbrig 1994). To this simple definition, it is necessary to add another dimension, indicating that "the concept involves the measurement of biotic richness in a given space and time" (Toledo 1994: 45). In this sense, this chapter focuses on the colonial period and the Andes, the approximate space dominated by the Incas and which under European rule constituted the Peruvian viceroyalty that roughly covers the current countries of Peru, Bolivia, Ecuador, Chile, and northern Argentina.

With the arrival of Europeans, the Andean territory was one of the most bioculturally diverse areas in the Americas. It undoubtedly resulted from the ecological heterogeneity of the Andean physical environment with its altitudinal microclimates, the diversity of its watersheds, and the marine currents along its coastline that generated particular climatic effects. Based on this biodiversity, anthropic action over the millennia domesticated a very wide variety of plants (about 180, including corn, various tubers, potatoes, beans, squash, etc.) and animals such as camelids, dogs, guinea pigs, and a variety of ducks that allowed the development of their ancient civilization. The Spanish chroniclers echoed the conquistadors' surprise and admiration in discovering the agricultural techniques (irrigation and terraces) and Andean pastoral development.

To paraphrase McNeill (2003: 23–26), the sixteenth century in Peru and the Americas was exceptional in terms of the magnitude of the changes and the intense human effort that brought them about. In the Andes, the Columbian Exchange (Crosby 1991) definitely involved, in addition to the exploitation of Andean agropastoral wealth by the Spaniards, the introduction of the main crops and animals of their agricultural inventory: the trilogy of wheat, grapevines, and olives – essential in the Mediterranean diet and culture – beans, bananas, and sugarcane, among others, as well as European livestock of varying size (equines, sheep, cattle, goats, pigs, gallinaceans) that demonstrated great ability to adapt and transform the local ecosystems. Other commensal (rats) and pathogenic species (malaria-carrying anopheline mosquitos), viruses, and bacteria, which wreaked havoc on unimmunized Indigenous human and animal populations, were also introduced (Gade 2015). This chapter will focus particularly on the effects of the relatively rapid expansion of Eurasian livestock, a topic that will help to better illustrate these changes.

While having many points in common with the other American spaces, the introduction of livestock to the Andes acquired original features. First, the Andean space was the only one in all of America with a millennial pastoral tradition that, like the Hispanic, functioned as a complementary strategy to agriculture. In addition to the presence of wild camelids (guanacos and vicuñas), archaeology testifies to an ancient tradition of llama and alpaca breeding, crucial in the pre-Hispanic Andean economy to carry out the exchanges of goods structured by the complementarity of the Andean ecological floors (Murra 1972) and as producers of meat, wool, and manure.

Second, the Andean area became a crucial mining center for the local and world economy (Assadourian 1982). In the twentieth century, Assadourian's model of the Potosí-centric colonial economy was consistent with that of Wallerstein known as the world economy or capitalist world-system. In the first decades of the twenty-first century, a new interpretive paradigm, the ecology-world system (Moore 2020), emphasized how this productive system appropriates nature and "co-produces it (both human and animal nature, plant, etc.), putting it at the service of accumulation" or "creates an ecology that expands along the planet across borders, driven by forces of infinite accumulation" (Molinero and Avalone 2020). The paradigmatic case of Potosí has allowed Moore to suggest the use of the term Capitalocene versus Anthropocene, assigning the capitalist system (gestated in the West and by a capitalist economic sector) – and not to the human species as a whole – responsibility for the acceleration of ecological deterioration and changes in the biosphere. In the Potosí boom, fundamental to the nascent world capitalist system, livestock were key for providing food, energy, transport, and raw materials. Livestock intensification created by mining (which took on an unprecedented scale) caused changes not only in biota and ecosystems, but also in the economic and social strategies of Indigenous and European people.

The chapter is organized into four sections that allow the reader to appreciate the trajectories of these biotic organisms introduced by the Spaniards. The first (1530–1550) focuses on showing the role that Andean and European livestock played in the defeat of the Incas. The second (1550–1600) historizes the unstoppable expansion of European livestock in the different Andean ecosystems and their importance in Hispanic colonization strategies. Although Indigenous and European livestock played a fundamental role in the cycles of conquest and colonization, many topics have not been precisely detailed for Peru: the stages and rates of introduction of the various Eurasian species, their effects and interaction with the Indigenous species, the way in which they were acclimatized (finding their particular ecological and productive niches), the uneven way in which they developed in the field, and the logics and interests that were behind the implementation and development of this utilization in the various situations that took place during that century. The modalities of European animal introduction followed the evolution of the forming colonial economy and society and the availability of Indigenous labor. With the mining boom in Potosí, livestock played an extremely important role in the colonial economy, a topic addressed in the third section of this chapter. Finally, particular attention is paid to the introduction of European livestock into Indigenous communities, a subject scarcely developed by historiography. In this last section, it is shown how the Indigenous population became familiar with foreign livestock, the mechanisms employed by the Crown and the Spanish settlers to induce them to breed, and the motivations that led to the development of European livestock becoming one of the fundamental bases for their corporate economy. Andean communities quickly adopted sheep, goats, and cattle, adapting their customs and livestock management to the new context.

Livestock and Conquest

Among domesticated animals in the Andes, ducks, dogs, guinea pigs, camelids, alpacas, and llamas were the most characteristic species of Andean civilization. Their domestication is dated between 4,600 and 4,000 years before present (Mengoni Golaños and Yacobaccio 2006). According to archaeology and zooarchaeology, llamas and alpacas come from two other camelids, the vicuña and the guanaco, which remained wild but were commonly hunted and captured for meat, fibers, and leather. Apparently, when Europeans arrived, the laminoids were numerous. Llamas functioned as pack animals, sources of fiber, and food. On the other hand, alpacas provided a higher quality fiber. The expansion of this livestock would have settled particularly during the period of the Incas who "created state herds, also promulgating a legal fiction according to which all the laminoids became state property" (Murra 1975: 160). A systematic methodology in the selection and reproduction processes took into account color, age, and sex to improve the species according to the needs of the rulers and the population, as chroniclers such as Cobo and Garcilaso de la Vega attest (Bustinza et al. 2021). The expansion of state livestock accompanied that of the empire, intensifying livestock production, whose development was carefully managed with *quipus* (knotted tally cords used as recording devices). Its textile (wool, fabrics) and food (*charqui*, a type of jerky) derivatives were abundant in the coves or warehouses located near the administrative and political centers of Tahuantinsuyu and along the *Qapac ñan* road network, where the Incas concentrated goods and food for their armies and their servants, as well as for their reciprocity and redistribution ceremonies (Murra 1975).

The process of laminoid expansion and occupation in the Andean territories from their (multiple) domestication areas is not clear (Goepfert et al. 2020). Although with a distinct occupation of space, they were present throughout the territory of Tahuantinsuyu at the time of the conquest. They had accompanied the Incas on their military expeditions, feeding the armies and moving provisions and weapons; and the flocks were strategically arranged at the border posts, according to the mid-sixteenth century chronicler Cieza de León (Borchart 1995: 155). The Incas would have introduced the breeding of state livestock farms to intensify livestock production that would revert into taxation and resources. This imperial economic strategy consisted of placing *mitimae* settlers in the territory of present-day Ecuador, where livestock were concentrated in the areas of greatest Inca presence (Bonavia 1996: 276–319; Borchart 1995). In the high altitudes of the Andean South, llamas and alpacas were indispensable capital for exchanging goods and ensuring social status. State herds were selected for slaughter at Andean ceremonies (Murra 1975).

Chroniclers document the presence of llamas and alpacas, "livestock of the land" or "sheep" or "rams of the land," as the Spaniards called them, throughout Tahuantinsuyu. Even in the first contact on the northern coast of Peru, the rams of the land surprised the conquerors. In Cajamarca, Cieza notes the wealth of the villages "full of maintenance, of precious clothing, with other wealth, many herds of sheep" (cited by Borchart 1995: 161), and Hernando Pizarro observed the same in the adjoining area of Callejón de Huaylas in his expedition to Cuzco. In the central area, native livestock were numerous in the Junín highlands, the Titicaca area, and the southern Andean highlands, where their density was evident in the 1530s and during the sixteenth century. The speculative calculations of Jesús Lara (1966: 253) are usually mentioned (repeated), a quantity of 23 million llamas and 7 million alpacas in the Tahuantinsuyu. This does not allow an accurate assessment of the total number of animals (Bonavia 1996: 331), so it is impossible to see the effects of conquest on the size of the laminoid population.

Historians, biologists, and zootechnicians highlight the drastic fall that would have occurred in this population during the first decades of the conquest. They see this decline as one of the most important effects in assessing the environmental impact of European contact. This decrease is explained by the killing and looting of conquest and civil wars and the intensive and forced uses of livestock in this juncture of great military movements before and after the conquest (Bustinza et al. 2021). It also evokes the policy of "scorched earth" at the beginning of conquest and indiscriminate hunting simply for hobby or sport (Borchart 1995: 163). In multiple passages, the chronicler Cieza de León notes the desolation that Spaniards provoked in the livestock of the land (*The Chronicle of Peru*, Chapter CXI). Girolamo Benzoni characterized the Spanish as the leprosy that had almost completely destroyed the Andean livestock (Borchart 1995: 162). For this initial period, the competition of European animals must be minimized or eliminated, since their introduction would have occurred first slowly and then more rapidly from the second half of the sixteenth century.

The conquistadors depended on Andean livestock. On every route to Cuzco through the northern mountains and Pachacamac, Hernando Pizarro received abundant indigenous livestock (Bonavia 1996: 299). This dependency is evidenced by the record the Jauja *caciques* made in their quipus of the property that was taken by force (*rancheados*) or voluntarily surrendered to their allies, the Spanish conquistadors, between the years 1533 to 1548 (Espinoza 1971; Murra 1975; Assadourian 1995; Scott 2005). In fifteen years, the careful accounting of the Huanca had recorded the delivery of 4,352 camelids (plus 930 on the way out), 12,168 rams for consumption (plus fourteen on the way out), sixty lambs, 161 pigs, and 456 hens; as well, they had forcibly taken 46,503 sheep, rams, and llamas; some chickens; and many eggs (Murra 1975). This bloodletting of livestock was also seen in Cuzco after the city was retaken by the Spanish after the encirclement of 1536, when there was a shortage of food, particularly meat (Bonavia 1996: 341). Disease also decimated the camelids. Some qualitative assessments indicate that before 1550 in an outbreak of scabies, or *carache* as the Indians called it, much of the native livestock would have perished (Bustinza et al. 2021: 5; Bonavia 1996: 353). According to Garcilaso de la Vega (1976: 184), this plague "dispatched, with great wonder and terror of Indians and Spaniards, two thirds of the livestock of varying size, llama, and guanaco." According to Sumar, this mortality was due to the neglect of camelid upbringing, since this disease already existed in the time of the Incas (1997: 212, 214).

The conquistadors were accompanied from the beginning by domesticated European animals that, for the first time, encountered domesticated South American animals. Like the Andean inhabitants, the Iberians were part of a millennial farming culture. The Spanish monarchy explicitly and legally protected all livestock in Castile without distinction since the thirteenth century. To defend their interests and with royal support, the ranchers joined the Mesta, a supracommunal association, which would have a starring role in Castilian economic and social life throughout the Early Modern Age. Over time, the privileges granted by the Crown to this association focused on transhumant livestock (glens, pastures) and the expansion of the merino industry: privileged by the Crown that maintained a strict monopoly on its management, as the fine wool was exported to European textile markets at great benefit to producers and the king's coffers. In the sixteenth century, this activity came under severe pressure from the decline of common pastures due to population growth and consequent agrarian expansion, which destabilized in the peninsula the precarious balance between livestock and agrarian uses (Melón Jiménez 2004).

It was at this juncture in Iberia that livestock and many of the associated norms, culture, and institutions began to be exported to America. In Peru, the meeting between Andean and Hispanic livestock species could be symbolically located at the exact moment of Indo-Spanish contact in these territories and is shown in the first gift exchange from representatives of both agropastoral societies, a metaphor for the Columbian Exchange. In 1528, during Pizarro's second voyage, when the Isla del Gallo conquistadors sighted the first Indigenous "city" from their boat, some Indians came out on their rafts to meet the strange newcomers carrying with them exquisite delicacies such as fruits, fish, drinks, and, among them, a lamb. In return, Pizarro gave the presiding noble man of the embassy a sow, a boar, four European hens, and a rooster (Cieza de León 1987: 53–54).

Three European species stand out in the conquest process: dogs, equines (mainly horses), and pigs, animals indispensable in any conquering campaign. The powerful Spanish bulldog that accompanied the conquistadors had mostly warrior functions. In the offensive, they rounded up enemies and were used to punish or kill Indians who did not obey the Spanish. In the defensive field, they were excellent lookouts, helping in the exploration of territories. In the rear, they guarded pig herds and other supplies and their fine hearing and sense of smell prevented possible ambushes. In times of famine, they were excellent supplies of protein for the Spanish, whether from hunting animals or their own meat. Gonzalo Pizarro took almost a thousand on his exploration in the Cinnamon Country that, at critical moments, were almost entirely eaten. The Crown, alerted by critics of the conquest, issued in 1541 a ballot addressed to Pizarro and Vaca de Castro forbidding cruel execution by dogs (Piqueras 2006; Bueno Jiménez 2011).

Equine livestock was in high demand in the conquest (the conquest's vanguard), in the Peruvian civil wars between Almagro and Pizarro and in the rebellion of Gonzalo Pizarro. Essential for war, horses were also a source of prestige and power. Their "import" was very expensive. The cost was nine hundred pesos in 1535 and still almost six hundred in 1567 (Ramírez 1991: 33). The cycle of horses reduced in the second half of the sixteenth century. However, their importance manifests itself in the periphery of the viceroyalty, in the extensive pampas surrounding Buenos Aires where, after the failed foundation of 1534, horses were abandoned or escaped. They multiplied in the pampas and occupied vast spaces spreading over a larger area, shaping the landscape and transforming the economy, the material culture and the lives of the populations that inhabited these territories (Pedrotta 2016).

Another essential animal species in the conquest were swine (Del Río 1996: 13–29). Fundamental to the Peninsular diet, the pig was a Christian cultural symbol against Muslims (Gade 1987). The success of the conquest would not have been possible without the incorporation of swine herds in the army's routes. They offered many advantages: their cost was reduced by their rapid acclimatization, high reproductive capacity, and their spread in American territories. They required little care and scarce manpower. Being omnivores, pigs could be fed under any circumstances. By the 1530s, at the time of the conquest of Peru, Granada, and León, Nicaragua's main colonial centers, had become pig supply centers that exported to Peru via Panama (Del Río 1996: 22). They expanded through the lands near the first cities founded in Peru in the 1530s and, although their diet was based on the natural plants of the countryside, their upbringing was, according to Fray Vicente de Valverde, as if they ate acorn. According to other testimonies, better bacon and *pernil* were produced in the mountains than in Castile (Del Río 1996: 26). In 1536 in the barely founded Lima, a pig was slaughtered daily. For reasons of hygiene it had been prohibited by the ordinances to have pigs in houses (Del Río 1996: 28). In 1538, the Cabildo of Quito forbade the residents to have more than ten heads for their consumption, and in 1541, it was able to deliver Gonzalo Pizarro about 3,000 for his expedition to the Cinnamon Country (Del Río 1996: 17). Although the abundance of these livestock at times favored their lower relative cost, prices fluctuated due to the instability generated by the cycles of wars in Peru. According to Del Río, prices were reduced from 675 *maravedís* for an *arrelde* (1,820 kg) in 1536 to 337 in January 1538 and three months later to 280. However, the price increased again due first to the civil wars and then to the increased demand from the urban and mining markets.

The Expansion of European Livestock in the Second Half of the Sixteenth Century

The relative stability that occurred in the Peruvian viceroyalty in the 1550s shifted the role of dogs and horses to the background. Other species began to play a fundamental role in the colonization processes of the second half of the sixteenth century. Undoubtedly, this period saw the introduction, development, and multiplication of European livestock take on more intensity, acceleration, and expansion. The initiatives of the Hispanic population living in Peru and the Indigenous population contributed to the generalization of European species. The efforts of the Spaniards to expand their livestock herds were favored by cultural inclinations, the logics of economic and commercial gain (the demand for products from the mining and urban economy), and the policies of the Crown. Indeed, Europeans wanted to reproduce their way of life and diet, a factor of body transformation and social distinction (Earle 2012; Saldarriaga 2012). Indigenous people had to shore up their economy in the new colonial context by adapting new species to their social reproduction strategies. Traditional Castilian livestock, whether small (sheep and goats but also pigs) or large (bovines and equines, e.g., donkeys and mules, as well as horses and oxen), expanded unevenly in the Andean territories. These animals were transcendental in the strategies of appropriation and exploitation of the resources of the various territories that made up the vast space controlled by the viceroys of Peru. Their development involved productive, legal, environmental, and social aspects and, of course, affected not only the biodiversity and competition between livestock, but also the lives and relationships of the various populations living together in Peru.

In the second half of the sixteenth century, the Crown sought to take control of power and the direction of colonization. Its policies directly and indirectly impacted livestock expansion. This was produced in stages in response to the different situations that would push livestock production. There were three fundamental milestones in this process during the sixteenth century. The first was the policy of decreasing *encomienda* rates in the 1550s and 60s, which pushed encomiendas to focus on business activity, causing increased demand and livestock production. The second was the implementation of Indigenous reductions in the 1570s which, by concentrating the diminished Indigenous population in delimited villages, left "free" spaces that the Spaniards occupied with their livestock. The third was the implementation of the first land compositions in the 1590s which, by granting firm property rights to the initially precarious European occupiers, sealed their expansion.

Among the factors that converged and favored livestock expansion in the 1550s and 1560s were the monarch's alliance with the religious aligned with Bartolomé de Las Casas to eliminate or substantially reduce the personal service of the Indians; the strong economic boost promoted by enterprises (all of them demanding livestock) on the part of Spanish *encomenderos* and settlers; and the policy of restitution. This effort by the authorities to abolish personal service and the demographic decline caused by wars and diseases had an indirect effect on livestock demand. One solution to this problem was to replace much of the human energy provided by Indians with animal energy, which was essential to expand the economy and make its investments profitable. It was in this context that the acclimatization of African camelids in Peru was attempted without lasting success, with the mule eventually becoming the most efficient means for transport. The importer, the trader Cebrián de Caritate, justified his request to the Crown to license the introduction of camels "because they were very necessary for the service of the land, since there was no longer personal service there" (Taboada 2017: 193–195).

The encomienda crisis in the 1550s due to the defeat of the encomenderos, commanded first by Gonzalo Pizarro and then by Hernández Girón, prompted the expansion of European livestock. The Crown's disciplinary policies and the limitation of its income (reduction in the appraisal of goods and money) forced encomenderos to compensate for losses by setting up new enterprises. This indirectly encouraged livestock, as they sought alternative profits through various ventures they had already started in the previous decades. They had the advantages of knowledge of the terrain, direct relationships with the caciques, and the possibility of access to the increasingly scarce workforce. With the demographic decline of these decades, the encomenderos obtained – almost without cost – the land to set up their *obrajes* (workshops), expand their livestock herds, build mills, and sow cereals, vineyards, and olive groves (by purchase, *mercedes* [grants], or illegally). A favorable market and a demand to replace costly imports further enhanced these business initiatives.

The main areas in which they invested were mining, agriculture, ranching, and manufacturing (sugar mills and textile manufacturing), increasing the production and expansion of livestock. In addition to enterprises specializing in the production and marketing of livestock, textile obrajes, whose main input was wool as raw material, and transport businesses that profited from the use of bulk animals, other business activities required varying degrees of animal power and derivatives to be able to produce their goods: agriculture demanded oxen, mules, horses, and animal fertilizers; mining and sugarcane production used oxen and/or mules to operate mills; mules and llamas for the movement of materials and products circulating in these extensive productive units; meat from various animals was necessary for the feeding of workers; and many of their derivatives (leathers, candles, etc.) were essential for furnishing homes and for production itself (Assadourian 1982; Moore 2020).

One of the mechanisms through which the encomenderos tried to encourage the breeding of European livestock, usually sheep, in Indian villages was restitution. Pressured by Dominican religious in the 1550s and 1560s, encomenderos made donations and *obras pías* (pious works) as restitution (Maldavsky 2019; Fulcrand Terrisse 2004: 76–82). This was to compensate for thefts committed during the conquests or excesses in the collection of tribute. The religious, who demanded restitution in exchange for acquittal, participated in the obras pías created to manage the restored livestock. In 1562, the encomendero of Pocsi, near Arequipa, Alonso de Cáceres, restored 200 sheep from Castile to the Indians of his encomienda, leaving the management of the herd to his heir and the prior of the Franciscans of Arequipa. Gómez de Solís, ten years after reimbursing money in 1552 for having collected too much tribute from the Indians of the region of Trujillo, organized an obra pía similar to that of Cáceres, but with 3,000 sheep and 200 cattle distributed between the encomiendas of Tapacarí and Huamachuco (Del Río 2005: 223). In the highlands, Lorenzo de Aldana, encomendero of Paria, donated more than 2,000 sheep and about 250 cattle to found two hospitals, entrusted to various religious orders, for the Indians of his encomienda in 1557 (Del Río 2005: 22). He also agreed with the Augustinians to keep four religious in charge and gave them 300 sheep and 200 llamas, in addition to a lifetime stipend of 1,000 pesos that would exempt the Indians and the encomendero from making any payment to the religious in charge of evangelization. Ten years later, in 1568, Aldana organized a hospitable obra pía entrusted exclusively to the Augustinians. In the region of Huamanga, the encomendero Hernán Guillén de Mendoza, owner of a construction site, stipulated in his 1594 will that 300 sheep from Castile, out of the 9,000 he owned, be given to the Indians of his encomienda (Salas de Coloma 1998: 75–82).

This imposition of European livestock on the Indigenous population in the 1550s and 1560s coincided with the expansion of Spanish ranches. It was in the northern area that European livestock expanded most rapidly, particularly pigs, goats, sheep, and, to a lesser extent, cows. In the mountains near Lima (Huaylas, Conchucos, Cajatambo, Canta, Huánuco), sheep production provided wool to the booming textile sector that expanded in these areas to meet the growing demand of the urban and mining sectors (Silva Santisteban 1964; Salas 1998; León 2002; Chocano 2016a; Chocano 2016b). The coast specialized in the exploitation of pigs, sheep, and goats to produce meat and some processed materials such as soap, tallow, hides, and *cordobanes* at a lower price than those imported from Europe, selling them in the markets of Lima and Panama. The encomenderos of the north coast had chosen to invest in ranches since 1550 primarily due to their low cost (Schlüpmann 2022; Aldana 1989; Ramírez 1991). The scarce labor they required was cheap, and the ranches occupied vacant land, whose use, while not giving them legal rights, allowed them the "de facto" appropriation of the property of corrals built to fence in livestock (Ramírez 1991: 65). Excessive prices for animal products imported from the Peninsula and increasing demand from urban markets in Trujillo and Potosí were additional incentives to invest in livestock farming. On the other hand, livestock investment did not require great dedication. Encomenderos appeared once a year to round up and mark the animals (Ramírez 1991: 63-64).

The policy of reductions introduced in the 1570s by Viceroy Toledo intensified livestock farming. While the reductions in principle did not involve the loss of land by the Indians, the concentration of the Indigenous population led to the abandonment of land and facilitated its use by the Spanish. In the case of Lambayeque, the movement of Indigenous peoples to the lower areas of the valleys displaced them to less productive areas due to unfavorable climatic conditions, less fertile land, and water scarcity. The best land was left available to the Spaniards, which generated a sharp increase in agricultural and livestock production (Ramírez 1991:96). Toledo granted *mita* workers at the request of the ranchers (Zuloaga 2012; Zuloaga 2022). Livestock activity increased and expanded in scale and complexity. The ranches in Lambayeque incorporated manufacturing processes to produce soap and hides, becoming livestock-industrial complexes that required a larger labor force and more specialized workers (Ramírez 1991: 100−101). In the mountainous areas, the increase in livestock production after Toledo is apparent in the visit of Archbishop Mogrovejo in 1593, according to which, in Conchucos and Huaylas, ranches and wool textile obrajes predominated over agricultural farms. As many as seventy ranches existed in Huaylas, the two largest having 20,000 and 12,000 heads respectively and the smallest ones only 15. Livestock ownership was widely distributed among large (prominent encomenderos and residents), medium, and small Spanish encomenderos and residents, as well as mixed-race and Indian owners, especially caciques and principals, but also commoners. Indigenous institutions (the community, its churches, poor people's houses, and hospitals) and a Dominican convent were financed by their livestock (Zuloaga 2012). In the region of Conchucos, caciques and principals had established eight chaplaincies based on sheep farming, and even one common Indian, Inés Truzopampa, owned her own sheep farm (Chocano 2016: 118, 128).

In the mid-1590s, the policy of land composition served the Crown to legalize the lands occupied "de facto" by the ranchers and to enable them to acquire others by paying financial compensation to the Royal Treasury. From occupiers they became owners. In Lambayeque, this process generated a great boom in agriculture to the detriment of livestock that went into crisis in the late sixteenth and early seventeenth centuries due to various factors: the fact that the titles of composition did not include property rights over pastures and forests, the growth of the fiscal costs of the sale of livestock, the complaints of Spanish and Indigenous farmers, and the decrease in the prices of soap and tallow. The crisis was resolved by restructuring livestock, replacing pigs with goats that required less investment, expanding the production scale by merging several ranches into one, the diversification of production within ranches, and the conditioning of part of the land for cultivation (Ramírez 1991: 119–144).

In the Andean South, the expansion of European livestock and the colonial importance of the Andean region played key roles in strengthening the main pole of world economic growth in the sixteenth century: Potosí, where mining activity required livestock intensification.

Livestock and the Rise of the Colonial Mining Economy: Potosí and the Andean South (1570–1600)

Mining was increasingly livestock dependent in the second period of colonial exploitation of Potosí when Viceroy Toledo, in the early 1570s, promoted the industrial system of amalgamation for silver refinement, while establishing the mining mita to ensure labor. At the end of the sixteenth century the Potosí mine produced about 74 percent of the world's silver (Machado and Rossi 2017).

In the 1970s and 1980s, Assadourian demonstrated the modernity of the colonial economy, when most historians were denouncing its dependence, backwardness, and feudality. Peruvian colonial economic space formed a dynamic and commoditized domestic market. The various productive regions specialized and provided a multiplicity of products to the mining and urban markets of the viceroyalty's large territory. Trade, through maritime and land transport, supported by animal energy, linked this space with the external market. It allowed Peruvian silver to flow throughout the Americas, across the Peninsula, Europe, and Asia (Assadourian 1982). According to the world-ecology paradigm, the boom in Potosí was based not only on the application of technological innovations and labor systems but also on "a global mode of appropriation of vital energies" (Machado 2017: 43). Livestock exploitation proved fundamental in this first phase of the accumulation of early modern capitalism and world-ecology.

The incorporation of products, animals, and new techniques required in economic specializations significantly affected the biota and abiotic resources in which they operated. Large-scale mining in Potosí, one of the world's most populous urban centers, required the adoption of complex economic and socio-environmental strategies and technologies, involving the construction of large infrastructure works, government technologies, massive supply systems for goods and services, the coercive use of human and animal labor, as well as complex intellectual and legal constructions to justify the system (Machado 2017: 38–39). There were processes of land transfers from Indigenous to Hispanic people (Assadourian 1982) and material and energy exchanges between both rural and urban areas and different parts of the Americas, Europe, and the East (Moore 2020). In all these processes, Indigenous people and native and newly introduced European livestock played a leading role. Animals were essential to mining, producing material for both mineral exploitation and the urban population, and transporting goods.

Around 8,000 llamas transported the ore from the hilltop mines to the Potosí mills where amalgamation was carried out (Contreras 2021; Moore 2020). The installation of hydraulic or animal-driven mills industrialized ore milling. Of the 111 in Potosí at the end of the sixteenth century, a quarter required the energy of oxen, horses, or mules (Salas et al. 2022: 5–6). Feeding livestock was a challenge given the decline of pastures in nearby areas and the increasing cost of fodder (Contreras 2021, 81).

Many of the necessary inputs came from livestock exploitation: leather for transporting mercury and ore or used as hinges and shock absorbers in machinery, tallow for candles that lit galleries, or manure used as fuel. The growing urban population depended directly and indirectly on livestock products. With 120,000 inhabitants in 1570 and 160,000 in 1610, Potosí became one of the largest urban centers of the time, outgrowing Venice, Seville, Amsterdam, or London (Machado 2017: 41). Housing required leather furniture, cordobanes, and candles. People fed on local and European livestock meat (lard, chickens, guinea pigs), among other products. Soap came from converting tallow into detergent, and obrajes produced large-scale textiles with sheep and alpaca wool (Assadourian 1982: 179–189). In 1603, 2,000 llamas and 1,000 sheep entered weekly, and annually, 4,000 cattle and 1,200 Indians produced coal and candles. The mining mita nurtured this mobilization of people (estimated about 60,000); each mita worker moved with his family and llamas that could carry necessities and provide a source of food (Moore 2020: 133–134).

In the colonial economic system, the intensity of traffic and the difficulty of moving products in the Andean topography made transport a strategic activity. Moving mercury, salt, and other amalgamation inputs in Potosi; transporting silver to the rest of Peru, the Americas, and the world; and the growing trade in products demanded by mining and urban markets all required intensified land traffic. This was based on the intensive use of indigenous and foreign animals and was highly dependent on road infrastructure and the wisdom of Andean shepherds and llama herders (Assadourian 1982; Moore 2020; Sánchez Albornoz 2020; Gabelmann 2015: 35–36).

The geopolitical importance of the routes used for the transfer of the mercury and silver sparked the Crown's interest to ensure its control and optimal functioning. Towards the last third of the sixteenth century, the authorities arranged more efficient and safer routes for transfers, Viceroy Toledo opting for a route through the port of Arica. The logistics of these trips were complex but saved distance and time (Contreras 2021; Orche and Amaré 2015). In the port of Arica, large animal reserves (more than 2,000 mules and 12,000 llamas in the first third of the seventeenth century) were needed to carry the goods received to Potosi. Being a very dry area, pastures were used more than 200 km away, which created serious problems of synchronizing with the boats. For most of the sixteenth century, there was a favorable cultural disposition towards the breeding and use of llamas, since they were abundant and cheap (Orché and Amaré 2015). They came from communal farms in the high Aymara Andean regions. The demand for their animals and their services as llama herders placed the Indians of these communities in a strategic position, since they were incorporated into the intense commercial traffic that was created between the Potosí-Huancavelica and Potosí-Lima axes. Many Aymara caciques reconciled commercial activities and new economic opportunities with their traditional duties to their communities. Aymara llama herders knew the dietary, physiological, and rest needs of this livestock (Orche and Amaré 2015). However, traffic intensity decreased as demand increased, making trade more expensive. Llamas died from tiredness and lack of pasture and water, as well as from diseases (parasites) they contracted in coastal areas or from accidents while transporting mercury. The economy required denser and heavier transit, whereas the llamas were slow (only travelling about three leagues – 16 km – a day) and had a low carrying capacity (Orche and Amaré 2015; Sánchez Albornoz and 2020).

More versatile and resilient, mules could carry up to two hundred kilograms. They endured many kilometers of travel (about five leagues, or 28 km) and were docile and reliable. They adapted very well to the winding and rugged Andean roads and were very efficient (Orche and Amaré 2015; Sánchez Albornoz 2020). Therefore, they rapidly expanded across the continent along with the other equines (horses and donkeys), surpassing llamas and porters in carrying capacity and endurance. The high growth of freight traffic encouraged the inhabitants of Córdoba to endeavor into mule production. The animal's reproduction depended on breeders, and its maintenance was more demanding and abundant than with llamas. The mule trade involved a large economic space from the Río de la Plata – through Córdoba, Jujuy, and Salta – to Potosí. Between 1610 and 1620, at least fifteen livestock enterprises specializing in breeding the hybrid were created in the area. Córdoba's ranches had abundant wild livestock that had not been appraised so far (Assadourian 1982: 33–38). From the end of the sixteenth century, the specialization in mules occupied the large empty plains of the current Argentine northwest and the central Chilean valley, which were integrated into the Potosí circuit with the production and marketing of the mules.

The Reception of European Livestock by Indigenous People

With the notable exception of Celestino and Meyer's work (1981), which focuses on the last colonial century, classical and more recent historiography on colonial livestock have neglected the issue of the Indian peoples' adoption of European animals and its multiple consequences. However, it is essential to understand the precise modalities of the introduction, imposition, and reception of European animals in the Americas beyond their capacity to self-breed noted by Crosby (1991). Researching the livestock initiatives of Spaniards is imperative to understand essential socioeconomic, cultural, and colonial Andean biodiversity aspects. However, the motivations, the modes of livestock incorporation, and their effects on Indians' agricultural organization and/or reorganization in their ecosystems and their material and symbolic reproduction strategies are equally important and even less studied. To better appreciate the introduction and impact of this new development on the economic, family, and social life of peasants and Indigenous communities, this section establishes two stages: the first covers the decades from 1550 to 1570, when the introduction is slow and encouraged by the Spaniards; and the second, between 1570 and 1600, when the breeding and development of European livestock expands considerably within Indian villages becoming one of the main pillars of community finance.

Factors of compulsion and timing govern the incorporation of European-origin products (Lorandi 1995: 406). European livestock breeding was introduced through the requirements of Hispanic species in the taxes of the encomienda, as well as in the work with the herds of the encomenderos and when it was imposed under restitution. From the mid-sixteenth century, traditional Andean and Hispanic uses were combined. The demand for Hispanic livestock in product appraisals proved very relevant for its introduction. The desire to reproduce the European way of life in the American context therefore explains why the Spaniards very soon demanded the payment of a tax in goods from Indigenous peoples that took into account the European diet. This explains the presence of wheat and gallinaceans in the first lists of goods that the Andean populations had to pay to the encomenderos. In the seventeenth century, the Jesuit Barnabé Cobo notes that the Spaniards "imposed on the Indians who submitted, among other tributes, a certain amount of wheat and other seeds and so many head of Castile livestock, as to force them with this to be applied to the raising and tilling of our livestock and seeds" (Cobo 1956: 377). In the annual tribute rate of Ichoc Pincos in Conchucos (a mountainous area of northern Peru) of 1549, thirty camelids were requested and no sheep, in addition to twenty pigs, 200 units of poultry, and 1,040 units of eggs. In turn, the Indians of Ichoc Pincos were to give their priest twelve sheep, 208 units of poultry, 2,502 units of eggs, and two pigs annually. In the tribute of 1557, only ten camelids, twenty-six pigs, and 500 units of birds were requested. In the annual rate of tributes of Tauca or Conchucos de Mori in 1550, they were taxed fifteen sheep (although it is not specified if these were sheep [ovejas de Castilla] or camelids [ovejas de la tierra]), thirty pigs, and 1,024 units of eggs, in addition to 300 poultry. The priest had to be given twelve sheep, 120 poultry, 624 eggs, and six pigs (Chocano 2016: 319–321). Even if gallinaceans could eventually compete with guinea pigs – because they were small and easy to raise – the biggest competition between local and European animals was probably sheep. But their adoption in Indigenous economies does not appear to have been immediate. Unlike in Mesoamerica, in the Andes, the ancient tradition of camelid farming was indicative of the Andean agropastoral experience, but did not guarantee an interest in sheep.

Therefore, the restitution of ill-gotten property was a way of imposing European livestock breeding on Indigenous economies, since it is not clear that the interest of Andean communities coincided with these transactions, with the exception of some caciques or certain contexts. In his restitution of 200 sheep to the Indians of Pocsi, near Arequipa, in 1562, the encomendero Alonso de Cáceres detailed the obra pía and commissioned the patrons "to take care that these are brought in part where they will not die like has happened with the others that have been given to them" (Testament of Alonso de Cáceres, National Library of Peru, Manuscripts Z1264, f.376v). This warning shows that in the Pocsi area, at 3,000 msm, where camelid farming was the norm, the sheep of Castile were not spontaneously taken in. It required that the restituted livestock not be sold before some growth and that they only be used collectively to pay tribute, clothe the poor of the community, and feed the encomienda priest. The legal instrument of the obra pía shows that Spaniards assimilated their donations of European livestock to the collective flocks with religious purpose present in the Andes before the conquest. Sheep thus assumed a sacred dimension. This statute, at the same time separate and collective, continues at the end of the sixteenth century, through the assets of the brotherhoods and communities, which structure the management and use of sheep by the Andean population.

It is difficult to assess the success or failure of the Spaniards initial strategy to force the Indians to raise livestock, whether Andean or European, through taxes or restitutions. Success is evident, for example, in the view of Huánuco of 1562: thirty years after the arrival of the Spaniards, many sheep from Castile had already appeared (100 heads) compared to llamas, which numbered only 152. This low number of llamas can be explained by the pressure exerted on them at the time of the conquest. Additionally, they were part of the tribute to the encomendero, giving over 104 heads annually in 1549 (Mellafe 1972). However, in some *repartamientos*, the fact that fixed livestock taxes were established did not imply that the local population produced them. Negotiations with encomenderos to deliver fewer products, including livestock, were common. Instead, the caciques gave money or replaced livestock not given by units of other goods (Trelles Aréstegui 1982: 219). The Indians of Allauca Huaraz declared in 1555 that they did not raise the livestock that belonged to them from the levy, but obtained it from other groups (*parcialidades*) in exchange for corn, wool, and sheep (Zuloaga 2022: 94).

Without denying European pressures for the incorporation of their livestock into the Indigenous economy, in many cases, some European livestock was voluntarily welcomed from the outset. Indigenous populations would have weighed several considerations for incorporating or rejecting European crops and livestock: that the new species would find a favorable environment for acclimatization, that it would not hinder subsistence production, that there would be no or minimal requirements for technology or skilled workers, that species would complement their own agricultural and livestock cycles, or that they would use ecosystems not already used by native crops or livestock (Lorandi 1995: 407). Chickens met these requirements and were therefore perhaps the earliest introduced species among the Indigenous population. In addition to being included in the lists of European species for tribute to their encomenderos and priests, the Castile birds would have been quickly incorporated by the Indians into their domestic economy. They were easy to raise and feed, and their egg supply made them a daily food source, reproductively surpassing Andean domestic ducks (Gade 2015: 33–34). There are records of chicken farming by Indigenous populations from 1537 in which they appear in very small numbers (five) given to Alonso de Alvarado, but shortly before the Inca general Quizpe Yupanque had taken 811 eggs as he passed through the Huanca's territory. In the travels of Governor Vaca de Castro to and from Cuzco in 1542, he received 132 chickens and almost 3,000 eggs. Also pigs were raised by Indians in their villages from very early on. In the same list, the Huanca recorded the delivery of pigs (twenty-three) in 1542 to Governor Vaca de Castro, another twenty to Gonzalo Pizarro during his uprising, and 141 to Pacificador La Gasca (Murra 1975: 256–260).

During the 1570s, Viceroy Toledo, while concentrating the Indigenous population in villages, paid close attention to the communal heritage of Indian peoples composed mainly of land and livestock. These resources, managed by the caciques, covered essential expenses for the life and reproduction of the community. Toledo had these assets located and registered to establish control mechanisms and detract from the autonomy of the Indigenous authorities. The major component of community property was livestock: whether of indigenous origin, preserved and reappropriated from the Inca and the sun; or of European origin, incorporated into the Indigenous economy through restitution. The viceroy's advisor, Juan de Matienzo, had written that the Indians of some *repartamientos* had "10,000 head of livestock, and 1,000 to 2,000 cows, and 1,000 sheep and rams of the land" that, according to him, the caciques had appropriated (Matienzo 1967: 71). Once the community assets of the Indians were registered, Toledo placed the wealthiest estates under the supervision of Spanish administrators. Before Toledo in 1567, Garcí Díez, the visitor of Chucuito, had counted 48,441 head of community livestock: both camelids and "certain amounts of livestock from Castile" (sheep). Everything was placed by his successor under the administration of a Spaniard (Lucht 2004: 183–184). The measures implemented by Toledo were applied to the entire territory of the viceroyalty and in service to the mining economy (Zuloaga 2010: 423; Del Río 1990: 189; Presta 2015). In addition, Toledo created a communal treasury (a three-key ark created for that purpose) to centralize the community's public finances with the total amount of tax collection and the proceeds earned by Indians from their community property. These revenues could no longer be managed by the caciques autonomously. The mayors of *cabildos* and the *corregidores* (royal authorities installed at regional and local levels) were to be involved in its administration. Toledo secularized community assets for ecclesiastical purposes, used and administered by priests through the assets of churches, hospitals, and confraternities. They became dependent on *corregidores* and *Audiencias* for control and administration. This reform undermined the peoples' economic autonomy and the maintenance of their traditional social reproduction mechanisms. The corregidores and other Spaniards appropriated the property.

Faced with difficulties in meeting their collective expenses, the Indians reorganized their community property under the cover of religious institutions that had economic capacity. Churches, religious brotherhoods, and hospitals returned to ecclesiastical jurisdiction after a long legal battle fought in the late sixteenth century (Zuloaga 2010; Zuloaga 2012; Zuloaga 2017). With the complicity of ecclesiastical authorities, the Indians increased their community livestock heritage with sheep, goats, and, to a lesser extent, cattle, ascribing it to property of ecclesiastical jurisdiction. The "census" of the detailed ecclesiastical visits made by the Archbishop of Lima between 1593 and 1605 shows that most villages of Indians had community herds distributed mostly in hospitals, churches, and brotherhoods. This livestock was sheep (in the serrain regions) and, to a lesser extent, goats (in the coastal areas). The extent of laminoid distribution in these areas before the conquest is unknown, but it is significant that livestock is not mentioned in the 1590s. It could show the retreat of increasingly scarce indigenous livestock faced with the foreign animals that were becoming widespread in the northern landscapes. Southern Andean Indian communities also introduced European livestock into their organization. The Kuraka of Asillo, whose community had benefited from a restitution by their encomendero in European wool livestock, had created a collective ranch at the end of the sixteenth century composed of 4,000 sheep from Castile who shared common pastures with the llamas (Glave 1989: 286–289).

European livestock, particularly sheep, became the economic pillar of the peoples' communal economy and central to their ability to reproduce symbolically and materially from the end of the sixteenth century. Its adoption would have been the logical response to demographic decline because of the danger of losing untapped land. In the 1590s, the campaign of land compositions facilitated their legal transfer to Spaniards, and the Indian peoples themselves used the mechanism to "legalize" and acquire full property rights in their own territories. Extensive livestock development could retain large amounts of land with minimal investment and limited labor. They were suitable territories for the acclimatization and breeding of sheep, goats, and cattle, and also had livestock specialists and pre-Hispanic pastoral management experience. This sustained the high costs of ritualistic and festive community celebrations that reinforced the traditional authority of the caciques, then much contested, and were the main bulwarks of the recreated Indigenous identity in colonial times. During the seventeenth century, European livestock continued to take hold in Indian villages as a fundamental resource for their subsistence and reproduction as a group. The brotherhoods acquired prominence as recipients of community livestock, ahead of hospitals and churches. Brotherhoods more easily avoided the growing greed of religious authorities and could be administered more autonomously. Therefore, the Indians from 1610 preferred to give their livestock to the brotherhoods, and this trend remained throughout the colonial era.

The high demand for wool from the colonial mercantile economy, particularly textiles, explains this choice, which probably involved, although little researched, cohabitation, complementarity, and perhaps competition between sheep and laminoids, as well as the mobilization of Indigenous knowledge and new imported techniques. This activity was previously dependent in the Andes on the rearing of native cattle and diversified with European sheep. Although the textile obrajes were an initiative of the encomenderos to expand their activities (Silva 1964; Salas 1998), the Indigenous communities worked in and for them, with labor and livestock raising. Just as European and indigenous livestock cohabited in pastures, their wools cohabited in the process of manufacturing. The cohabitation in the pasture is clear in the case of Asillo, with local llamas and returned sheep in a stay managed by the Kuraka and two ranches of the encomendero with cattle and sheep (Glave 1989: 286, 291). According to Fulcrand Terrisse (2004: 232–237), sheep have a selective diet that allows associating with various animals and do not damage the landscape more than llamas or alpacas. However, there is a lack of precise studies dedicated to the analysis of this cohabitation in livestock management and its consequences on the landscape.

It is not known exactly how the wool was distributed according to the fabrics being manufactured. Pre-Hispanic textile techniques were not only retained for domestic consumption but also for making more luxurious fabrics: the *cumbis* of colonial native elites. Sheep wool was, however, introduced into the manufacture of traditional tunics called *unku*, alongside camelid fibers. One of the changes observed is the greater variety of drawings in colonial designs, along with a probably lower quality (Pillsbury 2002: 77- 93). If Inca manufacturing structures were not maintained, the production of fine textiles was instead stimulated by urban demand and mining centers and carried out by weavers from Indian villages and traveling artisans working for individuals (Ramos 2010). While the *cumbi* incorporated sheep wool in the obrajes, it was also woven with camelid fibers, which were preferred. The obrajes made rustic fabrics, useful for dressing miners and ordinary people, as well as for use in transportation. They were rarely dyed, and when they were, local techniques were privileged (Salas 1998: 248). In the obrajes, in addition to Castilian sheep wool, local fibers like vicuña were used for hats, as well (Silva 1964: 33–34). This fiber was employed in traditional looms in the Arequipa region at the end of the eighteenth century, where "llama" fibers were also used in traditional waist looms (Silva 1964: 140–144). At this time, in Abancay, thin blankets of sheep and alpaca were woven (Silva 1964: 149). All this indicates that Andean weaving techniques coexisted with imported Spanish ones, in addition to maintaining local fibers. There is a lack of specific studies interested in this coexistence of fibers. Although the compatibility of sheep, alpacas, and llamas in the same space is observed, their differentiated or joint management in colonial times remains to be investigated.

Conclusion

As in the rest of America – though even more complex because of the pastoral tradition of the Andes – the introduction of European livestock linked with a complete package of economic, political, and social changes brought about a profound transformation of the precolonial Andes. It would also become one of the most important developments for both colonizing society and the Andean population. Livestock development was one of the fundamental engines and vehicles in the European strategy of occupation and appropriation of the space, utilized as an instrument of the Hispanic agrarian frontier's expansion against the Indigenous and a means to acquire legal property rights over the land by the Spaniards. Also the indigenous Andean pastoral and livestock culture, techniques, and ancestral knowledge were exploited by the Europeans to lay the foundations of the new mercantile system that was emerging, in which the Indigenous population itself became actively involved. The introduction of European livestock into Indian villages was a fundamental strategy in their modes of social reproduction, land conservation, surplus production, and corporate security, as well as fostering the combination of technologies and ways of managing and exploiting Andean and Hispanic traditions.

However, the degree of transformation generated by European animals remains under study. "We lack a global study of Andean pastoralism from the colony as well as landscapes at the end of pre-Hispanic times and during colonial times. We recognize that the structures and practices imposed by the Spanish must have contributed to profound changes in the Andean landscape, but we are not in a position to currently measure this impact" (Fulcrand Terrisse 2004: 195). Research into the effects of the European livestock introduction into the Andes is scarce. For some authors such as Flores Ochoa (Bonavia 1996: 526–528), the introduction of European livestock, particularly sheep, was an ecological catastrophe whose effects remain: not only because of the displacement of camelids and the diseases they brought (Webb 2015: 64–65), but also for its ability to destroy plant cover and generate erosion in an already fragile and slowly recovering environment. On the contrary, Fulcrand argues that the introduction of new animal species would have enriched biological diversity and consequently constituted more complex ecosystems, contributing to their stability (Fulcrand Terrisse 2004: 215–217). The first approach is in tune with the catastrophic paradigm that has dominated specialized historiography on the effects of the European livestock introduction in Mexico stimulated by Melville's (2012) classic work on the Valley of Mexico, who showed that extensive sheep rearing wiped out sophisticated farming systems as early as the sixteenth century. However, the catastrophic view is being nuanced in light of new research in other areas of Mexico and elsewhere on the continent. Case and regional studies show a variety of effects and situations ranging from reduced to little environmental impacts (Huasteca potosina or in the tropical lowlands of Veracruz) to the economic strengthening of Indigenous Mapuche populations in Chile, the Argentine Chaco, or the Durango Indians who used the control of European wild livestock (horses and cows especially) to resist Hispanic colonizers (Hernández 2001).

In addition to a study of the transformations of grazing techniques and landscapes, much remains to be done and investigated to understand the full consequences of the bioeconomic and cultural change that caused this upheaval. More bioarchaeological data, combined with an accurate mapping of the progress of European livestock in the Andes, are needed to better document the evolution we have presented in broad terms. In the case of northern Peru, everything seems to suggest that the ratio between European and Andean animals was reversed as the sixteenth century progressed, noting Miller's (2007) assessment of the Amerindian demographic catastrophe that "the biological conquest of America is more accurately seen as the replacement of Indians not with Europeans [or Africans] or microbes, but with cows, sheep, pigs, chicken, and hundreds of other new nonhuman species, in addition to the resurgence of native wildlife" (Miller 2007: 20). In the Andean south, the importance of llamas in transport preserved the survival of camelids, despite the imposed competition of the mule from the end of the sixteenth century. The driving force used in mining development and the competition and complementarity between European and local livestock in the textile field exemplify the benefits derived from the introduction of European species and characterize biological diversification and the radical economic and social impact it had. However, there is a lack of more precise studies on changes and exchanges of practical knowledge, for example in textile techniques and leather work, such as in the penetration of milk processing. In the cultural and religious sphere, there is also a lack of specific studies on the representations of European animals that Andean populations gradually integrated into their cultural universe. Research into little-studied sources in Indigenous languages could help develop this.

Translated by Eric Rummelhoff and revised by Omar Sierra Cháves.

References

Aldana, Susana. 1989. *Empresas coloniales. Las tinas de jabón en Piura.* Lima: Instituto de Estudios Peruanos/Centro de Investigación y Promoción del Campesinado.

Assadourian, Carlos S. 1982. *El sistema de la economía colonial: mercado interno, regiones y espacio económico.* Lima: Instituto de Estudios Peruanos.

———. 1994. *Transiciones hacia el sistema colonial andino.* Mexico City/Lima: Colegio de México/Instituto de Estudios Peruanos.

Bonavia, Duccio. 1996. *Los camélidos sudamericanos. Una introducción a su estudio.* Lima: Instituto Francés de Estudios Andinos.

Borchart de Moreno, Christiana. 1995. "Llamas y ovejas: el desarrollo del ganado lanar en la audiencia de Quito." In *Colonización agrícola y ganadera en América, siglos XVI-XVIII: su impacto en la población aborigen,* ed. Laura Escobari de Querejazu, 153–191. Quito: Abya-Yala.

Bueno Jiménez, Alfredo. 2011. "Los perros en la conquista de América: historia e iconografía." *Chronica Nova* 37: 177–204.

Bustinza Choque, Alfonso Víctor, Virgilio Machaca Machaca, Víctor Cano Fuentes, et al. 2021. "Evolución y desarrollo de las razas de Alpaca: Suri y Huacaya." *Revista de Investigaciones Veterinarias del Perú* 32, no. 5: 1–17.

Cáceres, Alonso de. 1562. *Testamento,* Manuscritos Z1264, f. 376v. Lima: Biblioteca Nacional del Perú.

Celestino, Olinda, and Albert Meyers. 1981. *Las cofradías en el Perú: región central.* Frankfurt: Vervuert.

Chocano, Magdalena. 2016a. *Una historia regional de la colonia a la república: territorio, población y economía.* Lima: Biblioteca del Congreso del Perú.

———. 2016b. "Perfiles de la producción textil en un espacio regional: Conchucos, Ancash, Perú entre 1593 y 1876." *Revista de Economía* 39, no. 77: 229–249.

Cieza de León, Pedro. 1987. *Crónica del Perú. Tercera Parte.* Lima: Pontificia Universidad Católica del Perú. Orig. pub. 1553.

Cobo, Bernabé. 1964. *Historia del Nuevo Mundo*. Vol. 1. Madrid: Ediciones Atlas/ Biblioteca de autores españoles. Orig. pub. 1654.

Contreras, Carlos. 2021. *Historia económica del Perú. Desde la conquista española hasta el presente*. Lima: Instituto de Estudios Peruanos.

Crosby, Alfred W. 1991. *El intercambio transoceánico: consecuencias biológicas y culturales a partir de 1492*. Mexico City: UNAM/Instituto de Investigaciones Históricas.

Del Río, María de las Mercedes. 1990. "La tributación indígena en el repartimiento de Paria (siglo XVI)." *Revista de Indias* 50, no. 189: 397–429.

———. 2005. *Etnicidad, territorialidad y colonialismo en los Andes: tradición y cambio entre los Soras de los siglos XVI y XVII, Bolivia*. Lima: Instituto Francés de Estudios Andinos.

Del Río Moreno, Justo. 1996. "El cerdo. Historia de un elemento esencial de la cultura castellana en la conquista y colonización de América (siglo XVI)." *Anuario de estudios americanos* 53, no. 1: 13–35.

Earle, Rebecca. 2012. *The body of the conquistador: food, race and the colonial experience in Spanish America, 1492–1700*. Cambridge: Cambridge University Press.

Espinoza Soriano, Waldemar. 1971. *Los huancas, aliados de la conquista: tres informaciones inéditas sobre la participación indígena en la conquista del Perú*. Huancayo: Universidad Nacional del Centro del Perú.

Fulcrand Terrisse, Bernardo. 2004. *Las ovejas de San Juan. Una visión histórico-antropológica de la introducción del ovino español y su repercusión en la sociedad rural andina*. Cusco: Asociación Arariwa.

Gabelmann, Olga. 2015. "Caminando con llamas. Caravanas actuales y analogías para el tráfico e intercambio prehispánico en Bolivia." *Revista de Estudios Sociales del Noa* 15: 33–58.

Gade, Daniel W. 1987. "The iberian pig in the Central Andes." *Journal of Cultural Geography* 7, no. 9: 35–49.

———. 2015. "Particularizing the Columbian exchange: Old World biota to Peru." *Journal of Historical Geography* 48: 26–35.

Glave, Luis Miguel. 1989. "Un curacazgo andino y la sociedad campesina en el siglo XVII el caso de Bartolomé Túpac Hallicalla, curaca de Asillo." In *Trajinantes. Caminos indígenas en la sociedad colonial. Siglos XVI y XVII*, ed. Luis Miguel Glave, 281–304. Lima: Instituto de Apoyo Agrario.

Goepfert, Nicolas, Elise Dufour, Gabriel Prieto, et al. 2020. "Herds for the gods? Selection criteria and herd management at the mass sacrifice site of Huanchaquito-Las Llamas during the Chimú period, northern coast of Peru." *Environmental Archaeology* 25, no. 3: 296–309.

Hernández, Lucila. 2001. *Historia ambiental de la ganadería en México*. Xalapa: IRD/ Instituto de Ecología.

Lara, Jesus. 1966. *La cultura de los Incas: El Tawantinsuyu*. Vol. 1. La Paz: Los Amigos del Libro.

León, Miguel. 2002. *Paños e hidalguía: Encomenderos y sociedad colonial en Huánuco: 1540–1640*. Lima: Instituto de Estudios Peruanos.

Lorandi, Ana María. 1995. "Complementariedad económica en los valles Calchaquíes y del Cajón." In *Colonización agrícola y ganadera en América. Siglos XVI al XVIII. Su impacto en la población aborigen*, ed. Laura Escobari de Querejazu, 385–415. Quito: Abya Yala.

Lucht, Roswitha. 2004. "Una nueva lectura de la Visita de Chucuito (1567): Interrelaciones múltiples y el ganado de la comunidad." *Indiana* 21: 175–194.

McNeill, John R. 2003. *Algo nuevo bajo el sol. Historia medioambiental del mundo en el siglo XX*. Madrid: Alianza Editorial.

Machado Aráoz, Horacio. 2017. "Potosí y los orígenes del extractivismo." *Voces en el Fénix* 60: 36–43.

Machado Aráoz, Horacio, and Leonardo J. Rossi. 2017. "Extractivismo minero y fractura sociometabólica." *RevIISE – Revista de Ciencias Sociales y Humanas* 10, no. 10: 273–286.

Maldavsky, Aliocha. 2019. "Teología moral, restitución y sociedad colonial en los Andes en el siglo XVI." *Revista portuguesa de filosofía* 75, no. 2: 1125–1148.

Matienzo, Juan de. 1967. *Gobierno del Perú*. Ed. Guillermo Lhomann Villena. Lima: Instituto Francés de Estudios Andinos. Orig. pub. 1567.

Mellafe, Rolando. 1967. "Consideraciones históricas sobre la visita de Iñigo Ortiz de Zúñiga." In *Visita de la provincia de León de Huánuco en 1562*, ed. John V. Murra, 325–344. Huánuco: Universidad Nacional Hermilio Valdizan.

Melón Jiménez, Miguel Ángel. 2004. "La ganadería española en la Edad Moderna. Apuntes para su estudio." In *El mundo rural en la España Moderna. Actas de la VII Reunión Científica de la Fundación Española de Historia Moderna*, ed. Francisco José Aranda Pérez, 727–770. Cuenca: Universidad de Castilla-La Mancha.

Melville, Elinor G. K. 2012. *A Plague of Sheep: Environmental Consequences of the Conquest of Mexico*. Cambridge: Cambridge University Press. Orig. pub. 1994.

Mengoni Golaños, Guillermo L., and Hugo D. Yacobaccio. 2006. "The Domestication of South American Camelids: A View from the South-Central Andes." In *Documenting domestication. New genetic and archeological paradigms*, ed. Melinda A. Zeder, Daniel G. Bradley, Eve Emshwiller, et al., 228–244. Berkeley: University of California Press.

Miller, Shawn W. 2007. *An Environmental History of Latin America*. Cambridge: Cambridge University Press.

Molinero, Yoan, Avallone G. 2020. "Ecología-mundo un nuevo paradigma para el estudio de las migraciones." *Revista de Metodología de Ciencias Sociales* 46: 23–44.

Moore, Jason W. 2020. "Esta elevada montaña de plata podría conquistar el mundo entero: Potosí y la ecología política del subdesarrollo, 1545–1800." In *La trama de la vida en los umbrales del capitaloceno. El pensamiento de Jason W. Moore*, ed. Mina

Lorena Navarro and Horacio Machado Araoz, 115–156. Mexico City: Bajo Tierra Ediciones.

Murra, John V. 1972. "El control vertical de un máximo de pisos ecológicos en la economía de las sociedades andinas." In *Visita de la provincia de León de Huánuco en 1562*, ed. John V. Murra, 427–476. Huánuco: Universidad Nacional Hermilio Valdizan.

———. 1975. *Formaciones económicas y políticas del mundo andino*. Lima: Instituto de Estudios Peruanos.

Núñez, Irima, Edgar González Gaudiano, and Ana Barahona. 2003. "La biodiversidad: historia y contexto de un concepto." *Interciencia* 28, no. 7: 387–393.

Orche, Enrique, and Maria Pilar Amaré. 2015. "Transporte de mercurio desde Huancavelica a Potosí en el Perú colonial." *De Re Metallica* 25: 53–74.

Pedrotta, Victoria. 2016. "Estrategias indígenas de captura y manejo del ganado cimarrón en las Sierras Septentrionales bonaerenses: las construcciones de piedra Cerro Guacho I y Cerro Guacho II." *Arqueología* 22, no. 2: 269–289.

Piqueras Céspedes, Ricardo. 2006. "Los perros de la guerra o el canibalismo canino en la conquista." *Boletín Americanista* 56: 187–202.

Pillsbury, Joanne. 2002. "Inka Unku: Strategy and Design in Colonial Peru." *Cleveland Studies in the History of Art* 7: 68–103.

Presta, Ana María. 2015. "La compañía del trajín de azogues de Potosí. Un capítulo inédito de la financiación de los repartimientos indígenas surandinos al desarrollo de la minería colonial." *Boletin del Instituto de Historia Argentina y Americana "Dr. Emilio Ravignani"* 43: 1–18.

Ramírez, Susan. 1991. *Patriarcas provinciales: la tenencia de la tierra y la economía del poder en el Perú colonial*. Madrid: Alianza editorial.

Ramos, Gabriela. 2010. "Los tejidos y la sociedad colonial andina." *Colonial Latin American Review* 19, no. 1: 115–149.

Salas de Coloma, Miriam. 1998. *Estructura colonial del poder español en el Perú Huamanga (Ayacucho) a través de sus obrajes. Siglos XVI-XVIII*. Vol. 1. Lima: Pontificia Universidad Católica del Perú/Instituto Francés de Estudios Andinos.

Salas, Alejandro, Natalia Andrea Soto González, Marisol Videla, et al. 2022. "Molinos y tahonas en Charcas, Córdoba y Buenos Aires (1550–1600)." *Estudios Atacameños. Arqueología y Antropología Surandinas* 68: 1–23.

Saldarriaga, Gregorio. 2012. *Alimentación e identidades en el Nuevo Reino de Granada, siglos XVI y XVII*. Bogotá: Ministerio de Cultura.

Sánchez Albornoz, Nicolás. 2020. "Las mulas en Indias: balance del primer siglo." In *Trabajo y migraciones indígenas en los Andes coloniales*, Nicolás Sánchez Albornoz, 193–209. Lima: Instituto de Estudios Peruanos.

Scott, Heidi V. 2005. "Más allá del texto: recuperando las influencias indígenas en las experiencias españolas del Perú." In *Más allá de la dominación y la resistencia. Estu-*

dios de historia peruana, siglos XVI-XX, ed. Paulo Drinot and Leo Garofalo, 23–47. Lima: Instituto de Estudios Peruanos.

Schlüpmann, Jakob. 2022. *La estructura agraria y el desarrollo de una sociedad regional en el Norte del Perú. Piura, 1588–1854*. Lima: Instituto de Estudios Peruanos.

Silva Santiesteban, Fernando. 1964. *Los obrajes en el virreinato del Perú*. Lima: Publicaciones del Museo Nacional de Historia.

Solbrig, Otto. 1994. "Biodiversity. An introduction." In *Biodiversity and global change*, ed. Otto Solbrig, Helmut van Emden, and Pieter Gregorius Willem Johannes van Oordt. Wallington: CAB international.

Sumar Kalinowski, Julio. 1997. "Evolución y desarrollo de la ganadería camélida en el altiplano latinoamericano." In *El Altiplano. Ciencia y conciencia en los Andes*, ed. Reynaldo Charrier González, Patricio Aceituno Gutiérrez, Milka Castro Lucic, et al., 211–221. Santiago de Chile: Universidad de Chile.

Taboada, Hernán G. H. 2017. *Extrañas presencias en nuestra América*. Mexico City: Centro de Investigaciones sobre América Latina y el Caribe.

Toledo, Víctor M. 1994. "La diversidad biológica de México. Nuevos retos para la investigación en los noventa." *Ciencias* 34: 43–59.

Trelles Aréstegui, Efraín. 1982. *Lucas Martínez Vegazo: funcionamiento de una encomienda inicial*. Lima: Pontificia Universidad Católica del Perú.

Vega, Garcilaso de la. 1976. *Comentarios reales de los Incas*. Vol. 2. Caracas: Biblioteca Ayacucho. Orig. pub. 1609.

Webb, James L. A. 2015. "Globalization of disease, 1400–1900." In *The Cambridge World History. The construction of a global world, 1400–1800*. Vol. 6, ed. Jerry H. Bentley, Sanjay Subrahmanyam, and Merry E. Wiesner-Hanks, 54–75. Cambridge: Cambridge University Press.

Zuloaga, Marina. 2010. "Evolución de los bienes de comunidad en Huaylas entre 1562 y 1610." In *Guerra, Finanzas y regiones en la historia económica del Perú*, ed. Carlos Contreras, Cristina Mazzeo, and Francisco Quiroz, 413–455. Lima: Instituto de Estudios Peruanos.

———. 2012. *La conquista negociada: guarangas, autoridades e imperio en Huaylas Perú, 1530–1610*. Lima: Instituto de Estudios Peruanos/Instituto Francés de Estudios Andinos.

———. 2017. "Las reducciones: el proyecto, su aplicación y su evolución en Huaylas." In *Reducciones. La concentración forzada de las poblaciones indígenas en el virreinato del Perú*, ed. Claudia Rosas and Akira Saito, 307–347. Lima: Pontificia Universidad Católica del Perú.

———. 2022. "El periodo colonial temprano de la historia económica de la región central." In *Historia económica del Perú Central*, ed. Carlos Contreras, 71–145. Lima: Banco Central de Reserva/Instituto de Estudios Peruanos.

Biodiversity in the Amazon in the Colonial Period

Neil Safier

The roots of the staggering biodiversity of the Amazon River basin in South America stretch back millions of years before the common era. Indeed, it may have been with the Big Bang itself that the matter, which would eventually come to form the rich raw materials of this region, came together. According to scientific theories accumulated in the past fifty years, the Amazon region's extraordinary biodiversity can only have meaning on a geological timescale. Over the course of millions of years of shifting, rising, settling, and adjusting, momentary bursts of speciation are thought to have taken place, adapting to changing circumstances and rushing to fill voids and niches where an opportunity for adaptive success and survival was possible. One of the leading theories currently being debated about the Amazon speculates that a massive maritime intrusion into northern South America from what is today the Caribbean Sea created a network of islands and wetlands that led to spikes in diversity, as these aquatic spaces of freshwater and saltwater melded with distinctive terrestrial landforms and provided new spaces for species to thrive. Scientists who abide by this theory point to fossils of plankton, mollusks, and other aquatic animals – not only fish but also dolphins – that speak to the presence of an estuary system that existed and was subjected to multiple episodes of flooding during most of the Miocene period (roughly 23 to 5 million years ago) (Wade 2015).

It is challenging to say whether the Amazon River region – either defined politically as a territorial conglomerate across nine South American nations that stretch on either side of the equatorial line or ecologically as a watershed region crossing over diverse biomes and distinct configurations of urban, rural, and Indigenous communities – has been a net contributor or net detractor to the accelerating human-centered activities of the Anthropocene, a powerful model for conceptualizing both ecological and geological change in the contemporary era. At one level, the sheer number of commodified products explored and exploited in the past several hundred years – rubber, most famously, but also natural products like açaí, Brazil nuts, sarsaparilla, and turtle eggs as well as mineral resources including bauxite, manganese, iron, and zinc – would lead to the conclusion that the Amazon both participated in and was massively affected by the extraction of natural products and their introduction into a global economic system. Almost without exception, however, the minerals cited above began to be mined only in the twentieth century. As a result, the social and material processes that led to their eventual extraction generally fall outside the temporal purview of an earlier phase of Amazonian exploitation, one that was affected most forcefully through the dynamics of colonialism and serves as the focus of this chapter.

As Claudia Leal makes clear in her incisive article about the temporal transformations of tropical forest environments, deforestation appears to have increased dramatically at precisely the moment when minerals like bauxite and iron began to be extracted *en masse* – that is, during the twentieth century (2018; see also Leal 2013). The extraction of rubber and valuable hardwoods from across the Amazon region caused analogous damage in the nineteenth century, but not nearly to the same degree. It is indisputable that the most significant set of ecological changes – and destruction of wildlife habitats – were set in motion within the Amazonia during the post-colonial period by miners, cattle ranchers, and agro-industrial farmers, with a dramatic increase in soybean production as one of the leading causes of the latter. One understudied prism, however, is the extent to which those communities that are at present most affected by these extractive processes and most vulnerable to their destructive practices originated in a much earlier period because of these practices: communities such as those around the Mineração do Rio Norte's Boa Vista mine that were formed when groups of enslaved Africans subject to conditions of coerced servitude fled from harsh plantation environments in the late-eighteenth century (Arregui 2015). These communities became the front line of a system of racial capitalism, emerging as a direct result of exploitative practices by European colonial powers in what academics traditionally call the early modern period (1450–1800). Even if the Great Acceleration is understood as an ecological process that started to manifest in the middle of the twentieth century, the building blocks for these activities were already clearly visible in this earlier period (Steffen et al. 2015). This chapter sets forth the idea that anthropogenic transformations in the natural world of the Amazon River basin did not begin with the late arrival of these cataclysmic transformations to equatorial South America. Rather, the gestures that early inhabitants of the Amazon engaged in were very relevant to what would eventually be considered the Anthropocene era, formed and shaped into a distinctive – though not globally unique – Amazonian iteration. As a rule, environmental history has been slow to take hold in the Amazon – due to some degree to the powerful disciplinary influences of archaeology and anthropology, which have dominated scholarly interest in the region – but several important articles have made great strides in this direction in recent years (Cleary 2001; Raffles and Winkler Prins 2003; Leal 2018; Hecht and Cockburn: 2011; Hecht 2013).

Human engagement in the Amazon necessarily begins with the Holocene period, the geological epoch that began at the end of the Ice Age or Pleistocene (some 12–13 thousand years ago). With the arrival of human populations around this time, the biodiversity of the Amazon region did not diminish; instead, it increased. In recent decades, anthropologists and archaeologists of the Amazon River region have highlighted how Indigenous populations throughout the Americas were, in this period, already using and manipulating early forest environments. In so doing, these scholars entered – and directly challenged – a broadening debate about when human intervention began to affect the world's natural environments. The Anthropocene – understood in simple terms as the geological epoch when human activity began to shape global environmental patterns – is shorthand for describing a period of unprecedented human intervention through industry, population growth, and the deliberate reshaping of a planet's landscape, temperature, or climate. Moreover, the utility of the Anthropocene as an interpretative mechanism for understanding South America's ecological history lies in ascertaining the extent to which human endeavors in early environments across equatorial South America contributed to a global climate crisis that accelerated in the mid-nineteenth century and that continues perilously to our day.

Using material analyses based on soil characteristics, plant distribution, and stylistic features of pottery, among other techniques, archaeologists of the Amazon region have argued convincingly that native peoples of the South American tropics proactively managed their local environments during the Holocene (Neves 2022; Rapp Py-Daniel 2015; Rostain 2017). Likewise, Amazonian ethnohistorians have shown the innovative strategies Indigenous populations engaged in to retain their autonomy while seeking access to new commodities, new instruments, and new knowledge in an ever-evolving Amazonian economy (Roller 2021; Harris 2010; Kawa 2016). Finally, historians of science have modeled new methods for reading the literary, material, and cartographic sources of early modern exploration against the grain, highlighting evidence that has accrued for the history of human interaction with the natural world from an imperial as well as an Indigenous perspective (Domingues 2019; Safier 2017; Gómez 2014). These insights into the critical ways historical journals, manuscripts, and maps can be used to contribute to contemporary environmental debates – and even engage with environmental activism – have inspired recent scholarship regarding the lengthier environmental history of the Amazon and its relationship to more recent changes in the land. Although the focus of this chapter is on the Brazilian Amazon, for reasons that relate largely (though not exclusively) to the kind of sources that chronicle the textual data that lie at the heart of this analysis, such national distinctions (and geographical boundaries) hardly existed in the period under question, and thus beg the question of how a regional or linguistic approach can even work to recount the history of such a vast and diverse equatorial expanse.

Early Gestures: The Arrival of Spaniards and Portuguese during the Colonial Period

So what were the earliest "gestures" or commentaries made by Europeans regarding the nature of the Amazonian ecosystem? Throughout the colonial period – from the earliest sightings of the Amazon headwaters by the Spanish navigator Vicente Yáñez Pinzón to the keen interest of Alexander von Humboldt in geopolitical developments – mercenaries, military officers, missionaries, and naturalists expressed wonder and admiration for Amazonian flora and the fauna in the late eighteenth century. Early on in the European exploration of the Amazon River basin, servants of the Portuguese and Spanish Crowns traveled along the waterways and floodplains (*várzeas*) extensively. Even before the time of Pedro de Teixeira's demarcation mission in 1637–39 (during a period of joint Spanish and Portuguese rule in the Iberian Peninsula, and hence in their American colonial possessions as well), expeditions fanned out along the various tributaries of the Amazon, Marañón, and Solimões rivers in an attempt to gain control over the native populations and begin to catalog the natural resources that existed in the dense, dark forested expanse. A discourse of natural abundance was not immediate. Still, bit by bit, one began to take shape as new observers arrived to assess and assay the land, its natural products, and its non-human and human populations. The Portuguese expeditionary Diogo Nunes – little recognized as having seen the Amazon basin before the Spaniard Francisco de Orellana (still acknowledged generally as its first explorer) – may have been the first to comment on the animal life in the Amazon basin. During his journey to the Peruvian region of "Machifalo" in 1538, Nunes gazed upon a region through which "the great river of the Amazons flowed," commenting on the "bounty of its resources [*mantimentos*]" and the "many islands populated by luminous peoples [*gente bem luzidia*]." Nunes later went on to describe these products in greater detail, including "milho" and "caçabe," which served as a kind of bread. However, special attention was given as well to the "mountain meats" such as "deer, tapirs, mountain pigs, ducks, and a multitude of other species [*castas*]," not to mention the ubiquitous "sheep like those in Peru." In Gaspar de Carvajal's account, a mixture of observed and unobserved insects, reptiles, birds, and fish emerged, from the "abundance of mosquitos" to the "many turtles as large as shields." A panoply of manatees, ostriches, cats, and monkeys paraded textually amongst the pages of the friar's mid-sixteenth-century account, as well as exotic birds that included "papagayos" and "guacamayos" that certain natives used to provide female Amazonian warriors with feathers that adorned their roofs and other interior domestic spaces (Papavero et al. 2002).

In many ways, the size of the animals was more noteworthy than their quantity in the relations of European travelers (with the exception of the mosquitos, whose ubiquitous presence was duly noted day and night by early travelers to the region). According to the chronicler Francisco Vázquez (who had accompanied Pedro de

Ursúa and Lope de Aguirre on their now-infamous journey from Lima into the Amazon River valley by way of the Marañón River), "there are many large turtles and birds that gather along the beaches, and many large fish that are quite tasty" (Papavero et al. 2002: 45). According to some later seventeenth century chroniclers, the Spaniards who first arrived along the western coasts of South America were eager simply to learn more about this region whose "fertility of the land" and "wealth of the people" were renowned (Gomberville 1684). Spanish Jesuits in the sixteenth century characterized the region as vast interior lands that had not yet been conquered, providing Francisco Pizarro, his brother Gonzalo, and others with ample justification for their own interior incursions. After discussing the descent of several large and significant rivers into the Amazon River basin, one of the river's most important seventeenth-century chroniclers, Cristóbal de Acuña, went on to record some of the natural features that contributed to the river's abundance, including the existence of small islands "nourished [*fertilizadas*] by the river that bathes them, [and] which allows the Native peoples [*naturales*] to use them for their seedbeds, since they have their houses [*habitaciones*] in the largest [of these islands]." According to Acuña, the constant flooding of the river "with its muds" fertilized the river and prevented their waters from ever being understood as "sterile." The primary resources that grew along the river's banks were corn ("Mayz") and manioc ("Iuca"), which Acuña called the "common sustenance of everyone, which is overabundant" (Papavero et al. 2002: 169–205).

The first individual to offer a more formal account of the biodiversity of the Amazon region was the Franciscan friar Cristóvão de Lisboa, whose *História Natural e Moral do Maranhão* – which may have begun as a broader history of the Maranhão region – ended up as a compendium "with ample information about all Geography... with [information about] plants, animals, and humans, [including] their customs and behaviors" (Papavero et al. 2002: 99; see also: Lisboa 2000; Marques 1996; Asúa and French 2005). Although there remains some suspicion (and indeed a great likelihood) that the manuscripts on which he drew derived from an earlier French presence in São Luís (and may have been penned by the French Franciscan missionary Claude d'Abbeville himself), Frei Cristóvão's extensive annotations and wealth of knowledge gleaned from Tupi sources served as a veritable encyclopedia of knowledge regarding (especially) the fish and fowl of the Amazon basin. Long lists of names such as "Guratimguaosu" and "Ynambuasu" to describe birds from the equatorial regions of the South American continent highlight the extent to which French knowledge was at the base of these manuscript annotations (the "-ouassou" suffix is a strong hint that the author was transliterating the Tupi suffix "-guasú" into French). But the dozens and dozens of native terms and their associated images seemingly drawn from life inaugurated an empirical approach to listing and cataloging diverse animal species without necessary reference to European precursors. Even more so than the highly influential *Historia Naturalis Brasiliae* (Leiden 1648),

Frei Cristóvão's *Historia dos animais e árvores do Maranhão* brought to life in vivid detail some of the most striking biodiversity to be found in the region, derived in no small manner from Indigenous sources that were in later centuries suppressed or ignored (Safier 2014).

The arrival of Europeans to the Amazon basin not only brought observations in European languages about the rich flora and fauna, but also wide-ranging ecological changes to the region, if perhaps less abruptly and with fewer immediate effects than in the Caribbean, Andes, and Mesoamerica. The successive waves of Spanish and Portuguese penetration into the interior of equatorial South America made only halting progress due to a confluence of factors, including the location of European settlements (mostly in the high Andes and along the coasts, where maritime connections to other parts of the globe prevailed); abrupt topography; thickness of the tropical forest cover; and Europeans' own inappropriate instruments and attire (it may be useful here to imagine the opening scene from Werner Herzog's film "Aguirre, Wrath of the Gods," where ill-outfitted soldiers descend with tremendous difficulty from the high mountains of the Andes into the Amazonian basin and valleys below). The subsequent introduction of horses, pigs, chickens, and sheep into the region tended at first to be limited. However, it later increased as colonists and native peoples alike recognized the burgeoning need to provision for an expanding European, Euro-Indigenous, and African-descended population in the Amazon.

How Europeans Registered Biological Diversity in the Amazon

As Europeans arrived in greater numbers and with greater frequency, they employed new textual technologies to manage a renewed interest in natural products from equatorial South America. Out of an abiding fascination with books describing natural environments imagined or encountered, an early modern "catalog of nature" emerged whereby Indigenous foodstuffs, woods, and dyes became transformative commodities with an impact far beyond the local environment where they were originally cultivated and collected. This catalog became the blueprint for later exploitation under the capitalist regimes of the twentieth century. By focusing on "technologies of registration" – the natural history catalog, lists of natural products observed and collected in situ, and narrative practices – this chapter provides detailed textual evidence of a new tool for approaching more significant questions of environmental history and the idea of human-induced environmental transformations in particular (Safier 2011). These practices shed light on what environmental history might have meant in the awkward moment between the heyday of imperial expansion in the sixteenth and seventeenth centuries – the so-called Columbian Exchange – and the emergence of environmental awareness as a counterpoint to rapid industrialization in the late nineteenth and twentieth centuries. Objects were circulating across vast distances and eclectic political frontiers. However, their more proximate portability – in the cultivated landscapes and cultural forests of the Amazon – may have had the most impact on perceptions of biodiversity from the eighteenth century well into the twenty-first.

The regimes that sought to extract these commodities did not, of course, emerge *ex nihilo*. Rather, they were the fruits of systems of plantation agriculture that grew out of the early Atlantic world, transplanted into northeastern Brazil and later into the French and English Caribbean, making their way back to Brazil (and, to some degree, back to the Amazon region) in the second half of the eighteenth century. During the colonial period, the Amazonian economy depended largely on products extracted from the forest, including cacao, clove bark, sarsparilla, copaiba oil, turtle shells, Brazil nuts, and rubber (Chambouleyron and Cardoso 2022). By the late eighteenth century, these more localized products had ceded pride of place to three more globally acknowledged commodities: rice, cotton, and cacao. Nevertheless, another commodity forces one to rethink the place of Amazonian biodiversity within a larger global frame. The trade of Amazonian clove bark, or *"cravo da Amazônia,"* exhibits a set of commercial relationships disconnected from the more traditional (and almost always slave-based) Atlantic economy. Instead, the cultivation and circulation of clove bark can only be understood as a Portuguese response to their broader imperial concerns, in which the Amazon – and its plant biodiversity – was to be used to substitute the limited availability of spices and foodstuffs from other sites within the larger Portuguese world (including, in this case, Asia). Although not nearly as successful a commodity as sugar or cotton would become (or coffee in the nineteenth century), the presence of Amazonian clove bark in the global market makes an argument against what was previously understood to be a Brazilian economy that was only reliant on monocultural agricultural exports that depended on the enslaved labor of Africans (Chambouleyron 2022). Other Amazonian crops and other natural products also became global commodities in the seventeenth and eighteenth centuries.

Even with the early success of Amazonian clove bark in global commercial trade routes, it was during the eighteenth century that the Spanish and Portuguese began to take the Amazon region's extraordinary diversity and potential commercial value seriously. By that time, Iberian agents and naturalists, with the assistance of Indigenous guides, traveled far from the central rivers and into the hinterlands in search of plants and minerals (Roller 2014; Giraldo 1993; Pelayo and Puig-Samper 1992). Spurred at least in part by eighteenth-century observations that recognized the abundance of the Amazon River region's natural resources, there was also a desire to integrate the Amazon region into a broader set of commercial relationships on a global scale. Spanish and Portuguese travelers answered this call to examine the tremendous diversity found within the Amazon basin. Activities in far-flung regions were carried out not only by naturalists but also (and especially) by Iberians administrators, artists, military officers, jurists, and engineers, whose interest was not so much to bring back material objects to Madrid and Lisbon as to categorize and catalog the riches of the New World for use *in situ*.

The second half of the eighteenth century saw a significant increase in the number of such expeditions sent by Spain and Portugal in the wake of the Treaty of Madrid (1750). As these expeditions moved across vast portions of South America, their goal was to establish more fixed and mutually recognizable boundaries between the two Iberian nations and to create, where possible, circumstances that would favor the development of commercial treaties in the region – including with Indigenous communities. Along the Spanish and Portuguese frontier, military barracks and fortresses arose where a modicum of scientific activity could also take place. Antonio de Ulloa and Jorge Juan provided background to Spain's territorial pretensions across equatorial South America in their *Dissertación historica, y geográphica sobre el meridiano de Demarcación entre los Dominios de España, y Portugal* (Madrid, 1749) which outlined how the expansive territories claimed by the Portuguese along the Amazon River had extended beyond what they should have been, based on incorrect assumptions in the political treaties between the Spanish and the Portuguese centuries before. Prior to 1750, descriptions of the social and political situation in the Amazon were left for religious authors such as the Jesuits Samuel Fritz, Jean Magnin, Pablo Maroni, and Juan Baptista Julián (Gómez 2014). In the wake of the Treaty of Madrid (1750), a host of Spanish expeditions were sent to establish these frontiers in a more scientific (or instrumental) vein, which included the work of such Spanish administrator-astronomers such as José de Iturriaga, Francisco Javier Haller, and Francisco Requena (Gómez 2014; Beerman 1996; Giraldo 1993). These border expeditions, which lasted until the final decade of the eighteenth century, did not so much transform the natural landscape as reorient some of the political divisions between Spanish and Portuguese America. At the same time, they enabled individuals such as Pedro Löfling – a naturalist-agent of the Spanish king and disciple of Carolus Linnaeus – to make elaborate sketches of the flora and fauna of the region known today as Venezuela, especially in the realm of zoology (Pelayo and Puig-Samper 1992).

On the Portuguese side of the border, Francisco Xavier de Mendonça Furtado, the brother of the Portuguese minister plenipotentiary, the Marquês de Pombal, arrived in the region in 1751 to the post of Governor General of the captaincy of Grão-Pará e Maranhão. Through this new agent, the Portuguese crown implemented a series of practices and policies to exert ever greater dominion over its Amazonian territories. One of the centerpieces of these policies was the establishment of the Companhia Geral de Grão-Pará e Maranhão (1755), whose purpose was to reestablish the centrality of the Portuguese in transatlantic commerce and to increase the workforce with free Indians and enslaved Africans. There was, however, also an intense campaign of agricultural development and experimentation with various species of plants and trees. It is within this broader context that Portuguese administrative agents began to include in their manuscript reports to the Portuguese crown registers of plants, herbs, resins, fruits, trees, and other natural objects that might assist in fulfilling these broader political and economic goals.

One of the regions in which much of this natural reconnaissance work took place in the second half of the eighteenth century was along the Rio Branco, an important fork of the Rio Negro entering just east of Barcelos which was itself one of the principal tributaries of the Solimões, or Amazon river (the Rio Branco finds itself situated in the present-day Brazilian state of Roraima, but during the colonial period, it sat in the borderlands between the captaincy of Rio Negro, the Spanish province of New Granada, and the Guianas). The Ouvidor Francisco Xavier Ribeiro de Sampaio visited this region while conducting an administrative journey along the Rio Negro from 1774 to 1775, and it is to his textual account and travel narrative that this chapter now turns. Sampaio, a Portuguese jurist, received training that was largely bureaucratic in nature, focusing on the management and statistical enumeration of Indigenous population centers throughout the captaincy of São José do Rio Negro. His task was to carry out a "correction" [*correição*], which entailed seeing whether the colonial officials had fulfilled their duties to the local populations. During this period, Sampaio also took an interest in the historical realities of the Rio Branco, the administrative capital, and a valley that had been under some scrutiny since Spanish and other European populations sought to encroach upon Portuguese dominion (Safier 2000).

Sampaio began his report on the Rio Branco with a geographical and climatic portrait of the region. He referred to the Rio Branco as a "New Mesopotamia," seeing in the "island" between the Amazon and Orinoco rivers an American version of the region between the Tigris and the Euphrates. Within this context, Sampaio characterized the region around the Rio Branco as enjoying a "perpetual springtime," but its circumstances belied an expectation of an inhospitable "torrid" landscape that suffers beneath extraordinary heat (1850: 204). Sampaio's account of the exploration of the Rio Branco also provided a historical window onto Portuguese colonization in the region, making explicit the political project undertaken by the crown to make contact with native populations in these "vast regions of this part of America" and to subject them to Portuguese governance and Catholic religious doctrine. One of the underlying motivations in writing such a report in the wake of the Treaty of Madrid, especially of a region that lay at the limit of Portuguese authority, was to demonstrate the uninterrupted possession of these territories through active cultivation: to show, in Sampaio's own words, "the continued use that the Portuguese had always made of the Rio Branco" and to narrate the consequent Spanish "invasions" of the Rio Branco territory. However, while this political conflict was central to Sampaio's goals, he also unveiled the natural features of the landscape, demonstrating that one of the central goals of Portuguese colonization was, in fact, to gain access

112 Colonial Period

to the abundant resources present along the river's edge and in the forested interiors: "The forests of the Rio Branco," Sampaio wrote, "abound with cacao: their waters, profuse with fish and turtles, which in the right season make their way to the beaches of that river to produce rich deposits of eggs, invite the region's inhabitants to take advantage of that voluntary surplus in order to produce oil that is extracted from the[se] same [animals]" (1850: 207).

The broader context of natural historical inquiry in eighteenth-century Europe might have shaped Sampaio's interest in the forest's natural features and its inhabitants' cultural characteristics. Sampaio left Portugal in 1767, five years before the Marquês de Pombal instituted the university reforms and renewal of scientific institutions that would transform the face of Portuguese natural history. Brigola (2003) writes about the reform of Portuguese scientific institutions and museums. Sampaio regularly cited Buffon and Montesquieu and was well versed in various works of scientific communication such as Abbé Pluche's *Spectacle de la Nature* or Hennebert and Beaurieu's *Cours d'Histoire Naturelle, ou Tableau de la Nature. Considérée dans l'Homme, les Quadrupédes, les Oiseaux, les Poissons & les Insectes* (Paris, 1770).

Nevertheless, Indigenous ingenuity helped shape this interest as well. When discussing the Pariána nation, for example, Sampaio enthusiastically described the "abundance with which they live: [their houses are] filled with flours [*farinhas*], fruits, and fish; their grills are filled with *jacarés*, or crocodiles" (Sampaio 1850: 61). This attention to the material realities of the local populations – their diets, especially, and the manner in which they were able to procure their vital necessities from the forest around them – transformed the philosophical discourse he employed in other parts of his "Diario" into a paean to Indigenous knowledge and to their ability to manipulate their environmental surroundings. In this instance, he wrote that the Pariána were "extremely inclined toward agriculture and gifted at fishing and hunting [...] Through their labor and industry," he concluded, "they live in abundance" (Sampaio 1850: 61).

In order to describe these material realities of the forest to a distant audience, Sampaio chose to register the natural products of the Rio Branco region using a list or catalog. In chapter ten of his "Relação," Sampaio enumerated the "nomenclature of the animals, plants, and minerals that can be found in the territory of the Rio Branco," alerting his reader that he would not provide a technical account of these objects such as one might find in a standard treatise of natural history. Instead, Sampaio emphasized that he would construct "a simple catalog" that would "give an idea of everything", dividing his subjects into animal, vegetable, and mineral kingdoms and subdividing each section into smaller categories, still. What this meant, in practice, was that Sampaio would follow a strategy that depended on information provided by native informants: providing the name in the Indigenous language and, where applicable, the local population's use of the animal, vegetable, or mineral product. Native knowledge was thus at the root of all European knowledge of Amazonian biodiversity. This meant, however, that certain objects would be represented by little more than their name, while others would be listed alongside the useful ways these products could be employed. For the section on aquatic birds, for instance, he divided them into white, "flesh-colored," red, black, and those "of varied colors," beneath which he listed grey seagulls, the fish-hawk, four types of "Socó," two kinds of "Marrecão," the "Maguarí" (large and small), two kinds of "Marreca," four species of "Maçarico," and three species of the "Guararimá." Little information appears other than the name, the color, the size, and (occasionally) the number of species contained within that denomination.

The vegetable kingdom, on the other hand, was both the most diverse and complete, subdivided into nine categories that described the uses and genres of the Rio Branco's wide-ranging vegetable material: timber trees; fruit-bearing trees; medicinal trees; dye trees; plants and herbs; barks; resins; lianas; and aquatic plants. Because of the sheer "variety" and "immensity" of these materials, Sampaio asked the reader to "forgive [him] from needing to reduce the trees, plants, bushes, lianas, and resins of the forests of the Rio Branco to a catalog," one that emphasized those species that the local inhabitants most commonly used. This focus on the utility of these botanical varietals was evident across the categories, including the Cumarú ("the hardest wood known to man"), the palm trees Patauá, Uaçaí, and Ubacába ("its fruit is a berry, which is infused into a drink"), the Muquém ("excellent blood thinner [...] It's a pity this drug was not sent to Europe"), Maniba and Macaxeira ("the roots of the latter two are used to make the flour known as *pão* or *mandióca*."), and several herbs that were "known to be antidotes to poison." Although much of the information collected by Sampaio related to the utility of these specimens derived from Indigenous sources, placing these objects into a catalog decontextualized this information from that origin. They moved from being specimens in the forest, with millennial historical interactions with local human populations, to being terms in a catalog where the historical ecology of their situation – their relationship to the native communities that cultivated and harvested them – was entirely removed.

For Sampaio, the extraordinary nature of Amazonian biodiversity served to underline the observation that had been made by earlier travelers to the region that an infinite number of botanists could never describe the plants and trees along the Amazon River. This was also true, Sampaio wrote, of the Rio Branco region: "In America, nature is so fertile, especially in its vegetable productions, that any intent [to capture it] is an arduous task and difficult to carry out" (1850: 262). Sampaio likened this overabundance of organic matter to a "vegetable monster," a kind of Amazonian hydra that "takes many forms" and diversifies into a "multiplicity of species." He ended his description of the vegetable kingdom with an appeal to abundance with a whirl of rhetorical hyperbole: "Who," Sampaio writes, "armed with a small shell would be capable of emptying the vastness of the sea? [...] Botany is an inexhaustible task in this part of the New World" (1850: 265). The sense of wonder and amazement at this profusion of organic species – what would come to be called the marvel of Amazonian biodiversity in the twentieth century – is apparent at this early stage of natural, historical examination, but it appeared in the context of a discrete attention to the enumeration of material objects that comprised the cornucopia of Amazonian nature: whereby each species – large and small, grey and multicolored, fruit-bearing and dye-producing, terrestrial and aquatic – needed to be granted their own position in a list or catalog that corresponded to the eighteenth-century botanical garden. Only then did the extent of this "inexhaustible" diversity begin to become clear. The appreciation of modern biodiversity from a European vantage point, then, may owe its origins as much to the technical registers of natural species in the eighteenth century as it did to the nineteenth-century discipline of biology. At the very least, the history of the Amazonian environment and the ecological thought that has maintained it over the centuries needs to consider the history of the Indigenous-inspired, European-executed catalog in its manuscript and printed forms, which served as the organizational media for containing the vast array of natural products that abounded in the eyes of eighteenth-century European observers.

Prior to turning to a different (but related) European account, it is important to note that there have always been other social actors who engaged with the Amazonian environment in ways that were far more direct and pragmatic than Sampaio. Two categories of communities that have received important attention in recent years are essential to underline: *Caboclos* and *Quilombolas*. For anthropologist Mark Harris, caboclos are "riverine peasantries" that pre-existed the event that brought them to the fore in Amazonian history – the Cabanagem: a series of revolts from 1835–40 that represented broad resistance to the newly installed regional government in Pará and throughout the northern Amazon region. While not representative of an ethnic unit per se, Caboclos were understood as a cultural group placed somewhere between the Portuguese officials and administrators, predominantly white, and the Indigenous-mestizo communities that regularly served as pilots, traders, and rowers along the river's edge. They were, according to Harris, "laborers, farmers, hunters, fishermen, administrators, and traders" who navigated life between the river and land, peasant communities that supported the broader colonial economy (Harris 2010: 40–41).

Meanwhile, enslaved Africans also composed a small but significant percentage of the social fabric of Luso-Amazonian life along the Lower Amazon. What would become the Amazonian communities of Santarém, Alenquer, and Óbidos had been founded in the seventeenth century by missionaries from the Jesuits and Franciscans, and these important sites for cacao production in the late-eighteenth century saw an increased number of enslaved Africans introduced as a result of Portuguese authorities' engagement and the newly established *Companhia Geral de Comércio do Grão-Pará e Maranhão* (1755) (Alden 1976). By 1799 at the latest, this region had become significant for fugitive groups of Indigenous Mura and African maroons, who built significant settlements along and around the Rio Trombetas throughout the early nineteenth century (De la Torre 2018). Although constraints limit the extent to which these two groups can be addressed in this chapter, both played significant roles in transforming local environmental conditions to adapt to the exigencies of imperial export agriculture, on the one hand, and provide subsistence gardens for the fugitives' sustenance on the other (Barickman 1994).

Natural Knowledge as Political Argument

This chapter now comes to the final example of the European technologies of registration discussed earlier in the context of Ouvidor Sampaio. The military engineer and colonel Lobo d'Almada, who would later become governor of the Rio Negro captaincy, used his *"Descripção relativa ao Rio Branco"* to advocate on behalf of the Portuguese crown against the rhetorical and military pretensions of the Spanish. The "Descrição" was, like Sampaio's account, a catalog discussing notions of the political frontier, Indigenous populations, and the presence of natural resources as part of a unified discourse of colonial administration. It was congruent with a larger strategy of using lists, charts, and "population maps" to gain numerical and administrative control over vast regions under dubious control by the Iberian powers. The previous governor of the captaincy of São José do Rio Negro, Joaquim Tinoco Valente, had made it clear that one vital aspect of the rights claimed by Portugal to possession of these territories was their history of extracting important natural products from the lands under dispute. Lobo d'Almada indicated that Portugal could claim the right of dominion because of their having "established factories [*feitorias*] for preserving fish, collecting butter from turtle eggs, and the many other products [*generos*] that those lands usually produce" (1861: 644). But it was his suggestion that the region be opened for cattle ranching that had both the most immediate as well as the most devastating ecological impact on the region.

Akin to planting an environmental time bomb, Lobo d'Almada reproduced this argument against the Spanish in his description of the Rio Branco. But in an article on the region's "natural products," he went even further in outlining its extraordinary commercial importance by discussing those natural products that would provide "commercial utility, or that could serve the needs and facilitate [human] life" (1861: 660). In order to do this, he listed the many vegetable products that could be found there, including cacao, sarsaparilla, vanilla, white and yellow species of the *semauma* tree, cupauba oil, the nut "vulgarly called Maranhão" (and known today as the *"castanha-do-pará"* or, in English, the Brazil nut), and woods of various kinds and colors, including orange wood – especially useful for household furniture, according to Lobo d'Almada – and redwood, which was good for the same purpose. As for inks and dyes, they included the *caapiranga* plant (for red ink), the carajura for a deep purple ink, and *jutaycica* resin as a varnish. Finally, Lobo d'Almada concluded this extensive list by enumerating those "diverse fruits [...] created without agriculture [*sem cultura*]," which included the cashew, the *abiurana*, the *cupuahi*, and "many others with fabulous tastes and smells, which would be highly prized if cultivated" (1861: 661). Similar descriptions appeared for the natural products of the animal kingdom: "the country," Lobo d'Almada wrote, "abounds in game," while birds (particularly "mutuns" and ducks) were innumerable. The number of turtles was "extremely abundant [*abundantissimo*]." Geography and accessibility also play a central role in Lobo d'Almada's discourse. In comparing cacao and sarsaparilla, he remarked that cacao "is always to be found on both banks of the river upstream," forging a connection between the specific region of the Rio Branco where cacao is found and the "fertile fields [...] covered with excellent grasses for cattle" (1861: 661). This mixture of emphasizing the natural products and suggesting where colonial projects might augment them became a hallmark of Lobo d'Almada's "Descripção."

The arguments Lobo d'Almada put forward in favor of the introduction of cattle into this region, however, were his most forceful, especially considering that he employed conservationist rhetoric even as he advocated for the introduction of a species that would ultimately have a devastating effect on the region's natural resources. Lobo d'Almada made the arguments that cattle would provide meat products to the capital, which would diminish the "waste" [*estrago*] of turtles; that these meat products would provide sustenance for those involved in indigo extraction; and, finally, that taxes on heads of cattle would provide critical income to the royal coffers. Once again referring to the "immense and fertile fields of the Rio Branco," Lobo d'Almada presented the introduction of cattle as a "convenient and necessary" means to take economic control of the tropical landscape, in conjunction with the commercial strategies he put forward to turn other natural products into valuable sources of income. In this way, the production of turtles, indigo, and taxes would be augmented (or preserved) by the introduction of a foreign species, and, by this same logic, the Portuguese would be improving the landscape, protecting its natural features, and profiting at the same time.

Lobo d'Almada produced conservationist rhetoric in defending the improved management of certain natural resources along the Rio Branco, as well. According to him, the "prodigious quantity of butter" or lard extracted from Amazonian turtles was essential to the commercial and economic well-being of the Rio Branco and the nearby Rio Solimões (Amazon). But the "disordered killing" of these defenseless creatures was putting this line of industry in jeopardy, and Lobo d'Almada resorted to a language of conservation in order to advocate for their protection. He spoke of "budgeting prudently" so that the turtles would not cease to lay their eggs entirely and railed against those practices that caused the turtles to become "extremely thin, to taste bad, and to die" prematurely (1861: 664).

He was all the more aggressive when it came to two other resources: cotton and indigo. In the case of the former, Lobo d'Almada insisted that cotton was already abundant in the region and that "all of the Indians [*gentilidade*] of that territory have cotton plants in their gardens." But Lobo d'Almada offered a prescription for the expansion of cotton fields in the region by suggesting that they should "belong proprietarily to village Indians" and that Amerindian women might learn to use the cotton wheel, which would enable them, within one year, according to him, to manufacture their own cloth. In this way, the natives would save themselves from the exorbitant price of cloth to cover their private parts, and there would, at the same time, emerge from the Indian villages a "commercial line" that would benefit both the Indians and the captaincy alike. In the case of indigo Lobo d'Almada justified its expansion as a commodity not because of its benefits to the Indigenous economy but because it was a native product that could be easily transported throughout the captaincy. To prove his point, he narrated an episode in which he transformed two bundles of indigo into a quantity that was as "precious" as that from the Rio Negro. Insisting on the eyewitness nature of his narrative, he commented that "no other type of culture would provide so many advantages or would be better placed as an object of commerce" (Lobo d'Almada 1861: 668). It was the material condition of the indigo plant and its ability to circulate that Lobo d'Almada emphasized, in addition to its being "beautiful and attractive as can be seen from the sample I submitted." The idea that a small, easily transportable volume of indigo could be sold for a "good price" was an even greater reason that the naturally occurring plant should be grown – and transported – throughout the land (1861: 666). Lobo d'Almada ended his entry on indigo with a moral tone, insisting that many "unscrupulous" colonists wished to profit from the work of others, especially "at the cost of tears and blood of the miserable and persecuted Indians," but that his proposal was different: despite their being "lazy, inconstant, and weak," his idea was that the Indians could be put to good use and that they were, in the end, also "our brothers."

Although they are far from being the only social actors that came to leave an impact on Amazonian biodiversity, Ribeiro de Sampaio and Lobo d'Almada were united in employing the catalog as a technology for registering that diversity: a way of textually controlling the overabundance of natural products they hoped to present to the crown as viable, exploitable resources. Each saw the need to go beyond the bounds of a traditional narrative format to present their administrative superiors with a portrait of the natural world in the Rio Branco region. In both instances, the catalog as a tool sought to contain an overabundant, seemingly inexhaustible natural world and place it comfortably within the confines of a single text, organized into chapters and – perhaps most importantly – expressed with coherence and authority without necessarily being complete or exhaustive. These two texts by Sampaio and Lobo d'Almada, albeit imperfectly, provided a portrait of the natural landscapes through which the two had passed, enabling others to imagine this usable landscape by bringing attention to its material realities. In and of themselves, these texts did not transform biodiversity. Still, they did provide blueprints for a capital- and commodity-infused world that would be picked up later by European and South American economic actors alike. Both Sampaio and Lobo d'Almada thus provided ammunition for European empires seeking to increase their knowledge of the natural contours of South American's interior regions and unwittingly accelerated ecological exploitation in one of the most sensitive spots of human-induced ecological change, a position that the Brazilian state and some of its Amazonian neighbors would take up with gusto in later centuries.

Conclusion

This essay has focused attention on the tools used by European imperial agents and administrators to capture in print the extraordinary diversity of the Amazon region, even as it has gestured toward the much wider range of social actors that should be considered in any conception of human-induced ecological change, including native groups, African-descended slaves and Quilombolas, riverine populations, and peasant communities more generally. While the examples given in this chapter cohere primarily (although not exclusively) around Portuguese America during the colonial period (which represents today approximately 60 percent of the Amazon basin), the conclusions reached are equally applicable to the "Spanish American" Amazon as well – that is, those spaces that would eventually become the Colombian, Peruvian, Ecuadorian, or Bolivian Amazon. Naturalists on the Spanish-American side of the frontier also relied increasingly on textual devices during the colonial period. Perhaps most famously, Alexander von Humboldt described the Amazon River region in print after spending several years traveling along its Spanish American perimeter without ever setting foot in Portuguese territory. He relied on the writings not only of Jesuit, Mercederian, and Capuchin missionaries who had spent extensive periods in the Spanish missions but also on the experiences of Indigenous and Euro-American Creoles whose knowledge he highlighted in his written texts. The conceptual library of ideas that Humboldt would amass following his return to Europe was comprised – if not invented – on the basis of their writings and experiences (Thurner and Cañizares-Esguerra 2022).

But it was the Brazilian naturalist Alexandre Rodrigues Ferreira – sometimes referred to anomalously as the Brazilian Humboldt – who made the most explicit comment about the relationship between the equatorial jungle and print when he wrote that every day he traveled through the Amazon basin was as if he was turning a page in the book of nature, hearkening back to the primeval world created by divine intervention and revealed on the pages of the holiest book of all (Safier 2007). But divine intervention, we also now know, did not save the Amazon region from the damage inflicted upon it in the 200 years since the opening up of the colonial world. Rampant exploitation in the last two centuries has simply accelerated the practices that were already taking place during the colonial period. It will take more than lists and names to reverse the cycle of devastation that has taken its place. It may take a far closer look at the ecological practices of the Amazon's earliest inhabitants, in fact, to stop the sky from falling, in the words of Davi Kopenawa Yanomami (2013).

The eighteenth-century examples drawn from the history of the Amazon's colonial-era exploration and exploitation demonstrate the efforts made to take stock of the abundance and diversity of the Amazon River region well before the modern era. The natural riches of this unique environment and the consequent efforts of the Spanish and Portuguese crowns to take advantage of their overseas resources – in an increasingly desperate fashion – led colonial agents to create lists and other forms of knowledge-producing technologies. Following the itineraries of these objects and writings – and especially of the individuals involved in creating them and the animals, insects, and floral bounty that functioned as the protagonists – allows a new way of understanding the history of science and ecology in the Amazonian world. It transforms the region not into an island, as Ribeiro de Sampaio imagined when he referred to the region as a "New Mesopotamia," but rather as a land of intersecting pathways, open to the world and nourished – and eventually destroyed – by its exchanges and transplantations. It is these circulating stories that the natural objects of the Amazon have hidden so effectively for centuries. Just like the inexhaustible sources of vegetative life that Sampaio struggled to count as he enumerated the many species he had found in this extraordinary new world of equatorial nature, these histories also seem to have no limits, even as we increasingly recognize the limited capacity of the Amazon River region itself to rebuff the destructive assaults that have been foisted upon it in recent times and, in many ways, throughout its centuries-long history.

References

Alden, Dauril. 1976. "The Significance of Cacao Production in the Amazon Region during the Late Colonial Period: An Essay in Comparative Economic History." *Proceedings of the American Philosophical Society* 120: 103–35.

Arregui, Aníbal. 2015. "Amazonian quilombolas and the technopolitics of aluminum." *Journal of Material Culture* 20, no. 3: 249–272.

Asúa, Miguel de, and Roger French, ed. 2005. *A New World of Animals: Early Modern Europeans on the Creatures of Iberian America*. Aldershot: Ashgate.

Barickman, Bert J. 1994. "'A Bit of Land, Which They Call Roça': Slave Provision Grounds in the Bahian Recôncavo, 1780–1860." *Hispanic American Historical Review* 74, no. 4: 649–687.

Beerman, Eric. 1996. *Francisco Requena: la expedición de límites. Amazonia, 1779–1795*. Madrid: Compañía Literaria.

Brigola, João Carlos. 2003. *Colecções, Gabinetes e Museus em Portugal no século XVIII*. Lisbon: Fundação Calouste Gulbenkian.

Chambouleyron, Rafael. 2022. "O «cravo do Maranhão» e a Amazônia global (séculos XVII-XVIII)". *Revista de Indias* 82, no. 285: 329–361.

Chambouleyron, Rafael, and Alírio Cardoso. 2022. "Economia da Amazonia Colonial: um balanço historiográfico." In *História econômica do Brasi: colonia*, ed. Fábio Pesavento and Fernando Carlos G. Cerqueira Lima. Niterói: EDUFF.

Cleary, David. 2001. "Towards an Environmental History of the Amazon: From Prehistory to the Nineteenth Century." *Latin American Research Review* 36, no. 2: 64–96.

De la Torre, Oscar. 2018. *The People of the River: Nature and Identity in Black Amazonia, 1835–1945*. Chapel Hill: University of North Carolina Press.

Domingues, Ângela. 2019. "Museus, coleccionismo e viagens científicas em Portugal de finais de Setecentos." *Asclepio* 71, no. 2: 1–19.

Giraldo, Manuel Lucena. 1993. *Laboratório Tropical. La expedición de límites al Orinoco, 1750–1767*. Madrid: CSIC.

Gomberville, Marin le Roy de. 1684. *La Doctrine des Moeurs*. Paris.

Gómez, Sebastián. 2014. *Frontera selvática. Españoles, portugueses y su disputa por el noroccidente amazónico*. Bogotá: Instituto Colombiano de Antropología e História.

Harris, Mark. 2010. *Rebellion on the Amazon: The Cabanagem, Race, and Popular Culture in the North of Brazil, 1798–1840*. Cambridge: Cambridge University Press.

Hecht, Susanna. 2013. *The Scramble for the Amazon and the Lost Paradise of Euclides da Cunha*. Chicago: University of Chicago Press.

Hecht, Susanna, and Alexander Cockburn. 2011. *The Fate of the Forest: Developers, Destroyers, and Defenders of the Amazon*. Chicago: University of Chicago Press.

Kawa, Nicholas C. 2016. *Amazonia in the Anthropocene: People, Soils, Plants, Forests*. Austin: University of Texas Press.

Kopenawa Yanomami, Davi. 2013. *The Falling Sky: Words of a Yanomami Shaman*. Cambridge: Harvard University Press.

Leal, Claudia. 2013. "Rainforest Frontiers." *RCC Perspectives* 7: 51–57.

———. 2018. "From Threatening to Threatened Jungles." In *A Living Past*, ed. Claudia Leal, José Augusto Pádua, and John Soluri. New York: Berghahn Books.

Lisboa, Cristóvão de. 2000. *História dos animais e árvores do Maranhão*. Lisbon: Commissão Nacional para a Comemoração dos Descobrimentos Portugueses.

Lobo d'Almada, Manoel da Gama. 1861. "Descripção relativa ao Rio Branco, e seu territorio." *Revista trimensal do Instituto Histórico e Geográfico Brasileiro* 24: 617–683.

Marques, João Francisco. 1996. "Frei Cristovão de Lisboa, missionário no Maranhão e Grão-Pará (1624–1635), e a defesa dos índios brasileiros." *Revista da Faculdade de Letras. História* 13: 323–352.

Neves, Eduardo. 2022. *Sob os Tempos do Equinócio: Oito mil anos de história na Amazônia central*. São Paulo: Ubu Editora.

Papavero, Nelson, Dante Martins Teixeira, William Leslie Overal, et al., ed. 2002. *O Novo Éden: A Fauna da Amazônia Brasileia nos Relatos de Viajantes e Cronistas desde a Descoberta do Rio Amazonas por Pinzón (1500) até o Tratado de Santo Ildefonso (1777)*. Belém: Museu Paraense Emílio Goeldi.

Pelayo, Francisco, and Miguel-Ángel Puig-Samper. 1992. *La obra científica de Löfling en Venezuela*. Caracas: Departamento de Asuntos Públicos de Lagoven.

Raffles, Hugh, and Antoinette M.G.A. Winkler Prins. 2003. "Further Reflections on Amazonian Environmental History: Transformations of Rivers and Streams." *Latin American Research Review* 38, no. 3: 165–187.

Rapp Py-Daniel, Anne. 2015. "Os contextos funerários na arqueologia da calha do rio Amazonas." PhD diss., University of São Paulo.

Roller, Heather. 2014. *Amazonian Routes: Indigenous Mobility and Colonial Communities in Northern Brazil*. Redwood: Stanford University Press.

———. 2021. *Contact Strategies: Histories of Native Autonomy in Brazil*. Redwood: Stanford University Press.

Rostain, Stéphen. 2017. *Amazonie: les 12 travaux des civilisations précolombiennes*. Paris: Belin.

Safier, Neil. 2000. "O Diario da viagem do Ouvidor Sampaio (1774–1775): as práticas narrativas de uma viagem administrativa na América Portuguesa." *LEITURAS: Revista da Biblioteca Nacional de Lisboa* 6: 123–148.

———. 2007. "'Every day that I travel... is a Page that I Turn': Reading and Observing in Eighteenth-Century Amazonia." *Huntington Library Quarterly* 70, no. 1: 103–128.

———. 2011. "Transformations de la zone torride: les repertoires de la nature tropicale à l'époque des Lumières." *Annales. Histoire, sciences sociales* 66, no. 1: 143–172.

———. 2014. "Beyond Brazilian Nature: The Editorial Itineraries of Marcgraf and Piso's *Historia Naturalis Brasiliae*." In *The Legacy of Dutch Brazil*, ed. Michiel Van Groesen, 168–186. Cambridge: Cambridge University Press.

———. 2017. "Masked observers and mask collectors: entangled visions from the eighteenth-century Amazon." *Colonial Latin American Review* 26, no. 1: 104–130.

Sampaio, Francisco Xavier Ribeiro de. 1850. "Relação Geographica-Historica do Rio Branco da America Portugueza." *Revista Trimensal de História e Geographia do Jornal do Instituto Histórico e Geográphico Brazileiro* 13, no. 18: 200–250.

Steffen, Will, Wendy Broadgate, Lisa Deutsch, et al. 2015. "The trajectory of the Anthropocene: The Great Acceleration." *The Anthropocene Review* 2, no. 1: 81–98.

Thurner, Mark, and Jorge Cañizares-Esguerra, ed. 2022. *The Invention of Humboldt*. London: Routledge.

Wade, Lizzie. 2015. "How the Amazon became a crucible of life." *Science*. October 28.

Biodiversity in Mesoamerica in the Colonial Period

Christopher Valesey and Martha Few

There is a general consensus among scholars that European colonialism – beginning with the encounter and invasions in the Americas and sharply accelerating throughout the Industrial Revolution – marks a watershed in humankind's imprint on the planet (Crosby 1972; Mann 2011; Lewis and Maslin 2015; Jones et al. 2023). Since then, the biodiversity boundary, part of the nine planetary boundaries theory to ensure a safe operating space for humanity, has been transgressed more than any other (Rockström et al. 2009; Mace et al. 2014). This chapter utilizes this periodization of three major environmental transformations of the Anthropocene in Mexico recently discussed by Jones et al. (2023): the first, from 11,000 to 1600 BCE, is marked by the "development of agriculture and greater social organization and technology of human indigenous societies" (5); the second begins with the rise of Olmec civilization ca. 1600 BCE and continues until the Mexican Revolution in early twentieth century; the third starts with changes in land use in post-revolutionary Mexican politics and society. This chapter spotlights the second stage as it relates to colonial Mesoamerica, a cultural and historical region that stretches from northern Mexico through much of Central America and that includes the Mayas, Mexica, Nahuas, and other ethno-linguistic cultures more broadly, highlighting patterns of exchange between Spanish colonists and various Indigenous populations, resource exploitation, deforestation, and changes to land usage.

In colonial-era Mesoamerica, pre-existing understandings of human-animal relationships not only informed engagement with new species but also reshaped global biodiversity, a steady but uneven process over time and space. Some Indigenous populations resisted both Spanish colonial domestic animal-related practices like cattle ranching and pastoralism, while others quickly adapted them for personal, economic, or communal benefit. Ultimately, the combination of the introduction of Hispanic animal husbandry alongside an increasingly exploitative colonial system resulted in significant changes in nature-society relations among populations under Spanish rule in Mesoamerica. This exploitative tendency of resource extraction, a key characteristic of Iberian expansion to the Americas and European colonialism more generally, was an early and significant step toward transgressing the biodiversity boundary of the planetary boundaries theory.

Encounter, Colonization, and Impacts on Mesoamerican Biodiversity

Traditional models of scholarship attributed possession of Old World domesticates as a teleological step towards "civilization" and one of the reasons why European expansion succeeded (Crosby 1972). Such thinking – long unconvincing – can be linked back to Spanish colonial writings like that of the Jesuit José de Acosta who remarked on what he perceived as the lack of domesticated animals and "useless beasts" (Acosta 2002: 65). Archaeological evidence demonstrates that even in ancient Teotihuacan (1–550 CE), residents bred cottontail and jackrabbits, and captured carnivorous predators for ritualistic purposes (Somerville et al. 2016; Sugiyama, Somerville, and Schoeninger 2015). Although Mesoamerican cultures did not domesticate ungulates prior to contact with Europe, they did hold other models of human-animal interactions that did not follow European-based models of domestication: they raised turkeys and dogs as part of household production, and cultivated insects such as cochineal and stingless honeybees (Valadez Azúa 2003; Thornton et al. 2012; White et al. 2004; Norton 2015). Across Mesoamerica, this labor was largely gendered labor, part of women's joint responsibilities in agricultural production and animal husbandry (Sousa 2017: 211). Moreover, Mesoamerican populations regularly hunted a wide variety of local aquatic, aviary, and land-based animals. Pre-contact Mesoamericans were breeders, trap-setting farmers, and collectors who exploited a wide variety of ecosystems for nonhuman animals – not just hunters who supplemented agricultural production (Valadez Azúa and Galicia 2014; Rojas Rabiela 1990).

In fact, biodiverse spaces of pre-contact Mesoamerica included not only wilderness and forest areas, but also urban centers that functioned as bases of empire. Tenochtitlan, the capital of the Mexica Empire, was particularly rich in biodiversity. In Hernán Cortés' second letter to King Charles V, he described the breeding of "rabbits, hares, deer and small dogs that they raise to eat" in the marketplaces, as well as a street "where they sell all types of birds" (1522). Emperor Motecuhzoma II (c. 1466–1520) maintained a magnificent zoo and aviary with exotic species procured through tribute, trade, and diplomatic exchanges, all of which was supported by hundreds of workers. Archeological excavations at the Templo Mayor have uncovered over four hundred species – fish, crocodiles, snakes, turtles, toucans, quetzals, and jaguars – in sixty offerings to Tlaloc and Huitzilopochtli. Tenochtitlan, and later Mexico City, markets teemed with aquatic beings for food consumption harvested and hunted from Lake Texcoco that surrounded the capital as well, not only fish but also salamanders, dragonfly larvae, shrimps and crawfish, and the waterbug *axayacatl* and its eggs (López Luján 1993; López Luján et al. 2012). As demonstrated by the Templo Mayor excavations, animal sacrifice and the interment of their remains frequently took place during ceremonies. There were close connections between the sacrificial practices using animals like deer and human sacrifice: they were carried out the same way, created filial bonds, and allowed for species regeneration (Olivier 2015).

In the early modern Iberian Peninsula, animals were similarly connected to culture, religion, and the economy. Moreover, these creatures also participated in imperial expansion long before Europeans set foot in the Americas. The need for new sheep pastures during the *Reconquista* was so intense that it "gave a stronger impulse" to Christian expansion (O'Callaghan 1983:183). Castilians colonized the newly reconquered Guadiana Basin frontier during the thirteenth century in large part through cattle ranching (Bishko 1963). Old-world species then participated in Iberian cross-Atlantic travel. The horses, dogs, pigs, cattle, chickens, sheep, and goats that accompanied Columbus on his second voyage to the Antilles in 1493 were the first to arrive in the Western Hemisphere. Spaniards left animals like domesticated pigs in some areas prior to colonization to ensure a food source as they went feral and could be hunted by future conquistadors and colonists (Archivo General de Indias 1546: L.10, fs. 41r-41v). Throughout the late fifteenth and early sixteenth centuries, Spaniards across the New World frequently sent letters to officials in Spain to request a greater livestock supply (Orden 1993:78). As well, live animals captured that were indigenous to the Americas, as objects of science, trade, and curiosity, quickly made their way to the European metropole, helping to shape ocean-going shipboard environments and early zoos, disrupting systemic human attempts to construct them as colonial animals who functioned solely as scientific or material objects in empire making (Few 2020).

Spain's colonial expansion, first to the Caribbean in the 1490s and then to Mesoamerica, in the 1510s, represented the first significant European presence in the Western Hemisphere, and one that began a period of profound global ecological transformations. Spaniards relied on the presence of Old World domesticates like cattle, sheep, goats, pigs, and chickens as they expanded their imperial domain. Diverse Indigenous peoples of Mesoamerica, which includes the Mexica, Nahuas, Mayas, and other ethno-linguistic cultures engaged with Spanish colonialism, and what has come to be known as the Columbian exchange of animal, bird, and plant species, at different times and degrees of intensity over the course of the colonial period.

While Alfred Crosby's Columbian exchange model has proved resilient (1972; 1986), the "animal turn" in recent historiography has shifted the focus in ways that challenge the historical construction of human-animal boundaries within the processes of ecological change. For Latin America, scholars have proposed alternative models that bring animals back into history to analyze local understandings of the natural world in the shift to colonial rule and center animals in historical narratives of Latin America, perspectives that require critical approaches to the archives by focusing on the ways that these sources at times reveal, and other times obscure, what Marcy Norton has called "modes of interaction" among species (Derby 2011; Domínguez 2017; Few and Tortorici 2013; Norton 2013: 53).

For Central Mexico, where archival sources exist in far greater numbers than other regions of colonial Mesoamerica, especially for the sixteenth century, scholars have contested the significance of the ecological footprint left by ungulates Europeans brought with them starting with Columbus' second voyage to the Americas in 1493. Some argue that an explosive rise in livestock population densities led to intense environmental degradation, while others assert that increases in herd sizes paralleled the sharp decline in Indigenous populations and environmental recovery (Toledo 1990; Melville 1994; Butzer and Butzer 1995; Sluyter 1998).

In either case, the encounter between Europe and Mesoamerica dramatically transformed both parties' knowledge of the natural world and the non-human animals of Mesoamerica's ecosystems. On the one hand, Mesoamericans met not just Spaniards but a variety of domesticated species common to civilizations across Eurasia that were deeply embedded in European institutions, religion, and culture (Alves 2011). On the other hand, European imperialism resulted in the realization that undiscovered, and perhaps even mythological creatures awaited discovery in the New World, species that could be collected and displayed in curiosity cabinets, exploited for their fur, feathers, and other body parts, or consumed as food and drugs, and in the process, changing global diets. Monarchs and colonial bureaucracies expressed great interest in learning about, acquiring, and profiting from as many New World species as possible, which they frequently did through often unacknowledged collaboration and exploitation with Indigenous peoples of Mesoamerica and their ecological knowledge, a process that continued throughout the colonial period and beyond.

From the start Spanish colonial officials facilitated the introduction of European domesticates across New Spain and even encouraged animal husbandry among the local population. Both Bishop Juan de Zumárraga and Viceroy Antonio de Mendoza asserted that the local population should be acculturated to animal husbandry and that sheep were particularly well suited for the pre-existing textile industry (Zumárraga 1534–1536; Mendoza 1543: fs. 7v-8r). In Oaxaca, political and religious officials introduced the Mixtec and Zapotec peoples to silkworm raising, which colonial officials could then exploit through forced tribute labor and taxation of these Indigenous cultures (Borah 1943).

Upon arrival, these animals – many of which were completely unknown to Indigenous populations in the Western Hemisphere – catalyzed a great deal of change in all aspects of social, cultural, and economic life in colonial Mesoamerica. Old World domesticates like cattle, sheep, horses, donkeys, pigs, goats, and chickens did not just supplement diets. Hispanic modes of animal husbandry like cattle ranching and sheep pastoralism transformed local economies and cultures. Complications from this sudden change in biodiversity across Mesoamerica in the sixteenth century and the introduction of European domesticated animals caused tension between Europeans and colonial populations, and at the same time also created opportunities for Indigenous people to creatively adapt, absorb, and transform human-animal-environment connections. In the earliest decades of Spanish colonialism, most Indigenous people interacted with introduced species in both rural and urban settings of European settlement. Wealthy Spaniards commanded large herds of livestock, yet Indigenous laborers, African slaves, and the emerging free mixed race (*casta*) populations provided the bulk of care. Over time, encounters between Indigenous laborers and livestock also increasingly occurred at estates owned by Indigenous or *mestizo* elites (Chance 2011; Hoekstra 2010; Villella 2016: 29–72). Serving livestock meant learning novel ways of interacting with animals based on husbandry practices throughout Eurasia, such as shoeing, hobbling, saddling, shearing, and castration.

Wandering domesticated animals such as sheep, pigs, and cattle thrust colonists into conflict with local populations, perhaps more than any other single factor. This occurred when owners did not properly pen the animals, or when formerly domesticated pigs went feral, resulting in encroachment on Indigenous-owned land, consumption of food crops, environmental degradation, deforestation, and contamination of water supplies (Anderson 2004: 177). In fact, one of the great ironies of the expansion of animal husbandry in many parts of the Americas is the misconception that indigenous populations lacked notions of territorial boundaries while Europeans clearly demarcated their property. On the contrary, due to Western European practice of "commonage" (communal grazing lands on open pastures) in combination with long-distance transhumance, Spaniards' uncontrolled livestock constantly wandered into Indigenous farms and gardens possessing clear and well-known boundaries (Butzer 1988). Animal husbandry, first practiced by Spaniards and later mastered by local populations, placed intense demands on a community's agrarian and water supplies (Barteet 2015: 184).

For Mesoamericans, a primary mechanism to cope with conflict during the early colonial period included engagement with the Spanish petition-and-response legal system. Conceptualized as vassals to the Spanish Crown, Indigenous elites and communities protested colonial policies, the behavior of municipal and religious officials, or advocated for a return to pre-contact styles of governance (Owensby 2008; Masters 2018). Thus began a centuries-long process in which New Spain's colonial officials adjudicated trespassing disputes between Indigenous communities and Spaniards who failed to monitor their herds. Such conflict was enough to incentivize local elites to engage with the early Spanish colonial government. Although Indigenous plaintiffs experienced mixed success, the depth of the archival record demonstrates that colonial officials took livestock encroachment seriously throughout the early colonial period.

Petitions against livestock encroachment did not frame the conflict as an environmental crisis. Instead, plaintiffs were primarily concerned with ambitious colonists who disregarded communal boundaries at the expense of community food crop production. Therefore, local elites took greater issue with Spanish herd owners who did not honor seasonal planting and harvesting schedules than they did with the livestock themselves. Like other petitions on behalf of Mesoamerica elites or communities, those that discussed livestock encroachment presented what scholars describe as an idiomatic language of submission and inferiority to the king to receive assistance. In doing so, locals capitalized on the rhetoric of *amparos* (protective judicial orders) promoted by Viceroy Luis de Velasco II, who characterized natives as *personas miserables* (wretched persons) and in need of protection (Owensby 2008). Rather than decrying an environmental catastrophe, local elites instead took advantage of the notion of a subordinate yet reciprocal relationship with the Spanish Crown to deal with issues with colonists and their livestock. Some sources indicate that Indigenous communities went to great lengths to deter livestock, but they likely belie ulterior political motives. For both Indigenous people and Spaniards, scapegoating livestock could be strategic if it furthered their greater agenda.

Not all resistance in Mesoamerica consisted of engagement with the legal system. Most notably, Mesoamericans adapted to horses to resist Spanish imperial expansion. Throughout the Chichimeca War (c. 1550–1590) in north and northwestern Mexico, mounted Chichimecas raided Spanish estates, mines, and livestock trains or ranches around the *Camino Real* (Royal Road) between Mexico City and Zacatecas. Even with fortified towns, advanced weaponry, and Indigenous allies, Spaniards were plagued by Chichimeca attacks throughout the latter half of the sixteenth century, whose power and mobility rested on the adoption of horses and their utilization for warfare against colonial authorities (Gradie 2017; Poole 2017).

Of all the introduced species, Mesoamericans adopted horses most quickly. As conquest expeditions spread outward from Tenochtitlan after the Spanish-Mexica War's conclusion in 1521, local elites bartered military collaboration for equine companions. Indigenous elites quickly recognized horses as Spanish symbols of social status, yet these animals were also used to carry trade goods or expedite travel through hostile territory. Spanish law theoretically prevented non-elite Indigenous people from owning horses throughout the sixteenth century; however, this practice was largely ignored, especially in more remote parts of Mesoamerica (Restall 1997: 103–104, 181; Terraciano 2001: 135; Villella 2016: 44).

Mesoamericans easily integrated chickens into their households due to their similarities with autochthonous turkeys. As with turkeys, women commonly raised chickens for consumption, trade, or tribute (Sousa 2015). King Philip II's sixteenth-century geographic survey, the *Relaciones Geográficas*, are inundated with examples of Mesoamerican households breeding them. These small, familiar, profitable, and rapidly procreating birds are frequently mentioned in mundane Indigenous-language texts, especially in the sixteenth century (Lockhart 1992: 201).

In Central Mexico, local populations began adopting large herds of sheep and goats by the middle of the sixteenth century. The Tlaxcalans – the foremost allies to the Spaniards during the Spanish-Mexica War – were likely the first to engage intensively with pastoralism. Their *cabildo* (city council) minutes contain multiple references to the ownership and maintenance of sheep. Not only did Tlaxcalans command large herds of sheep, they also monitored the sizes of herds in their tributary towns and hired local Spaniards to demonstrate how to most productively increase breeding and wool and cheese production (Lockhart, Berdan, and Anderson 1986). Although other Indigenous-language sources are scant, there are over a thousand viceregal grants for Indigenous communities and elites to procure herds of sheep throughout the sixteenth century. Similar adaptations to animal husbandry gradually expanded throughout Mesoamerica as colonization intensified and the number of domesticates increased (Alexander 2012; Baskes 1996: 11; Forde 2017; Thompson 2000).

In contrast, the archival record indicates that Mesoamericans did not petition the colonial bureaucracy to own cattle to nearly the same degree as they did for sheep. If they did, they did not do so successfully, as there are not many extant viceregal grants for all Mexico in the early colonial period. In urban settings, Mesoamericans witnessed the use of cattle in festivals that featured bullfighting (Garcia and Celestino 1992, see also Benson Library, Genaro García Collection, G2, Anales de Tecamachalco, f. 35v). However, Indigenous populations mostly engaged with them on Spanish-owned estates for fieldwork like plowing. The lack of Indigenous ownership of cattle, at least in the sixteenth century can likely be attributed to the fact that they are more expensive to maintain and take longer to breed than smaller domesticates like goats or sheep (Abbass 1993: 179).

The rise of muleteering among Indigenous, Black, and casta groups coincided with the opening of trading networks across Mexico and Central America starting in the 1530s and 1540s, linking port cities first on the Atlantic, and then on the Pacific to growing urban markets and sites of colonial economic production. Perhaps the most lucrative was the beginning of Manila Galleon trade between the Philippines to the port of Acapulco in 1565. Beforehand, most muleteers were Spaniards trading between Mexico City and Veracruz; afterward, Indigenous towns between Acapulco and Mexico City became "staging posts for pack animals" where local muleteers rented their beasts of burden to itinerant merchants, and some towns like Tepoztlan specialized in long-distance trade (Hassig 1985: 194; Seijas 2016). Indigenous communities also employed draft animals to carry cargo across the Royal Road between the lucrative silver mines in Zacatecas and Mexico City.

The introduction of animal-related vocabulary to Mesoamerican languages represents some of the earliest linguistic adaptations to Spanish. Nahuatl philologist

James Lockhart compared these linguistic transformations to the way that children learn language, explaining, "a preoccupation with animals plays a large role in a child's acquisition of a language, and the same phenomenon appeared in the early stages of the linguistic reaction of Nahuatl to the Spanish presence" (Lockhart 1992: 280–281). Mesoamericans used autochthonous wildlife as reference points when identifying new species whenever possible (Lockhart 1992: 280; Restall 1999: 181; Terraciano 2002: 85–86; Few and Tortorici 2013: 9). Afterward, Indigenous linguistic adaptations to European animals reflect meaningful cultural changes that began in the early colonial period. Human-animal interactions such as shoeing, shearing, bullfighting, jousting, and more encouraged new vocabulary and symbolized changes to Mesoamericans' interactions with the natural world. Across Mesoamerica, the timing of the borrowing of Spanish loanwords or the creation of new terminology depended on the pace and intensity of colonization.

Of course, novel ways of engaging with introduced species were not limited to animal husbandry, pastoralism, or the sensational activities seen during festivals – it also included adaptation of some of the newly introduced animals into food consumption and rituals in colonial society. Prior to contact with Europe, many Mesoamerican civilizations featured merchants who sold animals like deer, dogs, turkeys, fish, and birds as food. Although the early transition to beef, mutton, and pork was not unanimous (Garagarza 2013), Indigenous merchants and market sellers quickly incorporated the flesh of livestock into their inventories and their prepared food offerings. In Mexico City, archeologists of the Templo Mayor unearthed over 3,500 bone fragments of pigs, cattle, and sheep alongside streets adjacent to the main temple precinct, all of which are waste from butcher shops (Mejía et al. 2018). This acquired taste for beef, mutton, and pork was not focused exclusively in the colonial capital of New Spain; in fact, numerous geographic surveys requested by King Philip II in the late sixteenth century refer to Indigenous towns in which the populace bred and consumed livestock (Acuña 1985).

Drawing on humoral theory, Spanish colonial officials paradoxically believed that Indigenous people should adopt a European diet to acculturate yet warned that doing so quickly would be devastating to their health (Earle 2012: 168). They sporadically attempted to control Indigenous consumption of beef and mutton throughout the early colonial period. During seasons in which livestock herds were small, Spaniards accused Mesoamericans of overconsuming meat. In 1550, Mexico City cabildo officials wrote that excessive indulgence of meat led Indigenous people to be "sick and lazy" (Ayuntamiento de la Ciudad de México 1889: 454). During one particularly intense shortage in 1568, the Royal Audiencia of Mexico temporarily banned the operation of slaughterhouses in Indigenous pueblos throughout New Spain (Villavicencio 2014: 170). Like the movement of the living livestock, the circulation of their flesh could also be politically charged. For Mesoamericans, engagement with unfamiliar species was a consequence of the introduction of Hispanic modes of animal husbandry and pastoralism into the New World. Introduced species could be disruptive in local communities, but they could also be adapted for myriad personal or communal reasons. In contrast, Spaniards oriented research into local flora and fauna toward broader imperial or evangelization efforts. Identifying and cataloging new species was not just a matter of accruing more encyclopedic knowledge of the natural world; it informed proselytization and facilitated the exploitation of resources.

Colonial natural histories, all of which contain an abundance of information about flora and fauna, can be subdivided by their different purposes. José Pardo-Tomás distinguished three types of natural histories composed in colonial New Spain: those spurred by the Crown, those produced by mestizos and intended primarily for local audiences, and those aimed to assist with evangelization. The first category, a far-reaching imperial project that is most relevant for this chapter, was intended to collect information about territories within Spanish America. Authors based their research on documentary material made available as well as testimony from Indigenous and Spanish witnesses. Colonial officials dispersed detailed questionnaires across the colonies to determine information about local populations and nearby resources (Pardo Tomás 2016: 32–35). Antonio Barrera-Osorio described the institutionalization of empirical practices by the Spanish Crown via the House of Trade and Council of the Indies as an "early scientific revolution" (2016: 11).

During the mid to late-colonial period, Mesoamerica faced increased challenges related to ongoing epidemics, food shortages and famine, and insect infestations and plagues. These challenges altered biodiversity in the region, a complicated process and an area of current active research. The era known as the "Great Dying" (ca. 1492–1800) brought with it death on a massive scale: a 50–90 percent mortality rate for Indigenous peoples in Mesoamerica (Lovell and Lutz 1993: 134; Alchon 2003). This demographic collapse of Indigenous peoples from epidemics, violence and warfare, famine, and slavery had measurable atmospheric effects in carbon (CO_2) on the Earth's System, and thus caused "human-driven global impact on the Earth System in the two centuries prior to the Industrial Revolution" (Koch et al. 2019: 13).

Colonial models for the development of agricultural commodities for export to global markets transformed landscapes, as well as accelerated deforestation and its connected declines in local species, a pattern that continued in Mesoamerica until the Mexican Revolution in the early twentieth century. Heavy Spanish colonial tribute demands transformed Soconusco, a region along the Pacific coastal plain known in the Late Post-classic and colonial eras for its high-quality cacao beans in high demand in global markets. Though production largely remained in Indigenous hands during and after the conquest period, the effects of heavy colonial emphasis on cacao production led to deforestation, erosion, and habitat loss for animals in the region. Because of this emphasis. Less space was devoted to growing food crops especially staple crops like maize, and the colonial town, the center of cacao distribution in the region, Huehuetlan, had to import basic food stuffs. This, combined with labor shortages in part due to the demographic effects of the Great Dying, led cacao cultivators increasingly abandoned their cacao groves in this area in the seventeenth century, land that did not revert back to forests but instead transformed into grasslands and was used for grazing animals (Gasco 1999).

The cultivation of indigo as a key agricultural export commodity in colonial Mesoamerica nicely illustrates both ongoing attempts to exploit natural resources as well as often unsuccessful efforts to control the natural world and nonhuman animals in the region. Indigo had been cultivated as an export commodity under Spanish colonialism in Mesoamerica, and over the centuries of colonial rule, experienced a series of boom/bust cycles in production. After a stagnant period of production in the seventeenth century, indigo cultivation rebounded along the Pacific coastal plains of Central America, especially in the region that is now El Salvador, part of the profound socioeconomic and environmental changes generated especially after 1700 as part of the Bourbon Reforms (MacLeod 1973: 183). The processing of indigo plants after the harvest was a labor-intensive process that generated huge amounts of wet, rotting plant waste – *begasse* – that served as a breeding ground for flies that bit humans and animals, bringing with it multiple diseases and leading to the deaths, from the infected fly bites, of mules and other animals who helped power the indigo processing (Moziño 1799: 33–34). The problem was so dire that the President of the Audiencia of Guatemala passed a decree in 1799 ordering that all begasse be burned to deprive the flies of their breeding grounds (Rubio Sánchez 1976: 320). This boom period in indigo production brought locusts attracted to the young plant as an abundant food source, leading to waves of locusts plagues and infestations all along the indigo growing areas from Nicaragua up into southern Mexico, where locusts ate not only indigo but staple food crops like corn and cacao (Arrioja Díaz Viruell 2019). These led to reactive and largely ineffectual locust eradication campaigns of using forced Indigenous labor to kill the locusts by burning or crushing the insects as they swarmed, as well as the labor of domesticated animals such as pigs, turkeys, and other animals released into infested fields dig up and crush locust eggs sacs before they emerged from their egg sacs. Colonial-directed locust eradication campaigns can be seen as rooted in Spanish colonial attempts to control Mesoamerican landscapes and the nonhuman animals that inhabited them (Few 2013).

Final Remarks

The encounter between Europe and the Americas resulted in profound changes in biodiversity within both continent's respective ecosystems. In Mesoamerica, Old World domesticates like cattle, sheep, goats, pigs, and chickens catalyzed meaningful, and perhaps the earliest, engagement between local populations and Spanish colonists. This process did not occur as a single, sweeping event across Mesoamerica, but rather depended on the particular time and pace of colonization. Nevertheless, control over the movement and ownership of livestock was among the most controversial issues of the early colonial period. Although many Indigenous communities resisted or retaliated against livestock that encroached into their towns, trampled crops, or drained water supplies, many recognized that introduced species offered an opportunity to participate in the developing colonial order. Even though labor obligations were forced on Spanish *encomiendas* and *haciendas*, countless Indigenous elites and communities adapted their lifestyles and diets to animals that had never existed in their ecosystems prior to contact with Europe. It is strange to think about Mesoamerica without the flavorful meats and cheeses that often define local cuisine.

It is also important to emphasize the exploitative dimension of colonial Spain's interest in Mesoamerican biodiversity, as well as the detrimental impact that Iberian animal husbandry had on the environment. Even if environmental degradation – outside of crops for consumption or tribute – was not typically mentioned in Indigenous petitions against Spanish colonists and their herds, overgrazing and ungulate eruptions did occur. Moreover, investigating and cataloging Mesoamerican wildlife was part of a broader effort to profit from resources across the Americas. The Spanish monarchy and colonial officials sought to control the environment to facilitate trade and tribute more efficiently, which, as demonstrated by sporadic locust plagues in Guatemala, was not always possible. The effects of European colonial expansion profoundly impacted nature-society relations across Mesoamerica, a key step toward transgressing the biodiversity boundary of the planetary boundary's theory in the Earth's current Anthropocene era.

References

Abbass, D. Kathy. 1993. "Herd Development in the New World Spanish Colonies: Conquistadors and Peasants." In *Themes in Rural History of the Western World*, ed. Richard Herr, 165–193. Ames: Iowa State University Press.

Acosta, José de. 2002. *Natural and Moral History of the Indies*. Ed. Jane M. Mangan, trans. Frances M. López- Morillas. Durham: Duke University Press. Orig. pub. 1589.

Ayuntamiento de la Ciudad de México. 1889. *Actas de cabildo del Ayuntamiento de la ciudad de Mexico*. Vol. 6. Mexico City: Ayuntamiento de la Ciudad de México.

Acuña, René, ed. 1985. *Relaciones Geográficas del Siglo XVI*. 3 vols. Mexico City: UNAM.

Alchon, Suzanne Austin. 2003. *A Pest in the Land: New World Epidemics in a Global Perspective*. Albuquerque: University of New Mexico Press.

Alexander, Rani. 2012. "Prohibido Tocar Este Cenote: The Archaeological Basis for the Titles of Ebtún." *International Journal of Archaeology* 16, no. 1: 1–24

Alves, Abel. 2011. *The Animals of Spain: An Introduction to Imperial Perceptions and Human Interaction with Other Animals, 1492–1826.* Leiden: Brill Academic Publishing.

Anderson, Virginia DeJohn. 2004. *Creatures of Empire: How Domestic Animals Transformed Early America.* Oxford: Oxford University Press.

Archivo General de Indias. 1546. "Envio de ganado del marqués del Valle." June 5th, Seville.

Arrioja Díaz Viruell, Luis Alberto. 2019. *Bajo el crepúsculo de los insectos: Clima, plagas y trastornos sociales en el Reino de Guatemala (1768–1805).* Michoacán: El Colegio de Michoacán.

Barrera-Osorio, Antonio. 2006. *Experiencing Nature: The Spanish American Empire and the Early Scientific Revolution.* Austin: University of Texas Press.

Barteet, C. Cody. 2015. *"Títulos de Ebtún*, Yucatan, Mexico: Mapping Maya Colonial Identity in a Colonial Spanish Notarial Context." *Imago Mundi* 67, no. 2: 179–200.

Baskes, Jeremy. 1996. "Coerced or Voluntary? The Repartimiento and Market Participation of Peasants in Late Colonial Oaxaca." *Journal of Latin American Studies* 28, no. 1: 1–28.

Bishko, Charles Julian. 1963. "The Castilian as Plainsman: The Medieval Ranching Frontier in La Mancha and Extremadura." In *The New World Looks at its History*, ed. Archibald L. Lewis and Thomas F. McGann, 47–69. Austin: Literary Licensing LLC.

Borah, Woodrow. 1943. *Silk Raising in Colonial Mexico.* Berkeley: University of California Press.

Butzer, Karl W. 1988. "Cattle and Sheep from Old to New Spain: Historical Antecedents." *Annals of the Association of American Geographers* 78, no. 1: 29–56.

Butzer, Karl W., and Elizabeth K. Butzer. 1995. "Transfer of the Mediterranean Livestock Economy to New Spain: Adaptation and Ecological Consequences." In *Global Land Use Change: A Perspective from the Columbian Encounter*, ed. Billie Lee Turner II, Antonio Gómez Sal, Fernando González Bernáldez, et al., 151–193. Madrid: Consejo Superior de Investigaciones Científicas.

Chance, John K. 2011. "Los Villagómez de Suchitepec, Oaxaca: un cacicazgo mixteco, 1701-1860." *Revista Española de Antropología Americana* 41, no. 2: 501–520.

Cortés, Hernan. 1522. "Carta de relacio[n] e[m]biada a su S. Majestad [etc.]" National Library of Spain, Madrid. https://www.wdl.org/en/item/7335/view/1/29/.

Crosby, Alfred. 1972. *The Columbian Exchange: Biological and Cultural Consequences of 1492.* Westport: Greenwood Publishing Group.

———. 1986. *Ecological Imperialism: The Biological Expansion of Europe, 900–1900.* Cambridge: Cambridge University Press.

Derby, Lauren. 2011. "Bringing the Animals Back in: Writing Quadrupeds into Caribbean History." *History Compass* 9, no. 8: 602–621.

Domínguez, Daisy. 2017. "At the Intersection of Animal and Area Studies: Fostering Latin Americanist and Caribbeanist Animal Studies." *Humanimalia* 8, no. 1: 66–92.

Earle, Rebecca. 2012. *The Body of the Conquistador: Food, Race, and the Colonial Experience in Spanish America, 1492–1700*. Cambridge: Cambridge University Press.

Few, Martha. 2013. "Killing Locusts in Colonial Guatemala." In *Centering Animals in Latin American History*, ed. Martha Few and Zeb Tortorici, 62–92. Durham: Duke University Press.

———. 2020. "The Lives and Deaths of Caged Birds: Transatlantic Voyages of Wild Creatures from the Americas to Spain, 1740s-1790s." *Ethnohistory* 67, no. 1: 481–501.

Few, Martha, and Zeb Tortorici, ed. 2013. *Centering Animals in Latin American History*. Durham: Duke University Press.

Forde, Jaime E. 2017. "Volcanic Glass and Iron Nails: Networks of Exchange and Material Entanglements at Late Prehispanic and Early Colonial Achiutla, Oaxaca, Mexico." *International Journal of Historical Archaeology* 21, no. 2: 1–27.

Garagarza, León García. 2013. "The Year the People Turned into Cattle: The End of the World in New Spain, 1558." In *Centering Animals in Latin American History*, ed. Martha Few and Zeb Tortorici, 31–61. Durham: Duke University Press.

García, Luis Reyes, and Eustaquio Celestino. 1992. *Anales de Tecamachalco, 1398–1590*. Mexico City: CIESAS.

Gasco, Janine. 2006. "Soconusco Cacao Farmers Past and Present: Continuity and Change in an Ancient Way of Life." In *Chocolate in Mesoamerica: A Cultural History of Cacao*, ed. Cameron L. McNeill, 322–337. Gainesville: University Press of Florida.

Gradie, Charlotte M. 2017. "Discovering the Chichimecas." *The Americas* 74, no. 2: 67–88.

Hassig, Ross. 1985. *Trade, Tribute, and Transportation: The Sixteenth-Century Political Economy of the Valley of Mexico*. Norman: University of Oklahoma Press.

Hoekstra, Rik. 2010. "A Colonial Cacicazgo: The Mendozas of Seventeenth-Century Tepexí de la Seda." *European Review of Latin American and Caribbean Studies* 89: 87–106.

Jones, Robert W., C. Patricia Ornelas-García, Rubén Pineda-López, et al., ed. 2023. *Mexican Fauna in the Anthropocene*. Cham: Springer Nature.

Koch, Alexander, Chris Brierley, Mark M. Maslin, et al. 2019. "Earth System Impacts of the European Arrival and Great Dying in the Americas after 1492." *Quaternary Science Reviews* 207: 13–36.

Lewis, Simon L., and Mark A. Maslin. 2015. "Defining the Anthropocene." *Nature* 519: 171–180.

Lockhart, James. 1992. *The Nahuas After the Conquest: A Social and Cultural History of the Indians of Central Mexico, Sixteenth Through Eighteenth Centuries*. Redwood: Stanford University Press.

Lockhart, James, Frances Berdan, and Arthur J.O. Anderson, ed. 1986. *The Tlaxcalan Actas: A Compendium of the Records of the Cabildo of Tlaxcala, 1545–1627.* Salt Lake City: University of Utah Press.

López Luján, Leonardo. 1993. *Las ofrendas del Templo Mayor de Tenochtitlan.* Mexico City: Instituto Nacional de Antropología e Historia.

López Luján, Leonardo, Ximena Chávez Balderas, Belem Zúñiga-Arellano, et al. 2012. "Un portal al inframundo. Ofrendas de animales sepultadas al pie del Templo Mayor de Tenochtitlan." *Estudios de cultura náhuatl* 44: 9–40.

Lovell, W. George, and Christopher H. Lutz. 1994. "Conquest and Population: Maya Demography in Historical Perspective." *Latin American Research Review* 29, no. 2: 133–140.

Mace, Georgina M., Belinda Reyers, Rob Alkemade, et al. 2014. "Approaches to defining a planetary boundary for biodiversity." *Global Environmental Change* 28: 289–297.

MacLeod, Murdo. 1973. *Spanish Central America.* Berkeley: University of California Press.

Mann, Charles C. 2011. *1493: How the Ecological Collision of Europe and the Americas Gave Rise to the Modern World.* London: Granta Publications.

Masters, Adrian. 2018. "A Thousand Invisible Architects: Vassals, the Petition and Response System, and the Creation of Spanish Imperial Caste Leglisation." *Hispanic American Historical Review* 98, no. 3: 377–406.

Mejía, Fabiola Montserrat Morales, Edsel Rafael Robles Martínez, Jorge León Valdez Martínez, et al. 2018. "Estudio tafonómico de algunos mamíferos en contextos coloniales del Centro Histórico de la Ciudad de México." Paper presented at the conference Los animales del recinto sagrado de Tenochtitlan: Biología, arqueología, historia y conservación, El Colegio Nacional, Mexico City, November 7–9.

Melville, Elinor G. K. 1994. *A Plague of Sheep: Environmental Consequences of the Conquest of Mexico.* Cambridge: Cambridge University Press.

Mendoza, Don Antonio de. 1543. "Fragmento de la Residencia de Don Antonio de Mendoza." Austin: Joaquín García Icazbalceta Collection, Benson Library.

Moziño, José Mariano. 1799. *Tratado del xiquilite y añil de Guatemala.* Nueva Guatemala: Real Sociedad Económica.

Norton, Marcy. 2013. "Going to the Birds: Birds and Things and Beings in Early Modernity." In *Early Modern Things: Objects and Their Histories, 1500–1800,* ed. Paula Findlen, 55–83. London: Routledge.

———. 2015. "The Chicken or the Iegue: Human-Animal Relationships and the Columbian Exchange." *American Historical Review* 120, no. 1: 28–60.

O'Callaghan, Joseph F. 1983. *A History of Medieval Spain.* New York: Cornell University Press.

Olivier, Guilhem. 2015. *Cacería, Sacrificio y Poder en Mesoamérica: Tras Las Huellas de Mixcóatl, "Serpiente de Nube."* Mexico City: Fondo de Cultura Económica/UNAM.

Orden, José Tudela de la. 1993. *Historia de la ganadería hispanoamerica*. Madrid: Instituto de Cooperación Iberoamericana/Ediciones de Cultura Hispánica.

Owensby, Brian P. 2008. *Empire of Law and Indian Justice in Colonial Mexico*. Redwood: Stanford University Press.

Pardo-Tomás, José. 2016. "Making Natural History in New Spain, 1525–1590." In *The Globalization of Knowledge in the Iberian Colonial World*, ed. Helge Wendt, 29–51. Berlin: Max Planck Institute for the History of Science.

Poole, Stafford. 2017. "'War by Fire and Blood': The Church and the Chichimecas 1585." *The Americas* 74, no. 2: 115–137.

Restall, Matthew. 1997. *The Maya World: Yucatec Culture and Society, 1550–1850*. Redwood: Stanford University Press.

Rockström, Johan, Will Steffen, Kevin Noone, et al. 2009. "Planetary Boundaries: Exploring the Safe Operating Space for Humanity." *Ecology and Society* 14, no. 2: 1–33.

Rojas Rabiela, Teresa, ed. 1990. *La agricultura en tierras mexicanas desde sus orígenes hasta nuestros días*. Mexico City: Editorial Grijalbo-CONACULTA.

Rubio Sánchez, Manuel. 1976. *Historia de Añil o Xiquilite en Centro América*. 2 vols. San Salvador: Ministerio de Educación.

Seijas, Tatiana. 2016. "Inns, Mules, and Hardtack for the Voyage: The Local Economy of the Manila Galleon in Mexico." *Colonial Latin American Review* 25, no. 1: 56–76.

Sluyter, Andrew. 1997. "Landscape Change and Livestock in Sixteenth-Century New Spain." *Conference of Latin Americanist Geographers* 23: 27–39.

Somerville, Andrew D., Nawa Sugiyama, Linda R. Manzanilla, et al. 2016. "Animal Management at the Ancient Metropolis of Teotihuacan, Mexico: Stable Isotope Analysis of Leporid (Cottontail and Jackrabbit) Bone Mineral." *Plos One* 11, no. 8: 1–21.

Sousa, Lisa. 2017. *The Woman Who Turned into a Jaguar, and Other Narratives of Native Women in Archives of Colonial Mexico*. Redwood: Stanford University Press.

Sugiyama, Nawa, Andrew D. Somerville, and Margaret J. Schoeninger. 2015. "Stable Isotopes and Zooarchaeology at Teotihuacan, Mexico Reveal Earliest Evidence of Wild Carnivore Management in Mesoamerica." *Plos One* 10, no. 9.

Terraciano, Kevin. 2001. *The Mixtecs of Colonial Oaxaca: Ñudzahui History, Sixteenth through Eighteenth Centuries*. Redwood: Stanford University Press.

Thompson, Philip C. 2000. *Tekanto: A Maya Town in Colonial Yucatan*. New Orleans: Middle America Research Institute.

Thornton, Erin Kennedy, Kitty F. Emery, David W. Steadman, et al. 2012. "Earliest Mexican Turkeys (*Meleagris gallopavo*) in the Maya Region: Implications for Pre-Hispanic Animal Trade and the Timing of Turkey Domestication." *PLoS One* 7, no. 8: 1–8.

Toledo, Víctor M. 1990. "El proceso de ganaderización y la destrucción biológica y ecológica de México." In *Medio ambiente y desarrollo en México*, ed. Enrique Leff, 191–222. Mexico City: UNAM.

Valadez Azúa, Raúl. 2003. *La domesticación animal*. 2nd ed. Mexico City: UNAM.

Valadez Azúa, Raúl, and Bernardo Rodríguez Galicia. 2014. "Uso de la fauna, estudios arqueozoológicos y tendencias alimentarias en culturas prehispánicas del centro de México." *Anales de Antropología* 48, no. 1: 139–166.

Villavicencio, Maria Xóchitl Galindo. 2014. "Los 'señores de la tierra' y los mecanismos del abasto de carne en Tlaxcala en el siglo XVI." *Revista Complutense de Historia de América* 40: 155–177.

Villella, Peter. 2016. *Indigenous Elites and Creole Identity in Colonial Mexico, 1500–1800*. Cambridge: Cambridge University Press.

White, Christine, Mary D. Pohl, Henry Schwarcz, et al. 2004. "Field and Forest: Deer and Dog Diets at Lagarto and Copan." In *Maya Zooarchaeology: New Directions in Method and Theory*, ed. Kitty F. Emery, 141–158. Los Angeles: Cotsen Institute of Archaeology/UCLA.

Zumárraga, Bp. Juan de. c. 1534–1536. "Correspondance to the officials of Seville." Austin: Joaquín García Icazbalceta Collection, Benson Library.

Biodiversity in the Caribbean in the Colonial Period
Human–Animal Relations

Rodrigo C. Bulamah

"During slavery, the main thing was pig meat." In the first pages of *Biography of a Runaway Slave* (Barnet 1994), Esteban Montejo describes the value that pigs had in the diet and daily life of enslaved people in colonial Cuba. "Almost all slaves had their *conucos*. They were little strips of dirt for gardening. [...] [The slaves] grew everything there: sweet potato, squash, okra, corn, peas, horse beans, beans like limas, limes, yucca, and peanuts. They also raised piglets" (25–26). In the whole Caribbean world, these human-animal interactions helped shape both the possibility of colonialism as well as the lifeworld of Africans and their descendants. The conucos were provision grounds. As many Caribbean scholars have shown, these small portions of land that planters granted to the enslaved Africans and their descendants to reduce the costs of the colonial plantations were spaces in which enslaved people produced their own food while also developing techniques, practices, and concepts that worked both in complement and in opposition to the plantation (Lepkowski 1970; Mintz 1985a; Cardoso 1987; Castellano 2021; DeLoughrey 2011).

This literature, however, focuses mainly on land as the material ground in which these ideas of freedom were cultivated. Instead, this chapter intends to discuss how animals took a prominent role in these landscapes of coercion and autonomy, taking part in what Ángel Quintero-Rivera (1995), inspired by Jean Casimir (1992), dubs a dialectics of plantation and counter-plantation system (see also, Dubois and Turits 2019). These "creatures of empire" (Anderson 2004) were crucial to the formative moments of European expansion and the subsequent Conquest, playing a role in what Alfred Crosby (1972) famously called the "Columbian Exchange." The first pigs arrived on the island of Hispaniola, the site of the first European colonial settlement in the Americas, and were part of the initial phase of the "Atlantic Moment" that Trouillot defines as "a first moment of globality," in which it is possible to witness the "continuous centrality of the Atlantic as the revolving door of major global flows over four centuries" (2003: 29).

Although greatly inspired by Sidney Mintz's (1985b) important study on how sugar created global connections between labor, capital, and culinary habits, the aim here is to understand the ecological entanglements between animals, humans, and other beings. By "bringing animals back in," as Robin Derby (2011) provocatively puts it, this chapter also intends to go beyond metaphors that compare human and animal conditions. Much like Benedicte Boisseron in her fascinating book *Afro-Dog: Blackness and the Animal Question* (2018), this text is not exclusively interested in comparing human and animal forms of subjection and humiliation, but in understanding how humans and other-than-humans defied the colonial order through forging new alliances. By doing so, the hope is to engage with the new grand narrative that sees human agency as a geological force, epitomized by the idea of the Anthropocene, bringing its colonial history into focus to finally reflect on the afterlives of enslaved people's provision grounds and their human-animal alliances. Finally, the focus here will be on Hispaniola, nowadays divided between Haiti and the Dominican Republic, but wider Caribbean processes will be discussed whenever it is possible.

Plantation and Counter-Plantation Animalities

During the period of European voyages to the Caribbean and the Americas, vessels carried some food for crewmembers, who spent long periods on the high seas travelling from port to port. With the emergence of European settlements in the region, animals from the Old Continent were taken to the New World. Dogs, for example, were used for hunting and protection, and pigs became the first livestock, serving to Europeanize landscapes by transforming them into something increasingly familiar to colonizers (Alves 2011; Crosby 1986; Johnson 2012). Native animals, by contrast, were objects of fascination, subject to detailed descriptions that contributed to the construction of an Edenic vision of the New World (Paravisini-Gebert 2008). However, hunting and animal husbandry were the main paradigms in these human–animal interactions. According to historian Marcy Norton, in an extension of practices common to Europe, the native fauna of the Caribbean and the Americas at the beginning of Spanish expansion was viewed according to two prisms: hunting, a noble and elite activity; and livestock husbandry, an activity relegated to the plebeian level. Animal adoption, an Amerindian interspecies practice frequently described by travelers and colonial agents was therefore an enigma, one sometimes understood as husbandry. As Norton states, "Amerindian adoption was a cognate to forms of social life and intergroup conflict as European hunting and breeding were to rule and warfare" (2013: 22). Nonetheless, these multispecies encounters also gave rise, as will be shown, to new ecologies and interactions in those landscapes that empires tried to domesticate and control.

Pigs were particularly well-suited to the long sea voyages to the New World, as they constituted important sources of meat and fat and were omnivorous, requiring no special food. Furthermore, even though they were subjected to intense forms of confinement, discomfort, and suffering, they were hardy enough to survive (Donkin 1985). As Abbot Guillaume-Thomas Raynal (1770) noted at the end of the eighteenth century,

> America, at the time of the discovery, had no pigs, sheep, oxen, horses, or even any domestic animals. Columbus brought some of these useful animals to Saint-Domingue, where they spread everywhere [...]. They have multiplied there prodigiously. There are thousands of horned animals, whose skins have become the object of considerable exportation. The horses have degenerated, but the quality is compensated by the number. The lard of pigs is a substitute for butter. (53)

In Saint-Domingue, the French name for the island of Hispaniola, the abundance of animals Raynal described as "prodigious multiplication" occurred in large part between the sixteenth and seventeenth centuries, when the entire island was under Spanish rule. Herds of animals such as pigs, goats, oxen, horses, and dogs became feral after being abandoned or running away. Classified by the chroniclers of the time as *marrons, maroons* or *cimarróns*, or even *montaraces* (from the Spanish *monte*), these animals multiplied, above all, due to favorable interactions with the new landscapes. The mountain geography of the island's interior was less suitable for large plantations, and this, coupled with the lack of natural predators and the presence of dense forests, played a notable role in this expansion. *Marron* (or maroon), as explained by Tardieu (2006), is a term derived from Arawak language whose original meaning was "fugitive," but it was incorporated into the colonial lexicon of different empires to define native plants and animals that defied European domination, existing both in practical and ontological terms as something external to the European order. Over time, the term marronage also came to be used to define people who evaded captivity, as in the French expression *partir marron*, used in newspaper advertisements to search for enslaved runaways.

As in other Spanish colonies in the Caribbean, the productive activities undertaken on Hispaniola moved away from an initial focus on gold mining – employing native Arawak forced labor, Europeans under indentured contracts, and later enslaved Africans – to a small sugar production cycle that lasted until the beginning of the seventeenth century (Mintz 1996). The effective transition to a plantation economy happened later in the Spanish domains than in the other colonial territories of the Caribbean and Americas. In the Spanish colonial settlements, the exploitation of animal products (whether from herds or hunting), pearl fishing, growing ginger and tobacco, extracting salt to produce salted herring from the Baltic Sea, and producing timber were more important than cultivating sugar. Yet, despite sparse occupations, the Caribbean was the target of constant attention from the Spanish Crown due to the immense flow of wealth that connected its territories there to Europe, Africa, and Asia (Giusti-Cordero 2009).

Variations, conflicts, and fractures in the processes of occupation and the subsequent intensification of production, as well as a long list of diseases and a plurality of beings from diverse origins, eventually led to the development of a diverse "creole ecology" in which the plantation could thrive (McNeill 2010). While dogs were trained to hunt runaway enslaved people, which Boisseron (2018) argues reveals a proximity between animalization and racialization, European pigs, along with other non-humans, became part of a pool of "commons" that oriented early occupations as well as rhythms of settlement and colonization. Indeed, animals became part and parcel of a form of life that Malcom Ferdinand (2019) names "colonial inhabitation" (*l'habiter colonial*), a way of inhabiting the planet based on a form of racial violence in which the plantation was the organizing infrastructure. In fact, the French name for plantation, *habitation*, stresses exactly this exclusionary dimension, as only the white European settlers were subjects with rights – as Sybille Fischer (2016) notes – and therefore allowed to have proper life in the colonial setting, hence their designation as *habitants* (settlers). Paradoxically, as Creole animals that forged colonial landscapes in the New World, pigs gave rise to new forms of life based exactly on what was "uncommon" (Cadena and Blaser 2018), establishing new sociotechnical ecologies on the margins of the plantation machine.

The social and economic prevalence of slavery and monoculture led to a set of changes in the landscape as well as in the whole biodiversity of the Caribbean. Deforestation to install large sugarcane fields and irrigation systems, as well as the radical change in the demographics of the islands, forged an entirely new ecology. Nevertheless, the colonial landscape was also open to the forging of new landscapes in the margins of, or even against, the plantation. In fact, the agro-industrial order of Caribbean plantations went far beyond the generalized control and alienation efforts that define some classic and contemporary readings of the system. Anna Tsing, for instance, uses the sugarcane plantation that sustained colonial Brazil as a prototypical example to illustrate her definition of scalability: a project that could reproduce itself in different scales precisely because of its immutable frame, as it depended on "few interspecies relations" and "was comparatively self-contained [and] oblivious to encounter" (2015: 39). Moreover, continues the author, the enslaved Africans in this project "had no local social relations and thus no established routes for escape" (39) "Like the cane itself," Tsing concludes, "which had no history of either companion species or disease relations in the New World, [the enslaved people] *were isolated*" (39; emphasis added). By looking at historical sources, however, it can be seen that even in the face of immeasurable forms of violence and alienation, people found ways to recreate their lives and their ecologies even within the pervasiveness of the plantation.

Across the whole Caribbean in the seventeenth and eighteenth centuries, wealth assumed many forms, and the hunting of feral animals attracted the attention of pirates, smugglers, traders, adventurers, and other actors named "a masterless class" by Julius Scott (2018). There was great ambiguity in the practices of theft and smuggling, which always occupied an unstable position between legality and illegality, and *rescate* (as these activities were called) became profitable to the point of guiding exchanges, circulations, conflicts, and wars in the region (Andrews 1978; Brown 2020). Known as buccaneers, due to their habit of smoking game meat in a wood grill (from *boucan*, in French), or filibusters (possibly derived from "light boats," *vrijbuiter*, in Dutch), pirates and merchants occupied specific islands and regions of the archipelago for long periods of time. Among those islands was Tortuga (*Île de la Tortue*), off the northwest coast of Saint-Domingue. Jules Lecomte's (1837) historical novel *L'Île de la Tortue: Roman Maritime* illustrates this moment pretty well, describing hunting customs, same-sex marriages, and exchanges between pirates, privateers, and merchants who, at the time, might or might not have been linked to great European empires. Comparing them with the *habitans*, Lecomte highlights:

> Settlers [*habitans*] were those whose aptitude seemed more peculiar to constructions and plantations; people of peaceful morals and mood. The Buccaneers declared themselves hunters; the pursuit of oxen and wild boars in the woods of Saint-Domingue, *the preparation of hides and salted meats which constituted their daily occupations, later offered society the first elements of its trade and commerce.* [...] Finally, the Filibusters, or Corsairs, formed the third class of Adventurers by increasing their chase after Spanish ships. (18–20, emphasis added)

The hunting of feral pigs and cows and the trade in their hides, meat, and fat constituted the central activities of pirates and adventurers – something that historian Claudio de Majo (2022) interestingly identified as a "coevolutionary relation."

Extending Stephen Greenblatt (1991) and Alida Metcalf's (2005) concept of "go-betweens" to non-humans, it could be said that pigs, cows, and other animals were active mediators of relationships between Europeans and native populations in the Caribbean islands and the American continent (Vander Velden 2018). Escape, adaptation, and husbandry of European species led effectively to the occupation and formation of living settlements and trading posts in different parts of the region. Concurrent with the genocide and assimilation of Amerindian populations, the presence of these animals also motivated the settlement of buccaneers and corsairs, who started to raise animals for meat and use in transport and traction engines, thereby becoming settlers (Oexmelín 1930). It was exactly the establishment of settlements in the western part of Hispaniola, mainly by groups of Frenchmen, which motivated the concession of a third share of the colony to the French Crown by the Treaty of Ryswick in 1697. However, between the two colonies, the circulation of traders, animals, and wealth remained intense.

Traveling in Hispaniola in the late eighteenth century, the famous Martinique-born lawyer and writer Louis-Élie Moreau de Saint-Méry (1958) noted that, particularly along the northern coast of Saint-Domingue, "forests are a refuge for feral pigs [*cochons marons*]" before adding a geographical description of the north of the island and of its occupation. Except for villages such as Monte-Cristi, Puerto-Plata, and Samaná, he writes, "the northern share of the Spanish part is almost uninhabited" (207). "However," he continued, "every land close to the sea is granted [by the Crown], not in small lots, [...] but in large portions. In a way, it is for fishing that such concessions are requested, *but even more for hunting the feral pig*" (Moreau de Saint-Méry 1958), emphasis added). The interactions between hunters, dogs, pigs, and plants attracted Moreau de St-Méry's attention, and he described them in detail:

> The time of this hunt is defined by the time when a species of palm produces its seeds, which form a cluster – and which the animal is extremely fond of. A Spaniard, if he is alone with some dogs, goes armed with a spear, a machete, and a knife into the parts of the forest which contain the palm. When he sees a feral pig, the dogs circle it and distract it by barking until the hunter comes to kill him with his spear. The beast is then opened and emptied, the head and feet are thrown away, and the hunter takes care of the body, which he sometimes cuts to facilitate transport. (207–208, emphasis removed)

When hunters went to the forest collectively, Moreau de St-Méry's remarked:

> They choose a place where they believe the prey would be abundant; they build a small hut or *ajoupa* there, covered with stains or palm leaves, and they place several forks with crossbars to salt and dry the feral pig halves or to pile them up when they are ready. Quite often, transportation is by sea at least if the result is a considerable hunt. (208, emphasis in the original)

Whether individually or collectively organized, this dynamic of hunting, drying, and salting the meat, as well as its transportation and trade, dominated the economy of northern Hispaniola, making the border between Saint-Domingue and the Spanish Captaincy General of Santo Domingo a very fluid landscape. Moreau de St-Méry brings to light the poverty in the Spanish portion of the island, quite unlike the thriving colonial society that he saw on the western side. Observing the town of Cotuy, close to the gold mines of the Cibao province, he states that the region, "as the Spanish portion in general, was not in a situation of less neglect and misery" at the beginning of the eighteenth century (213). The poor settlers of Cibao, "descendants of primitive European owners," (Moreau de Saint-Méry 1958) most of them French, were known as *actionnaires* on account of their being in possession of a deed of concession (*acte de concession*) and were rarely counted in colonial censuses.

The topographical formation of the eastern part of the island made it poorly adapted to large-scale agriculture, unlike the northwestern part, where Cap Français or Le Cap, the capital of French Saint-Domingue, was located in the Plaine du Nord.

For the residents of the central and northeastern region, their only option was to care for their herds, which they could own in limited quantities, and go hunting (*monteria*), which was allowed only on certain days.

"It is to the education of animals, especially pigs that the inhabitants of Cotuy dedicate themselves almost exclusively, and these animals need intense care" (214), highlights Moreau de St-Méry, calling attention to the constant tension between domestication and feralization. Even with dedicated attention to food and care, pigs "were attracted to the woods with the hope of finding roots, fruits, and insects [...] but they did not always return [home] at night, going far away to the point of becoming wild, at times, in high numbers" (215). The miserable fate of those that raised them was to be "constantly betrayed in his wait [...] limited to hunting those he once believed were domesticated" (215). These accounts reveal that domestication was indeed as practical a problem as it was a metaphysical one during those early times in the Caribbean. Domestication was (and is) an unstable practice, rather difficult to define when it comes to human–animal ecologies. Although some authors tend to dismiss the concept due to its Eurocentric genealogy, this text sides with recent efforts that call for a more empirical critique of human–animal encounters that can amplify domestication's semantic field (Vander Velden 2012; Norton 2015; Sautchuk 2018).

Instabilities between domestication and feralization, expressed in tensions between breeding and hunting, helped shape a fundamental part of the economy of the Caribbean that was not centered on the plantation but was associated with it through circuits of provision, both at sea, in exchange circuits between the islands, and on land, as in the case of the divided island of Hispaniola. This disparity between plantation colonies and provision territories has been seen by many historians as an indication of a particular type of backwardness in Spanish colonies in the Caribbean. Having not moved towards the "plantation complex" discussed by Philip Curtin (1990) or gone through the "plantation revolution" identified by Ira Berlin (1998), these colonies, especially between the seventeenth and eighteenth centuries, seem to have been left out of history (or historiography), as Juan Giusti-Cordero (2009) convincingly argues. Animals and their interactions with humans reveal the limits of these overly schematic conclusions, which sometimes leave aside the transcolonial connections and flows that linked different spaces without necessarily involving the metropolis (Johnson 2012). Even though not initially oriented towards the plantation, the economic importance of the Spanish Caribbean and its animal economies prompted attempted raids, wars, and invasions by other European imperial powers. And such initiatives did not go unanswered by the Spanish Crown.

Provision Grounds and the Ambiguous Materiality of Freedom

In describing the French settlers in the north of Saint-Domingue, Moreau de Saint-Méry speaks of a "disapproval of the coarse customs and the non-social character" of Cotuy's inhabitants. "Perhaps", he continues, "the habit of a life whose care almost always has animals as an object makes it acquire a certain rudeness that shocks those who do not share it" (1958: 216). But this trait may still have been the result of a history of disputes over territories, something that was acquired through the participation of animals as agents in this geography of warfare. "Maybe there is still a precaution in this judgment, proper to the Frenchman who still remember, a century later, the massacre of his countrymen in Samaná" (2016) suggests Moreau de St-Méry, referring to the *ravages* or *devastaciones* – the massacres of animal livestock with the aim of relocating or expelling settlers – that took place in the region at the end of the seventeenth century (Moya Pons 2007: 40–43). The result of these *ravages*, however, has always proved to be quite insufficient (Giusti-Cordero 2014: 20).

These same French settlements were established to grow tobacco, whose production lasted until the end of the seventeenth century, when, after the decisive assignment of the western part of the island to France in 1697, sugar production assumed an increasing importance. Thus, the many landscapes of Hispaniola were shaped by a set of social, material, and ecological interactions in which animals were used in transportation and mechanical work on the plantation and, with the help of hunting, supplied meat and leather to the colonies and, not uncommonly, to European cities as well. At the beginning of the eighteenth century, as stated by the governor of Cap Français, Monsieur de Charitte, "[the Spaniards] know that, in relation to our sugar plantations, we cannot do without their cattle, since our herds are not sufficiently populated to supply what we need" (cited in Moya Pons 1977: 233).

As has been seen, pigs and other beings played a central role in the production of this Creole landscape and influenced travelers, pirates, settlers, captives, Europeans, and Africans, motivating occupations and disputes as well as interacting in different ways with colonial society and the class and racial divides that came to be a central part of it. But these interactions went far beyond the plantation. At the end of the eighteenth century, in opposing the abolitionist theses of the newly created Society of Friends of Blacks in Paris (*Société des Amis des Noirs de Paris*), Crublier de Saint-Cyran (1790) describes the houses and parcels of land managed by slave families in Saint-Domingue, saying that their working conditions were "generally less harsh than that of workers in France" (4). He further adds, "there is no [enslaved person] who does not have a house and land for himself and his family, who does not have chickens, pigs, and other properties, which are always carefully respected by the master" (5).

Reports by colonial officials or travelers like Saint-Cyran should be read with caution. Produced in a period that saw conditions of extreme violence, repression, and dispossession of Black people, such reports had specific political goals within the abolitionist debate that was taking place in different parts of the Atlantic. However, it is in the cracks of these historical sources that important descriptions can be found that, when read against, as well as along, the grain (Stoler 2009), provide fragments of the forms of sociality, conceptions, and daily practices of enslaved people. Moreover, such documents aid in the understanding of not only the changing attitudes of different human groups towards the "natural world," as Keith Thomas (1996) famously put it, but also the way in which animals shared an experience of place while materially creating new agrarian landscapes within and against the plantation.

Saint-Cyran's quick description of the houses and plots designated to enslaved people in Saint-Domingue confirms a general policy in the French, Spanish, and British colonies of granting portions of land that would serve for the production of food for subsistence and, sometimes, for commercial exchange in regional markets, allowing the enslaved a form of social mobility. At the same time, the concession of a space for growing food and raising animals largely benefited the plantation economy and served the colonial system by promoting the immobility of enslaved people and preventing them from becoming *marrons*. "Nothing is more adequate to retain [the enslaved] and prevent them from escaping than to provide them with something from which they can derive some benefit, such as birds, pigs, a tobacco plantation, cotton, herbs or the like," noted the Reverend Jean-Baptiste Labat (1724: 50), writing from the French colony of Martinique at the beginning of the eighteenth century. He then added that "the seizure [of these lands and animals] is sufficient to prevent, perhaps for good, that all Blacks on a plantation [*habitation*] try such an escape" (50).

Within the socioeconomic order of plantations, these lands, named "provision grounds" (*habitation* or *place à vivres*, in French, and *conucos*, in Spanish), enabled the development of labor techniques, agricultural practices, and forms of exchange between enslaved and free people. They helped shape what Lepkowski (1970) calls the "peasant breach" in his classical study of colonial Saint-Domingue, understood as a collective experience distinct from the slave order, an experience that, even if it "united them to the plantation and prevented escapes," can be seen as reflecting "cracks in the apparent solid edifice of the slave agro-industrial system" (62). According to historian Dale Tomich: "the slaves, in a complex mixture of accommodation and resistance, struggled both within and against the framework dictated to them and, in the course of their struggle, developed other values, ideas, and cultural forms." (2004: 150) As Mintz remarks,

> estate slaves commonly grew their own subsistence on plantation uplands, using lands judged unsuitable for the major plantation crops. It was on such lands that the slaves acquired or perfected their horticultural skill, developed their own standardized agricultural practices, learned the characteristics of Caribbean soils,

mastered the cultivation of new crops, and otherwise prepared themselves for their *reconstitution as peasantries*. (1989: 236, emphasis added)

Variations in the size of the plantation, its geography, and its main culture (which determined the quantity and seasonality of labor) could still confer a greater or lesser degree of productive autonomy to the enslaved, as compellingly argued by Trouillot (1993) of the coffee plantations in Saint-Domingue. For this reason, it was exactly on the outskirts of the plains where sugar flourished, in the mountain and marginal landscapes surrounding the plantation geography, that such techniques and skills were developed during slavery, both among the enslaved people who were guaranteed the chance to plant in this steep terrain, unsuitable for sugarcane, and among the maroon communities that thrived in the colony's interior (Price 1979). Mintz's argument focuses, above all, on agricultural practices, from soil preparation to harvest and, from there, to the processing, storage, conservation, and selection of seeds, leaving aside the technical knowledge developed in relation to game animals or husbandry. The historical source that Mintz used in his analysis was the well-known travel account of John Stewart (1823), whose observations centered on colonial Jamaica. The passage of particular interest to Sidney Mintz was as follows:

> Adjoining to the [enslaved] house is usually a small spot of ground, laid out into a sort of garden, and shaded by various fruit-trees. Here the family deposit their dead, to whose memory they invariably, if they can afford it, erect a rude tomb. Each slave has besides this spot, a piece of ground (about half an acre) allotted to him as a *provision-ground*. (Stewart 1823: 267, quoted in Mintz 1989: 187, emphasis added)

In these provision grounds, enslaved people grew roots, bananas, fruits, and peppers. Any surplus was destined for local exchanges and for sale in the markets, which guaranteed the enslaved access to cash and, therefore, to some social mobility, particularly in the case of enslaved women. But in or close to these spaces, creatures such as pigs and birds also coexisted. John Stewart continued his account of the provision grounds in Jamaica:

> This is the principal means of [slave's] support; and so productive is the soil, where it is good and the seasons regular, that this plot will not only furnish him with sufficient food for his own consumption, but an over-plus to carry to market. By means of this ground, as of the hogs and poultry which he may raise (most of which he sells), an industrious negro may not only support himself comfortably but save something. (1823: 267, quoted in Mintz 1989: 187, emphasis added)

Stewart notes that other species, such as horses, cows, sheep, and, on most estates, goats, were forbidden to people subjected to slavery. This is explained, possibly, both by the high value of these animals and by the space and intensive care they needed. Pigs, however, were forbidden to walk freely on the land under the planter's rule; but, like birds, they played a crucial role on the provision grounds. Thus, it is remarkable that throughout the Caribbean common social histories produced countless similarities among these early peasantries, and, due to their diversity of traditions and cultural influences, "originated in good measure from a common history of slavery and forced labor, the domination of the plantation system, and the narrow range of economic alternatives available to those who resisted that system by developing lifestyles outside it" (1989: 225).

Through the study of cultural practices in the early Caribbean, Sidney Mintz and Richard Price (1976) developed a very influential theory about the sociotechnical genesis of African-American cultures that became known as "creolization." With a strong materialist approach combined with the cultural ecology discussions of the time, the authors renewed perspectives on cultural and social formations in the Atlantic basin. Mintz and Price generalizations have been challenged by Africanists since the 1990s, but their empirical approach prompted further developments about cultural contact and ethnogenesis not only in the Americas but also in precolonial Africa and Europe. For a recent appreciation of this debate, see Sidbury and Cañizares-Esguerra (2011). This chapter puts forward the argument – adding something distinct to the creolization thesis – that human–animal alliances were crucial to the new life-worlds forged inside the provision grounds. In these gray zones on the margins of, and within, the plantation itself, spaces and techniques of cultivation and animal husbandry ensured other-than-human encounters in which new political horizons gave rise to what Wynter termed the "plot system" that, in opposition to the plantation, was "the focus of resistance to the market system and market values" (1971: 99). Similar to what Casimir called the "counter-plantation," the plot was oriented "towards the protection and regeneration of the community" (2018: 101).

In a context where property was extremely racialized and social mobility was restricted, people who lived under the burden of captivity experienced, even if in very limited forms, degrees of freedom through affective and material ensembles, recalling notions of dignity and autonomy that were not lost in the Middle Passage and forging – in a sort of "becoming with," to borrow a proposition from Haraway (2010) – new landscapes, futures, and possibilities of life. It was at this point that the peasant breach made possible the emergence of new ecologies from practices, affects, and techniques developed in the relationship with land, plants, as well as game and livestock animals, particularly pigs. "Furthermore," notes Trouillot, "as the richer planters became increasingly involved in sugar, and as the coffee revolution absorbed both those whites with more limited resources and those free blacks who had hitherto engaged in foodstuff production, ever larger segments of the growing population came to depend on the agricultural and craft products of slave families." (1990: 39)

With slave uprisings gaining momentum in the north of the colony, "rebelling slaves did not ask for an end to slavery, but merely for additional days to cultivate their plots" (39). In this process, the use of land and its property was closely related to the notion of freedom; or, as historian Carolyn Fick puts it, for the black laborers, "a personal claim to the land upon which one labored and from which to derive and express one's individuality was [...] a necessary and an essential element in their vision of freedom." "For without this concrete economic and social reality," the author concludes, "freedom for the ex-slaves was little more than a legal abstraction" (1990: 249).

From the beginning, in the set of events that would lead to the Haitian Revolution, redefining the cartography of Atlantic warfare for good, defiant alliances with other-than-human agents inside provision grounds played an important role (Boisseron 2018). Organized on the outskirts of the city of Le Cap, between mid and late August 1791, the *Bwa Kayman* ceremony is seen by popular historiographical and academic traditions as an event that prefigures the Haitian Revolution (Fick 1990; Dubois 2004: 99–102). In this ceremony, a great alliance was sealed involving enslaved Africans and their descendants, freedmen (*affranchis*), and free people of color (*gens de couleur*). In an act of sacrifice, they killed a pig in a service to the spirits known as the *lwa*. For Maurice Etienne, a popular Haitian historian, this ceremony was a moment of awareness for the enslaved Africans, "an achievement of conscience" that created the possibility of revolt: "to acquire the morale they needed, they sacrificed a pig and believed that if they drank his blood, the pig would make them invincible". With this sacrifice, pigs mediated an alliance with spirits, and those fighting for freedom gained strength to carry out a counter-plantation project, destabilizing the institution of slavery, reversing the Atlantic colonial order, and creating the path to the country's independence.

In the image below, the painter Jean-Baptiste Jean reproduces the celebration of 200 years of *Bwa Kayman*: a pig is sacrificed in a great ceremony surrounded by people dressed in handkerchiefs that, when tied on the heads or waist, reveal possession by a spirit. Three drums are beaten while a man blows a shell, the main symbol of collective action in Haiti. People dance and Haitian flags appear in the hands of some. A bowl of blood is placed on the floor, reflecting the sacrifice of the pig in the story of the *Bwa Kayman* ceremony. In the center of the painting, a reproduction of the original scene appears in a curious *mise en abîme*. In the ritual that gave birth to an independent country, pigs that were once *marrons* became *kreyòl* (Creole), a term that came to define the cuisine, the language, and the society of Haiti as a whole. The creole pigs were, as Michelet Delima, a senior peasant from the north of Haiti, said, the backbone of the house economy (*se sou kochon kreyòl ke lekonomi lakay te chita*) (Bulamah 2020). Through this process, the plantation or the *habitation* was subverted, and those who were once denied the right to inhabit finally became known, in Haitian Creole, as the new *abitan* (Fischer 2016).

Fig. 1: Celebration of 200 years of the Bois-Caïman, 1791–1991

Source: Jean-Baptiste Jean (1993). Author's collection.

Counter-Plantation Futures

In 2000, Crutzen and Stoermer proposed a new geological marker that could take into account the effective force of humankind as a geophysical force redefining not only human history but also the history of the planet as a whole. We have reached the Anthropocene. Although many scientists had already recognized the geological and morphological impacts of human activity, the effect of Crutzen and Stoermer's proposition was felt in many academic fields and has been particularly fruitful in the humanities and social sciences. For the authors, the onset of the Anthropocene could be located around "the latter part of the eighteenth century," coinciding with James Watt's invention of the steam engine, a symbol of the Industrial Revolution (2000: 17–18). For other scholars, however, a more appropriate name for this new era would be the Plantationocene, a concept that would shed light on colonization and the plantation infrastructure as the model and motor of modern forms of extracting Earth's resources that shaped our contemporary world (Haraway et al. 2016).

As has been argued here, the plantation was an enterprise viscerally linked to a wide range of other-than-human beings, including the land itself, plants, animals, and spirits. On the one hand, while the hunting of wild and feral animals and animal husbandry played an important role in the formation of new landscapes by pirates and settlers, colonial society depended on controlling the lives of animals, fungi, and plants, as their labor was crucial in monoculture production. On the other hand, Africans and their descendants, enslaved or runaways, interacted with these and other beings inside and outside the plantation, either in the provision grounds and animal pens or in the maroon communities, producing forms of counter-plantation alliances that materially defined territories, lives, and futures beyond the plantation. In post-revolutionary Haiti, these provision grounds and the small family compounds known as *lakou* became the center of a new Creole world (Bastien 1951; Dubois 2012: 107–109).

If the history of the world is, in a way, the history of the plantation, the role of more-than-human beings in forging new alliances and alternative futures should be taken into account. Animals, as well as other beings, with their own intentions and projects, played a crucial role in the technogenesis of these agrarian landscapes and in the ontogenesis of modern ideas such as freedom, understood here not only as a sociological dimension of peasantry as a class, but as a fundamental value of modernity. Therefore, if modern infrastructures, such as the plantation, have a crucial role in contemporary forms of inhabiting the world, the many counter-plantation practices and the plot systems that created other forms of dwelling cannot be disregarded. To bring Casimir (2018) back into the conversation, these practices protected and regenerated not only the community but also the world at large. They were not only forms of resistance but the materialization of new ecologies in practice: a work of regeneration for a time that is now known as the Anthropocene.

References

Alves, Abel A. 2011. *The Animals of Spain: An Introduction to Imperial Perceptions and Human Interaction with Other Animals, 1492–1826.* Boston: Brill.

Anderson, Virginia DeJohn. 2004. *Creatures of Empire: How Domestic Animals Transformed Early America.* Oxford: Oxford University Press.

Andrews, Kenneth Raymond. 1978. *The Spanish Caribbean: Trade and Plunder, 1530–1630.* New Haven: Yale University Press.

Bastien, Rémy. 1951. *La familia rural haitiana, Valle de Marbial.* Mexico City: Libra.

Barnet, Miguel. 1994. *Biography of a Runaway Slave.* Willimantic: Curbstone Press.

Berlin, Ira. 1998. *Many Thousands Gone. The First Two Centuries of Slavery in North America*. Cambridge: Harvard University Press.

Boisseron, Bénédicte. 2018. *Afro-Dog: Blackness and the Animal Question*. New York: Columbia University Press.

Brown, Vincent. 2020. *Tacky's Revolt: The Story of an Atlantic Slave War*. Cambridge: Harvard University Press.

Bulamah, Rodrigo C. 2020. "Pode Um Porco Falar? Doença, Sistemas e Sacrifício No Caribe." *Horizontes Antropológicos* 26, no. 57: 57–92.

Cadena, Marisol de la, and Mario Blaser, ed. 2018. *A World of Many Worlds*. Durham: Duke University Press.

Cardoso, Ciro Flamarion Santana. 1987. *Escravo ou camponês?: o protocampesinato negro nas Américas*. São Paulo: Editora Brasiliense.

Casimir, Jean. 1992. *The Caribbean: One and Divisible*. Santiago de Chile: United Nations/ Economic Commission for Latin America and the Caribbean.

———. 2018. "Une Lecture Décoloniale de l'histoire Du Peuple Haïtien de 1697 à 1915." *Rencontre* 34: 95–105.

Castellano, Katey. 2021. "Provision Grounds Against the Plantation: Robert Wedderburn's Axe Laid to the Root." *Small Axe* 25, no. 1: 15–27.

Crosby, Alfred W. 1972. *The Columbian Exchange: Biological and Cultural Consequences of 1492*. Westport: Greenwood Publishing Group.

———. 1986. *Ecological Imperialism: The Biological Expansion of Europe, 900–1900*. Cambridge: Cambridge University Press.

Crublier de Saint-Cyran, Paul-Edme. 1790. *Réfutation du Projet des Amis des Noirs, Sur La Suppression de La Traite Des Nègres et Sur l'abolition de l'esclavage Dans Nos Colonies*. Paris: Imprimerie de Devaux.

Crutzen, Paul, and Eugene Stoermer. 2000. "The 'Anthropocene'." *Global Change Newsletter* 41: 17–18.

Curtin, Philip D. 1990. *The Rise and Fall of the Plantation Complex: Essays in Atlantic History*. Cambridge: Cambridge University Press.

DeLoughrey, Elizabeth. 2011. "Yam, Roots, and Rot: Allegories of the Provision Grounds." *Small Axe* 15, no. 1: 58–75.

Derby, Lauren. 2011. "Bringing the Animals Back in: Writing Quadrupeds into the Environmental History of Latin America and the Caribbean." *History Compass* 9, no. 8: 602–621.

Donkin, Robin Arthur. 1985. *The Peccary: With Observations on the Introduction of Pigs to the New World*. Philadelphia: The American Philosophical Society.

Dubois, Laurent. 2004. *Avengers of the New World: The Story of the Haitian Revolution*. Cambridge: Harvard University Press.

———. 2012. *Haiti: The Aftershocks of History*. New York: Picador.

Dubois, Laurent, and Richard Lee Turits. 2019. *Freedom Roots: Histories from the Caribbean*. Chapel Hill: University of North Carolina Press.

Ferdinand, Malcom. 2019. *Une écologie décoloniale: penser l'écologie depuis le monde caribéen*. Paris: Éditions du Seuil.

Fick, Carolyn E. 1990. *The Making of Haiti: The Saint Domingue Revolution from Below*. Knoxville: University of Tennessee Press.

Fischer, Sibylle. 2016. "Inhabiting Rights." *L'Esprit Créateur* 56, no. 1: 52–67.

Giusti-Cordero, Juan. 2009. "Beyond sugar revolutions: rethinking the Spanish Caribbean in the seventeenth and eighteenth century." In *Empirical Futures: Anthropologists and Historians Engage the Work of Sidney W. Mintz*, ed. Aisha Khan, George Baca, and Stephan Palmié, 58–83. Chapel Hill: University of North Carolina Press.

———. 2014. "Sugar and Livestock: Contraband Networks in Hispaniola and the Continental Caribbean in the Eighteenth Century." *Revista Brasileira do Caribe* 15, no. 29: 13–41.

Greenblatt, Stephen. 1991. *Marvelous Possessions: The Wonder of the New World*. Chicago: University of Chicago Press.

Haraway, Donna, Noboru Ishikawa, Scott F. Gilbert, et al. 2016. "Anthropologists Are Talking – About the Anthropocene." *Ethnos* 81, no. 3: 535–564.

Haraway, Donna. 2010. *When Species Meet*. Minneapolis: University of Minnesota Press.

Jean, Jean-Baptiste. 1993. *Celebration of 200 years of the Bois-Caïman, 1791–1991* [Painting].

Johnson, Sara E. 2012. *The Fear of French Negroes: Transcolonial Collaboration in the Revolutionary Americas*. Berkeley: University of California Press.

Labat, Jean-Baptiste. 1724. *Nouveau Voyage Aux Isles de l'Amérique*. Vol. 1. The Hague: P. Husson editeur. http://catalogue.bnf.fr/ark:/12148/cb30701887x.

Lecomte, Jules. 1837. *L'Île de la Tortue: roman maritime*. Vol. 1, *Histoire des flibustiers*. Paris: Hyppolite Souverain. http://gallica.bnf.fr/ark:/12148/bpt6k56864353.

Lepkowski, Tadeusz. 1970. *Haiti*. Havana: Casa de las Américas.

Majo, Claudio de. 2022. "Creole Ecologies, Feral Customs: A Coevolutionary History of Buccaneering in Hispaniola During the Seventeenth Century." *Historia Ambiental Latinoamericana y Caribeña (HALAC)* 12, no. 1: 353–387.

McNeill, John Robert. 2010. *Mosquito Empires: Ecology and War in the Greater Caribbean, 1620–1914*. Cambridge: Cambridge University Press.

Metcalf, Alida C. 2005. *Go-Betweens and the Colonization of Brazil, 1500–1600*. Austin: University of Texas Press.

Mintz, Sidney W. 1985a. "From Plantations to Peasantries in the Caribbean." In *Caribbean Countours*, ed. Sidney W Mintz and Sally Price, 127–153. Baltimore: Johns Hopkins University Press.

———. 1985b. *Sweetness and power: the place of sugar in modern history*. New York: Penguin.

———. 1989. *Caribbean Transformations*. New York: Columbia University Press.

———. 1996. "Enduring Substances, Trying Theories: The Caribbean Region as Oikoumene." *The Journal of the Royal Anthropological Institute* 2, no. 2: 289–311.

Mintz, Sidney W, and Richard Price. 1976. *An Anthropological Approach to the Afro-American Past: A Caribbean Perspective*. Philadelphia: ISHI.

Moreau de Saint-Méry, M. Louis-Élie. 1958. *Description Topographique, Physique, Civile, Politique et Histoire de La Partie Française de l'Isle Saint-Domingue*. Vol. 1. Paris: Société de l'Histoire des Colonies Françaises et Librarie Larose. Orig. pub. 1796.

Moya Pons, Frank. 1977. *Historia colonial de Santo Domingo*. Santiago de los Caballeros: Universidad Católica Madre y Maestra.

———. 2007. *History of the Caribbean: Plantations, Trade, and War in the Atlantic World*. Princeton: Markus Wiener Publishers.

Norton, Marcy. 2013. "Animals in Spain and Spanish Americas." In *Lexikon of the Hispanic Baroque: Transatlantic Exchange and Transformation*, ed. Kenneth Mills and Evonne Levy, 17–23. Austin: University of Texas Press.

———. 2015. "The Chicken or the Iegue: Human-Animal Relationships and the Columbian Exchange." *The American Historical Review* 120, no. 1: 28–60.

Oexmelín, Alexandre. 1930. *Les Aventuriers et les Boucaniers d'Amérique, par Alexandre Oexmelín, chirurgien des aventuriers de 1666 à 1672*. Ed. Bertrand Guégan. Paris: Aux Editions du Carrefour.

Paravisini-Gebert, Lizabeth. 2008. "Endangered Species: Caribbean Ecology and the Discourse of the Nation." In *Displacements and Transformations in Caribbean Cultures*, ed. Lizabeth Paravisini-Gebert and Ivette Romero-Cesareo, 8–23. Gainesville: University Press of Florida.

Price, Richard. 1979. *Maroon societies: rebel slave communities in the americas*. Baltimore: Johns Hopkins University Press.

Quintero-Rivera, Angel. 1995. "The Caribbean Counter-Plantation: Rural Formation Heritage and the Contemporary Search for Fundamentals." In *The Search for Fundamentals: The Process of Modernisation and the Quest for Meaning*, ed. Lieteke van Vucht Tijssen, Jan Berting, and Frank J Lechner, 175–186. Dordrecht: Kluwer Academic Publishers.

Raynal, Guillaume-Thomas. 1770. *Histoire Philosophique et Politique Des Établissemens et Du Commerce Des Européens Dans Les Deux Indes*. Vol. 3. Amsterdam: Imprimeru de la Ville & de l'Académie.

Sautchuk, Carlos E. 2018. "Os Antropólogos e a Domesticação: Derivações e Ressurgências de Um Conceito." In *Políticas Etnográficas No Campo Da Ciência e Das Tecnologias Da Vida*, ed. Jean Segata and Theophilos Rifiotis, 85–108. Porto Alegre: Editora da UFRGS.

Scott, Julius Sherrard. 2018. *The Common Wind: Afro-American Currents in the Age of the Haitian Revolution*. London: Verso.

Sidbury, James, and Jorge Cañizares-Esguerra. 2011. "Mapping Ethnogenesis in the Early Modern Atlantic." *The William and Mary Quarterly* 68, no. 2: 181–208.

Stewart, John. 1823. *View of the Past and Present State of the Island of Jamaica with Remarks of the Moral and Physical Conditions of the Slaves, and on the Abolition of Slavery in the Colonies.* Edinburgh: Oliver & Boid, Tweeddale-House.

Stoler, Ann Laura. 2009. *Along the Archival Grain: Epistemic Anxieties and Colonial Common Sense.* Princeton: Princeton University Press.

Tardieu, Jean-Pierre. 2006. "Cimarrón-Maroon-Marron: Note Épistemologique." *Outres-Mers* 93, no. 350/351: 237–247.

Thomas, Keith. 1996. *Homem e o mundo natural: mudanças de atitude em relação as plantas e aos animais (1500–1800).* Trans. João Roberto Martins Filho. São Paulo: Companhia das Letras.

Tomich, Dale. 2004. *Through the Prism of Slavery: Labor, Capital, and World Economy.* Lanham: Rowman & Littlefield.

Trouillot, Michel-Rolph. 1990. *Haiti, State against Nation: The Origins and Legacy of Duvalierism.* New York: Monthly Review Press.

———. 1993. "Coffee Planters and Coffee Slaves in the Antilles: The Impact of a Secondary Crop." In *Cultivation and Culture: Labor and the Shaping of Slave Life in the Americas,* ed. Ira Berlin and Philip Morgan, 124–137. Charlottesville: University Press of Virginia.

———. 2003. *Global Transformations: Anthropology and the Modern World.* New York: Palgrave Macmillan.

Tsing, Anna L. 2015. *Mushroom at the End of the World: On the Possibilities of Life in Capitalist Ruins.* Princeton: Princeton University Press.

Vander Velden, Felipe Ferreira. 2012. "As galinhas incontáveis. Tupis, europeus e aves domésticas na conquista no Brasil." *Journal de la Société des américanistes* 98, no. 2: 97–104.

———. 2018. "Os primeiros cachorros: encontros interétnicos e multiespecíficos no Sudoeste da Amazônia." *Revista Brasileira de Ciências Sociais* 33: 1–23.

Wynter, Sylvia. 1971. "Novel and History, Plot and Plantation." *Savacou* 5: 95–102.

From the Mid-Nineteenth Century to 1950

Source: Fernando Efrén Sandoval (2021)

Introduction: Biodiversity and the Anthropocene in Latin America from the Mid-Nineteenth Century to 1950

Olaf Kaltmeier, Antoine Acker, León Enrique Ávila Romero and Regina Horta Duarte

In the midst of the nineteenth century, new dynamics can be observed in dealing with the biological diversity of flora and fauna in Latin America, both quantitatively – with regard to the scientific and political-economic penetration of ecosystems – and qualitatively – above all with regard to a changed understanding of nature – although they vary greatly from region to region. In the Amazon and Orinoco basins, the ideas of an exuberant wild nature have been revived. After the genocide of the Conquista, to which more than 90 percent of the Indigenous population fell victim, the rainforest spread out and presented itself to the explorers, settlers, and researchers of the nineteenth century – in contrast to the conquerors of the colonial era – as virtually untouched nature. This regeneration of nature was the biological-material basis for the emergence of the "pristine myth" (Denevan 1992). However, not all species benefited equally from this situation. Amazonian agricultural plants, which had been cultivated by the Indigenous societies to harvest fruits, nuts, and other useful items, declined.

In the age of high imperialism in the last third of the nineteenth century, the European powers sought to wipe all previously unknown white spots – including the areas marked as wilderness – off the map and subjugate them. In many peripheral and inaccessible areas, the first economic exploitation took place through simple forms of extractivism, which were largely driven forward with extreme violence and ecological ruthlessness. In the tri-border region of Paraguay, Argentina, and Brazil, the wild yerba mate – the knowledge of the Jesuits' cultivation techniques had been lost – was exploited before plantations were established again from the 1890s onwards. In the Amazon basin, driven by European and U.S. demand, the exploitation of wild rubber trees, based on the slave-like exploitation of the Indigenous population, increased in importance and became a booming industry that drove the further development of the region (Coomes and Bradford 1994). Individual animal species also became targets of extractivism, such as exotic birds for their feathers or chinchillas for their skins to supply Western luxury consumption, bringing them to the brink of extinction as early as the end of the nineteenth century. Paradoxically, this simple capitalist extractivism also brought early conservation measures, such as protecting the seabirds that produced guano – which was used as fertilizer for increasingly intensive agricultural production worldwide (Cushman 2014).

However, the image of exuberant natural biodiversity no longer applied to every region of Latin America, even in the nineteenth century. Especially in the early conquered and colonized areas of the Caribbean and parts of the Atlantic coast, immense biological degradation can be observed, particularly through deforestation, which reduced natural habitats. The socio-metabolic rift caused by the plantation economy was the main cause of this. The colonial plantation system underwent a renewal in the nineteenth century, which led to a neo-Columbian exchange. New species, such as coffee or zebu, were specifically introduced for plantation farming under scientific supervision (McCook 2011). Even before 1800, there were signs of the extinction of several native land and marine species in the Lesser Antilles, as well as the rapid spread of invasive plant and animal species (Watts 1986). In Barbados, no monkey species survived the sugar plantations and of the 529 uncultivated plant species on the island, only 11 percent are of native origin (Miller 2007: 85). The plantation economy also continued to spread in other coastal areas on the tropical Pacific side of Ecuador and in Mesoamerica. The end of the nineteenth century marked the rise of U.S. American imperialism in the Western hemisphere and U.S. capital became increasingly important in Latin America. From 1899 onwards, the United Fruit Company turned large parts of the forests of Costa Rica, Nicaragua, Colombia, and Panama into banana plantations (Soluri 2005).

The introduction of Eurasian animal species and, as a result, zoonoses, is one of the most central elements of the Columbian Exchange, which significantly changed pre-Columbian biodiversity (Crosby 1972). In the Andean region, llamas were increasingly displaced by sheep and goats, and in the Southern Cone, cattle and horses introduced during the colonial period had spread freely and run wild. The settler colonization that began in the middle of the nineteenth century, especially in the Southern Cone, which partly had the biopolitical objective of improving the national body and the supposed civilization of the peripheral areas, was accompanied by a profound change in biodiversity, which contemporary natural scientists already described as the "Europeanization of the landscape" (Hauman 1916). At the beginning of the nineteenth century, the waters were also biologically colonized by the introduction of salmonids and carp species (Kaltmeier 2021: 163–172).

In the nineteenth century, expeditions to explore and economically develop the flora and fauna of Latin America became increasingly important and provoked new insights that circulated worldwide. Alongside the early journeys of Johan Baptist Spix and Carl Friedrich von Martius, the research trip of the Prussian naturalist Alexander von Humboldt and the French botanist Aimé Bonpland between 1799 and 1804 was a milestone and catalyst for a veritable scientific euphoria about Latin

America. Even if it is rightly pointed out today that Humboldt's studies were based on the research of Ibero-American contemporaries such as Francisco José de Caldas (Thurner and Cañizares-Esguerra 2023), Humboldt placed such results in a broad conceptual framework and disseminated it in the scientific community of the time. Humboldt is considered one of the leading founders of vegetation geography, which not only classifies plants but also places them in their ecosystem (Lack 2018: 9). This approach also made it possible to address anthropogenic landscape change, as Humboldt saw plant geography as a link between plant and human history (Päßler 2020: 8). In geography, this work on vegetation zones had a lasting effect so that by the end of the nineteenth century a series of vegetation geography works and maps were published in and about Latin America.

The introduction of historicity into biology was a central epistemological upheaval in the nineteenth century. Previously, species had been fixed on the tableau according to the classification system introduced by Carl von Linné. This system based the naming of flora and fauna solely at the discretion of white Western men of science and ignored Indigenous names and naming practices. While this classification system of taxonomy was maintained, its epistemological foundations were partly shaken. The philosopher Michel Foucault worked out from the history of Western European thought that biologists now did not just stare at superficial differences between animals, but compared them anatomically by dissecting their hidden organ systems. In doing so, they also noticed the historicity of life (Foucault 1996: 279–287; Bondi and La Vergata 2017). The French naturalist Jean-Baptiste Lamarck was one of the first scientists to propose an evolutionary explanation of biodiversity that followed the philosophical principle of higher development. However, the real breakthrough in the theory of evolution was achieved by Charles Darwin, who developed his ideas on the origin of species and their mutability due to adaptation and selection to specific environmental conditions on the basis of his world voyage (1831–36), with significant stopovers in South America. As Elizabeth Kolbert (2016: 62) emphasizes, the theory of the origin of species is also a theory of their extinction. This is because natural selection can lead to the disappearance of species over a long period of time. Darwin himself was also quite aware that species can become extinct due to the influence of humans, although extinction was no conceptual or ethical problem for him.

However, at the end of the XIX Century evolutionism was by no means undisputed. The Swiss-American naturalist Louis Agassiz came to the Amazon region as late as 1867 to refute Darwin's theory of evolution. Based on the Christian doctrine of creation, Agassiz argued that God had established "zoological provinces" in which specific new species had been created.

Simultaneously with Darwin, another natural scientist, Alfred Russel Wallace, who had explored the Amazon region from 1848 to 1852, developed an evolutionary theory of the origin of species based on the struggle for survival. However, Wallace lost a large part of his South American collection. Further significant collecting activities and research trips in the context of the imperial penetration of the world were carried out by Henry Walter Bates (1825–1892) and Richard Spruce (1817–1893), who – unlike Humboldt – did not belong to the social elite and financed their travels by selling specimens to museums, botanical gardens, and private collectors (Stepan 2001, Hemming 2015). This form of scientific extractivism was partly promoted by deliberately ordered biopiracy. For example, Spruce was commissioned by the British government to collect cinchona seeds from Ecuador so that this important substance could be cultivated in India to combat malaria in order to advance the imperial project there. In 1876, the British naturalist Henry Wickham smuggled rubber seeds from Brazil to London on behalf of Kew Gardens. These could then be planted in Malaysia, breaking the Latin American rubber monopoly (Dean 1987).

Beyond the question of species diversity and its origin, botanists and plant geographers have also been concerned with neophytes. The term neophyte was first introduced in 1918 by the Swiss botanist Albert Thellung in a study on ruderal and adventive species. In 1877, the German-Argentine botanist Carlos Berg identified 154 non-native European plant species in the province of Buenos Aires and the region of Patagonia that were increasingly displacing the native ones (Berg 1877: 183). Accordingly, Otto Reiche (1907) argued that the European neophytes in the temperate regions of other continents, including Latin America, were particularly successful in their acclimatization and aggressive towards the native species. In general, however, it was also evident to the natural scientists of the time that this dramatic change in biodiversity since the second half of the nineteenth century was due to human activities (Kaltmeier 2021: 140–147). Humans – and the intentional as well as unintentional introduction of new species as a result of their activities – are the central vector in the modification of vegetation geography and the loss of biodiversity.

While the habitats of native species were increasingly restricted by the massive expansion of the modern technosphere, including resource-intensive agriculture and the introduction and spread of alien species, nature simultaneously became one of the foundations of the nation-building of the independent republics, which were increasingly oriented towards Enlightenment France, England, and Prussia. The foundation of the *Museo Nacional de Historia Natural* in Mexico (1790), the Royal Acclimation Garden (1808), and the Royal Museum (1818) in what is now Brazil were still based on the imperial claims of the Iberian colonial powers, but in the other countries of the region, the republican aspirations became more and more prevalent. In Chile, the Natural History Museum was founded in 1830, in Uruguay the *Museo Nacional de Historia Natural* in 1838, in Brazil the *Museo Paraense Emílio Goeldi* in 1866 with a special focus on the Amazonía, in Argentina the *Museo General de La Plata* in 1884, and in Venezuela the *Museo de la Ciencia* in 1875, to name just a few of the most important. Usually, Western European natural scientists (Claudio Gay in Chile, Carlos Thays and Carl-Curt Hosseus in Argentina, Emílio Goeldi in Brazil, Federico Albert and Rodulfo Philippi in Chile, Henri Pittier in Venezuela) were involved in founding and establishing these institutions and often became citizens of the respective Latin American countries. But Creole natural scientists (Maximo Martínez in Mexico or Francisco Pascasio Moreno in Argentina) also emerged and founded some of the first scientific journals and societies dedicated to biodiversity issues. Concepts and measures for the protection of native flora, fauna, and landscape were also discussed in this period. Many representatives emphasized not only the scientific aspect but also the aesthetic and affective value of nature, as expressed in Humboldt's ideas. In the Southern Cone, for example, the social elites founded civil society nature conservation organizations such as the Amigos del Árbol.

An important reference for institutional, state-run nature conservation was the national park legislation in the U.S. based on the model of Yellowstone National Park, which was established in 1872 and considered to be the first national park in the world. However, other nature conservation models, primarily from Western Europe, were also discussed in Latin America. In the Southern Cone, in particular, national parks and protected areas were established remarkably early by international standards. The first national parks were established in Argentina and Chile in the 1920s, and a national park authority was also set up in Argentina in the 1930s – based on the U.S. model (Kaltmeier 2021). These initiatives were clearly recognized internationally. For example, an Argentinian delegation was represented at the first international nature conservation conference, which took place in Bern in 1913. This led to the founding of an Advisory Commission for International Nature Conservation, a forerunner of today's International Union for Conservation of Nature (IUCN).

The establishment of national parks in Latin America was not exclusively geared towards protecting biodiversity, however. In Argentina, national parks were seen as poles of development that were intended to integrate peripheral areas into the nation through tourism. In Mexico – in contrast to the U.S. American idea of wilderness and parks without people – the establishment of national parks during the administration of Lázaro Cárdenas (1934–1940) related to aspects of agrarian reform, cultural heritage, education, and local economic development over and above nature conservation (Wakild 2011; Durand 2017).

A milestone in the inter-American efforts to protect nature was the Pan-American Convention for the Protection of Fauna, Flora, and Natural Beauty, which was adopted in 1940 and based largely on the U.S. national park model. This convention created one of the first legal frameworks for the double continent, which aimed to protect and preserve the environment and natural species. In the years that followed, almost all Latin American countries ratified the convention and subsequently established nature reserves and other conservation measures, particularly for the protection of migratory birds. As important as this convention is for international nature conservation, it also clearly marks the U.S. hegemony established at the beginning of the twentieth century with regard to environmental protection and biodiversity in the Americas. This hegemony increasingly extended to the interpretation and control of the tropics. The completion of the Panama Canal in 1914, which accelerated the exchange of biota by connecting the Atlantic and Pacific Oceans, can be seen as a materialization of this "conquest of the tropics." Accompanied by scientific research – above all to combat malaria and yellow fever – this large-scale project created the framework conditions for the development of tropical biology based on experimental stations in an expanded Caribbean region (Raby 2017).

In this U.S. academic-political milieu, which largely ignored the achievements and contributions of Latin American science and Indigenous knowledge, the foundations for the invention of the concept of biodiversity were laid in 1986 at the conference of the National Forum on BioDiversity in Washington. The idea was then popularized in particular by the 1992 Rio de Janeiro Conference on the Environment and the Convention on Biological Diversity (CBD) and, from 2010, by the International Year of Biodiversity and the subsequent U.N. Decade on Biodiversity (2011–2020).

References

Berg, Carlos. 1877. "Enumeración de las plantas européas que se hallan como silvestres en la provincia de Buenos Aires y en Patagonia." *Sociedad científica argentina* 3: 182–206.

Bondi, Roberto, and Antonello La Vergata. 2017. *Naturaleza*. Mexico City: UNAM.

Coomes, Oliver T., and Bradford L. Barham. 1994. "The Amazon rubber boom: labor control, resistance, and failed plantation development revisited." *The Hispanic American Historical Review* 74, no. 2: 231–257.

Crosby, Alfred W. 1972. *The Columbian Exchange: Biological and Social Consequences of 1492*. Westport: Greenwood Publishing Group.

Cushman, Gregory. 2014. *Guano and the Opening of the Pacific World: a Global Ecological History*. Cambridge: Cambridge University Press.

Dean, Warren. 1987. *Brazil and the Struggle for Rubber: A Study in Environmental History*. Cambridge: Cambridge University Press.

Denevan, William. 1992. "The Pristine Myth: The Landscape of the Americas in 1492." *Annals of the Association of American Geographers* 82, no. 3: 369–385.

Durand, Leticia. 2017. *Naturalezas desiguales. Discursos sobre la conservación de la biodiversidad en México*. Cuernavaca: UNAM.

Foucault, Michel. 1996. *Die Ordnung der Dinge*. Frankfurt: Suhrkamp.

Hauman, Lucién. 1916. *La Forêt Valdivienne et ses Limites. Notes de Geographique Botanique*. Buenos Aires: Trabajos del Instituto de Botanica y Farmacologia.

Hemming, John. 2015. *Naturalists in Paradise. Wallace, Bates and Spruce in the Amazon*. London: Thames & Hudson.

Kaltmeier, Olaf. 2021. *National Parks from North to South: An Entangled History of Conservation and Colonization in Argentina*. New Orleans/Trier: University of New Orleans Press/Wissenschaftlicher Verlag Trier.

Kolbert, Elizabeth. 2016. *Das 6. Sterben*. Frankfurt: Suhrkamp.

Lack, Walter. 2018. *Alexander von Humboldt und die botanische Erforschung Amerikas*. Munich: Prestel.

McCook, Stuart. 2011. "The Neo-Columbian Exchange: The Second Conquest of the Greater Caribbean, 1720–1930." *Latin American Research Review* [Special Issue] 46: 11–31.

Miller, Shawn William. 2007. *An Environmental History of Latin America*. Cambridge: Cambridge University Press.

Päßler, Ulrich. 2020. "Im freyen Spiel dynamischer Kräfte: Pflanzengeographische Schriften, Manuskripte und Korrespondenzen Alexander von Humboldts." In *Alexander von Humboldt: Geographie der Pflanzen. Unveröffentlichte Schriften aus dem Nachlass*, ed. Ulrich Päßler, 3–26. Berlin: Metzler.

Raby, Megan. 2017. *American Tropics. The Caribbean Roots of Biodiversity Science*. Chapel Hill: University of North Carolina Press.

Reiche, Karl. 1907. *Grundzüge der Pflanzenverbreitung in Chile*. Leipzig: Verlag von Wilhelm Engelmann.

Soluri, John. 2005. *Banana Cultures. Agriculture, Consumption, and Environmental Change in Honduras and the United States*. Austin: Texas University Press.

Stepan, Nancy L. 2001. *Picturing Tropical Nature*. London: Reaktion Books.

Thurner, Mark, and Jorge Cañizares-Esguerra. 2023. "Introduction: Under Humboldt's Footsteps." In *The Invention of Humboldt: On the Geopolitics of Knowledge*, ed. Mark Thurner and Jorge Cañizares-Esguerra, 1–13. London: Routledge.

Wakild, Emily. 2011. *Revolutionary Parks. Conservation, Social Justice, and Mexico's National Parks, 1910–1940*. Tucson: University of Arizona Press.

Watts, David. 1986. *The West Indies: Patterns of Development, Culture and Environment Change since 1492*. Cambridge: Cambridge University Press.

Biodiversity in the Southern Cone from the Mid-Nineteenth Century to 1950
Second Conquest and First Acceleration in the Genealogy of the Anthropocene

Olaf Kaltmeier and Eduardo Relly

In the Southern Cone – Chile, Argentina, Uruguay, Paraguay, southern Brazil and Bolivia – the Age of Empire manifested itself in a veritable Second Conquest (Kaltmeier 2022), visible in the appropriation and control of peripheral, often Indigenous territories and biomes. This conquest was epitomized by the Chilean *Pacificacción de la Araucanía* (1861–1883) and the Argentinean *Campaña del desierto* (1878–1885) against the Mapuche, and the raids conducted by the Uruguayan military that culminated in the *Matanza del Salsipuedes* in 1831. In the case of southern Brazil, the provinces of Santa Catarina and Rio Grande do Sul established either paramilitary forces and founded indigenous reservations to deal with the Indigenous population (Rinke 2018). The Chaco-War (1932–35), fought mainly between Bolivia and Paraguay, affected Guaraní communities deeply and has been understood in environmental terms as an "Anthropocene hyperobject" (Breithoff 2020), which, through warfare, created an anthroposcenic landscape.

Also of paramount importance for anthroposcenic landscape change was settler colonialism. Especially in the mid-nineteenth century, the Southern Cone states recruited massive amounts of European-born settlers from Germany, Italy, Scandinavia, Croatia, the Russian Empire, Scotland, and Wales. From a European perspective, mass emigration functioned as a biopolitical outlet for rural populations that had been made redundant by industrialization. In addition to seeds, viruses, livestock, vermin, weeds, and other biotic elements, these settlers brought with them Western ideas about ecosystem transformation and "civilization."

Within this process of the nation-state's violent geopolitical expansion and its integration into the accelerated globalization of the capitalist world-system, vast regions and biomes were biologically transformed. In the Caribbean, Mesoamerica, and the Andean region the first conquest in the long sixteenth century had enormous influences on (socio-)ecosystems that have led environmental historians to understand this period as a starting point for the Anthropocene's genealogy. With respect to the biological aspect of the Anthropocene, Alfred Crosby's concept of the "Columbian exchange" deserves mention, as well as its further development by Charles Mann into the "Homogenocene" – the worldwide convergence of biological worlds driven by anthropocenic vectors. Others locate Latin and Mesoamerican regions in an anthroposcenic genealogy within the "Plantationocene" in the extended Caribbean and northern Brazil or the global ecological influence of mining in the central Andes and Mexico (Machado 2022). Some of these aspects are also found in the Southern Cone, but only on a small scale. It is not until the mid-nineteenth century that large parts of the region enter the Anthropocene's genealogy through the Second Conquest. This occurred during a period referred to as the first acceleration phase of the Anthropocene (Bonneuil and Fressoz 2016: 50–1), associated with the transition to the fossil fuel energy regime, the Industrial Revolution, technological innovations, and capitalist penetration. For many regions of the Southern Cone, this meant rapidly accelerated change in socio-ecological metabolisms and radical transformation of biomes. This fundamentally changed biodiversity, both in terms of individual species – species extinction with the simultaneous introduction of neophytes (Second Columbian Exchange) – and of biomes themselves, whose landscapes and ecology were cultivated and Europeanized. Surpassing the ecologic boundaries of local ecosystems, as well as the desacralization of cosmologic and holistic views on land, also characterizes this first acceleration phase of the Anthropocene in the Southern Cone.

This chapter presents an overview of the most pressing activities that created social and ecological changes in the Southern Cone region, as well as resilience strategies and even adaptations to the impending modernization that were employed in the nineteenth century. Of course, the present aim is not to exhaust the issue but rather to offer the reader a glimpse at some examples of the acceleration, intensification, and commodification of human ecologies in the Southern Cone through a few specific activities under a macroregional perspective.

Environmental Knowledge

In the course of military conquest, the geographic registration and surveying of the last "white spots" that had not yet been colonized began. In the Southern Cone, this included, above all, the phytogeographical classification and mapping as well as the identification of animal and plant species by primarily Western European natural scientists. Natural science, especially in Argentina, was explicitly involved in a colonial-military project of conquering peripheral parts of the country, above all the pampas of northern Patagonia, which were controlled by the Indigenous population. Thus, a scientific commission (with Adolfo Doering as zoologist and Paul Günther Lorentz as botanist) was an integral part of the military operation led by General Roca, who defeated the Mapuche in a genocidal war of extermination. This marked the beginning of intensive natural history research in Argentina, in part also encompassing Uruguay as well as the border regions with Paraguay.

These naturalists, mainly of German and French origin, reconfigured and reclassified the region's biodiversity following nineteenth-century academic standards of the West. In Chile, Karl Reiche's *Grundzüge der Pflanzenverbreitung in Chile* provided a comprehensive scientific description and cataloging of the phytogeographic zones. Reiche segmented the country from north to south along lines of latitude, dividing the land into northern, central, and southern Chile along the 4,200 km stretch from the Atacama Desert to the Antarctica with each of these areas in turn divided into subareas (Fig. 1). This division along climate zones is complemented by a longitudinal axis that runs between the coastal region and the Andean Cordillera. In this way, Reiche (1907: 274–282) identified seventeen phytogeographical zones to which he assigns specific indicator plants. The geographic insularity through the desert, Antarctica, the Andean Cordillera, and the Pacific Ocean favors a high number of endemic species. Today, half of Chilean plant species, or 90 percent of seed plants, are considered endemic (Ministerio de Medio Ambiente, Tomo I, 2008: 56). In Brazil, the *Flora Brasiliensis* by Carl Friedrich Philipp von Martius and others (published between 1840 and 1906) was the main reference for its phytogeography. The chartering of complex organic systems accompanied state-building and provided data/inventories for a myriad of actors worldwide. On behalf of the Argentine Central Committee for the Philadelphia World's Fair, Richard Napp published the volume *Die Argentinische Republik* in 1876, containing the first comprehensive phytogeographical map of Argentina. This work was added to by botanist Paul Günther Lorentz and extends remarkably far beyond the borders of the Argentine Republic to include Chile, Uruguay, southern Brazil, Paraguay, and parts of Bolivia, demonstrating that biomes do not correspond necessarily with national borders.

170   From the Mid-Nineteenth Century to 1950

Fig. 1: "Chile: Die pflanzengeographische Einteilung"

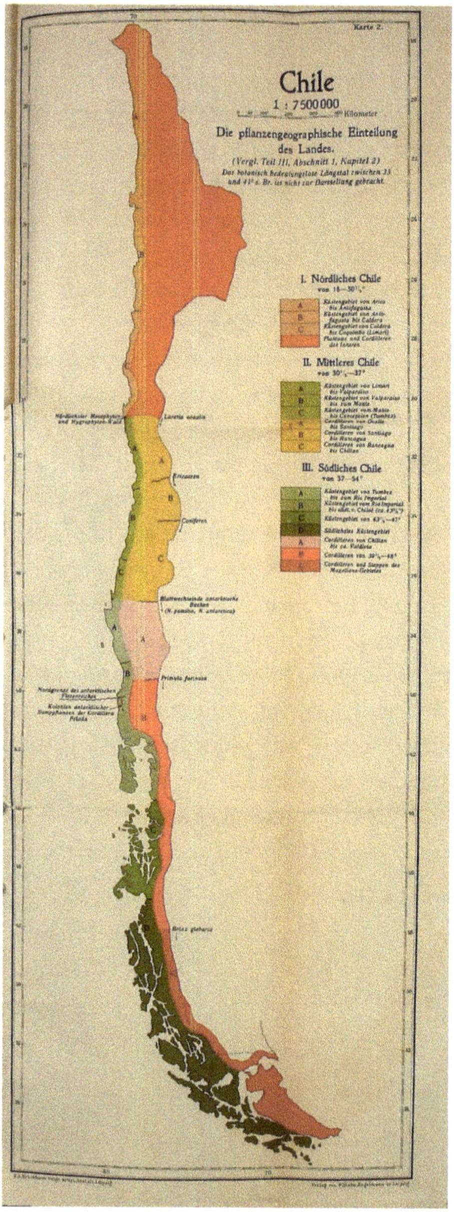

Source: Reiche (1907).

Fig. 2: Lorentz: "Mapa fitogeográfico de la República Argentina"

Source: Ricardo Napp (1876).

However, Western scientific classification of biodiversity along vegetation zones was not the only ordering grid. By the last third of the eighteenth century, in a process of ethnogenesis that began in the mid-seventeenth century, identity-territorial Mapuche units (*futamapu*) emerged with particular geomorphological and biocultural characteristics (Kaltmeier 2022, 78–9). The *lafquenmapu* is characterized by proximity to the sea and dominated by fishing, seafood gathering, and seaweed harvesting (*kollofe* or in Quechua *cochayuyu*) (Mösbach 1992). The *lelfünmapu* of the Central Valley is characterized by vegetable cultivation, livestock, and simple extractivism in the nothofagus forests, while in the *inapiremapu* of the Andean foothills land uses were already changing and were strongly influenced by the araucaria (Aldunate and Villagrán 1992). In the *piremapu* – the land of the snow – lived the Pehuenche, whose identitarian self-nomination is composed of *pehuén* (= cone of the araucaria) and *che* (= human being). On the lower lands of the Paraná-Paraguay river basin, the Guarani dominated vast swathes of deciduous and semievergreen forests and established an intricate network of *tekohá*, settlements ordained more on the matter of the people/families who live in a determined place than on a bounded area. Living in a world created by *Nhanderu reta*, the father of all Guarani who not only created the *yvy vai* (the earthly world) but rather the paths that enable each creature to follow its own way, the Guarani have in the last two millennia traversed several ecological zones porting with them specific biota for the maintenance and construction of their *yvy porã* (good land where *tekohá* may be built) (Noelli et al. 2021; Ladeira 2001). These Indigenous (and maroon) expressions of understanding the land dispute the viewpoint of Western-based powers. In a critical manner, these struggles will be brought into conversation with the current concept of biodiversity.

Extracting Plants and Animals

This chapter understands extractivism according to the whole gradient of meanings given by Gudynas (2015); extractivism may range from the local collection, for instance, of timber or fibers for personal or community use up to extractive industries like oil for exportation. It is a relation between integration to markets (local, national, exports) and intensity of resource exploitation (low, intermediate, high). Yerba mate took outstanding precedence in Paraguay, Brazil, and Argentina from the nineteenth century onwards. Conservation of *yerbales* became crucial since the extraction of the resource demanded the continuous management of the standing forests. Conservation measures began very early on, and municipalities were the first instances where such policies gained effect. As showcased previously, extractivism of yerba-mate scaled up, receiving the dedicated attention of national and provincial governments in the early twentieth century. Paraguay, early on, was the center of commercialization of yerba-mate in the whole region (Kleinpenning 2003). Heavily influenced by Guarani knowledge, *yerbales* distribution stretched from eastern Paraguay through the Argentinean province of Misiones, finally engulfing the three southmost states of Brazil (Gerhardt 2013). Plans to transform the yerba into a global commodity were pioneered in the early 1820s by Aimé Bonpland, a travel fellow of Alexander von Humboldt (Bell 2010). With commercial exit, especially in regional markets, yerba-mate extractivism was increasingly monopolized and relied on the forced labor of Guarani and impoverished popular segments of the population. After a solution for germinating mate seeds was found at the end of the nineteenth century, there was a system change from mate extractivism to a plantation culture.

Beginning in the mid-nineteenth century, animal extractivism mounted to the new dynamics of accelerated colonization. Hunting, especially at the beginning of clearing a new rural lot, was an activity to which families dedicated themselves diligently among the agrarian colonies of European origin that splintered across the whole region. As herds increased and agricultural production was consolidated, the recourse to hunting and fishing as a basic supply of protein decreased significantly (Porzelt 1937). Nevertheless, other accounts indicate the persistence of hunting even in the face of a more economically structured framework. Hunting of native "exotic" species also encountered high demand in U.S. American and European museums, zoologic collections, and fashion, creating permanent international commerce for furs, feathers, and stuffed animals. Commercial hunting of chinchillas began in northern Chile, Bolivia, Peru, and northwestern Argentina in the early 1820s, as their furs fetched high prices in Europe and the United States. Between 1900 and 1909, more than half a million furs were officially exported annually from Chile alone, bringing the population of the two existing chinchilla species to the brink of extinction. Thus, the chinchilla boom in Chile reached its peak in 1917. The endangerment of the species had already been recognized in the 1890s. In 1910, there was transnational regulation of the chinchilla fur trade between Chile, Bolivia, Peru, and Argentina, while Chile passed its own protection laws in 1898 and 1929. However, the actual enforcement of the laws remained problematic, especially because bans drove up prices and poaching increased. As late as 1960, some biologists considered chinchillas to be extinct in Chile. However, marginal populations were able to survive (Jiménez 1996). Furthermore, the vicuña was a highly commercial wild animal in the nineteenth century, despite being officially protected as early as 1825 through a law passed by the liberator Simón Bolívar.

The hunting of sea lions by the British and U.S. Americans began in the late seventeenth century, with an estimated 5 million killed during that time in Chile. By the mid-nineteenth century, there were already more than 400 ships hunting sea lions on the Chilean coast, which almost led to their extinction. As well, this population decline of sea lions certainly acted as a central factor in the extinction of Indigenous peoples of the Magallanes region, who depended on the species for more than seventy percent of their food. Similarly, within only a few decades, the Juan Fernández elephant seal was extirpated in the 1840s (Torres, Aguayo-Lobo, and Acevedo 2000). This phase of sea lion exploitation was followed by whaling, beginning in the late 1800s. By 1860, populations of the southern right whale had greatly diminished, and whaling began to shift further south. Shortly after independence in 1810, there were six whaling stations in Chile between Iquique and the Strait of Magellan (Aguayo et al. 1998). The greatest whaling activity in the Strait of Magellan occurred in the first years of the twentieth century after stocks in the North Atlantic were drastically reduced.

Beekeeping has been an elementary activity of native societies that had dealt for centuries with the stingless *Melipona bees* that occur in the neotropical regions. The first effective introduction of European bees (*Apis mellifera*) in South America is presumed to have been done by the catholic priest Antonio Carneiro in Rio de Janeiro in 1839. Nevertheless, the most accepted hypothesis on the original introduction of European bees in the Southern Cone involves the early German colonization of Rio Grande do Sul as of 1824. The *Apis Melifera* that first entered Brazil came from the Grand Duchy of Mecklenburg-Schwerin and substituted the wild honey produced by native bees. In the second Brazilian national exposition held in Rio de Janeiro in 1866, German-Brazilian honey was nationally praised (Schenck 1932). In Argentina, accounts of honey extraction go back to the reports of Ulrich Schmiedl, whose precise description of the Guarani use of the Melipona bees is remarkable. Honey production was led by political personalities like the former presidents Bernardino Rivadavia and Domingo Sarmiento. The province of Mendoza received European bees from Chile in 1855. This created two main zones of beekeeping, Buenos Aires and Mendoza, that, up to the 1950s, were the centers of honey production in Argentina. The debates on whether bees could alter local ecosystems, thereby hazarding fruit and crop production, were intense (Bierzychudek 1979).

Agriculture and Rural Colonization

Rural migration or colonization prevailed in the forests, and by the early twentieth century, the southern cone region made up a multicultural agrarian landscape as Germans, Italians, Poles, Ukrainians, Croatians, Scandinavians, Jewish, and Russian colonists settled in scattered plots of lands causing radical ecological change, as genetic fluxes, labor, and some capital permitted either the introduction of new crops or intensified the utilization of native plants (Zarth 2006). In general, the introduction of plants often assumed gendered roles as women were commonly in charge of transporting seeds of vegetables, fruits, and tea, reflecting the sexual divisions of European peasant and agrarian societies. In southern Brazil, it was not until 1880 that European seeds became broadly available and advertised in the popular rural calendars, which were very popular among the German colonies. The diffusion of the now widely popular tea, chamomile, which was called back then by Luso-Brazilian communities "German-chamomile," may best exemplify women's role in biodiversity change (Steffen 2010). In addition, analysts like Friedrich Gerstäcker and managers of colonies like Martin Buff ventured to affirm that vegetable gardens were a German idiosyncrasy deeply connected to the working experiences of rural women and girls (Gierus 2006). In Paraguay, in the areas around Asunción, the boom of *"naranja dulces"* was explicitly carried out by women (Kleinpenning 2003: 971). On the opposite spectrum of gender, grapes were seen as manly. Male migrants from western Germany and northern Italy had behind them a long history of regional specialization, and wine production played the role of a classic cash crop and aided integration into European markets. In southern Brazil, Italians excelled in wine production by using the North American variety *Isabella* on the slopes of the Atlantic Rainforest (Moretto and de Majo 2021). Outside of Brazil, wine both in Argentina and Chile was in the hands of seemingly aristocratic elites who could link the ascension of their families back to colonial times. French varieties like the *Cabernet Sauvignon* thrived and still frame production in these regions to the present day (Del Pozo 2014).

Following the thread of external genetic fluxes to the region, the introduction or diffusion of the European-Asiatic agronomic repertoire was pivotal. Grains like wheat, rye, barley, and oats made up the hopes of political classes who aspired for agrarian modernization, permanent occupation of land, and additional revenues for the treasury. Chile and Argentina fulfilled this role in Latin America; the former turned into a successful player in market integration since Chilean wheat production rapidly reached the Pacific coast of the United States, fueling the Gold Rush in California and legitimating German colonization of southern Chile (Kaltmeier 2022: 89–90). In Argentina, wheat cultivation became a huge success, and by the late 1880s, Argentinean wheat could feed European masses and change agrarian policies in the old continent. Wheat cultivation in the Argentinean Pampa was associated with the use of the plow and the grid, tools that were absent in the forested areas and accounted for technical progress. Cereal production gained pace in the 1890s with the help of railways, granaries, U.S. American machinery, and the non-protectionist policies in Europe. Wheat thrived, especially in the *Pampa húmeda*, and its trade was structured onto a concentrated commercial network, which relied on the infrastructures provided by the modernization of the cattle ranching system.

Brazil's world leadership in coffee exports jeopardized cereal production in the south; in 1891, Brazil signed a commercial treaty with the United States, securing the wheat market for North American farmers in exchange for privileged coffee exports (Pesavento 1983). Notwithstanding such hazards, German and Italian colonists, with the help of interested groups, resorted to widespread genetic exchange. In 1870, one could find in the German colony of Santa Cruz, for instance, wheat seeds from Egypt, Chile, Australia, Spain, and the United States. Unlike Argentina and Chile, Brazil's cereal successes were limited, thwarting the expectations of a whole generation of both Brazilian and European politicians who engaged in the policies of settler colonialism (Klug 2013). Rice had a dissimilar history because it served the interests of local elites to modernize rather than being an option for newly arrived colonists whose lack of capital could not afford irrigation, labor costs, and the great extension of land necessary for the crop. In Rio Grande do Sul and Uruguay, rice offered an alternative to cattle breeding, and rice clusters observable to this day are partially the result of people like the Brazilian stateman Assis Brasil, the German geneticist Alfredo Boelger, and their involvement with national associations for the progress of agriculture (Caetano 2019).

Agricultural research institutions, schools, and agronomic stations have taken an active part in framing the adoption of exotic crops, especially following French and German examples and approaches (Curi 2019). The subtropical and temperate characteristics of the northern Southern Cone played a distinctive role in the imperial agrarian sciences of the time because, unlike the efforts of imperial powers in fostering tropical agriculture in their tropical colonies, scientific investments in the Southern Cone turned to the adaptation of Euro-Asiatic crops in the local subtropical climates. However, a central focus on tropical plantations in Brazil remained influential within agricultural research (Oliver 2009). In Argentina, agricultural instruction and research accompanied the politics of rural colonization. Landed elites, especially around Buenos Aires, were active participants in both international commerce and the cattle ranching economy, which, at that time, dominated the agenda and thereby sidelined agriculture. The former president Domingo Faustino Sarmiento is seen as the initiator of agricultural education-research in Argentina especially for his public stance that it was a precondition for modernization. In the National Parks, agricultural research stations and tree nurseries were planned right from their beginnings in the 1900s (Kaltmeier 2021). The national government failed miserably in this endeavor, and provincial initiatives – like the investments carried out by Entre Rios between 1896 and 1910 – attempted to fill the void of a national commitment; in this latter case, teaching for newly arrived colonists and the focus on temperate exotic crops (cereals especially) prevailed (Cian 2018).

Although the introduction of plants and crops has characterized agriculture in the Southern Cone and thereby made salient the claims of modernization, native crops and plants (e.g., black beans and native pumpkins in the subtropical region) played a significant role in family farming, continuing to be the corollary of traditional agriculture/horticulture. With the expulsion of traditional communities from their lands, their ecologies were largely useful in setting agriculture afoot. Some crops like the potato, tobacco, and corn were, to a greater or lesser degree, already known about in nineteenth-century Europe. However, the productive weight they acquired in southern South America was unprecedented. Only the potato could not match the production of central and eastern Europe, since the latter was a cornerstone of technological agrarian modernization in the old continent. Prior to the arrival of migrants, the cultivation and consumption of potatoes was greatly limited to its original center of domestication (the Andean altiplano and the Chiloe Islands). Germans then introduced the potato with greater emphasis in Brazilian agriculture and, in a certain way, reamericanized it given the conditions of its diffusion (Relly and de Majo 2020). Corn retained its position since it could be sowed immediately after the first clear-cuts of forests and functioned both as a cash and subsistence crop. As soon as colonists acquired pigs, the grain was used for feed. Corn followed deforestation and turned out to be one of the main drivers of land change. Especially in Brazil, eastern Paraguay, and northeast Argentina, cassava found good reception like corn as local populations took advantage of Guarani agronomic domestication and the hybrid societies that followed them. Germans renewed the production of the tuber since cultivation was trending down in southeast Brazil. In 1842, Germans from Sao Leopoldo in Brazil could supply the whole provincial markets, especially through the commercialization of cassava flour (Roche 1969). Tobacco cultivation, mostly a cash crop, was extremely successful among Prussian colonists in central Rio Grande do Sul; the development of the tobacco industry was rampant in the twentieth century, and by the 1950s, tobacco cultivation consolidated to the region around Santa Cruz do Sul in Brazil (Da Cunha 1995).

Forestry and Deforestation

The widespread forest colonization – especially in Brazil, Chile, and the Argentinean province of Misiones – along with the expansion of agrarian commodities pushed members of the respective ethnic intelligentsia (Germans, Italians, etc.) and national liberal progressive-minded politicians to express European and North American sensibilities on nature. Some important figures openly contested the agrarian policies which permitted deforestation. German forestry was highly praised especially in the case of southern Brazil when 1848ers started directing German colonies and tried to motivate colonists to behave "rationally" towards the forests by adapting more intensive agricultural methods like crop rotation (Sellin 1875; Sellin 1876). These appeals were insistently published in the German-Brazilian press which has been around in Brazil since the 1850s. Newspapers reached the fringes of the German agrarian frontier, but quite often articles were written by German urban dwellers who pleaded for conservationist rationale in the whole region; the German *Forstwirtschaft* and its emphasis on tree-cutting cycles, afforestation with conifers, and quantitative methods became a model for many (Rambo 1994). By the turn of the twentieth century, forestry debates had become more urgent as railways accelerated colonization and provided the infrastructure for lumber commercialization for the first time.

In Chile, geographic conditions favored the early use of timber stocks; however, intensification and environmental degradation seem to have mostly taken place between 1880 and 1940. In order to make the conquered areas usable for agriculture, the unbridled use of slash-and-burn agriculture was deployed. Against this background, extensive centuries-old virgin forests were destroyed by the unregulated practice. In 1850, Federico Albert had estimated Chilean forest cover to be between 24 and 28.7 million hectares. The largest forest stands were located in southern Chile, despite Albert probably overestimating the forest stands in Magallanes. In 1914, on the other hand, Albert recorded only 15.7 million hectares. Thus, in half a century, Chile's forest cover had decreased by 13 million hectares. In 1944, the U.S. American Haig Mission made another forestry survey and estimated the land area covered with forest at 7.28 million of which, however, only 4.3 million hectares were covered with natural forest (Otero 2006).

Another important factor concerns the biodiversity of the forest standards. In northeast Argentina, southern Brazil, and eastern Paraguay, evergreen and semievergreen forests were prevalent; it was only on the slopes of the Brazilian plateau that Araucaria or *Curi* covered vast expanses of land facilitating extraction and transport. Furthermore, the European forestry practices and economic culture of colonists from Germany and northern Italy could cope better with less biodiverse woods. In general, semi-evergreen forests were considered agricultural forests, not only because colonists were used to a particular (deciduous) forest-field management that had existed in central Europe since medieval times, but rather because they hampered standardization. Epiphytes, lianas, and other plants like the bamboo-like *quila* in Southern Chile proved to be an extra challenge for the cutting of marketed species since they completely changed the methods of cutting (Relly 2020).

In the case of Paraguay, state monopolization of lumber stocks and yerba-mate prior to the War of the Triple Alliance empowered Asunción to create a more centralized forest policy. By the time of Solano López, reforestation in public lands succeeded by expanding the area of *Araucaria angustifolia* northwards. In 1846 and 1855, decrees were issued both to declare a monopoly on select species and to criminalize private cutters who previously accessed state forests. In the postbellum period, conservation measures were lifted, and forests became privatized; Quebracho trees came into the spotlight due to their utilization in tannin industries, creating a reliable source of revenue for the country in its national reconstruction effort (Brezzo 2019).

In Brazil, the plea for a structured forestry policy accompanied political discourses during the process of independence from Portugal and echoed Enlightenment voices coming from the Portuguese Empire (Pádua 2004). However, customary rights regarding land tenure, migration, and even some legislation discouraged concrete steps in that direction. The German and Italian colonies celebrated the free use of timber resources since colonists escaped rigid rules pertaining to forestry practices both in Germany, as in northern Italy. By the turn of the century, forestry became tantamount, inasmuch as the damages made to the forests became visible. Edmundo Navarro was an especially enthusiastic proponent of the adoption of Australasian neophytes (especially the genus *Eucalyptus* and *Acacia*) in order to supply fuel locomotive engines and timber for railroad ties as well as avoid erosion and fulfill broader economic ends. His idea prevailed as his influential book *A cultura do*

Eucaliypto nos Estados Unidos (1908) was warmly received by many advocates of both conservation and forestry (Franco and Drummond 2009).

President Nicolás Avellaneda in Argentina bundled forestry, conservation, and colonization together in Decree N. 1054, issued in 1879 and aimed at national expansion towards the Chaco. Like Brazil (especially in the southern states) and Paraguay, Argentina maintained a particular forestry policy that intended to harmonize the extraction of both timber (lumber and tannin) and non-timber resources (especially yerba-mate), radically differing from the highly influential tradition of German forestry and its strict focus on wood. Yerba-mate extraction and forestry were officially and administratively separated only during the *Década Infame* (1930–1943). Since the 1930s, the introduction and afforestation of exotic tree species have become pivotal, but – similar to Brazil during this time (and in spite of Navarro's influence) – national forestry was in charge of analyzing endemic species and their potential to aid national economic growth. The introduction of exotic biota in the realm of forestry is responsible, especially for conifers and the Salicaceae botanic family (Peri, Martinez Pastur, and Schlichter 2021).

Cattle and Animal Husbandry

Cattle bolstered colonial expansion toward native territories and ecologies; since the national independence movements of the nineteenth century, this process intensified, and livestock expanded to areas that were either owned by Indigenous groups or simply uninhabited at an unprecedented pace. Nevertheless, Indigenous peoples, such as the Mapuche, also appropriated cattle, horses, and sheep in the seventeenth and eighteenth centuries into their daily lives and economy, establishing international trade routes (Montalba and Stephens 2014). However, the proliferation of these neophytes put local biodiversity under pressure. Strikingly enough, the native animal husbandry of camelids (Guanaco and Vicuña) and llamas survived the incursion of cattle in the Andean altiplano. However, even remote places like Easter Island, where sheep were introduced by the *Compañía Explotadora de la Isla de Pascua* (a subsidiary of the Scottish company Williamson-Balfour) at the expense of the Rapa Nui people, or the Islas Malvinas, where sheep farming took enormous pace as of the 1860s thanks to British imperialism and the arrival of colonists from Scotland, witnessed augmented genetic fluxes and managerial intensification (Diamond 2011). In southern Patagonia, the sheep farming boom in the grasslands of the Chilean province Magallanes corresponded to a swift demand for wool and dairy in the northern countries; ecological changes were massive, and in Patagonia, the manure of sheep eutrophied several lakes and waterways. Cattle also advanced into forested areas following the European colonists' movement in the southern Brazilian states, opening up possibilities for newcomers to trade dairy products instead of hides, meat, jerky, and other products that were long part of the revenues of the landed elites. Colonists from central Europe excelled in pig farming, and in countries like Chile, Brazil, and Argentina, they founded successful companies that processed pork, changing not only local ecological balances but also national and local food cultures (Adam 2017).

As of the late nineteenth century, the La Plata region hosted a sophisticated cluster of meat production and meatpacking industries whose development relied mainly on the natural endowments of the Pampa bioregion and on the preexistent cattle ranching and meat processing practices of *Saladeros* and *Charqueadas* established in the La Plata region since colonial times. *Saladeros* (both in Uruguay and Argentina) and *charqueadas* (in Brazil) resulted in managerial improvements in workforce allocation (especially by resorting to black slavery) and resources (with a concentration of land tenure) that later were often converted into capitalist industries that attempted to respond to an inelastic demand in the industrialized countries. Refrigeration, developed by the French engineer Charles Tellier on behalf of the Argentinean government in 1868, allowed for the conservation of meat for longer periods of time. Industrial plants and ships were soon equipped with the technology. The international meat trade skyrocketed as the French-born Eugenio Terrason converted his *saladero* in San Nicolás de los Arroyos into a meatpacking plant.

Global genetic markets emerged in the late nineteenth century, and Argentina and its landed elites took advantage of it. The *Asociacón de Criadores* and the *Sociedad Rural Argentina* imported cattle belonging to the British pedigrees Shorthorn, Hereford, and Aberdeen Angus, developing the knowledge of genetic development further and solidifying the conversion of natural pastures into planted ones (Champredonde, Cara, and Hernández 2000). Brazilian experts introduced the Asiatic Zebu on a mass scale with astonishing success in the Cerrado (Wilcox and Van Ausdal 2018). In the Chilean South, descendants of German migrants and nationals took the upper hand in modernizing cattle ranching systems. German connections facilitated the import of cattle belonging to German and Dutch pedigrees developed for milk production like the Holsten Frisean. German merchants also acted as intermediaries for imports from other European markets like Britain (Gallardo Martínez 2017).

Additionally, grasses participated in the effort of modernizing a seemingly old economic activity that had taken place in the region since early colonial times. The first organized efforts in the region concerning the use of exotic grasses to foster livestock production materialized in Argentina. Although introduced back in the early times of the Iberian colonies in South America, alfalfa or lucerne (*Medicago sativa*) came to the fore during the 1860s and initiated the extraordinary agrarian development of the country during the transition to the twentieth century and beyond, as the *Medicago sativa* was transversally used in livestock breeding, dairy industries championed by European colonists, and as an instrument of nitrogen fixation in the arable soil. In Argentina, its diffusion happened through the *Región Cuyana* (via Chile) and reached Buenos Aires in the eighteenth century. In 1926, Argentina ranked second in global production (Basigalup 2007). In Brazil, alfalfa's introduction and cultivation had succeeded through different vectors and was established especially during the 1860's. Alfalfa remained dominant in the subtropical areas of South America while African species like Guineafowl, Pangola, the *Melinis minutiflora* ("capim gordura" or molasses grass) along with the genre Brachiaria, introduced especially to dry-tropical landscapes like the Brazilian Cerrado (Kluthcouski et al. 2013).

Fish Farming

As hunting swung between the use of local and exotic species, so too did fishing. Practices of fish farming like water tanks and reproduction techniques (the *hipofisação* technique was discovered by the German-Brazilian Rodolpho von Ihering, best known as the "father of the Brazilian fish farming") became more and more available (Ihering 1925), giving rise to a greater emphasis on the management of exotic fishes.

The first attempts to introduce alien fish species into Chilean waters can be traced back to the German Stephan Ludwig Jacobi in 1725. However, the real worldwide boom in fish farming began in the mid-nineteenth century, starting mainly in France and Germany. Initially, carp species were introduced in Chile, including the goldfish in 1856, considered an ornamental fish. By the end of the nineteenth century, the common carp, bred for consumption, was also introduced. The introduction of salmonids proved to be more difficult. After several failed attempts of acclimatization – whether private individuals or a large aquarium set up at the *Quinta Normal* agricultural school in Santiago – the introduction of various salmonids from Europe succeeded, mainly through the state-financed fish farm on the Río Blanco. The hatchery was founded by Federico Albert – who had thoroughly studied European fish farms – and managed by Pedro Golusda. In 1905, the first fish spawn arrived from Germany. By 1910 alone, ten more shipments of salmonoid spawn were imported, raised, and distributed throughout Chile's rivers and lakes. Also, in 1941, the *Asociación de Pesca y Caza* introduced in Chile the Argentine *Odonthestes bonarensis* as an alien species (Camus and Jaksic 2009: 61–62).

In Argentine Patagonia, the geographer and explorer Francisco P. Moreno invited the French ichthyologist Fernando Lahille to join him in 1892 to examine the possibility for the introduction of new species. In 1900, the Ministry of Agriculture also began to study the introduction of fish species and hired experts who contacted the U.S. Bureau of Fisheries, and in 1904, after a fifty-day journey, the first shipment of salmonid spawn arrived at the newly established fish hatchery near Lake Nahuel Huapi in northern Patagonia. By 1930, approximately 9 million fish eggs of alien species had been imported from Europe and the USA (Kaltmeier 2021: 163–165; Marini 1936)

In both countries, the colonization of the waters was carried out by state authorities, who primarily sought economic benefits. However, difficult market access prevented the commercial expansion of fish farming in Argentina. In Chile and Argentina, on the other hand, sport fishing – fueled by the national parks in northern Patagonia and the luxury hotels in Bariloche, Pucón, and Puerto Varas – experienced a heyday in the first half of the twentieth century.

With the massive introduction of new species, numerous problems arose. In Chile, in particular, fishing with dynamite, poison, large nets, or fixed traps was a central problem until the 1960s, despite the use of dynamite and poison being banned as early as 1898 and again in 1912. These regulations also introduced closed seasons. In Chile, moreover, the goldfish – but other carp species as well – became invasive and pushed back native species on a mass scale. Also, in Argentina, the first studies that demonstrated the native *puyen* (*Galaxia maculatus*) was a preferred prey fish of the introduced salmonids emerged in the 1940s. In general terms, a process of taxonomic homogenization of fish fauna set in across the countries of Patagonia, which could still lead to the extinction of native species (Rojas et al. 2021), something that fish farmer Marini (1936: 7) noted in Argentina as early as the 1930s: "The faunas, both terrestrial and aquatic, will converge over time."

Neobiotic Transformations

The colonization of large parts of the Southern Cone in the second half of the nineteenth century led to a new acceleration of the circulation of neo-biota. Beyond the intentional introduction and acclimatization of species of Eurasian and African origin, unintentional dissemination was also highly significant. Anthropogenic transformations of the regional biodiversity through neophytes were reflected especially in the studies of contemporary natural scientists. Instead of biological invasions, the nineteenth-century scientists have chosen a more neutral denomination of the neophyte, speaking of "*flore adventice*" (Hauman 1928), "*flora advena*" (Reiche 1906: 326), "*vegetales exóticos,*" "*plantas introducidas,*" "*plantas transmarinas*" (Berg 1877). The concept of neophytes was introduced first by Swiss botanist Albert Thellung in 1918 in a study on Montpellier. The first list of neophytes in Patagonia can probably be found in an essay by the German scientist Carlos Berg from 1877, which identified 154 European nonnative plants in the province of Buenos Aires and Patagonia (183). For botanists and natural scientists of the time, it was clear that this dramatic change in biodiversity from the second half of the nineteenth century was due to human activities. Berg, for example, distinguished between voluntary and involuntary introduction, seeing the port city of Buenos Aires and the La Plata region as a gateway for the introduction of neophytes. In the context of Chile, Karl Reiche argued that European species had been more aggressive and successful in their acclimatization in the temperate regions of the Americas. Consequently, a change in the biodiversity present even on remote islands in the nineteenth century can be observed, as Federico Johow (1896) discovered on Juán Fernández Island. While seventy-six autochthonous plant species could still be found at the beginning of the century, by the end of the 1800s, the flora had gone extinct or been displaced to marginal areas. Overall, the unintentional introduction of neophytes has probably been just as important as the intentional. Recently, anthropologist Terry Hunt (2007) has argued that the collapse of Rapa Nui society is not due to supposed un-adapted religious-societal practices that drove deforestation in order to erect moai, but to contact with Western travelers who introduced rats and disease. The former ate the seeds of the palm trees to the extent that their reproduction was impossible.

A further systematic discussion of the neophyte phenomenon in the Southern Cone was proposed by Lucién Hauman (1928) in *Essai de géobotanique humaine. Les modifications de la flore argentine sous l'action de la civilization* Hauman sketched a comprehensive classification model of the man-made transformations of flora. He categorically distinguishes between the intended and unintended introduction of neophytes. Each of these categories is then differentiated according to the geobotanical consequences. But – as Hauman makes clear – these direct anthropogenic interventions are only of locally limited scope. Instead, it is the indirect factors – "less visible, but even more interesting" – that have an extremely influential effect on flora change (Hauman 1928: 9). He also introduces the phytogeographic concept of translation, which he defines as "the transport of species indirectly caused by human activity" that possibly can create new habitats like waysides, walls, fertilized soils, or rough meadows created by grazing. Hauman left no doubt, however, that – in his estimation – anthropogenic landscape change certainly serves general social progress, which the primeval forest, in particular, is considered to be *"l'ennemie de l'homme civilisé"* (1928: 5).

The Protection of Biodiversity

Today, national parks and other protected areas are considered effective tools for protecting the biodiversity of species and ecosystems. Globally, the Southern Cone, after North America, was the region where the first national parks began to be established. In Argentina, the history of national parks begins in 1897, when a Brazilian officer Edmundo de Barros erected a sign on the Argentine-Brazilian border area near the Iguazú Falls in the south of Brazil declaring the area to be a national park.

Concerned about the integration of this northern border area, the *Gobernación del Territorio de Misiones* and the Ministry of the Interior commissioned the renowned landscape architect and botanist Carlos Thays to travel to Iguazú in order to study the creation of a national park. The core of Thays' 1902 plan for the establishment of a national park was a project for urban development and a military colony. The project was never realized, and ten years later, Thays revised the plans and presented a report illustrated with photographs entitled *Parque Nacional de Iguazú*, which was also unrealized and hardly implemented (Kaltmeier 2021: 6–21, Freitas 2021: 23–32). A second hotspot for the national park debate in Argentina was the region around Lake Nahuel Huapí in northern Patagonia. Francisco P. Moreno donated an area of three-square leagues to the Argentine state with the stipulation that a national park be established there. The donation was accepted on February 1, 1904, and the area was declared a national park. However, concrete implementation of the national park project remained unclear until the U.S. geologist Bailey Willis, who was conducting hydrological studies in Patagonia on behalf of the Argentine government, was commissioned by the Minister of Agriculture to prepare a study on a national park in the region. This study appeared in 1913 and was disseminated to the public, just as Thays presented his national park ideas internationally in that same year. However, due to domestic political tensions and the world political crisis caused by World War I, the plans were not pursued further.

At the beginning of the twentieth century, a civil society movement for environmental protection had developed in Argentina that was also firmly anchored among the elite. The recently founded *Sociedad Argentina de Ciencias Naturales* and *Academia Argentina de Ciencias Naturales,* pushed the creation of national parks with publications like *El proyectado parque nacional del Sud* in 1916 by Carl Curt Hosseus and *La protección de la naturaleza en la República de Argentina* in 1922 by Lucién Hauman (Kaltmeier 2021: 22–58). Regional initiatives to create parks flourished in Tucumán, Córdoba, and Río de la Plata. The Parque Nacional del Sud (today Nahuel Huapi) was officially established on April 8, 1922, in a decree by President Hipolíto Yrigoyen. With a protected area of 828,000 hectares in 1924, the park encompasses more than 100 times the area originally donated by Moreno, making it almost as large as Yellowstone National Park.

Another significant moment of institutionalization occurred with the passage of the Argentine National Parks Law on September 30, 1934, pushed by Exequiel Bustillo. This law established a national park authority, the Dirección Nacional de Parques Nacionales (DPN) –after the U.S. National Park Bureau – the second institution of its kind worldwide. Bustillo himself, however, vehemently opposed U.S. ideas of conservation that he described as an "orthodox tendency." Instead, Bustillo understood the national park as an "instrument of colonization" (Bustillo 1997: 15), of "border nationalization" (Freitas 2021: 8), and an engine of development. Accordingly, large infrastructure and urban development projects took place in the parks under Bustillo, as well as a touristification of the landscape, according to aristo-cratic-European criteria (hunting and sport fishing), which was epitomized by the introduction of neophytes such as red deer, pheasants, and rainbow trout in Nahuel Huapi National Park (Kaltmeier 2021: 140–172).

After the establishment of Iguazú and Nahuel Huapí National Parks, the DPN presented plans as early as 1937 for the creation of other national parks, especially in the south, which would be quickly implemented in the case of the Lanín, Los Alerces, Perito Francisco P. Moreno, and Los Glaciares National Parks. Bustillo resigned in 1944, and with the rise of Peronism from 1946, the national park movement became dedicated to promoting popular mass tourism (Scarzanella 2002: 16–17). At the same time, however, an increasingly explicit conservation-oriented national park policy based on the U.S. model of "parks without people" took hold in the 1950s. Key reasons for this stronger focus on conservation were the growing international debates and conventions surrounding the issue, beginning with the 1940 Convention for Nature Protection and Wildlife Preservation in the Western Hemisphere of the Pan-American Union signed by Argentina in 1941. In the 1960s, this trend of international standardization was to increase further and lead to internationally binding standards, especially through the efforts of the International Union of the Conservation of Nature (IUCN), founded in 1948.

The establishment of the Iguazú National Park on the Argentine side of the emblematic waterfalls fueled Brazilian nationalism. Brazil then "played catch-up" by establishing Iguaçu National Park in 1939, following the Argentine path of development, but was not able to establish a national park authority (Freitas 2021: 61–62). Nevertheless, the efforts to establish a park go back further in Brazil. As early as 1876, the abolitionist André Rebouças had pushed for the establishment of a park based on the U.S. model, and the aforementioned Edmundo de Barros had drawn up a plan for a national park on the Brazilian side of Iguazú Falls in 1897 (Freitas 2021: 62–66). Concurrent with Iguazú Park, Serra dos Órgãos National Park was established in 1939, while Itatiaia National Park, established in 1937, became the first Brazilian national park. These other two focus on the protection of the *Mata Atlântica* (Atlantic Forest) along the Brazilian southeastern coast. Between 1959 and 1961, there was another great wave of park foundations, also focused on the protection of the Atlantic Coast biomes – Mata Atlântica, Caatinga, and Cerrado. These regions were the most anthropized Brazilian biomes until 1960, when the "Great Acceleration" took off in Brazil (Pádua 2024).

In Chile, there was intense debate about forest protection as early as the mid-nineteenth century in the face of massive slash-and-burn agriculture in the south and deforestation for mining in the north. Decrees and laws regulating the use of forests in the course of agricultural colonization were issued in 1859, 1871, 1872, and 1873. Then, in 1879, the first attempt to establish state forest protection zones took place with the creation of a 10 km wide zone along the Andean Cordillera and a similar 1 km wide zone along the Coastal Cordillera, each approximately 500 km long (Cabeza 1988: 4). This project, however, was not realized, but in 1907 the *Reserva Forestal Malleco* was established in a much more reduced area of the Coastal Cordillera. In 1913, seven to eight *reservas forestales* (forest reserves) were established in the south, which on paper were supposed to protect an area of approximately 650,000 hectares, but half of these reserves disappeared. The *Inspección General de Bosques, Pesca, y Caza* (General Inspection of Forestry, Fishing, and Hunting), established in 1911 with the German-born natural scientist Federico Albert at its head, developed as a hub for conservation measures. Albert is considered both the father of national parks and of modern forestry in Chile (Camus 2006: 153–157). He pushed through a new *Ley de Bosques* that was modeled on German imperial forest legislation in Africa, as well as a hunting law (1929) to protect endangered species. However, as in Brazil, Chile failed to establish a national park authority. The first national park inaugurated in Chile was the Parque Nacional Benjamin Vicuña Mackenna in 1925; however, it only lasted until 1929. In 1926, the Vicente Perez National Park, which still exists today, was established. Both were created as *parques nacionales de turismo* (national tourist parks), firmly with the goal of developing national tourism, without being able to match the rigor of the Argentine model.

While the first protected areas were promoted under governmental and scientific aegis, there have been civil society initiatives for national park foundations since the 1930s, such as the *Amigos del Arbol*, which established the local national park Cerro Ñielol (1939) in Temuco, or the Touring Club Magallanes and the Club Andino for the later Torres del Paine National Park. In addition, international conferences also promoted the creation of parks. For example, in the Pan-Pacific Scientific Congress of 1933 in Vancouver, Chile committed to establishing the following protected areas with special flora and fauna on the Pacific ridge: Forest of Fray Jorge, certain areas in the region of Magallanes, Guiatecas cypress forests around Chiloe, along with Rapa Nui Island and the Juan Fernández Archipelago. These parks were successfully established between 1932 and 1941. From the 1930s to the 1950s, reservas nacionales continued to be established, especially in the south, following the utilitarian criteria of resource protection. Some disappear again as soon as they are created. In general, the history of protected areas in Chile is characterized by changes in land use from forest reserves to national parks, as well as protected areas that are founded and disappear again (García and Mulrennan 2020: 204–209). From the mid-1960s onward, there is another wave to establish protected areas, increasingly aligned with international standards and citing conservation concerns in particular.

Impacting Socio-Biodiversity:
Conquest, Colonization, and First Acceleration

The Southern Cone is a geopolitical territorial concept that encompasses different ecological systems as well as political-cultural regions in what are now the states of (southern) Brazil, Chile, Argentina, Uruguay, and Paraguay. Despite the immense socio-biological diversity, there have been socio-ecological changes that encompassed the entire region. In the second half of the nineteenth century, a veritable second conquest and large-scale colonization occurred in this vast South American region, understood as a central location of the first acceleration phase of the Anthropocene. After extensive military campaigns against the Indigenous peoples of the region, European-born settlers, some of whom were actively recruited by national governments with biopolitical, often racist social Darwinist agendas, became the essential actors of colonization. Comparable to the first *conquista*, this process had ethnocidal features, due also to the dynamics of biological colonization. After their military conquest in 1883, the Mapuche were victims of major measles and cholera epidemics that reduced some populations up to 20 percent (Bengoa 1996, 338–9); in 1888/9, leprosy was introduced to Easter Island (Rapa Nui), after which the Chilean state turned the island into a veritable prison camp for lepers starting in the 1910s (Foerster and Montecino 2012). Conquest and colonization destroyed the evolved human-environment relationships and the socio-ecological metabolism of the region. In southern Patagonia and Tierra del Fuego, the Selk'nam, who had a symbiotic relationship with the maritime fauna, were victims of genocide by European sheep farmers. In Mato Grosso, Guaraní were forced into slave-like conditions for mate production. Ethnocide was also accompanied by ecocide, the extent of which has not yet been systematically recorded. But Indigenous peoples were not only "guardians" or "keepers" of local biodiversity, the Mapuche integrated foreign cultural elements, including neophytes, into their own culture and developed a new socio-ecological metabolism based on the extensive breeding of horses, cattle, and sheep. Also, the diffusion of neophytes, such as the introduction of the European apple in northern Patagonia, has been traced back to routes across the Andes. Noncapitalist human ecologies, now, have primarily been forced into hard-to-reach marginal lands.

Western colonization – understood then as civilization – brought about a rapid and profound, large-scale transformation of regional biodiversity. As early as 1916, the Belgian botanist Lucién Hauman summed up this large-scale landscape transformation, referring to what he saw in the Valdivian Forest in Chile as Europeanization: "Agricultural colonization has remarkably 'Europeanized' certain regions of this beautiful geobotanical area" (Hauman 1916: 20). Thus, the geomorphological and phytogeographical appearance changed in such a way that agriculture, forestry, and livestock breeding created anthroposcenic landscapes. This is also expressed in the change of biodiversity. In this way, a significant shift in biomass can be observed from wild plants and animals to farm ones. These non-local species, which have been optimized for use through selective breeding, generally cannot survive without human control and care. While the processes of early colonization were still oriented toward small-scale subsistence and local markets, towards the end of the nineteenth century, the commodification of natural resources and their integration into economies of accumulation and growth increasingly prevailed on the basis of an optimism about progress and an instrumental understanding of nature, enabling new and aggressive forms of economic exploitation of nature and people. This Southern Cone of the nineteenth century continues into the present.

Parallel to the planned and controlled transformation of biodiversity, the unintentional processes are also central. Especially regarding the expansion of the infrastructural technosphere (roads, railroads, ports), neophytes spread on a mass scale in the region. In part, local species were displaced; in part, new, largely neutral symbioses were formed.

Unlike the first *conquista*, the second *conquista* was accompanied by the tools of modern scientific knowledge whose premise centered on improvement, intensification, and transformations of existing settings. Yet, Scientists were aware of the biological consequences of colonization. Natural scientists reflected upon the anthropogenic transformation of floral biodiversity, arguing that the progress of European civilization had significantly and profoundly changed the environment in which they lived in the areas of soil, water, flora, and, above all, fauna. Hauman even put the regional transformation he observed in Chile and Argentina in a global, "general process of transforming the vegetation of our Earth" (1928: 4) and thus made an important argument on what this chapter would call the biological Anthropocene, finding its expression later in the concepts of "homogenocene" (Mann 2019) or a "new Pangaea" (Kolbert 2016: 197–220). Nevertheless, in the countries of the Southern Cone, some influential individuals reacted to the biological, second conquest differently; the Swiss naturalist Moises Bertoni, who spent most of his life in Paraguay, claimed in the early twentieth century the superiority of Guarani ecologies and environmental knowledge, basing his version of Paraguayan indigenism on this assumption. In Brazil, at this same time, the biologist Frederico Hoehne argued for nature reserves in which solely Brazilian biodiversity should be represented, thereby linking nature conservation with the emerging national-statist political movement (Relly 2023).

Affirmatively, national elites enthusiastically used technological means to modernize and integrate their countries into global capitalism. Universities and research institutes, experiments with indigenous/foreign biota, and huge crop acclimatization programs were established. Other natural science approaches were limited to an assumed value-neutral description of the loss of local biodiversity. In part, these approaches echo a Darwinian fatalism, according to which the stronger species prevail in the evolutionary struggle. Still, other approaches use the knowledge of the possibility of species extinction and the loss of local biomes to exert political pressure via social organizations and movements to enforce conservation laws and nature reserves. Similar to the U.S., a thoroughly successful national park movement was also established parallel to the benefit-oriented, aggressive, and ethnocidal settler colonialism, but unlike in the U.S., it was not buttressed by transcendental and sublime ideas of wilderness.

There is no doubt, however, that the intensification of production, world market integration, and commercialization of natural resources and land observed from the mid-nineteenth century to the end of World War II had a role in the emerging global trend toward the transgression of the planetary boundaries of ecosystems that characterize the Anthropocene.

References

Adam, Paulo Rogerio Friedrichs. 2017. "A banha no Rio Grande do Sul: final do século XIX e primeira metade do século XX." *Estudios Históricos* 18, no. 1: 1–25.

Aldunate, Carlos, and Carolina Villagrán, ed. 1992. *Botánica indígena de Chile*. Santiago de Chile: Editorial Andrés Bello.

Basigalup, Daniel H. 2007. *El cultivo de la alfalfa en la Argentina*. Buenos Aires: INTA.

Bell, Stephen. 2010. *A Life in Shadow: Aimé Bonpland in Southern South America, 1817–1858*. Redwood: Stanford University Press.

Bengoa, José. 1996. *Historia del pueblo mapuche*. Santiago de Chile: Ediciones Sur.

Berg, Carlos. 1877. "Enumeración de las plantas européas que se hallan como silvestres en la provincia de Buenos Aires y en Patagonia." *Sociedad científica argentina* 3: 182–206

Bierzychudek, Antonio. 1979. *Historia de la apicultura argentina*. Buenos Aires: Mattone.

Bonneuil, Christophe, and Jean-Baptiste Fressoz. 2016. *The Shock of the Anthropocene*. London: Verso.

Breithoff, Esther. 2020. *Conflict, heritage and world-making in the Chaco*. London: University College London.

Brezzo, Liliana M. 2019. "Reconstrucción, poder político y revoluciones. 1870–1920." In *Historia del Paraguay*, ed. Ignacio Telesca, 199–224. Buenos Aires: Debolsillo.

Bustillo, Exequiel. 1997. *El despertar de Bariloche*. Buenos Aires: Editorial Sudamericana. Orig. pub. 1968.

Cabeza, Angel. 1988. *Aspectos históricos de la legislación forestal vinculada a la conservación, la evolución de las áreas silvestres protegidas de la zona de Villarrica y la creación del primer parque nacional de Chile*. Santiago de Chile: Conaf.

Caetano, Gerardo, ed. 2019. *Ciencia, tecnología y producción agropecuaria: Historia de la cooperación bilateral entre Alemania y Uruguay. 1856–2018.* Montevideo: Instituto Nacional de Investigación Agropecuaria Uruguay.

Camus Gayán, Pablo. 2006. *Ambientes, bosques y gestión forestal en Chile, 1541–2005.* Santiago de Chile: Lom.

Camus Gayán, Pablo, and Fabián Jaksic. 2009. *Piscicultura en Chile. Entre la productividad y el deterioro ambiental.* Santiago de Chile: Geolibros-Caseb.

Champredonde, Marcelo, Roberto Bustos Cara, and Horacio Hernández. 2000. "Territorio y sociedad en la construcción de la genética: un ejemplo en bovinos para carne en la región pampeana." *Revista Universitaria de Geografía de l'U.N.S* 9: 81–109.

Cian, Janet Priscila. 2018. "Orígenes de las escuelas agropecuarias en la provincia de Entre Ríos, Argentina. 1896–1910." *Mundo agrario* 19: 42.

Crosby, Alfred W. 1972. *The Columbian Exchange: Biological and Cultural Consequences of 1492.* Westport: Greenwood Publishing Group.

Cunha, Jorge Luiz da. 1995. *Rio Grande do Sul y la colonización alemana. Ein Beitrag zur Geschichte der deutsch-brasilianischen Auswanderung und der deutschen Siedlung in Südbrasilien zwischen 1824 und 1914.* Santa Cruz do Sul: Leo Quadtke UNISC.

Curi, Alcides Beretta. 2019. "Terratenientes, Estado y conocimiento agronómico. la Asociación Rural del Uruguay y los tempranos vínculos con la ciencia y la agronomía alemanas, 1871–1901." In *Ciencia, tecnología y producción agropecuaria: historia de la cooperación bilateral entre Alemania y Uruguay. (1856–2018)*, ed. Gerardo Caetano, 45–120. Montevideo: Instituto Nacional de Investigación Agropecuaria Uruguay.

Del Pozo, José. 2014. *La historia del vino chileno: Desde la época colonial hasta hoy.* Santiago de Chile: Lom Ediciones.

Diamond, Jared M. 2011. *Collapse: How Societies Choose to Fail or Succeed.* New York: Penguin.

Foerster González, Rolf, and Sonia Montecino Aguirre. 2012. "Rapa Nui: la lepra y sus derivados." *Escrituras Americanas* 1: 270–353.

Franco, Joao Luís de Andrade, and José Augusto Drummond. 2009. *Proteção à natureza e identidade nacional no Brasil, anos 1920 – 1940.* Rio de Janeiro: Editora FIOCRUZ.

Freitas, Frederico. 2021. *Nationalizing Nature. Iguazu Falls and National Parks at the Brazil-Argentina Border.* Cambridge: Cambridge University Press.

Gallardo Martínez, Eduardo P. 2017. "Modernización ganadera en el sur de Chile: Osorno y sus contactos chileno-alemanes en perspectiva transnacional,1917-1939." PhD diss., Free University of Berlin.

García, Magdalena, and Mónica E. Mulrennan. 2020. "Siguiendo la historia de las áreas protegidas en Chile: Estrategias de territorialización y racionalidades estatales cambiantes." *Revista de Geografía Latinoamericana* 19, no. 4: 199–234.

Gerhardt, Marcos. 2013. "História ambiental da erva-mate." PhD diss., Universidade Federal de Santa Catarina.

Gierus, Renate. 2006. "'Além das grandes águas'. mulheres alemãs imigrantes que vem ao sul do Brasil a partir de 1850: Uma proposta teórico-metodológica de historiografia feminista a partir de jornais e cartas." PhD diss., Escola Superior de Teologia.

Gudynas, Eduardo. 2015. *Extractivismos. Ecología, economía y política de un modo de entender el desarrollo y la Naturaleza*. La Paz: Centro de Documentación e Información Bolivia.

Hauman, Lucién. 1916. *La Forêt Valdivienne et ses Limites. Notes de Geographique Botanique*. Buenos Aires: Trabajos del Instituto de Botánica y Farmacologia.

———. 1928. *Les modifications de la flore argentine sous l'action de la civilisation. Essai de géobotanique humaine*. Brussels: M. Hayez, Imprimeur de l'Académie Royale de Belgique

Hunt, Terry L. 2007. "Repensar la catástrofe ecológica de la Isla de Pascua." *Journal of Archaeological Science* 34, no. 3: 485–502.

Ihering, Rodolpho von. 1925. *Da vida dos peixes: ensaios e scenas de pescaria*. São Paulo: Melhoramentos.

Jiménez, Jaime E. 1996. "The extirpation and current status of wild chinchillas *Chinchilla lanigera* and *C. brevicaudata*." *Biological Conservation* 77, no. 1: 1–6.

Johow, Federico. 1896. *Estudios sobre la flora de las Islas de Juan Fernández*. Santiago de Chile: Imprenta Cervantes.

Kaltmeier, Olaf. 2021. *National Parks from North to South. An Entangled History of Colonization and Conservation in Argentina*. New Orleans/Trier: University of New Orleans Press/Wissenschaftlicher Verlag Trier.

———. 2022. *Resistencia mapuche. Reflexiones en torno al poder. Siglos XVI a XXI*. Santiago de Chile: Pehuén.

Kolbert, Elizabeth. 2016. *Das 6. Sterben*. Frankfurt: Suhrkamp.

Kleinpenning, Jan. M. G. 2003. *Paraguay 1515–1870. Una geografía temática de su desarrollo*. Madrid: Iberoamericana.

Klug, João. 2013. "Imigração, colônias e colonos no Brasil imperial: uma análise das propostas de Abrantes, Decosterd e Tavares Bastos." In *Colonos, colônias & colonizadores: aspectos da territorialização agrária no Sul do Brasil*, ed. João Carlos Tedesco and Rosane Marcia Neumann, 11–25. Porto Alegre: NEMEC.

Kluthcouski, Joao, Luiz Adriano Maia Cordeiro, Gessí Ceccon, et al. 2013. "Braquiária na agropecuária brasileira: uma história de sucesso." In *Consórcio milho-braquiária*, ed. Gessí Ceccon, 17–26. Brasília: EMBRAPA-SPI.

Ladeira, Maria I. 2001. *Espaço Geográfico Guarani-mbya: significado constituição e uso*. São Paulo: Edusp.

Machado Aráoz, Horacio. 2022. "America(n)-Nature, conquestual habitus and the origins of the 'Anthropocene'. Mine, Plantation and their geological (and anthropological) impacts." *DIE ERDE – Journal of the Geographical Society of Berlin* 153, no. 3: 162–177.

Majo, Claudio de, and Eduardo Relly. 2020. "American vines, European potatoes: An evolutionary history of European migrations in southern Brazil." *International Review of Environmental History* 6, no.1: 5–29.

Majo, Claudio de, and Samira Peruchi Moretto. 2021. "From slash and burn to winemaking: the historical trajectory of Italian colonos in the uplands of Rio Grande do Sul, Brazil." *Modern Italia* 26, no. 2: 141–158.

Mann, Charles C. 2019. "Columbian Exchange." In *The Routledge Handbook to the History and Society of the Americas*, ed. Olaf Kaltmeier, Josef Raab, Mike Foley, et al., 67–74. London: Routledge.

Marini, Tomás L. 1936. *Los salmónidos en nuestro Parque Nacional de Nahuel Huapi. Comentarios a los trabajos de Piscicultura realizados en nuestro país*. Buenos Aires: Ministerio de Agricultura – División Piscicultura

Mösbach, Ernesto Wilhem de. 1992. *Etnobotanica de Chile*. Santiago de Chile: Editorial Andrés Bello.

Montalba, René, and Stephens, Niall. 2014. "Ecological Change and the 'Ecological Mapuche': A Historical Sketch of the Human Ecology of Chile's Araucania Region." *Human Ecology* 42, no. 4: 637–643.

Napp, Ricardo. 1876. *Die Argentinische Republik*. Buenos Aires: Dampfbuchdruckerei der Sociedad Anónima.

Noelli, Francisco Silva, Francisco Silva Noelli, Giovana Cadorin Votre, et al. 2019. "Ñande reko: fundamentos dos conhecimentos tradicionais ambientais Guaraní." *Revista Brasileira De Linguística Antropológica* 11, no. 1: 13–45.

Pádua, José Augusto. 2024. "Situando la historia del Antropoceno: El caso de Brasil." In *Los cuidados en y más allá del Antropoceno: Un recorrido interdisciplinario ante las crisis socio-ecológicas*, ed. Philipp Wolfesberger, Olaf Kaltmeier and Ann-Kathrin Volmer, 43–60. Buenos Aires: CALAS-CLACSO.

———. 2004. *Um sopro de destruição: pensamento político e crítica ambiental no Brasil escravista, 1786–1888*. Rio de Janeiro: Jorge Zahar

Pesavento, Sandra Jatahy. 1983. *RS: agropecuária colonial e industrialização*. Porto Alegre: Mercado Aberto.

Oliver, Graciela de Souza. 2009. *Institucionalização das ciências agrícolas e seu ensino no Brasil, 1930–1950*. São Paulo: FAPESP.

Otero, Luis. 2006. *La huella del fuego: Historia de los bosques nativos: poblamiento y cambios en el paisaje del sur de Chile*. Santiago de Chile: Pehuén.

Peri, Pablo Luis, Guillermo José Martinez Pastur, and Tomas Miguel Schlichter. 2021. *Uso sostenible del bosque: Aportes desde la Silvicultura Argentina*. Buenos Aires: Ministerio de Ambiente y Desarrollo Sostenible de la Nación.

Porzelt, Hans Martin. 1937. *Der deutsche Bauer in Rio Grande do Sul*. Ochsenfurt am Main: Fritz & Rappert.

Rambo, Arthur Blásio. 1994. "Imigração alemã e ecologia." *Estudos Leopoldenses* 30, no. 136: 71–92.

Reiche, Karl. 1907. *Grundzüge der Pflanzenverbreitung in Chile (Die Vegetation der Erde)*. Leipzig: Editorial de Wilhelm Engelmann.

Relly, Eduardo. 2020. "A agricultura e floresta dos alemães no Brasil: mobilidade, conhecimentos e transfers no Urwald (século XIX)." *Estudios Ibero-Americanos* 46, no. 1: 1–16.

———. 2023. "Recursos genéticos e bioprospecção no Brasil: capitaloceno, protagonismo e os (des)caminhos até o Protocolo de Nagoya (2010)." *Caravelle* 119: 89–106.

Rinke, Stefan. 2018. "'No alternative to extermination': Germans and their 'savages' in Southern Brazil at the turn of the nineteenth century." In *Savage Worlds*, ed. Matthew P. Fitzpatrick and Peter Monteath, 21–41. Manchester: Manchester University Press.

Roche, Jean. 1969. *Colonização alemã e o Rio Grande do Sul*. Porto Alegre: Globo.

Scarzanella, Eugenia. 2002. "Las bellezas naturales y la nación: Los parques nacionales en Argentina en la primera mitad del siglo XX." *Revista Europea de Estudios Latinoamericanos y del Caribe* 73: 5–21.

Schenck, Emil. 1932. "Beiträge zur Geschichte der brasilianischen Bienenzucht." *Der Landwirt* 1/2: 4–5.

Sellin, Albrecht W. 1875. "Die Errungenschaften der modernen Landwirtschaft und das Verhalten unserer Colonien zu denselben." *Koseritz' Deutscher Volkskalender für die Provinz Rio Grande do Sul* 2: 73–94.

———. 1876. "Was sollen wir pflanzen?." *Koseritz' Deutscher Volkskalender für die Provinz Rio Grande do Sul* 3: 99–131.

Steffen, Clemente J. 2010. *Plantas medicinales: usos populares tradicionales*. São Leopoldo: Instituto Anchietano de Pesquisas.

Torres, Daniel, Anelio Aguayo-Lobo, and Jorge Acevedo. 2000. "Mamíferos Marinos de Chile. II. Carnivora." *Serie Científica INACH* 50: 25–103.

Wilcox, Robert W., and Shawn van Ausdal. 2018. "Hoofprints: Cattle Ranching and Landscape Transformation." In *A Living Past: Environmental Histories of Modern Latin America*, ed. John Soluri, Claudia Leal, and José Augusto Pádua, 183–204. New York: Berghahn Books.

Zarth, Paulo. 2006. "A estrutura agrária." In *História geral do Rio Grande do Sul*. Vol. 2, *Império*, ed. Helga Iracema Landgraf Piccolo and Maria Medianeira Padoin, 187–214. Passo Fundo: Méritos.

Biodiversity in the Andes from the Mid-Nineteenth Century to 1950
Tropical Andes in the Key of the Anthropocene

Tyanif Rico Rodríguez and Olaf Kaltmeier

In the tropical Andes, the question of biodiversity can hardly be discussed without mention of the landscape's anthropogenic modification by Indigenous peoples since at least 2,500 BCE. The tropical Andes, with the exception of the northern part of Colombia, the Colombian Pacific coast, and southern Venezuela, coincide with the area of the Inca Empire's political influence – the Tahuantinsuyu – a historically pluriethnic cultural region. This was a central aspect of Andean cultures, which developed an extraordinary capacity to utilize vertical ecological diversity and link it through diverse exchange relationships (Moseley 1992; Murra 2002). In this context, the relationship of Andean human groups with the natural environment is key to understanding Andean societies (Spalding 1984). Thus, the intensive relationship between humans and the environment has given rise to an anthropogenic biodiversity that finds its expression, for example, in more than 4,000 varieties of potato, 100 varieties of quinoa, beans, tomatoes, etc., i.e., in crops that respond to long-standing domestication processes (Graves 2006).

The Spanish Conquest marked a sociocultural and metabolic rift in the Andean world and an early spark of the Anthropocene. This rupture was caused by the transformation of the relations of production and social organization through the introduction of animals, especially sheep, goats, cows, and horses, as well as plants such as wheat or grapes. The *hacienda*, as well as mega-mining, promoted deforestation and consolidated forms of spatial organization that would completely transform the landscape and social relations in the Andes. Although Andean land use patterns were massively altered, Indigenous-peasant (bio)diversity persisted in many communities through territorial, kinship, and organizational figures until the mid-nineteenth century.

The struggles for political independence since the 1810s and the republican period were characterized by political and economic instability. The literature for this period has focused on the socio-political and economic dynamics. Still, little attention has been paid to the relationship with the environment and the pressure on nature, in which there seems to be a continuity with the dynamics of the colonial period. However, at the regional level, economic bonanzas through the extraction and advancement over forests and jungles had an impact on the spatial distribution of the population and, therefore, led to changes in the landscape, the distribution of productive activities, and the demand for labor.

These changes deepened that metabolic rift, especially after 1850, when a drastic and accelerated process of transformation took place in which the Enlightenment and European industry began to shape the dynamics of time, work, and relations with nature. Liberal encroachments on subsistence forms of agriculture and communal land ownership altered the material and symbolic links of Indigenous peasant communities with their environment to a degree comparable to that of the first conquest (Larson 2004: 21).

On the coast and western slopes of the Andes, plantation economies were established with non-endemic products such as bananas in Ecuador, sugarcane in Peru, and coffee in Colombia. However, plantations were also established with native species, such as cotton and cacao, and even tobacco cultivation expanded. One of the consequences of this process was the massive loss of habitats and ecological niches of native flora and fauna. In the Andean highlands, laws prohibiting Indigenous communal lands led to widespread expropriation of land and its transfer to the hacienda system, which in turn was oriented towards the world market – for example, with sheep wool production. This progressively pushed the agricultural frontier and weakened the sensitive ecosystem of the páramos as important water reservoirs.

This chapter proposes some keys for reading the processes that make up the metabolic rift of the regional dimensions that affected the tropical Andes. The advance of capitalism in the nineteenth century, with its ruptures, was based on the imposition of industrial time on the dynamics of agriculture and life, the processes of constant deterritorialization-reterritorialization through the advance of the agricultural frontier, the establishment of technologies of power and occupation, the projects of the nation-state suppressing Indigenous communities, and the displacement and appropriation of local knowledge through rational and instrumental dominion over nature. These ruptures make up some of the characteristics of the Anthropocene in the Andes in the period under study and are present in interconnected ways in the processes described here. This chapter proposes these keys to create a broader notion of the Anthropocene that, while studying biodiversity, nature, and its rhythms, also pays attention to history, social relations, and the geopolitics of power, thus enabling an understanding of the particularities of the metabolic regime that took shape or asserted itself in the period under study in the tropical Andes.

Naming, Controlling, and Classifying the Biodiversity of the Tropical Andes

Expert knowledge played a central role in the multiple strategies to order and classify a territory that, since colonial times, has been interpreted through the tension between its condition as an infinite source of exotic riches – ready to be extracted, known, and named – and, on the other hand, its inhospitable character as wild nature that must be tamed. The displacement and appropriation of knowledge through rational and expert dominion over nature was one of the ruptures generated by the medical-scientific expeditions of the time. It was also the case with the implementation of technologies of power and occupation as part of the nation-state projects, evidenced by the close relationship between scientific practices and the political concerns of the elites. The role of these expeditions and their travelers – a group of "experts," including physicians, geographers, and traders –was key to territorial expansion in search of resources, as well as to the development of scientific knowledge, both of which defined the foundations of modern science and the place that nature and the peoples of the tropics would have.

Especially in the last two decades of the eighteenth century, there was a real wave of large-scale scientific expeditions in Latin America (Bustamante Ponce 2016). Throughout the nineteenth century – with the exception of the revolutionary years – there was continuous extraction of biological material by European expeditions and travelers (Jorgensen 1999). The knowledge enterprise in the tropics developed an inventory of the flora, which prioritized plants useful for industry, medicine, and commerce. The study of cinchona, its varieties, and therapeutic properties was one of those that received the greatest impetus. The expedition in New Granada initiated by José Celestino Mutis and Francisco José de Caldas during the colonial era played a fundamental role in the review of the virtues of cinchona and in the advancement of the territory and the species present there. It is worth mentioning that botanical exploration was part of the huge European project to reorder the world. Like many others, Mutis was "an 'imperial ambassador' taking part in an enormous project of classification, whose most solid representative is Linnaeus" (Nieto Olarte 2006: 168). The systematization of nature was a European project, whose focus on the exploration of the interior of the continents was accompanied by the imposition of particular values and culture (Pratt 2010).

The work of the naturalist classifying and naming natural objects would facilitate the control not only of nature but also of other cultures. In addition to replacing local medicinal practices, the order of nature proper to the different peoples was also denied. The European-Christian vision of nature never abandoned the idea that the purpose of creation and of each of its objects was for the benefit of man. There has always been a teleological and functional vision of nature as if it had been created especially for man and specifically for European man (Nieto Olarte 2006: 164). This ideal of progress, on which the enlightened science rests, gave way to multiple efforts to incorporate the "wastelands" (*baldíos*) into the nation through cartographic mapping. An example of this was the Chorographic Commission in Colombia, commissioned to Agustín Codazzi during the 1850s, which allowed the elites to figure out more precisely which lands were owned by the Church and which belonged to Indigenous communities (Palacio Castañeda 2006: 40). Both the Mutis Expedition and the Codazzi Commission were closely linked to the efforts of the colonial state, and later the republican state, to make a detailed assessment of the riches contained in its territories (Restrepo 2023: 260).

In the first decades of the nineteenth century, the future promoters and disseminators of the political and scientific practices of the European Enlightenment after independence can be found among the Creole elite agents and beneficiaries of the colonial government. This was the role of Francisco José de Caldas, who was part of that "community of Creoles in whose hands natural history, medicine, geography, and astronomy became the expression of their own political interests" (Nieto Olarte 2022: 10). In Peru, for example, the expeditions led by botanists Hipólito Ruiz and Joseph Pavón at the end of the eighteenth century stand out, in which a large number of species were collected and deposited in the Botanical Garden and the Cabinet of Natural History in Madrid (Díaz and Arana 2016). Likewise, in the mid-nineteenth century, Antonio Raimondi, who led studies on the economic potential of saltpeter and guano, is noteworthy. The economic boom of the latter also benefited his expeditions, financed by state resources. The interest of Western European explorers and naturalists in socio-biological diversity was of such magnitude that the Andes region became a place from which new environmental knowledge was being generated.

During the transition from the eighteenth to the nineteenth century, which in Latin America was also accompanied by the political process of breaking away from the Spanish Empire and the transition to independent republics, Alexander von Humboldt and Aimé Bonpland's voyage of exploration left a lasting impact on the transatlantic space between Western Europe and the Americas. The myth of Humboldt as the "scientific father of political independence" was promoted by the independence fighters, especially by Simón Bolívar himself (Zeuske 2000: 129), and would serve to position the new republics in an enlightened current of universal progress. Humboldt and especially Bonpland identified a considerable number of new species; Humboldt himself estimated that they had collected more than 4,500 plant species, of which 3,600 were considered undescribed (Lack 2018: 63).

Plant- or phytogeography was one of the key concepts proposed by Humboldt to describe the diversity of habitats in the interaction between the plant world and various ecological factors, embodied in "Ideen zu einer Geographie der Pflanzen nebst einem Naturgemälde der Tropenländer" (Ideas for a Geography of Plants together with a Natural History of Tropical Countries) of 1807. This concept made it possible to address anthropogenic landscape change, as Humboldt understood plant geography as a connection between plant history and human history (Päßler 2020: 8).

Fig. 1: Tableau physique des Andes et pays voisins

Source: Humboldt (1807). Peter H. Raven Library/Missouri Botanical Garden (CC BY-NC-SA 4.0), Biodiversity Heritage Library

The natural landscape of tropical countries is described along an idealized altitudinal profile (see Fig. 1). From the Ecuadorian volcanoes Chimborazo (at the left) and Cotopaxi (at the right), Humboldt identifies different vegetation zones according to altitude, which can be characterized by indicator plants. For this piece, Humboldt resorted to work done by Creole researchers such as Francisco José de Caldas, who had conducted studies on the cinchona tree through the five classic altitude levels of the Andes (*Tierra caliente* [hot land], *Tierra templada* [temperate land], *Tierra fría* [cold land], *Tierra helada* [frozen land], *Tierra nevada* [above snow line]) and on the vegetation floors of Imbabura.

In the field of geography, this notion of vegetation zones had a lasting effect. An example of this was the work of Carl Troll, who carried out geographical studies of vegetation in the Andes in the 1920s through a scientific-cultural interpretation of the theory of controlling a maximum of ecological floors that John Murra used in his ethnohistorical studies of Andean societies. Murra identified in the Andean world a sophisticated system of organization that was structured on the basis of "vertical archipelagos," which were sustained in complex interdependence with the landscape through exchanges along the altitudinal gradient and whose social base was anchored to communal relations of tenure, property, and subsistence-oriented work. In the Andes, the main medium of exchange was not metals but textiles and vegetables (Murra 2002: 360).

Fig. 2: Landscape Zones of the Tropical Andes

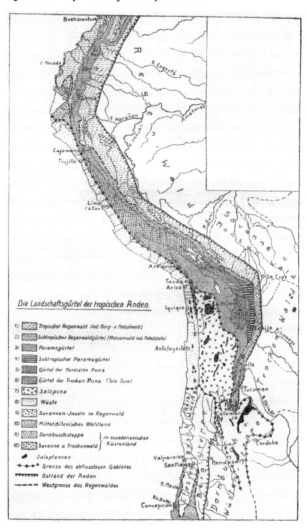

Source: Carl Troll (1931: 273)

Troll's view of ecological floors (Fig.2) was anchored in the everyday knowledge of Andean societies and its practical application. His work provides a transnational understanding of the entire breadth of the tropical Andes' central region, basically following the maximum extension of the Tahuantinsuyo. Troll analyzed the "most intimate connection between land and culture in soil culture" (1931: 260). The author recognizes pre-Hispanic achievements in agriculture – especially in the cultivation of corn and tubers, as well as the domestication of camelids such as llamas and alpacas – and farming methods. In this context, Troll also emphasizes the "highly developed cultivation of varieties," important for the focus on biodiversity (1931: 271). By identifying landscape zones in the central Andean region, Troll links the physiogeographical characteristics of each zone with their respective (agro)cultural use in the Inca empire.

Charles Darwin's trip to South America and Australia (1831–1836) and the foundation of the theory of evolution marked a turning point in the understanding of nature, which until then had been based on a creationist and divine view, that is, as something given and static. On the contrary, the idea was put forward that nature itself is subject to its own processes of historical transformation. This includes the eminently important realization that species evolve over time and that new species can emerge through adaptation to ecological niches. In parallel, the view that species can become extinct also took hold in the early nineteenth century.

Beyond catastrophism, which attributes extinction in historical periods to external environmental catastrophes, Darwin defended the gradual disappearance of less adapted species in the struggle for existence. His theory does not advocate the protection of species, but considers that the principle of perfection also applies to those species that become rare and disappear as a consequence of human influence. For example, the giant tortoise (*Chelonoidis niger niger*), which Darwin described in detail in his travel diary for its usefulness to humans, became extinct just ten years after his visit due to overexploitation and habitat degradation by introduced species (Darwin 1839). The same can be said of *Nesoryzomys darwini* or Darwin's mouse of the Galapagos, which has been considered extinct since the early twentieth century.

Scientific expeditions such as those of Humboldt or Darwin were by no means new to the region. Beyond the already mentioned contributions to the Western scientific understanding of biodiversity and nature, these activities were always linked to mechanisms of civilization of nature and to colonial and imperial processes of intellectual and material appropriation through practices of control and classification. The expeditions and the work of outstanding scientists worldwide were decisive for the production of knowledge not only about the Andes region – which today are understood as a megabiodiversity hotspot – but also about natural processes on a planetary scale. Despite this, however, there was a lack of understanding of how this biodiversity was linked to the use of landscapes by Indigenous peoples and peasant communities based on the diverse uses and conceptions of nature that define and sustain the tropical Andes.

Exploiting Biodiversity: Plantations and Extractive Enclaves

The dynamics of the republican period, the independence struggles, and the nation-state projects – which were in tension with the expansive and extractive dynamics left over from the agenda of the Viceroyalty – impacted the landscape and the population in varied and violent ways. The imposition of industrial time on the dynamics of agriculture and life, as well as the deterritorialization processes that this created, are key to understanding how the aspects described here contributed to the metabolic rupture that marks the Anthropocene in the tropical Andes.

The first decade of the nineteenth century was a period of independence struggles in the region (Bolivia and Ecuador in 1809, Colombia in 1810, and Peru in 1821). With financial and military challenges that implied undertaking different strategies to know and control a space of national sovereignty, the republican projects needed to consolidate a territorial and political identity. The close relationship between scientific practices and political concerns shaped the nation-state projects in the nascent republics. These processes took place in the midst of extractive dynamics, the advance of the agricultural frontier and tensions over land use and ownership, with a high dependence on the international market. The socio-political and social order was exclusionary, segmented, one that would not completely break with the colonial system. There, European industry –which demanded raw materials, as well as a socio-spatial organization functional to an extractive work model – defined a way of working and relating to biodiversity through expansive extraction and the plantation model.

The internal regional division shows how the transformation of the landscape and the development of infrastructure and economic exploitation were interdependent processes. Whether sugarcane, cacao, or bananas, these products were the result of regional booms that linked the economies of these countries with the international market through the establishment of monocultures. These booms had an impact similar to that of mining, although they hardly articulated the country internally or generated the conditions for the construction of a national state project. In general terms, different processes of extraction and use of biodiversity can be distinguished between the coast, the sierra, and the east. Distinguishing between these regions shows how the ecosystemic and landscape differences were deeply related to the social, political, and ideological proposals that were developed in those areas. The *latifundio* monoculture was a technique not only of production but also of power that changed scale, social relations, and hierarchy, imposing slave labor through racial matrices.

Coast

The Ecuadorian economy, like that of other countries in the region, was in crisis throughout this period. However, industrial development, related to cacao and sugarcane plantation systems, occurred mainly on the coast, attracting a significant flow of labor and initiating a moderate industrialization process (Botero 2013). Ecuador's cacao (*Theobroma cacao*) exports grew slowly but steadily. Between 1895 and 1914, Ecuador accounted for 20 to 25 percent of the world's cacao production, constituting about 70 percent of its exports (Larrea Maldonado 2006: 47).

Subsequently, due to the increase in prices of some inputs in the context of World War II, banana production – which had replaced cacao plantations – had favorable trading conditions, contributing to its boom between 1948 and 1964. The transformation of the Ecuadorian coastal landscape by monocultures was a key dynamic of this period to understand the impact on biodiversity. This process promoted an accelerated expansion of the agricultural frontier and the rapid destruction of the remaining humid and dry forests, until their near disappearance.

During this period in Peru, products such as cotton (*Gossypium arboreum*) and sugarcane (*Saccharum officinarum*) played a key role both in attracting internal and migrant labor and in the advance of deforestation based on hacienda economies. Peruvian cotton emerged as an important export crop due to the decline in U.S. production. At this juncture, producers increased the cultivated area by importing machinery and building railroad lines that connected the haciendas with nearby ports (Gonzales 1991). This same productive infrastructure would become useful for the commercialization of sugarcane. The allocation of land – previously owned by religious orders – to members of the Creole elite or foreign immigrants promoted this expansion process both in the highlands and on the coast. The productive organization promoted by local elites and experts allowed the agricultural frontier to advance; this spawned multiple deterritorialization processes, affecting both the inhabitants of these spaces and the migrant labor force, as well as the landscape, all of which soon had consequences for crops and ecosystems (Larrea Maldonado 2006).

Another product for European industry obtained from the coasts of the tropical Andes by means of extractive processes was guano. It is a fertilizer made from dried seabird droppings, which during the second half of the nineteenth century, was massively extracted from the coasts and islands of Peru. These islands were rich in guano due to their diversity of birds, such as gulls, pelicans, gannets, and guanay cormorants, among other species that nested there due to the high presence of Peruvian anchovetas (*Engraulis ringens*) in the cold currents of the Pacific (Duffy 1994). The extraction and trade of this product to supply the demand for fertilizers in Europe took place under deplorable working conditions. The pressure on ecosystems, birds, and the soil from which it was extracted had very serious impacts on the reduction of entire animal populations. The fact that this natural resource was located near the capital of Peru meant that it required practically no investment or inputs and was easy to exploit, which facilitated the monopoly of its extraction. Through guano, Peru would financially consolidate a political project anchored to extractive logics and the interests of regional elites (Aguirre 2002). After artificial nitrogen fertilizer began to be produced in Norway and Germany from 1905 onwards, the exploitation of guano was reduced, although it remained an important commodity. The conservative "Aristocratic Republic" (1895–1919) gave rise to a technocratic model of guano management. In 1909, the *Compañía Administradora del Guano* was created, which scientifically managed the guano islands and transformed them into ecological laboratories, in order to demonstrate the effectiveness of a technocratic regime in the control of ecosystems for capitalist exploitation. The objective during this time was to preserve the three species of pelicans that produced guano to ensure their exploitation, while other species, such as the Humboldt penguin, were culled (Cushman 2013).

Sierra

The central Andes have historically been the most populated region. It is also from here that the expansion towards the coast or the eastern Amazon took place. The Indigenous settlements in the central Andes and the dynamics of the republican period favored the extension of the latifundio, in tension with agriculture and communal lands. In Peru, for example, since the colonial period, the introduction of new species and products, such as wheat, grapes, sheep, and pigs, among others, shaped trade relations in terms of supplying international demand, causing the displacement of both native species and cultivation practices and giving rise to new production relations (Dollfus 1981).

Indigenous tribute and slave labor were structures and sources of income inherited from the colonial regime, which were abolished only in the mid-nineteenth century. Some authors argue that while this was a period of economic and financial instability, there was also a process of economic and demographic re-indigenization (Contreras 2011; Pierce 2017) due to the complex relationship between hacienda structures, communal lands, and labor for extractive activities. In the mid-nineteenth century, liberal reforms were promoted throughout the region to generate a land market, which affected not only community land tenure, but also the regional authority structure. For the mestizo elites, this was an essential step for the development of "agrarian capitalism," a necessary complement to large-scale mining for export. The new property system would consist of the extension of individual titles to both communities, such as ayllus, and hacienda owners, whose lands no longer depended on communal control (Platt 2016).

In Ecuador, subsistence production predominated in the smallholdings and *huasipungos* (small plot of land given by a hacienda owner to a forced laborer), while in the sierran haciendas, which had expanded in the nineteenth century, cereals, potatoes, milk, and wool were produced for the domestic market (Kaltmeier 2021). The complex interaction between haciendas, crops, and regional booms was determined by geomorphological conditions. In Colombia, located at the bifurcation of the three branches of the Andes Mountains, the altitudinal gradient was an important condition for the productive organization of the mountain regions. Due to the variety of existing climates, from the mid-nineteenth century onwards, some products achieved relative success in international markets due to the transportation possibilities offered by the Magdalena River. These products include tobacco, cinchona, indigo, cotton, and, by the end of the nineteenth century, coffee (Palacios 2009).

These crops expanded through the complex interrelationship between haciendas, plantation economies, landowner interests, and landscape structure. This relationship defined the production and commercialization zones based on the communication possibilities through the rivers, the small Indigenous settlements, and later colonists, in addition to the continuous expansion of landowners based on cattle raising. Tobacco was one of the most important products, whose viceroyal monopoly was inherited by the Republic through the *rentas estancadas* (rents derived from articles whose exclusive commercialization was reserved for the state). Its production demanded fleets and navigation routes with steamboats on the Magdalena River, and railroads in the Caribbean savannas for transportation to the port (Sastoque 2011). This led to the construction of storage and marketing infrastructure, which contributed to the expansion of its cultivation in the areas surrounding the Magdalena Valley. Tobacco, as well as indigo, cinchona, or rubber, were crops that required low investment costs but large extensions for their extraction. They were also produced by labor under precarious conditions. Expansion into the forests was progressive and, along with the clearing for these crops, cattle were introduced as a mechanism of control and land grabbing.

In the region opened up by the colonization of Antioquia in Colombia, indigo was part of another regional boom in the same areas as tobacco production. The expansion of its extraction was due to the demand of the English textile industry (Alarcón and Arias 1987: 171). Extensive control over land had an impact not only on forests, but also on the tenure structure and landscape transformation (Alarcón and Arias 1987). This was a parallel process to the one described by Van Ausdal (2009), where grasses of the African varieties pará (*Brachiaria mutica*) and guinea (*Panicum maximum*) were introduced due to their ability to suppress the regeneration of recently cleared forest areas with the end goal of establishing cattle herds. The search for or cultivation of these products (tobacco, rubber, cinchona, indigo, etc.) led to an advance towards the Amazon regions and the east of the mountain range; regions that the expeditionaries and travelers helped to make visible as exploitable territories.

Traditional plants, such as coca (*Erythroxylum coca*), were also important crops. Coca was produced in Bolivia, especially on the haciendas established in previous centuries in the subtropical valleys of the Yungas, located near La Paz and part of a region of Andean forest and mountain jungle along the eastern flank of the central Andes (Lema 1992).

Eastern Piedmont

The cinchona or *quina* was a highly valued medicinal plant during this period, used as an antiseptic to control fever. Since the botanical expeditions of Mutis and Caldas, its extraction and commercialization generated profound socio-spatial transformations in Bolivia, Peru, Ecuador, and Colombia. After gold and silver, cinchona was one of the most sought-after American products. The demand for cinchona was particularly strong in those countries with colonial interests in places of endemic fevers, such as England and Holland (Nieto Olarte 2006: 147). The demand and the type of extraction (separation of the bark from the tree) led to the depredation of forests and jungles north of the equator. Petitjean (1992), based on a review of Mutis' notes and work on the Botanical Expedition, notes that to obtain 20,000 arrobas of husk bark, it was necessary to cut 300,000 trees. It is estimated that between 1752 and 1796 alone more than 11 million trees were felled (Díaz and Arana 2016: 205).

The extraction of cinchona and rubber (*Hevea brasiliensis* and *Hevea benthamiana*, respectively) in the Caquetá-Putumayo piedmont region was a clear example of this expansive model that involved multiple deterritorialization processes and an instance of the forms of knowledge appropriation about American plants and products through the idea of rational and expert dominion over nature. Although, as Sandoval and Echandía (1986) point out, the cultivation of cinchona had competed with tobacco for labor and capital, while also mobilizing resources by offering much higher wages than other agricultural activities. The *quineros* (bark strippers) of the upper Putumayo quickly became rubber tappers, reusing the infrastructure inherited from the exploitation of the cinchona for this new extractive boom (Mongua Calderón 2022).

The cinchona and rubber boom articulated the Andean-Amazonian piedmont with both national and international economies, promoted the settlement processes in the east, and laid the foundations for new modalities of articulation and integration of trade routes along the Putumayo River with steam navigation (Zarate 2001). This allowed the export of cinchona to the main Brazilian ports, improving the relations between traders and Indigenous people and the circulation of merchandise, which encouraged the arrival of new demographic cycles. The rise of steam engines promoted a metabolic rupture of planetary scope, in particular through the idea that the work process would acquire "the rhythm we would like" (Porto Gonçalves 2016: 297).

The extraction of cinchona and later rubber, the technological developments of the steam engine, and the growing interest of scientists and European travelers – whose frequent expeditions can be explained within the context of the industrial boom of the time – promoted the search for and control of new raw materials (Gómez López 2003). Hundreds of Indigenous people and peasants from Putumayo, Gran Cauca, the lowlands of Bolivia, as well as the Amazonian regions of Peru and the Sucumbíos region of Ecuador, contributed their labor to the work involved in the search, extraction, packaging, and commercialization of the bark. Guides, *macheteros*, cargo men, cooks, rowers, sailors, pilots, administrators, etc. gave life to one of the most ambitious and brutal enterprises of the time, established through a culture of terror and violence over bodies and nature (Taussig 1991). The rubber boom only lasted between 1872 and 1924, ending due to a decline in price and the competition from larger scale production in the plantations of Southeast Asia driven by the British Empire.

The use of peasant labor to open cultivation areas was a common practice that created important internal migration processes, giving rise to the settlement of new regions. As territory under the dominion of hacienda owners and landholders expanded, dispersed peasant settlements formed in the peripheries of these large extensions, generating disputes over lands between settlers and the landholders who claimed ownership.

Biodiversity and Andean Subsistence Agriculture

The role of Indigenous and peasant economies in the provision of goods for subsistence is an important vein for the analysis of transformations and continuities in the dynamics that affected biodiversity in the Andes, especially when focusing on the deterritorialization processes resulting from the agricultural frontier's advance and the implementation of modes of organization and production based on plantation crops and enclave economies. However, the role of Indigenous and peasant economies has been a topic that has received little attention from a historical perspective. In particular, the contribution of smallholder agriculture to agrobiodiversity, related both to the variety of crops or "planned diversity" and to the uncultivated flora and fauna found on or near agricultural land, deserves mention (Soluri 2013).

The processes of anthropic landscape and ecosystem intervention in the Andes were carried out, in general terms, through two types of agriculture: first, peasant and Indigenous agriculture concerning the processes of domestication and colonization of land, and second, enclave economies concerning the agricultural fron-

208   From the Mid-Nineteenth Century to 1950

tier's advance. The peasant and Indigenous subsistence economies played a key role in sustaining the labor force that migrated to the areas of expansion and work opportunities, as well as – until the mid-nineteenth century – the payment of taxes for national finances. These systems operated in the central Andes largely based on high biodiversity and management that reduced the risk of crop failure by employing species specialized to certain ecological niches and micro-climatic conditions.

Domestication Processes

The subsistence strategies that developed in the Andes are inseparable from the forms of social organization. Forest-related agricultural development, such as agrosilvopastoral systems, has been one of the least explored fields in research, despite being able to demonstrate that the extensive grass steppes characteristic of the Central Andean puna, for example, are landscapes transformed as a result of long-term anthropogenic changes (Herrera and Ali 2009).

Thus, it is important to understand the role of animals and plants and their relationship to subsistence practices and economies. Plant and animal domestication has been a parallel process to cultural and demographic development. The soil of the tropical Andes is home to 182 species of native domesticated plants such as the potato, of which there are about 200 species (and nearly 4,000 varieties), most being distributed in the Andean region of Peru, Ecuador, Colombia, Bolivia, and northern Argentina. The most common potato species (*Solanum tuberosum*) was domesticated in the Lake Titicaca region more than 8,000 years ago (Spooner et al. 2005). Foods such as oyuco (*Ullucus tuberosus*), oca (*Oxalis tuberosa*), quinoa (*Chenopodium quinoa*), sweet potato (*Ipomoea batatas*), pumpkin (*Curcubita ficifolia*), yucca (*Manihot esculenta*), among others, also have their origin in the central Andes. In this region, since pre-Hispanic times, the nuclei of population and power were both centers of cultivation and areas for grazing animals and conserving staple foods. They also handled water management, with irrigation ditches, aqueducts, and supply sources (Escobar-Mamami and Pulido Capurro 2021), and provided areas for the care of camelid herds. Llamas (*Lama glama*) and alpacas (*Lama pacos*) were used to carry loads and as a source of food.

The advance over the jungle and the access of travelers, scientists, and expeditionaries to many regions was facilitated by Indigenous collaborators, settlers, and peasants. Local knowledge about dyes, medicinal plants, natural medical products, and an infinity of raw materials demanded by the growing industrial production in Europe were key to the advance and extraction of products such as tagua (*Phytelephas macrocarpa*), used to manufacture of buttons, combs, etc (Peralta and Díaz 2022). The displacement and appropriation of local knowledge through rational and expert dominion over nature was evident in this relationship between local settlers, colonists, travelers, and production elites.

With coffee cultivation's consolidation in the haciendas and its expansion in the twentieth century in Colombia, through small-scale peasant production, two types of relationships arose that helped to promote biological diversity, while at the same time deepening several environmental tensions. First, as an understory crop, small-scale production incorporated various types of plants such as bananas and other fruit trees to create shade. Secondly, food crops as a subsistence base in the midst of montane forests allowed for the sustenance of native species.

It should be noted that montane forests are the natural habitat of many of the fruit varieties that are wild relatives of Andean crops. Debouck and Libreros Ferla (1995) identified twelve wild genera associated with Andean crops, such as papaya (*Carica papaya*), tomato (*Lycopersicon esculentum*), tamarillo (*Cyphomandra betaceum*), several species related to passion fruit and curuba (*Passiflora sp.*), avocado (*Persea americana*), legumes of the genus *Phaseolus vulgaris*, Andean blackberry (*Rubus glaucus.*), and sweet cucumber (*Solanum muricatum*). This is evidence of the variety and diversity of crops for the food base (Cuesta et al. 2012).

Continuing tensions with ecosystems have been related to the agricultural frontier's continuous expansion. The advance over forests, páramos, rainforests and Indigenous territories occurred through deforestation, colonization processes, and other violent mechanisms, favoring the development of subsistence economies along with cash crops. These processes are common in the Pacific plains, the Patía region, or the Orinoquía in Colombia, as well as on the Ecuadorian coast, the Amazon in Peru and Bolivia – particularly in places such as Pando or Beni and later Chapare and the Yungas – and in the páramo ecosystems north of the Andes mountain range. The loss of agrobiodiversity is clearly linked to the history of the peasant's articulation with markets and nation-states, but the exact nature and functioning of these links still needs to be better understood. Hence the importance of revealing the hidden history of agrodiversity in Latin America and the Caribbean (Soluri 2013: 73), a pending agenda in studies for this period.

The Advance over the Agricultural Frontier

During the Republican period, deforestation progressed along with the cultivation of species such as eucalyptus (*Eucalyptus globulus*) and pines (*Pinus sylvestris*), which rapidly invaded the native forest soils. The introduction of eucalyptus produced severe changes in the sierra landscape, where forests would continuously disappear to supply the energy needs of the cities and the railroad (Larrea Maldonado 2006: 55).

Since colonial times, chronicles leave no doubt that the decline of forests was directly linked to the demand for fuel for blacksmiths, brick kilns, bakeries, and kitchens, giving rise to an alarming situation. The forms of spatial organization as well as the consumption of resources have changed radically since then. However, with the expansion of a productive model from the regional elites and international capital, the idea of the tropics as an inexhaustible source of resources had a severe impact on the decrease of native biomass, putting endemic species such as cedar (*Cedrela odorata*), carob (*Prosopis sp*), or guaiac (*Tabebuia chrysotricha*) in a very vulnerable situation. Likewise, in the high mountain ecosystems, the advance over punas and páramos was sustained, to the point of being one of the most threatened areas in the northern and central Andes. The biota of these ecosystems, particularly the páramos, represents a unique evolutionary phenomenon, with grasslands that extend from the limit of arboreal vegetation to the altitudinal limit of vegetation, isolated from each other in a matrix of humid forest dominated by a variety of espeletia trees, commonly known as frailejones. It is a unique plant because of its role in water retention through the condensation of mist, conserving water and fixing it to the soil by capillarity (Galvis-Hernández and Ungar 2021). These high mountain ecosystems are home to unique marsupial species of the *Coenolestidae* family and the dwarf deer (*Pudu mephistopheles*).

On the other hand, the clearing and colonization of humid and tropical regions and the development of subsistence practices in tension with the forest and the fauna that inhabit them were produced by what Palacios (2009) calls the "ethos of the axe": a way of gaining ground in the jungle with the force of the machete and slash-and-burn techniques, reducing to ashes the logs and stubble that remained after the clearing. This also controlled the presence of insects, spiders, and snakes, and kept away other animals, including tigers, bears, and monkeys, which were detrimental to domestic animals and orchards (Jiménez 2015). This undoubtedly had profound consequences on ecosystems, landscape connectivity, the habitats of multiple species and, above all, built a relationship with the domesticated landscape and fauna considered dangerous. The jaguar (*Panthera onca*) and the Andean bear (*Tremarctos ornatus*), among other predators, had to bear this burden in the colonization of the Cordillera. The conversion of the Carare forests into oil wells and the consolidation of the colonization of the slopes in other areas of the Andean region in the first two decades of the twentieth century ended up delineating the few strongholds in which the jaguar survives today in the Andes (Jiménez 2015: 114).

This process has also generated the vulnerability of entire ecosystems, endangering species such as the condor (*Vultus gryphus*), countless mammal species such as the mountain tapir (*Tapirus pinchaque*), primates such as the yellow-tailed woolly monkey (*Lagothrix flavicauda*), the Andean night monkey (*Aotus miconax*), the black-headed spider monkey (*Ateles fusciceps*), or the cotton-top tamarin (*Saguinus Oedipus*), and birds such as the plate-billed mountain toucan (*Andigena Laminirostris*) or the green-naped tanager (*Tangara fucosa*), among many others that have been put at risk, particularly by the loss of their habitat. All this, not to mention the alarming decline in insect populations (Wagner et al. 2021).

The dynamics of land grabbing on which the haciendas were established were based on the notion of these spaces as "wastelands," "empty spaces," or "virgin forests," displacing their inhabitants. The search for exotic products for exploitation by travelers and regional elites was always in tension between the generalized perception of the tropics as unhealthy places or as an inexhaustible source of inputs, whose exploitation was possible thanks to the denial of the historical trajectory of their original populations; this same denial also allowed travelers and Creole elites to use the Indigenous as cheap labor (Peralta and Díaz 2021). In Bolivia, for example, this view of the territory helped shape the view that the Indigenous peoples of the eastern lowlands in relation and status were inferior to the white-mestizo settlers (Von Stosch 2014). After the implementation of the Bohan Plan in 1942, the idea began form that the white-mestizo colonizers had the mission of productive development in opposition to the Indigenous populations, legitimizing their property through demonstrating productive activity and care for the borders of the state (Kaltmeier 1999; Benavides 2022). The establishment of extractive cycles and the rapid environmental transformation of the temperate and lowland areas of the Andean region in the nineteenth century was possible thanks to the vast environmental resources that existed there.

Conservation Strategies and the Development of Protected Areas

In the face of progressive land grabbing in the second half of the nineteenth century, the issue of natural resource conservation and the protection of vulnerable ecosystems also became a concern for states. In the southern Andes, laws were enacted to protect endangered species. In the 1820s, commercial hunting of chinchillas began in the border region between Bolivia, Peru, Argentina, and Chile, and their pelts fetched high prices in the U.S. and European markets. Hunting was so ruthless that, by the 1890s, both chinchilla species were considered to be in serious danger of extinction. Therefore, in 1910, a transnational species protection law was passed between the four countries mentioned above to regulate the hunting of this animal. However, its application remained precarious (Jiménez 1996).

The first protected areas and national parks in the Andean region were created in the 1930s. At the Pan-Pacific Scientific Congress held in Vancouver, Canada, in 1933, the countries of the Pacific coast committed themselves to creating national parks. In this context, the creation of a nature reserve in the Galapagos Islands was also decided in 1936. More than twenty years later, in 1958, this area was declared Ecuador's first national park, with an area of 7,995.4 km². The legacy of scientific and research work in these areas had an impact on the incipient development of protected areas, as most of the national park systems in this region were not created until the 1960s.

Sajama National Park was created in Bolivia on August 2, 1939 through a Supreme Decree issued by President Germán Busch, but it was not until 1945 that its creation was ratified. This was done with the objective of protecting the high altitude *queñoa* forest (*Polylepis tarapacana*), a species known worldwide because its distribution reaches higher altitudes than any other tree; a range between 3,900 and 4,700 meters above sea level. In turn, Colombia opted for the establishment of forest reserves in important public or private lands to preserve water reservoirs, starting in 1938. Through this initiative, the Forest Reserves of Rio Guabas, Rio Cali, and Cerro Dapa-Carisucio in Valle del Cauca were created to supply the sugar mills (Rojas Lenis 2014: 163).

However, until 1940, there were only isolated state and private initiatives to protect biodiversity, including technocratic initiatives to control the guano production ecosystem. The 1940 Pan American Convention on Nature Protection and Wild Life Preservation in the Western Hemisphere established one of the first regulatory frameworks for the region with the objective of protecting and conserving the environment and natural species. The ratification of the convention had some early effects in the tropical Andes.

In Colombia, the La Macarena Biological Reserve was declared in 1948, which includes 629,280 km² in the most extensive geological uplift to the west of the Guiana Shield – a very old geological formation disconnected from the Andes mountain range, where multiple ecosystems such as rainforests, flood forests, in addition to herbaceous vegetation of Amazonian savannah are found (Leal 2019). Research on yellow fever and other tropical diseases led doctors and zoologists to note the existence of this mountain range. Its designation, still novel, was based on fortuitous initiatives of influential actors and rested on ambiguous institutional ground (Leal 2022: 32). However, a great boom of national parks in the Andes began in the 1960s and 1970s. In Peru, the first national park was created in 1961, and La Macarena Biological Reserve was designated as a national park in 1971.

Nature conservation strategies were developed in tandem with the development of scientific research and the importance of spaces for its promotion. The incipient development of botanical gardens in this period was a sign of this. In Bogotá, the Botanical Garden in honor of Mutis' legacy, which would bear his name, was established as a scientific institution in 1955 by the city council.

Although the creation of parks and protection strategies in this period corresponded to scientific interest in conservation and knowledge, it is also important to note that there were conflicts due to institutional ambiguity and lack of knowledge about these spaces (Leal 2022). As a consequence, many of the declared areas within the conservation zones have historically been inhabited by Indigenous and peasant communities that have had multiple relationships with these spaces, even playing a key role in their preservation. This would be one of the conflicts provoked by the creation of these conservation areas starting in the 1960s, and which still today has crucial resonances in the definition of conservation strategies and the definition of the role of human settlements in this process.

Conclusions

The impacts of the dynamics of this period on biodiversity were decisive. The metabolic rift that entailed the transformation of the landscape and labor relations, as well as the construction of national projects based on extractive and exporting economies of resources, nature, and people, occurred in complex relation between actors and scales. The encroachment on nature and the territories of peasant and Indigenous communities would not be possible without the intervention of several factors. On the one hand, political conjunctures and disputes over the constitution of forms of national identity had an influence. On the other hand, the voracity of extractive capital and the sustained European demand for inputs, as well as the imaginary of the tropics and the Americas as an exotic place of great natural wealth to be exploited – which scientists, travelers, and expeditionaries would contribute to create – played a key role.

The relationship between scientific agendas, national projects, and extractive capital propitiated and financed the expansion into the interior of the jungles and forests, establishing not only extractive economies, but a whole order of meaning that would sustain a type of relationship with nature at the cost of its domination and extinction. The expansion of the forests also sacrificed subsistence economies, and these, in turn, moved towards new forest areas in a perpetual movement and expansion of the agricultural frontier.

During this period, the foundations were laid for the relationships and conflicts that today cause multiple crises for biodiversity, ecosystems, and the populations that inhabit these regions. The keys to reading this period are the implementation of technologies of power and occupation; the deterritorialization, appropriation, and displacement of local knowledge through the rational domination of nature; and the imposition of industrial time as the guiding axis of production relations and technologies of power and occupation, such as the plantation. These keys help demonstrate how the processes described here shaped a metabolic rupture that demonstrates the Anthropocene's expression in the tropical Andes.

In the midst of multiple tensions and views on territories and populations as wild, this region produced knowledge that had a global impact on the understanding of nature and the cycles that sustain the conditions of biodiversity on the planet. However, this knowledge came at the cost of the lives of hundreds of species of animals and plants that were left behind with the advance of the voracity of capital, demographic pressure, and extractivism.

What will the jaguars tell from the remaining patches of jungle about their history in the mountains of the cordillera? What will the bears say to each other among frailejones and potato crops? How have the guano birds recomposed themselves? Who wonders about the relationships that were broken in the forest and jungles when the cinchona, ceibas, and guayacanes fell after the advance of "progress?" The "ethos of the axe" is undoubtedly a good metaphor to understand the relationships that were established with biodiversity in this period and, above all, to ask ourselves about the continuities that mark our historical time.

Translated by Eric Rummelhoff and revised by Omar Sierra Cháves.

References

Aguirre, Carlos. 2002. "La historia social del Perú republicano (1821–1930)." *Historica* 26, no. 2: 445–501.

Alarcón, Francisco José, and Daniel Gustavo Arias Buitrago. 1987. "La producción y comercialización del añil en Colombia 1850–1880." *Anuario Colombiano de Historia Social y de la Cultura* 15: 195–209.

Benavides, Jean Paul. 2022. "Territorios indígenas versus colonizadores campesinos en Bolivia." *Debates en sociología* 54: 115–141.

Botero, Luis. 2013. "Ecuador siglos XIX y XX. República, 'construcción' del indio e imágenes contestadas." *Gazeta de Antropología* 1, no. 29.

Bustamante Ponce, Teodoro. 2016. *Historia de la conservación ambiental en Ecuador.* Quito: Flacso.

Contreras, Carlos. 2011. "Menos plata pero más papas: consecuencias económicas de la independencia en el Perú." *Histórica* 35, no. 2: 101–132.

Cuesta, Francisco, Priscilla Muriel, Stephan G. Beck, et al., ed. 2012. *Biodiversidad y Cambio Climático en los Andes Tropicales – Conformación de una red de investigación para monitorear sus impactos y delinear acciones de adaptación.* Lima/Quito: Red Gloria-Andes.

Cushman, Gregory T. 2013. *Guano and the Opening of the Pacific World: A Global Ecological History.* Cambridge: Cambridge University Press.

Darwin, Charles. 1839. *Narrative of the surveying voyages of His Majesty's Ships Adventure and Beagle between the years 1826 and 1836.* London: Henry Colburn, Great Marlborough Street.

Díaz Palacios, Julio, and Martín Arana Cardó, ed. 2016. *Historia ambiental del Perú. Siglos XVIII y XIX.* Lima: Ministerio del Ambiente/Universidad Nacional Agraria La Molina/Pontificia Universidad Católica del Perú.

Debouck, Daniel G., and Dimary Libreros Ferla. 1995. "Neotropical montane forest: A fragile home of genetic resources of wild relatives of New World crops." In *Biodiversity and Conservation of Neotropical Montane Forests*, ed. Steven P. Churchill, Henrik Balslev, Enrique Forero, et al., 561–577. New York: New York Botanical Garden.

Dollfus, Oliver. 1981. *El reto del espacio andino*. Lima: Instituto de Estudios Peruanos.

Duffy, David. 1994. "The guano islands of Peru: the once and future management of a renewable resource." *BirdLife Conservation Series* 1: 68–76.

Escobar-Mamani, Fortunato, and Victor Pulido Capurro. 2021. "Biodiversidad y científicos viajeros. Una visión desde los Andes." *Revista de Investigaciones Altoandinas* 23, no. 1: 5–9.

Galvis-Hernández, Marcela, and Paola María Ungar, ed. 2021. *Páramos Colombia: biodiversidad y gestión*. Bogotá: Instituto de Investigación de Recursos Biológicos Alexander von Humboldt.

Gonzales, Michael J. 1991. "The Rise of Cotton Tenant Farming in Peru, 1890–1920: The Condor Valley." *Agricultural History* 65, no. 1: 51–71.

Graves, Christine, ed. 2006. *La papa, tesoro de los Andes*. Lima: Centro Internacional de la Papa.

Gómez López, Augusto. 2003. "La explotación quinera en el piedemonte amazónico. Auge y crisis." *Revista Medicina* 25, no. 2: 131–134.

Humboldt, Alexander von. 1807. *Tableau physique des Andes et pays voisins*. Peter H. Raven Library/Missouri Botanical Garden.

Herrera, Alexander, and Maurizio Ali. 2009. "Paisajes del desarrollo: la ecología de las tecnologías andinas." *Antípoda. Revista de Antropología y Arqueología* 8: 169–194.

Jiménez, Jaime E. 1996. "The extirpation and current status of wild chinchillas Chinchilla lanigera and C. brevicaudata." *Biological Conservation* 77, no. 1: 1–6.

Jiménez Viña, José Arturo. 2015. "Rugidos entre los Andes. una historia del jaguar en la región andina (1820–1910)." Master's Thesis, Universidad Nacional de Colombia.

Jorgensen, Peter. 1999. "Historia de las colecciones botánicas." In *Catálogo de las plantas vasculares del Ecuador*, ed. Peter Jorgensen and Susana León, 25–43. Saint Louis: Missouri Botanical Garden.

Kaltmeier, Olaf. 1999. *Im Widerstreit der Ordnungen. Kulturelle Identität, Subsistenz und Ökologie in Bolivien*. Wiesbaden: Deutscher Universitätsverlag.

———. 2021. *Resistencia indígena y formación del Estado. Saquisilí del siglo XVI al XXI*. Quito: Corporación Editora Nacional.

Lack, Walter. 2018. *Alexander von Humboldt und die botanische Erforschung Amerikas*. Munich: Prestel.

Larrea Maldonado, Carlos. 2006. *Hacia una historia ecológica del Ecuador. Propuestas para el debate*. Quito: Corporación Editora Nacional/Universidad Andina Simón Bolivar.

Larson, Brooke. 2004. *Trials of Nation Making: Liberalism, Race, and Ethnicity in the Andes, 1810–1910*. Cambridge: Cambridge University Press.

Leal, Claudia. 2019. "Un tesoro reservado para la ciencia. El inusual comienzo de la conservación de la naturaleza en Colombia (décadas de 1940 y 1950)." *Historia Crítica* 74: 95–126.

———. 2022. "Breve historia de los parques nacionales de Colombia, 1948–2003." *Naturaleza y Sociedad. Desafíos Medioambientales* 22: 23–49.

Lema, Ana María. 1992. "Profesíon: cocalero. Historia de la defensa de la coca, XVI-XX." In *Etnicidad, economía y simbolismo en los Andes: II congreso internacional de etnohistoria. Coroico*, ed. Silvia Arze, Rossana Barragán, Laura Escobari, et al., 387–400. Lima: Institut français d'études andines.

Mongua Calderón, Camilo. 2022. *Los rostros de un estado delegado. Religiosos, indígenas y comerciantes en el Putumayo, 1845–1904*. Bogotá/Quito: Editorial Universidad del Rosario/FLACSO Ecuador.

Moseley, Michael. 1992. *The Incas and their Ancestors: The Archaeology of Peru*. New York: Thames and Hudson.

Murra, John V. 2002. "El control vertical de un máximo de pisos ecológicos en la economía de las sociedades andinas." In *El mundo andino. Población, medio ambiente y economía*, ed. John Murra, 85–125. Lima: Pontificia Universidad Católica del Perú/Instituto de Estudios Peruanos.

Nieto Olarte, Mauricio. 2006. *Remedios para el imperio*. Bogotá: Universidad de los Andes.

———. 2022. "Capítulo 2: Francisco José de Caldas: Geografía y Política en el Semanario del Nuevo Reyno de Granada." *Nuevas Lecturas de Historia* 39: 21–37.

Palacio Castañeda, Germán A. 2006. *Fiebre de tierra caliente. Una historia ambiental de Colombia 1850–1930*. Bogotá: ILSA.

Palacios, Marco. 2009. *El café en Colombia, 1850–1970: una historia económica, social y política*. 4th ed. Mexico City: El Colegio de México.

Päßler, Ulrich. 2020. "Im freyen Spiel dynamischer Kräfte: Pflanzengeographische Schriften, Manuskripte und Korrespondenzen Alexander von Humboldts." In *Alexander von Humboldt: Geographie der Pflanzen. Unveröffentlichte Schriften aus dem Nachlass*, ed. Ulrich Päßler, 3–26. Berlin: Metzler.

Peralta Agudelo, Jaime Andrés, and Margarita Rosa Díaz Benjumea. 2022. "Entre bosques tropicales y comunidades negras. El Platviajero del siglo XIX frente a la otredad del Pacífico colombiano." *Apuntes* 91: 133–158.

Platt, Tristán. 2016. *Estado boliviano y ayllu andino. Tierra y tributo en el norte de Potosí. Primera edición en esta colección*. La Paz: Vicepresidencia del Estado Plurinacional.

Pierce, Adrian. 2017. "Reindigenización y Economía en los Andes 1820–1870, desde la mirada europea." *Historia Mexicana* 67, no. 1: 233–293.

Petitjean, Patrick, Catherine Jami, and Anne Marie Moulin, ed. 1992. *Science and Empires: Historical Studies about Scientific Development and European Expansion*. New York: Kluwer Academic Publishers.

Porto-Gonçalves, Carlos. 2016. "Lucha por la Tierra. Ruptura metabólica y reapropiación social de la naturaleza." *Polis* 15, no. 45: 291–316.

Pratt, Mary Louise. 2010. *Ojos imperiales. Literatura de viajes y transculturación*. Mexico City: Fondo de Cultura Económica.

Restrepo, Eduardo. 2023. "Expedicion Humana, a la zaga de la 'Colombia oculta'. Diversidad genética, arrogancia científica e imaginarios de nación." *Tabula rasa* 47: 239–273.

Rojas Lenis, Yazmín. 2014. "La historia de las áreas protegidas, sus firmas de gobierno y las alternativas para la gobernanza." *Sociedad y Economía* 27: 155–176.

Sandoval, Yesid, and Camilo Echandía. 1986. "La historia de La Quina desde una perspectiva regional. Colombia, 1850 – 1882." *Anuario Colombiano de Historia Social y de la Cultura* 13/14: 53–187.

Sastoque, Edna Carolina. 2011. "Tabaco, quina y añil en el siglo XIX." *Revista Credencial*. https://www.revistacredencial.com/historia/temas/tabaco-quina-y-anil-en-el-siglo-xix.

Soluri, John. 2013. "Los campesinos y la historia oculta de la biodiversidad. Nuevas historias ambientales de América Latina y el Caribe." *RCC Perspectives* 7: 67–74.

Spalding, Karen. 1984. *Huarochiri: An Andean Society Under Inca and Spanish Rule*. Redwood: Stanford University Press.

Spooner, David M., Karen McLean, Gavin Ramsay, et al. 2005. "A single domestication for potato based on multilocus amplfied fragment length polymorphism genotyping." *PNAS* 102: 14694–14699.

Taussig, Michael. 1991. *Shamanism, Colonialism, and the Wild Man: A Study in Terror and Healing*. Chicago: University of Chicago Press.

Troll, Carl. 1931. Die geographischen Grundlagen der andinen Kulturen des Incareiches. *Ibero-amerikanisches Archiv* 5, no. 3: 258–294.

Van Ausdal, Shawn. 2009. "Potereros, ganancias y poder. Una historia ambiental de la ganadería en Colombia, 1850 -1950." *Historia Crítica* 362: 126–149.

Von Stosch, Kristina. 2014. *Indígenas y campesinos en Alto Beni. Diferentes visiones en torno a tierra, territorio y recursos naturales*. La Paz: Tierra.

Wagner, David, Eliza M. Grames, Matthew L. Forister, et al. 2021. "Insect decline in the Anthropocene. Death by a thousand cuts." *PNAS* 118, no. 2.

Zárate, Carlos. 2001. *Extracción de quina: la configuración del espacio andino-amazónico de fines del siglo XIX*. Leticia: Universidad Nacional de Colombia.

Zeuske, Michael. 2000. "Humboldt und Bolívar." In *Alexander von Humboldt. Netzwerke des Wissens*, ed. Frank Holl, 128–129. Berlin/Bonn: Akat.

Biodiversity in the Amazon from the Mid-Nineteenth Century to 1950
Science in the History of Amazon Megadiversity

Magali Romero Sá, Dominichi Miranda de Sá and Lorelai Kury

The term "Amazon" now refers to the region defined by the Amazon River basin, covered by a tropical forest that extends for approximately 7 million km² from the Atlantic Ocean to the Andes Mountains, encompassing nine South American countries: Brazil, Colombia, Venezuela, Peru, Bolivia, Ecuador, Guyana, Suriname, and French Guiana. About 70 percent of the Amazon is in Brazil, representing nearly 60 percent of the country's territory.

Home to hundreds of different Indigenous peoples, traditional populations, and millions of inhabitants residing in major urban centers such as Manaus and Belém, the region is primarily described in superlatives related to the natural world: the largest watershed, the largest freshwater reservoir, the most complex drainage network, and the largest tropical forest in the world. It is also one of the richest terrestrial biomes on Earth for most taxonomic groups, housing approximately 30 percent of the world's plant and animal species. The region also hosts 70 percent of continental protected areas (Capobianco 2001; Stegmann et al. 2024). Due to its unique geomorphological situation, the Amazon region has unique climatic and ecological conditions, with great topographic diversity, various distinct ecosystems, and pronounced variations in geomorphology, soils, flora, and fauna (Salati 1990; Ab'Saber 2003).

Chroniclers, travelers, naturalists, colonial agents, science practitioners, and scientists, both European and neo-European, who traversed the region since the sixteenth century, contributed to elucidating the biological dynamics of the Amazon's grandeur in their fieldwork. Their records and analyses condense physiographic, biogeographic, geomorphological, political, cultural, and historical observations, with an emphasis on understanding the natural world. This is because their research also focused on investigating the commercial potential of natural elements, which should be converted into "economic resources."

The scientific framework of boundless natural abundance gave significance to the conquest and occupation processes that are the origins of the environmental devastation history of the Amazon. However, science has also established its role in global climate regulation through carbon storage and sequestration, and hydrological cycles. According to Earth system scientists, who warn of the unprecedented risks of the forest's transformation into a climate emergency, this should be the greatest global concern today (Nobre et al. 2021). Thus, sciences have been central both in the processes of meticulous scrutiny and commodification of nature, as well as in understanding anthropogenic transformations on the planet. Therefore, they play a leading role in the Anthropocene.

The contradictory role of knowledge and exploration that science has played in the march toward the Anthropocene has been the subject of reflection and studies by different analysts (Arias-Maldonado 2019; Charbonnier 2017; Latour 2020; Renn 2020; Schemmel 2020; Silva 2022; Stengers 2023; Stengers 2015; Trischler 2016; Tsing et al. 2021; Tsing 2019). Anthropologist Anna Tsing has called for theorists to investigate what she termed the "science of failure," i.e., to conduct studies with strong ethical content seeking to understand "what went wrong" in the expertise that supported human infrastructures that ended up "functioning" as true "Anthropocene triggers" (Tsing et al. 2021). Historian Mattias Schemmel argues that "the Anthropocene is not just a problem of policy, the application of science, or scientific policy; it is also a problem of science itself. [...] It must extend its rationality to include its own interaction with society and nature" (Schemmel 2020: 6). Therefore, it should reflect on the social and ecological effects of its findings.

This is precisely the reflection proposed in this chapter: what were the outcomes of the knowledge produced for economic exploration of the Brazilian Amazon in the nineteenth and twentieth centuries when expeditions and scientific voyages to the region intensified? This chapter follows authors who argue that this knowledge is associated with the process of transforming the Amazon into a microcosm of the Anthropocene (Brondizio 2013; Silva 2022). The Amazon catalyzes the transformations in socio-economic and biogeochemical processes characterizing this geohistorical event, defined by the global impact of human activity on the planet. The discussion here will focus on how scientific knowledge about the Amazon's megadiversity was produced in association with colonial empires and the Brazilian national state, culminating in a complete transformation of the forest. It will demonstrate that the sciences permeated the main processes of understanding and international circulation of knowledge about the ecological dynamics of the Amazon. However, these sciences also participated in the commodification of biodiversity and its integration into global chains of trade and biopiracy, the unilateral use of Indigenous knowledge, and strong propaganda for transforming the forest into arable land.

The proposal to analyze the ambivalence of sciences in the Anthropocene does not imply anti-scientific sentiment in any way. On the contrary, it underscores the significance of sciences in the discourse surrounding the planet's future and advocates for politically aware and responsible scientific practices regarding the knowledge they generate (Stengers 2023).

Amazon: The Gestation of a World

Euclides da Cunha (1866–1909), renowned for his book *Os Sertões* (1902), delivered a speech at the Brazilian Academy of Letters in 1903 entitled "Amazon: The Gestation of a World," where he narrated the emotion he felt when entering the Amazon. He described an excess of skies above an excess of waters, indecisive shallows, islands, or pre-islands partially dissolved in the tidal flats. He claimed to have finally understood why the Spanish priest Cristóbal de Acuña considered that the great river should have originated in Paradise (Cunha 1986; Foot Hardman 2007; Foot Hardman 2001).

The vision conveyed by ancient chroniclers and explorers about the region's rich potential fueled the colonizers' greed, with the possibility that extensive commercial and catechizing investment in the name of the King and God would yield them wealth and the expansion of Christianity (Mafra 2012). The spiritual conquest, aiming at the pacification and incorporation of Indigenous peoples, was associated with the search for plant species of commercial interest for food, pharmacopeia, and various industrial uses. The discovery and identification of numerous plant varieties with commercial value became part of the activities of those who ventured into the region with the fundamental assistance of the Indigenous people (Costa 2002).

Bioprospecting in the Amazon region began with trade networks and the actions of colonial agents, without the contribution of cumulative systematization made public. Europeans and neo-Europeans established the use and circulation of the so-called "drugs of the hinterland" through means that did not involve experts in natural history or medicine. The methodical inventory of Indigenous and traditional knowledge began to be published mainly in the nineteenth century, leading to the arrival in the region of naturalists and explorers from various countries.

Between 1799 and 1804, the Spanish colonies in the Americas (Venezuela, Cuba, Colombia, Peru, Ecuador, Mexico) were explored by the Prussian naturalist Alexander von Humboldt (1769–1859) in the company of the French botanist Aimée Bonpland (1773–1858). The exploration of the Venezuelan Amazon led him to coin the term "Hyleia," taken from the writings of Herodotus (484–425 BC) for equatorial forests. In addition to the numerous new specimens of plants and animals collected in the places visited by the two explorers, Humboldt left in his writings important accounts of the geographical and geological experiences during the journey. In his publications, he introduced a new style of describing scientific journeys through a poetic treatment of nature (Lisboa 1997: 42; Kohlhepp 2006).

Strongly influenced by the travel accounts of the Prussian naturalist in the Spanish colonies of America, German naturalists Carl Friedrich Philip von Martius (1794–1868) and Johann Baptist von Spix (1781–1826) arrived in Brazil. Humboldt's Amazonian Hyleia would become part of the imaginary and exploration desire of numerous foreign naturalists over the years (Browne 1983; Lisboa 1997). Despite the current questioning of Humboldt's pioneering role in relation to studies already being developed by Hispanic scholars at the time, which he completely erased in his descriptions and publications, (Thurner and Cañizares-Esguerra 2022), it cannot be denied that, for European and North American naturalists of the nineteenth and twentieth centuries, Humboldt's writings were motivating and highly inspiring. His perspective on the varied distribution of life on the planet, the idea of the special vigor of the natural world in warm climates, and the importance of scientific excursions for understanding natural spaces were fundamental (Dettelbach 1996).

Carl Martius, a Bavarian botanist who participated in an expedition to Brazil between 1817 and 1820, was one of the main naturalists of the nineteenth century who ventured into the Amazon. In his travel account, co-written with zoologist Johann Baptist Spix, they outlined a kind of balance of what was known about the Amazon from the European perspective. According to them, no research on the Amazon River had been conducted since the Frenchman La Condamine (1701–1774). The expeditions undertaken since the sixteenth century by Spaniards and Portuguese did not provide geographical clarifications. Many reports were difficult to access, as publicity was not in the interest of the Spanish and Portuguese crowns. A significant part of the expeditions, including that of Brazilian naturalist Alexandre Rodrigues Ferreira (1756–1815), who traveled through the Amazon region and Mato Grosso between 1783 and 1792, was remembered by the inhabitants, but there was nothing tangible the two scientists could benefit from. Furthermore, they claimed that the names of locations had been changed and no longer corresponded to the old reports. They navigated by a map of the French Academy from La Condamine's time and one from Arrowsmith. In other words, even the major river that allowed Europeans to penetrate the forest was poorly mapped for outsiders. Thus, they were "entirely at the mercy of an Indian, our guide" (Spix and Martius 1831: 965).

Spix and Martius provided an interesting description of the city of Belém in the early nineteenth century, animated by the influx of boats with forest products turned into commodities, such as sugar, cachaça, coffee, cocoa, vanilla, cotton, copaiba balsam, tow, tar, copal, many types of woodworking and construction timber, tobacco, piassava, sarsaparilla, tapioca, puxuri, cumaru, tamarind, Maranhão clove, indigo, annatto, Brazil nut, guarana, and amber:

> trade [...] depends mainly on the articles it receives from the most active places in the interior of the province: Cametá, Gurupá, Santarém, and the Rio Negro province. As soon as the commerce canoes from these regions arrive, the city

streets come alive, and half-naked Indians can be seen busy carrying the precious articles to the customs, and from there to the various warehouses scattered throughout the city. (Spix and Martius 1831: 912)

Outside of this time, everything would be quiet and lifeless. This rhythm observed by Spix and Martius changed from 1853 onward, when steam navigation began on the Amazon. Until that time, sailboats took at least sixty days to travel from Belém to Manaus, a journey that from then on took about ten days. This acceleration facilitated travel in the region – which was extremely difficult and exhausting – and the export of products, including rubber.

Martius' research was important for the understanding of the specificity of the Amazon in relation to global biomes. In the book *Historia naturalis palmarum*, published between 1823 and 1850, the Amazon region is portrayed as one of the "floristic empires" of the planet, comprising the Amazon and Orinoco basins, which he calls megapotamic or Amazonian-Orinocan. In this region, there is a concentration of palms only comparable to its counterpart in the Old World, the region of South Asia and Malaysia. Martius' geobotanical research also led him to elaborate phytogeographic divisions of Brazil, which he named after Greek nymphs. The Amazon rainforest was associated with the Naiads, of rivers and waters, as a hot and humid region of the Amazon and Orinoco. In 1858, Martius organized his biogeographic classification of Brazil on a map, entitled *Tabula geographica quinque provincias Florae brasiliensis ilustrans*. This representation of Brazilian biomes is still considered valid in its general lines (Kury 2022).

Martius' multiple interests and talent for large syntheses made his work pioneering in various areas. Like him, some other naturalists, despite specializing in a branch of natural history, maintained a comprehensive view of the natural and human framework of the regions they visited. The connections between social, cultural, physical, and natural phenomena could be themselves a theme of reflection, as seen in the studies of Alexander von Humboldt, who traveled through the Americas and Russia. Others, such as Charles Darwin (1809–1882) and Alfred Russel Wallace (1823–1913) – who visited Brazil – sought to relate time and space to the diversity of living organisms. During the first half of the nineteenth century, in a fundamentally fixist scientific environment, believing in the immutability of species, one of the major challenges for research was to engage in a dialogue between the forms of living beings and the environments they inhabited.

Martius also envisioned a prosperous future for the Amazon region, impressed by the abundance of natural resources and "its fertile lands," foreseeing its elevation to civilization and industry ensured by the most beautiful and generous nature (Spix and Martius 1981: 143). This vision was widely disseminated in the scientific community due to the special interest among men of science in the epistemology of

From the Mid-Nineteenth Century to 1950

the immediate knowledge of travelers who "saw with their own eyes" the exuberance of the rainforest (Kury 2001a).

Collections and Commerce: Amazonian Biodiversity as Economic and Scientific Value in Validating New Scientific Theories

The tropical forest provided economic goods for many naturalists who explored it. The demand for exotic specimens to enrich private collections and European and North American museums led to the funding by numerous collectors and amateurs who ventured into specimen collection and sold their collections to scientific institutions and individuals. Many naturalists depended on this form of commerce for their survival. In 1848, two British naturalists, Alfred Russel Wallace and Henry Walter Bates (1825–1892), arrived in the Amazon region to explore its natural history, understand the origin of species, and collect and send natural history specimens for commercialization by their agent Samuel Stevens (1817–1899). Collections from "exotic" places had enormous value, and, as Nancy Stepan (2001) notes, many young naturalists, unable to travel but deeply interested in natural history, saw specimen collection as a great opportunity to fulfill their desires and vocations. This was the case for Alfred Russel Wallace, Henry Walter Bates, and Richard Spruce (1817–1893). Not belonging to the British elite, with low economic prospects, selling specimens became a great opportunity to pursue their interests. The certainty that they would find buyers for their collections was decisive in realizing a scientific adventure in the Amazon rainforest (Stepan 2001).

Samuel Stevens founded the Natural History Agency in London in the same year the two naturalists were traveling to the Amazon. He advanced the payment to Bates and Wallace so they could start the journey and for the future shipment of specimens, and he would sell the natural history specimens to collectors and museums, charging a 20 percent commission with an additional 5 percent for insurance and transportation. Stevens promoted the collections at meetings of the Entomological Society of London and the Linnaean Society, displaying the material collected by the naturalists, hence contributing to the promotion of the richness of the Amazonian fauna, especially insects, which was his specialty (Ashworth 2021; Stevenson 2010).

Bates spent eleven years exploring the Amazon rainforest and, between 1848 and 1859, collected more than 14,000 species of insects, of which 8,000 were considered new to science. These specimens were sent to collectors, British institutions, and Samuel Stevens. In addition to the assembled collections, Bates (1944) masterfully described the sociobiodiversity of the Amazon through the publication of his travel book and contributed to the acceptance of Darwin's theory of natural selection through his research on mimicry in Amazonian insects (Antunes 2019; Sá 2022). Wallace returned to England four years later and, in 1854, ventured into the lush forests of the Malay Archipelago, where he spent eight years until 1862, exploring and collecting specimens. There, he developed the theory of natural selection simultaneously with Darwin in Europe. His contribution to the knowledge of Amazonian biodiversity was of enormous relevance, and his research and observations are still followed and discussed today (Ribas 2023). To explain the origin of biodiversity in the Amazon, Wallace considered rivers as barriers. Observing the primates of the region, Wallace detected that primates of different species were restricted to geographically isolated regions by rivers, and each region and habitat type contained a distinct set of species, forming an area of endemism (Wallace 1854; Knapp 1999; Papavero and Santos 2014). According to his hypothesis, when the drainage network of the major Amazonian rivers formed, ancestral animal populations that previously occupied a certain area would have been divided and isolated into subpopulations, undergoing speciation processes on opposite riverbanks. His observations still influence studies on the biodiversity of the region (Knapp 1999; Nunes 2018; Ribas 2023). From his studies, the notion arises that each area includes endemic species, which are affected differently by anthropogenic interventions such as deforestation, fires, and infrastructure development. This understanding is part of current debates on the Anthropocene with the significant impact that Amazonian biodiversity has been undergoing due to aggressive economic exploitation. Another noteworthy aspect of Wallace's considerations was the emphasis he placed on the knowledge of traditional populations. Without them, the observations and collections of the British naturalist (Wallace 1979) would have been impossible.

British naturalists were not the only ones to rely on knowledge passed down by natives and local inhabitants; this had been a common practice since the arrival of the Europeans in the Americas. Antonio Barrera-Osorio and Mauricio Olarte, in their work on the Ibero-American world and the role of Indigenous knowledge in the emergence of modern science, demonstrate that the knowledge and survival of New World explorers were only possible due to the wisdom and experience of natives and local inhabitants regarding animals, plants, and their medicinal uses (Barrera-Osorio and Olarte 2019: 7).

In the view that the Brazilian Amazon would be the privileged locus for the study of biodiversity, the Swiss-American naturalist Louis Agassiz (1807–1873) arrived in the region in 1867. He aimed to prove his creationist-based theories and that Darwin was wrong in his postulation of the theory of evolution (Santos 2005).

Agassiz, although widely recognized intellectually by U.S. authorities and the public, began to be questioned by young U.S. American naturalists who rejected his interpretations, deemed them too theological, and criticized his racist conceptions. In this context, the opportunity arose for Agassiz to undertake a scientific expedition to the Amazon, a kind of Promised Land for ichthyologists. With the publicity guaranteed by such a trip, the geological observations, and the material collected in this immense region, the zoologist believed he could obtain strong allies to refute evolutionary ideas and defend the fixity of species and successive creations. As Agassiz explained, the principal scientific problem to be elucidated by the expedition was the origin of species (Agassiz and Agassiz 1975; Kury 2001b).

In the Amazon region, Agassiz dedicated himself to finding evidence of a recent glaciation (Pleistocene), which would have marked a rupture between current and extinct species. The Swiss naturalist had already tried to prove that there were glaciations in Europe and the United States. If he could show evidence of a relatively recent ice age in the Amazon, Agassiz would make the phenomenon global, not just localized. Contemporary works (such as those of Bates and Wallace) did not share this opinion. Hartt, his companion on the Thayer expedition, gradually distanced himself from Agassiz's glacial hypothesis. Nowadays, it is considered that the glacial period in the region dates back to much earlier periods, millions of years before Agassiz had estimated (Kury 2001b).

In addition to the extinction and recreation of faunas, Agassiz also advocated that God had created "zoological provinces." As the boundaries of these provinces would be quite narrow, the Amazon Valley would contain several provinces. Regarding fish – his main area of study – Agassiz believed that the species found varied along the length of the Amazon and were different for each tributary. In contrast to Darwin, he thought that variability within each species was practically non-existent. Thus, what is considered a variety today, Agassiz regarded as a new species. Various passages from his travel account confirm his quest for extreme species differentiation.

At the end of the expedition, despite failing to prove his theory regarding natural selection and the origin of species, Agassiz brought a considerable collection of Amazonian fauna, especially fish, to U.S. American museums.

Prospecting Amazonian Biodiversity

The search for natural products of economic value has always been part of naturalists' research. Even when traveling with diverse purposes, plants and animals used in the economy and pharmacopeia by Indigenous people and riverine communities were collected and taken to major European centers or their colonies to be acclimatized and cultivated.

Londa Schiebinger (2004) has drawn attention to the complexity of bioprospecting in the Atlantic space in the eighteenth century. In line with the implementation of Linnaean natural history, certain species and expertise were valued, while others were erased. The imperial selective logic pointed out by the author developed throughout the nineteenth century, intensifying the commodification of plants and silencing local practices, including in the Amazon. Naturalists positioned themselves as authorities on the use of natural products.

In Martius and Spix's travel instructions, one of Martius' responsibilities was to conduct rigorous research on plant medicines and all other plant materials whose utility for arts and industries could be proven, comparing them with those used in his home country (Spix and Martius 1981: 26).

The arrival of the British naturalist Richard Spruce (1817–1893) in the region in 1849 – who, like his compatriots Bates and Wallace, went to the Amazon with the task of collecting botanical material to be sent to England and, with these sales, sustain himself in the region – led to intensive bioprospecting of the Amazonian flora not only in Brazil but also in the Venezuelan, Peruvian, and Ecuadorian Amazon. Spruce's main task was to collect material for the Royal Botanical Garden, Kew. His trip would be financed by the sale of botanical specimens brokered by the botanist George Bentham (1800–1884), who committed to receiving all his botanical collections, naming the already described species, arranging them into sets under their various genera, and sending them to various collectors in England and other European countries who had registered to receive the specimens (Spruce 1908: xxxiii). Spruce received instructions from Kew's director, William Hooker (1785–1865), on collecting useful plant products and Indigenous artifacts of economic value for the newly created Museum of Economic Botany at Kew (Martins 2021: 24). During the fifteen years he spent exploring the Amazon and Andes, between 1849 and 1864, Spruce collected about 14,000 botanical specimens and around 350 ethnobotanical artifacts, in addition to making observations on various native practices in plant use, recognizing their economic potential, and even mapping the plants used in hallucinogenic ceremonies in Indigenous rituals (Araújo 2018; Cabalzar et al. 2017; Schultes 1983; Seaward 2000).

In 1855, Spruce took advantage of the newly created Amazon Navigation and Trade Company and sailed from Manaus to Peru. From Nauta, he traveled up the Huallaga River to Chasuta and then overland to Tarapoto. After two years exploring the region, Spruce received a request from the British government through the Indian Foreign Office to travel to Ecuador to obtain quinine seeds to be sent for cultivation in India. The idea to make this request to Spruce came from Clement Markham (1830–1916), a geographer linked to the Indian Office who was familiar with the region and local quinine exploration. Markham was responsible for quinine production, an alkaloid extracted from the tree and used in the treatment of malaria. Cultivating cinchona was of great importance to European countries as malaria was a significant problem in the colonies. As pointed out by Nicolás Cuvi, as early as the late eighteenth and early nineteenth centuries, the Ecuadorian physician Eugenio Espejo and the Colombian Francisco José de Caldas highlighted the urgent need for reforestation of the cinchona tree due to overexploitation, leading to the assumption in Europe that these plants were on the verge of extinction (Cuvi 2018: 6). Breaking the monopoly on its production in the Americas was the main goal of the British government. Markham was responsible for this colonial endeavor to transfer cinchona seeds and, later, rubber tree seeds (Philips 1995; Dewees 2023).

To assist Spruce in collecting, Markham sent Kew's gardener, Robert Mackenzie Cross (1836–1911), recommended by William Hooker. Cross would later be sent to Brazil to assist Wickham in collecting Hevea seeds. Spruce found and identified the most productive species that produced seeds at the ideal planting stage. After two years, he sent about one hundred thousand mature seeds to Kew Gardens and over six hundred cuttings and seedlings. The plants were later sent to India and cultivated there. The success of the venture contributed to strengthening British control in India. Although Spruce was not directly involved in obtaining Hevea seeds for British colonies, he contributed to the understanding of the most suitable species for domestication through the extensive and detailed study he conducted on different Hevea species, having discovered eight new species (Bentham 1854; Spruce 1855; Gonçalves, Cardoso, and Ortolani 1990).

The success of biopiracy in Ecuador further piqued the interest of the British in cultivating rubber trees in their Asian colonies. In Brazil, as the demand for rubber grew and exports increased, some members of the elite began to recommend encouraging rubber tree cultivation. Among them was João Martins da Silva Coutinho (1830–1889), whose participation in the 1867 Universal Exhibition in Paris, according to Warren Dean (1989), contributed to the transfer of Hevea seeds. In his report, Coutinho discussed the superiority of Pará rubber tree and estimated the cost of operating a plantation. The Coutinho's data were described in an article published in 1869 by James Collins (1846–1900), curator of the Pharmaceutical Society of London, on different types of latex-producing species worldwide. Collins, based on the works of Spruce, Bentham, and Coutinho's report, concluded his article by encouraging the acclimatization of Pará rubber, following the success of the cinchona transfer, asserting its superiority over others and its higher market price (Dean 1989: 34; Dean 1991: 35; Collins 1869: 91; Sá 1998: 162). In 1871, Collins was commissioned by Clements Markham (1830–1916), secretary of the Royal Geographical Society, to survey the rubber industry worldwide. His report published in 1872, once again recommending the introduction of Hevea in India for trade, sparked the interest of the Indian Foreign Office and Kew Gardens, through its director Joseph Hooker. Hooker mobilized by reaching out to contacts in Brazil, and English travelers heading to the Amazon were recruited to send Hevea seeds to Kew (Desmond 1995; Sá 1998). Henry Wickham (1846–1928), an Englishman resident of Santarém who made a living from the trade of animals and a small coffee plantation, had presented to Kew, during this period, some plants that might be of interest to the Empire. The book Wickham had published in 1872 about his journey through the Caribbean and Pará, with drawings of Hevea, accredited him to be commissioned to collect rubber. After lengthy negotiations with the Indian Office regarding the best collection method and his payment, Wickham began the collection with the help of Indigenous people. With a steamboat for transport, he managed to dispatch over 60,000 seeds to Kew Gardens. At that time, he was also assisted by Robert Cross (1836–1911), sent to the Amazon by Markham. Of the seeds sent, 4 percent germinated, and 1,900 were transferred to Ceylon. Cross also dispatched over a thousand Hevea seeds to Kew, of which 400 remained in Kew and 100 were sent to Ceylon. Thus began the domestication of *Hevea brasiliensis* in the British colonies and the downfall of the rubber trade in Brazil (Desmond 1995: 256–257; Schultes 1984: 9–10).

During the period when Hevea was being mapped in the region for seed collection, the Brazilian naturalist João Barbosa Rodrigues (1842–1909) arrived in the Amazon. Commissioned by the imperial government to study especially the region's palms and orchids, Rodrigues spent three and a half years in the Amazon, exploring various rivers and mountains in the lower Amazon, such as the Capim, Tocantins, Tapajós, Xingu, Trombetas, Jamundá, Uatumã, Jatapú, and Urubu rivers, as well as the Curumu, Ereré, and Parintins mountains (Sá 2001; Rodrigues 2012). During this period, he acquired knowledge of the local flora – especially regarding the region's palms – in medicine, cuisine, and housing, as well as conducted studies in ethnobotany and archaeology. He assimilated the art of curare, a paralyzing poison, dark red in color, resinous in appearance, and soluble in water extracted from the bark of certain vines, mainly belonging to two different families of plants. Some Indigenous societies used it to poison their arrows for hunting, and he learned about the antidote, along with other Indigenous and local knowledge (Sá 2012; Sá 2004; Soentgena and Hilbert 2016).

Barbosa Rodrigues returned to the region some years later to be the director of the newly created Botanical Museum of the Amazon, inaugurated in 1883 and closed in 1890 after the Proclamation of the Republic of Brazil in 1889. The Botanical Museum was designed by him to be a modern institution similar to museums in Europe and the United States. In addition to taxonomic studies of botanical and ethnographic collections gathered in the Amazon region, the museum was also dedicated to the study of botany applied to medicine and industry. With the closure of the Botanical Museum, Barbosa Rodrigues was appointed director of the Rio de Janeiro Botanical Garden in 1892. The knowledge acquired during his stay in the Amazon with the Pariqui (an Indigenous society living on the banks of the Jatapu River, a tributary of the Uatumã River in Pará) about the medicinal use of an herbaceous plant of the Nictaginaceae family, was patented by him in 1893 as a new medicine used in hepatic treatment and called "Pariquyna" in homage to this people (Sá 2001: 912). The use of such medicine gained wide popular acceptance and was marketed until the 1940s. In 1899, already as director of the Rio de Janeiro Botanical Garden, Barbosa Rodrigues was commissioned by the Ministry of Industry, Transportation and Public Works to respond to the request of the Ministry of Foreign Affairs of the Republic of El Salvador, Central America, about "rubber gum" (Barbosa Rodrigues 1900; Domingues 2022). Fresh from the Amazon and a great connoisseur of the region's flora, the Brazilian naturalist published a detailed work on Hevea and the superiority of *Hevea brasiliensis* (Barbosa Rodrigues 1900).

He then reported on the terrible working conditions of rubber tappers and the damage caused to the trees. Critical of how latex collection was being carried out, with the death of numerous rubber trees along the rivers, he described the method to keep the trees healthy with continuous latex production. He also discussed the best planting method, the appropriate environment, such as soil nature, and the time needed to extract latex (Barbosa Rodrigues 1900: 60; Domingues 2022: 9). As Domingues pointed out, Rodrigues' work went beyond the initial goal of responding to a foreign government's diplomatic request for information on rubber gum. His work affirmed the relevance of rubber cultivation in the Amazon region, considering the species' ecological dynamics and traditional knowledge holders.

In this same period, Jacques Huber (1867–1914), a researcher at the Emílio Goeldi Paraense Museum, was developing studies on the Amazonian flora and mainly on the latex extraction industry. The Paraense Museum, created in 1866 by Domingos Soares Ferreira Penna (1818–1888), was then under the direction of Swiss zoologist Emílio Goeldi (1859–1917). Invited to the directorship of the Amazonian Museum in 1894, Goeldi arrived in Belém from Rio de Janeiro, where he had held the position of subdirector of the zoology section at the National Museum ten years earlier (Sanjad 2010: 174). With the proclamation of the Brazilian Republic and internal disputes at the Museum in Rio de Janeiro, Goeldi's contract was canceled, and he accepted the invitation from the government of Pará to lead the Paraense Museum. The Swiss naturalist helped consolidate the Museum in Pará, integrating it into the national and international scientific movement with a clear and coherent scientific project for the Amazon. He increased the formation of scientific collections of natural history and ethnology, launched the Bulletin of the Paraense Museum, promoted the creation of the botanical garden and zoo, and facilitated intense scientific exchanges between experts and national and foreign institutions (Sanjad 2006; Sanjad 2010). In 1900, after an important diplomatic role during the Franco-Brazilian Dispute, he was honored by having his name included in the museum, which became known as the Emílio Goeldi Paraense Museum.

One of Goeldi's first initiatives was to bring his friend Jacques Huber from Switzerland to head the botanical section. Huber arrived in the region in 1895 and immediately began important studies related to the Amazonian flora, especially on rubber-producing species. Starting in 1897, he extensively published on the subject, mapping and describing new species of rubber trees. Rubber exports were driving the regional economy. From the port of Belém, between 1895, the year Huber arrived, and 1900, rubber exports increased from 15,461 tons to 19,252 tons (Weinstein 1993: 225). Studies on rubber trees were becoming increasingly relevant, and through his research, Huber became the leading expert on latex-producing trees from both a botanical and utilitarian perspective (Cunha 2009: 495; Castro, Sanjad, and Romeiro 2009: 506).

In 1907, Huber assumed the directorship of the Paraense Museum after Emílio Goeldi's return to Europe. During this period, rubber production in the east began to show increasing economic results, and concerns about the decline in exports led to Huber being appointed to conduct technical studies on rubber production in Asian countries. Between 1911 and 1912, Huber traveled through plantations in Ceylon, Sumatra, Java, and the Malay Peninsula. Upon his return, he submitted a 116-page report with detailed descriptions of planting methods, soil types, climate, latex extraction methods, production cost values, and comparisons between plantations in the east and the Amazon. As Barbosa Rodrigues had pointed out years before in his report, Huber also noted that for the rubber industry to succeed it would be necessary to consider the ecological, geographical, social, economic, political, and administrative specificities of the region, a warning that local governments ignored (Castro, Sanjad, and Romeiro 2009: 509, 511). New attempts to recover the rubber economy in the Amazon would still be implemented in the first half of the twentieth century.

The "Goblin of the Amazon"

The scientific exploration expeditions through Brazil, which had initially commenced as a European endeavor to secure colonial possession and dominance, were redefined by Brazilians between the nineteenth and twentieth centuries to chart the "natural wealth" of the territory, following a logic of pursuing national economic self-sufficiency. Additionally, they supported state-led modernization projects and the construction of energy, transportation, and communication infrastructure, including hydroelectric plants, railways, and the expansion of the telegraphic network. With the consolidation of national institutions such as the National Museum (MN), the Brazilian Historical and Geographic Institute (IHGB), and the Oswaldo Cruz Institute (IOC), they also became an important part of the efforts to build a "national science," that is, research on Brazilian themes conducted by Brazilians. They were responsible for elaborating mappings of the natural conditions of the different localities visited – botanical, zoological, geological, mineralogical, and astronomical inventories; studies of soil, climatic, epidemiological, and socioeconomic conditions; navigability of rivers; distribution of indigenous populations; and availability of groundwater.

Among these expeditions, carried out in association with the political Independence (1822) and the proclamation of the Brazilian Republic (1889), it is important to mention the Scientific Exploration Commission (1856), Imperial Geological Commission (1875), Imperial Hydrographic Commission (1879), Exploratory Commission of the Central Plateau of Brazil (1892–1894), Rondon Commission (1907–1930); and the medical-scientific expeditions of the Oswaldo Cruz Institute, which are discussed later in this chapter. These expeditions also traversed the Brazilian Amazon (Lima 2013; Benchimol and Silva 2008).

This initiative aimed at systematically inventorying the region's nature and attempting to convert "territorial funds" and areas of international boundary disputes into "utilized territories" or effective political domains (Moraes 2007). These efforts were accompanied by attempts to restructure the rubber economy and regional development works.

One of these works was the construction of the Madeira-Mamoré Railway, famously known as the "Devil's Railroad," as thousands of workers died during the construction. Original plans and failed construction attempts, dating back to the nineteenth century, were proposed by Bolivia and envisioned as a route to access international markets, aiming to reach the Atlantic Ocean through the Amazon basin. In the definitive project in the early twentieth century, with Brazilian and American participation, the railroad aimed to boost local and international rubber trade and stimulate the occupation of Acre, a territory ceded to Brazil by Bolivia in 1903 through a diplomatic agreement. Its primary objective was to navigate through the most challenging and waterfall-ridden section of the Madeira River, to facilitate the transportation of Bolivian and Brazilian rubber for exportation (Foot Hardman 1991).

Local malaria outbreaks hindered the progress of the project, leading the Madeira-Mamoré Railway Company to hire the IOC in 1909. The hope was that the IOC's medical-scientific evaluation and prescriptions would finally enable the completion of the railway. The then director of the IOC, Oswaldo Cruz (1872–1917), coordinated the study that resulted in the report "General Considerations on the Sanitary Conditions of the Madeira River" (1910). The trip occurred from June 16 to August 29, 1910, and the report describes the expedition through the Madeira River region, undertaken by Cruz along with the physician Belisário Penna (1868–1939), to evaluate the sanitary conditions of the river and its banks, where the railway was being constructed (Schweickardt and Lima 2007).

In the document, Oswaldo Cruz defined malaria as the "goblin of the Amazon," leaving the entire population in a state of chronic, permanent illness. Local disease conditions were associated with ecological variations (climate, water, river floods, and interactions with animals, especially insects), living conditions (mainly related to work in rubber plantations), and the impact of environmental changes in the region, as documented by doctors, rubber tappers, and local populations (Schweickardt and Lima 2007).

Cruz suggested several investments in infrastructure and sanitation to spread and modernize cities around the Madeira-Mamoré: sewers, piped water, lighting, garbage collection, and street paving, as rough roads turned into "dangerous swamps" and created ideal conditions for Anopheles mosquitoes (malaria-transmitting insects) to "spread death." With the sanitary recommendations of the IOC, the railway could be completed, connecting Porto Velho to Guajará-Mirim, two cities in the current state of Rondônia, founded respectively at the beginning and end of the project: 1907 and 1912 (Schweickardt and Lima 2007: 24).

The rubber economy prompted a second medical-scientific expedition by the IOC to the Amazon. Between October 1912 and April 1913, a new expedition was conducted, with a commission comprising Carlos Chagas (1879–1934), Antônio Pacheco Leão (1872–1931), and João Pedro de Albuquerque (1874–1934). The resulting report, "Medical-Sanitary Conditions of the Amazon Valley," released in 1913, included 334 photographs, maps, and suggestions for medical-sanitary facilities in the region. Sponsored by the newly created Rubber Defense Superintendence, linked to the Ministry of Agriculture, Industry and Commerce of Brazil, the commission traveled through the rivers Solimões, Juruá, Purus, Acre, Iaco, Negro, and the lower Rio Branco.

The report highlighted the epidemiology of the Amazon Valley, the dwellings, landscapes, and Indigenous groups of the regions traversed, as well as the history of the Brazil-Bolivia conflict in the occupation of Acre. The scientists attributed a decisive role in the salvation of the rubber industry to public health, with an emphasis on worker health. To achieve this, they advocated for vigorous action to confront malaria in the heart of the Amazon rainforest, including the free or low-cost distribution of medicines, the establishment of health posts and hospitals based on criteria such as the importance of localities in rubber extraction, population concentration, distance from major centers, and navigational conditions of the rivers linking the main production points. They also suggested the creation of a local research institute for the development of specific diagnostics and detailed investigation of atypical cases, as it would lead to many "unprecedented discoveries" for science. In the Amazon, diseases were believed to exhibit "anarchized" symptoms (Schweickardt and Lima 2007).

In these scientific expeditions, the initial aim was the total socio-natural management of health-disease processes, with malaria qualification as a symbol of the "backwardness" of the Amazon region and as a technical problem to be overcome through medical intervention, involving hospitals and medications. However, within the same process, the local involvement of these scientists allowed for the deepening of ecological studies, which were pivotal for the consolidation of the tropical medicine research agenda at the IOC, exploring intricate relationships among diseases, environments, parasites, vectors, hosts, and human populations (Schweickardt and Lima 2007; Benchimol and Silva 2008). Consequently, clear associations emerged between disease incidence and alterations in local hydrological regimes, which fostered the proliferation of malaria-transmitting Anopheles mosquitoes. This was a result of the implementation of new economic activities such as deforestation and agriculture, the influx of new settlers susceptible to the disease and their portable biotas, the simplification of local sociobiodiversity, and new interspecific interactions – typical human disturbances of the Anthropocene. The interventions of technoscience coexisted with ecological approaches and contributed both to the production and explanation of the prevailing health situation: the Amazon region currently reports 99 percent of malaria cases in Brazil (Packard 2007; Benchimol and Silva 2008).

In the following decades, the diagnosis of the "economic delay" in the Amazon region, especially from the 1930s onward, led to the creation of new federal policies, programs, and institutions dedicated to regional development (Andrade 2023). During this time, one of the main institutions created was the Agronomic Institute of the North (IAN) in 1939. A hallmark of this institution was scientific research focused on the agricultural utilization of the Amazon, with an emphasis on trials into the domestication of animal and plant species (Sá and Silva 2019). The IAN aimed to transform the Amazon into a laboratory and farm (Garfield 2009: 30; Garfield 2014), projecting it as the world's granary and a solution to global hunger. The key instrument for this transformation was the comprehensive understanding of its ecology for the implementation of multiculture agricultural practices and the introduction of livestock (Sá and Silva 2019). Once again, Amazonian ecology was the goblin that scientists persisted in attempting to domesticate.

Final Considerations

From the 1960s onward, during the military dictatorship in Brazil, there was an acceleration of interventions presented as symbols of development, modernization, and the occupation of the supposed "demographic void." Construction of highways (such as the Trans-Amazonian), mining projects, hydroelectric plants, and large-scale colonization and agrarian modernization programs led, from the 1970s onward, to the most intense destruction of the forest on record. Simultaneously, it triggered international reactions from environmentalists, scientists, NGOs, and multilateral agencies. The Amazon rainforest became a symbol of the emerging environmental movement (Hecht and Cockburn 1990; Pádua 2005; Pádua 2015; Acker 2014; Acker 2017; Rojas 2016; Silva 2022; Pereira and Sá 2022). In recent years, activists, Indigenous and traditional communities, and scientists from various fields have argued that the Brazilian Amazon is currently the "center of the world" (Brum 2021) due to its megadiversity and its role in global climate regulation.

Symbolizing the ambivalent role of sciences, this knowledge about the uses of Amazonian megadiversity, which places it at the center of current debates about the planet's future, has been indebted to other historically marginalized knowledge, notably Indigenous knowledge. Despite being generically mentioned in the works of some scientists and travelers analyzed in this chapter, the contributions of their knowledge have never received due credit. This is due to the excessive historical valorization of written sources, such as articles and scientific texts, in which their names and those of their peoples were ignored. These are material supports of ideas that they did not produce, as they have different cultural expressions. However, by analyzing the efforts required for the execution of scientific journeys and expeditions, a broader array of historical actors contributing to our current understanding of the Amazon emerges. Strictly speaking, the very Amazonian megadiversity, according to recent research in anthropology and archaeology, is the result of millenary coevolution between Indigenous peoples and the forest (Neves et al. 2021; Pardini 2020; Kawa 2016).

An ethical scientific production should, in any field of knowledge, first recognize the ambivalence of sciences in the histories of the Anthropocene. It should also acknowledge the important historical collaboration of Indigenous knowledge, including in the formulation of ecological hypotheses. It is time to reverse the colonial relationship with other forms of knowledge, meaning scientists need to learn and become proficient in Indigenous knowledge, from which they have always benefited (Kimmerer and Artelle 2024). Historians of science and social scientists dedicated to the debate on the Anthropocene have highlighted its potential as a "negotiation zone" and epistemological collaboration, at the intersection of different knowledges (Trischler 2016). They also reinforce the important role of alternative epistemologies in problematizing new savior techniques, such as geoengineering, which propose to "reverse" the climate catastrophe in an update of the most unrealistic and aggressive technological utopias of the twentieth century (Hamilton 2016). There are even authors who advocate for a necessary scientific indomitability of the Anthropocene in order to maintain its permanent capacity to induce new reflections and transformations, not only of knowledge but also of existential ones (Taddei, Scarso, and Castanheira 2020). Faced with the imminent fall of the sky (Kopenawa and Albert 2015) and the intrusion of Gaia (Stengers 2015), only with a new interspecific sensitivity and cooperation between different ecological knowledge can we address the challenges of habitability in the Anthropocene (Tsing 2019).

If there is a world to come (Danowski and Castro 2017), it will not be built upon the marginalization of Indigenous knowledge, which is inseparable from the history and future of the Amazon as the center of the world and a microcosm of the Anthropocene. It will also not adhere to the epistemological pattern of science from past centuries: guided by a singular expertise and positioned hierarchically, cognitively, and culturally superior to others (Danowski and Castro 2017; Tsing et al. 2021; Tsing 2019; Stengers 2023; Krenak 2019). As Danowski and Castro argue (2017: 159), engaging in dialogue with Indigenous knowledge represents the only viable future, not a remnant of the past. In updating Spix and Martius and facing the crossroads of the Anthropocene, Indigenous peoples will need to be our guides once again.

References

Ab'Saber, Aziz Nacib. 2003. *Os domínios de natureza no Brasil: potencialidades paisagísticas*. São Paulo: Ateliê Editorial.

Acker, Antoine. 2014. "'O maior incêndio do planeta': como a Volkswagen e o regime militar brasileiro acidentalmente ajudaram a transformar a Amazônia em uma arena política global." *Revista Brasileira de História* 34, no. 68: 13–33.

———. 2017. *Volkswagen in the Amazon: The Tragedy of Global Development in Modern Brazil*. Cambridge: Cambridge University Press.

Agassiz, Elizabeth Cary, and Louis Agassiz. 1975. *Viagem ao Brasil*. Belo Horizonte/São Paulo: Itatiaia/EDUSP.

Andrade, Rômulo de Paula. 2023. *Em busca do desenvolvimento: saúde, políticas e destruição na Amazônia 1930–1966*. Manaus/Rio de Janeiro: Editora UEA/Editora Fiocruz.

Antunes, Anderson Pereira. 2019. "Um naturalista e seus colaboradores na Amazônia: a expedição de Henry Walter Bates no Brasil (1848–1859)." Master's thesis, Oswald Cruz Foundation.

Araújo, Wladimyr Sena. 2018. "Richard Spruce e Alfred Russel Wallace: naturalistas do século XIX e o encontro com o caapi." *Jamaxi* 2, no. 2: 143–158.

Arias-Maldonado, M. 2019. "The 'Anthropocene' in Philosophy: The Neo-material Turn and the Question of Nature." In *Anthropocene Encounters: New Directions in Green Political Thinking*, ed. Frank Biermann and Eva Lövbrand, 50–66. Cambridge: Cambridge University Press.

Ashworth, William B. 2021. "Scientist of the day: Samuel Stevens." *Linda Hall Library*. March 11. https://www.lindahall.org/about/news/scientist-of-the-day-samuel-stevens/.

Bates, Walter Henry. 1944. *O naturalista no rio Amazonas*. Trans. Cândido de Mello-Leitão. São Paulo/Rio de Janeiro: Companhia Editora Nacional.

Barrera-Osorio, Antonio, and Mauricio Nieto Olarte. 2019. "Ciencia, tecnología, saberes locales e imperio en el mundo atlántico, siglos XV-XIX." *Historia Crítica* 73: 3–20.

Barbosa Rodrigues, João. 1900. *As Heveas ou seringueiras – Informações*. Rio de Janeiro: Imprensa Nacional.

Benchimol, Jaime Larry, and André Felipe Cândido da Silva. 2008. "Ferrovias, doenças e medicina tropical no Brasil da Primeira República." *História, Ciências, Saúde-Manguinhos* 15, no. 3: 719–762.

Bentham, George. 1854. "On the North Brazilian Euphorbiaceae in the collection of Mr. Spruce." *Hooker´s Journal of Botany and Kew Gardens Miscellany* 6: 321–333/363-376.

Brondizio, Eduardo Sonnewend. 2013. "A microcosm of the Anthropocene: Socioecological complexity and social theory in the Amazon." *Perspectives: Journal de la Reseaux Francaise d'Institut d'études avancées* 10: 10–13.

Browne, Janet. 1983. *The secular ark: studies in the history of biogeography.* New Haven: Yale University Press.

Brum, Eliane. 2021. *Banzeiro òkòtó: Uma viagem à Amazônia Centro do Mundo.* São Paulo: Companhia das Letras.

Cabalzar, Aloiso, Viviane Stern da Fonseca-Kruel, Luciana Martins et al., ed. 2017. *Manual de etnobotânica: plantas, artefatos e conhecimentos indígenas.* São Paulo/São Gabriel da Cachoeira: Instituto Socioambiental/Federação das Organizações Indígenas do Rio Negro.

Capobianco, João Paulo, ed. 2001. *Biodiversidade na Amazônia Brasileira.* São Paulo: Instituto Socioambiental.

Castro, Anna Raquel de Matos, Nelson Sanjad, and Doralice dos Santos Romeiro. 2009. "Da pátria da seringueira à borracha de plantação: Jacques Huber e seus estudos sobre a cultura das heveas no Oriente (1911–1912)." *Boletim do Museu Paraense Emílio Goeldi. Ciências Humanas* 4, no. 3: 503–545.

Charbonnier, Pierre. 2017. "Généalogie de l'Anthropocène La fin du risque et des limites." *Annales HSS* 72, no. 2: 301–328.

Collins, James. 1869. "On India-rubber, its history, commerce and supply." *Journal of the Society of Arts* 18: 81–93.

Costa, Kelerson Semerene. 2002. "Homens e natureza na Amazônia brasileira: dimensões (1616–1920)." PhD diss., Universidade de Brasília.

Cunha, Euclides da. 1986. "Amazônia: a gestação de um mundo." In *Euclides da cunha. Um Paraíso Perdido*, ed. Leandro Tocantins. Rio de Janeiro: José Olympio Editor.

Cunha, Osvaldo Rodrigues da. 2009. "Jacques Huber (1867–1914)." *Boletim do Museu Paraense Emílio Goeldi. Ciências Humanas* 4, no. 3: 489–502.

Cuvi, Nicolás. 2018. "Tecnociencia y colonialismo en la historia de las Cinchona." *Asclepio. Revista de Historia de la Medicina y de la Ciencia* 70, no. 1: 1–13.

Danowski, Déborah, and Eduardo Viveiros de Castro. 2017. *Há mundo por vir? Ensaio sobre os medos e os fins.* Florianópolis: Cultura e Barbárie/Instituto Socioambiental.

Dean, Warren. 1989. *A Luta pela Borracha no Brasil.* São Paulo: Nobel.

———. 1991. "A botânica e a politica imperial: a introdução e a domesticação de plantas no Brasil." *Estudos Históricos* 4, no. 8: 216–228.

Desmond, Ray. 1995. *The History of the Royal Botanic Gardens, Kew.* London: The Harvill Press.

Dettelbach, Michael. 1996. "Global physics and aesthetic empire: Humboldt's physical portrait of the tropics." In *Visions of empire: voyages, botany, and representations of nature*, ed. David Philip Miller and Peter Hanns Reill, 258–292. Cambridge: Cambridge University Press.

Dewees, Jacob. 2023. "Bittersweet Empire: Clements Robert Markham, Cinchona, and Botanical Exploitation." PhD diss., Wesleyan University.

Domingues, Heloisa M. Bertol. 2022. "João Barbosa Rodrigues and 'Queen Rubber:' An innovative scientific culture." *Rodriguésia* 73: 1–12.

Foot Hardman, Francisco. 1991. *Trem fantasma: a modernidade na selva*. São Paulo: Companhia das Letras.

———. 2001. "A vingança da Hiléia: os sertões amazônicos de Euclides." *Tempo Brasileiro* 144: 29–61.

———. 2007. "Amazônia como voragem da história: impasses de uma representação literária." *Estudos de Literatura Brasileira Contemporânea* 15: 207–221.

Garfield, Seth. 2009. "A Amazônia no imaginário norte americano em tempo de guerra." *Revista Brasileira de História* 29, no. 57: 19–65.

———. 2014. *In search of the Amazon: Brazil, the United States, and the nature of a region*. Durham: Duke University Press.

Gonçalves, Paulo de S., Mário Cardoso, and Altino A Ortolani. 1990. "Origem, variabilidade e domesticação da Hevea; uma revisão." *Pesquisa agropecuária brasileira* 25, no. 2: 135–156.

Hamilton, Clive. 2016. "The Anthropocene as Rupture." *The Anthropocene Review* 3, no. 2: 93–106.

Hecht, Susanna, and Alexander Cockburn. 1990. *The Fate of the Forest: Developers, Destroyers and Defenders of the Amazon*. Chicago: Chicago University Press.

Kawa, Nicholas C. 2016. *Amazonia in the Anthropocene: People, Soil, Plants, Forests*. Austin: University of Texas Press.

Kimmerer, Robin Wall, and Kyle A. Artelle. 2024. "Time to support Indigenous science." *Science* 383: 243–243.

Knapp, Sandra. 1999. *Footsteps in the Forest: Alfred Russel Wallace in the Amazon*. London: Natural History Museum.

Kohlhepp, Gerd. 2006. "Descobertas científicas da Expedição de Alexander von Humboldt na América Espanhola (1799–1804) sob ponto de vista geográfico." *Revista de Biologia e Ciências da Terra* 6, no. 1: 260–278.

Kopenawa, Davi, and Bruce Albert. 2015. *A queda do céu: palavras de um xamã yanomami*. São Paulo: Companhia das Letras.

Krenak, Ailton. 2019. *Ideias para adiar o fim do mundo*. São Paulo: Companhia das Letras.

Kury, Lorelai. 2001a. "Viajantes-naturalistas no Brasil oitocentista: experiência, relato e imagem." *História, Ciências, Saúde-Manguinhos* 8: 863–880.

———. 2001b. "A sereia amazônica dos Agassiz: zoologia e racismo na Viagem ao Brasil." *Revista Brasileira de História* 21, no. 41: 157–172.

———. 2022. "Os viajantes e a paisagem natural do Brasil Tabula geographica Brasiliae, Carl von Martius, 1858." In *História do Brasil em 25 mapas*, ed. Andréa Doré and Junia F. Furtado. São Paulo: Companhia das Letras.

Latour, Bruno. 2020. *Diante de Gaia: oito conferências sobre a natureza no Antropoceno.* São Paulo/Rio de Janeiro: Ubu Editora/Ateliê Editorial.

Lima, Nísia Trindade. 2013. *Um sertão chamado Brasil.* 2nd ed. São Paulo: Hucitec.

Lisboa, Karen Macknow. 1997. *A nova Atlântida de Spix e Martius: natureza e civilização na Viagem pelo Brasil (1817–1820).* São Paulo: Hucitec/Fapesp.

Mafra, Sandoval da Silva. 2012. "A visão da Amazônia do Pe. Cristóbal de Acuña. Da viagem à invenção da Amazônia." *Língua e Literatura* 30: 217–234.

Moraes, Antonio Carlos Robert. 2007. "Território, região e formação colonial. Apontamentos em torno da geografia histórica da independência brasileira." *Ciência &Ambiente* 33: 9–16.

Martins, Luciana. 2021. "Plant artefacts then and now: reconnecting biocultural collections in Amazonia." In *Mobile Museums: Collections in circulation,* ed. Felix Driver, Mark Nesbitt, and Caroline Cornish, 21–43. London: UCL Press.

Neves, Eduardo Goés, Laura Furquim, Carolina Levis, et al.. 2021. "Peoples of the Amazon before European colonization." In *Amazon Assessment Report 2021,* ed. Carlos Nobre et al., 1–40. New York: United Nations Sustainable Development Solutions Network.

Nobre, Carlos, Andrea C. Encalada, Elizabeth Anderson, et al., ed. 2021. *Amazon Assessment Report 2021.* New York: United Nations Sustainable Development Solutions Network.

Nunes, Ingrid de Souza. 2018. "Estruturação filogenética e diversificação de lagartos amazônicos." Master's thesis, Instituto Nacional de Pesquisas da Amazônia.

Packard, Randall M. 2007. *The Making of a Tropical Disease: a Short History of Malaria.* Baltimore: John Hopkins University Press.

Pádua, José Augusto. 2005. "Arrastados por uma Cega Avareza: as origens da crítica à destruição dos recursos naturais amazônicos." *Ciência e Ambiente* 31: 131–146.

———. 2009. "Natureza e Sociedade no Brasil Monárquico." In *O Brasil Imperial,* ed. Keila Grinberg and Ricardo Salles, 313–365. Rio de Janeiro: Civilização Brasileira.

———. 2015. "Tropical Forests in Brazilian Political Culture: From Economic Hindrance to Endangered Treasure." In *Endangerment, Biodiversity and Culture,* ed. Fernando Vidal and Nélia Dias, 148–171. London: Routledge.

Papavero, Nelson, and Christian Fausto Moraes dos Santos. 2014. "Evolucionismo darwinista? Contribuições de Alfred Russel Wallace à Teoria da Evolução." *Revista de História* 34, no. 67: 159–180.

Pardini, Patrick. 2020. "Amazônia indígena: a floresta como sujeito." *Boletim do Museu Paraense Emílio Goeldi. Ciências Humanas* 15, no. 1: 1–11.

Pereira, Vanessa, and Dominichi Miranda de Sá. 2022. "Science and the Green Revolution in the Brazilian Amazon: The Establishment of Embrapa during of the Civilian-Military Dictatorship and the Emergence of Environmental Movements (1972–1991)." *Historia Ambiental Latinoamericana y Caribeña (HALAC)* 12: 170–216.

Philips, Kavita. 1995. "Imperial Science Rescues a Tree: Global Botanic Networks, Local Knowledge and the Transcontinental Transplantation of Cinchona." *Environmental History* 1, no. 2: 173–200.

Renn, Jürgen. 2020. *The Evolution of Knowledge: Rethinking Science for the Anthropocene.* Princeton: Princeton University Press.

Ribas, Camila C. 2023. "Escapando da sombra de Darwin: como Alfred Russel Wallace inspira pesquisadores indígenas." *Nature* 613: 24–26.

Rodrigues, William Antonio. 2012. "Barbosa Rodrigues e os estudos botânicos na Amazônia." *Revista Brasileira de História da Ciência* 5: 31–40.

Rojas, David. 2016. "Climate Politics in the Anthropocene and Environmentalism: Beyond Nature and Culture in Brazilian Amazonia." *PoLAR: Political and Legal Anthropology Review* 39, no. 1: 16–32.

Sá, Dominichi Miranda de, and André Felipe Cândido da Silva. 2019. "Amazônia brasileira, celeiro do mundo." *Revista de História (USP)* 178: 1–26.

Sá, Magali Romero. 1998. "James William Trail: a British Naturalist in Nineteenth-century Amazonia." *Historia Naturalis* 1: 99–254.

———. 2001. "O botânico e o mecenas: João Barbosa rodrigues e a ciência no Brasil na segunda metade do século XIX." *História, Ciências, Saúde – Manguinhos* 3: 899–924.

———. 2004. "Paulo Carneiro e o curare: em busca do princípio ativo." In *Ciência, política e relações internacionais: ensaios sobre Paulo Carneiro*, ed. Marcos Chor Maio, 43–65. Rio de Janeiro: Editora Fiocruz/UNESCO.

———. 2012. "Do veneno ao antídoto. Barbosa Rodrigues e os estudos e controvérsias científicas sobre o curare." *Revista Brasileira de História da Ciência* 5: 12–21.

———. 2022. "Mimetismo, Disfarces, Ambiguidades." In *Nas fronteiras da natureza*, ed. Lorelai Kury. Rio de Janeiro: Andrea Jakobsson Estudio.

Salati, Enéas. 1990. "Modificações da Amazônia nos últimos 300 anos: suas consequências sociais e ecológicas." In *Desafio amazônico: o futuro da civilização dos trópicos*, ed. *Sérgio de Salvo Brito*, 23–46. Brasília: Editora Universidade de Brasília: CNPq.

Sanjad, Nelson. 2006. "Emílio Goeldi e a Institucionalização das Ciências Naturais na Amazônia." *Revista Brasileira de Inovação* 5, no. 2: 455–477.

———. 2010. *A Coruja da Minerva: O Museu Paraense entre o Império e a República (1866–1907)*. Brasília/Belém/Rio de Janeiro: Instituto Brasileiro de Museus/ Museu Paraense Emílio Goeldi/Fundação Oswaldo Cruz.

Santos, Fabiane V. dos. 2005. "'Brincos de ouro, saias de chita:' mulher e civilização na Amazônia segundo Elizabeth Agassiz em Viagem ao Brasil (1865–1866)." *História, Ciência, Saúde -Manguinhos* 12, no. 1: 1–21.

Schemmel, Matthias. 2020. "Global history of science as a knowledge resource for the Anthropocene." *Global Sustainability* 3: 1–8.

Schiebinger, Londa. 2004. *Plants and Empire: Colonial Bioprospecting in the Atlantic World*. Cambridge: Harvard University Press.

Schultes, Richard Evans. 1983. "Richard Spruce: an early ethnobotanist and explorer of the northwest Amazon." *Journal of Ethnobiology* 2: 139–147.

———— 1984. "The Tree that Changed the World in One Century." *Arnoldia* 44, no. 2: 3–16.

Schweickardt, Júlio César, and Nísia Trindade Lima. 2007. "Os cientistas brasileiros visitam a Amazônia: as viagens científicas de Oswaldo Cruz e Carlos Chagas (1910–1913)." *História, Ciências, Saúde-Manguinhos* 14:15-50.

Seaward, Mark R. D. 2000. "Richard Spruce, botânico e desbravador da América do Sul." *História, Ciências, Saúde – Manguinhos* 7, no. 2: 377–388.

Silva, André Felipe Cândido da. 2022. "A Amazônia como microcosmo do Antropoceno: a história das pesquisas transnacionais em ecologia amazônica e os impactos ambientais da Grande Aceleração (1952–2002). Projeto de Pesquisa." Rio de Janeiro: Casa de Oswaldo Cruz.

Soentgena, Jens, and Klaus Hilbert. 2016. "A química dos povos indígenas da América do Sul." *Quimica Nova* 39, no. 9: 1141–1150.

Spix, Johann-Baptist von, and Carl von Martius. 1831. *Reise in Brasilien*. Vol. 3. Munich: C. Wolf.

————. 1981. *Viagem pelo Brasil 1817–1820*. Vol. 3. São Paulo: EDUSP.

Spruce, Richard. 1855. "Note on the Indian Rubber of the Amazon." *Hooker´s Journal of Botany and Kew Gardens Miscellany* 7: 193–196.

————. 1908. *Notes of a botanist on the Amazon and Andes*. Ed. Alfred Russel Wallace, 2 vols. London: Macmillan.

Stegmann, Lis, Filipe M. Franc, Raquel L. Carvalho, et al. 2024. "Brazilian public funding for biodiversity research in the Amazon." *Perspectives in Ecology and Conservation* 22, no. 1: 1–7.

Stepan, Nancy Leys. 2001. *Picturing Tropical Nature*. London: Reaktion Books.

Stengers, Isabelle. 2015. *No tempo das catástrofes: resistir à barbárie que se aproxima*. São Paulo: Cosac Naify.

————. 2023. *Uma outra ciência é possível: manifesto por uma desaceleração das ciências*. Rio de Janeiro: Bazar do Tempo.

Stevenson, Brian. 2010. "Samuel Stevens, 1817–1899." http://microscopist.net/StevenssS.html.

Taddei, Renzo, Davide Scarso, and Nuno Castanheira. 2020. "A necessária indomesticabilidade de termos como 'Antropoceno:' desafios epistemológicos e ontologia relacional." *Revista Opinião Filosófica* 11, no. 3: 1–19.

Thurner, Mark, and Jorge Cañizares-Esguerra, ed. 2022. *The Invention of Humboldt: On the Geopolitics of Knowledge*. London: Routledge.

Trischler, Helmuth. 2016. "The Anthropocene: A Challenge for the History of Science, Technology, and the Environment." *NTM* 24, no. 3: 309–335.

Tsing, Anna L. 2019. *Viver nas ruínas: paisagens multiespécie no Antropoceno*. Brasília: IEB Mil Folhas.

Tsing, Anna L., Jennifer Deger, Alder Keleman Saxena, et al., ed. 2021. *Feral Atlas: The More-Than-Human Anthropocene*. Redwood: Stanford University Press.

Wallace, Alfred Russel. 1854. "On the monkeys of the Amazon." *Annals Magazine of Natural History* 14: 451–454.

Wallace, Alfred Russel. 1979. *Viagens pelo Amazonas e Rio Negro*. Belo Horizonte/São Paulo: Itatiaia/Universidade de São Paulo.

Weinstein, Barbara. 1993. *A borracha na Amazônia: expansão e decadência, 1850–1920*. São Paulo: Hucitec/Edusp.

Biodiversity in Mesoamerica from the Mid-Nineteenth Century to 1950
Dialectics between the Capitalinian and Communian Ages

Alberto Betancourt Posada

Biodiversity involves all varieties of life in their different forms, levels, combinations, and scales. It is expressed in the existence of different ecosystems, species, and varieties within a species. Biodiversity can occur in ecology (biogeographical realms, biomes, provinces, ecoregions, ecosystems), the diversity of organisms (order, genus, family, species, population), or genetics (populations, individuals, chromosomes, genes, nucleotides). Human activity affects, reduces, or enhances biological diversity. This was also the case in Mesoamerica between 1800 and 1950, when two models of relation to and use of biodiversity coexisted and rivaled (and in fact remain in competition): the agroecological communitarian model and the nature-reifying capitalist model. The first has been driven by native peoples and peasant communities. Communitarian and subaltern, it has conserved but also increased biodiversity by diversifying ecosystems, species, populations, and genes. The other colonizing hegemonic model has been implemented by the external and internal ruling classes, which have promoted the region's subsumption into the capitalist economic system and enacted a way of producing and relating to nature that has created acute crises on various scales of biodiversity, brought ecosystems to the brink of collapse, reduced biodiversity, and eroded genetic diversity. In short, Mesoamerica experienced the confrontation between an agroecological economy and a pecuniary economy. However, first, the geographic area of study must be defined.

The XXVII International Congress of Americanists, held in 1939, commissioned Paul Kirchoff to delimit the area made up of the southern half of Mexico and almost all of Central America (except for a small eastern strip). The distinguished anthropologist postulated the existence of a cultural superarea that he called Mesoamerica, formed by culturally and linguistically diverse societies of superior cultivators, which shared, among others, the following features: common agricultural practices; the organization into *calpulli*-like clans; the use of a calendar of eighteen months, twenty days, and five additional days; and the existence of numerous domestication and diversification processes that gave rise to numerous varieties of corn, beans, chili peppers, pumpkins, nopals, sapotes, avocados, quintoniles, purslane, and green tomatoes, as well as more than 5,000 edible, medicinal, cosmetic, and ornamental plants. The domestication and diversification processes developed by the native peoples: a) have contributed to the diversification of landscapes (Casas 2016); b) have invented agroforestry systems with low ecological impact (Moreno 2016); c) have generated abundant agrodiversity (Boege 2008); d) have produced real germplasm banks; and e) have created species with enormous plasticity and genetic richness. It is, therefore, possible to affirm that Indigenous peoples have become a true diversifying evolutionary force (Casas 2016). Consequently, both at the beginning of the nineteenth century and today, the diversity of ecosystems, species, populations, and genes in Mesoamerica is the result not only of the confluence of the nearctic and neotropical bioregions, but also of a *long history*, in which the native civilization has been modifying and enriching the environment. In this way, as Moreno rightly points out, native peoples have developed agroforestry systems that have allowed them to co-create biocultural landscapes, such as the florid deserts of Tehuacán, Puebla, the diversified fog forests of the Altos de Chiapas, the agrodiverse rainforests of the Lacandona Forest, or the oak pine forests of the Purépecha Plateau. The same can be said of many of the Central American landscapes among which the following can be highlighted: "Petén-Veracruz moist forests (Guatemala), Isthmian-Atlantic moist forests (Honduras, Nicaragua, Costa Rica), Talamancan montane forests (Costa Rica, Panama), Central American pine-oak forests (Guatemala-Honduras), the Belize Pine Forest (Belize-Guatemala), the Chirripó páramo (Costa Rica), the flooded forests of El Petén (Guatemala), Chocó-Darién moist forests (Panama), [and] the Caribbean mangroves (Honduras, Costa Rica, Nicaragua, Panama)." (McCarthy and Salas 1999: 26)

The Clash between Two Models of Relationship with Nature

Between 1800 and 1950, Mesoamerica experienced tension between two different models of relating to nature and specifically biodiversity. On the one hand, native peoples and peasant communities maintained the pre-Hispanic Mesoamerican civilizational matrix: nature's sacral character; low ecosystem impact agroforestry systems; crop rotation; multiple land use; and agrodiversification processes. At the turn of the nineteenth century, *deep Mesoamerica* (Indigenous people and their culture) remained (as it is today) a true telluric force, in the sense that it changed the face of the earth by contributing to the diversification of landscapes, species, and genes. Native peoples continued to exist, remain active, and struggle to persist, update, re-exist, and flourish.

In counterpoint, the capitalist-neocolonial civilizational model conceived of nature as a commodity and natural resource; extracted strong amounts of raw materials from ecosystems (e.g., railroad sleeper wood); overexploited aquifers; sowed monocultures; contaminated soils, water, and land with agrochemicals; and built large urban systems.

The clash between these two models involved the duel between two possible futures, the agroecological economy vs. the pecuniary economy, or in other words, the Capitalinian Age (currently dominant) vs. the Communian Age. To explain the latter terms, it is useful to refer to John Bellamy Foster and Brett Clark (2018), who propose considering the Anthropocene as a new geological and historical epoch, which begins with what they call the Capitalinian Age, characterized by the exploitation of human beings and nature, a series of environmental compulsions caused by the insatiable reproduction of capital (well described by Rosa Luxemburg), the acceleration of species extinction, and the real risk of the extinction of the human species, for example by a nuclear holocaust. Their text is very suggestive because it posits the chance of moving to a second Anthropocene Age, called the Communian, which would only be possible in the event of a revolution of consciousness and productive practices, giving rise to the common good and care for nature. Taking up this conceptualization of the Anthropocene, this text proposes that, between 1800 and 1950, Mesoamerica was the scene of a collision between two civilizational models: the capitalist-colonial-patriarchal project or a destructive Anthropocene and the agroecological project sustained by the native peoples or a positive Anthropocene. The latter might have been the germ of another possible future and the potential bearer of a Communian Age, as it was less anthropocentric and more harmonious with the diversity of life on Earth, coinciding with what the native peoples consider *buen vivir* (good living) or *lekil kux far* (in Tseltal Maya).

Two Ways to Relate to Biodiversity: Mesoamerican Civilization vs. European Colonialism

Three thousand years before the arrival of the Spanish, Mesoamerica constituted one of the agricultural centers of origin (Vavilov 2012). The region developed important processes for the domestication and diversification of landscapes (intervened with domesticated trees, for example, sapote), ecosystems, plants (e.g., more than 1,100 varieties of maize and many varieties of nopals), animals (such as turkey), and microorganisms (e.g., bacteria for the production of pulque or huitlacoche, a delicacy based on maize fungi). Although they were interrupted and sabotaged during the colonial period, domestication processes remained alive in 1821 with the declaration of independence of New Spain and the Captaincy of Guatemala. Domestication practices involved the production of a robust *corpus* of knowledge about the area's landscapes and ecosystems, the creation of agrodiversity, the establishment of community forms of agricultural production compatible with the preservation of wilderness, and the development of intergenerational plant breeding processes. Mesoamerican farmers and, notably, women practiced long intergenerational seed selection processes, which fostered the artificial emergence of many varieties of the same species (e.g., nopals, tomatoes, magueys, beans, and chilies, among many others). The production of plant varieties encouraged the genetic enrichment of species and varieties and the formation of rich germplasm banks. To this must be added the consolidation of a super-strong sustainable system of production of highly nutritious, tasty, and accessible food (Casas 2016). During the conquest, colonial period, and independence, the European and Mesoamerican elites perceived Mesoamerican landscapes and ecosystems, especially tropical ones, as pristine, but in reality, they were co-creations. Despite the destruction caused by three centuries of colonial rule, the Indigenous population had intervened in and regenerated ecosystems to the extent that "soils, forests, water sources, and wildlife were greater in the 1800s than in 1850" (Goebel McDermott 2019).

At the beginning of the nineteenth century, many native peoples and peasant communities kept alive the civilizational matrix that allowed them to conserve wild biodiversity, generate new domesticated biological diversity, and genetically enrich organisms. At the end of the viceroyalty, the Mexican empire (which fleetingly included all of Central America) had a population of 6 million Indigenous people, dispersed in approximately 4,000 towns, constituting 60 percent of the population, 22 percent mixed race and Afro-descendants, and 18 percent listed as white (Falcón 2015). During the independent period, liberalism's implementation and vision of progress implied the refunctionalization of the Mesoamerican territory in the service of the U.S. American and European markets. The new economy led to drastic changes in the way nature was related to and caused significant changes in the territory. According to Challenger (2009), with the consummation of independence in Mexico and Central America, some colonial-origin trends were accentuated that negatively affected a wide variety of ecosystems. The expansion of the livestock industry, uncontrolled grazing, and feral animals, for example, drastically altered the grasslands. Forests suffered from the expansion of mining and the installation of smelters (*beneficios mineros*). The emergence of incipient proto-industrial processes – especially within the hacienda – increased the demand for mesquite and other wood species that could be used as firewood to feed an increasing number of boilers. Desert areas experienced overhunting of pronghorn and bighorn sheep. The moist forests were ravaged by the continuous looting of precious woods, such as cedar and mahogany, for the construction of beautiful houses and furniture in various countries and cities in Europe (Challenger 2009). The intensive use of these woods in London mansions stands out as a significant example. As noted by Gómez López (2022), between 1840 and 1950, the logging activities began with the clearing of chechen, dyewood (*palo de tinte*), and pochote from the rainforests of La Chontalpa, located in Tabasco, transporting the wood across the Usumacinta, Mezcalapa, and

Grijalva rivers. The logs, poles, or planks were shipped to Europe from Coatzacoalcos, Minatitlan, and the port of Veracruz. The rapid deterioration of the jungles of Tabasco forced the loggers to move to the Lacandon jungle, in Chiapas. On the borders between Tabasco and Chiapas, there were extensive and fragrant mahogany forests. Large farms dedicated to the exploitation of cacao, tobacco, sugarcane, rubber, and woods were soon built in the region, which exploited mainly rubber, gum, mahogany, and cedar (Gómez López 2022), dramatically transfiguring the jungle.

In contrast, while the neocolonial enclave economy spoiled temperate forests, jungles, grasslands, and deserts, many native communities and peoples maintained highly diversified agricultural production practices and even continued important processes of diversifying landscapes, ecosystems, species, and genes.

In addition, biodiversity was enriched when a form of *mestizo* agrodiversity developed, adapting species from Europe. For example, in El Salvador, indigo, sugar, and balsam were sown and adapted to new climatic conditions. The mestizo landscapes increased the biological versatility of the territory. "IIn many towns wheat, corn, rice, beans, chickpeas, potatoes, bananas, cassava, cacao, indigo, avocados, cochineal, among other products were grown. Fruits such as coconuts, mangoes, annonas, watermelons, melons, jocotes, etc. Livestock were raised, and woods such as mahogany, cedar, pine, laurel, oak, oak, cypress, courbaril, balsam were produced, some of which were valued for construction." (Bernal Ramírez 2009:15)

As Goebel Mc Dermott (2019) has rightly pointed out, at the beginning of the nineteenth century, Latin America and, especially Central America, "became the most modern of the new Europes as the predatory economy determined the relationship between society and nature." At the same time, however, native peoples resisted the imposition of this model that damaged ecosystems. For example, many of the crops and animals of the nineteenth century had as their center of origin Mesoamerica, including maguey, corn, epazote, copals, turkey, chapulines, purple snail, or grana cochinilla; others were brought by Europeans and required adaptation and/or diversification processes in Mesoamerica, such as carrot, onion, cauliflower, rice, spinach, garlic, and wheat, to name just a few.

Foundations of Mesoamerican Environmental Thinking

The defense of ecosystems and biodiversity emerged in Mesoamerica even earlier than in the United States (Simonian 1999). Since late colonial times, and during the first years of independent life, several thinkers raised the need to develop their own biological knowledge, apart from Europeans. That is, a national science different from colonial science and based on Indigenous knowledge of nature. Maria Eugenia Constantino (2019) notes the eagerness of scientist José Antonio Alzate to rectify European truths through knowledge rooted in the American context. In his studies on hummingbirds published in the *Gaceta de Literatura de México*, he questioned the purely bookish European knowledge that lacked empirical verification on the ground. He also questioned the lack of direct observation of (American) nature and the lack of awareness of local knowledge. His appreciation of traditional knowledge makes him a precursor to ethnobiology and, specifically, *Mesoamerican ethnobiology*. The Novohispanic naturalist also advocated science based on empirical observation from America. To cite one case, he captured a hummingbird that was brooding, collected its nest and made various observations about its breeding process. According to Constantino, Alzate captured a bird that "was brooding two eggs; he had collected it with everything, including its nest, to weigh, observe, and then write a detailed description of the place where it had nested" (2019: 467). His observation allowed him to detect and analyze the nest materials, incubation time, feeding process, appearance, and development of the chicks and, from that point on, challenge European ornithology.

Another important effort to learn about American biodiversity and revalue local knowledge that would allow for its conservation and rational use was undertaken by the German scientist and naturalist Alexander von Humboldt. His findings, obtained through his valuable botanical expeditions, were recognized as an invaluable contribution to the (American's) self-knowledge of nature and its inhabitants. On December 22, 1854, the Mexican government awarded him the Grand Cross. When Humboldt died on May 6, 1859, Benito Juárez, then a refugee in Veracruz, said that Mexico "owed him special gratitude for the studies he made on the nature and products of its soil" (Ortega and Medina 2015).

Community Agroforestry Systems in Resistance to Intensive Resource Extraction

In Mesoamerica, during the second half of the nineteenth century, approximately seven out of ten people lived in the countryside. The population's robust Indigenous substratum and the persistence of common lands led to the conservation and diversification of ways of life: multiple land use; the promotion of complex agroforestry systems; the planting of crowded family gardens with abundant species; and the continuous exchange between wild and domesticated nature, carried out for example through practices such as beekeeping, mushroom harvesting, and the collection of wild plants. The communal lands maintained what might be called community reserves raided by girls and boys who "cooperated with their families by collecting firewood, zacate, medicinal herbs, stones, fruits" (Falcón 2015: 112).

At the beginning of the second half of the nineteenth century, the boom in haciendas and the liberal economy stripped many communities of their lands, waters, and mountains; it also increased pressure on a wide variety of ecosystems. In Mexico, the reform laws and the promulgation of the Constitution of 1857 imposed the secularization of church property, encouraged an intense process of appropriation of Indigenous territories, and sharply concentrated land ownership. In 1876, at the beginning of the Porfiriato, there were 8,000 farms, which imposed semi-slavery conditions on their workers, drastically changed land use, and implemented a productive model that overexploited numerous ecosystems. In the Yucatán, henequen haciendas, sugar mills, and the construction of infrastructure for export seized the communal lands; the violence sparked the Mayan rebellion of *las Cruces Parlantes* (Reina 2021). In Chihuahua, immense haciendas for livestock were formed. Coffee haciendas flourished in Chiapas (Falcón 2021). The haciendas' consolidation transformed the ways of producing, required new materials, and gave rise to other types of jobs: large cane plants, coal manufacturers, cattle ranches, fishing fleets, and copper industries emerged. Additionally, modern mines and proto-factories (within the hacienda) emerged. For example, in Morelos, *trapiches* (animal-powered mills) were used to obtain sugar and spirit; in the Yucatán, large areas of henequen were sown to satisfy the demand of industrial facilities where fabric and jute ropes were manufactured (Falcón 2021). The haciendas disrupted everything: landscapes, land uses, water consumption, labor relations, and even food.

Railway construction drastically affected the vast majority of Mexican ecosystems; it involved a huge demand for wood for the manufacture of sleepers that led to the clearing of forests and the intensive use of water in blast furnaces where rails and machines were produced. The construction of the Mexican Central Railway, the Mexican National Railway, and the Sonora Railway, to take a few examples, set off the immoderate exploitation of trees, converting vast sites "into bare and barren lands" "with hot and dry climate." This process destroyed the beneficial climate that once prevailed in these regions. Demand for timber unleashed the greed of many companies that paid paltry sums for its extraction, such as the Compañía Industrial de Michoacán S. A. (Pérez 2022).

The second half of the nineteenth century was characterized by the clearing of vacant territories (all those that did not belong to a single individual) and the dispossession of community land. Many Indigenous and peasant families lost land, forests, waters, and mountains. The loss of their lands and commons generated an intense process of mass proletarization, peonage, and the growth of cities. The communities tenaciously defended their lands, natural resources, and biodiversity. Resistance was sometimes legal and peaceful, but on many occasions, in the absence of a response, it turned into violent riots. Many communities managed to conserve at least part of their lands, forests, grasslands, lakes, rivers, bodies of water, and mountains as working commons (Falcón 2021).

Towards the last third of the nineteenth century, authoritarian governments led by dictators rose to power in Mexico and Central America and promoted modernization processes from above to hook the region to the locomotive of progress. In practice, their modernizing vision involved refunctionalizing the territory of the region to subsume it into the capital reproduction cycles of the United States, Britain, Germany, and other core countries of the world economy. In Mexico, Porfirio Díaz (1876–1910) came to power; in Nicaragua, José Santos Zelaya (1892–1909), and in Guatemala, Manuel Estrada Cabrera (1898–1920). In El Salvador, Rafael Saldívar (1876–1885) ruled during the so-called Coffee Republic (1876–1991).

In Mexico, the productive changes of Porfiriato greatly affected ecosystems. As Ezcurra, Montaña, Carrillo, and Delhoume (1988) have rightly pointed out, the region's reorientation toward the U.S. market stimulated the extensive breeding of cattle to satisfy demand, causing a profound alteration of prairie ecosystems. The way livestock were managed caused a serious deterioration of vegetation, soil, and hydraulic dynamics.

On the other hand, forest clearing for coffee planting and timber extraction for railroad sleepers was very destructive for mountain cloud forests (*bosques mesófilos*) and temperate broadleaf-coniferous forests. Landslides and dispossession of land from Yaqui Indians affected diversity on the fertile banks of the Yaqui and Mayo rivers.

The Claim to Traditional Knowledge: Ethno-Botany and Ethno-Agroecology

In Mexico, during Porfiriato, systematic racism was practiced, "theoretically justified" by the positivism of so-called "scientists." However, intellectuals also claimed the sophistication, value, and usefulness of traditional knowledge. Francisco del Paso y Troncoso, a Mexican humanist, made a thesis entitled *Historia de la Medicina*, in which he enthusiastically extolled the knowledge of "the medical matter in the ancient Mexicans," emphasizing the achievements of the Indian peoples "whose intelligence is of the greatest interest." Moreover, another work of his, *La Botánica entre los nahuas*, "addresses the botanical gardens of the Nahuas, their Synonymy, Linguistics, Iconography, Nomenclature, and Taxonomy. In his text, he put into play his talents as a keen Nahuatl scholar, documentarian, and librarian" (Museo Nacional de Arqueología, Historia y Etnografía 1992: 308).

Francisco del Paso y Troncoso's passion for knowledge of Nahuatl earned him an invitation from naturalist Alfonso Herrera to teach a course on this subject at the *Escuela Nacional Preparatoria*. On August 21, 1887, he made a speech before the statue of Cuauhtémoc. When the president removed the veil, he began his speech in Nahuatl describing the rise, reign, and fall of the last Aztec emperor and said:

> At the very high level reached by the knowledge acquired by the civilized peoples of ancient Anahuac in the scientific branches that depend on observation, espe-

cially nature. Thus, it is known to all that Natural History and Astronomy were cultivated by the Indians with the greatest care. Netzahualcoyotl, the Acolhua king, had reportedly drawn in his palaces all the rare plants and animals that existed in his domains. (Museo Nacional de Arqueología, Historia y Etnografía 1992: 357)

Francisco del Paso's research vindicated the existence of a proper Nahuatl taxonomy, nomenclature, and pharmaceuticals. Nahuatl medicine, he argued, was based on the empirical knowledge produced in the botanical gardens.

Agrarian Capitalism and the Americanization of the Central American Landscape

In 1899, the United Fruit Company installed plantations in Costa Rica, Nicaragua, and Panama, causing drastic changes in landscape and biodiversity. In the Central American countries where the United Fruit Company penetrated, the forests were cleared, the lands were drained, canals were introduced, and banana monocultures were planted. Historian John Soluri (2005) presents photographs from the fruit company archive showing workers swarming the Costa Rican tropical forest. In that country, the construction of railway tracks went hand in hand with the banana plantation. The compulsive planting of this fruit had numerous consequences in Panama, to cite another case: it turned extensive forests into large monocultures and practiced an intensive use of chemicals in crops; the ecological imbalance led to a greater presence of malaria, an extensive outbreak of the pathogen black sigatoka and the proliferation of terciopelo snakes in crops (Soluri 2005). In Honduras, concessions to railway companies to remove bananas were accompanied by permits for massive timber harvesting, water use, and mineral extraction.

Mesoamerican peoples had cultivated forests rich in biodiversity and had modified them (along with productive practices) to support a larger population in a fragile ecological balance, managing to maintain forests abundant in precious wood trees. In contrast, the global demand for timber and colonization underwent an abrupt biophysical rearrangement that intensively extracted precious timber, for example, on the banks of Honduras (Goebel McDermott 2019).

In 1901, under Manuel Estrada Cabrera, the United Fruit Company planted large areas of coffee in Guatemala. Beginning in 1904, Minor Keith signed a contract with the dictator to build the first railroad line between Antigua Guatemala and Puerto Barrios, creating conditions for the establishment of the banana and coffee plantations that would spread throughout the territory. Rainforests were dismantled and transformed into banana plantation plains. Keith boasted of "turning virgin land into productive soil." Traditional Mayan agriculture, which had maintained biodiversity so effectively that the forest seemed pristine, was replaced by "scientific methods of agriculture." Monoculture replaced the Mayan *milpa* (polyculture). Crop rotation was displaced by the exploitation of soils until they were exhausted. Gradually an agrarian capitalism was consolidated based on an export coffee economy driven by the dictatorship of Justo Rufino Barrios: "In 1905, for example, Guatemala exported 36.6 million kilos of coffee, and before World War I, the figure rose to 50.2 million kilos" (Torres 1984: 141). During that period, a core of German landowners (*latifundistas*) linked to the trading and banking houses of Hamburg and Bremen consolidated in the Verapaces region: "For example, in 1913, the 170 German-owned model farms produced 39 percent of the exportable crop (out of a total of 40.5 million kilos)" (Torres 1984: 142). In the midst of this ocean of destruction, some islets of conservation remained. In 1870, the Astilleros Municipales were protected as natural forests (Mc Carthy and Salas 1999).

In Nicaragua, between 1870 and 1909, an agro-export model was introduced that drastically altered the relations between society and nature. "The land's hunger for coffee" drastically altered the relations hacienda owners, ranchers, coffee growers, and merchants had with Indigenous peoples and small farming communities. Many Indigenous people became day laborers in semi-slavery. The supply of coffee for American tables caused a continuous abandonment of food production for the local population and generated food vulnerability. The outward orientation of Latin American economic policies towards the world markets – the *desarrollo hacia afuera* – destroyed both *ejidos* and privatized communal land, introducing intensive cultivation of rubber, cacao, vanilla, and sugarcane (Sola 2007).

In Panama, the construction of the canal involved, among other things, the creation of the reservoir Lake Gatun between 1907 and 1913, transforming numerous summits into islands and causing a significant loss of biodiversity. According to Bennet (1998), recent research showed that when Barro Colorado was a summit it housed 108 mammal species, but when it became an island, only forty-five species survived. The contraction of space decreased the predators of peccaries and pizotes (also called white-nosed coati) causing overpopulation; as a result, the nests of numerous species suffered furious attacks.

Environmental Apocalypse, Mexican Revolution, and Conservation Policies

Between 1910 and 1950, various changes were made in the productive structure of Latin America, leading to a developmental model that increased pressure on biodiversity (Infante-Amate, Urrego and Tello 2020), the emergence of various socioenvironmental conflicts, and the birth of important public policies of biodiversity conservation. The damage to biodiversity had different causes. Increased net exports of materials, biomass, fossil fuels, metals, and non-metallic minerals destroyed large areas of forest and vegetation. Extraction of oil, minerals, and timber led to territories of predation, social conflicts, and dysfunctional institutions. Monocultures depleted soils and contaminated water sources.

In 1910, the Mexican Revolution broke out as a result of numerous political, economic, and socio-environmental conflicts. One of the most active sectors during this important social movement was Indigenous peoples. For example, the movement headed by Emiliano Zapata took up arms to demand the restitution of lands, waters, mountains, and forests that were common property. Many of the peoples who joined the rebellion against the dictatorship of Porfirio Díaz were imbued with a strong communist spirit: "when the Diaz government fell, not a few towns still had at least some of their lands and waters, especially forests, mountains, lakes and other assets that should continue to be exploited by all of them" (Falcón 2021: 117–118).

The vindication of the commons, Indigenous values, knowledge, and practices was also expressed in the field of science. Maximino Martínez pioneered ethnobotany, agroecology, and biodiversity conservation based on the defense of Indigenous knowledge. According to researchers María del Consuelo Cuevas Cardona and Carmen López Ramírez, Maximino Martínez, who started his career as a schoolteacher, organized a school garden on the street La Piedad, exemplary in many ways, by forming crews of youth agriculturists who worked the land, while learning agriculture and practical botany: "Half of the harvest would be distributed among the children to take home and the other half would be sold to buy tools and supplies for school" (Cuevas Cardona and López Ramírez 2009: 981) The example was found in many surrounding schools. Later, Martínez participated with Alfonso Herrera in the Biological Studies Division. From there, Martínez promoted biodiversity conservation and participated in an expedition to various islands and bays of Baja California that resulted in a presidential decree of Álvaro Obregón to protect Guadalupe Island, located west of the peninsula. The measure banned the hunting of elephant seals, saving them from aggression by hunters and allowing them to spread across the peninsula. In addition, Maximino Martínez participated actively in the Botanical Garden and was in charge of creating the National Herbarium and receiving the collections from the aforementioned institutions. Among them, for example, the collection from the National Medical Institute is noteworthy. Founded in 1885, it had gathered about 15,000 specimens. In 1933, he published *Las plantas medicinales de México*, a text that collected much of the research on medicinal plants used by different Indigenous communities in Mexico (Cuevas Cardona and López Ramírez 2009: 981). Later, now in the Ministry of Development, Maximinio Martínez explains his argument regarding the importance of Mexican biogeography and its multiple uses: "To have data at any time on whether this or that plant exists in Mexico, in what places, its growing area, how much it is harvested or can be exploited, the possibility of being grown in a certain region, etc." (cited in Cuevas Cardona and López Ramírez 2009: 990)

In 1934, when General Lázaro Cárdenas' regime began, he carried out major agrarian reform, endowed land to numerous ejidos, and allowed for the emergence of a Mexican model of biodiversity conservation. His government was prodigious in experimenting with various forms of restitution of common property and in creating public property, for example through the creation of national parks. It also formulated conservation policies that simultaneously proposed biodiversity conservation, community empowerment, and the economic development of forests. Similarly, new models of agricultural, agro-industrial, and agroforestry production were introduced. According to Emily Wakild (2011), in her book *Revolutionary Parks*, during the government of General Lázaro Cárdenas a highly original model of public natural parks was formulated in Mexico, aimed at preserving natural cultural heritage and biodiversity, as well as intersecting economic production with social justice. While preservation was among its goals, the government achieved this by promoting the enjoyment of nature among the Mexican population. Parks became an environmental education space. *Revolutionary Parks* analyses four cases of iconic national parks: Lagunas de Zempoala (1936), aimed at tourism, social welfare, and environmental restoration; Izta-Popo (1937), created to stop the clearing of the oyamel fir forest, predated by the San Rafael paper industry; La Malinche, focused on preserving the forest to maintain the watershed and avoid intercommunal conflicts over resources; and finally, El Tepozteco, emblematic of the relationship between nature and culture, a space where the archaeological zone and the forest become observatories that resist, challenge, and offer alternatives to modernity (Tortolero 2014).

Conservation Efforts in Central America

Central America is home to around fifty-one native peoples. Its presence in the area dates back more than 11,000 years, during which these peoples have changed the plant composition of their forests that still had a mixture of wild vegetation and introduced or modified species at the beginning of the century. The Indigenous presence has changed forests through the practice of tilling, felling, and burning; the introduction of species; and the construction of canals. Nevertheless, it has also preserved them through the construction of terraces that conserve soils, the multiple use of their territories, and the practice of orchards and family gardens, which establish a coexistence between wild and domesticated. In El Darien, Panama, to cite one case, there are significant remnants of tropical forests that have enjoyed secondary plant succession for the past 350 years. Many traditional agricultural landscapes contributed to biodiversity conservation, peasant income, preservation of forested areas, preservation of riparian areas, and maintenance of floristic complexity (Harvey 2008). In the second half of the nineteenth century, many native peoples of Central America continued to maintain the Mesoamerican tradition of respectfully relating to nature. For example, the Q'echi' of Guatemala, in the Alta Verapaz region, continued to produce valuable ethnobotanical and ethnozoological knowledge based on careful observation and interaction with the environment. Thanks to this sophisticated ecological knowledge, they contributed to conserving the biodiversity of the ecoregion (Velázquez 2021). The reservation of Bosawas, an Indigenous territory, is notable in Nicaragua. There were also important conservation efforts from the Embera-Wounaan and the Ngäbe, in Lake Chiriquí and Bahia Almirante, Panama.

In counterpoint, between 1899 and 1930, the United Fruit Company became the largest agricultural enterprise in the world and completely transformed the landscape of Central America and the Caribbean. It appropriated 525,000 acres of tropical landscape, altering them drastically and profoundly. In addition, it leased another 3 million acres chiefly to produce bananas. This land use change turned huge areas of tropical rainforests into "savannas" of large-scale mono-plantations, americanized the landscape, and reinforced the expansion of the "progress" frontier by clearing of forests that had remained in excellent conservation condition. The agroexport, aristocratic agriculture (so called because of its concentration in a few hands) wiped out "virgin lands" (although as already mentioned these were mostly landscapes co-created by communities); it changed weather patterns, topography, and soil composition. This activity brought many ecosystems to a head on the verge of no longer being able to reproduce. Starting in 1910, the company, in full control of production, started large-scale plantations and promoted the construction of export infrastructure. The discourse legitimizing its activities led to the denigration of the agricultural practices and knowledge of the local inhabitants, a representation of the territory as waste (*baldío*), the use of intensive land plowing with machinery, the deployment of mass fencing, and the construction of roads. According to Justine Holme (2013), U.S. Americans conceived of the conquest of Central America in a spirit similar to the conquest of the West:

> Seeking the successful creation of neo-American environments, United Fruit 'attacked' the jungle landscapes while simultaneously developing widespread sanitation programs to eliminate the prevalence of tropical disease. Carving their way into the jungle, United Fruit labourers under the guidance ofCompany engineers removed dense underbrush, felled forests, cleared pathways for rail lines, and excavated intricate drainage systems designed to empty swamps and lower water levels. Acre after acre fell under the relentless blades of Company workers who were charged with eliminating environmental obstacles and paving the way for a new Americanized version of Nature. (Holmes 2013: 13–14)

The creation of this New American landscape, in its effort to dry swamps and clear the jungle, unintentionally created conditions for the reproduction of the *Aegis Agypti* and *Anopheles* mosquitoes, which spread yellow fever and malaria.

In El Salvador, at the turn of the century, the area of coffee production expanded markedly and twelve families took over almost all production. In Honduras, the Tela Rail Company, a subsidiary of United Fruit, owned 400 acres for banana cultivation. Almost the entire north coast was occupied by three companies that drastically transformed the landscape (Arenas 1990). In Costa Rica, coffee production fell by 50 percent between 1926 and 1929 (Arenas 1990).

During the 1940s, in Honduras and Costa Rica, where large fruit companies owned 20 percent of the agricultural area, some coffee and banana crops were abandoned in order to introduce the production of cacao, abaca, and oil palms. Costa Rica and Guatemala also expanded the area under sugar and cotton cultivation (Arenas 1990).

Despite the damage caused, there were also conservation efforts in some regions of Central America that resulted in achievements; for example, in 1928, the Half-Moon Cay area of Belize was declared Crown Reserve. As Domínguez Molina (2021) rightly points out, in 1952, Faustino Miranda published his book *La vegetación de Chiapas* about the flora of that region, in which he gives an account of the antiquity, abundance, and sophistication of the botanical knowledge of the native Mesoamerican peoples of Central America. At a later time, the Nicaraguan Ministry of the Environment and Natural Resources published Alfredo Grijalva Pineda's book, *Flora útil etnobotánica de Nicaragua* (2006), which reflects the importance of the botanical, pharmaceutical, and agronomic knowledge of the peoples of the region in the first half of the twentieth century.

Conclusions

During the period 1800–1950, two very different ways of relating to nature and ecosystems coexisted. On the one hand, native peoples and peasant communities continued landscape domestication and diversification processes; the domestication of plant and animal species; the diversification of plant species; multiple land use; the promotion of agrodiversity; the formation of germplasm banks; and the protection of mountains, rivers, and soils. In contrast, the new colonization models, now liberal, promoted the extraction of raw materials; the overexploitation of resources; and the implementation of an agricultural model based on the continuous expansion of the agrarian frontier, founded on large landholdings and the use of fertilizers and pesticides. In addition, it promoted the growth of monocultures; water pressure; an increasing extraction of large volumes of wood; urban growth; and the overdomestication of plants and animals. At the beginning of the second half of the twentieth century, the Capitalinian Age, as a colonizing project, was a hegemonic force in the Mesoamerican territory. Its development-colonization model perpetuated the dispossession of peasant communities, promoted an agroexport model, and fostered excessive urban growth and the production of difficult-to-degrade materials. This "civilizing" project resulted in the loss of large layers of vegetation, loss of biodiversity, erosion of genetic wealth and critical degradation of numerous ecosystems.

However, in Mesoamerica, native peoples continued to practice forms of relationship with nature based on super-strong sustainability. There is still an alive and vibrant deep Mesoamerica, practicing sustainable ways of production, resacralizing land, preserving wild diversity, increasing agrodiversity, and diversifying landscapes. As Arturo Escobar (1993) has rightly pointed out, formulating a "theory from below" entails not only recognizing the existence of capitalism, but also detecting and mapping the forces that oppose it. This cartographic act implies the challenge of contrasting the capitalist vision that expands across the globe, finding no other economic way to resist it, with a new imaginary that includes an academic dimension – an epistemology of the South – that shows the persistence of other forms of economic organization alternative to capitalism and that are capable of producing worlds of life or, if you will, possible beautiful worlds.

The Mesoamerican peoples developed and kept alive an ecological economy that Joan Martínez Alier (2004) calls authentic *oikonomia*, much more sustainable than the pecuniary economy. If today there is potentially the possibility of building a higher civilization that defends life and not profit, it is thanks to the social resistance that kept alive an alternative model. This impulse for life constitutes an important contribution of Mesoamerica in the struggle to transform the Capitalinian Age, the negative age of the Anthropocene, into a positive age – the Communian, to use the terms of Foster and Clark (2018). It cannot be known what trend will prevail globally. Sometimes market forces and their self-destructive compulsions seem unstoppable, but in the face of a situation of danger (environmental and civilizational), historical optimism, in the sense of assuming the responsibility of imagining a better and viable world, is a responsibility and a way to practice the principle of hope posited by Ernst Bloch (2006): to take note in the present the possibilities for a better future.

Translated by Eric Rummelhoff and revised by Omar Sierra Cháves.

References

Arenas, Clara. 1990. *Centroamérica en el vértice de la historia.* Guatemala City: CLACSO.

Bennet, Andrew F. 1998. *Enlazando el paisaje. El papel de los corredores y la conectividad en la conservación de la vida silvestre.* San José de Costa Rica: Unión Mundial para la Naturaleza.

Bernal Ramírez, Luis Guillermo. 2009. *Historia de El Salvador.* San Salvador: Ministerio de Educación.

Bloch, Ernst. 2006. *El Principio Esperanza.* Madrid: Editorial Trotta.

Boege, Eckart. 2008. *El patrimonio biocultural de los pueblos indígenas de México. Hacia la conservación in situ de la biodiversidad y agrodiversidad en los territorios indígenas.* Mexico City: INAH.

Casas, Alejandro, Juan Torres-Guevara, and Fabiola Parra, ed. 2016. *Domesticación en el continente americano.* Vol. 1, *Manejo de biodiversidad y evolución dirigida por las culturas del Nuevo Mundo.* Mexico City: UNAM.

Challenger, Antony, and Rodolfo Dirzo. 2009. "Factores de cambio y estado de la biodiversidad." In *Capital natural de México.* Vol. 2, *Estado de conservación y tendencias de cambio*, ed. Rodolfo Dirzo, Renée González, and Ignacio J. March, 37–73. Mexico City: Conabio.

Constantino, María Eugenia. 2019. "José Antonio Alzate, instrumentos animales y conocimiento fiable en Nueva España, siglo XVIII." *História, Ciências, Saúde-manguinhos* 26, no. 2: 465–481.

Cuevas Cardona, Consuelo, and Carmen López Ramírez. 2009. "Cambios de gobierno en la vida de un botánico mexicano: Maximino Martínez (1888–1964)." *Historia Mexicana* 58, no. 3: 973–1004.

Domínguez Molina, Leydi, Carlos Uriel del Carpio-Penagos, Eduardo Estanislao Espinoza-Medinilla, et al. 2021. "Algunas especies de plantas y animales de la Depresión Central y Costa del Pacífico de Chiapas y Centroamérica, y su relación con sociedades de filiación otomangue." *Revista Etnobiología* 20, no. 2.

Escobar, Arturo. 1993. "El lugar de la naturaleza y la naturaleza del lugar: ¿globalización o postdesarrollo?." In *La colonialidad del saber: eurocentrismo y ciencias sociales*, ed. Edgardo Lander, 113–143. Buenos Aires: CLACSO.

Falcón, Romana. 2021. "En el fondo de la pirámide social." In *Historia del pueblo mexicano*, ed. Coordinación de Memoria Histórica y Cultural de México, 111–120. Mexico City: INHERM.

Foster, John Bellamy, and Brett Clark. 2018. "El Capitaliano la Primera Edad Geológica del Antropoceno." *Alianza Global Jus Semper.* https://jussemper.org/Inicio/Rec ursos/Info.%20econ/Resources/JBellamyFoster+BClark-ElCapitaliniano.pdf.

Goebel Mc Dermott, Anthony. 2019. "Exportando bosques, importando insustentabilidad. Comercio forestal y transformaciones socio-ambientales en Centroamérica: una aproximación desde la historia global, siglos XVIII al XX." *Diálogos* 23, no. 1: 5–45.

Gómez López, Marco Antonio. 2022. "Entre el comercio maderero y la exportación, una reconstrucción histórica de la compañía Bulnes Hermanos." Master's thesis, Universidad de Ciencias y Artes de Chiapas.

Grijalva Pineda, Alfredo. 2006. *Flora útil etnobotánica de Nicaragua*. Managua: MARENA.

Harvey, Celia A., Oliver Komar, Robin Chazdon, et al. 2008. "Integration Agricultural Landscapes with Biodiversity Conservation in the Mesoamerica Hotspots." *Conservation Biology* 22, no. 1: 8–15.

Holme, Justine. 2013. "Creating Wealth Out of the World's Waste Spots': The United Fruit Company and the Story of Frontiers, Environment, and American Legacy 1899–1930." Master's thesis, Montreal University.

Infante-Amate, Juan, Alexander Urrego Mesa, and Enri Tello Aragay. 2020. "Las venas abiertas de América Latina. En la era del antropoceno. Un estudio biofísico del comercio exterior (1900–2016)." *Diálogos. Revista electrónica de Historia* 21, no. 2: 177–214.

Martínez Alier, Joan. 2004. *El ecologismo de los pobres. Conflictos ambientales y lenguajes de valoración*. Barcelona: Icaria Antrazyt/Flacso.

McCarthy, Ronald, and Alberto. Salas 1999. Las áreas protegidas de Centroamérica. *Revista De Ciencias Ambientales* 16, no. 1: 26–39.

Montaña, Carlos, Exequiel Ezcurra, Antonio Carrillo, and Jean-Pierre Delhoume. 1988. "The decomposition of litter in grasslands of northern Mexico: a comparison between arid and non-arid environments." *Journal of Arid Environments* 14: 55–60.

Moreno, Isabel, Alejandro Casas, Víctor M. Toledo, et al. 2016. *Etnoagroforestería en México*. Mexico City: UNAM.

Museo Nacional de Arqueología, Historia y Etnografía. 1992. *Anales del Museo Nacional de Arqueología, Historia y Etnografía. A la memoria de Don Francisco del Paso y Troncoso. Su vida y sus obras. Núm. 18 Tomo I (1922) Cuarta Época (1922–1933)*. Mexico City: Instituto Nacional de Antropología e Historia.

Ortega y Medina, Juan A. 2015. *Humboldt desde México*. Mexico City: UNAM.

Pérez Talavera, Víctor Manuel. 2022. "Bosques, deforestación, medio ambiente y factores sociales durante el Porfiriato en México." *Historia y Espacio* 18, no. 58.

Pineda-Posadas, Emily, Usi´j Bá-Velásquez, Julio Morales-Álvarez, et al. 2021. "Uso y conocimiento de la fauna silvestre de la comunidad q'echi' de Santa Lucía Lachúa, Alta Verapaz, Guatemala: un abordaje etnozoológico." *Ciencias sociales y humanidades* 8, no. 1: 7–24.

Reina, Leticia. 2021. "Guerra de Castas y rebeliones campesinas en el siglo XIX." In *Historia del pueblo mexicano*, ed. Coordinación de Memoria Histórica y Cultural de México, 121–129. Mexico City: INHERM.

Simonian, Lane. 1999. *La defensa de la tierra del jaguar. Una historia de la conservación en México*. Mexico City: Instituto Nacional de Ecología-SEMARNAP.

Soluri, John. 2005. *Banana cultures. Agriculture, Consumption and Environmental Change in Honduras and the United States*. Austin: University of Texas Press.

Torres Rivas, Edelberto. 1984. "Guatemala, medio siglo de historia política." In *América Latina: Historia de medio siglo*. Vol. 2, *México Centroamérica y el Caribe*, ed. Pablo Gonzales Casanova, 139–173. Mexico City: Siglo XXI.

Tortolero Villaseñor, Alejandro. 2014. "Review: Emily Wakild, Revolutionary Parks. 2011. Conservation, Social Justice, and Mexico's National Parks, 1910- 1940, USA: The University of Arizona Press." *Secuencia* 89: 227–231.

Vavilov, Nikolai. 2012. "México y Centroamérica como centro básico de origen de las plantas cultivadas del Nuevo Mundo." *Etnobiología* 10, no. 4: 28–43.

Wakild, Emily. 2011. *Parques revolucionarios. Conservación, justicia social y parques nacionales en México: 1910–1940*. Mexico City: La Cigarra.

Biodiversity in the Caribbean from the Mid-Nineteenth Century to 1950

Reinaldo Funes Monzote

The Caribbean region is generally considered one of the most bioculturally diverse regions on the planet, regardless of its geographic or geopolitical delimitation. Here the chapter limits itself to the most conventional conceptualization: the islands in the sea that gives it its name and the Bahamas (the Antilles Arch), together with continental territories marked by the legacy of African slavery, such as Belize and the Guyanas (in the Anglo-Saxon denomination West Indies). The inclusion of the Hispanic nations of the continent around the basin usually has less consensus, although there are many common socioeconomic and cultural patterns that gave rise to the so-called Greater Caribbean (Gaztambide-Géygel 2014: 23–51).

The growing geopolitical influence of the United States, and its conversion into the hegemonic power first in the Americas and then globally marks this long period in the history of the region. It is no coincidence that the Caribbean Sea, together with the Gulf of Mexico, formed part of what was then known as the "American Mediterranean," a sort of Mare Nostrum of the northern republic as a key piece of the Monroe Doctrine. The declaration of war on Spain to intervene in the war of independence being waged in Cuba and the military occupation of the island, along with Puerto Rico, the Philippines, and Guam in 1898, can be considered the formal birth of U.S. imperialism. One of its greatest symbols was the completion of the Panama Canal in 1914, a majestic work of modern engineering seen as the materialization of the "conquest of the tropics" by and for the "white man." This encounter with the Circum-Caribbean region, as Megan Raby (2017) argues, created the basis for the development of tropical biology through the creation of experimental stations that proved instrumental in the emergence of the modern science of ecology and biodiversity.

These pages will address three dimensions of the concept of biodiversity for the Caribbean region. On the one hand, the process of the destruction of flora and fauna as a consequence of the expansion of agriculture and livestock through plantations for export or socioeconomic activities for local consumption; on the other hand, the introduction of plant and animal species that contributed to configure new domesticated landscapes; and finally, the efforts from science and government actions to contain the accelerated loss of local biological resources or to diversify them in order to offer viable alternatives through the creation of scientific institutions or conservationist provisions.

Factors such as the location in the tropical belt, the impact of climatic events such as hurricanes or droughts, or the socioeconomic processes associated with the plantation system are key to any study of the region's biocultural diversity. But reference to them in other chapters and the existing literature free us to deal with their implications for issues related to biodiversity (Schwartz 2015; Morgan et al. 2022: 187–252). At the same time, it should be kept in mind that the insular Caribbean was early on one of the territories most transformed by European colonialism. The massive modification of the landscapes found in the Lesser Antilles – occupied since the beginning of the seventeenth century by England, France, Holland, Denmark, and Sweden – preceded one of the great milestones of what is now called the Anthropocene era, the Industrial Revolution with its epicenter in England. In this sense, the sugar revolution that began in 1640 in the small island territories of the eastern Caribbean, which Spain had discarded as "useless," was decisive (Higman 2000).

The first plantations in the Caribbean appeared in Hispaniola and in other Hispanic islands as early as 1518 to process sugar cane. But that initial growth was limited in scale in the midst of larger territories. This was not the case with the new plantation model promoted by other European metropolises in the Lesser Antilles, which, partly because of the limited space, soon became the dominant element of an economy centered on agricultural products of high commercial value. The starting point for this sugar revolution was the English Barbados (440 km²) and the then French St. Kitts (176 km²), whose most accessible forested areas of were replaced by sugarcane plantations in less than two decades.

With the advance of sugar, the socio-environmental changes that would transform the ecology and society of the "sugar and slave islands," as Alexander von Humboldt (2011[1826]) called them, accelerated. The plantations can be considered to have contributed to the cultural heterogeneity of the region due to the complex amalgamation of European colonizers, enslaved Africans, and later arrivals of hired laborers, together with the few remnants of pre-Columbian populations. Similarly, the impact on biodiversity can be assessed both in terms of the degradation of the ecosystems found in 1492 and the new biota introduced consciously or by chance after that date. European colonization and the plantation economy favored the arrival of new plants and domestic animals that provided traction and food, while encouraging the introduction of grasses and forages that were more nutritious than the local grasses. In a certain way, more diverse agroecosystems emerged with the contribution of species brought from the Old World and especially from other tropical territories of Asia, Africa, and the so-called American neotropics, although at the same time these introductions were key to the simplification of local ecologies or the disappearance of more sustainable native cultivation techniques.

This stage that it is our task to analyze is part of what Stuart McCook (2011) has called the Neo-Columbian Exchange, with the boom in the transfer of plants, animals and pathogens from Asia, the Pacific, and Africa to the European colonies in the New World from the eighteenth century until 1930. With respect to the first introductions that followed the conquest of America, several innovations contributed to the acceleration of these transoceanic exchanges. These include deliberate efforts to boost the agro-export economy in the Greater Caribbean, the existence of international public and private scientific networks such as botanical gardens and agricultural stations, new transportation technologies of the steam age, and direct exchanges with other tropical regions in an increasingly intertwined world.

However, the extension of agriculture in general, and plantation agriculture in particular, has at the same time posed a serious threat to native plant and animal biodiversity. Before 1800, the Lesser Antilles already showed evidence of extinction of several local terrestrial and aquatic species, along with the rapid proliferation of invasive plant or animal species (Watts 1986). The same pattern of socio-environmental change was repeated in other Caribbean islands between the late seventeenth and eighteenth centuries. From the initial nucleus in the Lesser Antilles, the epicenter of the plantations moved to the English island of Jamaica and the western part of Hispaniola where the French established the colony of Saint-Domingue or Haiti. Both replicated the same processes of massive deforestation in flat areas near the coasts and inland valleys for the production of sugar cane, cotton, coffee and indigo in the mountainous areas. At the end of the eighteenth century, Haiti was considered the richest colony in the world by European standards, being the largest exporter of sugar, coffee and other tropical crops.

Logging

The sugar revolution and the plantation system were made possible by the massive importation of slaves from Africa or hired laborers from other regions (India, Java, China, Spain), together with the local resources of soil and biomass. The traditional farming system relied heavily on slash-and-burn forest to obtain high agricultural yields with the organic matter stored in the soil after land clearing. However, the rapid deforestation of the smaller island territories led early on to the emergence of innovations aimed at restoring land fertility, through the use of manure; or saving fuel, using sugarcane bagasse.

Although much of the forest wealth of the insular Caribbean was destroyed to make way for plantations, it was also an important resource for local construction, energy supply, and the trade in timber and other by-products. Until the end of the eighteenth century, the region's precious woods, particularly mahogany and cedar, were sent to European courts or allowed the construction of strategically important activities such as shipbuilding in Havana (Funes 2008: 39–82). Among the Caribbean forest by-products most in demand during the colonial period were the dyes extracted from trees such as the campeche wood (*Haematoxilum campechanun*) or the smoke tree (*Chlorophora tinctoria*).

Mahogany trees, whose timber would be considered the most valuable in the tropics, were subject to intense selective logging during the eighteenth and nineteenth centuries (Anderson 2012). The Caribbean region had an abundance of two of its three species in the Americas: Jamaican, Spanish, Cuban, or Dominican mahogany (*Swietenia mahogani*) and Honduran mahogany (*Swietenia macrophylla*). The popular names express the main sources of origin of the precious wood obtained from mahogany for international trade, although the distribution was wider and included other islands of the Greater Antilles, South Florida, and the Central American coast from Mexico to the Amazon basin.

The best example of the high value achieved by mahogany was the establishment of Belize as a British colony. The first settlements of British subjects from the Antilles date back to the seventeenth century after receiving concessions from the Spanish crown to exploit the campeche wood, which produced a dye in great demand in the wool industry. These territories were also abundant in Spanish cedar (*Cederela odorata*) and Honduran mahogany, which were another source of wealth, used for shipbuilding and cabinetmaking. Since the end of the eighteenth century, mahogany became the main and almost the only source of income for Belize, gaining formal status as a British colony in 1840 under the name British Honduras. In the 1920s an expert on tropical forests and timber wrote about their economics: "The people in general think in terms of timber, and timber is now almost synonymous with mahogany. From the time of its earliest settlement the only important source of revenue has been the forest" (Record 1926: 562).

Cuba and Hispaniola also participated in the mahogany trade, replacing the supply from other islands, such as Jamaica and the Bahamas, the main sources during the eighteenth century (Morgan 2022: 97). After Central America's independence, the Republic of Honduras' interest in promoting the mahogany trade, which boomed between the 1850s and 1860s, led to frequent conflicts with British Honduras over control of the forests. With the extension of supplies from Central and South America, it was in the last quarter of the nineteenth century that the American mahogany trade reached its peak (Revels 2002).

Hispaniola saw a major boost to the timber industry after Haiti's independence in 1804 and in the context of the Haitian occupation of the entire island between 1822 and 1844. Along with coffee, forestry products became a main export item for the Haitian side of the island. Until the middle of the century, there was an expansive commercial phase in campeche wood, as well as mahogany and *guayacán* (*Lignum vitae*) (*Guaiacum officinale/Guaiacumsanctum*), which were part of the payment of the debt imposed by France on the new Republic for its emancipation. On the Dominican side, timber extraction continued to increase after Haitian independence. Its mahogany was one of the most prized in the market and large quantities of campeche and fustete wood were also extracted, as well as guayacán. When several of these species became scarce at the beginning of the twentieth century, the focus of logging interests turned to the extensive pine forests of the central mountain range (Moya Pons 2010).

There was also a timber boom in Cuba during the nineteenth century in areas where cattle ranching still prevailed or, in a more ephemeral manner, in those areas occupied by sugar plantations. The island was rich in mahogany, cedar, guayacán, and fustete trees, which were in great demand in the United States and Europe. However, sugar represented the main source of wealth, and most of the forest cover was eliminated to make way for the sugar mills, which were large consumers of firewood (Funes 2008: 127–178). Puerto Rico had a similar process in its coastal plains, and due to its smaller territorial extension and high population density, the percentage of deforested area was higher at the end of the nineteenth century (Domínguez 2000).

Forest exploitation was generally carried out through selective logging. However, after the larger specimens were exhausted, the remaining smaller tress were cut down as well. This was helped by new technologies applied to this industry, such as steam engines in sawmills and tractors, which made it possible to penetrate to more distant places. After the advent of the airplane, aerial observation was introduced to detect the presence of mahogany or other species of high commercial value. Later, the chainsaw made it possible to intensify the rate of logging even more, although there was not much left of the abundant forest wealth found by the Europeans in the insular Caribbean.

A book by U.S. forester Tom Gill (1931) sponsored by the Tropical Plant Research Foundation on the tropical forests of the Caribbean placed Trinidad, Haiti, Puerto Rico and most of Cuba in the group of countries that had lost almost all of their valuable forest cover of the past. The continental areas bordering the Caribbean, on the other hand, belonged to the group that still possessed enormous virgin forests and were emerging as a great source of timber for future exports. Deforestation in the first group included the high demand for firewood and charcoal for domestic and industrial uses.

The destruction of the forests of the insular Caribbean in the nineteenth century and first half of the twentieth century did not go unnoticed by scientists and authorities. As timber stocks dwindled and agriculture encroached on the forest frontier, concern grew about its economic and ecological future. The main objective was to introduce a modern forestry administration, as occurred with the implementation of the *Ordenanzas de Montes para Cuba y Puerto Rico* by Spain in 1876. Similarly, in 1922, a Forest Department was created in Belize to establish scientific management of the Crown's forests in the British colony.

It should be added that it is not only the exploitation of precious wood or hard-wood forests, but also of other types of forest formations present in the Antilles and the continental Caribbean. As more accessible forest resources disappeared, the use of ecosystems initially considered marginal expanded. This was the case with the mangrove areas that began to be exploited for charcoal and firewood production, not to mention the numerous dewatering projects that proliferated throughout the region in the twentieth century to eliminate wetland areas.

Agroecosystems: Between Plantations and Smallholdings

The slave revolution in Haiti in 1791 and the proclamation of its independence in 1804 marked the symbolic end of the pre-industrial slave plantation. Jamaica replaced the French colony as the leading exporter of sugar. Around 1805, it produced the largest sugarcane harvest with some 100,000 mt of sugar, more than the 78,696 mt obtained in the Haitian plantations at the outbreak of the uprising. This event also catapulted Cuba as a major sugar producer, although it remained behind Jamaica until the late 1820s. No other Caribbean island was in a better position than the largest of the Antilles to capitalize on the new conditions of the sugar market in the context of the industrial revolution in England, Europe, and the United States.

One of the reasons was the maintenance of the slave system against the policies promoted by the British Empire for the abolition of the slave trade and slavery, which it dictated for its colonies in 1807 and 1834, respectively. In Cuba, on the other hand, the slave trade, prohibited since 1820, continued illegally until 1866. Two decades later, slavery was definitively abolished, several years after it was abolished in Puerto Rico (1873). Another fundamental reason was the abundance of natural resources and forests in the vast Cuban plains, as opposed to the levels of environmental degradation that the English and French colonies in the area faced in proportion to their size.

But the decisive factor was the early irruption in Cuba of the technologies of the steam era, which allowed a great increase in production in the context of the so-called "second slavery." This was the beginning of industrialized agriculture in the tropics, with the broadening of steam engines in the refineries to power the mill since 1820. Shortly afterwards, although more slowly, vacuum evaporators were introduced in the boiler house, starting in the 1840s, and centrifuges in the following decade, which completed the process of mechanizing the factory.

Added to this process was the transportation revolution with the use of steamships to take the product to foreign markets and, above all, the early use of railroads to transport it to the ports. Cuba was one of the first countries and the second in America (after the United States) to have this means of transport on its sugar plains, starting in 1837–38. This made it possible to penetrate into the interior more quickly and occupy the forest frontier to establish plantations. Forests were synonymous with timber, firewood for boilers and fertile soils with abundant organic matter that allowed high yielding crops. This system was referred to as portable or transhumant, similar to an open pit mine. With steam and fossil fuel technologies, the occupation of space and the consequent loss of biodiversity accelerated. The rapid reduction of avifauna observed by travelers and naturalists was one of the most visible consequences (Funes 2020a: 147–151).

The combination of slavery and the technologies of the industrial revolution allowed sugar production in Cuba to increase tenfold between the 1820s and 1870s. The relationship with the United States was decisive as the main market and supplier of much of the technology, raw materials, and foodstuffs that cemented the sugar specialization of the Greater Antilles. Under the same design, sugar occupied a large part of the coastal plains of Puerto Rico, then the second largest exporter in the insular Caribbean. Other European colonies experienced periods of sugar resurgence, such as Guadeloupe, Martinique, and Barbados in the second half of the nineteenth century on the basis of steam engines, the appearance of central mills, and railroad networks. It is worth noting that during the modernization process of sugar agribusiness, hybrid varieties of sugar cane rich in sucrose were created to replace the traditional Bourbon and Cristalina varieties that were attacked by pests and had decreasing yields. Barbados became the center of this innovation in the Caribbean following John Redman Bovell's research at the Dood Botanical Garden, established in Barbados in 1885, which produced new varieties that spread rapidly throughout the Caribbean region (Galloway 1996).

Due to the territorial scale demanded by modern sugar factories (known as the central), their greatest success was in the Spanish Antilles. This had to do, of course, with the growing hegemony of the United States over the region. The declaration of war on Spain and the occupation of Cuba (1898–1902) and Puerto Rico (1898 to the present), followed by the Dominican Republic (1916–1924) and Haiti (1915–1934), were the foundation for a new expansion of sugar in these countries. Through massive investments, U.S. companies became the main producers of sugar in the Antilles.

This new sugar boom was linked to the so-called "conquest of the tropics," an idea that was widespread in North Atlantic circles of power at the time. It was first and foremost a material "conquest" of tropical ecosystems for the benefit of industrialized countries or the "white man," as it was called at the time. But also from the development of science to deepen the knowledge of these regions, which gave rise to "tropicalized" sub-disciplines within the agricultural sciences, geography or forestry studies (*dasonomía*) and the emergence of concepts such as neotropics or biodiversity. A central role in this regard was played by the founding of experimental agronomic stations following the U.S. model for botanical and agricultural research, in support of the new sugar boom in the Antilles and the banana plantations on the continental coasts of the Caribbean basin (McCook 2009).

The new Cuban sugar expansion took place in the plains of the eastern half of the country (Camagüey and Oriente provinces), where extensive cattle raising and wooded landscapes still predominated. The so-called "giants," twenty-seven new power plants owned by large U.S. corporations, were erected in both countries. Following the traditional slash-and-burn system, their owners preferred to occupy the forest frontier, thus contributing to the most intense deforestation in Cuba's history. The First World War was a high point, when the existing capacity doubled in just a few years. The 1914 harvest was 2,244,500 mt; in 1925, it reached 5,200,800 mt.

It is not difficult to imagine the serious damage caused to biodiversity in those regions opened to cultivation in order to guarantee sugar cane to the modern central factories, which formed huge estates with their own railway networks and private docks. The remaining forests in the Dominican plains also underwent intense defor- estation, although their sugar growth was less spectacular, from 51,000 mt in 1899 to some 400,000 mt in 1935. In Puerto Rico, after its inclusion as a U.S. tariff territory in 1901, sugar production increased from some 50,000 mt at the beginning of the century to more than 1 million mt in 1934. With no land available to expand plant- ings, this sugar boom depended more on the use of fertilizers and irrigation. Other Caribbean territories experienced a recovery of their agro-industry during the same period, as was the case of Jamaica, which in 1941 produced 175,000 mt of sugar, re- sponsible for 15 to 20 percent of exports.

The increase in scale in modern U.S. technology and capital-intensive factories accentuated the historical trend toward land devoted to export crops rather than food for the domestic market. Even some in the latter category, such as bananas, began to be produced in the form of plantations destined for the foreign market. The continental Caribbean was the realm of the banana plantations, but they also had a presence in the West Indies in Jamaica, the Dominican Republic, and Trinidad. In contrast to previous stages, medium or small landowners had access to sugarcane and banana plantations, which reinforced the trend towards homogenization of the rural landscape (Striffler and Moberg 2003).

Other export crops enjoyed boom periods during this period. Coffee occupied mostly mountainous areas, although there were exceptions such as the coffee boom in the plains of western Cuba in the 1820s and 1830s. In Haiti, unlike the failure to re- activate the sugar plantations, coffee production was resumed through small peas- ant farms in the mountains. During most of the nineteenth century and the major- ity of the twentieth century, the country remained the main regional exporter based on family farming and artisanal techniques. By the 1880s, this peasant colonization movement reached the physical limit of arable land and there was an increasing frag- mentation of the farms (D'Ans 2011).

In the last third of the nineteenth century, coffee plantations penetrated the mountainous zones of central and western Puerto Rico. Regarding environmental impacts, aspects such as changes in the constitution of the forests, greater vulnerability to hurricanes and problems with soil depletion and erosion are mentioned in texts. The intensive cultivation of coffee trees, which reached its zenith in the 1880s and 1890s, led to the neglect of subsistence crops and animal husbandry, increasing dependence on food imports and the impoverishment of the workers' diet (Picó 1979).

Cocoa was another export crop with a significant presence in the region. The island of Trinidad had its heyday between 1880 and 1920. In the Cibao area of the Dominican Republic, the same trend began in the 1880s and by the end of the century there were a few large-scale plantations controlled by foreign firms. However, most of the cocoa farms belonged to peasant families who accumulated money from tobacco cultivation, by then in decline. Cocoa and coffee maintained their presence in Dominican exports until the fall in prices that began in 1930.

The aforementioned export crops were the most widespread in several of the Antillean islands between the end of the nineteenth century and the beginning of the twentieth century. But other crops were more localized, such as cotton and arrowroot in St. Vincent, nutmeg in Grenada, ginger in Barbados, Nevis, and Jamaica or campeche and pepper in Jamaica (Watts 1986). Tobacco plantations in Cuba and the Dominican Republic or the citrus plantations promoted by Americans on the Isle of Pines, the second largest island in the Cuban archipelago, at the beginning of the twentieth century could also be added to this list.

At many times, peasant populations were key to sustaining exports, as was the case with coffee in Haiti after independence. They also participated in the supply of sugarcane to the Cuban sugar mills through the *colonato*. However, agricultural diversity on the farms depended in part on the characteristics of the crop. Descriptions of coffee or cocoa plantations usually reflect the existence of intercropping or polycultures, as opposed to the more specialized sugar or banana plantations. However, both plantations and small farms were vital for the multiplication of new plants that began to multiply in the Caribbean landscapes since the nineteenth century, such as mangoes, breadfruit, cinnamon, flame, and eucalyptus trees.

Smallholdings were predominant in peasant production, which tended to occupy marginal areas not suitable for plantations. This explains their concentration in mountainous areas, or in soils with low agricultural potential, which could contribute to increased erosion. Farmers dedicated to subsistence crops or livestock were vital for the supply of local markets. Its greatest boom was linked to times of plantation decline or economic crisis, as occurred after the abolition of slavery in Jamaica and other British islands. Smallholdings could contribute to crop diversity and greater food availability, but were highly vulnerable to fertility decline, lack of resources, population pressure, and migration to cities or abroad (Soluri 2019).

Livestock and Animals

Until the end of the eighteenth century, sugar, coffee or cotton plantations were the main factor of environmental transformation in the British and French West Indies. However, the Hispanic Antilles maintained most of its territories dedicated to extensive cattle raising, which supplied local demand and in many cases supplied specimens to foreign colonies that lacked the necessary space to raise animals on a larger scale (Moscoso 2020). Because of its larger size, the exception among the islands belonging to other European powers was Jamaica, where cattle ranching was developed as a complementary activity to sugar expansion. This is how the important sector of the paddock owners, mostly Creoles, was forged.

After the abolition of slavery and the decline of Jamaican plantations, cattle ranching had a renaissance linked to the meat and milk market, such that the number of paddocks increased from 378 to 604 between 1844 and 1881. Many of the original sugar estates were converted into animal husbandry units for horses, swine, sheep, and goats. This change was further amplified towards the end of the nineteenth century due to the possibilities of supplying the domestic market and the demand from Cuba after the wars of independence and at the beginning of the twentieth century due to the sugar boom, as well as to supply horses to other British islands (Shepherd 2009).

Jamaica was one of the first territories to have pastures of African origin, such as guinea grass (*Panicum maximun*) and animals from other tropical zones, such as the zebu (*Boss indicus*), which contributed to revolutionize cattle raising in the American tropics. The former arrived on the island in the eighteenth century, coming from Barbados or introduced directly by trafficking ships, and the latter was introduced in the mid-nineteenth century from India. In both cases, Jamaica was the probable origin of the dispersion to Cuba and the other Hispanic Antilles.

Extensive cattle ranching or free-ranging remained the main economic activity in several areas of the insular Hispanic Caribbean until the nineteenth century, along with logging and agriculture for the local market (Funes and Piqueras 2023). Its impact on biodiversity was relatively minor, although it represented the basis for the generalization of mammals and other domesticated species brought from the Old World. Despite the use of fire to create pasture areas, which gave rise to anthropic savannahs, the low animal load made possible the appearance of secondary forest or scrubs.

This situation began to change in the nineteenth century as Cuba, Puerto Rico, and later, the Dominican Republic specialized in the sugar agroindustry. As in Jamaica, cattle ranching was largely subsidiary to the plantations through the installation of paddocks, with fenced land and the planting of artificial pastures. Outside of the planting areas, traditional cattle ranching gave way to pastures specialized in raising and fattening animals. It was on these farms where the greatest efforts were made to reform livestock farming through the importation of European cattle breeds for beef such as the Shorthorn or Durham (Funes 2020b).

Towards the end of the nineteenth century, the importation of new breeds such as the Holstein for dairy cattle, whose origin in cold climates demanded greater attention, began. However, extensive cattle ranching continued to predominate, and during the twentieth century, zebu cattle gained popularity due to their greater resistance to the tropical climate. Starting in the 1930s, with the gradual rise of automobile transportation, the production of animal protein became the main focus of cattle farming.

Domesticated European species were not the only source of animal protein in the Caribbean. Native fauna was an alternative in many territories in the initial phases of colonization. In the herding economy, for example, selective logging coexisted with hunting and fishing. During the opening phase of the plantations, the capture of animals and their disappearance from the deforested areas was more intense. Hutias, the most abundant mammal, was used as food for the slaves. By the end of the eighteenth century they could be considered to have disappeared from the Windward Islands (Watts 1986: 439). Shortly thereafter in Cuba it became a prized food once again for the enslaved during the expansion of the sugar plantations towards the forested frontier throughout the nineteenth century.

The avifauna was among the most affected by deforestation and legal or illegal hunting. For example, several species of macaws endemic to the Caribbean can be considered extinct, including the Cuban macaw (*Ara tricolor*) in the second half of the nineteenth century. Among shorebirds, the case of flamingos is emblematic. From an original area that included Florida, the Bahamas, Jamaica, Hispaniola, and Puerto Rico, by the early 1930s, the only wild populations remained in a few marshes and shallow saltwater lagoons in the center north Cuba and perhaps some islands of the Bahamas. More than habitat destruction, the cause was excessive hunting to capture their eggs or live specimens for their colorful plumage.

During this period (1810–1950), hunting of terrestrial and marine species for commercial purposes boomed. Among the former are the American crocodile (*Crocodylus acutus*), which has a wide distribution throughout the Caribbean Basin, and the Cuban crocodile (*Crocodylus rhombifer*), whose habitat is limited to the Zapata Swamp in Cuba. Crocodile skin was highly prized in Europe and the United States for making items such as women's handbags, wallets, shoes, belts, and coats. The latter include several species of sponges, which had their main extraction areas in the Bahamas, with a center in Nassau, and in Cuba, especially in the Gulf of Batabanó, the nucleus of exports in the first half of the twentieth century. Most of them went to the New York market, but they were also destined to France, Germany and other countries such as Argentina and Japan (Corfield 1938).

The green turtle (*Chelonia mydas*), hawksbill turtle (*Eretmochelys imbricata*), and loggerhead turtle (*Caretta caretta*) have been widely exploited in the Caribbean since the seventeenth century as food for their meat and eggs, as well as for their shells. The most important center of turtle fishing developed around the Cayman Islands, but overexploitation decimated the nesting sites by the end of the eighteenth century. From then on, the turtle farmers began a new phase of turtle consumption with their expansion to other territories, such as the keys of southern Cuba and the Central American Caribbean coasts.

This change entailed greater investment of capital by the Cayman elite for vessels of greater range and tonnage. The most prized species were the green turtle for its meat and the hawksbill turtle for its shell, with the main foreign market in England until the end of the nineteenth century. Thereafter, the United States began to absorb most of the purchases. Turtle soup and turtle steak (especially green turtle) became fashionable in wealthy men's clubs. At the same time in the interwar period, industrial processing of products such as canned turtle soup began, expanding consumption among the middle class (Crawford 2020).

The economic activities surrounding the animals had a high incidence in the decline of their populations in the Caribbean region. Overexploitation put the species involved at risk of becoming extinct, giving rise to a growing need for conservation action, as in the case of the West Indian or Caribbean manatee (*Tricherus manatus*), which is widely used for its fat, meat, and skin (Harris 2020). In other cases, such concerns came late, as was the case with the Caribbean monk seal (*Monachus tropicalis*), also known as the Jamaican seal, last seen in 1952. There is debate about whether or not it was an abundant species in the area at the arrival of Europeans and about the causes of its extinction (Baisre 2013). Whether the starting point was hunting for oil or the capture of specimens to be sent to natural history museums since the mid-nineteenth century, both activities contributed to it being considered today the second marine mammal to disappear in the modern era (Jøgersen 2021).

Another of the marine mammals with a major presence in the region in the past were the whales, which were widely exploited during the nineteenth and twentieth centuries. The nuclei of whaling activity were established in the areas of the Lesser Antilles, in a staggered manner in the islands of Trinidad (1830–1862), Barbados (1879–1910), and Grenada (1920–1926). Another important center developed in the seas near St. Vincent and the Grenadines with their own economic cycles since 1875. The presence of U.S. whalers in these areas between 1866 and 1887 had a high impact on humpback whales (*Megaptera novaeangliae*), estimated at 2,491 individuals captured.

In parallel, artisanal fishing from the coasts of the aforementioned islands contributed to the elimination of no less than 1,400 whales of the same species, which led to the cessation of whaling in several of the islands. For example, in southern Grenada between 1925 and 1926, a Norwegian whaling company erected a modern building for processing cetaceans and brought steamboats to the island to develop the activity on an industrial scale. However, after the killing of about 180 whales in two years, operations ceased soon after due to a shortage of whales (Romero and Creswell 2005).

There is an idea that Caribbean islands consume little fish despite being surrounded by water, but it should be taken into account that tropical seas can be rich in variety of species and not so in density. In most of the Antillean arc, island shelves are narrow and nutrient-poor, so they cannot support large fish populations. In the twentieth century the region was affected by overfishing, especially where industrial methods were used, in addition to the destruction of marine habitats, contamination of coastal waters, and displacement of fishing villages by other economic activities (Valdés-Pizzini 2011).

Protection of Flora and Fauna

In the face of the rapid ecological transformation of the Lesser Antilles by the slave plantations, scientists and civil servants were early advocates of conservationist actions. In the second half of the eighteenth century, the creation of botanical gardens and forest reserves began in several of the English and French islands, regarded as an expression of the beginnings of modern conservation policies and laws (Anderson, Grove, and Hiebert 2006). Their objectives were both economic, to introduce new species with agricultural and medicinal potential, as they were ecological, to cope with changes in the local climate due to the lack of rainfall.

In the Hispanic Caribbean, the first Botanical Garden was established in Havana in 1817. Later, in the 1880s, the Havana Acclimatization Garden was created. As part of a growing interest in scientific agriculture, towards the end of the century, teaching centers and agronomic stations were founded in Puerto Rico and Cuba (Fernández 2005). More than just work to protect nature, the interest was to contribute to crop diversification or improved yields.

In some of the institutions created in the nineteenth century, topics related to the conservation of flora and fauna began to appear, such as the Real Academia de Ciencias Médicas, Físicas y Naturales de La Habana, inaugurated in 1861. Among the academics were the island's leading naturalists, who were already warning of the dangers of accelerated forest destruction and the disappearance of native species. This type of concern was also present among the members of the *Sociedad Protectora de Animales y Plantas de la Isla de Cuba*, active in Havana between 1882 and 1891.

The constant decrease in forested areas influenced the adoption of concrete measures. In the case of the aforementioned *Ordenanzas de Montes para el servicio del ramo en Cuba y Puerto Rico*, promulgated in 1876, the action was focused on the few forests owned by the State, less than ten percent of the territory in both archipelagos. In the Dominican Republic, a law for the conservation of forests and jungles was passed in 1884, in the midst of the danger posed by the advance of sugarcane plantations. However, the situation seemed more critical in Puerto Rico, where the first forest reserve was created in the Luquillo forests in 1902, which became a National Forest in 1907. During the Great Depression the New Deal programs reached the island through the Civilian Conservation Corps, which, between 1933 and 1942, undertook large plans to restore forests for recreational and landscape purposes (Valdés-Pizzini, González, and Martínez 2011).

In the midst of the great expansion of the sugar frontier in the Hispanic Caribbean during the first decades of the twentieth century, the demand for forest protection grew. Influential Dominican intellectuals denounced the accelerated deforestation and its effects on the source of the rivers, a call that resulted in the creation in 1926 of an Aquatic and Forest Reserve to protect the Yaque del Norte River. In Cuba, that same year, the planting of sugar cane was prohibited in areas of high forest, although little remained of the original forests in flat and hilly areas. In 1930, this provision was converted into law and the first forest reserve, the Sierra de Cristal National Park, was created. In Haiti, the San Rafael National Forest was established in 1936 (Atwood 1941).

Beyond saving or restoring forest wealth, steps were taken to protect specific species. One of the first measures of this type appeared in Saint Vincent with The Bird and Fish Protection Ordinance of 1901. In addition to imposing penalties for illegal capture or trade of species such as turtles, it protected the endemic parrot (St. Vincent's Amazona/*Amazona guildingii*), later designated as a national bird (Anderson, Grove, and Hiebert 2006: 14).

Hunting and fishing laws attempted to establish regulations. One enacted in Cuba in 1909, to replace the one in force since 1879, copied from Spanish legislation on the matter, introduced the novelty of proclaiming the right of ownership over wild animals. The objective was to cut down on the excesses committed by private landowners, who would henceforth have to request a license to hunt or fish on their properties. Similarly, in the Dominican Republic, a hunting law was passed in 1916 prohibiting the destruction of animals that were not harmful to agriculture and livestock, reinforced by another law in 1931.

However, the tendency was to create areas as a refuge for hunting or fishing, or the protection of species in their natural habitat. One example was the creation of a National Flamingo Refuge on the north coast of Camagüey, by presidential decree in June 1933. It was developed after bird lovers approached the government to ask for the conservation of the species, and the visit of the president of the New-York-based National Audubon Society, Gilbert Pearson, who was informed about the existence of flocks of flamingos in a primitive state on the island.

According to the decree, the extinction of the species in the rest of America was an incentive, since the vigilance and punishment for violators would make the country the only one to conserve such an original and colorful bird. It was felt that the protection zone would be more effective than an outright ban on flamingo hunting throughout the country. Three years later, the refuge area was extended to the entire north and south coast of the provinces of Camagüey and Las Villas.

Around the same time, three other conservation zones were established in Cuba. In 1936, the National Hunting and Fishing Refuge in the Zapata Swamp; in 1939 the Topes de Collantes National Park and Forest Reserve; and in 1941 the Juan Gundlach National Hunting and Fishing Refuge, in a wide area around Havana. The implementation did not meet expectations, but its emergence is indicative of a growing awareness of the effects of destroying biodiversity.

The main warnings were issued by local and foreign naturalists, but also by institutions dedicated to the study of agriculture and tropical ecosystems. For example, in 1900, the U.S. Congress authorized the creation of an experimental station in Mayagüez, Puerto Rico. In 1910, the island's association of sugar plantation owners established a new station in Río Piedras, which in 1914 passed to the administration of the island government as the Río Piedras Agricultural Experimental Station. In Cuba, the Santiago de las Vegas Agronomic Experimental Station was inaugurated in 1904 and sugar interests supported the opening of a private agricultural station at the Baraguá plant, which was short-lived (McCook 2009). This model of institution focused on solving the problems of plantation agriculture and played an important role in the dissemination of new hybrid sugarcane varieties as alternatives against plagues such as the mosaic virus.

Other institutions created under the influence of the U.S. model played a fundamental role in the proliferation of studies on tropical ecosystems and, as mentioned above, in the creation of the concept of biodiversity. These were the cases of the Harvard Botanical Station for Tropical Research and Sugarcane Investigation, in Cienguegos, Cuba, created in 1899 in areas of the Soledad sugar mill, owned by the U.S. American Edwin Atkins; and the Chinchona Botanical Station, established in 1903 in Jamaica, initially affiliated with the New York Botanical Garden. Another example is the Tropical Forest Experimental Station founded in Puerto Rico in 1939 (Raby 2017).

The insular Caribbean was one of the first regions in the tropics to suffer the socio-environmental consequences of the irruption of plantations and agribusiness into its ecosystems. It could even be said that until the mid-twentieth century its degree of anthropization would be one of the most widespread in the tropical area, both because of the centuries of European colonization and because it was the first frontier in the expansion of U.S. industrial metabolism. In any case, it could be said that the interest in studying its tropical nature since the beginning of the twentieth century was largely due not so much to its former splendor as to its increasing deterioration. More than the fruit of biodiversity resulting from natural selection, the landscapes of the Antilles at the end of this period were the consequence of an intense process of biocultural change that made the Caribbean one of the initial nuclei of the globalization process since 1492.

Translated by Eric Rummelhoff and revised by Omar Sierra Cháves.

References

Anderson, Jennifer L. 2012. *Mahogany: The Cost of Luxury in Early America*. Cambridge: Harvard University Press.

Anderson, Robert S., Richard Grove, and Karis Hiebert, ed. 2006. *Islands, Forest and Gardens in the Caribbean: Conservation and Conflict in Environmental History*. London: Macmillan Caribbean.

Atwood, Wallace W. 1941. *La protección de la naturaleza en las Américas*. Mexico City: Editorial Cultura.

Baisre, Julio A. 2013. "Shifting Baselines and the Extinction of the Caribbean Monk Seal." *Conservation Biology* 27, no. 5: 927–935.

Corfield, George S. 1938. "Sponge Industry of the Caribbean Area." *Economic Geography* 14, no. 2: 201–206.

Crawford, Shakira D. 2020. *The Last Turtlemen of the Caribbean: Waterscapes of Labor, Conservation, and Boundary Making*. Chapel Hill: University of North Carolina Press.

D'Ans, André-Marcel. 2011. *Haití. Paisaje y Sociedad*. Santiago de Cuba: Editorial Oriente.

Domínguez Cristóbal, Carlos. 2000. *Panorama histórico forestal de Puerto Rico*. Río Piedras: Editorial de la Universidad de Puerto Rico.

Fernández, Leida. 2005. *Cuba agrícola: mito y tradición (1878–1920)*. Madrid: Consejo Superior de Investigaciones Científicas.

Funes Monzote, Reinaldo. 2008. *From Rainforest to Cane Field in Cuba. An Environmental History since 1492*. Chapel Hill: University of North Carolina Press.

———. 2020a. "Revolución azucarera y cambio socioambiental en Cuba en tiempos de la Segunda Esclavitud." *Revista UFMG* 27, no. 1: 124–161.

———. 2020b. "'Un arcoíris en medio de la tempestad.' Visiones del potrero cubano en el siglo XIX." *Mundo Agrario* 21, no. 46.

Funes Monzote, Reinaldo, and José A. Piqueras, ed. 2023. *Usos agrarios, mensura y representación en Cuba. Siglo XIX*. Havana: Editorial Imagen Contemporánea.

Galloway, John Herbert. 1996. "Botany in the Service of Empire: The Barbados Cane-Breeding Program and the Revival of the Caribbean Sugar Industry, 1880s-1930s." *Annals of the Association of American Geographers* 86, no. 4: 682–706.

Gaztambide-Géigel, Antonio. 2014. *Tan lejos de Dios... Las relaciones del Caribe con Estados Unidos*. Santiago de Cuba: Editorial Oriente.

Gill, Tom. 1931. *Tropical Forests of the Caribbean*. Baltimore: Tropical Plant Research Foundation.

Harris, Lynn B. 2020. "Maritime cultural encounters and consumerism of turtles and manatees: An environmental history of the Caribbean." *The International Journal of Maritime History* 32, no. 4: 789–807.

Higman, Barry. 2000. "The Sugar Revolution." *Economic History Review* 53, no. 2: 213–236.

Humboldt, Alexander von. 2011. *Political Essay on the Island of Cuba*. Trans. J. Bradford Anderson, Vera M. Kutzinski, and Anja Becker. Chicago: University of Chicago Press. Orig. pub. 1826.

Jøgersen, Dolly. 2021. "Erasing the extinct: the hunt for Caribbean monk seals and museum collection practices." *História, Ciência, Saúde – Manghinos* 28, no. 10: 161–183.

McCook, Stuart. 2009. "The World was my Garden. Tropical Botany and Cosmopolitism in American Science, 1898–1935." In *Colonial Crucible. Empire in the Making of the Modern American State*, ed. Alfred W. McCoy and Francisco A. Scarano, 499–507. Madison: University of Wisconsin Press.

———. 2011. "The Neo-Columbian Exchange: The Second Conquest of the Greater Caribbean: 1720–1930." *Latin American Research Review* 46, 11–31.

Morgan, Philip D., John R. McNeill, Matthew Mulcahy, et al. 2022. *Sea & Land. An Environmental History of the Caribbean*. Oxford: Oxford University Press.

Morgan, Philip D. 2022. "The Caribbean Environment to 1850." In *Sea & Land. An Environmental History of the Caribbean*, ed. Philip D. Morgan, John R. McNeill, Matthew Mulcahy, et al., 19–129. Oxford: Oxford University Press.

Moscoso, Francisco. 2020. *El hato: latifundio ganadero y mercantilismo en Puerto Rico: siglos 16 al 18*. Río Piedras: Publicaciones Gaviota.

Moya Pons, Frank, ed. 2010. *Historia de la Republica Dominicana*. Madrid: CSIC.

Picó, Fernando. 1979. "Deshumanización del trabajo, cosificación de la naturaleza. Los comienzos del auge del café en el Utuado del Siglo XIX." *Cuadernos de la Facultad de Humanidades* 2: 55–70.

Raby, Megan. 2017. *American Tropics: The Caribbean Roots of Biodiversity Science*. Chapel Hill: University of North Carolina Press.

Record, Samuel J. 1926. "Forestry in British Honduras." *Journal of Forestry* 24, no. 5: 562–568.

Revels, Craig S. 2002. "Timber, Trade, and Transformation: A Historical Geography of Mahogany in Honduras." PhD diss., Lousiana State University.

Romero, Aldemaro, and Joel Creswell. 2005. "In the land of the mermaid: How culture, not ecology, influenced marine mammal exploitation in the Southeastern Caribbean." In *Environmental Issues in Latin America and the Caribbean*, ed. Aldemaro Romero and Sarah E. West, 3–30. Dordrecht: Springer.

Schwartz, Stuart. 2015. *Sea of Storms: A History of Hurricanes in the Greater Caribbean from Columbus to Katrina*. Princeton: Princeton University Press.

Shepherd, Verenne. 2009. *Livestock, Sugar and Slavery. Contested Terrain in Colonial Jamaica*. Kingston: Ian Randle Publishers.

Striffler, Steve, and Mark Moberg, ed. 2003. *Banana Wars. Power, Production, and History in the Americas*. Durham: Duke University Press.

Soluri, John. 2019. "Cocina casera: campesinos, cocina y diversidad agrícola." In *Un pasado vivo. Dos siglos de historia ambiental latinoamericana*, ed. Claudia Leal, John Soluri, and José A. Pádua, 179–199. Bogotá: Fondo de Cultura Económica.

Valdés-Pizzini, Manuel. 2011. *Una mirada al mundo de los pescadores en Puerto Rico. Una perspectiva global*. Mayagüez: Centro Interdisciplinario de Estudios del Litoral.

Valdés-Pizzini, Manuel, Michael González Cruz, and José Eduardo Martínez Reyes. 2011. *La transformación del paisaje puertorriqueño y la disciplina del Cuerpo Civil de Conservación, 1933–1942*. San Juan: Universidad de Puerto Rico.

Watts, David. 1986. *The West Indies: Patterns of Development, Culture and Environment Change since 1492*. Cambridge: Cambridge University Press.

From 1950 to the Present

Source: Fernando Efrén Sandoval (2021)

Introduction: Biodiversity and the Anthropocene in Latin America from 1950 to the Present

Antoine Acker, Léon Enrique Ávila Romero, Regina Horta Duarte and Olaf Kaltmeier

In *The Falling Sky*, the Yanomami shaman Davi Kopenawa writes about his "discovery of the Whites" in the 1960s in the Upper Orinoco when he was a little kid. Yanomami adults had known these strangers for some time already (Kopenawa and Albert 2013), yet Kopenawa's perspective as a child allows him to convey this first encounter with a frightening alien group in a genuine light that strongly resonates with the shock that resulted from the arrival of early colonizers on the shores of Mexico, Brazil, or the Caribbean islands in the sixteenth century. The world of the Whites discovered by Kopenawa was mineral, plastic, and electric. He wondered what their shoes, glasses, watches, and flashlights were and was afraid of and disgusted by the sound of their motors, the voices on their radios, and the smell of their gasoline (2013: 176). These textures, sounds, and smells came right out of world markets and capitalist societies obsessed with technological progress and consumption. In young Davi's view, the Whites had no notion of the vegetal, animal, spiritual, and aquatic lives interacting in the forest, yet these strangers brought their own tragic "contribution" to biodiversity by spreading pathogens, creating epidemics that caused a dramatic loss of life among the Yanomami (2013: 252). Only years later did Kopenawa finally understand the Whites' landscape-changing project, which amounted to a massive reduction of biodiversity: "I came to understand that they wanted to know [the forest] and plot its limits to take possession of it. [...] It is the anger that makes me fight today against those outsiders who think only of burning the forest's trees and soiling its rivers like hordes of peccaries!" (2013: 177).

The destruction of an ecosystem's diversity, interconnections, and balance, experienced as the end of the world, is not only clear in reports of the Indigenous perception of the sixteenth-century colonial conquests. It has been an ongoing process, intensively rekindled in the second half of the twentieth century by the operations of internal colonization and the joint politics of state and capital development established by modern Latin American countries, often with the support of international loans and expertise. Mapuche communities have been threatened by the expansion of forest plantations since the Pinochet dictatorship and its infrastructure projects like the dams at the BioBío River. The Maya fought against the dam flooding of their land in Guatemala in the late 1970s as well as the Emberá Katío in Colombia, two decades later. All these peoples may have experienced a similar, world-ending feeling like Kopenawa described before (Kaltmeier 2022; Cabrera Becerra, Calvo, and Rubio 1999; Leguizamón Castillo 2015; Einbinder 2017; Lynch 2019; Torres-Salinas et al. 2016; Valencia-Hernández et al. 2017).

Kopenawa was born in the Amazon, a tropical forest biome in the heart of Latin America, which has endured a stunning loss of forest cover. Still in their infancy in the post-war decades, infrastructure projects became widespread in the Amazon from the late 1960s onwards: hydroelectric dams, mining, ports, and in the following decades, even oil concessions in Ecuador and Suriname. Even more spectacular, though never completed, were the "Pharaonic" highway projects such as the Marginal de la Selva (announced in 1963), which was to connect the Colombian, Ecuadorian, Peruvian, Venezuelan, and Bolivian Amazonia, and the Transamazônica that crosses Brazil from east to west (1970). Ignoring the populations already settled in the region and exercising multiple forms of ecological violence, Latin American governments, often with the support of the United States and international development banks, encouraged both the establishment of rural colonies (Kaltmeier 1999) and large-scale agricultural estates (in particular, cattle farms) to fill the "demographic void" of the "virgin forest" (Acker 2022). In this context, the Amazon transformed into a globally watched mirror of the world's destruction, and the alarming rate of biodiversity reduction became a symbol of the Great Acceleration (Acker 2017).

Since World War II, the consumption of materials and energy has increased (Fernández Durán and González Reyes 2018). This period has been called The Great Acceleration. Its central aspects have been a greater accumulation of carbon dioxide in the atmosphere and a substantial increase in the number of automobiles, which went from 40 million in the mid-twentieth century to 850 million in the twenty-first century. Another outstanding aspect has been the increase in the production of plastic: in 1950, there were about 1 million tons, while in 2015, there were 300 million (McNeill and Engleke 2016). In general, the use of agrochemicals in the so-called Green Revolution increased significantly. Synthetic nitrogen use in agricultural production went from 4 million to 85 million tons in the same period of analysis. In addition to these data, the twentieth century saw the impressive growth of infrastructure works expanding the technosphere at the biosphere's expense: dams, roads, power plants, extraction machines, and an increase in environmental predatory methods, such as fishing with trawl nets.

In this context, biodiversity as a term appeared in 1986 when U.S. natural scientists and politicians applied it in the "National Forum on Bio-Diversity." This neologism, however, has its historical roots in the United States' neo-imperial conquest of the Caribbean and Mesoamerican tropics in the late nineteenth century (Raby 2017). This technoscientific concept, which rapidly made its entrance into international and local politics, reveals how a growing interest and concern for species diversity and its future grew out of the exponential turn taken by the Anthropocene in that period. It was precisely during the Great Acceleration that Latin American states began developing ambitious politics of preservation, notably through the proliferation of national parks. Although the first in Latin America were created in the 1930s in Argentina, Chile, Mexico, and Brazil (Kaltmeier 2021; Freitas, Leal, and Wakild 2024), it was in the 1960s that many countries in the region faced a veritable boom of national parks and, since 1971, U.N. biosphere reserves to protect flora, fauna, and landscapes. With over 4,000 threatened species, Latin America is at the top of the "Red List" established by the International Union for the Conservation of Nature, and Latin American states exert sovereignty over biodiversity contexts that are vital to the entire planet (Moreno 2013).

Especially in U.S. conservationism, the protection of nature – in an imagined state of wilderness – is a genuine ethos of protected areas, often in conflict with the uses of Indigenous peoples and peasant communities, as it envisions "parks without peoples." This approach is also represented in the Convention on Nature Protection and Wildlife Preservation in the Western Hemisphere, a milestone established by the Organization of American States as early as 1940. Despite all these efforts to protect biodiversity, we are living in a moment when the survival of thousands of species is threatened by anthropogenic actions. This moment, called the sixth extinction, is possibly the greatest phenomenon of terrestrial and marine species disappearance in over 65 million years. There have been episodes of mass extinction in different periods of the planet's history, wiping out up to 98 percent of life on Earth, but the sixth extinction is the only one that has been attributed to anthropogenic causes, with climate change and the loss of habitat being its main vectors (Kolbert 2019). And indeed, climate-change-driven megafires are the ultimate threat to Latin American wildlife in the Great Acceleration. In the Pantanal wetland region at the borders of Brazil, Bolivia, and Paraguay – sheltering jaguars, tapirs, and hundreds of species of rare amphibians, fish, and birds as well as over 1700 known species of plants – about seventeen million animals were killed by fire in 2023 (WWF-Brazil 2023).

Throughout Latin America, the human-driven fall in faunal, as well as floral, diversity has been amplified by various factors during the Great Acceleration. During the second half of the twentieth century, rural-urban migration accelerated the pace of urbanization. While, in 1950, only 40 percent of the population lived in cities, today, the urbanization rate is around 80 percent (CEPAL 2012). Mexico City's sprawling urbanization has led to the destruction of surrounding forests and wetlands and threatened numerous endemic species, such as the axolotl, a well-known amphibian native to the region (Méndez, Binnqüist, and Méndez 2019; Román Suárez 2022). The expansion of Bogotá, in turn, has resulted in the conversion of surrounding *páramo* ecosystems into urban areas, depriving species of bears and local plants like the frailejón of their much-needed water (Preciado Beltrán, Leal Pulido, and Almanza Castañeda 2005). Many other examples will be explored systematically in the following chapters of this section.

Yet Latin America's biodiversity has been, above all, a victim of the continent's structural position as a provider of natural resources transformed into primary goods and commodified since the 1980s in the realm of the neoliberal theorem of selective world market integration. This has been a central element in a renewed process of biodiversity's oversimplification for the needs of international markets, especially around the so-called Green Revolution: the modernization of the Global South's farming sector since the 1960s and 1970s. Mexico and Brazil played pioneering roles in this event, particularly in the development and dissemination of high-yielding crop varieties and agricultural technologies. By the early 1940s, U.S. American agronomists started to work closely with Mexican scientists and governments, thanks to the financial as well as technical support of international organizations such as the Rockefeller Foundation. They established targeted strategies to improve corn (maize) and wheat species' adaptability to national and global markets. New varieties that rapidly gained the name "miracle seeds" were resistant to diseases, pests, and environmental stresses, leading not only to significant increases in crop yields but also to the disappearance of many corn species, with a negative effect on the human diet (Azpíroz 2019; Turrent Fernández 2018). From the early 1990s, the manipulation of farming crops took on an accelerated dimension through the emergence of genetically modified organisms (GMOs), with the Southern Cone being one of the global "laboratories" for their massive propagation, mostly soy and corn (Bravo 2014). By 2000, Argentina was the world's second-largest producer of GMOs, concentrating 18 percent of global land use for transgenic farming (Solbrig 2004).

In strong and large Latin American states such as Mexico, Brazil, and Argentina, the Green Revolution was indeed a successful process of technological transfer that boosted economic growth and showed a previously unseen mobilization capacity by Latin American nations. Yet, paradoxically, it also accentuated the role of the continent as a primary goods export reserve, a role once assigned by the colonial project. Latin America's semi-peripheral integration into global economic processes happened at the expense of its biodiversity. The "Plantationocene," Donna Haraway (2015) and Ana Tsing's proposed alternative to the Anthropocene, which characterizes the oversimplification of biodiversity through the creation of export agrarian economies, may have been born in the colonial context of the Atlantic space. Yet, it has taken its full modern form in the (Latin) American monocultures and pastures of the Great Acceleration meant to produce fruits, soy, and meat for the world. In the vast Brazilian *cerrado* (central savannahs), this accelerated expansion of agribusiness since the 1970s has unleashed alarming rates of deforestation, by far surpassing those of the much-observed Amazon rainforest (Dutra e Silva 2017). In the Southern Cone, the expansion of the fruit export sector and forest plantations has become one of the main drivers of biocultural simplification of landscapes. In several regions of Mesoamerica, the spread of avocado cultures in lands formerly alien to this plant played a similar role, while also generating imbalances in the surrounding aquifers – as avocados require water all year round, unlike the native flora adapted to seasonal rainfall variations (Hernández Fernández 2023).

The technologically driven transformations of this new Plantationocene enabled capitalism to make radical changes and replacements in the interspecies configuration of Latin American ecosystems never achieved in previous epochs. Earlier in the twentieth century, the most resourceful multinational companies, such as Ford, hit brick walls trying to implement monocultures in the Amazon, fighting a losing battle against resilient fungi, weeds, and insects (Grandin 2010). Brazilian agronomists, in turn, invented a soy variety that worked well on some of the most complex tropical soils, bringing the Plantationocene into the most resistant rainforest environments (Silva and de Majo 2022). Transgenic forms of massively cultivated crops such as soy, corn, or sugarcane – while thought to improve resistance to diseases and pests as well as increase productivity and quality to adapt to market demands – have contributed to accelerating deforestation and biodiversity loss (Atencio et al. 2020; Blum et al. 2009; Centurión Mereles 2011; Molina and Melgar Morales 2014). In this vein, Svampa connects the debate on the Anthropocene with the critique of (neo)extractivism: "Consequently, it is possible to establish a relationship between neo-extractivism (as a dominant development dynamic) and Anthropocene (as a critique of a certain model of modernity)" (2019: 29).

To be sure, this new regime of interspecies relations resulted from power relations much more complex than in colonial times. On the one hand, agrarian modernization still aimed at fulfilling international trade demand and firmly kept Latin America on a path of dependency linked to the evolution of primary good prices. It is safe to speak, at least in part, about lingering imperialist structures that sometimes took on the form of blatantly neocolonial relations of power. One famous example is the 1954 CIA-backed *coup d'état* in Guatemala, in which the United Fruit agribusiness multinational corporation is known to have played a notable (though not central) role (Gleijeses 1991). Another can be seen in the introduction of the forest-export model in Chile by the neoliberal Pinochet-dictatorship. But the so-called progressive regimes of the 2000s and 2010s also supported the agroindustrial commodities boom (Svampa 2019). Since the 1970s, the oversimplification of biodiversity underpinning the Green Revolution was in great part designed by (white) Latin American biologists, agronomists, and engineers, and funded by Latin American (democratic and authoritarian) governments. It enriched a very powerful new agrobusiness class, playing a significant role in the making and unmaking of Latin American governments.

Another advancing threat has been tourism, especially since the 1960s. Latin American beaches came to be sold as paradise on Earth by Western travel agencies. Coastal developments for resorts and recreational activities have destroyed coral reefs, mangroves, and nesting sites for marine turtles. Cruise ship tourism in the Caribbean has been linked to issues such as pollution from waste disposal and damage to fragile marine ecosystems.

Nevertheless, there has also been a paradox present in Latin American biodiversity during the Great Acceleration: the greater the threat against it, the greater its symbolic value as a collective heritage that the elites invite Latin American people to identify with. The iguana represented in the logo of the Colombian oil company Ecopetrol since 2003 is a case in point, as it serves to both greenwash communication (iguanas being a direct victim of the drier climate engendered by the Great Acceleration's unsustainable use of fossil fuels) and to symbolize tropical patriotism (Gutiérrez 2019). Latin American states and even social movements have also started to use biodiversity very consciously as a vehicle to defend their interests on the global stage. Likewise, Indigenous peoples throughout the continent have allied with global environmental NGOs to defend their livelihood and survival (Acker, Kaltmeier, and Tittor 2020; Arambiza and Painter 2013; Chicchón 2009). Ecuador's 2007 initiative demanding global compensation at the U.N. for missing oil revenues in exchange for leaving Amazon oil in the ground and protecting the biodiversity of the Yasuní park was a spectacular political move that illustrates the complexity of the Great Acceleration (Gallardo Fierro 2017). It showed the ambiguous relation of Latin American governments to biodiversity, which in the past decades has become both a heritage to preserve and a bargaining chip to promote economic interests.

But biodiversity protection does not only belong to nation-making in Latin America. The continent has also played a major role in shaping global politics in the matter, at least since the Earth Summit of Rio de Janeiro in 1992, an event in which biodiversity loss and climate change were discussed for the first time by U.N. countries as related phenomena. In this conference, the international Convention of Biological Diversity (CBD) was presented and ratified by all Latin American countries. In 2010, the United Nations declared the International Year of Biodiversity as the starting point for the U.N. Decade on Biodiversity. Left-wing ecological activism and governments have pushed this intersectional approach of the U.N. even further in their attempt to propose an alternative global environmental diplomacy, such as during the World People's Conference on Climate Change and the Rights of Mother Earth organized in Cochambamba, Bolivia, in 2010 (World People's Conference on Climate Change and the Rights of Mother Earth 2010). In the last decades Indigenous, Afro-descendent, and peasant movements have introduced new forms of relationships between humans and more-than-humans into the political debate. Building on Indigenous cosmovisions, these demands are based in a defense of life and ideas of an abundant, full life – like the Kichwa *sumak kawsay* (Kaltmeier 2024).

In this context, in some countries like Ecuador and – on a local level – Colombia, the rights of nature are introduced, recognizing it or its elements, like rivers, as juridical subjects (Acosta 2019).

Politically, this new relation with the non-human world finds its expression in an "ecoterritorial turn" in Latin American social movements (Svampa 2019), which includes the defense of the different territories' socio-biodiversity. Since the late 1980s, Latin American constitutions have increasingly incorporated special land regimes with collective, bottom-up management, with strict limitations to or the interdiction of mining and export farming activities to preserve the sustainable relationships between humans and other species. This has been an uneven process, largely incomplete, and affected by numerous setbacks. The continuous fight of Afro-descendant communities, Indigenous peoples, and peasants for their rights to practice multispecies agriculture, the reasonable collection of vegetal resources, and moderate hunting – often socially ritualized in a spiritual exchange with non-human animals – has been an essential condition for calling attention towards biodiversity's future in the region. Even in the urban context, marginalized and socially disadvantaged communities are at the forefront of biodiversity's restoration, for example in the reforestation project of the Morro de Babilônia *favela* of Rio de Janeiro or in the "green terraces" of Medellín's Comuna 13 (Sedrez and Barbosa 2023). At a time in which an increased vegetal presence is globally considered an indispensable condition for urban life to survive on a warmer planet, Latin America's social margins, combined with the continent's multicultural traditions and its plurality of cosmogonies, are proving to be major assets.

(Indigenous) socio-ecological activists as well as social anthropologists have questioned the great defining division of European cosmology that separates nature from culture. Instead of starting from the classificatory separation of nature and culture, there is a "dizzying otherness of the existent" (Latour 2017: 68). To establish a relationship within this diversity, what is needed now is not a quasi-religious and pantheistic re-enchantment of the world, but new ontologies of inhabiting it. Rather than isolating oneself from the web of life in the self-created technosphere, humans should accept their being-in-this-world and understand themselves, as well as other co-inhabitants, as earthlings. However, from an Andean point of view, the question remains open as to whom to include in this group. In many Indigenous perspectives, it is obvious to include animals and plants – which might even be considered human (Kohn 2021; Descola 2014) – while in Andean cosmovisions even earth beings, such as the mountains (*apus*) should also be included (De la Cadena 2010). The preservation of life and the ontology of inhabiting the earth are central aspects of this worldview, which challenges the modern understanding of a biodiversity external to human society.

References

Acker, Antoine. 2017. *Volkswagen in the Amazon: The Tragedy of Global Development in Modern Brazil*. Cambridge: Cambridge University Press.

———. 2022. "Les lieux du XXe siècle: l'Amazonie." In *Histoire du XXe siècle*, ed. Nicolas Beaupré and Florian Louis, 687–690. Paris: Presses Universitaires de France.

Acker, Antoine, Olaf Kaltmeier, and Anne Tittor. 2020. "Nature." In *The Routledge Handbook to the Political Economy and Governance of the Americas*, ed. Olaf Kaltmeier, Anne Tittor, Daniel Hawkins, et al, 418–432. London: Routledge.

Acosta, Alberto. 2019. "Construcción constituyente de los Derechos de la Naturaleza. Repasando una historia con mucho futuro." In *La Naturaleza como sujeto de derechos en el constitucionalismo democrático*, ed. Liliana Estupiñán Achury, Claudia Storini, Rubén Martínez Dalmau, et al., 155–206. Quito: Universidad Andina Simón Bolívar.

Arambiza, Evelio, and Michael Painter. 2013. "Biodiversity Conservation and the Quality of Life of Indigenous people in the Bolivian Chaco." *Human Organization* 65, no. 1: 20–34.

Atencio, Randy, François-Régis Goebel, José Daniel Salazar, et al. 2020 "Biotecnología aplicada a la producción de caña de azúcar en Panamá: Una visión general." *Centros: Revista Científica Universitaria* 9, no. 2: 128–143.

Azpíroz, María-Luisa. 2019. "Maíz transgénico vs agricultura ecológica: un análisis del discurso de Greenpeace México en torno a la seguridad alimentaria, la soberanía alimentaria y el derecho a la alimentación (2007–2017)." *Estudios sociales. Revista de alimentación contemporánea y desarrollo regional* 29, no. 54: 1–28.

Blum, Alfredo, Ignacio Narbondo, Gabriel Oyhantçabal Benelli, et al. 2008. *Soja transgénica y sus impactos en Uruguay. La nueva colonización*. Montevideo: RAP-AL Uruguay.

Bravo, Elizabeth. 2014 "Los cultivos transgénicos en América Latina." In *América Latina: La transgénesis de un continente. Visión crítica de una expansión descontrolada*, ed. María Isabel Manzur, Georgina Catacora, and María Isabel Cárcamo, et al., 14–17. Santiago de Chile: Ediciones Böll.

Cabrera Becerra, Gabriel, Carlos Calvo, and Dany Rubio. 1999. *Los níkak: nómadas de la Amazonia colombiana*. Bogotá: Editorial Universidad Nacional.

Centurión Mereles, Hugo Florencio. 2011. "Cultivo de soja transgénica. Efectos en comunidades campesinas e indígenas del este Paraguayo." *Ra Ximhai* 7, no. 3: 347–354.

CEPAL. 2012. *Población, territorio y desarrollo sostenible*. Santiago de Chile: Comisión Económica para América Latina y el Caribe.

Chicchón, Avecita. 2009. "Working with Indigenous Peoples to Conserve Nature: Examples from Latin America." *Conservation and Society* 7, no. 1: 15–20.

De la Cadena, Marisol. 2010. "Indigenous cosmopolitics in the Andes: conceptual reflections beyond 'politics'." *Cultural Anthropology* 25, no. 2: 334–370.

Descola, Philippe. 2014. *Die Ökologie der Anderen*. Berlin: Matthes & Seitz.

Dutra e Silva, Sandro. 2017. *No Oeste, a Terra o Céu: a Expansão da Fronteira Agrícola no Brasil Central*. Rio de Janeiro: Mauad X.

Einbinder, Nathan. 2017. *Dams, Displacement, and Development: Perspectives from Río Negro, Guatemala*. Cham: Springer.

Fernández Durán, Ramón, and Luis González Reyes. 2018. *En la espiral de la energía. Vol. 2, Colapso del capitalismo global y civilizatorio*. Madrid: Libros en acción – Baladre.

Freitas, Frederico, Claudia Leal, and Emily Wakild. 2024. "Before Biodiversity: Trajectories of National Parks in Latin America (1930s–1980s)." *Latin American Research Review*: 1–20.

Gallardo Fierro, Lucía. 2017. "Re-Thinking Oil: Compensation for Non-Production in Yasuní National Park Challenging Sumak Kawsay and Degrowth." *Sustainability Science* 12, no. 2: 263–274.

Gleijeses, Piero. 1991. *Shattered Hope: The Guatemalan Revolution and the United States, 1944–1954*. Princeton: Princeton University Press.

Grandin, Greg. 2010. *Fordlandia: The Rise and Fall of Henry Ford's Forgotten Jungle City*. New York: Henry Holt and Company.

Gutiérrez, María Margarita. 2019. "El logo, el branding y su influencia en la marca. Caso de estudio: el logosímbolo de Ecopetrol 2003." *Signo y Pensamiento* 38, no. 75.

Haraway, Donna. 2015. "Anthropocene, Capitalocene, Plantationocene, Chthulucene: Making Kin." *Environmental Humanities* 6, no. 1: 159–165.

Hernández Fernández, Viridiana. 2023. "Esperanzas crecientes, negociaciones secas: Las industrias mexicanas y estadounidense del aguacate en la era del Tratado de Libre Comercio y el cambio climático." *Sillares Revista de Estudios Históricos* 2, no. 4: 119–173.

Kaltmeier, Olaf. 1999. *Im Widerstreit der Ordnungen. Kulturelle Identität, Subsistenz und Ökologie in Bolivien*. Wiesbaden: Deutscher Universitätsverlag.

———. 2021. *National Parks from North to South: An Entangled History of Conservation and Colonization in Argentina*. New Orleans/Trier: University of New Orleans Press/Wissenschaftlicher Verlag Trier.

———. 2022. *Resistencia mapuche. Reflexiones en torno al poder. Siglos XVI a XXI*. Santiago de Chile: Pehuén.

———. 2024. "¡Cuidado!, el Antropoceno. Entre exaltación de la vida y necropolítica." In *Los cuidados en y más allá del Antropoceno: Un recorrido interdisciplinario ante las crisis socio-ecológicas*, ed. Philipp Wolfesberger, Olaf Kaltmeier, and Ann-Kathrin Volmer, 13–26. Buenos Aires: CALAS-CLACSO.

Kohn, Eduardo. 2021. *Cómo piensan los bosques*. Quito: Abya Yala.

Kolbert, Elizabeth. 2019. *La sexta extinción*. Barcelona: Editorial Crítica.

Kopenawa, Davi, and Bruce Albert. 2013. *The Falling Sky. Words of a Yanomami Shaman*. Trans. Nicholas Elliot and Alison Dundy. Cambridge: Harvard University Press.

Leguizamón Castillo, Yeimmy Rocío. 2015. "Conflictos ambientales y movimientos sociales: el caso del movimiento embera katío en respuesta a la construcción de la represa Urrá (1994–2008)." *Memoria y Sociedad* 19, no. 39: 94–105.

Lynch, Barbara Deutsch. 2019. "What Hirschman's Hiding Hand Hid in San Lorenzo and Chixoy." *Water* 11, no. 3: 1–18.

McNeill, John R., and Peter Engelke. 2016. *The Great Acceleration: An Environmental History of the Anthropocene since 1945*. Cambridge: Harvard University Press.

Méndez, Ma Guadalupe, Gilberto Sven Binnqüist, and Sergio A. Méndez. 2019. "Riesgo, vulnerabilidad y cambio climático en suelo de conservación ecológica de la Ciudad de México. El caso de los humedales de Tláhuac." *Veredas. Revista del Pensamiento Sociológico* 36: 13–45.

Molina, Luis, and Mario Melgar Morales. 2014. "Biotecnología Aplicada al Cultivo de la Caña de Azúcar." In *El cultivo de la caña de azúcar en Guatemala*, ed. Mario Melgar, Adlai Meneses, Héctor Orozco, et al., 79–106. Guatemala City: CENGICAÑA.

Moreno, Verónica, ed. 2013. *Conservación ahora*. Quito: International Union for Conservation of Nature.

Preciado Beltrán, Jair, Robert Orlando Leal Pulido, and Cecilia Almanza Castañeda. 2005 *Historia ambiental de Bogotá, Siglo XX: Elementos históricos para la formulación del medio ambiente urbano*. Bogotá: Fondo de Publicaciones Universidad Distrital Francisco José de Caldas.

Raby, Megan. 2017. *American Tropics. The Caribbean Roots of Biodiversity Science*. Chapel Hill: University of North Carolina Press.

Román Suárez, Hermax Rubén. 2022. "La Sierra de Santa Catarina: extractivismo, urbanización, gentrificación y construcción social de alternativas en el oriente de la CDMX." *Diversidad* 23: 81–91.

Sedrez, Lise, and Natasha Augusto Barbosa. 2023. "Narratives on Babylon Hill: Exploring the making of a community and its urban forest through oral and environmental history (1985–2015)." In *Urban Movements and Climate Change. Loss, Damage and Radical Adaptation*, ed. Marco Armiero, Ethemcan Turhan, and Salvatore Paolo De Rosa, 143–160. Amsterdam: Amsterdam University Press.

Silva, Claiton Marcio da, and Claudio de Majo, ed. 2022. *The Age of the Soybean: An Environmental History of Soy During the Great Acceleration*. Cambridge: White Horse Press.

Solbrig, Otto T. 2004. "Ventajas y desventajas de la agrobiotecnología." In *Los transgénicos en América Latina y el Caribe: un debate abierto*, ed. Alicia Bárcena, Jorge Katz, Marianne Schaper, et al., 33–69. Santiago de Chile: Comisión Económica para América Latina y el Caribe.

Svampa, Maristella. 2019. *Las fronteras del neoextractivismo en América Latina: conflictos socioambientales, giro ecoterritorial y nuevas dependencias.* Bielefeld: Bielefeld University Press.

Torres-Salinas, Robinson, Gerardo Azócar García, Noelia Carrasco Henríquez, et al. 2016. "Desarrollo Forestal, Escasez Hídrica, y La Protesta Social Mapuche por la Justicia Ambiental en Chile." *Ambiente & Sociedade* 19, no. 1: 121–145.

Turrent Fernández, Antonio. 2018. "El maíz transgénico, posible amenaza de la biodiversidad del maíz nativo mexicano." *Agro Productividad* 1, no. 2: 6–9.

Valencia-Hernández, Javier Gonzaga, Erika-Milena Muñoz-Villarreal, et al. 2017. "El Extractivismo Minero a Gran Escala. Una Amenaza Neocolonial Frente a La Pervivencia Del Pueblo Embera." *Revista Luna Azul* 45: 419–445.

World People's Conference on Climate Change and the Rights of Mother Earth. 2010. "People's Agreement of Cochabamba." Climate Emergency Institute. April 24. https://www.climateemergencyinstitute.com/uploads/Peoples_climate_ag reement.pdf.

WWF-Brazil. 2023. "Pantanal has record number of fire outbreaks in the first 20 days of November." November 22. https://www.wwf.org.br/?87282/Pantanal-has-rec ord-number-of-fire-outbreaks-in-the-first-20-days-of-November.

Biodiversity in the Southern Cone from 1950 to the Present

John Soluri

For more than thirty years, scientists and a wide array of other communities, ranging from Mapuche healers to German bug collectors, have assembled compelling evidence that the Earth is undergoing a sharp decline in biological diversity due to the actions of people including intensive agriculture, energy production, mining, forestry, and urbanization (Faundes 2010; Hallmann et al. 2017). The magnitude of extinctions of vertebrate species "exploded" in the 1980s, affecting taxa both old and new (McCallum 2015; Cowie, Bouchet, and Fountaine 2022). This was the context in which the term "biodiversity" emerged as an important scientific and political concept. First deployed – in the English language – by U.S. biologists who did field research in Latin America, "biodiversity" (*biodiversidad* or *biodiversidade*) quickly gained influence among Latin American scientists, policymakers, and activists. The concept was institutionalized at the 1992 United Nations Conference on Environment and Development (UNCED), where delegates drafted the Convention on Biological Diversity (Sarandón 2010; McCook 2018).

The Convention on Biological Diversity offered a definition of biodiversity that went beyond species to include both genetic material (intraspecific diversity) and ecological complexes (interspecific diversity). Biodiversity, therefore, is not merely the sum total of life forms or species. This chapter builds on the Convention's definition in order to emphasize that biodiversity is best understood as an array of dynamic ecological relationships or assemblages that result from life forms interacting with one another and non-living materials. Ultimately, these assemblages are vital for reproducing the wondrous variety of life on the planet Earth. That said, there is little scientific or philosophical consensus over how to define a species, much less agreement on how many species exist (Richards 2010).

The scientific and vernacular names given to flora and fauna are documents that reflect the historical contexts in which organisms – and their classifiers – have lived. In Chile, nearly half of all contemporary vernacular names and eight scientific names to identify temperate forest birds are derived from the Mapuche language Mapuzugun. In addition, the names of many of Chile's forest birds are onomatopoeias, an indication that fauna was not only identified by sight or morphology (Ibarra, Benavides, and Caviedes 2020). This kind of cultural borrowing/appropriation reveals the often-hidden ways that scientific knowledge is derived from sources other than European cultures. The names used to describe life forms, therefore, serve as reminders of the challenges of separating biological diversity from cultural diversity.

In the area now known as the Southern Cone, people have made material and symbolic use of plants and animals for thousands of years. Since 1950, however, people have exploited living organisms at unprecedented rates and scales, generating equally unprecedented threats to biodiversity. As in many other parts of the twentieth-century world, states, business corporations, financial institutions, and research institutes in the Southern Cone promoted models of agriculture, forestry, mining, energy production, livestock raising, and fishing that privileged short-term yields – extraction – over the nurturing of biological diversity. In other words, people and institutions in the Southern Cone have not merely "experienced" ecological crises; they have provoked them by extracting and consuming material resources often at the expense of Indigenous societies or rural inhabitants who lack power over resources (Harambour Ross 2019; Klubock 2014).

The 1992 UNCED Conference brought together not only representatives of nation-states, but also a fairly diverse conglomeration of civil organizations (NGOs) that proliferated following the end of Cold War-era military dictatorships that ruled Paraguay (1954–1989), Argentina (1966–1973; 1976–1983), Chile (1973–1990), and Uruguay (1973–1985). These authoritarian states repressed political dissent of all kinds by torturing, killing, or disappearing tens of thousands of people. Post-Cold War neoliberal democratization opened up economies to the rapacious exploitation of people and resources while simultaneously creating political and social spaces for organizing movements and research efforts to challenge state and corporate control over biodiversity and water and mineral resources.

This entry focuses largely on threats to biodiversity posed by the expansion of three kinds of monocultures – soybean farms, tree plantations, and salmon aquaculture – which have generated both large profits and loud protests. Monocultures were no strangers in the Southern Cone; the exploitation of grasslands for the production of wheat, maize, or wool in the nineteenth and early twentieth centuries served to dispossess Indigenous societies, bolster nation-states, and enrich capitalists. Although contemporary critics often associate today's monocultures with "neoliberal extractivism," monocultures can also be understood as the continuation of a "long Green Revolution" that began in the early twentieth century and was characterized by high-density cultivation of selectively bred crop plants and animals (Gudynas 2015; Patel 2013).

The recent histories of soy farms, pine and eucalyptus plantations, and salmon aquaculture illustrate how monocultures simultaneously eroded biodiversity at the regional level while also appropriating it on a global scale. First domesticated in

China, soybeans (*Glycine max*), including a genetically modified variety developed in the United States, have replaced native grasslands and forests in Argentina, Brazil, Paraguay, and Uruguay; Monterrey pine (*Pinus radiata*) from California and blue eucaliptus (*Eucalyptus globulus*) from Australia have formed the basis of tree plantations in Chile and Uruguay that have replaced native forests and grasslands; and Atlantic salmon (*Salmo salar*) sourced from Norway spawned ecological change in aquatic ecosystems in southern Chile.

Monocultures have generated large profits for relatively small groups of investors while creating employment and boosting consumption for working- and middle-class people (Tinsman 2014; Leguizamón 2020; Song et al. 2021). At the same time, the expansion of monocultures has engendered challenges and opposition from local actors including Indigenous people, peasants, fishers, and residents of working-class neighborhoods. These groups have often struck alliances with academic researchers, medical doctors, and lawyers in order to engage with state and corporate entities. In academic and political realms, agroecologists have challenged the primacy of agronomists; conservation biologists have identified hazards posed by engineers' designs for dams; and social scientists using concepts and evidence from political ecology and environmental history have exposed the ways that capitalism (and sometimes socialism) accelerated the consumption of life-sustaining resources while exacerbating inequalities along lines of class, gender, and ethno-racial identities (Alimonda 2017; Baigorrotegui 2019; Merlinsky and Wagner 2019; Sicard and Altieri 2010).

In Argentina, Brazil, and Chile, a wide range of fruit and vegetable industries have utilized intensive monocropping as a production model; in Brazil and Paraguay, cattle ranching drove – and still drives – deforestation. In addition, large-scale mining and energy projects have posed threats to biodiversity by damming rivers, flooding forests, and building roads. Critics of monocultures and other kinds of megaprojects often refer to the areas in which these activities take place as "sacrifice zones" – places where governments choose to destroy biodiversity and transform local livelihoods in the name of economic growth or national development.

"Sacrifice zones" are often contrasted to "spared lands" – state-sanctioned protected areas such as national parks. After exploring biodiversity loss and conflict associated with monocultures, this chapter briefly examines the post-1950s expansion of both public and private protected areas in the Southern Cone. Since the creation of the Convention on Biological Diversity, both state and private initiatives to create protected areas have been increasingly framed in an international, scientific language of "protecting" or "conserving" biodiversity. The ability of protected areas to foster biodiversity and reduce rates of extinction is not clear, particularly when such "land sparing" co-exists alongside high-input monocultures, massive mines, and fossil fuel extraction. Moreover, major political and biological challenges exist for ensuring that protected areas are established in locations and at sufficient scales to sustain ecological relationships without displacing people in the biocultural mosaic that is the Southern Cone.

The Southern Cone as Biocultural Mosaic

The Southern Cone is a multinational region in South America that typically includes Argentina (2.8 million km²), Chile (0.75 million km²), and Uruguay (0.17 million km²). In this volume, the Southern Cone also encompasses Paraguay (0.4 million km²) and southern Brazil (approx. 2.5 million km²). This conglomeration of territorial states is not as rich in plant and animal life as "megadiverse" macroregions like the Amazon or Mesoamerica, but the Southern Cone includes eight of the world's fifteen identified biome types. Paraguay alone contains seven major eco-regions while straddling tropical and temperate biomes. From the Atacama Desert to Cape Horn, the region includes some of Earth's driest and wettest terrestrial ecosystems. There are subtropical dry forests, including the immense Chaco in Paraguay and Argentina, as well as temperate rain forests in southern Chile. Grassland ecosystems include the humid Pampas in Argentina and Uruguay, subtropical savannas in the Chaco and Mato Grosso, and semi-arid, windswept steppe in Patagonia. Finally, Argentina, Chile, and Uruguay's coastal zones contain extremely abundant and diverse life, including fish, mollusks, marine mammals, and a plethora of birds (Güller and Zelaya 2017). This ecological diversity undermines the coherency implied in the name Southern Cone, a term rooted more firmly in Cold War geopolitical imaginaries than biocultural materialities (Marchesi 2019).

On an organismic level, southern Argentina and Chile are characterized by high rates of endemism – life forms found nowhere else on the planet. In the territory claimed by Chile, twenty mammals are endemic, as are nearly forty percent (2,145 of 5,471) of the cataloged vascular plants (Rodríguez et al. 2018). Argentina has eighty-nine endemic mammals; an estimated 17 percent of ten thousand vascular plants in its national territory are endemic (Zuolaga and Belgrano 2015). Paraguay and Uruguay have significantly fewer species of flora and fauna than their much larger neighbors, but they are comparatively rich in avian life: Uruguay has as many different kinds of birds (approx. 450) as Chile in spite of being less than one-quarter the size. Paraguay, whose territory is about half that of Chile, is home to 689 species of birds.

According to the International Union for the Conservation of Nature (IUCN), there are 206 endangered and 110 critically endangered species in Argentina, Chile, Paraguay, and Uruguay. This list includes 103 endemic species in Chile and seventy endemic species in Argentina. In addition, 4.4 percent (187) of Argentina's life forms are listed as "vulnerable," a status that the IUCN assigns to species whose populations are estimated to have declined by 30 to 50 percent in recent history and/or whose geographic range is small or shrinking. Chile has a similar percentage (4.3 percent) of vulnerable species; Paraguay (2.5 percent) and Uruguay (2.3 percent) have significantly lower percentages of vulnerable species (IUCN 2021).

Since 1950, urban environments have expanded significantly in the Southern Cone, while the number of peasants – small-scale producers of food for both auto-consumption and exchange – has declined sharply since the 1980s (Soluri 2019). In 2020, approximately 90 percent of the 70 million people residing in Argentina, Chile, or Uruguay inhabited places that were defined as urban (World Bank 2022). In southern Brazil, more than 80 percent of the 30 million people inhabiting the region were urbanites. The percentage of Paraguay's 7 million inhabitants who lived in urban areas in 2020 was significantly less (62 percent) than that of its neighbors, yet exceeded the global rate of urbanization (~55 percent). The growth of large metropolitan areas in grasslands, including the capital cities of Buenos Aires, Santiago, and Montevideo, concentrated people, private wealth, state resources, and political power. At the same time, regional cities like Temuco, Chile or Salta, Argentina were among the fastest-growing urban areas in the Southern Cone. Today, small and medium-sized urbanizations can be found in every biome, including deserts, semi-arid steppe, mountains, and forests.

Contemporary cities in the Southern Cone are characterized by dense populations of people inhabiting spaces characterized by impermeable surfaces (e.g., cement); channeled or buried waterways; and air, water, noise, and light pollution generated by industry and homes as well as modes of transport (notably private automobiles) and sewer systems. Such conditions tend to sever ecological relationships and create new ones based on flora and fauna adapted to urban ecologies (McKinney 2008; Moño-Pacheco and Villaseñor 2022). Suburban areas have also grown tremendously in recent decades. In some cases, suburbs have produced an increase in the variety of plants and animals due to the introduction of ornamental plants and animals at rates that exceed those of documented local extinctions. This does not mean that suburban landscapes do not alter ecologies in ways that threaten native species or long-standing ecological relationships (Hernández, Rodríguez, and Gallo 2009).

In recent decades, cities in the Southern Cone have become more interconnected, linked by roads and high-speed highways that facilitated suburbanization while creating ecological conditions that favor the propagation of introduced plant species (Sedrez and Horta 2018). They have also become centers of energy consumption, specifically electricity and fossil fuels for transportation, heating, and cooking. The need to create and maintain energy services for growing urban populations prompted governments to undertake projects like gas drilling, hydroelectric dams, and transmission infrastructures that degraded or destroyed habitats for plants and animals (Milanesio 2013).

City lights should not blind us to the reality that, from Atacama to Patagonia, rural areas have been – and continue to be – home to important populations of Indigenous and non-Indigenous people (Zarrilli 2016). To a large degree, the expansion of capital-intensive monocultures, biodiversity loss, and urbanization have been linked in a mutually reinforcing dynamic that drives life throughout the Southern Cone including in the vast region dubbed *"La República de la Soja."*

"The Republic of Soy"

World production of soybeans increased more than any other crop between 1970 and 2020, skyrocketing from less than 30 million tons to more than 300 million tons. Soybeans covered an estimated 100 million hectares of land in 2020 (Soutullo, Zladúa, and Teixerira-de-Mello 2020). Brazil is by far the leading producer and exporter of soybeans in South America; soybeans are also a leading crop in Argentina, Paraguay, and Uruguay (Céspedes-Payret et al. 2009). Rising consumption of cooking oils in China and India, the two largest importers of soybean oil in the 2010s, largely drove the expansion of international markets, along with rising rates of meat consumption – soy being a raw material for animal feed (Turzi 2017). For more than twenty years, soy cultivation in the Americas has utilized genetically modified varieties of soybeans that are resistant to the broad-spectrum herbicide glyphosate, popularly known as Roundup. In addition to generating profits for Monsanto, "Roundup Ready" soy has enabled till-free methods of cultivation that have reduced labor costs and soil erosion rates while giving rise to "superweeds" including *Amaranthus hybridus* that are 100 times more resistant to glyphosate than susceptible populations (Vazquez et al. 2017; García et al. 2019). Extremely heavy application rates of Roundup have also exposed people to suspected carcinogens.

In Argentina, where commercial soybean cultivation began in the 1940s, the crop had already covered hundreds of thousands of hectares of land by the 1970s. Production boomed in the 1990s following the adoption of favorable policy measures, including approval of the use of genetically modified varieties. Land in soybean monocultures rose nearly 500 percent and production increased by 700 percent between 1985 and 2015 (Turzi 2017; Leguizamón 2020; Zarrilli 2016). By the early 2010s, soy covered 20 million hectares in Argentina, including provinces with long histories of monocropping (Buenos Aires and Córdoba) as well as provinces in north and northwest Argentina (Chaco, Entre Ríos, Salta, and Tucumán) that had previously been on the margins of capital-intensive agriculture.

In the Pampas of Argentina, the expansion of soy turned an agroscape formed by livestock and annual crop production into a homogeneous, continuously-cropped landscape characterized by little planned or associated agrodiversity; by the early twenty-first century, 90 percent of the Pampas were converted to crops or pasture.

As might be expected, monocultures and livestock raising have severely depleted populations of large predators and herbivores leading to regional extinctions (e.g., puma and jaguar) or vulnerable situations (e.g., deer and guanacos). Soy expansion has also negatively impacted the diversity of rodents and some insects. Effects on avian life has been varied: the decline of the migratory raptor Swainson's Hawk (*Buteo swainsoni*) due to pesticide exposure drew international attention (Medan et al. 2011). In the Argentine Chaco, including the province of Salta, soy monocultures increased from 100,000 to 600,000 hectares between 1990–2010. Analyses of LANDSAT data indicate extensive deforestation and fragmentation of the region's dry forests indicating that changes in socio-ecological relationships are unfolding along with rising social conflicts (Gasparri and Grau 2009; Vallejos et al. 2022).

Brazilian soybean production began in Rio Grande do Sul, before spreading to the states of Paraná, Santa Catarina, Mato Grosso, and beyond; between 1985–86 and 2015–16, cropland in soy rose from 9.4 million hectares to 33.3 million hectares; production increased from fourteen million to one hundred million metric tons (Turzi 2017). In Mato Grosso, where the average soy farm occupied 3000 hectares, monocropping drove the highest regional rate of deforestation recorded in Brazil in the twenty-first century (Wittman et al. 2017). In Paraguay, soybeans surpassed cotton as the nation's top export crop in the mid-1980s. Cultivation began in the nation's eastern provinces before spreading west in the early twenty-first century. In the western Chaco, ranching and farming activities cleared more than 44,000 km² of forest between 1987 to 2012, rates of deforestation comparable to those in Latin America's tropical regions. Some researchers found that investors frequently purchased pastureland in the western Chaco for conversion to soy, suggesting that ranching may have been an intermediate stage of land use between forest and soybean farming (Baumann et al. 2017).

Nearly surrounded by soy-producing regions, Uruguay did not join the "Republic of Soy" until the early twenty-first century. Agribusinesses had planted approximately 1 million hectares of soybeans in 2020, an increase that coincided with big increases in imports of insecticides and herbicides, including endosulfan and glyphosate. Sampling studies carried out in Uruguay found agrochemicals present in soils, fish, and beehives in locations both adjacent to soy farms and in protected areas lying several kilometers from soy monocultures. These findings point to some of the challenges associated with the co-existence of biologically diverse ecosystems and intensive monocultures that rely on agrochemicals capable of migrating through soil or water (Soutullo, Zladúa, and Teixerira-de-Mello 2020).

In Argentina, political protests related to soy expansion have taken on distinct forms in different contexts. For example, in a working-class neighborhood surrounded by soy farms on the edge of the city of Córdoba, women launched one of Argentina's first organized protests against aerial herbicide spraying by invoking the idea of health as a human right. In 2002, the group Mothers from

Barrio Ituzaingo Anexo was formed in response to maternal and pediatric health concerns: respiratory illness, cancer, birth defects, and miscarriages. Working in collaboration with regional professionals, the Mothers created a "death map" (*mapa de la muerte*): an epidemiological study intended to call their neighbors' attention to connections between exposure to agrochemicals and local health problems. The group also engaged in public protests directed at local government officials and filed lawsuits against soy growers and pesticide applicators (Leguizamón 2016; and Leguizamón 2020: 112–138). In this instance, activists did not frame their concerns about monocultures in terms of local or planetary declines in biodiversity but rather in maternalist discourses and symbols that invoked reproductive health and children's wellbeing. Community organizers pressured local officials to establish buffer zones around their neighborhoods as a means to reduce exposure to pesticides, but they stopped short of calling for a ban on herbicide use or restriction on the location of soy monocultures.

In Malvinas, Córdoba – the poorest urban area in the province – residents organized a blockade and occupation of a site where the Monsanto Corporation sought to build a facility for producing genetically modified maize seed. The protests and occupations, which began in 2013, drew international attention and succeeded in compelling Monsanto, which had received an endorsement from Argentina's President Cristina Fernández de Kirchner, to abandon the project and sell the land in 2017. Working-class people struck alliances with scientists and other professionals in order to mobilize knowledge and resources in their struggles, but some local activists distanced themselves from national political parties or international movements (Leguizamón 2020).

Concerns for maternal and pediatric health did not always compel people in Argentina to protest the power of soy producers. In towns surrounded by soy where livelihoods and social status were rooted in the idea of living "off the countryside" (*del campo*), most middle-class women and men displayed an "acquiescence" to the risks posed by herbicide spraying; "murmurs" prevailed over social movements (Leguizamón 2020: 92–111). Through 2018, protests over agrochemical use on soy monocultures in Argentina failed to result in a federal law banning glyphosate fumigations in urban areas. State officials relied on well-worn strategies of authorizing scientific reviews that produce inconclusive findings and opening judicial proceedings that dragged on for years, often outliving the original plaintiffs (Leguizamón 2020: 131–137; Swistún and Auyero 2009).

Challenges to soybean monocultures were different in Argentina's northern Chaco region (provinces of Chaco, Formosa, Santiago del Estero, and Salta) where rural people including Indigenous groups (Kollas, Tobas, and Wichís) struggled against deforestation and dispossession of the land on which they farmed, raised livestock, hunted, and foraged (Schmidt 2019). In contrast to the national profile, one-third of the population in the Chaco region inhabited rural areas and relied on access to patchy habitats for their livelihoods (Zarrilli 2016). Organizations like the *Movimiento Campesino de Santiago del Estero* (MOCASE) represented thousands of rural families that frequently lacked legal titles to their land, leaving them vulnerable to dispossession by agribusinesses. MOCASE collaborated with both national peasant organizations (*Movimiento Nacional Campesino Indígena*) in Argentina and the international network *La Vía Campesina* to employ legal strategies to retain land while embracing a vision that rejects corporate monocultures in favor of agroecological approaches that value biodiversity in farming systems (Leguizamón 2020: 128–130; Pinto 2012; and Perfecto, Vandermeer, and Wright 2009).

In the western Chaco of Paraguay, cattle ranching and soy expansion have undermined Indigenous livelihoods notwithstanding provisions in Paraguay's 1992 Constitution protecting Indigenous land rights. For example, a state-sanctioned territory held by the Angaité (self-named Enenlhet) was surrounded by cattle ranches that entered the region in the early 2000s. The ensuing deforestation undermined Angaité foraging and hunting practices, compelling some Angaité to seek work on ranches in order to be able to hunt and forage (Glauser 2019). Some Angaité have received government aid while others have sold or leased land to ranchers. At the same time, Angaité communities have maintained hunting practices (*marisca*) and rituals that seem to resist the "transactional" politics practiced by state officials and NGOs; such rituals inscribe meanings on forests and their animal inhabitants that ranchers do not understand (Glauser 2018).

Foreign Forests and Indigenous Rights

Central-Southern Chile is home to temperate forests that include endemic or rare life forms including hundreds of plants such as the Ruil (*Nothofagus alessandri*), Keule (*Gomortega keule*), and monkey puzzle (*Araucaria araucana*) trees; mammals like Chinchillas (*Chinchilla lanigera*) and Darwins' fox (*Lycalopex fulvipes*); along with reptiles and amphibians. Currently, many of these forests are highly fragmented after nearly a century of state and private forestry projects. State support for tree plantations in Chile, which began in the 1930s, expanded under the reformist government of Eduardo Frei (1964–1970) whose administration directly and indirectly subsidized reforestation, including the re-seeding of areas where people had cleared native forests comprised of *Nothofagus* (including raulí, coigüe, lenga) and *Araucaria* with introduced species like Monterrey pine. Under Salvador Allende, the Popular Unity government (1970–1973) accelerated the nationalization of forest lands while maintaining a "developmentalist logic" that stressed the export-oriented industrialization of forests via partnerships with domestic and international investors (Klubock 2014: 216). Allende also created national parks, taking advantage of a clause in Chile's forestry law that empowered presidents to establish parks without undertaking protracted processes of expropriation and indemnification. Allende's policies slowed the deforestation of native araucaria forests in some regions, but his short-lived government also promoted the logging of native forests to provide a livelihood for Mapuche communities and reforestation with Monterrey Pine for pulp and paper production (Klubock 2014: 227).

Under the dictatorship of Augusto Pinochet (1973–1990), the Chilean state subsidized the establishment of tree plantations to such a degree that it became profitable to plant trees regardless of demand. Between 1974 and 1980, pine plantations grew by 1 million hectares, more than 75 percent of which were seeded by the Chilean government or via government subsidies (Montalba-Navarro and Carrasco 2003). In 1979, Chile was responsible for half of all the pine planted in the world (Klubock 2014: 239). Enthusiastic government backers declared timber to be the "new copper" an indication of both the scale of revenues generated by tree plantations and the extractivist mentality typical of neoliberal economic models.

State support for tree plantations outlived the Pinochet dictatorship; between 1995 and 2009, tree plantations expanded by more than one hundred thousand hectares annually; by 2015, mono-species forests covered 2.4 million hectares of land in southern Chile (Zamorano et al. 2015). In the Coastal Range of southern Central Chile, plantations expanded in areas previously occupied by forests or shrublands whose flora included at least two endemic tree species vulnerable to extinction (Nahuelhual et al. 2012). Today, fragments of forest are restricted to upper elevations in the Andean mountains; expansive tracts of native forest are also found in the southern portion of Chile's Coastal Range.

Tree plantations have not been restricted to Chile; the government of Uruguay, utilizing a 1987 forestry law, promoted the afforestation of grasslands in order to generate raw materials for pulp and paper production. As was the case in Chile, the Uruguayan state gave subsidies to private corporations to establish tree monocultures. By the early twenty-first century, pine and eucalyptus plantations covered nearly 1 million hectares of land or 5.6 percent of Uruguay's national territory; transnational companies owned one-half of the production (Cravino 2021). The long-term effects on biodiversity generated by the afforestation of grasslands are not clear, but field studies have documented a reduction in species richness among mammals in eucalyptus stands due mainly to the absence of native specialist animals found in grasslands. Most mammalian species found in tree plantations were in firebreaks – strips of grasslands intended to isolate tree stands (Cravino 2021). Research in Uruguay and elsewhere also indicates that the elevated rates of evapotranspiration associated with tree plantations led to a reduction in groundwater discharge (Paruelo 2012).

In Central-South Chile, forestry projects have been embroiled in social conflict since their inception. Mapuche and non-Indigenous rural dwellers have challenged state and private expropriations of land and loss of access to resources found in native forests. For example, in 1983, a Chilean peasant conveyed their impression of socio-ecological changes linked to tree monocultures: "Nobody claimed the forests in the cordillera; everyone depended on them and used their products but they did not belong to anyone. In our region, we see that plantations are fenced off, the roads are barred; the water of the Andalién, Bío-Bío, and Trongo rivers is contaminated because the landowners exploit the forests that grow on the banks of the watersheds and they do not care who uses the water below." (Klubock 2014: 255–256)

For the Mapuche, a significant portion of Chile's tree plantations lie within Wallmapu, the historical territory of a Mapuche nation that spanned the Andes and whose memory challenges the legitimacy of the territorial claims of both the Argentine and Chilean states. The forest, or *lemu*, is vital to Mapuche identity for both material and symbolic reasons; many Mapuche communities have linked the expansion of pine monocultures to a decline in their physical and spiritual well-being (Montalba-Navarro and Carrasco 2003; Torres-Salinas et al. 2016). For example, a Mapuche *machi*, Francisca Linconao Huircapan, filed a lawsuit against a forestry company in a regional court in Temuco in 2009 for the alleged removal of native flora from the banks of mountain springs situated on land adjacent to Mapuche lands. In addition to contending that the action violated the Chilean Forestry Law prohibiting the removal of vegetation in proximity to water sources, the suit invoked ILO Convention 169 on Indigenous and Tribal Peoples and the Convention of Biological Diversity to assert that the company's actions had degraded an ecosystem whose waters and medicinal plants held sacred meaning for Mapuche (Faundes 2010). In asking the court to compel the company to halt its activities on lands not legally owned by Mapuche, Linconao sought to assert rights to biocultural heritage over property rights. The regional court ruled in her favor, a decision that was later upheld by Chile's Supreme Court.

The story of Machi Linconao's activism has not concluded. In 2013, she was accused of participating in a deadly case of arson and arrested under Chile's anti-terrorism laws. Five years later, she was acquitted; in 2021, she served as an elected Mapuche representative to Chile's unsuccessful Constitutional Convention. Linconao's tumultuous relationship with the Chilean state captures the tensions and contradictions of neoliberal states whose legitimacy resides in protecting capitalism, cultural pluralism, and increasingly, biodiversity. The Chilean state has both supported and criminalized Mapuche efforts to assert power over biocultural resources. Mapuche organizations, in turn, have sometimes denied the legitimacy of state rule, while at other times leveraging courts and even forestry corporations to defend their territories, livelihoods, and language (Hale 2020). Faced with expanding forest plantations and decreasing access to water, some Mapuche have migrated to cities while others have cultivated small stands of forests that mix native and exotic species (González-Hidalgo, Fonk, and Toledo 2013).

Maritime Monocultures: Salmon Farms and Social Conflict

Beginning in the late 1980s, southern Chile became the epicenter of a new kind of monoculture in the Southern Cone: intensive fish farming. Spurred by government policies, changing consumer tastes, and transnational investors, the salmon industry became the most important economic sector in southern Chile, employing tens of thousands of workers (Vargas and Cárcamo 2022). For twenty years (1987 to 2007), salmon farming grew at a meteoric rate, turning the region into the world's second-leading producer and top exporter of Atlantic salmon to Japan and the United States. As was the case with soy and tree plantations, the expansion of aquaculture in Chile was part of a global phenomenon: in 2009, the U.N. Food and Agriculture Organization declared aquaculture to be the world's "fastest growing food production system" (Soluri 2011).

Salmon producers initially took advantage of southern Chile's relatively clean, fresh-water lakes to nurture juvenile salmon into adults for subsequent transport to sea pens situated in the protected ocean waters found in Ancúd Bay. Intensive aquaculture, therefore, posed risks to biodiversity in both fresh and marine water environments. The introduction and cultivation of millions of carnivorous fish to freshwater lakes threatened endemic species of fish; storms or other forces capable of damaging the sea pens used to contain salmon have caused unintentional releases of large quantities of salmon into the open sea. Following concerns about fish escapes and problems with freshwater parasites, salmon companies shifted from lakes to enclosed tanks for raising juvenile salmon. Atlantic salmon continued to mature in vertical sea pens some twenty to thirty meters deep. The dense concentration of fish added large quantities of organic waste to marine benthic zones; salmon monocultures also generated pollution in the forms of heavy metals like copper used to clean pens, parasiticides employed to control sea lice, and antibiotics utilized to inhibit infections that form in lesions created by sea lice (Gerhart 2017; Soluri 2011).

The network of Atlantic salmon monocultures that stretched from Norway to southern Chile facilitated a pandemic of infectious salmon anemia (ISA) in 2007–08 that compelled aquaculture companies in southern Chile to harvest fish prematurely, abandon sea pens, and lay off thousands of workers (Soluri 2011). The salmon industry responded to the economic risks posed by ISA by concentrating capital and expanding geographically, pushing further south in an effort to spread production sites without drastically reducing the density of fish raised in sea pens. Salmon aquaculture continued to nurture not only fish but also bacteria, parasites, and viruses; in 2014, the aquaculture industry used 563,000 kilograms of antibiotics (Gerhart 2017).

Unsurprisingly, social conflicts over salmon farming have had less to do with land tenure and more to do with the industry's ecological instability linked to pathogens and pollution that have contributed to periodic die-offs of fish and other aquatic organisms that are vital to livelihoods and cultures in southern Chile. In 2016, the island of Chiloé erupted in protest in response to a swath of mass die-offs of marine organisms ranging from shellfish to whales, including millions of farmed salmon. Aquaculture companies responded by laying off thousands of workers. Biologists connected the events to a red tide – toxic algal blooms – linked to warm ocean temperatures and possibly the enormous volume of organic waste generated by 400 hundred salmon farms. Led by unions of small-scale fishing people, protesters blockaded access to the island for two weeks while calling on the government to tighten regulations on the salmon industry and promote local fishing operations (Daughters 2016).

In many regards, salmon aquaculture (i.e., monocultures) has spawned similar dynamics to those created in terrestrial monocultures like soy and pine. Local people, both Indigenous and non-Indigenous have sometimes gained employment opportunities while almost always losing access to biological resources that formed the basis for foraging or hunting. In all cases, state policies have played critical roles in enabling monocultures to expand via subsidies and/or weak regulatory structures affecting both worker well-being and ecosystem health.

States, along with local and translocal actors, have also been key players in projects intended to conserve biological diversity in the Southern Cone. The expansion of public and private conservation areas since 1950 has generated new forms of social conflict.

Conserving Biodiversity

The Southern Cone is home to some of the earliest protected areas created in Latin America, including national parks such as Argentina's Nahuel Huapi (originally called National Park of the South) founded in 1922. Initiatives to establish national parks resulted from a complex set of influences, many of which resonated with European or U.S. ideas about scenic landscapes, forestry, and tourism. They also often functioned to promote nationalism by establishing a state presence near territorial boundaries and/or by erasing Indigenous histories (Freitas 2021; Kaltmeier 2021). These early parks sought to protect habitats of emblematic flora or fauna, an objective that was not seen as incompatible with the introduction of new plants and animals including red deer, trout, or the Douglas Fir (Kaltmeier 2021).

Following World War II, domestic and international forces (e.g., UNESCO) continued to promote state investments in protected areas with the dual goals of conserving flora and fauna while stimulating tourism. For example, local recreation enthusiasts in Punta Arenas convinced Chilean authorities to establish Torres del Paine National Park in 1959 (originally "Lago Grey" National Park). Torres del Paine expanded significantly between 1961 and 1980, due to actions taken by both Allende's socialist government and Pinochet's military dictatorship. Tourism, which grew slowly prior to the 1990s, remained a key objective for the national park as did the nurturing of native fauna, including the south Andean huemul, small numbers of which were introduced to the Torres del Paine from elsewhere in Chile (Alvarez et al. 1986).

The rate at which Southern Cone states established protected areas in both terrestrial and marine environments increased between 1970–2000, driven in part by the growing influence of conservation biologists who lobbied to shift the focus of protected areas from "natural attractions" to the conservation of biodiversity (Wakild 2018). National parks, however, continued to reinforce notions of wilderness (*desiertos*) that undergirded nationalist narratives and often excluded Indigenous and other rural dwellers. Nevertheless, beginning in the 1980s, conservation advocates began striking tenuous alliances with residents of these areas (Wakild 2018). In Argentina, these alliances became institutionalized in the early twenty-first century in the form of co-management of protected areas. This model, rooted in a vision of joint decision-making and management of resources involving government agencies and local, resident people, offered the potential to achieve intercultural dialogue and place different kinds of knowledge in conversation (Trentini 2011; Trentini 2012).

In practice, co-management has exposed – as well as created – contradictions that lay at the heart of struggles over biocultural diversity. For example, in 2008, conflict emerged in Nahuel Huapi when a Mapuche group attempted to re-occupy (*recuperar*) an area inside the park boundaries that government scientists had declared a "critical area" because it provided habitat for endemic species like the endangered south Andean huemul, an endemic plant (*Senecio carboniensis*), and a frog, *rana del Challhuaco* (*Atelognathus nitoi*). In this case, the knowledge of biologists was valued over that of Mapuche residents because the latter had returned to the area having been expelled decades earlier (Trentini 2011). The Mapuche lacked legitimacy due to their historical mobility that did not conform to notions of an "ancestral" presence. Although protected areas in the Southern Cone have not systematically expelled people from their boundaries, the establishment of national parks in territories historically controlled by Indigenous groups has left complicated legacies; attempts to co-manage protected areas often fail to conceptualize biodiversity in a manner that respects the complexity of Indigenous cosmologies and lived experiences.

National parks are by no means the only form of protected area in the Southern Cone; provincial and local conservation areas have also expanded, driven by grassroots and government actions. For example, in 2005, residents in a coastal community in the Atacama region of Chile, concerned about pollution from proposed industrial facilities, petitioned the government to establish a nature sanctuary in the Huasco River estuary, home to 180 types of flora and fauna. Some artist-activists used photography to call attention to the estuary's botanical diversity and encouraged people to identify endemic species, an example of citizen science that has become a popular tactic to mobilize supporters and generate evidence to present before government officials and mass media. Chile's Ministry of the Environment established a nature reserve (*sanctuario de la naturaleza*) "*Humedal Estuario del Río Huasco*" in 2020 – fifteen years after the initial proposal (Bolados, Morales, and Barraza 2021). The example of Río Huasco illustrates how meanings inscribed into local places undergird movements to value biocultural diversity.

The late-twentieth-century convergence of neoliberal policies and rising concerns about biodiversity in the Southern Cone materialized in the creation of very large, privately owned conservation areas, particularly in Argentine Patagonia and southern Chile. Patagonia began attracting the interest of international conservationists in the mid-twentieth century when organizations like the New York City-based Wilderness Conservation Society initiated projects in Argentine Patagonia focused on protecting marine and coastal wildlife (Conway 2005). In addition, outdoor enthusiasts like Yves Chouinard and Douglas Tompkins traveled to Patagonia in the 1960s prior to becoming major entrepreneurs. Tompkins, along with his spouse Kris, took advantage of both Pinochet-era laws to promote foreign investment and low property prices to begin purchasing land in 1991 eventually assembling a massive private reserve known as Parque Pumalín. After functioning for twelve years (2005–2017), Tompkins Conservation donated nearly 300,000 hectares to the government of Chile which established the National Park "Pumalín Douglas Tompkins." In the early 2000s, Kris Tomkins founded *Conservación Patagonia*, an organization that purchased former sheep ranches in Chile and Argentina and subsequently donated the properties for incorporation into two new national parks: Patagonia Park in Aysen, Chile; and Monte León National Park in Santa Cruz, Argentina (Jones and Gettinger 2016).

In addition, the Italian apparel company Benneton purchased large amounts of land in Argentine Patagonia. These private conservation initiatives generated controversy at regional and national levels; opposition was often framed in nationalist terms by ranchers and other rural people who were suspicious of foreign control and projects to "re-wild" Patagonia by removing wire fences that once contained sheep in order to nurture habitat for south Andean huemuls, pumas, guanacos, and rheas. In Argentina, the Mapuche Ancestral Resistance occupied lands titled to Benneton in Chubut, Argentina, until being violently removed by federal troops (Pannell 2017).

The ability of protected areas to nurture biodiversity and environmental justice remains unclear; climate change and the ability of pollutants to migrate through soil and water media limit the capacity of protected areas to spare plants and animals from hazards generated beyond their boundaries (Rodríguez-Jorquera et al. 2016). Ultimately, biodiversity in the Southern Cone will be influenced – for better or worse – by forces and actors operating beyond protected areas. This reality is made apparent by the recent history of one of Patagonia's oldest inhabitants: guanacos

(*Lama guanicoe*). The proliferation of sheep and other livestock in the early twentieth century led to a steady decline in guanacos due to habitat loss and commercial hunting. Guanaco populations began to increase in the early 1990s when export markets for furs largely disappeared following trade restrictions put in place by the Convention on International Trade in Endangered Species (CITES), an international agreement to curtail commerce in products derived from endangered or vulnerable plants and animals. In addition, a long-term decline in world demand for wool, along with regional pasture degradation, led to the abandonment of ranches in Patagonia that guanaco populations have "re-wilded" in recent decades (Soluri 2023). National parks-based tourism has helped to revalorize living guanacos, but the camelid's recent population increase resulted from a combination of international environmental politics and transnational fashion trends, affirming the importance of both local and trans-local forces in the conservation of biodiversity.

The Anthropocene and the Unforeseen

Since the mid-twentieth century, many forms of life have been threatened by the loss or alteration of their habitats due to the expansion of monocultures in the Southern Cone. These threats are not confined to the Southern Cone; they are variations on a planetary theme of large-scale socio-ecological change, including global warming, that led scientists studying Earth Systems in the early 2000s to coin the term "Anthropocene" in recognition of the leading role played by people in changing the Earth. Social scientists responded by offering alternative labels (e.g., "Capitalocene" and "Plantationocene") that questioned the Anthropocene's analytical power while implicitly acknowledging the term's growing influence (Selcer 2021).

The danger in using a term like Anthropocene, or the only slightly less-sweeping concepts it has spawned, is that they posit a coherency that tends to break down when units of analysis shift from the planetary to the regional or local. When analyzing the political ecologies of specific places, what often stands out is the unforeseen: the unpredictable and often contradictory ways that diverse people understand and respond to biodiversity. In the Southern Cone, the threats to biodiversity caused by the expansion of monocultures have led some people to organize campaigns that call on governments to address social and environmental injustices related to health and livelihood. For many Indigenous people, the loss of biodiversity is both a cultural and an ecological crisis that is frequently bound up with struggles to re-assert their territorial sovereignty. Finally, a significant set of social actors – including those whose livelihoods are closely tied to monocultures – have responded to biodiversity loss with ambivalence, resignation, or denial. Scholar-activists tend to pay limited attention to this rather diverse conglomeration of people, yet the ongoing struggles in Chile to create a new national constitution point to the profound political challenges associated with building legal structures that would promote biocultural diversity in the Southern Cone.

References

Alimonda, Héctor. 2017. "En Clave de sur: La ecología política latinoamericana y el pensamiento crítico." In *Ecología Política Latinoamericana* Vol. 2, ed. Hector Alimonda, Catalina Toro Pérez, and Facundo Martín, 33–49. Buenos Aires: CLAC-SO.

Alvarez, Marcelo, Claudio Cunazza, Santiago Gómez, et al. 1986. "Plan de manejo Parque Nacional Torres del Paine." Working Paper N° 78, CONAF, Santiago de Chile.

Baigorrotegui, Gloria. 2019. "Making Justice for Counter-Expertise and Doing Counter-Expertise for Justice." *Science as Culture* 28, no. 3: 375–382.

Baumann, Matthias, Christoph Israel, María Pique-Rodríguez, et al. 2017. "Deforestation and cattle expansion in the Paraguayan Chaco 1987–2012." *Regional Environmental Change* 17, no. 4: 1179–1191.

Bolados García, Paola, Valeska Morales Urbina, and Stephanie Barraza López. 2021. "Historia de las luchas por la justicia ambiental en las zonas de sacrificio en Chile." *Historia Ambiental Latinoamericana y Caribeña (HALAC)* 11, no. 3: 62–92.

Céspedes-Payret, Carlos, Gustavo Piñeiro, Marcela Achkar, et al. 2009. "The irruption of new agro-industrial technologies in Uruguay and their environmental impacts on soil, water supply, and biodiversity: a review." *International Journal of Environment and Health* 3, no. 2: 175–197.

Conway, William. 2005. *Act III in Patagonia. People and Wildlife*. Washington, D.C.: Island Press.

Cowie, Robert H., Philippe Bouchet, and Benoît Fontaine. 2022. "The Sixth Extinction: Fact, Fiction or Speculation?." *Biological Reviews* 97, no. 2: 640–663.

Cravino, Alexandra, and Alejandro Brazeiro. 2021. "Grassland afforestation in South America: Local scale impacts of eucalyptus plantations on Uruguayan mammals." *Forest Ecology and Management* 484: 1–9.

Daughters, Anton. 2016. "Fish Kills and Protests on the Island of Chiloé." *Anthropology News* 57, no. 5: 1–6.

Faundes, Juan Jorge. 2010. "Primera sentencia que aplica el convenio n° 169 de la OIT en Chile. Derecho a vivir en un medio ambiente libre de contaminación comprende el concepto de territorio, hábitat y protección de la cultura de los pueblos indígenas." *Revista Chilena de Derecho y Ciencia Política* 1, no. 1: 97–113.

Freitas, Federico. 2021. *Nationalizing Nature: Iguazu Falls and National Parks at the Brazil-Argentina Border*. Cambridge: Cambridge University Press.

García, Maria J., Candelario Palma-Bautista, Antonia M. Rojano-Delgado, et al. 2019. "The Triple Amino Acid Substitution TAP-IVS in the EPSPS Gene Confers High Glyphosate Resistance to the Superweed Amaranthus hybridus." *International Journal of Molecular Sciences* 20, no. 10: 1–15.

Gasparri, Nestor Ignacio, and Ricardo Grau. 2009. "Deforestation and fragmentation of Chaco dry forest in NW Argentina (1972–2007)." *Forest Ecology and Management* 258, no. 6: 913–921.

Gerhart, Andrew. 2017. "Petri dishes of an archipelago: the ecological rubble of the Chilean salmon farming industry." *Journal of Political Ecology* 24, no. 1: 726–742.

González-Hidalgo, Marien, Martín Fonk, and Gabriela Toledo. 2013. "Diversidad y biodiversidad como ejercicios de autonomía: alternativas locales ante el impacto de la industria forestal en Chile." *Ecología Política* 46: 73–77.

Glauser, Marcos. 2018. "Entendiendo las respuestas de un pueblo indígena del Chaco Paraguayo a la desposesión territorial." *Gestión y Ambiente* [Supplement 2] 21: 86–94.

———. 2019. *Angaité's responses to deforestation: Political ecology of the livelihood and land use strategies of an indigenous community from the Paraguayan Chaco*. Berlin: LIT Verlag Münster.

Gudynas, Eduardo 2015. *Extractivismos. Ecología, economía y política de un modo de entender el desarrollo y la naturaleza*. Cochabamba: CEDIB.

Güller, Marina, and Diego G. Zelaya. 2017. "A hot-spot of biodiversity in Northern Patagonia, Argentina." *Biodiversity and Conservation* 26: 3329–3342.

Hale, Charles R. 2020. "Using and Refusing the Law: Indigenous Struggles and Legal Strategies after Neoliberal Multiculturalism." *American Anthropologist* 122, no. 3: 618–631.

Hallmann, Caspar A., Martin Sorg, Eelke Jongejans, et al. 2017. "More than 75 percent decline over 27 years in total flying insect biomass in protected areas." *PLoS ONE* 12, no. 10: 1–13.

Harambour Ross, Alberto. 2019. *Soberanías Fronterizas: Estado y Capital en la Colonización de Patagonia (Argentina y Chile, 1830–1922)*. Valdivia: Ediciones UACh.

Hernández, Marcelo Paulo, Andrea Yanina Rodríguez, and Daniel José Gallo. 2009. "El Ombusillo. Una planta endémica en peligro de extinción." *Museo* 3, no. 23: 17–21.

International Union for Conservation of Nature [IUCN]. 2021. "The IUCN Red List of Threatened Species. Version 2021–3." https://www.iucnredlist.org.

Ibarra, José Tomás, Pelayo Benavides, and Julián Caviedes. 2020. "Winged voices: Mapuche ornithology from South American temperate forests." *Journal of Ethnobiology* 40, no. 1: 89–100.

Jones, Geoffrey, and Ben Gettinger. 2016. "Alternative Paths of Green Entrepreneurship: The Environmental Legacies of the North Face's Doug Tompkins and Patagonia's Yvon Chouinard." Working Paper No. 17–034, Harvard Business School, Boston.

Kaltmeier, Olaf. 2021. *National Parks from North to South: An Entangled History of Conservation and Colonization in Argentina*. New Orleans/Trier: University of New Orleans Press/Wissenschaftlicher Verlag Trier.

Klubock, Thomas M. 2014. *La Frontera: Forests and Ecological Conflict in Chile's Frontier Territory*. Durham: Duke University Press.

Leguizamón, Amalia. 2016. "Environmental Injustice in Argentina: Struggles against Genetically-modifed soy." *Journal of Agrarian Change* 16, no. 4: 684–692.

———. 2020. *Seeds of Power: Environmental Injustice and Genetically Modified Soybeans in Argentina*. Durham: Duke University Press.

Marchesi, Aldo. 2019 "Experiencia históre ideaidea del Cono Sur." *Conversaciones del Cono Sur* 4, no. 2: 11–23.

McCallum, Malcolm L. 2015. "Vertebrate biodiversity losses point to a sixth mass extinction." *Biodiversity and Conservation* 24, no. 10: 2497–2519.

McCook, Stuart. 2018. "Prodigality and Sustainability: The Environmental Sciences and the Quest for Development." In *A Living Past: Environmental Histories of Modern Latin America*, ed. John Soluri, Claudia Leal, and José Augusto Pádua, 226–245. New York: Berghahn Books.

McKinney, Michael L. 2008. "Effects of urbanization on species richness: A review of plants and animals." *Urban Ecosystems* 11, no. 2: 161–176.

Medan, Diego, Juan Pablo Torretta, Karina Hodara, et al. 2011. "Effects of agriculture expansion and intensification on the vertebrate and invertebrate diversity in the Pampas of Argentina." *Biodiversity and Conservation* 20: 3077–3100.

Merlinsky, Maria Gabriela, and Lucrecia Soledad Wagner. 2019. "'La memoria del agua' Megaminería y Conflictos Ambientales en Mendoza." *Espoiler*, December 9, 1–9.

Milanesio, Natalia. 2013. "The Liberating Flame: Natural Gas Production in Peronist Argentina." *Environmental History* 8, no. 3: 1–24.

Montalba-Navarro, René, and Noelia Carrasco. 2003. "Modelo forestal chileno y conflicto indígena ¿ecologismo cultural mapuche?." *Ecología Política* 26: 63–77.

Moño-Pacheco, Catalina B., and Nélida R. Villaseñor. 2022. "Avian species richness in cities: A review of the Spanish-language literature from the Southern Cone of South America." *Urban Ecosystems* 25: 601–616.

Nahuelhual, Laura, Alejandra Carmona, Antonio Lara, et al. 2012. "Land-cover change to forest plantations: Proximate causes and implications for the landscape in south-central Chile." *Landscape and Urban Planning* 107, no. 1: 12–20.

Pannell, Jack. 2017 "Benetton in Patagonia – The Oppression of Mapuche in the Argentine South." *Council on Hemispheric Affairs*, August 9. https://www.coha.org/b enetton-in-patagonia-the-oppression-of-mapuche-in-the-argentine-south/.

Paruelo, José M. 2012. "Ecosystem services and tree plantations in Uruguay: A reply to Vihervaara et al. (2012)." *Forest Policy and Economics* 22, 85–88.

Patel, Raj. 2013. "The Long Green Revolution." *Journal of Peasant Studies* 40, no. 1: 1–63.

Perfecto, Ivette, John Vandermeer, and Angus Wright. 2009. *Nature's Matrix: Linking Agriculture, Biodiversity Conservation, and Food Sovereignty*. London: Routledge.

Pinto, Lucas Henrique. 2012. "Problematizando el 'debate ambiental' desde la hegemonía neoliberal en Argentina: notas sobre la experiencia del Movimiento Nacional Campesino Indígena (MNCI)." In *Historia política y gestión ambiental: Perspectivas y debates*, ed. Alejandra Salomón and Adrián Zarrilli, 9–35. Buenos Aires: Ediciones Imago Mundi.

Richards, Richard A. 2010. *The Species Problem: A Philosophical Analysis*. Cambridge: Cambridge University Press.

Rodríguez, Roberto, Clodomiro Marticorena, Diego Alarcón, et al. 2018. "Catálogo de las plantas vasculares de Chile." *Gayana Botánica* 75, no. 1: 1–430.

Rodríguez-Jorquera, Ignacio A., Pablo Siroski, Winfred Espejo, et al. 2016. "Latin American Protected Areas: Protected from Chemical Pollution?." *Integrated Environmental Assessment and Management* 13, no. 2: 360–370.

Sarandón, Santiago J. 2010. "Biodiversidad, agrobiodiversidad, y agricultura sustenable: análisis del convenio sobre diversidad biológica." In *Vertientes del pensamiento agroecológico: fundamentos y aplicaciones*, ed. Tomás León Sicard and Miguel Angel Altieri, 105–129. Bogotá: Universidad Nacional de Colombia.

Schmidt, Mariana Andrea. 2019. "Injusticas ambientales, territoriales y socio-sanitarias en el Chaco salteño, Argentina." *Folia Histórica del Nordeste* 35: 7–26.

Sedrez, Lise, and Regina Horta Duarte. 2018. "The Ivy and the Wall: Environmental Narratives from an Urban Continent." In *A Living Past: Environmental Histories of Modern Latin America*, ed. John Soluri, Claudia Leal, and José Augusto Pádua, 138–162. New York: Berghahn Books.

Selcer, Perrin. 2021. "Anthropocene." In *Encyclopedia of the History of Science*. Pittsburgh: Carnegie Mellon University.

Sicard, Tomás León, and Miguel Angel Altieri, ed. 2010. *Vertientes del pensamiento agroecológico: fundamentos y aplicaciones*. Bogotá: Universidad de Colombia.

Soluri, John. 2011. "Something Fishy: Chile's Blue Revolution, Commodity Diseases, and the Problem of Sustainability." *Latin American Research Review* [Special issue] 46: 55–81.

———. 2019. "Cocina casera: campesinos, cocina, y diversidad agrícola." In *Un pasado vivo. Dos siglos de historia ambiental latinoamericana*, ed. Claudia Leal, John Soluri, and José Augusto Pádua. Bogotá: Fondo de Cultura Económica.

———. 2023. "The Wild Side: Hunting Guanacos in Patagonia." *Global Environments* 16, no 1: 40–56.

Song, Xiao-Peng, Matthew C. Hansen, Peter Potapov, et al. 2021. "Massive soybean expansion in South America since 2000 and implications for conservation." *Nature Sustainability* 4: 784–792.

Soutullo, Alvaro, Mariana Ríos, Natalia Zladúa, et al. 2020. "Soybean expansion and the challenge of the coexistence of agribusiness with local production and conservation initiatives: pesticides in a Ramsar site in Uruguay." *Environmental Conservation* 47: 97–103.

Swistún, Débora Alejandra, and Javier Auyero. 2009. *Flammable. Environmental Suffering in an Argentine Shantytown*. Oxford: Oxford University Press.

Tinsman, Heidi. 2014. *Buying into the Regime: Grapes and Consumption in Cold War Chile and the United States*. Durham: Duke University Press.

Torres-Salinas, Robinson, Gerardo Azócar García, Noleia Carrasco Henríquez, et al. 2016. "Forestry Development, Water Scarcity, and the Mapuche Protest for Environmental Justice in Chile." *Ambiente & Sociedade* 19, no. 1: 121–144.

Trentini, Florencia. 2012. "Ecologia Política y Conservación: el caso del 'co-manejo' del Parque Nacional Nahuel Huapi y el pueblo Mapuche." *Revista Pilquen* 15, no. 1: 1–11.

———. 2011. "Entre la Conservación y la legitimidad: el caso de la comunidad Maliqueo y el Parque Nacional Nahuel Huapi." *Revista Kula* 4: 61–75.

Turzi, Mariano. 2017. *The Political Economy of Agricultural Booms: Managing soybean production in Argentina, Brazil, and Paraguay*. Cham: Springer.

Vallejos, María, Melina Faingerch, Daniel Blum, et al. 2022. "'Winners' and 'losers' of the agricultural expansion in the Argentine Dry Chaco." *Landscape Research* 47, no. 6: 723–734.

Vargas Cárdenas, Marcela, and Nicole Cárcamo Velásquez. 2022. "'Del gualato al subcontrato salmonero', trayectorias laborales de campesinos y campesinas del sur austral de Chile (1970–1990)." *Cuadernos de historia* 56: 91–115.

Vazquez, Medardo Avila, Eduardo Maturano, Augustina Etchegoyen, et al. 2017. "Association between Cancer and Environmental Exposure to Glyphosate." *International Journal of Clinical Medicine* 8: 73–85.

Wakild, Emily. 2018. "A Panorama of Parks: Deep History, Depopulation, and the Cadence of Conserving Nature." In *A Living Past: Environmental Histories of Modern Latin America*, ed. John Soluri, Claudia Leal, and José Augusto Pádua, 246–265. New York: Berghahn Books.

World Bank. 2022. "Urban population (% of total population)". https://data.worldbank.org/indicator/SP.URB.TOTL.

Wittman, Hannah, Michael Jahi Chappell, David James Abson, et al. 2017. "A social–ecological perspective on harmonizing food security and biodiversity conservation." *Regional Environmental Change* 17: 1291–1301.

Zamorano-Elgueta, Carlos, José María Reyes Benayas, Luis Cayuela, Stijn Hantson and Dolors Armenteras. 2015. "Native forest replacement by exotic plantations in Southern Chile (1985–2011) and partial replacement by natural regeneration." *Forest Ecology and Management* 345: 10–20.

Zarrilli, Adrián Gustavo. 2016. "Nuevas formas de politización y conflictos socio-ambientales en el mundo rural Argentino: las provincias Chaco y Formosa frente a los procesos de deforestación y el avance de la frontera agrícola (1980–2010)." *Historia Ambiental Latinoamericana y Caribeña (HALAC)* 6, no. 1: 11–29.

Zuolaga, Fernando O., and Manuel J. Belgrano. 2015. "The Catalogue of Vascular Plants of the Southern Cone and the Flora of Argentina: their contribution to the World Flora." *Rodriguésia* 66, no. 4: 989–1024.

Biodiversity in the Andes from 1950 to the Present
The Tropical Andes and the Sixth Mass Extinction Event

Kenneth R. Young

Biological diversity includes all the species of the world, the manner in which they are distributed and interact, and their evolutionary interrelations. Species exist in populations, with genes interchanged and natural selection acting over time on overall genetic diversity, gene flow, and the origin of new lineages (Nosil 2012). Species also occur in assemblages and communities that collectively form ecosystems, with biotic and abiotic processes that can be associated with functions, some of which constitute ecosystem services directly or indirectly useful to humans (Chapin, Kofinas, and Folke 2009; Costanza et al. 2017). The loss of biodiversity can affect any of these phenomena from genes to the global ecosystem. That loss takes on special resonance when it occurs due to human decisions or values. The human role in causing species extinctions is of concern, as are additional human actions that are altering global climate parameters and their feedbacks on ecosystem functions and the dynamics of landscape mosaics.

The tropical Andes represent one of the world's biodiversity hotspots (Brooks et al. 2006), including hundreds of species of birds, mammals, reptiles, amphibians, and vascular plants, plus thousands of invertebrate species, among others. The mountainous terrain and equatorial position make for a high biophysical diversity of climates, soils, and ecosystem types. There are high mountain peaks, shrouded cloud forests, dry scrub hillsides, palm forests, and many areas converted from forest or shrubland into productive lands for farming and for the grazing of livestock. Located within these diverse landscapes are many species still unknown to science, and with rapid current changes caused by land use, much of that diversity is at risk (Wilson 1996; Ceballos et al. 2015).

Some of the biodiversity is associated with the number of species found in one place, an amount known as "alpha diversity," which can be quantified by species richness or as considered in indices calibrated by relative abundances of the species present (Millington, Schickhoff, and Blumler 2011). The species turnover found from place-to-place gives a measure of how different each place is in terms of species composition; the turnover is quantified through measures of "beta diversity." Finally, each species also has a place in an evolutionary (or phylogenetic) lineage, giving the means to evaluate distinctiveness among species in terms of shared DNA or time elapsed since speciation. All these spatial and temporal considerations influence how biodiversity can be evaluated and how its loss will be manifested. Biodiversity conservation strategies may choose to emphasize places with the highest species richness; alternatively, they may focus on species with genes linked with traits that are considered useful or those otherwise considered unique, charismatic, or rare.

Biogeography is the study of Earth's life, including the history and locations of species through time and the ecological processes involved with delimiting range distributions and affecting species dominance and abundance (Lomolino, Riddle, and Whittaker 2017). Traditionally, this academic discipline has investigated and synthesized descriptions of the biomes and biogeographic realms of the world, their changes in relation to evolution, plate tectonics, and climate change in the past, as well as the importance of biophysical gradients acting upon distributions of species and ecosystems. However, in addition to the taxa, places, and events important in affecting living organisms, increasingly it is clear that there must also be careful attention to the past, present, and future role of humans in altering biogeographical patterns and processes.

The goal of this chapter is to demarcate the challenges and opportunities associated with the loss of biological diversity in the tropical Andes, referring here to countries from Venezuela south to Bolivia and elevations above 1,000 m elevation with ecosystem types including grasslands, wetlands, shrublands, and forests (Young et al. 2007). Human influences are pervasive in some parts of the Andes, as seen in drained or managed wetlands, burned and grazed grasslands and shrublands, growing cities, and deforested landscapes with forest remnants and pine or eucalypt tree plantings.

This overview is done through an examination of the biophysical conditions associated with biodiversity maxima in the mountain ranges of northwest South America. Given the antiquity and prevalence of human-caused influences, this topic is augmented by consideration of the rather different complications posed by the biodiversity coevolved with humans giving rise to agrobiodiversity. Solutions to the biodiversity crisis may proceed from understanding the ongoing extinction trends provoked by the Great Acceleration of the 1950's and as framed by recognition of the Anthropocene (Crutzen 2006; Ellis 2015; Davies 2016) as a particularly potent means to understand human influences on the biosphere, including ancient land uses. An activist and applied approach would include species-rescue programs and may require rethinking goals of ecological restoration.

Biodiversity's Axes

There are three main biophysical gradients that affect biodiversity: temperature, precipitation, and water availability (Migliavacca et al. 2021). The first two are basic climate variables, while the third is influenced by those variables and by other features such as seasonality, type of soil for plants, and water chemistry for aquatic organisms or air pressure for terrestrial taxa. In the Andes Mountains, the most obvious gradient is a complex one of elevation (Körner 2021), along which temperatures drop upslope but where precipitation and water availability show more complicated spatial relationships. For example, topographic locations exposed to prevailing winds will be moister than those on leeward slopes, even though altitudes are identical (Fig. 1). Similarly, places with some kinds of bedrock will form deep soils for plants, with relatively high storage of soil moisture, while others at the same altitude may have rocky or even serpentine soils with limited edaphic resources for plant growth. As a broad generalization, less species richness, and hence less alpha diversity, is expected at higher elevations in the Andes or on harsher sites, with due consideration of the respective edaphic and topographic limitations that may be locally influential.

Fig. 1: Ridgeline in central Peru showing people for scale in center and shrublands to the left and fog and cloud forest to the right

Source: Photograph by author. This photograph illustrates the dramatic environmental gradients giving rise to high biodiversity, with abrupt changes in humidity, elevation, and topography.

Beta diversity may show more complicated expectations as it is influenced by place-to-place differences and by the sizes and shapes of species distributions (Sonne and Rahbek 2024). An endemic species is found in one place (Gaston 2003), but the Andes Mountains, with their thousands of kilometers of north-to-south interconnections, can have endemic species with long north-south distributions that are quite narrow east-west due to habitat specificity (Young 1995). Hence, sampling from place-to-place may include generalist, widely distributed species, which would reduce measures of beta diversity, or it could include endemic species, which would increase species turnover rates. Valuing biodiversity in terms of turnover would suggest that places that are more unique in terms of species composition or gradients that show especially high spatial turnover would be of more interest than places that are essentially duplicative in terms of species composition (Margules and Sarkar 2007). Generalizations might include expecting higher beta diversity in parts of the Andes with steep elevational gradients or with rapid spatial shifts leading to biogeographic barriers due to abrupt changes in climate/microclimates, soils, or topographic position.

Phylogenetic diversity will be highest in endemism hotspots (Shipley and McGuire 2022), although such maxima may be in harsh sites occupied by unique species or alternatively in refugia that maintained similar biophysical features in the past while surrounding areas changed (Fjeldså et al. 2012; Roberts and Hamann 2016). Neoendemics are recently evolved species with restricted distributions; the locations they occupy suggest active speciation processes are occurring, including those affecting species that have genetic variation patterns that are not (yet) sufficiently distinct for species recognition by taxonomists. Paleoendemics evolved long ago and would include those rare species that are considered "living fossils" due to their similarity to ancient taxa known from geological strata. Some neoendemic plants are located at the highest elevations in the Andes (Al-Shehbaz et al. 2013; Keeley, Cantley, and Gallaher 2021) with their nearest relatives within evolutionary clades found at lower elevations; presumably Andean uplift in the last 4 million years explains their evolutionary histories (Young et al. 2002; Antonelli et al. 2009). The paleoendemics are much older and may even encompass links to taxa that existed before the Andes formed and when South America was still part of Gondwana or Pangea 50 to 250 million years ago (Palma and Spotorno 1999 for marsupials).

An "Anthropocene" perspective on biodiversity (Young and Duchicela 2023) would suggest that humans have now assumed roles in shaping diversity patterns and processes that are of the same magnitude of importance and influence as have had temperature, moisture, and geographical connections over the eons. People, thus, should be added to the basic biogeographical axes affecting species distributions and composition. The human role includes direct alterations of land cover and the respective terrestrial and aquatic ecosystems but may also include legacies of past land uses that have lingering influences on the Andean biota.

For example, the megafauna that were important Andean ecosystem engineers, such as giant sloths, mastodons, and gomphotheres, vanished soon after humans colonized South America at the start of the Holocene (Bush et al. 2022; Dantas and Pausas 2022). Additional land cover change associated with the development of agriculture, pottery, and settlements (Quilter 2022) led to deforestation and likely many additional extinctions of forest-dependent species or other specialists that were eliminated deliberately or whose habitat was displaced by people. To illustrate this point, Young (1998) provided a long list of Andean tree genera with large-seeded fruits, specialized for dispersal by relatively large birds or mammals that are commonly found only in large expanses of non-fragmented forest, and are not found in highly fragmented forests where the seed dispersal agent would not be present. Fragmented forests and forest edges instead have many tree species with nonspecialized and small seeded-fruits or wind-dispersed seeds. Landscapes being progressively deforested would lose forest-dependent animals, not to mention the trees needing closed canopy to reproduce, plus understory and epiphytic herbs.

A further regime shift, known as the Columbian Exchange, was associated in the 1500s with colonization and the introduction of European, Asian, and African plant and animal species, along with novel land-use practices (Crosby 2003; Voeks 2019). Examples range from grazing systems with cattle, sheep, and goats to fields planted with wheat, barley, and alfalfa. Andean biotic landscapes are nowadays palimpsests of the original biota that survived those changes, accompanied by new species coming from different evolutionary lineages but pre-adapted to Andean climates or else brought as part of the toolkit of useful species utilized in farming and forestry systems.

More generally, reconceptualizing biogeographical studies to include human dimensions is challenging as seen in the case of the tropical Andes. It would seemingly need to include human history as part of the domain of study of Historical Biogeography, the social sciences to understand aspects of the ecological processes acting upon the biota in Ecological Biogeography, and the humanities for helping to understand the causalities of global change. Conservation Biogeography would include research topics on the dynamics of rare species or others considered of value, including the species domesticated for their usefulness.

Agrobiodiversity

Farmers and pastoralists create landscape mosaics that include patches of croplands and pasturelands, corridors of hedgerows, living fences, and riparian forests, as well as a background matrix land cover type that may restrict or facilitate movements of organisms across the landscape (Perfecto, Vandermeer, and Wright 2019). Many rural areas in the Andes have this kind of land cover (Young 2009), with natural vegetation scattered as habitat islands in inaccessible locations (Sylvester, Sylvester, and Kessler 2014). Here the biodiversity includes the species found in those mosaics, with alpha diversity of native species relatively low but beta diversity potentially high given the human-caused place-to-place heterogeneity. Many of the introduced ruderal species would presumably be weedy or invasive species coming from other continents (Richardson and Pyšek 2012), so their relative phylogenetic distinctiveness would be high, and their ecological impacts could be substantial (Vizentin-Bugoni et al. 2021). Consequently, many of the commonly used biodiversity measurements need to be made context specific in these humanized landscapes. High measures of alpha, beta, and phylogenetic diversity may simply indicate much human alteration if the species involved are nonnatives.

Fig. 2: *Maize hanging to dry after harvest in an Andean household*

Source: Photograph by author. This photograph illustrates the heterogeneity of the harvested maize, and the diverse nature of Andean agrobiodiversity more generally.

In addition, the Andean crops and livestock that were domesticated from native species constitute an additional biodiversity phenomenon. For example, the potato not only shows genetic lineages of half a dozen wild *Solanum* species (Spooner et al. 2014) but has ongoing introgression due to gene flow moving from wild species into domesticated landraces (Parra-Rondinel et al. 2021). The thousands of potato varieties are only in part natural entities, sharing an extended genotype with wild species, but are created and maintained by human artifice. Similar cases exist for alpaca breeds, tomato varieties, or heterogeneity in harvested maize (Fig. 2). In fact, the animal species that are legacies of European colonists also show many localized genetic differences, at least some of which are adaptive with free-ranging cattle able to survive on their own and an array of chicken varieties found among Andean households.

Humans, thus, create and maintain novel biodiversity through their land uses, and by means of domestication and ongoing cultural selection (Gepts et al. 2012; Radeloff et al. 2015). Humans can augment some measures of landscape heterogeneity with farming and pastoralism, while domesticated species are diversified for human needs and pleasure. Traditionally, agrobiodiversity has not been considered in tomes of Biogeography, but an Anthropocenic perspective would suggest that this inclusion is now essential. Given that humanity depends on a small list of plants and animals for most food, the additional diversity created by human action may well include many genes and functional traits that are either useful now or that could be essential for food security under differing conditions in the future.

Philosophically and practically, addressing agrobiodiversity requires very different responses than does the biodiversity of unutilized species. Whereas specialized conservation efforts aimed at endangered species may require population-level interventions or the establishment of protected areas and conservation corridors, the active conservation of agrobiodiversity uses gene and seed banks, farmer-centered programs (Shiva 2016), indigenous territories (Pironon et al. 2024), and now gene editing to prepare for the future (Kieu et al. 2021; Whitfield et al. 2021; Raza et al. 2023). Instead of aiming to maintain or facilitate natural ecological and evolutionary processes, the goal is to foster or to substitute for human behavior's role in originating or sustaining (agro)biodiversity. Research tools for evaluating the former might include genetic, population, or ecosystem monitoring, while the latter needs observations in fields and rural households where the future of agrobiodiversity will be decided.

Human knowledge is, thus, an important dimension for agrobiodiversity, meaning that agronomists and range scientists need the means to interact with anthropologists, geneticists, economists, and many others (Zimmerer et al. 2019). In fact, domestication might have lessons for more effective and inclusive ways of thinking about biodiversity conservation from an Anthropocene perspective, including more widespread use of citizen science approaches. Biogeography could become a more inclusive discipline by being informed by these phenomena and by more carefully including humans as agents of change in analyses.

Trends of the Great Acceleration

The Great Acceleration commenced in the 1950s with atomic weapons testing, accompanied by societal changes resulting in exponential increases in greenhouse gases and fertilizer use, and with similarly dramatic losses in forest cover and fish stocks (Smil 2021). Global climate change became noticeable, and globalization interconnected national and regional economies. Some have suggested that this time would be an effective start date for recognition of the beginning of the Anthropocene, although others posit earlier years for when human influences became significant and global in extent (Ruddiman 2003; Lewis and Maslin 2018). There were past times when human-caused extinctions were significant. Most conspicuously, early world colonization by *Homo sapiens* coincided with the loss of many megafaunal species (Barnosky et al. 2017) and island species (Steadman 2006), although these losses do not necessarily lend themselves to providing the conditions needed for recognizing the Anthropocene with stratigraphic criteria (Waters et al. 2016; Malhi 2017).

Nevertheless, the Great Acceleration does remind us of post-World War II neoliberal economic developments, along with a continued push for export agriculture and mining in the Global South, incentives for rural-to-urban migration, and the social transformations of farmers and pastoralists into workers and consumers (Green et al. 2019). This commodification can be observed in conservation approaches that now monetize carbon sequestration and water provision (Kosoy and Corbera 2010), making financial what was once simply biodiversity. Only some countries in the tropical Andes have resisted these efforts, most conspicuously in Ecuador where species other than humans are provided some constitutional rights (Lewis 2016). Many rural and indigenous communities can be said to value native species for their own intrinsic values, especially when they intertwine with belief systems (Sarmiento and Hitchner 2022). Thus, most nation-states in the Andes are promoting neoliberal means for biodiversity conservation, while substantial areas in those same countries, in fact, are governed environmentally with other values in mind. The social actors involved with neoliberal policies are governmental and some nongovernmental organizations, while resistance to those policies is to be found in the land use practices of Andean communities and in programs of some nongovernmental organizations.

Time periods before and after the Great Acceleration provide important indicators for biogeographic studies of the Anthropocene, reducing negative impacts caused by people is at the core of current biodiversity conservation activities. In some cases, restoration, reforestation, rewilding, or reintroductions of extirpated species may be desirable.

Extinction

Just as speciation results in more species over time (Harvey et al. 2020), extinction results in losses. Over geological time, extinction is the fate of species, but the time scales involved are five to ten orders of magnitude longer than human lifespans, meaning that extinction in the present is essentially an instantaneous and irreversible event. Often such background extinction is nearly invisible in the geological record, except for mass extinctions, the five largest of which were associated with global shifts in climate and the reordering of the composition and organization of biotas (Millington, Schickhoff, and Blumler 2011; Lomolino, Riddle, Whittaker 2017).

Given enough time, on the order of 10 to 30 million years, speciation, diversification, and adaptive radiation refill and modify ecological niches, as seen in the fossil record. An event that is disruptive and destructive in ecological time, may lead to increased diversity over millions of years. The most recent major global catastrophe led to the extinction of the dinosaurs 65 million years ago and the start of the current Cenozoic Era characterized by high mammalian diversity. It is difficult from the perspective of a species living immersed in the contexts of current extinction processes to declare definitively that we (i.e., humans) are causing yet another mass extinction of that magnitude, but most researchers who have evaluated the topic have been in the affirmative (Barnosky et al. 2017; Cowrie, Bouchet, Fontaine 2022).

There is also an important spatial dimension to extinction, with global extinction referring to the moment when no individuals of a particular species are alive, but which is usually preceded by a series of local extinctions as populations disappear locally one by one (Levin 2000). In fact, metapopulation models stress that such local extinctions are common as source habitats provide for recolonization of sink habitats that cannot maintain the species without immigration (Hanski 1998); similarly, the Equilibrium Theory of Island Biogeography (MacArthur and Wilson 2016) has species richness of an island dependent on both dispersal and extinction rates. These are important biogeographical approaches for being able to make predictions about the diversity and persistence of species on islands or in fragmented habitat types.

In the Andes Mountains and among its habitat archipelagos, extinction, thus, might best be considered the result of the overall loss of populations and inhabited habitat patches being greater than dispersal and recolonization rates, as suggested by those biogeographical frameworks. In turn, this points to the need for researchers to consider factors that limit dispersal, including the size of and distance among source populations, plus the resistance of landscape matrices to dispersal; and the factors that limit (re)colonization such as site-specific abiotic stresses, microbial processes or interspecific competition, predation, or herbivory. Conservationists would need to consider manipulating those variables, for example, by reintroducing locally extinct plants or animals, by managing vegetation structure to favor open habitat species with burning or mechanical disturbances, by limiting seed/seedling predation or augmenting seed dispersal, or by endangered species programs that include assessments of long-term population viability.

Current extinction processes act upon the legacies of past extinctions, which differentially eliminated larger animals (Dirzo et al. 2014; Barnosky et al. 2016), and those native species originally inhabiting lands with good soils and gentle topography that are(were) most preferred for crop agriculture. Lost first were the megafauna (replaced eventually by livestock) and predators, and then many additional species disappeared that were dependent on natural vegetation types. Those human-caused change processes increasingly act in novel ways, with modifications associated with pesticides, microplastics, monocultures, and soil erosion, not to mention the directional and unpredictable changes imposed by greenhouse gases and causing global climate shifts that need to be taken into consideration (Svenning and Sandel 2013; Lovejoy and Hannah 2019; Arneth et al. 2020). Important social actors include not only the rural inhabitants who carry out farming but also the people responding to the demand generated by growing urban populations who consume the products produced in the countryside.

Both modeling approaches of native ecosystems under future conditions (Tovar et al. 2013) and empirical observations done on mapped forest plots (Fadrique et al. 2018) have revealed spatial heterogeneity and showed unexpected dynamics, making simple predictions difficult. There are limitations on projecting future changes given the unknowns, the high place-to-place heterogeneity common in the Andes, and the likelihood of ecological and/or social surprises.

It is probable that future extinction trends will further accelerate. As an example, current dramatic losses of frog species to chytrid fungi-caused and other diseases (Seimon et al. 2017; Cohen et al. 2020) may well cause trophic cascades affecting the small invertebrates they once consumed. The species considered high-altitude specialists will be subject to mountaintop extinctions if they no longer have upward topography for dispersal and colonization (Freeman et al. 2018). Both examples are difficult to observe directly and may well take place undocumented and unwitnessed. Intervening to halt extinction may need to happen on a species-by-species basis unless place-based programs include steep elevational gradients or else locales that could function as refugia. Biogeography has classically been an observational and historical discipline (Millington, Schickhoff, and Blumler 2011; Lomolino, Riddle, Whittaker 2017); given these challenges, it may now need to become an activist discipline willing and able to intervene in the extinction processes. If humans unintentionally have become a biogeographical agent of note, perhaps using foresight to change trajectories is a reasonable option for society to consider. Frogs could be rescued and bred to be reintroduced someday; mountaintop extinctions could be limited by relocating doomed plant or bird species to higher mountain ranges.

The Great Acceleration's trends in environmental and socioeconomic criteria that began their exponential increase in the 1950s continue (Ripple et al. 2020) with only a few counterexamples of flattening slopes, such as global limits acting upon ozone-destroying chemicals and recent increases in marine aquaculture taking some pressures off global fish stocks; the other trend lines are all inclined sharply upward. In the Andes, rural-to-urban demographic shifts, in theory, could take environmental pressures off rural areas; in practice, there is no evidence that this is the case (Geldmann et al. 2019) given the increased needs of cities for water and food and the expansion of peri-urban environments with unique species assemblages (Hurtado-M et al. 2020).

Further complications to future trajectories due to greenhouse gases and climate change (Urrutia and Vuille 2009) are already visible in the loss of ice and glaciers (Masiokas et al. 2020), shifts upslope of both snowlines and some treelines (Young et al. 2017), and increased presence of woody plant species in vegetation formerly dominated by graminoids (Aide et al. 2019). The respective studies include methods from remote sensing, landscape monitoring, and glaciology. Tracking the metapopulation dynamics in the species facing extinction in landscape mosaics will be challenging as those processes act through changes at the scale of seeds and seedlings, or bird nest by bird nest. There need to be biodiversity monitoring programs in place that measure demographic processes in populations of plants and wildlife. In turn, these programs could be nurtured by further conceptual development of theory and practice for the prediction of extinctions.

The places occupied by neoendemic species may be priorities for place-based conservation efforts if those actions would protect not only the species of concern but also the potential for further diversification and speciation processes to occur. Places where new frog and lizard species have been found recently would be important sites for inclusion in protected area systems. The paleoendemic species may have such great phylogenetic value to society that they need be protected at the species level, including through intrusive rescue actions such as captive breeding and reintroduction programs. Typically, this kind of attention has been directed instead at charismatic flagship species such as the Andean bear (*Tremarctos ornatus*), the Andean condor (*Vultur gryphus*), and the giant *Puya raimondii* rosette plant.

Endangered species in general would also need such efforts but the sheer scope of future conservation needs is of a magnitude not yet addressed (e.g., Ter Steege et al. 2015 was done on more than 15,000 tree species in one study). For example, many of the smaller statured species among the approximately 3,500 plant species found in the páramo highlands of Ecuador and Colombia (Madriñán et al. 2013) may be at risk as they shift distributions upslope and get shaded out by taller rosette and shrub life forms that are also shifting upward (Duchicela et al. 2021). There likely is no feasible way to bring that number of species into botanical gardens (Griffith et al. 2021), so landscape management, including shrub removals, may be needed on the mountain slopes to keep local extinction processes from leading to global extinctions. Maybe Andean pastoralists in the future will be remunerated to combine their grazing systems with activities that keep habitats suitable for shade-intolerant plant species of conservation importance.

Conclusions

From the perspective of *Homo sapiens* in the 2020s, it is hard to be sure if current extinctions add up to what a geocentric perspective in the distant future will want to label as a mass extinction event. Nevertheless, many attempts to project current losses into future consequences seem in line with rates that would set back biodiversity processes on the order of 20 million years, based on the post-catastrophe recovery rates of other mass extinctions in the fossil record. Because these are geological time frames, it may be prudent to assume that loss trajectories are not sustainable if current species diversity is to be maintained, including phylogenetic diversity; if the services provided by natural environments depend at least in part on that diversity; and if agricultural and forestry systems could be improved upon through species breeding programs in a changing world. All of these are concerns in countries of the tropical Andes.

An Anthropocene perspective also implies a future global trajectory of continued increases in human influences, meaning also that pathway choices are present (Steffen et al. 2015; McKay et al. 2022) and the Global Tropics may have special importance and resonance for the planet (Roberts et al. 2023). If Andean species extinctions changed fundamentally at the start of the Holocene (Ruddiman et al. 2015), which seems to have been the case, then it may make sense to reimagine a Holocene with increasingly potent human alterations; this interpretation fits the histories of the more humanized landscapes of the tropical Andes, which show human colonization in the high elevations in the early Holocene, associated with burning and hunting/gathering livelihoods (Bush et al. 2022). The drier and more seasonal environments are where most agricultural and pastoral land use systems have replaced natural ecosystems, with the least impacted areas being the cloud forests where farming and habitation are most difficult (Young 2021). The decision can be made to intervene in scenarios of habitat loss and species extinction. Alternative livelihood trajectories for people that permit coexistence with other species can be considered.

Measurements of biodiversity do not capture all these nuances, as alpha diversity may be inflated by nonnative species, and beta diversity captures aspects of species turnover, but does not clarify which switches are due to land use, past and present. Phylogenetic uniqueness is of great value for prioritizing which species may be the most distinctive and of great historical importance. Nevertheless, it must be utilized with care to distinguish past biogeographical legacies from more recent human-associated jump dispersal events. For example, the *Anolis* lizard assemblages found among Caribbean Island archipelagos have been reshaped phylogenetically by the loss of native species and the gain of species colonizing with human assistance from elsewhere in the Americas (Helmus, Mahler, and Losos 2014). Humans today challenge plate tectonics itself in terms of the reorganization of Earth's biota (Baiser et al. 2012); Andean landscapes now include the biota of other continents.

The evolutionary toolkit of humans contains fire and other instruments of ecosystem engineering (Boivin et al. 2016; Archibald et al. 2018; Root-Bernstein and Ladle 2019), plus decision-making and cooperation, traits that have led first to landscape management, but now to planet-altering influences (Harari 2015; Young 2016). Perhaps an acceptance of this apparent need to "domesticate" nature can be utilized to create ecological spaces safe for human interests but not hostile to large numbers of native species. Rural Andean landscapes that continue to maintain both productive croplands and pasturelands for local people, and yet are embedded in a matrix with native herbs, shrubs, and trees, suggest this could be so. Management that lessens pesticide applications, pays careful attention to water use, and strives to give importance to fallowed areas and patches or corridors of natural vegetation fits into socioenvironmental goals, resonates with many traditional practices, and hence may be part of an Anthropocene perspective aiming for sustainable use of the half of the Earth meant for human uses.

It was Edward O. Wilson (2016) in his *Half-Earth* book who first proposed that half of the world be dedicated to human land uses and its equivalent in aquatic environments. The other half of the world (Dinerstein et al. 2019) would metaphorically belong to nature, whether protected through remoteness (Watson et al. 2016), in protected areas and on Indigenous territories, or creative combinations thereof (Bonebrake et al. 2019; Maxwell et al. 2020). Many innovations in biogeographical studies could result from focusing more attention on the effects of past and present land use. That is, Biogeography of the Andes Mountains would consider both managed and wild lands, from agricultural fields and pasturelands to national parks and wildlife refuges.

Ecological restoration can repair ecosystem services on degraded lands (Bastin et al. 2019); the goals may prioritize functional traits rather than focusing on the alpha diversity of native species. Ironically, "restoration" may not be the correct term anymore (Young and Duchicela 2021) as the system state needed in the future may no longer mirror the original state existing pre-Great Acceleration (Hobbs, Higgs, and Hall 2013). In places where natural processes are meant to predominate, then the maintenance of evolutionary potential seen in neoendemism hotspots can be utilized along with biodiversity hotpots to choose conservation priorities. Even here, however, it may well be necessary to intervene, especially in habitat fragments or on high mountains, with active habitat or species management. If humans have altered Biogeography's processes inadvertently, it is also possible to do so proactively.

References

Aide, T. Mitchell, H. Ricardo Grau, Jordan Graesser, et al. 2019. "Woody vegetation dynamics in the tropical and subtropical Andes from 2001 to 2014: Satellite image interpretation and expert validation." *Global Change Biology* 25, no. 6: 2112–2126.

Al-Shehbaz, Ihsan A., Asunción Cano, Huber Trinidad, et al. 2013. "New species of Brayopsis, Descurainia, Draba, Neuontobotrys and Weberbauera (Brassicaceae) from Peru." *Kew Bulletin* 68: 219–231.

Antonelli, Alexandre, Johan A.A. Nylander, Claes Persson, et al. 2009. "Tracing the impact of the Andean uplift on Neotropical plant evolution." *PNAS* 106, no. 24: 9749–9754.

Archibald, Sally, Caroline E.R. Lehmann, Claire M. Belcher, et al. 2018. "Biological and geophysical feedbacks with fire in the Earth system." *Environmental Research Letters* 13, no. 3: 1–18.

Arneth, Almut, Yunne-Jai Shin, Paul Leadley, et al. 2020. "Post-2020 biodiversity targets need to embrace climate change." *PNAS* 117, no. 49: 30882–30891.

Baiser, Benjamin, Julian D. Olden, Sydne Record, et al. 2012. "Pattern and process of biotic homogenization in the New Pangaea." *Proceedings of the Royal Society B: Biological Sciences* 279, no. 1748: 4772–4777.

Barnosky, Anthony D., Emily L. Lindsey, Natalia A. Villavicencio, et al. 2016. "Variable impact of late-Quaternary megafaunal extinction in causing ecological state shifts in North and South America." *PNAS* 113, no. 4: 856–861.

Barnosky, Anthony D., Elizabeth A. Hadly, Patrick Gonzalez, et al. 2017. "Merging paleobiology with conservation biology to guide the future of terrestrial ecosystems." *Science* 355, no. 6325: 1–10.

Bastin, Jean-Francois, Yelena Finegold, Claude Garcia, et al. 2019. "The global tree restoration potential." *Science* 365, no. 6448: 76–79.

Boivin, Nicole L., Melinda A. Zeder, Dorian Q. Fuller, et al. 2016. "Ecological consequences of human niche construction: Examining long-term anthropogenic shaping of global species distributions." *PNAS* 113, no. 23: 6388–6396.

Bonebrake, Timothy C., Fengyi Guo, Caroline Dingle, et al. 2019. "Integrating proximal and horizon threats to biodiversity for conservation." *Trends in Ecology & Evolution* 34, no. 9: 781–788.

Bush, Mark B., Angela Rozas-Davila, Marco F. Raczka, et al. 2022. "A palaeoecological perspective on the transformation of the tropical Andes by early human activity." *Philosophical Transactions of the Royal Society B: Biological Sciences* 377, no. 1849: 1–11.

Ceballos, Gerardo, Anne H. Ehrlich, and Paul R. Ehrlich. 2015. *The Annihilation of Nature: Human Extinction of Birds and Mammals.* Baltimore: Johns Hopkins University Press.

Chapin III, F. Stuart, Gary P. Kofinas, and Carl Folke, ed. 2009. *Principles of Ecosystem Stewardship: Resilience-Based Natural Resource Management in a Changing World*. Dordrecht: Springer Science & Business Media.

Cohen, Jeremy M., Erin L. Sauer, Olivia Santiago, et al. 2020. "Divergent impacts of warming weather on wildlife disease risk across climates." *Science* 370, no. 6519: 1–11.

Costanza, Robert, Rudolf De Groot, Leon Braat, et al. 2017. "Twenty years of ecosystem services: how far have we come and how far do we still need to go?." *Ecosystem Services* 28: 1–16.

Cowie, Robert H., Philippe Bouchet, and Benoît Fontaine. 2022. "The Sixth Mass Extinction: fact, fiction or speculation?." *Biological Reviews* 97, no. 2: 640–663.

Crosby, Alfred W. 2003. *The Columbian Exchange: Biological and Cultural Consequences of 1492*. Westport: Greenwood Publishing Group. Orig. pub. 1972.

Crutzen, Paul Josef. 2006. "The Anthropocene: the current human-dominated geological era." *Pontifical Academy of Sciences, Acta* 18: 199–293.

Dantas, Vinicius L., and Juli G. Pausas. 2022. "The legacy of the extinct Neotropical megafauna on plants and biomes." *Nature Communications* 13, no. 1: 1–13.

Davies, Jeremy. 2016. *The Birth of the Anthropocene*. Berkeley: University of California Press.

Dinerstein, Eric, Carly Vynne, Enric Sala, et al. 2019. "A global deal for nature: guiding principles, milestones, and targets." *Science Advances* 5, no. 4: 1–17.

Dirzo, Rodolfo, Hillary S. Young, Mauro Galetti, et al. 2014. "Defaunation in the Anthropocene." *Science* 345, no. 6195: 401–406.

Duchicela, Sisimac A., Francisco Cuesta, Carolina Tovar, et al. 2021. "Microclimatic warming leads to a decrease in species and growth form diversity: insights from a tropical alpine grassland." *Frontiers in Ecology and Evolution* 9: 1–15.

Ellis, Erle C. 2015. "Ecology in an anthropogenic biosphere." *Ecological Monographs* 85, no. 3: 287–331.

Fadrique, Belén, Selene Báez, Álvaro Duque, et al. 2018. "Widespread but heterogeneous responses of Andean forests to climate change." *Nature* 564, no. 7735: 207–212.

Fjeldså, Jon, Rauri C.K. Bowie, and Carsten Rahbek. 2012. "The role of mountain ranges in the diversification of birds." *Annual Review of Ecology, Evolution, and Systematics* 43: 249–265.

Freeman, Benjamin G., Micah N. Scholer, Viviana Ruiz-Gutierrez, et al. 2018. "Climate change causes upslope shifts and mountaintop extirpations in a tropical bird community." *PNAS* 115, no. 47: 11982–11987.

Gaston, Kevin J. 2003. *The Structure and Dynamics of Geographic Ranges*. Oxford: Oxford University Press.

Geldmann, Jonas, Andrea Manica, Neil D. Burgess, et al. 2019. "A global-level assessment of the effectiveness of protected areas at resisting anthropogenic pressures." *PNAS* 116, no. 46: 23209–23215.

Gepts, Paul, Thomas R. Famula, Robert L. Bettinger, et al., ed. 2012. *Biodiversity in Agriculture: Domestication, Evolution, and Sustainability*. Cambridge: Cambridge University Press.

Green, Jonathan M.H., Simon A. Croft, América P. Durán, et al. 2019. "Linking global drivers of agricultural trade to on-the-ground impacts on biodiversity." *PNAS* 116, no. 46: 23202–23208.

Griffith, M. Patrick, Falon Cartwright, Michael Dosmann, et al. 2021. "Ex situ conservation of large and small plant populations illustrates limitations of common conservation metrics." *International Journal of Plant Sciences* 182, no. 4: 263–276.

Hanski, Ilkka. 1998. "Metapopulation dynamics." *Nature* 396, no. 6706: 41–49.

Harari, Yuval Noah. 2014. *Sapiens: A Brief History of Humankind*. New York: Random House.

Harvey, Michael G., Gustavo A. Bravo, Santiago Claramunt, et al. 2020. "The evolution of a tropical biodiversity hotspot." *Science* 370, no. 6522: 1343–1348.

Helmus, Matthew R., D. Luke Mahler, and Jonathan B. Losos. 2014. "Island biogeography of the Anthropocene." *Nature* 513, no. 7519: 543–546.

Hobbs, Richard J., Eric S. Higgs, and Carol Hall. 2013. *Novel Ecosystems: Intervening in the new Ecological World Order*. Hoboken: John Wiley & Sons.

Hurtado-M, Ana Belén, María Ángela Echeverry-Galvis, Beatriz Salgado-Negret, et al. 2021. "Little trace of floristic homogenization in peri-urban Andean secondary forests despite high anthropogenic transformation." *Journal of Ecology* 109, no. 3: 1468–1478.

Keeley, Sterling C., Jason T. Cantley, and Timothy J. Gallaher. 2021. "The 'evil tribe' spreads across the land: a dated molecular phylogeny provides insight into dispersal, expansion, and biogeographic relationships within one of the largest tribes of the sunflower family (Vernonieae: Compositae)." *American Journal of Botany* 108, no. 3: 505–519.

Kieu, Nam Phuong, Marit Lenman, Eu Sheng Wang, et al. 2021. "Mutations introduced in susceptibility genes through CRISPR/Cas9 genome editing confer increased late blight resistance in potatoes." *Scientific Reports* 11, no. 1: 1–12.

Körner, Christian. 2021. *Alpine plant life: Functional Plant Ecology of high Mountain Ecosystems*. Cham: Springer Nature.

Kosoy, Nicolás, and Esteve Corbera. 2010. "Payments for ecosystem services as commodity fetishism." *Ecological Economics* 69, no. 6: 1228–1236.

Levin, Donald A. 2000. *The Origin, Expansion, and Demise of Plant Species*. Oxford: Oxford University Press.

Lewis, Simon L., and Mark A. Maslin. 2018. *The Human Planet: How we created the Anthropocene*. New Haven: Yale University Press.

Lewis, Tammy L. 2016. *Ecuador's Environmental Revolutions: Ecoimperialists, Ecodependents, and Ecoresisters*. Cambridge: MIT Press.

Lomolino, Mark V., Brett R. Riddle, and Robert J. Whittaker. 2017. *Biogeography*. Sunderland: Sinauer.

Lovejoy, Thomas E., and Lee Jay Hannah, ed. 2019. *Biodiversity and Climate Change*. New Haven: Yale University Press.

MacArthur, Robert H., and Edward O. Wilson. 2016. *The Theory of Island Biogeography*. Princeton: Princeton University Press.

Madriñán, Santiago, Andrés J. Cortés, and James E. Richardson. 2013. "Páramo is the world's fastest evolving and coolest biodiversity hotspot." *Frontiers in Genetics* 4: 1–7.

Margules, Chris R., and Sahotra Sarkar. 2007. *Systematic Conservation Planning*. Cambridge: Cambridge University Press.

Malhi, Yadvinder. 2017. "The concept of the Anthropocene." *Annual Review of Environment and Resources* 42: 77–104.

Masiokas, Mariano Hugo, Antoine Rabatel, Andres Rivera, et al. 2020. "A review of the current state and recent changes of the Andean cryosphere." *Frontiers in Earth Science* 8: 99.

Maxwell, Sean L., Victor Cazalis, Nigel Dudley, et al. 2020. "Area-based conservation in the twenty-first century." *Nature* 586, no. 7828: 217–227.

McKay, David I. Armstrong, Arie Staal, Jesse F. Abrams, et al. 2022. "Exceeding 1.5 C global warming could trigger multiple climate tipping points." *Science* 377, no. 6611: 1610–1613.

Migliavacca, Mirco, Talie Musavi, Miguel D. Mahecha, et al. 2021. "The three major axes of terrestrial ecosystem function." *Nature* 598, no. 7881: 468–472.

Millington, Andrew C., Udo Schickhoff, and Mark Blumler, ed. 2011. *The SAGE Handbook of Biogeography*. London: SAGE Publications.

Nosil, Patrik. 2012. *Ecological Speciation*. Oxford: Oxford University Press.

Palma, R. Eduardo, and Angel E. Spotorno. 1999. "Molecular systematics of marsupials based on the rRNA 12S mitochondrial gene: the phylogeny of Didelphimorphia and of the living fossil microbiotheriid Dromiciops gliroides Thomas." *Molecular phylogenetics and evolution* 13, no. 3: 525–535.

Parra-Rondinel, Fabiola, Alejandro Casas, Domingo Begazo, et al. 2021. "Natural and cultural processes influencing gene flow among wild (atoq papa), weedy (araq papa and k'ipa papa), and crop potatoes in the Andean region of southern Peru." *Frontiers in Ecology and Evolution* 9: 1–18.

Perfecto, Ivette, John Vandermeer, and Angus Wright. 2019. *Nature's Matrix: Linking Agriculture, Biodiversity Conservation and Food Sovereignty*. London: Routledge.

Pironon, Samuel, Ian Ondo, Mauricio Diazgranados, et al. 2024. "The global distribution of plants used by humans." *Science* 383, no. 6680: 293–297.

Quilter, Jeffrey. 2022. *The Ancient Central Andes*. 2nd ed. London: Taylor & Francis.

Radeloff, Volker C., John W. Williams, Brooke L. Bateman, et al. 2015. "The rise of novelty in ecosystems." *Ecological Applications* 25, no. 8: 2051–2068.

Raza, Ali, Abhishek Bohra, Vanika Garg, et al. 2023. "Back to wild relatives for future breeding through super-pangenome." *Molecular Plant* 16, no. 9: 1363–1365.

Richardson, David M., and Petr Pyšek. 2012. "Naturalization of introduced plants: ecological drivers of biogeographical patterns." *New Phytologist* 196, no. 2: 383–396.

Ripple, William J., Christopher Wolf, Thomas M. Newsome, et al. 2017. "World scientists' warning to humanity: a second notice." *BioScience* 67, no. 12: 1026–1028.

Roberts, David R., and Andreas Hamann. 2016. "Climate refugia and migration requirements in complex landscapes." *Ecography* 39, no. 12: 1238–1246.

Roberts, Patrick, Jed O. Kaplan, David Max Findley, et al. 2023. "Mapping our reliance on the tropics can reveal the roots of the Anthropocene." *Nature Ecology & Evolution* 7, no. 5: 632–636.

Root-Bernstein, Meredith, and Richard Ladle. 2019. "Ecology of a widespread large omnivore, Homo sapiens, and its impacts on ecosystem processes." *Ecology and Evolution* 9, no. 19: 10874–10894.

Ruddiman, William F. 2003. "The anthropogenic greenhouse era began thousands of years ago." *Climatic Change* 61, no. 3: 261–293.

Ruddiman, William F., Erle C. Ellis, Jed O. Kaplan, et al. 2015. "Defining the epoch we live in." *Science* 348, no. 6230: 38–39.

Sarmiento, Fausto, and Sarah Hitchner, ed. 2022. *Indigeneity and the Sacred: Indigenous Revival and the Conservation of Sacred Natural Sites in the Americas.* New York: Berghahn Books.

Seimon, Tracie A., Anton Seimon, Karina Yager, et al. 2017. "Long-term monitoring of tropical alpine habitat change, Andean anurans, and chytrid fungus in the Cordillera Vilcanota, Peru: Results from a decade of study." *Ecology and Evolution* 7, no. 5: 1527–1540.

Shipley, Benjamin R., and Jenny L. McGuire. 2022. "Interpreting and integrating multiple endemism metrics to identify hotspots for conservation priorities." *Biological Conservation* 265: 1–14.

Shiva, Vandana, ed. 2016. *Seed Sovereignty, Food security: Women in the Vanguard of the fight against GMOs and Corporate Agriculture.* Berkeley: North Atlantic Books.

Smil, Vaclav. 2021. *Grand Transitions: How the Modern World was made.* Oxford: Oxford University Press.

Sonne, Jesper, and Carsten Rahbek. 2024. "Idiosyncratic patterns of local species richness and turnover define global biodiversity hotspots." *PNAS* 121, no. 3: 1–7.

Spooner, David M., Marc Ghislain, Reinhard Simon, et al. 2014. "Systematics, diversity, genetics, and evolution of wild and cultivated potatoes." *The Botanical Review* 80: 283–383.

Steadman, David W. 2006. *Extinction and Biogeography of Tropical Pacific birds*. Chicago: University of Chicago Press.

Steffen, Will, Katherine Richardson, Johan Rockström, et al. 2015. "Planetary boundaries: Guiding human development on a changing planet." *Science* 347, no. 6223: 1–10.

Svenning, Jens-Christian, and Brody Sandel. 2013. "Disequilibrium vegetation dynamics under future climate change." *American Journal of Botany* 100, no. 7: 1266–1286.

Sylvester, Steven P., Mitsy D.P.V. Sylvester, and Michael Kessler. 2014. "Inaccessible ledges as refuges for the natural vegetation of the high Andes." *Journal of Vegetation Science* 25, no. 5: 1225–1234.

Ter Steege, Hans, Nigel C.A. Pitman, Timothy J. Killeen, et al. 2015. "Estimating the global conservation status of more than 15,000 Amazonian tree species." *Science Advances* 1, no. 10: 1–10.

Tovar, Carolina, Carlos Alberto Arnillas, Francisco Cuesta, et al. 2013. "Diverging responses of tropical Andean biomes under future climate conditions." *PloS one* 8, no. 5: 1–12.

Urrutia, Rocío, and Mathias Vuille. 2009. "Climate change projections for the tropical Andes using a regional climate model: Temperature and precipitation simulations for the end of the 21st century." *Journal of Geophysical Research: Atmospheres* 114, no. D2: 1–15.

Vizentin-Bugoni, Jeferson, Jinelle H. Sperry, J. Patrick Kelley, et al. 2021. "Ecological correlates of species' roles in highly invaded seed dispersal networks." *PNAS* 118, no. 4: 1–8.

Voeks, Robert A. 2019. *The Ethnobotany of Eden: Rethinking the Jungle Medicine Narrative*. Chicago: University of Chicago Press.

Waters, Colin N., Jan Zalasiewicz, Colin Summerhayes, et al. 2016. "The Anthropocene is functionally and stratigraphically distinct from the Holocene." *Science* 351, no. 6269: 1–10.

Watson, James E.M., Danielle F. Shanahan, Moreno Di Marco, et al. 2016. "Catastrophic declines in wilderness areas undermine global environment targets." *Current Biology* 26, no. 21: 2929–2934.

Whitfield, Stephen, Sarah Chapman, Marcelin Tonye Mahop, et al. 2021. "Exploring assumptions in crop breeding for climate resilience: opportunities and principles for integrating climate model projections." *Climatic Change* 164: 1–18.

Wilson, Edward O. 1996. *In Search of Nature*. Washington, D.C.: Island Press.

———. 2016. *Half-Earth: Our Planet's Fight for Life*. New York: W.W. Norton & Company.

Young, Kenneth R. 1995. "Biogeographical paradigms useful for the study of tropical montane forests and their biota". In *Biodiversity and Conservation of Neotropical*

Montane Forests, ed. Steven P. Churchill, Henrik Balslev, Enrique Forero, et al., 79–87. New York: New York Botanical Garden.

———. 1998. "Deforestation in landscapes with humid forests in the central Andes: patterns and processes". In *Nature's Geography: New Lessons for Conservation in Developing Countries*, ed. Karl S. Zimmerer and Kenneth R. Young, 75–99. Madison: University of Wisconsin Press.

———. 2009. "Andean land use and biodiversity: humanized landscapes in a time of change." *Annals of the Missouri Botanical Garden* 96, no. 3: 492–507.

———. 2016. "Biogeography of the Anthropocene: Domestication." *Progress in Physical Geography: Earth and Environment* 40, no. 1: 161–174.

———. 2021. "Ecology and human habitation of Andean forests." In *The Archaeology of the Upper Amazon: Complexity and Interaction in the Andean Tropical Forest*, ed. Ryan Clasby and Jason Nesbitt, 23–37. Gainesville: University of Florida Press.

Young, Kenneth R., and Sisimac Duchicela. 2021. "Abandoning Holocene dreams: Proactive biodiversity conservation in a changing world." *Annals of the American Association of Geographers* 111, no. 3: 880–888.

———. 2023. "Biodiversity and the Anthropocene." In *Encyclopedia of Biodiversity*. 3rd ed., ed. Samuel M. Scheiner. Cambridge: Elsevier.

Young, Kenneth R., Blanca León, Peter M. Jørgensen, and Carmen Ulloa Ulloa. 2007. "Tropical and subtropical landscapes of the Andes Mountains." In *The Physical Geography of South America*, ed. Thomas Veblen, Kenneth Young, and Antony Orme, 200–216. Oxford: Oxford University Press.

Young, Kenneth R., Carmen Ulloa Ulloa, James L. Luteyn, et al. 2002. "Plant Evolution and Endemism in Andean South America." *Botanical Review* 68, no. 1: 4–21.

Young, Kenneth R., Alexandra G. Ponette-González, Molly H. Polk, et al. 2017. "Snowlines and treelines in the tropical Andes." *Annals of the American Association of Geographers* 107, no. 2: 429–440.

Zimmerer, Karl S., Stef de Haan, Andrew D. Jones, et al. 2019. "The biodiversity of food and agriculture (Agrobiodiversity) in the Anthropocene: Research advances and conceptual framework." *Anthropocene* 25: 1–16.

Biodiversity in the Amazon from 1950 to the Present
Towards a Great Biocultural Simplification

Felipe Vander Velden

Amazonia is one of the planet's most biodiverse biomes; in over 7 million square kilometers of nine countries in South America, this region hosts an impressive variety of animal, vegetable, and microscopic life forms. Perhaps a third of all living species existing today have been verified here, among its roughly 40,000 species of plants, 1,300 birds, and over 1,000 amphibians (Capobianco 2001; Butler 2020; WWF 2020; WWF 2022). The region is a mosaic of different ecological zones with considerably distinct characteristics, some notable for an even more diverse collection of species and multispecies interactions (Orme et al. 2005; Zador 2021). The region's numerous aquatic environments make for impressive biodiversity: Amazonia is the world's largest river basin, holding roughly 20 percent of all the fresh water on the planet, and maybe home to the largest number of known fish species (WWF 2016; Val et al. 2017).

For approximately 14,000 years, this spectacular diversity of plants, animals, fungi, and microorganisms has lived alongside the human populations that occupy Amazonia (Heckenberger and Neves 2009; Pereira and Guapindaia 2010; Neves et al. 2021). Indeed, through activities that altered this same biodiversity, Amerindian peoples have been central to establishing the mosaic of Amazonian landscapes and the incalculable wealth of the beings that inhabit them, as ethnographic studies and research on the archeology and ecological history of this region have shown (Posey 1985; Descola 1994; Balée 1994; Balée 2013; Denevan 2001; Balée and Erickson 2006; Rostain 2014; Rostain 2016; Clement et al. 2015; Magalhães 2016). Of course, the Amazon is not an untouched natural environment free of people and formed without concerted human and other-than-human efforts, but instead an ecological complex of beings in which Amerindian societies and other human groups from Africa or Europe, since the fifteenth century, have comprised a disparate multitude of biotic and abiotic agents which have shaped and reshaped the immense forest and its many habitats for thousands of years (Raffles 2002; Kohn 2013; Kawa 2016; Neves and Heckenberger 2019).

The vast amounts of knowledge produced by indigenous and non-indigenous societies in and about the region and the many modes of interaction between humans and other-than-humans reflect the mutual processes of making the forest (which involve animals, plants, microorganisms, human groups, and other forces like the climate, rivers and lakes, and soils). In the case of animals, there is ample evidence of highly detailed knowledge about Amazonian fauna among the native populations of the Amazon, as well as sophisticated technical and conceptual developments for relating to this diversity of beings (Hames 1980; Hames and Vickers 1983; Jensen 1988; Correa 1993; Jara 1996; Ribeiro 1997; Marchand and Vander Velden 2017). It is no coincidence that recent innovative anthropological reflections on ontology (the "ontological turn") are framed within the Amazon and focus on the intimate interdependence between humans and other-than-humans, as in the case of animism (Descola 2005) and Amerindian perspectivism (Viveiros de Castro 1998), highlighting the centrality of animals in indigenous Amazonian sociocosmologies.

The same is true for extensive knowledge of Amazonia's botanical diversity, whether cultivated, managed, collected, protected, or wild (Clement 1999; Albert and Milliken 2009; Alexiades and Peluso 2009; Carneiro da Cunha and Morin de Lima 2017; Emperaire 2017). Afro-descendant populations in Amazonia also hold expansive botanical and ecological knowledge, and other communities that migrated to this region developed notably sophisticated expertise about this environment in a relatively short period – just over a century for rubber tappers in the western Amazon, for example (Carneiro da Cunha and Barbosa de Almeida 2002; Voeks and Rashford 2013). Scientific studies have long noted the extensive variety of cultivars farmed by indigenous and other traditional Amazonian peoples, which modern farmers in the region have even appropriated, as well as the various uses of this dazzling diversity of plants (Ribeiro 1987). Collaborative and innovative research involving indigenous and non-indigenous researchers and institutions in several countries has increasingly revealed this botanical wealth (Silveira 2012; Daly and Shepard Jr. 2019). Today we know that the creation and conservation of agricultural biodiversity in Amazonia is not restricted to Amerindian peoples but also found in traditional, peasant, and migrant communities, and in several cases, has taken place in association with researchers, particularly from the 1980s (Soluri 2018).

The arrival of Europeans in the late fifteenth century, accompanied by their notions of the immense natural area as "the green hell," sparsely populated by barbarous, backward, and unlearned peoples, clearly wrought enormous changes for life in the Amazon region (Stepan 2006). They endeavored to conquer the forest, subjecting it to European intentions by converting it into land (from a legal and geopolitical perspective) and transforming the beings that lived there into resources or merchandise: the famed "drugs of the sertão" (certain native spices and medicinal herbs), quinine, cocoa, rubber, animal skins and feathers, wood, pasture, and energy. Although some of these processes of extracting the "resources" of Amazonian flora and fauna during the first 450 years of non-indigenous occupation were impressive – for example, fishing for turtles and manatees to obtain meat, eggs, and oil as early as the seventeenth century (Batista 2007: 221–241; Fiori and Santos 2013), the rubber boom in western Amazon from the mid-1800s (Weinstein 1983; Dean 2002), and commercial hunting that yielded a significant volume of pelts in the first half of the twentieth century (Broad 1987; Antunes 2015; Antunes, Shepard, and Venticinque 2014) – the rhythm and extent of anthropogenic changes in the region shifted dramatically from 1945 onward during the "eccentric historical moment" designated the Great Acceleration (McNeill and Engelke 2016).

Considering these profound changes to the biome from the second half of the twentieth century, with particular attention to the impact provoked by Indigenous and traditional communities in the region (Hecht and Cockburn 2011), this chapter discusses Amazonian biodiversity concerning the *threats* it has faced since the 1950s while highlighting specific strategies to resist them, especially local or regional responses by social groups and various institutions in the countries that share this biome. This focus on the practices and processes that threaten life in Amazonia (and the region itself) results from the privileged view in this text of relationships between human and other-than-human beings (namely animals and plants). In this sense, human actions and practices transform biodiversity for better or worse along deeply interconnected historical paths; because of the biocultural perspective adopted here, researchers must not separate the human (culture) and the nonhuman (nature).

During the final moments of his monumental exploration of the Amazon River in 1541–1542, the Spanish explorer Francisco de Orellana described what he called the "province of São João" (near the mouth of the Trombetas River, in modern Pará, Brazil) and stated that the land was "ready to *raise cattle* since it has good fodder as in our Spain" (Carvajal 1992[1542], p. 261, my emphasis). Although we know there was no ranching in this part of South America at that time, let us consider cattle for a moment. If we label Orellana's dream of colonization as "opting for agribusiness," in the manner of Bolle (2010: 47), it seems anachronistic, perhaps heralding a far-off future when the group of other-than-human beings known as *cattle* spread into nearly every corner of the Amazon, accelerating a process of *ecological simplification* (Haraway 2016; Hopes and Perry 2019) of life or biological diversity in the forest characteristic of the post-1950 period. Cattle are certainly not the only agent of the recent profound changes in Amazonia's biodiversity and the relationships between humans and other-than-humans in the forest. Nevertheless, it seems appropriate to mention that, according to Crosby (2002), these animals have driven ecological imperialism in the region since the 1950s. In this way, like a new package of introduced species – which includes not only herd animals but also other beings like parasites, pets, trees for construction, exotic grasses, pathogens, and of course, all the sociocultural formations and practices that inevitably accompany them, in an accurate natural-cultural assemblage (Haraway 2003) – cattle and their advance are both a cause and a consequence of recent major transformations in Amazonia. Here, two processes that threaten Amazonian biodiversity need introduction, focusing first on the relationships these impacts have on other-than-human beings and then on their relation to indigenous and traditional peoples. Making the problem even more complex, the impacts suffered by human and other-than-human collectives show that the Amazon's biodiversity and sociodiversity are not separate.

The biocultural perspective does not allow the natural to be separate from the cultural (and consequently allows many different worlds to flourish). Thus, the study of animals, plants, and other-than-human beings in the Amazon extends far beyond what scientific biology studies. This understanding has been the banner of a contemporary anthropology that implements "multinaturalism" (Viveiros de Castro 1998) or the "plurality of worlds" (De la Cadena and Blaser 2018): not distinct visions of one single world, but different worlds inhabited by distinct human and other-than-human communities. The immense variety of other-than-human beings involved here extends far beyond the "real" species that zoology and botany catalog to include animals and plants from the mythologies and knowledge systems of indigenous and traditional peoples: animals that have been hunted, fished, captured, tamed, loved, hated, or scorned by the populations of the Amazon, whether native, migrant, rural, or urban; powerful, sacred medicinal plants of the indigenous peoples, river dwellers, rubber tappers, *caboclos*, *quilombolas*, and others; and even the exotic plant and animal species that they introduced, feral or feralized animals or those that comprise domestic diversity, all equally varied according to their place in villages, on small rural properties, settlements, farms, the urban centers and peripheries of the Amazon's cities, or on large agricultural estates scattered throughout this biome.

What must be maintained here is that a "species" like *Panthera onca*, the zoologists' jaguar, is just one of the many beings that inhabit the Amazon; there are many "other jaguars" that live in the forest, as many as the number of sociocultural and sociolinguistic formations that live alongside other-than-human beings and they cannot be reduced to a scientifically recognized species without the risk of stating that western science reigns supreme in revealing the "true" real world. This perspective naturally multiplies the problem of environmental devastation and the erosion of sociobiodiversity in Amazonia from the Great Acceleration, generating additional challenges for effective socioenvironmental policy to ensure its future.

Humans and Nonhumans in the Amazon since the Great Acceleration

Threats to Flora and Fauna from 1950 onward

The biodiversity of Amazonia has been attacked and eroded (while still being discovered) by a series of anthropogenic processes that began in the sixteenth century but accelerated massively in terms of impact and destruction after the middle of the twentieth century (most notably after 1970) as various countries looked to solidify their national identities, integrity, and sovereignty; defend distant and poorly defined frontiers; and incorporate new territories to advance capital. The spread of neoliberal policies from the 1990s reinvigorated these efforts. Aggressive deforestation from expanding pastures and monocultures like soy for export; increasingly uncontrollable forest fires; illegal logging and gold-panning; large-scale mining and petroleum ventures; proliferating highways, railways, and other transport infrastructure; increasing urbanization; as well as hydroelectric dam projects; and commercial and predatory hunting and fishing (among other threats) have put pressure on the entire forest, according to a recent and comprehensive report on this topic by a consortium of environmental organizations from six countries in the Amazon basin (RAISG 2021; Schmink and Wood 1991; Hébette 1991; Ribeiro 1992; Ricardo 1999; Vieira et al. 2008; Capozzoli 2008; Hecht and Cockburn 2011; Gallice, Larrea-Gallegos, and Vázquez-Rowe 2019, Larrea-Alcázar et al. 2021; CLACSO/CEDLA 2021).

In the early 1970s, the Brazilian Amazon still had approximately 99 percent of its original vegetation; today, the above operations have destroyed roughly 19 percent, around 760,000 km² (Pádua 2018: 102–107). In the early 1990s, neoliberal policies were definitively established in Brazil to encourage the intensification of this environmental devastation (Fearnside 2005). In the face of this sobering scenario, this chapter seeks to revisit relationships between human and other-than-human beings in the Amazon biome, particularly from the perspective of historical and anthropological studies, along with how their links to the growing processes of anthropization in this region. This involves observing what we know about interactions between humans and other-than-humans in post-1950s Amazonia, and how they are involved (as both causes and consequences) in the advancing destruction of the different ecosystems there. In this section, the focus will be on two threats to life in the Amazonia from a relational viewpoint, in other words, processes through which humans relate to other-than-humans and interactional dynamics that tend to be fatal for the latter. These processes include predation (hunting, fishing, and plant extractivism) and utilization (trade and consumption) of other-than-human beings and the introduction of exotic species, most dramatically seen in the growth of ranching and monoculture farming that comprise agribusiness.

Predation: Capture, Commerce, and Consumption

Subsistence hunting and fishing have been practiced for millennia by indigenous Amazonian peoples and more recently by other local traditional populations such as river dwellers, *caboclos*, rubber tappers, Brazil nut gatherers, *quilombolas*, *palenqueros*, and maroons (Carneiro da Cunha and Barbosa de Almeida 2002; Silvius, Bodmer, and Fragoso 2004; Alves de Figueiredo and Barros 2016; Saraiva and Corrêa 2016; Barros 2017) with historically lower impact, although some native populations have become increasingly involved with commercial hunting (Apaza et al. 2002; Puyol et al. 2010). However, although these traditional practices differ from commercial hunting and fishing in several ways, they have reached significant levels, particularly after the 1960s (Bennett and Robinson 2000). As various studies have shown, non-indigenous populations in the Amazon are large consumers of hunted meat (bush meat), even in the cities, where there is often a lively informal trade in the meat of animals and native fish, including endangered species (Rebêlo and Pezzuti 2000; Vliet et. al 2014; Mendes and Simonian 2016; Chaves et al. 2018; Mendes 2020). One investigation that took place in two cities in the state of Amazonas (Borba and Novo Aripuanã) in Brazil found that nearly all urban families consume wild fauna, including fish (99 percent), hunted meat (mammals and birds, 79 percent), turtles (48 percent), and crocodilian species (28 percent) (Parry, Barlow, and Pereira 2014). Recent studies affirm the need to consider the habits, preferences, and tastes of Amazonian populations, who enjoy game meat (Torres et al. 2021), but whose growth places great pressure on this fauna. These markets generate ferocious competition for resources, always to the detriment of traditional peoples, which is the case on the border between Brazil, Peru, and Colombia where local fishers are unable to compete with large fishing boats that sell substantial quantities of frozen fish (Pinto 2016).

Much of the emptying of native fauna from their Amazonian habitats has resulted from the violent process of human occupation seen especially in the 1960s and 1970s as large numbers of people from other regions migrated into the forest zones and demographic growth accelerated throughout the region, a dynamic encouraged in Brazil by the perverse alliance between the military dictatorship and elites who were anxious to occupy new territories and diversify their investments: today, roughly 65 percent of the population in the Amazon biome lives in cities (WWF 2016: 27). Many of these waves of migrants were (and in certain places still are) the result of large government projects designed, in the words of a former Brazilian military president, "to give land without men to men without land" (Velho 1972). These flows can be seen in the ever-climbing rates of urbanization in Amazonia: various studies (Browder and Godfrey 1997; Vicentini 2004) maintain that urbanization in this region cannot be ignored, since it includes not only overpopulated metropolises (like Belém, Manaus, and Iquitos) but also accelerated growth in small and medium-sized towns and villages (Pinedo-Vasquez and Padoch 2009; Arcila Niño 2011; Zárate Botía 2012). These neo-Amazonian urban agglomerations place increasing pressure on the fauna via unregulated deforestation, growing consumption of wild meat and fish, the capture of wild animals as pets or for various markets, and the introduction of invasive exotic species (Costa, Silva, and Rodrigues 2014; Silva and Lima 2014).

Pressure from hunting and fishing has contributed to a phenomenon known as the "empty forest," in which animals (particularly large mammals) disappear from regions where vegetation, however, appears to remain intact (Redford 1992). This also increasingly has become true of "empty rivers" where large fish and other aquatic animals are no longer found (Antunes et. al 2016). The indigenous peoples in these regions seem to have noticed this situation: although territories earmarked exclusively for use by indigenous peoples best protect the Amazon's vegetation and biological diversity (Nepstad et al. 2006; Rolla 2006; Valle 2010), some already have trouble accessing game animals. For example, the Karitiana in the southwestern Brazilian Amazon report that they increasingly have to "walk a lot" or "go far" (from their villages) to find game (Vander Velden 2016; see also Maruyama and Morioka 1998: 73). Further research is necessary to evaluate the impacts of commercial hunting and fishing throughout Amazonia, always considering native, indigenous, and local perceptions that create additional questions related to the richness of biodiversity according to a biocultural approach.

These same threats may also endanger the Amazon's immense botanical diversity in massive ways, such as accelerated deforestation and, more specifically, phenomena such as logging high-value species like cedar and mahogany and trafficking in rare plants like orchids and bromeliads (Martini, Rosa, and Uhl 2001; Macedo 2009; Servicio Nacional Forestal y de Fauna Silvestre 2020). These practices lead to intensive and selective searches for certain species that ultimately intensify pressure and, in turn, increase the risk that life in this region will become less diverse (Larrea-Alcázar et al. 2021). A debate has emerged around the sustainability of plant extractivism, but increasing scalability has revealed the vulnerability of certain individual species even as studies related to the cultivation of some of these plants have advanced (Homma 2014; Silva et al. 2016).

Hunting, fishing, and extractivism for human consumption have close links to the more recent phenomena of biopiracy and trafficking in wild species, which equally strike a blow to Amazonian biodiversity. While biopiracy in the Amazon has especially affected plant species with potential industrial and commercial applicability, as well as so-called "genetic resources" (Bensusan 2002; Ramos 2006), the illegal trade in animals to produce crafts, medications, and fashion (particularly from rare and threatened species) has continued to grow (Doughty and Myers 1971; Hennessey 2007; Alves and Santana 2008; Macleod and Hennessey 2011; Sinovas et al. 2017; Vander Velden 2018). Currently, knowledge is scarce about the local and regional microdynamics of this global business; more importantly, we need to learn more about the circulation of live wild animals on the edges of Amazonia itself and the reasons why populations capture, keep, and utilize these beings in captivity (Broad, Mulliken, and Roe 2003: 16; Costa, Silva, and Rodrigues 2014). Nevertheless, there is evidence of intensive exploitation (unfortunately, tending towards exhaustion) of the extensive variety of ornamental fish in various rivers in the region, for example, raising concern about the sustainability of certain rare or threatened species which, precisely for their scarcity, are highly coveted in Brazilian and foreign markets which support such predatory practices (Souza, Mello and Menezes 2009; Prang 2004; Moreau and Coomes 2008; Gonçalves et al. 2009).

In any case, one recent manifestation of neoextractivism in Amazonia (not only trafficking in wild beings but also activities including the illegal wood trade and illegal mining) is an association with organized crime networks in various countries and links to drug and gun trafficking, money laundering, tax evasion, and generalized corruption involving public officials and politically and economically powerful local elites (Couto 2020). Furthermore, international geopolitical interests in selling the air (through carbon sequestration policies) and water add new dimensions to neoextractivism in the forest and complicate the process that Bertha Becker (2005) called the mercantilization of nature, with the emergence and increasing value of natural capital which increasingly recasts the forest into a warehouse full of resources available for commodification and exploitation.

Introduction of Exotic Species

The introduction of exotic plants and animals has consequences in urban areas, but its impacts extend far beyond. Knowledge about the potential biotic and abiotic changes (such as the extinction of endemic species from predation, competition, or the spread of unknown pathogens) provoked by non-native species in Amazonian ecosystems, such as feral dogs (Lessa et al. 2016), tilapia (*Oreochromis* spp., originating in Africa) (Pérez et al. 2003; Pozzetti and Gasparini 2018); the giant brown freshwater prawn in Amazonian estuaries in Pará, Brazil (Barros and Silva 1997); and commercial plantations of teak (*Tectona grandis*), acacia (*Acacia mangium*), and eucalyptus (*Eucalyptus* spp.) – exotic trees that spread across the entire biome, including as part of reforestation projects (Conrado da Cruz et al. 2020) – still needs to be researched. However, attention to native perspectives on "biological invasion" may sometimes yield surprising results from a biocultural point of view, such as evidence that this process generates *greater* diversity of life forms instead of reducing it via its potential impacts. Various local populations debate the ecological and sociocultural effects of non-native species expansion; for example, the fish known as pirarucu (*Arapaima gigas*) escaped from local fish farmers into the Guaporé River where it did not naturally occur. The Kujubim Indians linked this development to the powers of the *eré*, the white men, and the changes resulting from their actions in indigenous lives associated with the river. Today these fish are integrated into economic and regional circuits that involve indigenous peoples and local fishermen on the Brazil/Bolivia border (Sanchez 2020).

Indigenous and peasant farmers who seek variety and diversity have incorporated and cultivated exotic plant species such as sugarcane, allochthonous bananas (Musaceae), and even much more recent arrivals into their fields (Carneiro da Cunha and Morim de Lima 2017: 64). On the other hand, the erosion of what is known as domestic biodiversity should also be noted: the disappearance of species and varieties of cultivated plants due to pressures including the standardization of very few varieties suited to consumer preferences and logistical requirements and the encroachment of monoculture farming into traditional horticultural areas (Emperaire 2001).

Certainly, the exotic species with significant past and present consequences in the current great simplification of Amazonia's biodiversity were introduced intentionally and had links to the significant development of agribusiness throughout the region over the past half-century. These include certain other-than-human species that should be considered in reflections on the erosion of biodiversity in the biome, such as palm oil (*Elaeis guineensis*) and the expansion of palm oil production in the Peruvian central Amazon (Anchirayco and Lasteros 2021) and the lower Amazon River in Brazil (Brandão and Schoneveld 2015). Another example is sugarcane (*Saccharum* spp.) for fuel production (Vieira et al. 2008: 951–952) and, of course, soy (*Glycine max*), which advances aggressively northward through the southern Amazon (Léna and Oliveira 1991; Simon and Garagorry 2005; Fearnside 2008). These are just some of the monocultures involving the catastrophic conversion of rich forest zones into monotonous landscapes dominated by a single planted species that characterize the Plantationocene (Hopes and Perry 2019), an alternative to the Anthropocene highlighting the drastic reduction in types of life forms. In general, an other-than-human, a particular animal, and the assemblages of beings that accompany it precedes the establishment of these plants in Amazonian contexts historically; the animal alluded to is cattle (*Bos taurus*), a central character in the neoextractivism destroying the Amazon through alliances between neoliberal policies and public and private actors, especially since the 1990s.

Ranching, particularly for beef production, is known to have created enormous momentum in various areas of the Amazon basin in recent decades, an explosion that first began after 1950 with a series of technical and technological advances in livestock production in the region (Valentim and Andrade 2009; Smeraldi and May 2008; Smeraldi and May 2009; Van Ausdal and Wilcox 2018). Forest vegetation was not suitable for ranching during the colonial period, leading to problems with adapting the animals and production techniques to dense forests or flooded areas, limiting the presence of cattle – even though ranching prospered in certain regions since at least the seventeenth century (Oliveira 1983: 255–257; Dias-Filho and Lopes 2020). Still, from the 1960s onward, the race to economically occupy the Amazon and large migrations to the region propelled land appropriation and more intensive clearing, always followed by the establishment of pasture and introduction of cattle, serving as a sign and a type of guarantee of land ownership. In Brazil, it is said that "land with cattle is land with an owner" (Fearnside 1989: 64).

Today ranching activity (most notably, cattle ranching) accounts for 84 percent of deforestation in the Amazon, and over 10 percent of the entire river basin has already been converted into pasture (Vieira et al. 2008: 951; RAISG 2020: 33). This expansion in ranching consequently ensures that lands which have been previously "tamed," occupied, and deforested are snapped up for export monocultures that follow the cattle, in a routine repeated across various areas of the biome (Botelho de Andrade 2005; Costa Silva 2015). Driven by powerful neoliberal agrarian elites in countries like Brazil, Bolivia, and Colombia (Pompéia 2021), cattle are majorly responsible for simplifying the variety of Amazonian biota, as well as in their connection to a variety of other-than-human species that share their pathways, such as the many wood species established in ranching facilities, exotic grass species for artificial pastures (Dias-Filho 2014), and other beings that generally follow cattle and the way of life they introduce: horses, pigs, sheep, chickens, commercially raised fish, Africanized honeybees, and fast-growing imported wood species.

So it is largely through cattle that the Amazon has been consumed since the second half of the twentieth century (Durães 2017); this animal is one of the main actors in simplifying life and ecological networks that we are discussing here (Ficek 2019). This process results from the growing global increase in meat consumption and continuing expansion of yields and economic performance for ranching, alongside aggressive public incentives and international investments (Hecht 1985; Flórez-Malagón 2008; van Ausdal 2009). Obviously, this has considerably impacted the native human populations in this biome. Recent studies have shown that traditional populations (rubber tappers and river dwellers) and smallholders have taken up small-scale cattle ranching, most notably as a form of savings and ensuring their land remains occupied, contributing to the development of local cattle raising techniques (Arima and Uhl 1996; Porto, Alvino de Mesquita, and Santos 2004; Toni et al. 2007; Wood, Tourrand, and Toni 2015; Pantoja, Costa, and Postigo 2009). To a certain extent, modest-scale ranching is here to stay (Hoelle 2014; Hoelle 2015), and many small-scale migrant producers have fallen back on cattle as a connection to "large-scale ranching operations and regional export economy," which in turn raises meaningful discussions about the socioenvironmental viability of these small herds (Pereira, Simmons, and Walker 2016). Alongside the growth of large ranches, we can discuss the accelerated process of ranchification in Amazonia (Smeraldi and May 2008; Walker et al. 2009).

It is no different for many indigenous peoples who live in the Amazon basin. Various native groups who have occupied natural grassland regions since the eighteenth century – such as the savannas between northern Brazil and the interior of Guyana – have adopted cattle (Rivière 1972). But the appeal of ranching, together with growing incentives (particularly after the turn of the twentieth century), triggered the introduction of ranching to many different peoples who had not been familiar with this mode of exploiting and living alongside other-than-human beings. Whether indigenous individuals made this decision or myriad governmental and non-governmental projects encouraged it, cattle began appearing in traditional territories throughout Amazonia, sometimes in small herds of just one or two animals. Nevertheless, the outcome was almost always discouraging since these peoples did not implement modern productive concepts, and in most places, the animals disappeared for various reasons or remained in and around the villages with little to no utility (Descola 1982; Baksh 1995; MacDonald 1997; Rudel, Bates, and Machinguiashi 2002).

Additionally, in certain territories, the presence of cattle has been seen to impact the local ecology and biodiversity (Fearnside 1989; MacDonald 1997: 326–327; Fiorello, Noss, and Deem 2006), but this does not seem to have decreased the enthusiasm among some indigenous societies in the Amazon for adopting, raising, and exploiting cattle (Hecht 1993; Amigos da Terra 2009). It is important to note that the relationships between Amazonian people and other other-than-human beings have a history that includes occasionally radical transformations in their cosmologies, which are not watertight (Fernández-Llamazares and Virtanen 2020). Examples of indigenous peoples adopting these exotic beings into their constantly changing cosmologies suggest that research on these issues of biodiversity and sociodiversity together must come from a biocultural perspective.

Sociobiodiversity and Biocultural Diversity in Amazonia

The two major threats to the Amazon's rich biodiversity described above, which follow the accelerated destruction of the forest, have attracted increasing global attention because of their effects on the climate and Earth's ecology as a whole within the current context known as the Anthropocene. Especially since the late 1980s, a close bond has been forged between the environment and resident communities, giving rise to the contemporary socioenvironmentalism visible in the reformulation of national legislation and creation of new modes of environmental conservation intended to work specifically with nature and culture, such as the establishment of extractivist reserves in Brazil (Carneiro da Cunha and Barbosa de Almeida 2002). From a local perspective (but certainly with increasing repercussions at the planetary level), indigenous leaders, peasants, scientists, and environmentalists have made their voices heard in striking critiques of the modern industrial approach to life in Amazonia, highlighting the intricate and ancestral relationships between the human and other-than-human communities that populate the biome, the values associated with what they consider the good life and the destruction of these ways of life catalyzed by the advance of large-scale capital. These voices introduce a growing socioenvironmental or biocultural dimension centered on this notion of the good life: *buen vivir* or *bem viver* (Kopenawa and Albert 2015; Suruí and Sombrun 2015; Baniwa 2019).

From these initiatives, recognized and emerging leaders are attempting to warn the world not only about the large-scale impacts but also the negative local and/or regional effects of the Great Acceleration on Amazonian populations. Although often demographically small, these groups preserve significant knowledge of life forms, their complex interactions, and their potential economic uses. In this way, they strongly critique the pillars of the capitalist system by demonstrating the inherent bias (racial, sociopolitical, gender, and species) of discourses that have supported notions such as development, progress, and civilization. Since the 1980s especially, complex alliances between environmentalists, indigenous and traditional peoples, and the forest itself have been constructed in order to fight environmental destruction and the genocide/ethnocide of those now known as the peoples of the forest (Albert 1997; Carneiro da Cunha and Almeida 2002). For example, indigenous efforts have intensified in recent years as they win local and even national offices (Verdum and Paula 2020). Alongside such developments, these guardians of the forest have become targets of the brutal violence in the region focused against indigenous leaders, environmentalists, journalists, public agents, and other actors dedicated to protecting human peoples and other-than-humans and their ways of life, such as the rubber tapper and leader Chico Mendes (1988), the nun Dorothy Stang (2005), and more recently (2022) the indigenist Bruno Pereira and journalist Dom Phillips, as well as many other indigenous leaders and social activists. Since 2009, over 300 deaths connected to land conflicts and deforestation have been reported in the Brazilian Amazon alone (Human Rights Watch 2019).

Incorporating local indigenous and non-indigenous reflections and viewpoints into our analysis of the environmental destruction and erosion of biodiversity in the Amazon, considering the ontological turn (De la Cadena and Blaser 2018), produces even more dramatic scenarios in which these changes damage not just one single world (through various destructive means) but instead destroy entire worlds, other worlds, and the worlds of others, obliterating the perspectives of populations marginalized from the places they occupied for millennia, and their everyday interactions with beings they have always known (Danowski and Viveiros de Castro 2017). In these Amazonian multiverses, living beings and knowledge about them cannot be separated and have an intimate connection to shared experience; in just one example, events that involve hunting and dismemberment of animals and distribution of their meat are not only classes in the anatomy, physiology, and/or etiology, but also classes of history, geography, politics, and many other areas of knowledge encapsulated in the relationships between humans and animals and practices developed over millennia. In this way, the disappearance of a species (even if localized) produces a gap that is not only ecological but also cultural or rather biocultural. Similarly, the extinction of native languages, practices, and knowledge leads to the disappearance of an entire group of beings that exist only in these singular worlds of words.

In this sense, as many authors have maintained for some time, the future of Amazonia and its exuberant biodiversity is intimately connected to protecting its social and cultural diversity (Fernández-Llamazares et al. 2021). The multiplicity of biological life forms and ways of living that are entwined in complex socio-ecological systems must be addressed as a group by science and policy (Mikkola 2021). Thus, to preserve the Amazon (its fauna, flora, microorganisms, ecology, waters, landscapes, and all of its global functions), it is essential to respect the knowledge, practices, and techniques of the peoples of the forest, considering the increasingly established acknowledgment that biological diversity and cultural diversity go hand in hand and mutually enrich each other (Maffi 2001; Athayde et al. 2021). From a biocultural perspective which does not contrast lived experience and ideas against each other, biodiversity in the Amazon is even more extraordinarily rich and significant than previously thought. There are myriad and even uncountable numbers of animals and plants in the Amazon, if we consider them through the various prisms as the inhabitants of many lived and conceived worlds. The general idea is that we must focus on understanding the interconnected or entangled worlds between humans and other-than-humans in socially and natural-culturally unique ways, along with engagement of human practices and knowledge with this world (or these worlds) in which they live and with the many life forms that comprise what is considered biodiversity. In this way, biodiversity is sociodiversity, and sociocultural worlds reflect and provide information on the endless possibilities resulting from human thought and practices that produce difference and variety in their entanglements with the world. Biological life forms and sociocultural ways of living mutually strengthen each other rather than opposing each other in the outdated dualist framework that posits nature and culture as opposites.

This perspective also invites us to recognize that the peoples of the Amazon, in their practices and multispecies engagements, actually boost local diversity through agriculture and by managing wild species and varieties (Carneiro da Cunha and Morim de Lima 2017; Carneiro da Cunha, Magalhães, and Adams 2021). The Amazon is currently home to roughly 410 indigenous peoples (RAISG 2021: 12), coordinated by the *Coordinadora de las Organizaciones Indígenas de la Cuenca Amazónica* (COICA), an organization founded in 1984 that spans nine national indigenous organizations in the region. This biome also is the home of numerous traditional populations, from Black communities who have occupied the forest for at least three centuries (Price 1996; Marin, Carvalho, and Almeida 2020) to small farmers, many migrants and settlers, who have sought a life for themselves in the region with many impacts that differ from (and are less drastic than) those caused by mega-scale ventures involving farming, mining, ranching, hydroelectric dams, and infrastructure projects, for example, and do not reduce or simplify (agro)biodiversity (Aragón Vaca 2005; Fleury 2016). The multispecies engagements between native people and their territories, the beings of the forest, and their biotic and abiotic components require a holistic approach to study and combat the grave threats faced by the Amazon, especially over the past fifty years during the Great Acceleration as well as the great simplification of life (Surralés and Hierro 2005; Velho et al. 2017).

Of course, all these suggestions are the result of a broad alliance between scientific research and environmental conservation (through relatively new environmental sciences), which began to blossom, especially in the Amazon during the 1970s and

1980s, when the notion of biodiversity began to take hold, and the tropical South American forest began to transform into a critical biome in conservationist debates around the world (McCook 2018). During this time as well, local, regional, and international NGOs began to proliferate in the region, creating a new model for institutionalizing relationships between society and nature that connects governments, nongovernment organizations, research institutions, and traditional peoples. Many of these NGOs bring together environmental and human rights (including indigenous rights), recognizing the profound alliance between humans and other-than-humans evident in the past and present and is also necessary for the future of Amazonia (Barbosa 2015). Of course, this movement also experienced violent reactions from powerful developmentalist and predatory interests opposing the preservation of both life forms and forms of life, which also cannot be considered separately.

Final Considerations

We can conclude this brief exploration of threats to Amazonian biodiversity after 1950 during the Great Acceleration as follows:

- The Amazonia is the biome with the greatest biodiversity on the planet, home to 10 to 15 percent of all known plant and animal species (Barroso et al. 2021); biologists as well as scholars of the humanities in the areas which inventory other worlds still discover new species (see Cozzuol et al. 2013 for a joint discovery involving both zoology and anthropology).
- This biome has rapidly experienced a simplification since 1950 to such a degree that over 8,000 plant species and 2,300 animal species are currently endangered (Nobre et al. 2021); the enormous native biodiversity of the forest is giving way to sterile pastures and monocultures and the relative homogeneity of urban ecosystems.
- From a scientific point of view, biodiversity loss involves over 10,000 botanical and zoological species (Nobre et al. 2021). Within a relational analysis that highlights the interactions between humans, plants, and animals, two processes are decisive in this erosion of biodiversity: predation and extractivism, and the introduction of exotic species epitomized in ranching and monoculture farming.
- Nevertheless, from a biocultural perspective, this loss is even greater since the disappearance of indigenous, traditional, and local peoples, languages, knowledge, techniques, and ways of life or their substitution by "modern" exploitative processes implies the loss of entire (ecological) worlds, and in turn, of "types" or "qualities" of different beings, since biodiversity and social diversity cannot be considered separately in these entangled worlds (Voort 2019). The effects of genocide, ethnocide, and erosion of biodiversity in Amazonia are virtually im-

possible to quantify from a biocultural point of view. However, its scale is visible in the many indigenous languages that have become extinct and the various others which are currently dying or at imminent risk of extinction in the region (Queixalós and Lescure 2000).

This process of large-scale biological simplification in Amazonia goes hand in hand with what we can call the simplification of social and cultural diversity (Picq 2013) within a multifaceted environmental crisis: the loss or deliberate and gradual erasure of a wide variety of indigenous languages, for example (Crevels 2012), or the growing conversion of local forms of productive organization and modes of relating to other-than-human alterities into the production of commodities and market-scale economies (Tsing 2004). This aspect of the Great Acceleration, molded within a set of predatory relationships between humans, animals, plants, and other beings explored above, brings with it grim consequences that spread across multiple levels, from local contexts of impoverished biodiversity and associated worlds (including the loss of genetic diversity) up to the global and planetary levels, with macro-scale ecological cycles disturbed by drastic and wide-reaching modifications to the world's largest tropical forest. Lamentably, it is the traditional and indigenous native Amazonian societies that experience an impact first and most strongly by these processes that have taken on catastrophic dimensions since the 1950s.

Amazonia, like the rest of the world, for millennia has been comprised of a "historical complex" that "involves human beings, plants, rivers, animals and artifacts, in processes that used to involve not just dominating the natural world, but previously [...] adaptation, the learning of meaning, of listening to the rhythms of the forest beings" (Duarte 2019: 24). While in the sixteenth century, Francisco de Orellana saw fields for raising cattle in the Amazonian wetlands, the many travelers and researchers who followed never stopped admiring the staggering variety of life in the region, whether biological or sociocultural. The cattle the Spanish *conquistador* foresaw did indeed appear and continue to arrive in large numbers, along with soybeans, palm oil, animal traffickers, exotic grasses, the outskirts of poor urban peripheries, and many other agents of simplification. Nevertheless, the Amazon Forest still holds myriad human and other-than-human inhabitants: animals, insects, plants, trees, microorganisms, viruses, rivers, lakes, mountains, spirits, *mapinguaris*, owners of the animals, and many more, all of which comprise the splendid richness of this threatened biome.

For these reasons, now more than ever, one must hear and make heard the voices of these beings, humans and other-than-humans alike, and at the same time, the voice of the river in the speech of the indigenous leader, the words of the river dweller through the fish, the language of the birds in the trees that disperse their seeds, or the spirit of the hunted animal. Only true *multispecies ethnographies* (cf. Kirksey and Helmreich 2010) that consider natural-cultural forms of mutual coproduction or co-constitution between the different beings that populate the many worlds will make it possible to describe this close dependence (and perhaps indiscernibility) between nature and culture in the Amazon, recognizing once and for all that humanity, modern western humans all around the globe, are not possible without the immense forest.

References

Albert, Bruce. 1997. "Territorialité, ethnopolitique et développement: a propos du mouvement indien en Amazonie brésilienne." *Cahiers des Amériques Latines* 23: 177–210.

Albert, Bruce, and William Milliken. 2009. *Urihi A – A terra-floresta Yanomami*. São Paulo: Instituto Socioambiental.

Alexiades, Miguel, and Daniela Peluso. 2009. "Plants 'of the ancestors', plants 'of the outsiders': Ese Eja history, migration and medicinal plants." In *Mobility and migration in Indigenous Amazonia: contemporary ethnoecological perspectives*, ed. Miguel Alexiades, 220–248. New York: Berghahn Books.

Alves de Figueiredo, Rodrigo, and Flávio Barros. 2016. "Caçar, preparar e comer o 'bicho do mato': práticas alimentares entre os quilombolas na Reserva Extrativista Ipaú-Anilzinho (Pará)." *Boletim do MPEG – Ciências Humanas* 11, no. 3: 691–713.

Alves, Rômulo, and Guindomar Santana. 2008. "Use and commercialization of *Podocnemis expansa* (Schweiger 1812) (Testudines: Podocnemididae) for medicinal purposes in two communities in North of Brazil." *Journal of Ethnobiology and Ethnomedicine* 4, no. 3: 1–6.

Amigos da Terra. 2009. *A hora da conta: pecuária, Amazônia e conjuntura*. São Paulo: Amigos da Terra – Amazônia Brasileira.

Anchirayco, Jorge, Efraín Paucar, and Natividad Quillahuaman Lasteros. 2021. "Ciclos de mercado, políticas económicas y marginalización de las economías propias del pueblo indígena Shipibo-Konibo por palma aceitera y minería aurífera en dos corredores económicos de la Amazonía peruana." In *Amazonía y expansión mercantil capitalista. Nueva frontera de recursos en el siglo XXI*, ed. Neyer Nogales, 195–255. Buenos Aires/La Paz: CLACSO/Centro de Estudios para el Desarrollo Laboral y Agrario-CEDLA.

Antunes, André, Glenn Shepard Jr, and Eduardo Venticinque. 2014. "O comércio internacional de peles silvestres na Amazônia brasileira no século XX." *Boletim d Museu paraense Emílio Goeldi – Ciências Humanas* 9, no. 2: 487–518.

Antunes, André. 2015. "Um século de caça comercial na Amazônia." PhD diss., Instituto Nacional de Pesquisas da Amazônia.

Antunes, André, Rachel Fewster, Eduardo Venticinque, et al. 2016. "Empty forest or empty rivers? A century of commercial hunting in Amazonia." *Science Advances* 2: 1–14.

Apaza, Lilian, David Wilkie, Elizabeth Byron, et al. 2002. "Meat prices influence the consumption of wildlife by the Tsimane' Amerindians of Bolivia." *Oryx* 36, no. 4: 382–388.

Aragón Vaca, Luis Eduardo, ed. 2005. *Populações da Pan-Amazônia*. Belém: NAEA/UFPA.

Arcila Niño, Oscar. 2011. *La Amazonia colombiana urbanizada: un análisis de sus asentamientos humanos*. Bogotá: Instituto Amazónico de Investigaciones Científicas-Sinchi.

Arima, Eugênio, and Christopher Uhl. 1996. *Pecuária na Amazônia oriental: desempenho atual e perspectivas futuras*. Belém: IMAZON.

Athayde, Simone, Glenn Shepard, Thiago Cardoso, et al. 2021. "Critical interconnections between cultural and biological diversity of Amazonian peoples and ecosystems." In *Amazon Assessment Report 2021*, ed. Carlos Nobre, Andrea C. Encalada, Elizabeth Anderson, et al., 10.1-10.34. New York: United Nations Sustainable Development Solutions Network.

Baksh, Michael. 1995. "Changes in Machiguenga quality of life." In *Indigenous peoples and the future of Amazonia: an ecological anthropology of an endangered world*, ed. Leslie Sponsel, 187–205. Tucson: University of Arizona Press.

Balée, William. 1994. *Footprints in the Forest: Ka'apor Ethnobotany – the Historical Ecology of Plant Utilization by an Amazonian People*. New York: Columbia University Press.

———. 2013. *Cultural Forests of the Amazon: a Historical Ecology of People and their Landscapes*. Tuscaloosa: The University of Alabama Press.

Balée, William, and Clark Erickson, ed. 2006. *Time and Complexity in Historical Ecology: Studies in the Neotropical Lowlands*. New York: Columbia University Press.

Baniwa, André. 2019. *Bem viver e viver bem segundo o povo Baniwa no noroeste amazônico*. Curitiba: Editora da UFPR.

Barbosa, Luiz. 2015. *Guardians of the Brazilian Amazon Rainforest: Environmental Organizations and Development*. London: Routledge.

Barros, Flávio Bezerra. 2017. "Os caçadores do Riozinho do Anfrísio: saberes e práticas culturais entre narrativas e imagens." *Muiraquitã* 5, no. 1: 152–186.

Barros, Marcelo, and Luis Maurício Silva. 1997. "Registro da introdução da espécie exótica *Macrobrachium rosenbergii* (De Man, 1879) (Crustacea, Decapoda, Palaemonidae), em águas do Estado do Pará, Brasil." *Boletim do Museu Paraense Emílio Goeldi* 13, no. 1: 31–37.

Barroso, Mário, Gabriel Costa, Mariana Ferreira, et al. 2012. *ARPA – Biodiversidade*. Brasília: WWF-Brasil.

Batista, Djalma. 2007. *O complexo da Amazônia: análise do processo de desenvolvimento*. Manaus: Editora INPA/Editora Valer/Edua.

Becker, Bertha. 2005. "Geopolítica da Amazônia." *Estudos Avançados* 19, no. 53: 71–86.

Bennett, Elizabeth, and John Robinson. 2000. *Hunting of wildlife in tropical forests: implications for biodiversity and forest peoples*. Washington, D.C.: The World Bank.

Bensusan, Nurit, ed. 2002. *Seria melhor mandar ladrilhar? Biodiversidade: como, para que, por quê*. Brasília: Instituto Socioambiental Universidade de Brasília.

Bolle, Willi. 2010. "A travessia pioneira da Amazônia (Francisco de Orellana, 1541–1542)." In *Amazônia: região universal e teatro do mundo*, ed. Willi Bolle, Edna Castro, and Marcel Vejmelka, 19–56. Rio de Janeiro, Editora Globo.

Botelho de Andrade, Emeleocípio, ed. 2005. *A geopolítica da soja na Amazônia*. Belém: Embrapa Amazônia Oriental/MPEG.

Brandão, Frederico, and George Schoneveld. 2015. *The state of oil palm development in the Brazilian Amazon*. Bogor: CIFOR.

Broad, Steven, Teresa Mulliken, and Dilys Roe. 2003. "The nature and extent of legal and illegal trade in wildlife." In *The trade in wildlife: regulation for conservation*, ed. Susan Oldfield, 3–22. London: Earthscan.

Broad, Steven. 1987. *The harvest of and trade in Latin American spotted cats (Felidae) and otters (Lutrinae)*. Cambridge: Wildlife Trade Monitoring Unit/IUCN Conservation Monitoring Centre.

Browder, John, and Brian Godfrey. 1997. *Rainforest cities: urbanization, development, and globalization of the Brazilian Amazon*. New York: Columbia University Press.

Butler, Rhett A. 2020. "The Amazon Rainforest: The World's Largest Rainforest." *Mongabay*. August 14. https://rainforests.mongabay.com/amazon/.

Capobianco, João Paulo, ed. 2001. *Biodiversidade na Amazônia Brasileira*. São Paulo: Instituto Socioambiental.

Capozzoli, Ulisses, ed. 2008. *Amazônia: destinos*. São Paulo: Duetto Editorial.

Carneiro da Cunha, Manuela, and Mauro W. Barbosa de Almeida, ed. 2002. *Enciclopédia da Floresta. O Alto Juruá: práticas e conhecimentos das populações*. São Paulo: Companhia das Letras.

Carneiro da Cunha, Manuela, and Ana Gabriela Morin de Lima. 2017. "How Amazonian indigenous peoples contribute to biodiversity". In *Knowing our lands and resources: indigenous and local knowledge of biodiversity and ecosystem services in the Americas*, ed. Brigitte Baptiste, Diego Pacheco, Manuela Carneiro da Cunha, et al., 62–80. Paris: UNESCO.

Carneiro da Cunha, Manuela, Sônia Magalhães, and Cristina Adams, ed. 2021. *Povos tradicionais e biodiversidade no Brasil: contribuição dos povos indígenas, quilombolas e comunidades tradicionais para a biodiversidade, políticas e ameaças*. São Paulo: SBPC.

Carvajal, Frei Gaspar de. 1992. *Descubrimiento del río de las Amazonas*. Valencia: EDYM. Orig. pub. 1542.

Chaves, Willandia, Francislane Cabral da Silva, Pedro Constantino, et al. 2018. "A caça e a conservação da fauna silvestre no estado do Acre." *Biodiversidade Brasileira* 8, no. 2: 130–148.

CLACSO/CEDLA. 2021. *Expansión mercantil capitalista y la Amazonía como nueva fronte-ra de recursos en el siglo XXI*. Buenos Aires: CLACSO.

Clement, Charles, William Denevan, Michael Heckenberger, et al. 2015 "The domestication of Amazonia before European conquest." *Proceedings of the Royal Society B* 282, no 1812: 1–9.

Clement, Charles. 1999. "1492 and the loss of Amazonian crop genetic resources I: The relation between domestication and human population decline." *Economic Botany* 53, no. 2: 188–202.

Conrado da Cruz, Denis, José Maria Benayas, Gracialda Ferreira, et al. 2020. "An overview of forest loss and restoration in the Brazilian Amazon." *New Forests* 52: 1–16.

Correa, François ed. 1993. *La selva humanizada: ecología alternativa en el trópico colombiano*. Bogotá: ICAN/CEREC.

Costa, Viviany, Maria Luisa Silva, and Angélica Rodrigues. 2014. *Aves silvestres mantidas como animais de estimação na Amazônia: aspectos culturais e etológicos*. Saarbrücken: Novas Edições Acadêmicas.

Costa Silva, Ricardo G. da. 2015. "Amazônia globalizada: da fronteira agrícola ao território do agronegócio – o exemplo de Rondônia." *Confins: Revue Franco-Brésilienne de Géographie* 23.

Couto, Aiala. 2020. "Ameaça e caráter transnacional do narcotráfico na Amazônia brasileira." *Confins: Revue Franco-Brésilienne de Géographie* 44.

Cozzuol, Mário Alberto, Camila L. Clozato, Elizete Holanda, et al. 2013. "A new species of tapir from the Amazon." *Journal of Mammalogy* 94, no. 6: 1331–1345.

Crevels, Mily. 2012. "Language endangerment in South America: the clock is ticking." In *The indigenous languages of South America: a comprehensive guide*, ed. Lyle Campbell and Verónica Grondona, 167–233. Berlin/Boston: De Gruyter Mouton.

Crosby, Alfred. 2002. *Imperialismo ecológico. A expansão biológica da Europa: 900–1900*. São Paulo: Companhia das Letras.

Daly, Lewis, and Glenn Shepard Jr. 2019. "Magic darts and messenger molecules: toward a phytoethnography of indigenous Amazonia." *Anthropology Today* 35, no. 2: 13–17.

Danowski, Déborah, and Eduardo Viveiros de Castro. 2017. *Há mundo por vir? Ensaio sobre os medos e os fins*. Florianópolis: Cultura e Barbárie/Instituto Socioambiental.

Dean, Warren. 2002. *Brazil and the struggle for rubber: a study in environmental history*. Cambridge: Cambridge University Press.

De la Cadena, Marisol, and Mario Blaser, ed. 2018. *A world of many worlds*. Durham: Duke University Press.

Denevan, William. 2001. *Cultivated landscapes of Native Amazonia and the Andes*. Oxford: Oxford University Press.

Descola, Philippe. 1982. "Territorial adjustments among the Achuar of Ecuador." *Social Science Information* 21, no. 2: 301–320.

———.1994. *In the society of nature: a native ecology in Amazonia*. Cambridge: Cambridge University Press.

———. 2005. *Par-delà nature et culture*. Paris: Éditions Gallimard.

Dias-Filho, Moacyr. 2014. *Reclaiming the Brazilian Amazon: the restoration and management of pasture lands*. Belém: Embrapa Amazônia Oriental.

Dias-Filho, Moacyr, and Monyck dos Santos Lopes. 2020. *História e desafios na pecuária bovina na Amazônia*. Belém: Embrapa Amazônia Oriental.

Doughty, Robin, and Norman Myers. 1971. "Notes on the Amazon wildlife trade." *Biological Conservation* 3, no. 4: 293–297.

Duarte, Regina Horta. 2019. "História dos animais no Brasil: tradições culturais, historiografia e transformação." *Historia Ambiental Latinoamericana y Caribeña (HALAC)* 9, no. 2: 16–44.

Durães, Francisco Batista. 2017. *A "pata do boi" e os impactos ambientais na região do Araguaia paraense*. Jundiaí: Paco.

Emperaire, Laure. 2001. "Elementos de discussão sobre a conservação da agrobiodiversidade: o exemplo da mandioca (*Manihot esculenta* Crantz) na Amazônia brasileira." In *Biodiversidade na Amazônia Brasileira*, ed. João Paulo Capobianco, 225–234. São Paulo: Instituto Socioambiental.

———. 2017. "Saberes tradicionais e diversidade das plantas cultivadas na Amazônia." In *Knowing our lands and resources: indigenous and local knowledge of biodiversity and ecosystem services in the Americas*, ed. Brigitte Baptiste, Diego Pacheco, Manuela Carneiro da Cunha, et al., 40–61. Paris: UNESCO.

Fearnside, Philip. 1989. *A ocupação humana de Rondônia: impactos, limites e planejamento*. Brasília: Programa Polonoroeste/SCT-PR/CNPq.

———. 2005. "Deforestation in Brazilian Amazonia: history, rates, and consequences". *Conservation Biology* 19, no. 3: 680–688.

———. 2008. "Ameaça da soja." In *Amazônia: destinos*, ed. Ulisses Capozzoli, 44–51. São Paulo: Duetto Editorial.

Fernández-Llamazares, Álvaro, and Pirjo Virtanen. 2020. "Game masters and Amazonian Indigenous views on sustainability." *Current Opinion in Environmental Sustainability* 43: 21–27.

Fernández-Llamazares, Álvaro, Dana Lepofsky, Ken Lertzman, et al. 2021. "Scientists' warning to humanity on threats to indigenous and local knowledge systems." *Journal of Ethnobiology* 41, no. 2: 144–169.

Ficek, Rosa E. 2019. "Cattle, capital, colonization: tracking creatures of the Anthropocene in and out of human projects." *Current Anthropology* 60 [Supplement 20]: S260–S271.

Fiorello, Christine, Andrew Noss, and Sharon Deem. 2006. "Demography, hunting ecology, and pathogen exposure of domestic dogs in the Isoso of Bolivia." *Conservation Biology* 20, no. 3: 762–771.

Fiori, Marlon Marcel, and Christian F. M. dos Santos. 2013. "Colonizadores portugueses, tartarugas e peixes-boi: uma história da busca por carne, gordura e combustível na Amazônia do século XVIII." *Diálogos* 17, no. 3: 1247–1257.

Fleury, Marie. 2016. "Agriculture itinérante sur brûlis (AIB) et plantes cultivés sur le haut Maroni: étude comparé chez les Aluku et les Wayana en Guyane française." *Boletim do Museu Paraense Emílio Goeldi – Ciências Humanas* 11, no. 2: 431–465.

Flórez-Malagón, Alberto, ed. 2008. *El poder de la carne: historias de ganaderías en la primera mitad del siglo XX en Colombia*. Bogotá: Editorial Pontificia Universidad Javeriana.

Gallice, Geoffrey, Gustavo Larrea-Gallegos, and Ian Vázquez-Rowe. 2019. "The threat of road expansion in the Peruvian Amazon." *Oryx* 53, no. 2: 284–292.

Gonçalves, Alany, Maurício Camargo, Cristiane Carneiro, et al. 2009. "A pesca de peixes ornamentais." In *Entre a terra, as águas e os pescadores do médio rio Xingu*, ed. Maurício Camargo and Rubens Ghilardi Jr., 235–261. Belém: UFPA/IFEPA.

Hames, Raymond, ed. 1980. *Studies in hunting and fishing in the Neotropics*. Working Papers on South American Indians no. 2. Bennington: Bennington College.

Hames, Raymond, and William Vickers, ed. 1983. *Adaptive responses of Native Amazonians*. Cambridge: Academic Press.

Haraway, Donna. 2003. *The Companion Species Manifesto: Dogs, People, and Significant Otherness*. Chicago: Prickly Paradigm Press.

———. 2016. *Staying with the Problem: Making Kin in the Chthulucene*. Durham: Duke University Press.

Hébette, Jean, ed. 1991. *O Cerco está se fechando*. Petrópolis: Vozes.

Hecht, Susanne. 1985. "Environment, development and politics: capital accumulation and the livestock sector in Eastern Amazonia." *World Development* 13, no. 6: 663–684.

———. 1993. "The logic of livestock and deforestation in Amazonia." *BioScience* 43, no. 10: 687–695.

Hecht, Susanne, and Alexander Cockburn. 2011. *The fate of the forest: developers, destroyers, and defenders of the Amazon*. Chicago: University of Chicago Press.

Heckenberger, Michael, and Eduardo Goés Neves. 2009. "Amazonian archaeology." *Annual Review of Archaeology* 38: 251–266.

Hennessey, Bennett. 2007. "Quantifying the illegal parrot trade in Santa Cruz de la Sierra, Bolivia, with emphasis on threatened species." *Bird Conservation International* 17: 295–300.

Hoelle, Jeffrey. 2014. "Cattle culture in the Brazilian Amazon." *Human Organization* 73, no. 4: 363–374.

———. 2015. *Rainforest cowboys: the rise of ranching and cattle culture in western Amazonia.* Austin: University of Texas Press.

Homma, Alfredo Oyama, ed. 2014. *Extrativismo vegetal na Amazônia: história, ecologia, economia e domesticação.* Brasília: EMBRAPA.

Hopes, Addie, and Laura Perry, ed. 2019. *Reflections on the Plantationocene: a conversation with Donna Haraway & Anna Tsing moderated by Greg Mittman.* Madison: Center for Culture, History, and Environment in the Nelson Institute at the University of Wisconsin-Madison.

Human Rights Watch. 2019. "Rainforest mafias: how violence and impunity fuel deforestation in Brazil's Amazon." September 17. https://www.hrw.org/report/2019/09/17/rainforest-mafias/how-violence-and-impunity-fuel-deforestation-brazils-amazon.

Jara, Fabiola. 1996. *El camino del kumu: ecologia y ritual entre los Akuriyó de Surinam.* Quito: Abya-Yala.

Jensen, Allen Arthur. 1988. *Sistemas indígenas de classificação de aves: aspectos comparativos, ecológicos e evolutivos.* Belém: MPEG.

Kawa, Nicholas. 2016. *Amazonia in the Anthropocene: peoples, soils, plants, forests.* Austin: University of Texas Press.

Kirksey, S. Eben, and Stefan Helmreich. 2010. "The emergence of multispecies ethnography." *Cultural Anthropology* 25, no. 4: 545–576.

Kohn, Eduardo. 2013. *How forests think: toward an anthropology beyond the human.* Berkeley: University of California Press.

Kopenawa, Davi, and Bruce Albert. 2015. *A queda do céu: palavras de um xamã yanomami.* São Paulo: Companhia das Letras.

Larrea-Alcázar, Daniel, Nicolás Cuvi, Judson Valentim, et al. 2021. "Economic drivers in the Amazon after European Colonization from the Nineteenth Century to the Middle of the Twentieth Century (the 1970s)." In *Amazon Assessment Report 2021*, ed. Carlos Nobre, Andrea C. Encalada, Elizabeth Anderson, et al., 11.1-11.25. New York: United Nations Sustainable Development Solutions Network.

Léna, Philippe, and Adélia Oliveira, ed. 1991. *Amazônia: a fronteira agrícola 20 anos depois.* Belém: Museu Paraense Emílio Goeldi.

Lessa, Isadora, Tainah Guimarães, Helena Bergallo, et al. 2016. "Domestic dogs in protected areas: a threat to Brazilian mammals?." *Natureza e Conservação* 14: 46–56.

MacDonald, Theodore. 1997. *De cazadores a ganaderos.* Quito: Abya-Yala.

Macedo, Marcus Vinícius. 2009. *Vida e morte na Amazônia indígena: as invasões madeireiras e os povos Ashaninka.* Rio Branco: Edufac.

Macleod, Ross, and Bennett Hennessey. 2011. "A study of the parrot trade in Peru and the potential importance of internal trade for threatened species." *Bird Conservation International* 21: 76–85.

Maffi, Luisa, ed. 2001. *On biocultural diversity: linking language, knowledge and the environment*. Washington, D.C.: Smithsonian Institution Press.

Magalhães, Marcos Pereira, ed. 2016. *Amazônia antropogênica*. Belém: Museu Paraense Emílio Goeldi.

Marchand, Guillaume, and Felipe Vander Velden, ed. 2017. *Olhares cruzados sobre as relações entre seres humanos e animais silvestres na Amazônia (Brasil, Guiana Francesa)*. Manaus: EDUA.

Marin, Rosa Acevedo, Cynthia Carvalho, and Alfredo W. Berno de Almeida, ed. 2020. *Cimarrones, marrons, quilombolas, boni, raizales, garifunas e palenqueros nas Américas*. Manaus: UEA Edições/PNCSA.

Martini, Adriana, Nelson de Araújo Rosa, and Christopher Uhl. 2001. "Espécies de árvores potencialmente ameaçadas pela atividade madeireira na Amazônia." In *Biodiversidade na Amazônia Brasileira*, ed. João Paulo Capobianco, 338–347. São Paulo: Instituto Socioambiental.

Maruyama, Megumi, and Noboru Morioka. 1998. "The impact of deforestation in Brazilian Amazonia – the indigenous peoples of Rondônia state." *Journal of Forest Planning* 4: 71–75.

McCook, Stuart. 2018. "Prodigality and sustainability: the environmental sciences and the quest for development." In *A living past: environmental histories of Modern Latin America*, ed. John Soluri, Claudia Leal, and José Augusto Pádua, 226–245. New York: Berghahn Books.

McNeill, John, and Peter Engelke. 2016. *The Great Acceleration: an environmental history of the Anthropocene Since 1945*. Cambridge: Harvard University Press.

Mendes, Fabricio de Siqueira. 2020. "Comercialização ilegal de carne de animais silvestres em feiras livres de algumas cidades do Estado do Amazonas (Brasil)." *Revista Colombiana de Ciencia Animal* 12, no. 2: 1–11.

Mendes, Fabricio de Siqueira, and Ligia Simonian. 2016. "Animais silvestres comercializados ilegalmente em algumas cidades do estado do Pará." *Revista Eletrônica do Mestrado em Educação Ambiental – FURG* 33, no. 1: 4–21.

Mikkola, Heimo, ed. 2021. *Ecosystem and biodiversity in Amazonia*. London: IntechOpen.

Moreau, Marie-Annick, and Oliver Coomes. 2008. "Structure and organization of small-scale freshwater fisheries: aquarium fish collection in Western Amazonia." *Human Ecology* 36: 309–323.

Nepstad, Daniel, Stephen Schwartzman, Barb Bamberger, et al. 2006. "Inhibition of Amazon deforestation and fire by parks and indigenous lands." *Conservation Biology* 20: 65–73.

Neves, Eduardo, and Michael Heckenberger. 2019. "The call of the wild: rethinking food production in ancient Amazonia." *Annual Review of Anthropology* 48: 371–388.

Neves, Eduardo Goés, Laura Furquim, Carolina Levis, et al. 2021. "Peoples of the Amazon before European colonization." In *Amazon Assessment Report 2021*, ed.

Carlos Nobre, Andrea C. Encalada, Elizabeth Anderson, et al., 8.1-8.40. New York: United Nations Sustainable Development Solutions Network.

Nobre, Carlos, Andrea C. Encalada, Elizabeth Anderson, et al., ed. 2021. *Amazon Assessment Report 2021*. New York: United Nations Sustainable Development Solutions Network.

Oliveira, Adélia E. de. 1983. "Ocupação humana." In *Amazônia: desenvolvimento, integração, ecologia*, ed. Eneas Salati, Herbertt Shubart, Wolfgang Junk, et al., 144–327. São Paulo/Brasília: Editora Brasiliense/CNPq.

Orme, C. David, Richard Davies, Malcolm Burgess, et al. 2005. "Global hotspots of species richness are not congruent with endemism or threat." *Nature* 436: 1016–1019.

Pádua, José Augusto. 2018. "The dilemma of the 'Splendid cradle': nature and territory in the construction of Brazil." In *A living past: environmental histories of Modern Latin America*, ed. John Soluri, Claudia Leal, and José Augusto Pádua, 91–114. New York: Berghahn Books.

Pantoja, Mariana Ciavatta, Elisa Lozano Costa, and Augusto Postigo. 2009. "A presença do gado em reservas extrativistas: algumas reflexões." *Revista Pós Ciências Sociais* 6, no. 12: 115–130.

Parry, Luke, Jos Barlow, and Heloisa Pereira. 2014. "Wildlife harvest and consumption in Amazonia's urbanized wilderness." *Conservation Letters* 7, no. 6: 565–574.

Pereira, Edithe, and Vera Guapindaia, ed. 2010. *Arqueologia Amazônica*. 2 vols. Belém: Museu Paraense Emílio Goeldi.

Pereira, Ritaumaria, Cynthia Simmons, and Robert Walker. 2016. "Smallholders, agrarian reform, and globalization in the Brazilian Amazon: cattle versus the environment." *Land* 5, no. 24.

Pérez, Julio, Sinatra Salazar, Carmen Alfonsi, et al. 2003. "Ictiofauna del Río Manzanares, a cuatro décadas de la introducción de *Oreochromis mossambicus* (Pisces: Cichlidae)." *Boletín del Instituto Oceanográfico de Venezuela* 42: 1–18.

Picq, Pascal. 2013. *De Darwin à Lévi-Strauss: l'homme et la diversité en danger*. Paris: Odile Jacob.

Pinedo-Vasquez, Miguel, and Christine Padoch. 2009. "Urban, rural and in-between: multi-sited households mobility and resource management in the Amazon flood plain." In *Mobility and migration in Indigenous Amazonia: contemporary ethnoecological perspectives*, ed. Miguel Alexiades, 86–96. New York: Berghahn Books.

Pinto, Moisés Tavares. 2016. *O mercado de caça e pescado na tríplice fronteira Brasil – Colômbia – Peru*. Manaus: Edua/Fapeam.

Pompéia, Caio. 2021. *Formação política do agronegócio*. São Paulo: Elefante.

Porto, Roberto, Benjamin Alvino de Mesquita, and Itaan Santos. 2004. *Expansão e Trajetórias da Pecuária na Amazônia: Maranhão, Brasil*. Brasília: Editora UnB.

Posey Darrell. 1985. "Indigenous management of tropical forest ecosystems: the case of the Kayapó Indians of the Brazilian Amazon." *Agroforestry Systems* 3, no. 2: 139–158.

Pozzetti, Valmir Cesar, and Mateus Papa Gasparini. 2018. "A Inserção de Peixe Exótico Tilápia nos Rios do Estado do Amazonas: Prejuízos Ambientais à Panamazônia." In *Anais do V Congresso Internacional de Direito Ambiental e Desenvolvimento Sustentável: Pan-Amazônia – Integrar e Proteger e do I Congresso da Rede Pan-Amazônia*, ed. Beatriz Souza Costa, 173–190. Belo Horizonte: Editora Dom Helder.

Prang, Gregory. 2004. "Social and economic change in Amazonia: the case of ornamental fish collection in the Rio Negro Basin." In *Some other Amazonians: perspectives on modern Amazonia*, ed. Stephen Nugent and Mark Harris, 57–80. London: Institute for the Study of the Americas.

Price, Richard, ed. 1996. *Maroon societies: rebel slave communities in the Americas*. Baltimore: Johns Hopkins University Press.

Puyol, Ana, Victor Hugo Inchausty, Bernardo Ortiz, et al. 2010. *Género, alternativas productivas y seguridad alimentario: la disminuición de la cacería comercial en Yasuní como una oportunidad para el mejoramiento de la gobernanza territorial*. London: International Union for Conservation of Nature/Traffic.

Queixalós, Francisco, and Odile Lescure, ed. 2000. *As línguas amazônicas hoje*. São Paulo: IRD/ISA/MPEG.

Raffles, Hugh. 2002. *In Amazonia – A Natural History*. Princeton: Princeton University Press.

RAISG [Rede Amazônica de Informação Socioambiental Georreferenciada]. 2021. *Amazônia sob pressão*. São Paulo: Instituto Socioambiental.

Ramos, Alcida Rita. 2006. "The commodification of the Indian." In *Human Impacts on Amazonia: The Role of Traditional Ecological Knowledge in Conservation and Development*, ed. Darrell A. Posey and Michael J. Balick, 248–272. New York: Columbia University Press.

Rebêlo, George, and Juarez Pezzuti. 2000. "Percepções sobre o consumo de quelônios na Amazônia: sustentabilidade e alternativas ao manejo atual." *Ambiente e Sociedade* 3, no. 6/7: 85–105.

Redford, Kent. 1992. "The empty forest." *BioScience* 42, no. 6: 412–422.

Ribeiro, Berta. 1987. *O índio na cultura brasileira*. Rio de Janeiro: UNIBRADE/UNESCO.

———. 1992. *Amazônia urgente: cinco séculos de história e ecologia*. Belo Horizonte: Itatiaia.

———, ed. 1997. *Suma Etnológica Brasileira*. Vol. 1, *Etnobiologia*. Belém: Editora Universitária da UFPA.

Ricardo, Fany, ed. 1999. *Interesses minerários em terras indígenas na Amazônia Legal brasileira*. São Paulo: Instituto Socioambiental.

Rivière, Peter. 1972. *The forgotten frontier: ranchers of North Brazil*. New York: Holt, Rinehart and Winston.

Rolla, Alicia. 2006. "Tis inibem o desmatamento na região da fronteira agrícola." In *Povos Indígenas no Brasil – 2001/2005*, ed. Carlos Alberto Ricardo and Fany Ricardo, 182–184. São Paulo: Instituto Socioambiental.

Rostain, Stéphen. 2014. *Islands in the Rainforest: Landscape Management in Pre-Columbian Amazonia*. London: Routledge.

———. 2016. *Amazonie: Un jardin naturel ou une forêt domestiquée*. Paris: Errance.

Rudel, Thomas, Diane Bates, and Rafael Machinguiashi. 2002. "Ecologically noble Amerindians: cattle ranching and cash cropping among Shuar and colonists in Ecuador." *Latin American Research Review* 37, no. 1: 144–159.

Sanchez, Gabriel. 2020. "Os Eré e 'o Tal do Pirarucu': equívocos epistemológicos e ontológicos a respeito de suas agências predatórias entre os Kujubim (Rondônia)." *Anthropológicas* 31, no. 1: 37–66.

Saraiva, Luis, and Jéssica Corrêa. 2016. "Reflexões sobre homens, manguezais e caranguejos em Bragança-PA." *Iluminuras* 17, no. 42: 270–287.

Schmink, Marianne, and Charles Wood, ed. 1991. *Frontier expansion in Amazonia*. Gainesville: University Press of Florida.

Servicio Nacional Forestal y de Fauna Silvestre. 2020. *Plan nacional de conservación de las orquideas amenazadas del Perú 2020-2029*. Lima: SERNAMP/Ministerio del Ambiente Perú.

Silva, Sumara Matos, and Renato Abreu Lima. 2014. "Levantamento da fauna silvestre no centro de reabilitação do batalhão da polícia ambiental nos anos de 2010 e 2013 no município de Candeias do Jamari-RO." *Revista do Centro de Ciências Naturais e Exatas – UFSM* 18, no.1: 296–311.

Silva, Danielle Wagner, Livio Sérgio Claudino, Carlos Douglas Oliveira, et al. 2016. "Extrativismo e desenvolvimento no contexto da Amazônia brasileira." *Desenvolvimento e Meio Ambiente* 38: 557–577.

Silveira, Diego. 2012. *Redes sociotécnicas na Amazônia: tradução de saberes no campo da biodiversidade*. Rio de Janeiro: Multifoco.

Silvius, Kirsten, Richard Bodmer, and José M. Fragoso, ed. 2004. *People in nature: wildlife conservation in South and Central America*. New York: Columbia University Press.

Simon, Marcelo, and Fernando Garagorry. 2005. "The expansion of agriculture in the Brazilian Amazon." *Environmental Conservation* 32, no. 3: 203–212.

Sinovas, Pablo, Becky Price, Emily King, et al. 2017. *Wildlife trade in the Amazon countries: an analysis of trade in CITES Listed Species*. Cambridge: Amazon Regional Program (BMZ/DGIS/GIZ)/UN Environment – World Conservation Monitoring Centre.

Smeraldi, Roberto, and Peter H. May. 2008. *O Reino do Gado: Uma nova fase da pecuarização da Amazônia*. São Paulo: Amigos da Terra – Amazônia Brasileira.

―――. 2009. *A hora da conta: pecuária, Amazônia e conjuntura*. São Paulo: Amigos da Terra – Amazônia Brasileira.

Soluri, John. 2018. "Home cooking campesinos, cuisine, and agrodiversity." In *A living past: environmental histories of Modern Latin America*, ed. John Soluri, Claudia Leal, and José Augusto Pádua, 163–182. New York: Berghahn Books.

Souza, Rosália, Ana Fátima Mello, and Rozani Menezes, ed. 2009. *Atividade extrativista do peixe ornamental – região do baixo Rio Branco – Roraima – Brasil*. Brasília: IBAMA/SEBRAE.

Stepan, Nancy Leys. 2006. "Constructing tropical nature". In *Human Impacts on Amazonia: The Role of Traditional Ecological Knowledge in Conservation and Development*, ed. Darrell A. Posey and Michael J. Balick, 17–32. New York: Columbia University Press.

Surralés, Alexandre, and Pedro Garcia Hierro, ed. 2005. *The land within: indigenous territory and the perception of environment*. Copenhagen: IWGIA.

Suruí, Almir, and Corine Sombrun. 2015. *Sauver la planète: Le message d'un chef indien d'Amazonie*. Paris: Albin Michel.

Toni, Fabiano, Jair Carvalho dos Santos, Ronei Sant'ana de Menezes, et al. 2007. *Expansão e trajetórias da pecuária na Amazônia: Acre, Brasil*. Brasília: Universidade de Brasília.

Torres, Patricia Carignano, Carla Morsello, and Renata Pardini. 2021. "Forest cover and social relations are more important than economic factors in driving hunting and bushmeat consumption in post-frontier Amazonia." *Biological Conservation* 253.

Tsing, Anna. 2004. *Friction – An ethnography of global connection*. Princeton: Princeton University Press.

Val, Adalberto, Vera F. de Almeida-Val, Philip Fearnside, et al. 2017. "Amazonia: water resources and sustainability." In *Waters of Brazil: strategic analysis*, ed. Carlos Eduardo Bicudo, José Tundisi, and Marcos Barnsley Scheuenstuhl, 73–88. Cham: Springer.

Valentim, Judson, and Carlos Maurício Andrade. 2009. "Tendências e perspectivas da pecuária bovina na Amazônia brasileira." *Amazônia: Ciência & Desenvolvimento* 4, no. 8: 9–32.

Valle, Raul Telles do, ed. 2010. *Desmatamento evitado (REDD) e povos indígenas: desafios e oportunidades no contexto amazônico*. São Paulo: Instituto Socioambiental; Washington: Forest Trends.

Van Ausdal, Shawn. 2009. "Potreros, ganancias y poder: una historia ambiental de la ganadería en Colombia, 1850–1950." *Historia Crítica* [Special Edition]: 126–149.

Van Ausdal, Shawn and Robert Wilcox. 2018. "Hoofprints: cattle ranching and landscape transformation." In *A living past: environmental histories of Modern Latin America*, ed. John Soluri, Claudia Leal, and José Augusto Pádua, 183–204. New York: Berghahn Books.

Vander Velden, Felipe. 2016. "Como se faz um cachorro caçador entre os Karitiana (Rondônia)?" *Teoria e Cultura* 11, no. 2: 25–35.

———. 2018. *Joias da floresta: antropologia do tráfico de animais.* São Carlos: Edufscar/Fapesp.

Velho, Otávio. 1972. *Frentes de expansão e estrutura agrária.* Rio de Janeiro: Zahar Editores.

Velho, Otávio, João Pacheco de Oliveira, Aurélio Viana Jr., et al. 2017. *Conhecimentos tradicionais e territórios na Pan-Amazônia.* Manaus: UEA Edições.

Verdum, Ricardo, and Luís Roberto de Paula, ed. 2020. *Antropologia da política indígena: experiências e dinâmicas de participação e protagonismo indígena em processos eleitorais municipais (Brasil-América Latina).* Rio de Janeiro: Associação Brasileira de Antropologia.

Vicentini, Yara. 2004. *Cidade e história na Amazônia.* Curitiba: Editora da UFPR.

Viveiros de Castro, Eduardo. 1998. "Cosmological deixis and Amerindian Perspectivism." *The Journal of The Royal Anthropological Institute* 4, no. 3: 469–488.

Vliet, Nathalie van, María Paula Quiceno, Daniel Cruz Antia, et al. 2014. *Carne de caça e segurança alimentar na zona da tríplice fronteira amazônica (Colômbia, Peru e Brasil).* Bogotá: CGIAR/USAID/CIFOR/Fundação Si/UFAM/Fundação Omacha.

Voeks, Robert, and John Rashford, ed. 2013. *African ethnobotany in the Americas.* Cham: Springer.

Voort, Hein van der. 2009. A relevância das línguas indígenas na biota amazônica. In *Museu Goeldi: 150 anos de ciência na Amazônia,* ed. Ana V. Galúcio and Ana Prudente, 352–385. Belém: MPEG.

Walker, Robert, John Browder, Eugenio Arima, et al. 2009. "Ranching and the new global range: Amazônia in the 21st century." *Geoforum* 40: 732–745.

Weinstein, Barbara. 1983. *The Amazon rubber boom, 1850–1920.* Redwood: Stanford University Press.

Wood, Charles, Jean François Tourrand, and Fabiano Toni. 2015. *Pecuária, uso da Terra e Desmatamento na Amazônia: um Estudo Comparativo do Brasil, do Equador e do Peru.* Brasília: Universidade de Brasília.

WWF. 2016. *Living Amazon Report 2016: A regional approach to conservation in the Amazon.* Brasília/Quito: WWF Living Amazon Initiative.

———. 2020. "From the boa to leafcutter ant, and back to red piranha, Amazon wildlife comes in all shapes and sizes." https://wwf.panda.org/discover/knowl edge_hub/where_we_work/amazon/about_the_amazon/wildlife_amazon/.

———. 2022. *Living Amazon Report 2022.* Quito: WWF.

Zador, Michele, ed. 2021. *Ecosystem Profile: Biodiversity Hotspot of the Tropical Andes.* Arlington: Critical Ecosystem Partnership Fund.

Zárate Botía, Carlos Gilberto ed. 2012. *Espacios urbanos y sociedades transfronterizas en la Amazonia.* Leticia: Universidad Nacional de Colombia Sede Amazonia/Instituto Amazónico de Colombia.

Biodiversity in Mesoamerica from 1950 to the Present
Alternatives and Conflicts

Yolanda Cristina Massieu Trigo

Nature and biodiversity in the Anthropocene are indispensable for human life, while very fragile and easy to destroy. The objective is to show Mesoamerica's situation as a biodiverse region experiencing difficulties in conserving its biological resources. To face this challenge, valuable experiences are documented in Mexico and Central America that embody alternative approaches, which can be understood as the transition to sustainable societies, although they have ancestral roots in the original groups and their territorial management practices.

This chapter seeks to sustain an analytical axis that includes questioning development paths in the face of the socio-environmental destruction characteristic of the Anthropocene. The important role of biodiversity in counteracting the ecological destruction that characterizes this era is evidenced by the Mesoamerican experiences described above, in which the social actors present in biodiverse territories have been able to propose their own self-managed alternatives, even under adverse conditions.

Biodiversity: the Theoretical-Historical Reflection on a Fragile Wealth

The use of the word "biodiversity" to name the variety of living beings and ecosystems on planet Earth is recent. It is a fundamental, complex, and general concept, which includes the entire biological organization of the earth, including human beings, with structural, functional, and compositional components and the scales of time and space (Toledo 1994). The origin of the term coincides with the recognition of environmental destruction (Núñez, González-Gaudiano, and Barahona 2003).

Latin America is one of the regions of the world with the greatest biodiversity and natural resources. Specifically, two of the seventeen megadiverse countries are located in Mesoamerica: Mexico and Costa Rica – the others on this list are Bolivia, Brazil, China, Colombia, Ecuador, the Philippines, India, Indonesia, Kenya, Madagascar, Malaysia, Peru, the Democratic Republic of the Congo, South Africa, and Venezuela, which contain 70 percent of the planet's biodiversity (Infobae 2014). In

Central America, the seven countries that make it up occupy only 0.51 percent of the planetary territory and are home to nine percent of the world's biological wealth, present in 206 ecosystems and more than 300 forms of landscape. There is a Central American System of Protected Areas (SICAP), derived from the Convention on Biodiversity, which has developed as the set of National Systems of Protected Areas (SINAP), made in 2003 of 557 legally established protected areas, comprising about 25 percent of Central American territory (SICAP 2003: 5, 7).

As for Mexico, protected natural areas (PNAs) throughout the country are made up of forty-five biosphere reserves, sixty-six national parks, thirty-nine flora and fauna protection areas, eight natural resource protection areas, five natural monuments, and eighteen sanctuaries. Specifically in the Mesoamerican area of the country (states of Aguascalientes, Campeche, Chiapas, Mexico City, Colima, State of Mexico, Guerrero, Hidalgo, Jalisco, Michoacán, Morelos, Nayarit, Oaxaca, Puebla, Quintana Roo, San Luis Potosí, Sinaloa, Tlaxcala, Veracruz and Yucatán) (Hispanoteca n.d.), there are 187 protected natural areas, covering 90,967,329 ha, most of the total protected areas of Mexico (CONANP 2023): all this in a context of socioeconomic inequality and environmental degradation – both in Mexico and Central America – with the constant loss of biodiversity due to fragmentation, habitat destruction, and species trafficking (Massieu 2018).

Castro (2017) distinguishes three historical periods in the society-nature relationship on the continent, which are seen in the reality of Mesoamerica. The first refers to the origins of human presence in the Americas, with a wide range of interactions with the natural environment over 15,500 years of societal evolution prior to the conquest, giving rise to important civilizational cycles in Mesoamerica, mainly the Maya, Mexica, Mixtec, and Zapotec societies. The second corresponds to the colonial era, with European control of Mesoamerican societies and territories, which operated until the nineteenth century when the independence processes took place. Colonial society began its decomposition due to the increase in rent extraction by the Spanish monarchy from the second half of the eighteenth century. The third period, of shorter duration but greater intensity, extends from 1850 to 1970 approximately, and is characterized by the development of capitalist forms of relationship between the social and natural systems of the region. Liberal Reform played a fundamental role, as it led to the creation of a land market and individualization of production since the nineteenth century, materializing as differences and nuances in Latin American countries. In the case of Mesoamerica, it stands out that, from 1950, there were intense processes of agricultural modernization with greater industrialization in the case of Mexico; from the 1940s, and more sharply between 1950 and 1970, the technology of the so-called Green Revolution was promoted, which led to the use of improved seeds, agrochemicals, and mechanization on irrigated land, something that was accessible only to large producers (Hewitt 1975). In the case of Central America, this agricultural modernization manifested itself as fruit-producing enclaves for export, led by large transnationals such as the United Fruit Company, with bananas as an emblematic product. Both in the generation of an agribusiness sector in Mexico and in the expansion of fruit cultivation for export in Central America, there was collaboration between national governments and the monoculture model with the use of agrochemicals and machinery generating a loss of biodiversity. In the Central American case, these processes were accompanied by the overexploitation of the labor force, and in the case of Mexico, the formation of a large sector of small-scale peasant producers who live in difficult conditions until today. In both cases, it can be affirmed that, to date, environmental deterioration and biodiversity loss continue (Hewitt 1975; Hewitt 2007; Massieu 2016; Hernández and Agudelo 2019).

In the 1980s, state intervention in the economy was almost totally eliminated, and a cycle of neoliberal policies began that privileged private capital and the free market as central protagonists, promoting the commodification of natural resources and common goods of the region under the growing domination of powerful multinational companies and increasing demand for raw materials and natural resources by the central powers. In Central America, a good example would be the forests of Costa Rica (Goebel McDermott 2013), which provided funds to liberal governments from the late nineteenth century to the first half of the twentieth century to finance an incipient industrialization and integrate into the world market. This change led to the withdrawal of the state from the promotion of agricultural technologies such as those described since 1950, leaving it in the hands of transnational companies to supply the inputs.

Biodiversity: the Difficulty of Conservation in National and International Policies

From the beginning of environmentalism, the question has arisen as to whether biological diversity is only valuable because of its usefulness to humans and whether only humans can confer such values. This utilitarian and mercantilist idea is contrasted by the idea of the intrinsic value of nature, according to which it deserves to be preserved without demonstrating any economic value.

The destruction of biodiversity has reached alarming levels and there is already talk of a sixth anthropogenic extinction (which coincides with the Anthropocene). According to the World Wild Foundation (WWF), between 1970 and 2014, 52 percent of vertebrate species became extinct, and in 2016, this figure increased to 57 percent (WWF 2014; WWF 2016). According to Turvey and Crees (2019), the extinction of a considerable number of species has been due to human action since the Holocene. The International Union for Conservation of Nature (IUCN) recognizes more than 28,000 species at risk of extinction, a figure that only reflects those that have been studied. Even the most conservative estimates in this regard estimate that this figure is 100 times higher than the previous (Turvey and Crees 2019: R985).

In the case of Mesoamerica, there are worrying figures in terms of species extinction. According to research by Londoño and Sánchez Cordero (2009) in Costa Rica, Nicaragua, and Panama, there are more than fifty threatened species in 0.5 percent of the area of each country. In these same three countries, twenty-one to fifty species of this status were found in more than 50 percent of their area. El Salvador and Honduras show eleven to twenty threatened species in more than 50 percent of their territory, and in Mexico, there are one to five endangered species in more than 50 percent of its surface. The distribution of these species in transformed areas (agriculture and urban areas) ranged from 11 to 30 percent; El Salvador, Panama, and Guatemala showed more than 50 percent of the distribution; Honduras and Mexico more than 40 percent; Belize less than 25 percent. El Salvador, Honduras, Panama, Nicaragua, and Mexico showed high percentages of distribution for the classes Amphibia, Liliopsida, Polipodiopsida, and the orders Asterales, Fabales, Laurales, Myrtales, Scrophulariales, and Rubiales. The authors argue that, while the PNAs fulfill their function of reducing rates of habitat loss, they are not necessarily representative of the rich biodiversity of the Central American region.

Since the approval of the Convention on Biological Diversity (CBD) of the United Nations Organization in 1992 (United Nations Environment Programme 1992), there has been an intense global debate regarding biodiversity, and its previous status as humanity's common heritage has been eliminated. This international agreement is the most important in terms of the protection of biological resources. The conservation policy emphasizes the creation of PNAs (Article 8 of the CBD), which has promoted the emergence of new markets, such as ecotourism, bioprospecting, and carbon credits. In 1962, there were a thousand PNAs in the world, covering three percent of the earth's surface; in 2003, the amount increased to 102,000, with 11.5 percent (Reyez 2016). The main threats to biodiversity are a) Fragmentation, loss of habitat, and deterioration in quality and integrity; b) Overexploitation of resources (hunting; extraction of resources such as eggs, pets, overuse for survival, illegal trafficking, and illegal logging; indiscriminate and uncontrolled use of genetic and biochemical resources; overexploitation of aquifers; toxic mining) and pollution; c) Gaps in the conservation of species and ecosystems that are not included in protected wild areas; d) Climate change, especially the lack of knowledge on the best measures to reduce the vulnerability of biodiversity. Conservation is conceived from biological and physical variables, the social aspect does not receive the same consideration despite being fundamental (Ovando and Herrera 2010).

It often happens that decreeing the PNAs implies that, outside these areas, predatory processes can occur without any control. Despite this, today many endemic species and conserved ecosystems are found in these areas. It is an ambivalent issue, and international regulation continues to privilege the creation of

PNAs as the main conservation measure. The CBD's Aichi targets emphasized this aspect, with the aspiration to reach 17 percent of the world's land surface and 10 percent of the world's marine surface as a protected area by 2020, an objective that was not met in the face of the unprecedented global pandemic (Aichi Biodiversity Targets n.d.).

It is questionable whether only decreeing PNAs is sufficient for the conservation of biodiversity. On the one hand, as Londoño and Sánchez Cordero (2009) propose, the speed of habitat loss can be controlled with this measure, but that does not necessarily mean protecting endangered species. The authors also provide evidence in their research of the presence of threatened species outside the PNAs. On the other hand, in the decrees of the PNAs, verticality often prevails: local populations that inhabit these territories are not participants in the decision, which often generates conflicts. In Mexico there is a long list of PNAs in this situation, to the detriment of conservation, such as the cases of the Monarch Butterfly Reserve in Michoacán (García 2009) or the Tehuacán-Cuicatlán reserve in Puebla and Oaxaca (Brunel 2009). When bioprospecting, collecting the knowledge associated with the living being is very important as it increases the possibility of obtaining a profitable result by 400 percent (Bravo 2013: 71).

Status of Mesoamerican Biodiversity

Central America

The region ranks first in terms of species diversity in the world and holds second place in plant density and first in birds and mammals. Costa Rica, Panama, and Guatemala rank in the top thirty-two places in terms of the number of vertebrate and plant species in the world, out of a list of 228 countries (Ovando and Herrera 2010: 17). Classification systems are not homogeneous, although the best known since the seventies is that of Holdridge life zones (Holdridge 1967).

In terms of ecosystems, Guatemala and Honduras are the countries with the greatest diversity, having nineteen and seventeen distinct ecosystems respectively, out of a total of twenty-two in the region (Ovando and Herrera 2010: 23). There is a paucity of studies on the genetic diversity of Central American species, the few studies refer to domesticated plants and contain almost no knowledge of wild flora and fauna. There is even less information on their conservation status. There are some lists in Guatemala, Nicaragua, Panama, and Costa Rica of existing and endangered species, but priority conservation tasks are pending (Ovando and Herrera 2010: 33).

There were 557 PNAs in Central America in 2003. El Salvador has been the latest to decree PNAs, starting in the eighties, and remains the country with the least protected area; Costa Rica, on the other hand, has the most PNAs, while those of Panama cover more surface. There is an advance in tourism related to the existence of biodiversity as an attraction, especially wildlife, which implies a different management of these vertebrates. This may lose potential in the face of ecosystem degradation and the management of "new" ecosystems, both results of human intervention.

On how to manage the PNAs, there is a great variety of strategies in Central America, which coincide with the categories of national park, biological reserve, and natural monument, as well as international categories (e.g., Ramsar Site, Biosphere Reserve, and Heritage Site). Many protected areas are jointly managed by NGOs, municipalities, community groups, and universities – private areas are also allowed in Costa Rica. Ex situ conservation (zoos, botanical gardens, arboretums, zoo hatcheries, scientific collections, and genebanks), in most cases, are private for exhibition purposes and do not conduct research. Despite their shortcomings, they play an important role in the environmental education of their visitors.

Of the existing lists, the countries with the highest number of threatened and endangered species are Panama, Costa Rica, and Guatemala. Panama accounts for 15 percent of the reported species of vertebrates and plants, Costa Rica 14 percent, and Guatemala 18 percent; there are no lists for Nicaragua. The Central American flora presents more threatened species than fauna. According to the Convention on International Trade in Endangered Species of Wild Fauna and Flora (CITES), there are 1,000 endangered in Costa Rica and Panama, 13 percent and 8 percent of the total species of vertebrates and plants. Of the vertebrates, birds stand out, of which the largest number are in Panama (271), followed by El Salvador (188), and Honduras (133); they are followed by mammals, with Guatemala and Belize with the largest number (11 species in each case), and amphibians, with more endangered species in Guatemala (93) and Costa Rica (90). In the latter country, there are two officially recognized extinctions: those of the golden toad and the Guanacaste hummingbird, but in all countries, species not sighted for more than ten years are mentioned without having been officially declared extinct. With regard to plants, in Central America, 524 species are located on the red lists of the International Union for Conservation of Nature (IUCN). From the existing information, it was found that out of a total of 359, 283 are in protected natural areas. The goal of the Global Strategy for Plant Conservation (GSCP) is that at least 60 percent of the world's threatened plant species are protected in situ (Ovando and Herrera 2020: 42–49).

Mexico

Mexico belongs to the group of megadiverse countries in the world, ranking 5th in global biodiversity (considering vascular plants, mammals, birds, reptiles, and amphibians), after Brazil, Colombia, China, and Indonesia, and stands out for the large number of species, high endemism, and great genetic variability of many taxonomic groups, due to evolution and cultural diversification. The native Mesoamerican peoples domesticated a large number of species and used many more, both wild and cultivated, for therapeutic, food, textile, religious, ornamental, and construction purposes. There is a close relationship between their great biological and cultural diversity, which is particularly evident in the case of cultivated species. It ranks first in the Americas and fifth in the world for the number of living languages: 291 (Sarukhán et al. 2009: 21). The areas of greatest biodiversity also correlate to a greater presence of Indigenous peoples speaking these languages (Boege 2008). In the territories of Indigenous communities (14.3 percent of the total area), almost all of Mexico's vegetation is found, including most of the humid forests, mesophilic forests, and humid temperate forests, all of them high in biodiversity. A third of the PNAs are federal and 26 percent of their surface includes Indigenous territories. Indigenous peoples make up almost 19 percent of the population of the PNAs (Sarukhán et al. 2009: 39–40).

Proportionally, the number of species that inhabit Mexico with respect to the world total (10–12 percent) is much higher than what the territory represents (1.4 percent) (Sarukhán et al. 2009: 23). It is one of the countries with the highest number of native mammal species, around 525 reported in 2006, and Sarukhán et al. recorded 535 in 2009 (Sarukhán et al. 2009; Arqueología mexicana 2006), only below Indonesia or Brazil, which have 560 and 540, respectively. There are 137 species of bats, 15 percent of a total of 927 in the world (Eguiarte 2006), and 2,184 species of fish, second only to Indonesia, the Philippines, Australia, and part of Papua New Guinea. In terms of terrestrial vertebrates, Mexico is in third place with 535 species, after Brazil and Colombia (667 and 578 species respectively). Of the endemic plants, the country has about 15,000 (between 50 and 60 percent of those known so far). Vertebrates, reptiles, and amphibians have the highest degree of endemism, with 57 and 65 percent exclusive to the country. Freshwater mammals and fish have 32 percent endemism in both cases (Sarukhán et al. 2009: 25).

This rich biodiversity is distributed in a heterogeneous and complex way in the territory, with greater variability of living beings in tropical areas – as in other countries– and with desert areas very abundant in cacti. Endemic species are fewer in the humid tropics, higher in the sub-humid tropics, and highest in arid and semi-arid regions. Sarukhán et al (2009) placed emphasis on sustainable and low-impact management in areas outside protected areas, something fundamental that has not been given the importance it deserves in the Mesoamerican area, as Londoño and Sánchez Cordero (2009) affirm for Central America.

Mexico had 25,628,239 hectares in 177 PNAs of federal management in 2009, in various modalities. In addition, there are 404,516.17 ha of certified protected areas voluntarily destined for conservation. In total, 26,032,755.17 hectares of surface are under some type of protection (CONANP 2018). Despite the fact that there are a series of conflicts and that there are other undecreed conserved areas, this situation presents an interesting platform for the observation and study of Mexican biodiversity, which still needs to be seriously evaluated. As stated above, most of these areas are in the Mesoamerican part of Mexico.

At the thirteenth Conference of the Parties (COP 13) of the Biodiversity Conference held in Cancun, Mexico, in 2016, then President Peña Nieto decreed four more protected natural areas, reaching a total of 91 million hectares. In theory, the PNAs should have a management program, which would be the guiding instrument of planning and regulation that establishes the activities, actions, and basic guidelines for their administration. In practice, this management is deficient: of the total of 177 PNAs recognized before the 2016 decree, seventy-five of them (42.4 percent) did not have a management program, with consequent risks to their preservation, restoration, and conservation. On the other hand, 104 of the PNAs prior to the decree (58.8 percent) did not comply with the international treaties on environmental matters signed by Mexico (Convention on Wetlands of International Importance; the Convention for the Protection of the World Natural and Cultural Heritage; the U.N. Convention on Climate Change and, in the case of the rights of Indigenous peoples and communities, International Labour Organization Convention 169). In addition, thirty-two PNAs did not have a published management program, and such programs are often urgently developed when megaprojects arise that affect these areas. Regarding the right to consultation of Indigenous communities on actions in their territory (Convention 169 of the International Labor Organization), according to the National Human Rights Commission (CNDH), in 2016, twenty-seven PNAs suffered the transformation or loss of original ecosystems, aquifer contamination, soil erosion, and deforestation and did not have financial resources for their administration, operation, and surveillance; thus, the elimination or modification of their declarations was recommended. It was also reported that in eighty PNAs, there is an Indigenous population (sometimes more than 90 percent), and in twenty-nine of them, there was no management program. According to the *Comisión Nacional de Áreas Naturales Protegidas* (CONANP) in 2016, fifty-one PNAs did not have the capacity to have such programs, so part of them were in the process of being repealed (Reyez 2016). There is a considerable deterioration in vegetation in general – not only in the PNAs; in 1993, the vegetation cover occupied only 54 percent of its original surface, and in 2009, it had been reduced by 62 percent, while the vegetation cover of forests and jungles in 2002 occupied only 38 percent, with greater loss in tropical regions (Sarukhán et al. 2009: 46).

Reyez (2016) reports that in another CONANP document (Estrategia 2014), the existence of illicit activities in the PNAs has been reported, such as hunting, clandestine logging, planting of illicit crops, and presence of criminal groups, partly because the Inspection and Surveillance Programs in PNAs are only present in fifty-five of them. For the optimal operation of CONANP, it is necessary to increase the budget by 17 percent per year, but the current government has significantly reduced spending for the environmental sector by 7 percent between 2019 and 2020, and 1.5 percent between 2020 and 2021. CONANP had a budget decrease of 3.7 percent between 2020 and 2021 (Muller et al. 2021). Another ominous indicator is that CONABIO (*Comisión*

Nacional para el Conocimiento y Uso de la Biodiversidad) went from being an autonomous entity to a dependency of the *Secretaría de Medio Ambiente y Recursos Naturales* (SERMARNAT) and has been allocated less and less budget. The reduced budget negatively affects all Mesoamerican biodiversity since CONABIO made important contributions to its study and was a key participant in the ambitious Mesoamerican conservation project called the *Corredor Biológico Mesoamericano*.

With respect to genetic diversity, although progress has been made in its study, knowledge is still very limited, since there is only accessible research on the genetic variation of forty-five of the 2,583 species – mainly plants of economic interest – listed in the respective standard of SERMARNAT (Sarukhán et al. 2009: 34). There is greater genetic variability in the centers of origin of the species, as is the case in Mexico for corn, cotton, and nitrogen-fixing microorganisms such as rhizobium.

Ecosystem fragmentation has detrimental effects on the genetic variability of populations, and more studies are needed to assess the consequences of habitat loss, particularly on species with reduced populations. Mexico is one of the largest centers of plant domestication in the world, with more than 15 percent of food species originating in the country (Sarukhán et al. 2009: 35–38). The remaining vegetation is fragmented and water ecosystems have suffered significant destruction. Another pervasive threat to biodiversity and conservation has been the increasing and disorderly urbanization. These threats become more acute with the manifestations of climate change. Mexico – like Central America – is particularly exposed to the destruction of regulating systems such as mangroves and deforestation due to its geographic location, with extensive coastal areas. The country is highly vulnerable to droughts and hurricanes, which are becoming more frequent and devastating.

In terms of endangered species and extinctions, it is known with certainty that 127 species have been lost, of which seventy-four were endemic. In 2001, there were nearly 2,500 species in some extinction risk category. Most of the extinct species are birds of the Mexican islands and amphibians, although their quantification is difficult (Sarukhán et al. 2009: 57). In 2018, CONANP data included 2,606 species in some risk category, of which 475 were in danger of extinction.

Experiences of Community Biodiversity Management in Mesoamerica

The Indigenous Peasant Coordinator of Community Agroforestry in Central America (ACICAFOC)

ACICAFOC is a non-profit organization that facilitates procedures for the access, use, and responsible management of natural resources, with the aim of contributing to the socio-productive development of Indigenous peoples and rural communities. It has its origins in the 1980s, when meetings of Indigenous and peasant organizations began to be organized in Central America. In 1993, with the support of the Forests, Trees and People Programme of the Food and Agriculture Organization of the United Nations (FAO), forestry and agroecological organizations met in various activities and workshops, which evidenced the need for greater coordination and established a temporary and flexible Coordinating Commission with representatives of several regional organizations (*Federación Hondureña de Cooperativas Agroforestales –* FECAHFOR, *Unión Nacional de Agricultores y Ganaderos de Nicaragua –* UNAG, and the *Junta Forestal Campesina –* Unaforca of Costa Rica) (ACICAFOC n.d.) and the support of the *Asociación de Organizaciones Campesinas Centroamericanas para la Cooperación y el Desarrollo* (ASOCODE).

In 1991, the Mesoamerican Workshop on Peasant and Indigenous Participation in the Decision-Making Process and Use of Forest Resources (*Taller Mesoamericano de Participación Campesina e Indígena en el Proceso de Toma de Decisiones y Aprovechamiento de los Recursos Forestales*) was held in Costa Rica, an activity that was carried out with a commission of two people from each country. In 1994, also in Costa Rica, the First Central American Meeting of Community Forestry (*Primer Encuentro Centroamericano de Forestería Comunitaria*) was held, with the support of IUCN, FAO, ASOCODE as well as a non-timber project CATIE (*Centro Agronómico Tropical de Investigación y Enseñanza de Costa Rica*).

In September 1994, the approach of the *Consejo Centroamericano de Bosques* was presented to the *Comisión Coordinadora Centroamericana de Forestería Comunitaria* (CCAB) and the FTP-FAO Advisory Committee. By 1996, four national coordinations had been formed with twenty-five organizations in Nicaragua and Honduras, fifteen in Guatemala and El Salvador, and developments underway in Costa Rica, Panama, and Belize. In January 1995, the San Ignacio de Acosta Agenda was drafted in Costa Rica, and national coordination processes began to be developed and financed, giving rise to the ACICAFOC, a management agency to obtain and administer funds from national and international institutions aimed at promoting community forestry. It has projects mainly in Central American countries: Belize, Costa Rica, El Salvador, Honduras, Nicaragua, and Panama, along with Argentina, Benin (Africa), Buthan (Asia), Colombia, and the Dominican Republic. These projects include

- Alternative sustainable agroforestry management in the North Atlantic region of Nicaragua, which was financed by the World Bank between 2010 and 2013, working with 1000 cocoa farmers to increase production levels.
- Development of technical capacities of Indigenous and peasant organizations. The capacities of organizations close to ACICAFOC were strengthened to join initiatives relevant to climate change. The area of work was all in Central America, with funding from the GIZ (German Society for International Cooperation) in 2011. Specifically, it sought integration into national processes of REDD+ (Redu-

cing Emissions from Deforestation and Forest Degradation), a program of FAO (FAO n.d.)

- Support for advocacy and defense of civil society. This focused on supporting civil society and vulnerable communities to influence negotiations in global climate change processes. It was carried out between 2011 and 2013 in Honduras, Guatemala, Nicaragua, and Bolivia, with funding from Red Suswatch (Sustainability Observatory). Its objective was the articulation of approaches from civil society organizations to the most effective dialogue with government entities, to influence the negotiation process in the UNFCCC (United Nations Framework Convention on Climate Change) and the definition and action regarding policies and strategies on climate change at the national and regional levels.
- A regional rainwater harvesting project, targeting seven municipalities in Guatemala, El Salvador, Honduras, and Nicaragua in force from 2011 to 2015, with funding from the AECID (*Agencia Española de Cooperación Internacional para el Desarrollo*) that aimed to increase the coverage of drinking water to improve the quality of life for inhabitants of municipalities that suffer prolonged droughts.
- National, regional, and local participation of peasant groups of civil society. Through an open public call, advice was provided on the consultation process for REDD+. This project was carried out in Costa Rica from 2012 to 2013 with resources from the *Fondo Nacional de Financiamiento Forestal*.
- A co-management process with ten grassroots community organizations, carried out in Belize in 2013, with the cooperation of RRI (Rights and Resources Initiative, an international body with more than twenty-one donors). Among its donors are AIPP (Asian Indigenous People Pact), AMPB (*Alianza Mesoamericana de Pueblos y Bosques*), CED (Center for Environment and Development), CIFOR (Center for International Forestry Research), COICA (*Coordinadora de Organizaciones Indígenas de la Cuenca Amazónica*), ISA (*Instituto Socioambiental*) and PCM (*Proceso de comunidades negras*) (RRI n.d.; ACICAFOC n.d.).

Cuetzalan, Mexico: Biodiversity, Culture, and Defense of the Territory

Cuetzalan is a highly marginalized municipality in the state of Puebla and most of its inhabitants are Indigenous: 38,926 of a total of 47,333 (CDI 2010), with the Nahua or Masehual group as the dominant majority. It is a biodiverse territory, not only because of the large number of plants and animals it houses, but also because of the culture and the richness of its natural resources such as water. The region was first occupied by the Totonac people in the fourth century AD and then by the Nahuas in the fifteenth century. The mestizos and Spaniards came later during the conquest. It is a stronghold of biodiversity with a combination of several ecosystems: the mountain mesophilic forest, pine and oak, and the sub-evergreen low forest are variegated in a pronounced and complex relief, ranging from 1,600 to 159 meters above sea level. It has the most precipitation in the country with an annual rainfall of 4,200 mm. It also has a karst geological system (mountain systems formed by calcareous rock or limestone), which creates a peculiar behavior of water and develops cave ecosystems.

The majority of the Nahua or Masehual population has managed to sustain a mode of agricultural production and use of flora and fauna respectful of nature based on a worldview that establishes that nature does not belong to human beings; rather, they must be integrated into it, as they belong to it (Meza 2014: 173). In an interview conducted in 2014, Ms. Rufina Villa, a local leader, said that animals have more right to live than humans, because "they do not threaten nature," and that humans do not have the right to take from nature more than they need and should not abuse it for profit (Villa 2014).

Without idealizing the conservation of biodiversity and water by the Masehuales and Totonacos as optimal just because they are Indigenous practices, it is necessary to recognize the capacity of management of natural resources of these native groups, despite population growth and power struggles in the region. The original cloud forest and jungles have almost completely disappeared, but a form of production based on shade coffee was recreated, which allowed water and biodiversity to be conserved. Despite this, poverty prevails in the region, even with the organizational and defense efforts described above. Historically, the Masehuales and Totonacos have managed to conserve a good part of the land, and many of their practices preserve the ecosystem in good condition, but there are also predatory practices. The ancient coniferous forests present in the bends and high mountainous areas are now areas of much smaller trees, and there are large portions with uncovered bedrock because the vegetation that supported the humus has been lost in a process of constant erosion.

The municipality and its people are currently going through an interesting process of planning and carrying out their own self-managed territorial ordering, embodied in a document with official recognition, achieved through a process of resistance against predatory projects that sought to impose themselves from the local and national governments, (mass and exclusive tourism, Walmart, mining, and hydroelectric). This document has been a very valuable instrument for the defense of the territory, and its gestation process demonstrates how territorial ordinances can not only be a means of government policy but also elaborated by the population itself in a democratic manner. The complex biocultural relationship of the Masehuales of Cuetzalan with their natural environment is expressed in their narratives, in which animals, water, lightning, the moon, and other natural elements are endowed with life and have a fairly horizontal, although not always harmonious, relationship with human beings. In the region, there is a belief that some natural elements have life, such as water, at which one must not throw stones, but respect. Another belief is that some animals have supernatural powers, such as the *serpiente cincuata*, considered the guardian of places and which should not be attacked because it attracts bad luck (Villa 2014).

For Beaucage (2012), the current Cuetzalteco ecosystem is explained by two major periods in regional history: the first was from the founding of the town as a republic of Indians in the sixteenth century, with the collective form of land tenure called *"el común de los naturales"* (the common of the natives). The second has been since the mid-nineteenth century when this collective form of tenure was dismantled with the Reform Laws and replaced by private property. It is in this second epoch when the current ecosystem is produced, and the Indigenous people adapted their way of life to the privatization of the land. This meant the establishment of individual private plots corresponding to the traditional indigenous coffee plantation, which, in contrast to the coffee plantation, is not a monoculture, but developed as a tree polyculture adapted to the tropical mountain environment that characterizes the region. The occupation of the territory mainly by Totonac and Nahuatlaca groups dates back more than 750 years and has generated biocultural processes that have transformed nature, expressed in the milpa (*milaj*), the mountain or intervened jungle (*kuojta*), the mountain in which it is produced (*kuojtakiloyan*), the potrero (*ixtautat*) or the coffee plantation under shade (*caffenta*), which forms a landscape of biological and cultural diversity.

Indigenous knowledge and the conception that implies the kuojtakiloyan (the forest where we produce) is one of the most notable examples in Mexico of sustainable community management of natural resources and biodiversity. It is a tangible sample of modern Indigenous knowledge with ancestral roots but elaborated, recreated, and practiced by the Totonac and Masehual peoples today. This is expressed through, although the original forests have been lost, the region retaining its richness in biodiversity and water. According to the CUPREDER (*Centro Universitario para la Prevención de Desastres Regionales*), of the *Benemérita Universidad Autónoma de Puebla*, the mountain mesophilic forest or high mountain, which originally covered 50 percent of the territory of the municipality, only occupied 14 percent in 2009; almost 50 percent was lost in thirty years. The medium evergreen forest, which occupied 40 percent of the surface, also in 2009, was only present in 0.81 percent of the area. Maize cultivation declined somewhat between 1979 and 2009, while coffee cultivation almost doubled (Fernández Lomelín 2013: 102).

The population is dense (275 people per square meter), with Nahuas in the west, south, and east, and Totonacs in the center of the territory. Farmers grow corn, beans, coffee, pepper, fruits such as oranges and mamey, and some sugar cane for sale. There is also the presence of cinnamon and vanilla in some of the orchards. The kuojtakiloyan preserves a great biodiversity in plants and other living beings, while also having a productive use. Between 1920 and 1990, Indigenous coffee plantations expanded, which for Beaucage (2012) created a "tree polyculture," and constituted for the peasants an ecological and productive way out of the rapid population growth, which increasingly hindered the previous way of subsistence based on the *milpa*.

The abundance of water is the subject of dispute and recent threats, since the exclusionary tourism project against which the inhabitants resisted in 2009 intended to monopolize the water of 18,000 people for a few. This tourism project, called "Cloud Forest," was promoted by the *Comisión para el Desarrollo de los Pueblos Indígenas* without consulting the inhabitants of the region, who mobilized and arrested it (Meza 2014: 175). Recently, they have wanted to impose mining and hydroelectric projects, which the population has resisted and cannot grow without limit according to territorial planning. All these projects relied on the abundance of water in order to be implemented. Precipitation and orography generate both groundwater and surface water, and the resurgence of underground currents forms pools and waterfalls. They are common in areas where there are steep and inaccessible slopes, which the inhabitants call *apa or ameyal* (Fernández Lomelín 2013: 108).

In all the toponymy of Cuetzalan, water is present. For Fernández Lomelí "water is alive, present in almost all place names" (2014). The mountain is very precious because it supplies water for 80 percent of the population. The idea of the earth on the water appears, a pre-Hispanic vision of the world where there are no caves, but these are the jaws of the jaguar, that is, the entrance to the *tlalocan*, which is another dimension, another world; the *taltipan* is the earth; the *inhuical* the sky, the place where we go when we die; and finally, the *ayotzi* is the turtle that generates water in springs and rivers (Fernández Lomelín 2014). The biodiversity, ecosystems, and people of Cuetzalan, briefly described, are those that are at risk from the threats of predatory projects that seek to impose themselves in the region, before which the municipality and its people are immersed in a process of defense of the territory. Among the threats that triggered this mobilization are first, the aforementioned exclusionary tourism project in 2009, which generated the collective elaboration of territorial planning; then, the threat to install a Walmart and later mining and hydroelectric megaprojects, which led to long-term resistance to date, and which has spread to other municipalities in the sierra (Hernández 2018). The Masehuales and Totonacos of Cuetzalan have advanced in the defense of their territory, rich in natural resources, and have prevented to date these megaprojects typical of the Anthropocene, with a self-managed approach. With the current Mexican government, many of the threats have disappeared or diminished since local organizations, notably the Tosepan Titataniske cooperative complex, have participated, to the extent that the current *Secretaría de Medio Ambiente y Recursos Naturales* belongs to this organization. The Tosepan Titataniske is a group of cooperatives that originated in the region in the late 1980s as a supply cooperative, and to date have expanded their range of activities to the production of organic coffee, pepper, honey, housing, microfinancing, and ecotourism, among others (Cobo, Paz Paredes, and Bartra 2018).

Santa María Yavesía, Sierra Juárez de Oaxaca: Forests and Commonality

The Sierra Juárez de Oaxaca is distinguished by the sustainable management of its forests, the result of a process of recovery of its territory since the late 1980s. The region has a remarkable biodiversity, given the varied altitudinal levels that it comprises, and is a great water collector, as the Papaloapan River – one of the largest in Mexico with 45 billion cubic meters per year – originates there (Merino 2008: 41). It is known as one of the most important conservation sites in the world, with the best and widest altitudinal gradient of wet vegetation in the country. It also influences its location as a watershed of the slopes of the Pacific Ocean and the Gulf of Mexico. It has areas covered with high evergreen forests, low evergreen forests, mesophilic forests, pine-oak forests, and subalpine grassland areas. In the Sierra, 50 percent of the plant species of Oaxaca are found, with high endemism. There are 168 thousand hectares of mesophilic forest or cloud forest, the most threatened in Mexico and Latin America (Avendaño 2009).

This section refers specifically to Santa María Yavesía, one of the three joint towns of the Sierra. For the analysis, it is necessary to consider the approach of communality (Díaz 2004; Martínez Luna 2015; Guerrero 2015; Nava 2018) and how this is expressed at the level of a community that owns an important natural resource (approximately 9,000 hectares of pine-oak forest), with its own project to obtain income through ecotourism managed under internal regulations. For Díaz (2004), a Mixe or Ayuuk author foundational to the approach of communality, this is the phenomenological manifestation of community, emphasizing the relationship of humans with nature and with individuals among themselves and highlighting their differences with Western society. For this author, the elements of communality thus conceived are a) the Earth as mother and as territory, b) consensus in assembly for decision-making, c) the free service or *tequio* as an exercise of authority, d) the collective work or *tequio* as an act of recreation, and e) the rites and ceremonies as an expression of the communal gift.

Martínez Luna (2015), a Zapotec or binnizá theorist of the Sierra Juárez and founding author of communality together with Díaz, distinguishes four moments of communal philosophy: a) nature, geography, territory, or land; (b) the society, community, family that inhabits that nature; (c) work carried out by society, community, or family in that territory; and d) what that society – the community that inhabits that soil – obtains or achieves as enjoyment, well-being, celebration, distraction, satisfaction, and fatigue with its work. For Nava (2018), there are differences and similarities in the two approaches: in Díaz and the Ayuuk, the territory and nature are more present, while in Martínez Luna and the Zapotecs or Binnizá of Sierra Juárez, greater weight is given to the party, coexistence, and service to the community.

Yavesía has its own ecotourism approach, which consists of maintaining its forest as a reserve and not exploiting it to obtain wood, as the neighboring towns do. This distinguishes this community from the Lachatao and Amatlán joint peoples, who practice ecotourism in parallel to logging exploitation, which has generated conflicts with Yavesía.

The relevance of the reflection on the management of the Yavesía forest is related to the situation of forests at the global level, since, given the official global recognition of climate change (which has not implied that effective measures are taken to counteract it), it is known that forests and reforestation (together with diversified peasant agriculture) are indispensable to "cool" the planet (Welch 2022: 42).

In Yavesía, the forest is communal, and it is the *comuneras* and the *comuneros* who have decision-making power over the actions to be taken in the management of natural assets (mainly forest and water). For its part, the citizen assembly (of all the inhabitants of the community) is the space where other issues are put on the table, agreements are made, and the direction of the projects is determined. In its forest, there is a great variety of animal species, some of them in danger of extinction (this is the case of mammals such as peccary, puma, deer, jaguar, and diverse birds). The inhabitants proudly state that their forest, not having been exploited, has become a refuge area for these animals.

The organization of the Mancomunado peoples dates back to the Mexican Revolution, when they organized self-defense groups to protect themselves from banditry (Chapela 2019). In 1962, this agrarian nucleus of unique characteristics was recognized by a national decree on October 20 and has a forest area of 20,849.3 hectares between the three joint villages. In addition to community management, there are commercial pressures, such as a forestry company that exploits the forests of Amatlán and Lachatao; Yavesía does not participate in this exploitation and has the explicit community purpose of maintaining its forest as a reserve. These notions were present in the workshop that the author of this text facilitated, giving rise to the reflection presented here.

The Zapotec or Binnizá inhabitants of the northern highlands have historically had a horizontal relationship with the natural assets of their region, which translates into the care of natural resources. The Pueblos Mancomunados of the northern highlands of Oaxaca are Santa Maria Yavesia, Santa Catarina Lachatao, Nevería, San Isidro Llano Grande, San Miguel Amatlán, San Antonio Cuajimoloyas, Santa Martha Latuvi, and Benito Juárez, which aim to establish shared activities for the use of natural assets for common use. This is not without conflicts: in the workshop taught, rivalry and anger were perceived with the neighboring peoples who, according to the participants, had deforested their forests and now invaded the Yavesía, both for ecotourism and for timber extraction. This is reflected in obstacles to joint community actions, expressed in the absence of Yavesía in the ecotourism project of joint peoples that has its office in the city of Oaxaca.

The inhabitants of Yavesía agree that it is necessary to take care of the mountains, as well as to continue the reforestation of the oak-pine forest and preserve the biodiversity of the mountains since there lies the well-being of the community. Therefore, the participants in the workshop and the authorities interviewed believe it is convenient to maintain an autonomous, community-based, relational tourism with their organizational practices. This is part of the pillars of its tourism construction, which has focused on the good state of conservation of its forest, so low-impact activities are promoted, such as running, hiking, and mountain biking tours. The inhabitants of Yavesía are clear that the people who visit their territory must be aware of the horizontal and respectful relationship that they themselves, as forest dwellers, have built over generations, as well as the internal communal regulations. There are no tourist cabins, as in other towns of the Sierra Juárez, visitors stay in the houses of the community, and the *Comité de Ecoturismo*, elected in assembly, decides which members of the community receive tourists, organizing shifts that allow the equitable distribution of benefits.

Their project is self-sustained and communal, which is reflected in the organization of the camps in the forest, of which there were several modalities: one includes the girls and boys of the primary school, the adolescents of the secondary school, and the youth to promote the forest care among the new generations. Camps for outsiders, such as mountain bikers and teachers from the Isthmus, have allowed the community to be known as an ecotourism destination. These events economically benefit different sectors of the community; for example, women take charge of the sale of food and take advantage to offer their products, such as jams, nuts, and canned fruits, among other things. Despite these advances, there are still areas of community forest management that are not regulated, such as hunting, and potential for the sale of local products is wasted without community agreements. However, Yavesía promotes a tourism that respects nature, fostering community pride in maintaining its forest, and thus contributing an approach that counteracts the serious characteristics of environmental damage of the Anthropocene.

Conclusions

From the brief theoretical-historical and contextual reflection, as well as the cases exposed, this chapter proposes some conclusions.

The debate remains as to whether nature and biodiversity should be conserved per se, or whether they need to be useful and profitable for humans. It is clear that the ecological deterioration and extinction of species challenge us to resolve this issue, although there is increasing evidence that the survival of humanity is dependent on the existence of ecosystems in good condition.

The discussions in international forums and the evidence shown in the cases presented lead us to reflect on the best way to conserve and the pertinence of this being done only in PNAs. The need to find ways of life and consumption that do not exceed the natural capacity for ecosystem restoration is evident. Mesoamerica, as a biodiverse region, has problems of lack of resources to conserve and use this wealth sustainably. This is compounded by the region's vulnerability to climate change.

The current socio-environmental risks are greater than those that were presented in the 1950s, although this chapter argues that this time period was when a form of food production and modernization began that led to many of the current damages, such as deforestation, soil impoverishment, and contamination with agrochemicals, in addition to damage to human and animal health. One must reflect on what has been considered "development" in the twentieth century and how, in the Anthropocene, environmental deterioration is bringing humanity and the planet to the brink of total destruction. Given this, it is important to document experiences such as those exposed, which occur in the history, context, and biological richness of the Mesoamerican region.

Although there is an important global institutional concern for the regulation and access to biodiversity, in a way that allows it to be conserved, the results are still incipient, in contrast to an extinction that advances by leaps and bounds. This chapter finds a very important potential for knowledge, cosmogony, and practices in the original peoples of Mesoamerica to find ways of conserving biodiversity and, at the same time, using it. This crosses several levels: the need to manage national and international funds for the benefit of Indigenous and peasant communities – of which ACICAFOC has valuable experience in Central America – and the experience of many Indigenous peoples of the region in terms of a respectful relationship with Nature that allows biodiversity to be conserved. The latter is frequently related to the processes of defense of the territory and the internal regulations to manage natural resources, as found in Cuetzalan and the Sierra Juárez.

In the experiences described, a paradox is observed: the civilizational approaches have ancient roots from native peoples and have advanced against the current with obstacles. The processes of defense of their territories have been key for these communities to have been able to realize their approaches. That is, the deep ancestral roots of their knowledge and cosmogony are valid, within the framework of an Anthropocene urged by solutions to civilizational and socio-environmental crises. In both cases, this chapter has described community management of important natural resources (water, forest, biodiversity) and the approaches that have emerged as a response to concrete threats.

It can be seen that the communality of the Sierra Juárez and the kuojtakiloyan of the Sierra Norte de Puebla as their own autonomous elaborations, civilizational proposals that deserve to be considered before the environmental devastation characteristic of the Anthropocene. In both cases, the intrinsic value of the natural environment is present since income is obtained through low-impact activities, not at the expense of Nature's destruction nor privileging the excessive obtaining of profit. These are the civilizational approaches that can counterbalance the socio-environmental damage characteristic of the Anthropocene. Likewise, the existence of their own peasant and Indigenous organizations and management spaces, such as ACCICAFOC, allow a moderate optimism about the conservation of biodiversity in the region, as they are linked to the existence of peasant and Indigenous organizations that have found the necessary support to manage their natural resources in a communal and sustainable manner.

Translated by Eric Rummelhoff and revised by Luisa Raquel Ellermeier.

References

ACICAFOC (Coordinadora indígena campesina de agroforestería comunitaria de Centroamérica). n.d. "ACICAFOC." https://www.acicafoc.org/.

Aichi Biodversity Targets. 2020. "Fliers." *Convention on Biological Diversity.* https://www.cbd.int/doc/strategic-plan/2011-2020/Aichi-Targets-ES.pdf.

Avendaño, Olga Rosario. 2009. "En la Sierra Norte de Oaxaca." *Society of Environmental Journalists.* https://www.sej.org/library/sej-espanol/en-la-sierra-norte-de-oaxaca.

Beaucage, Pierre. 2012. "Historia social y construcción de un ecosistema: la toponimia del ordenamiento territorial campesino indígena en Cuetzalan." *Kuojtakiloyan. El monte donde producimos* 12: 3–12.

Boege, Eckart. 2008. *El patrimonio biocultural de los pueblos indígenas de México. Hacia la conservación in situ de la biodiversidad y agrodiversidad en los territorios indígenas.* Mexico City: Instituto Nacional de Antropología e Historia/Comisión Nacional para el Desarrollo de los Pueblos Indígenas

Bravo, Elizabeth. 2013. *Apuntes sobre la biodiversidad del Ecuador.* Quito: Abya Yala/ Universidad Politécnica Salesiana.

Brunel, Claudia. 2016. "Desarrollo y conservación desde una mirada crítica: algunas reflexiones acerca de un matrimonio desunido. El caso de Santiago Quiotepec, en la Reserva de la Biosfera Tehuacán-Cuicatlán." In *El dilema de la conservación: tres experiencias de gestión comunitaria de recursos naturales*, ed. Yolanda Massieu Trigo, 38–87. Mexico City: Universidad Autónoma Metropolitana-Xochimilco.

Castro, Guillermo. 2017. "Nuestra América, los tiempos del tiempo." In *Ecología Política Latinoamericana. Pensamiento crítico, diferencia latinoamericana y rearticulación epistémica*, ed. Héctor Alimonda, Catalina Toro Pérez, and Facundo Martín, 95–102. Buenos Aires: CLACSO.

CDI (Comisión Nacional para el Desarrollo de los Pueblos Indígenas). 2010. Catálogo de Localidades Indígenas 2010. *Instituto Nacional de los Pueblos Indígenas*. Mexico City. https://www.inpi.gob.mx/localidades2010-gobmx/catalogo_de_local idades_indigenas_2010.xlsx.

Chapela, Francisco. 2019. Interview by author, Oaxaca, September 10.

Cobo, Rosario, Lorena Paz Paredes, and Armando Bartra. 2018. *Somos Tosepan. 40 años haciendo camino*. Mexico City: Rosa-Luxemburg-Stiftung/Unión de Cooperativas Tosepan.

CONANP (Comisión Nacional de Áreas Naturales Protegidas). 2018. "México cuida y protege especies prioritarias dentro de Áreas Naturales Protegidas." October 3. https://www.gob.mx/conanp/prensa/mexico-cuida-y-protege-especies-prio ritarias-dentro-de-areas-naturales-protegidas.

———. 2023. "Áreas Naturales Protegidas." May 8. https://www.gob.mx/conanp/do cumentos/areas-naturales-protegidas-278226?state=published.

Díaz, Floriberto. 2005. "Comunidad y comunalidad." In *Antología sobre culturas populares e indígenas. Lecturas del Seminario Diálogos en la Acción*, Vol. 2, ed. Lilian Scheffler Hudlet, Alejandro Agustin Guzman Contreras, Marina Anguiano Fernandez, et al., 365–373. Mexico City: Consejo Nacional para la Cultura y las Artes.

Eguiarte, Luis E. 2006. "Los murciélagos en México." *Arqueología Mexicana* 80: 24–25.

FAO (Organización de las Naciones Unidas para la Alimentación y la Agricultura). n.d. "REDD+ Reducción de las emisiones derivadas de la deforestación y la degradación de los bosques." https://www.fao.org/redd/overview/es/.

Fernández Lomelín, Luis Enrique. 2013. "Gestión Pluricultural del agua en un territorio indígena. El caso de Cuetzalan, Puebla: 1860–2011." PhD diss., El Colegio de Tlaxcala.

———. 2014. Interview by author, Cuetzalan, April 5.

García, Eligio. 2008. "La participación de comunidades mazahuas y otomíes en el manejo de los recursos naturales: conservación o deterioro en la Reserva de la Biosfera Mariposa Monarca (RBMM)." Master's tesis, Universidad Autónoma Metropolitana-Xochimilco.

Goebel McDermott, Anthony. 2013. *Los bosques del "progreso". Explotación forestal y régimen ambiental en Costa Rica: 1883–1955*. San José de Costa Rica: Universidad de Costa Rica.

Guerrero, Arturo. 2015. "La comunalidad como herramienta: una metáfora espiral." *Bajo el volcán* 15, no. 23: 113–129.

Hernández, Francisco Javier. 2018. "Los defensores de la vida contra los proyectos de muerte: Resistencias y Articulaciones frente a la industria extractiva en la Sierra Norte de Puebla." *Bajo el volcán* 18, no. 28: 109–143.

Hernández, Isabel Cristina, and Maria Alejandra Agudelo. 2019. "El pulpo que se alimenta de bananas, ¿continúa en centroamérica?." *Fragua* 12, no. 24: 45–62.

Hewitt de Alcantara, Cynthia. 1975. *La modernización de la agricultura mexicana. 1940–1970.* Mexico City: Siglo XXI Editores.

———. 2007. "Ensayo sobre los obstáculos al desarrollo rural en México. Retrospectiva y prospectiva." *Desacatos* 25: 79–10.

Hispanoteca. Lengua y cultura hispanas. n.d. "Mapa de las culturas mesoamericanas." http://hispanoteca.eu/Hispanoam%C3%A9rica/Mapa%20de%20Meso am%C3%A9rica.htm.

Holdridge, Leslie Ransselaer. 1967. *Life zone ecology.* San José de Costa Rica: Tropical Science Center

Infobae. 2014. "Mapa del día: descubre cuáles son los 17 países megadiversos." November 25. http://www.infobae.com/2014/09/09/1593463-mapa-del-dia-des cubre-cuales-sonlos-17-paises-megadiversos.

Londoño-Murcia, Maria Cecilia, and Victor Sánchez Cordero. 2011. "Distribución y conservación de especies amenazadas en Mesoamérica, Chocó y Andes tropicales." *Revista mexicana de biodiversidad* 82, no. 3: 926–950.

Martínez Luna, Jaime. 2015. "Conocimiento y comunalidad." *Bajo el Volcán* 15, no. 23: 99–112.

Massieu, Yolanda. 2016. "Sustentabilidad, soberanía alimentaria y políticas públicas en México: ¿misión imposible?." In *Reflexiones sobre seguridad alimentaria. Búsqueda y alternativas para el desarrollo de México,* ed. Felipe Torres Torres, María del Carmen del Valle, and Jessica Mariela Tolentin, 177–195. Mexico City: UNAM.

———. 2018. *Mirada de jaguar. Venturas y desventuras de la biodiversidad en América Latina.* Mexico City: Universidad Autónoma Metropolitana-Xochimilco.

Merino, Leticia. 2008. "Conservación comunitaria en la cuenca alta del Papaloapan, Sierra Norte de Oaxaca." *Nueva Antropología* 21, no. 68: 37–49.

Meza, Alejandra. 2014. "Masehuales y coyomes de Cuetzalan. Respuesta social: construcción de procesos en defensa del territorio." In *El México bárbaro del Siglo XXI,* ed. Carlos Rodríguez Wallenius and Ramsés Arturo Cruz Arenas, 169–181. Mexico City: Universidad Autónoma Metropolitana-Xochimilco.

Muller, Aldo, Gabriela Niño, Itzel Alcerreca, et al. "Análisis del presupuesto destinado a medio ambiente y cambio climpártico en el PEF 2021." *IKI Alliance México,* February 16. https://iki-alliance.mx/analisis-del-presupuesto-destinado-a-medio -ambiente-y-cambio-climatico-en-el-pef-2021/.

Nava, Elena. 2018. "La comunalidad oaxaqueña. Lucha y pensamiento indígena." In *Pensamiento indígena en Nuestramerica. Debates y propuestas en la mesa de hoy,* ed. Pedro Canales Tapia and Sebastião Vargas, 27–46. Santiago de Chile: Ariadna Ediciones.

Núñez, Irama, Edgar González Gaudiano, and Ana Barahona. 2003. "La biodiversidad. Historia y contexto de un concepto." *Interciencia* 28, no. 7: 387–393.

Ovando, Vilma, and Álvaro Herrera. 2010. *Conocimiento y conservación de la biodiversidad en Centroamérica*. San José de Costa Rica: Instituto Nacional de la Biodiversidad.

Reyez, José. 2016. "Áreas Naturales Protegidas, en el abandono." *Contralínea*, December 11. http://www.contralinea.com.mx/archivo-revista/index.php/2016/12/11/areas-naturales-protegidas-en-el-abandono/.

RRI (Rights + Resources). n.d. "The coalition. Partners and Colaborators." https://rightsandresources.org/who-we-are/the-coalition/partners-collaborators/.

Sarukhán, José, Patricia Koleff, Julia Carabias, et al. 2009. *Capital natural de México. Conocimiento actual, evaluación y perspectivas de sustentabilidad. Síntesis.* Mexico City: Comisión Nacional para el Conocimiento y Uso de la Biodiversidad.

SICAP [Sistema centroamericano de áreas protegidas]. 2003. *Informe regional del Convenio sobre la Diversidad Biológica*. Guatemala City.

Toledo, Víctor Manuel. 1994. "La diversidad biológica en México." *Ciencias* 34: 43–59.

Turvey, Samuel, and Jennifer Crees. 2019. "Extinction in the Anthropocene." *Current Biology* 29: R982-R986.

United Nations Environment Programme. 1992. *Convenio sobre la Diversidad Biológica*. May 22.

Villa, Rufina. 2018. Interview by author.

Welch, Craig. 2022. "Sin renacer de las cenizas: el cambio climático está terminando con los bosques nativos del planeta." *National Geographic*, May 1. https://www.ngenespanol.com/ecologia/bosques-como-los-afecta-el-cambio-climatico-y-sus-consecuencias/.

WWF (World Wildlife Fund). 2014. "Informe Planeta Vivo 2014." http://www.footprintnetwork.org/images/article_uploads/Informe-PlanetaVivo2014_LowRES.pdf.

———. 2016. "Informe Planeta Vivo 2016. Riesgo y resiliencia en una nueva era." https://wwflac.awsassets.panda.org/downloads/informe_planeta_vivo_2016_riesgo_y_resilencia_en_una_nueva_era.pdf.

Biodiversity in the Caribbean from 1950 to the Present

Ryan S. Mohammed and Lanya Fanovich

The Insular Caribbean has a great plethora of biodiversity. The Caribbean has been regarded as a biodiversity hotspot, with high levels of endemism in some northern regions and mainland species in some southern countries. The region's biodiversity has been documented since well before the 1950s, but knowledge transfer and sharing has been a persistent issue coupled with the major issue of biodiversity loss in the Great Acceleration (McNeill and Engelke 2016). Data and accurate documentation play an important role in species governance. First, much of the documentation was done by people who were not from the Caribbean, therefore, the information was taken with them when they returned to their home countries. Secondly, because several European countries claimed various Caribbean islands as overseas territories, data among islands was not exchanged. Finally, there was no data repository unless the species and specimens documented moved to a North American or European museum.

The Caribbean saw various periods of development and technological advancement that influenced biodiversity documentation. Several states had external owners and administrators from the 1950s to the 1960s, which had a direct impact on their actions. The Caribbean states were in a period of transition from the 1960s to the 1980s in which a number of islands had obtained independence from the United Kingdom and were creating their own economic base. From the 1980s to the 2000s, these countries were undergoing infrastructure stabilization and economic diversification. As communication and real-time documentation proliferated with the emergence of cyber technology in the 2000s, the global community shrank, resulting in the digitization of historic Caribbean records. The Global Biodiversity Information Facility (GBIF) is one such platform that has digitized these records. It is an international organization that focuses on making scientific data on biodiversity accessible online.

The GBIF has around 1 million records of digitized natural history specimens from the Caribbean. There are now 5 million data from the Caribbean from georeferenced images supplied via the citizen-science platforms iNaturalist and eBird (Sullivan et al. 2014). This is unsurprising given the region's high level of ecotourism.

Distant users of these digital datasets should be aware of potential biases related to tourist-derived data; for example, preserved specimens may have been obtained at different times and locations than tourist observations, and such biassed sampling can lead to inaccurate characterization of a species' biological niche (Boakes et al. 2010; Torres-Cristiani et al. 2020).

Several factors have led to the existence of biodiversity and its documentation in the Caribbean. These include governance, geography, geology, weather, and trade. To trace the changes in biodiversity documentation and distribution in the Caribbean, sixteen specific taxa have been chosen for discussion: *Anthozoans* (corals), *Elasmobranchs* (rays and sharks), *Cetaceans* (whales and dolphins), non-volant Mammals (non-flying terrestrials), Chiroptera (bats), *Anuran* (frogs and toads), *Boidae* (boas), Anolis lizards (Anole lizards), *Lepidopterans* (butterflies and moths), *Culicidae* (mosquitoes), *Macrobrachium* spp. (freshwater decapod Cretaceans), *Poeciliidae* fish (live-bearer fish), *Trochilidae* (hummingbirds), *Psittaciformes* (Parrots), *Rhizophora* spp. (mangroves), and *Arecaceae* (palms).

While it is possible to see a general trend of increased biodiversity documentation, one should not misinterpret this to imply there has been an increase in biodiversity densities or abundance. Additionally, with the recent advancements in taxonomy ranging from osteology to molecular biology, it would seem there has been an increase in species number, when in fact there has been a decrease in absolute species richness due to species loss. Also, the role of Indigenous and cultural influences on the acceptance and management of biodiversity cannot be negated, as entities such as IUCN (International Union for Conservation of Nature) and IPBES (Intergovernmental Science-Policy Platform on Biodiversity and Ecosystem Services) have recognized theses as avenues for traditional knowledge.

Political Governance and the Influences on Biodiversity Documentation

Between 1950 and 1960, most Caribbean Island states were governed by either European countries or the U.S. whilst most of the Greater Antilles had reached formal independence during the nineteenth century (Haiti 1804, Dominican Republic 1844, Cuba 1902). While the United States of America retained administrative control over the U.S. Virgin Islands and Puerto Rico, the other islands were possessed by the United Kingdom, France, or the Netherlands. During this decade, agriculture dominated the islands' economy, cultivating tobacco, cacao, coffee, and sugarcane. The plantation economy was built on agricultural mass production, typically of a few commodity crops produced on enormous farms toiled over by slaves or laborers. This had a direct impact on the landscape because slash and burn of primary forest for plantation production – inherited during the main colonial periods – was prevalent.

From 1954 to 2010, the Netherlands Antilles consisted of five Dutch island territories. From 1958 until 1962, the United Kingdom founded the West Indies Federation, a political union comprised of eleven English-speaking Caribbean nations, all of which were British dependencies at the time. This was short-lived, as most of the British holdings in the Caribbean achieved political independence between the 1960s and 1980s, beginning with Jamaica in 1962 as a consequence of the Jamaican Independence Act, followed by Trinidad and Tobago (1962), Barbados (1966), Bahamas (1973), Grenada (1974), Dominica (1978), St. Lucia (1979), St. Vincent (1979), Antigua and Barbuda (1981), and St. Kitts and Nevis (1983). Jamaica joined the Commonwealth of Nations as a Commonwealth realm after independence, a process that was followed by all other independent islands. With this, the Cayman Islands reverted to direct British authority from being a self-governing part of Jamaica. France and the Netherlands continue to have considerable Caribbean territories, followed by the United Kingdom and the United States of America.

Private collecting of specimens throughout the colonial period influenced where and how natural historical resources were stored, as well as who had access to them. Despite the importance of private collections in evolutionary biology, scientists have restricted access to them. For example, only three Dominican amber fossils of Anolis lizards have been described prior to the recent publication of seventeen privately-owned fossils of this species, demonstrating the stability of several these ecomorphs since the Miocene (Sherratt et al 2015). In other instances, although some private collections are vast (e.g., the Barcant butterfly collection in Angostura, Trinidad) and open to the public for viewing, not all are well-curated, and the lack of specimen metadata (e.g., locality, collection date) may limit their discoverability and research utility. Furthermore, historical data has influenced the distribution of some taxa because these earlier collections were based on proximity to core settlement or colonial operations. Another example is the Imperial College of Tropical Agriculture (ICTA) museum, which was founded in Trinidad in 1921 and focused on agricultural pests. In 1960, The University of the West Indies absorbed both the National Herbarium of Trinidad and the ICTA agricultural collection. However, thanks to the founding of ICTA, Trinidad and Tobago now have a close to 100,000 of locally curated specimens. The ICTA collection is now housed in the University of the West Indies Zoology Museum (UWIZM).

Caribbean's Biogeography

The West Indies are an archipelago with more than one thousand islands that separate the Atlantic Ocean from the Caribbean Sea and cover a distance of 2,700 km from Trinidad and Tobago to the most western tip of Cuba. They are not in contact with the continents although they are relatively close, at about a distance of 20 km between Trinidad and South America and 210 km between Cuba and Yucatan. These islands are generally divided into three smaller archipelagos with different topography and independent geological history, i.e., the Lesser Antilles, Greater Antilles, and the Bahamas Archipelago (Bahamas Islands + Turks and Caicos Islands). The Lesser Antilles belong to a small volcanic arc with about twenty-one main islands and numerous islets and keys dating from Mid Eocene (about 45 Myr.) with an approximate total area of 8,320 km². These islands are commonly referred to as the Windward and the Leeward Islands according to their position relative to the prevailing winds.

The geography and climate in the Caribbean region vary. Some islands in the region have relatively flat terrain of non-volcanic origin. These may comprise of carbonate substrate originating from ancient coral reefs. Aruba, Curaçao, Barbados, Bonaire, the Cayman Islands, Saint Croix, the Bahamas, and Antigua are among these coralline islands. The origins of several islands are volcanic as the Caribbean subduction plate moves eastward below the Atlantic resulting in the high elevation mountains of the Lesser Antilles. The active volcanic geology of Dominica, Montserrat, St. Vincent, and Grenada all contribute to the steep topography. In comparison to mountainous locations that have tropical rainforest conditions, flatter places are often drier and have savannah-type or desert conditions. The steep sided nature of these peaks usually give rise to dendritic natural drainages radiating towards the coastline. The combination of volcanic calcium carbonate geology also allows for the formation of cave networks on various islands, which also provide habitats for unique faunas. Trinidad is unique as it is considered a continental island since it connects to the South American tectonic plate and was joined to the mainland as recently as 10,000 years ago. Tobago was also connected to Trinidad as recently as 20,000 years ago based on Glyptodon scutes found there. Glyptodon, an extinct group of large, herbivorous armadillos of the genus of glyptodont, lived from the Pliocene, around 3.2 million years ago, to the early Holocene, around 11,000 years ago, in Brazil, Venezuela, Uruguay, Paraguay, Bolivia, Peru, Argentina, and Colombia.

Trinidad's recent connection to the mainland in geological time scale has also influenced its flora and fauna as they share hundreds of genera and both provide a neotropical habitat. Additionally, because of the north-flowing Atlantic Ocean's currents, colonizing events have occurred resulting in some the of Lesser Antillean Islands sharing similar taxa to the mainland. The larger islands of the Greater Antilles have not only tropical rain forest but also a high level of endemism. This is particularly true for the avifauna as Jamaica has twenty-eight single-island endemics, Dominican Republic thirty-three, and Puerto Rico eighteen.

Diversification is promoted by opportunities for allopatric divergence between islands, or within the large islands of the Greater Antilles, with a classic example provided by the Anolis lizards. The timing of colonization events using molecular clocks permits analysis of colonization–extinction dynamics by means of species accumulation curves. These indicate low rates of colonization and extinction for reptiles and amphibians in the Greater Antilles, with estimated average persistence times of lineages in the West Indies exceeding 30 Myr. Even though individual island bird populations might persist an average of 2 Myr on larger islands in the Lesser Antilles, recolonization from within the archipelago appears to maintain avian lineages within the island chain indefinitely. The Caribbean was fairly shielded from the impacts of the last ice age and benefited from some colonizing effects. However, birds of the Lesser Antilles also provide evidence of a mass extinction event within the past million years, emphasizing the time-heterogeneity of historical processes. Geographical dynamics are matched by ecological changes in the distribution of species within islands over time resulting from adaptive radiation and shifts in habitat, often following repeatable patterns.

Weather is another major contributor to the region's biodiversity. While the region is normally sunny most of the year, the wet season lasts from May to November, and the dry season lasts from December to April. The rainy season is counterintuitively warmer, although the air temperature is high for most of the year, ranging from 25 to 33°C between the two seasons. The hurricane season lasts from June to November, impacting islands with a hurricane belt that arcs to the northwest of Grenada and to the west of Barbados. While the frequency and intensity of storms peak in August and September and affect the Caribbean's northern islands more often, recorded data over the years have shown an increase in the intensity and frequency of tropical storms over the last decade. While there has been a cyclical association between the number of named tropical storms and years from 1950 to 2015, with an average of ten to fourteen systems per year, this has subsequently increased, with the average for the last five years (2019–2023) exceeding twenty. This can have a negative impact on biodiversity by shortening the recovery time for recolonization and population re-establishment. Additionally, pioneer species, also known as 'R' strategists, emerge first and are likely to have invasive species attributes.

For some islands, topography can influence localized weather, such as in Trinidad and Tobago. Multiple low-pressure cyclonic weather systems originating in the east are rejected by Trinidad's norther mountain range, which serves as a buffer for the entire island. This along with its proximity to South America, explains Trinidad's low number of named tropical storms.

Floral and Faunal Examples of Biodiversity within the Caribbean

Over 10,000 species have been identified in the Caribbean. The following taxonomic groupings were chosen because they represented a diverse range of biodiversity, including flora and fauna, as well as freshwater, marine, and terrestrial habitats.

These groups also exhibit spatial and temporal documentation trends. The data for these sixteen taxa was extracted from the GBIF database to assess their species richness over the years across the insular Caribbean as depicted in Figures 1a and 1b. The database includes confirmed recordings from the iNaturalist online platform as well as data from eBird. Both rely heavily on citizen-based and community science. Even with sources and confirmations from global taxonomists and its myriad of positive aspects, there are still shortcomings in this mega-global dataset. One persistent difficulty with many specimens accessioned at regional museums is that they have not been described or identified. The Lepidopterans are a notable example of this, with almost 2,000 unidentified entries in the GBIF database of 4,010 (for the insular Caribbean) noted. Additionally, the graphs presented utilize data sourced up till the incomplete 2024 year. Therefore, an unrealistic decrease in all graphs is noted.

Fig. 1a: Total number of observations for Anthozoa, Elasmobranchii, Cetaceans, Non-volant Mammals, Chiroptera, Anurans, Boas, and Anolis per year across the insular Caribbean

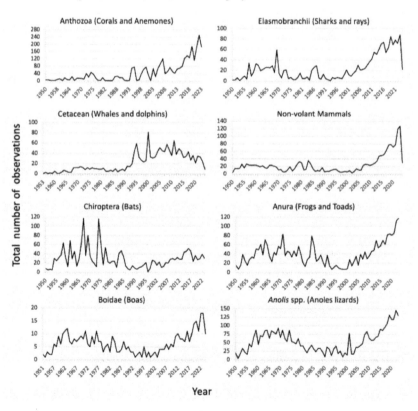

Source: Author's elaboration from GBIF data

Fig. 1b: Total number of observations for Lepidoptera, Culicidae, Macrobrachium, Poecilldae, Trochilidae, Psittaciformes, Rhizophora, and Arecaceae across the insular Caribbean

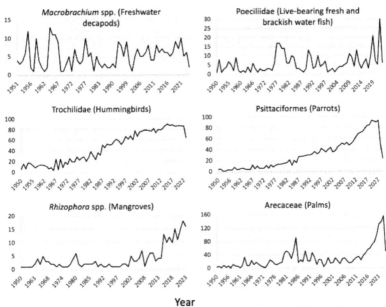

Source: Author's elaboration from GBIF data

The trends resulting from a paucity of data between 1950 and 1960 are instantly visible for all sixteen groups. During this time, however, Cuba, the Dominican Republic, and Haiti dominated species recording. This was due to the establishment of early museum collections in these countries. Trinidad also benefited from the ICTA collection, which focused on agricultural pests and pollinators. As a result, most Lepidopteran records during that time came from Trinidad. Culicidae (mosquitoes) collection were also from the CAREC (Caribbean Epidemiological Centre). The Caribbean Epidemiology Centre (CAREC) was established in January 1975 succeeding the Trinidad Regional Virus Laboratory (TRVL). The TRVL itself was established in 1952 by the Rockefeller Foundation in partnership with the Trinidad and Tobago Government. TRVL was engaged in much work on insect, tick, and mite-transmitted viruses, commonly called arboviruses. There was also a great focus on yellow fever, as well as the Mayaro and Oropouche viruses, the latter being mosquito-borne. This strongly influenced the peak of documented occurrences of mosquitoes during the 1950s to 1960s. The CAREC and ICTA collections have both been incorporated into the UWIZM collection. The UWIZM also houses insect collections of the Centre for Agriculture and Bioscience International (CABI) from the period of 1970s-90s.

Additionally, bat biodiversity was high on the scientific agenda during this period since a Trinidadian bacteriologist (Dr. Lennox Pawan) was the first to demonstrate that vampire bats could transmit rabies to other animals and people (Pawan 1936). Considering that most British colonies had small livestock holdings, this constituted a public health concern. Research in Caribbean bat populations continued for the next two decades, with most entries coming from Trinidad and Tobago. Non-volant mammals saw an increase in data entries after the 2000s as more reliable, cheaper, and portable camera trapping technology and devices became available. This was directly attributed to the digital storage of photographs via computer hard drives, SD card memories, and global cyber storage of information. These technological improvements also meant more cameras could be deployed for extended periods with increased resolution and sensitivities. The same could be said for shark data collection, as well. The Global Fin Print initiative has been using baited remote underwater videos (BRUV) for documentation, helping determine the density and diversity of sharks and rays (MacNeil et al. 2020; Simpfendorfer et al. 2023). Fanovich et al. (2017) also utilized citizen science to add to the distribution documentation of elasmobranchs in Tobago.

The documentation of marine mammals has had more emphasis within the last three decades. There has been increased concern for the effect of man-made noise pollution in the ocean, particularly upon cetaceans, which are known to be sensitive to sound. Several Caribbean countries usually mandate offshore industrial and commercial activities to have on board a Marine Mammal Observer (MMO). This has led to more data being collected for the Caribbean region. Also, Dominica created the world's first marine protected area for sperm whales in 2023, and the Bahamas now actively promotes community science for marine mammal documentation, resulting in recent spikes in whale documentation. These islands are home to at least twenty-five species of marine mammals in Abaco. Similarly, the Dutch Antillean islands established a shark and whale conservation region within the last decade. Collectively, Caribbean mammalian fauna now includes terrestrial and aquatic animals like global Cetaceans, bats, manatees, and the venomous Hispaniolan solenodon, making the region species rich in this taxonomic class (Fig. 2).

Fig. 2: Total Mammalian Species Richness for the Caribbean. GBIF data 1950 to 2022

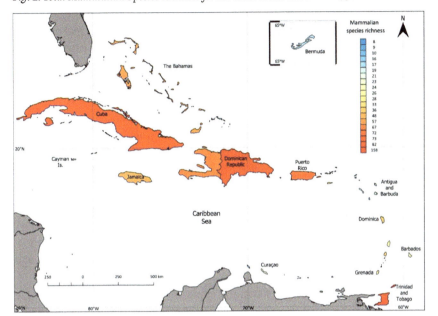

Source: GBIF (n.d.)

Between 1960 and 1980, the ICTA collections and recordings were transferred to the UWIZM, Trinidad. Herpetofauna, specifically anurans and lizards (especially *Anolis spp.*), were frequently documented by the Hispanic islands, including Puerto Rico. It should be noted that both Cuba and Hispaniola have a high level of endemism. As evidenced by the low number of species registrations with corals, there was minimal emphasis placed on marine and coastal biodiversity in the Caribbean.

Documentation of Lepidopterans reduced from the 1980s to the 2000s, since potentially only new species were recorded on the GBIF database. This pattern was also observed in Anurans and *Anolis spp*. The decrease during this time could be attributed to political challenges in Cuba and Haiti, as fewer resources were (probably) dedicated to biodiversity monitoring. However, data on hummingbird richness in the insular Caribbean continued to rise.

Overall, data entry increased in the 2000s. This is attributable to a few factors. For starters, the availability of the internet and computerized documentation enabled more data to be recorded and verified. In addition, the launch of the eBird online platform in 2002 resulted in citizen scientists playing an essential part in documenting bird diversity and distribution, for example hummingbird and parrot documentation benefitted from these platforms. iNaturalist, launched in 2008, also became an important tool for both researchers and amateur naturalists to access online taxonomic and species identification. During this time, genetic analysis technology reached its pinnacle.

New species were discovered by collecting expeditions as well as analyzing museum specimens. Because of this, poecilids and herpetofauna gained several new species. This can be seen in the records of the boas, anurans, and anoles. Murphy (1997) documented 129 species for Trinidad Tobago, however two decades later Murphy et al. (2018) were able to document 140 more. Since then, there has been both new discoveries in the wild as well as new classifications. Most recently the green anaconda has been re-classified into the original *Eunectes murinus*, or southern green anaconda, and *Eunectes akayima*, the northern green anaconda, which are genetically 5.5 percent different (Rivas et al. 2024). This validates molecular testing of Trinidad's green anaconda populations as there are distinct populations in the southwest as well as the east.

Some species, such as those belonging to the *Macrobrachium* decapod crustaceans or freshwater shrimp, were consistently low in recordings. This was mostly because the Caribbean has less than forty *Macrobrachium* species (Chase Jr. and Hobbs 1969).

While this new genetic evaluation method benefitted coral populations, the 2000s also raised climatic worries. The earliest literature on the Caribbean's coral – published in 1959 (See Goreau 1959) – already highlighted concerns in Jamaica's reef assemblages. Conversely, Guggenheim (2022) has highlighted some regional successes. Nonetheless, concerns about sea-level rise and the destruction of coastal districts began to emerge in the media and among the general public. The Caribbean's marine diversity was now being prioritized. This was demonstrated by the increase in the number of species recorded for both corals and *Rhizophora* mangrove species. The Greater Antilles mangrove ecoregion comprises various coastal areas in Cuba, Hispaniola, Puerto Rico, and Jamaica.

The Greater Antilles mangroves vary in development, from scrub vegetation found as coastal fringe to well-developed stands with heights of up to 25 m found at river mouths. Despite numerous floristic studies of the Caribbean region, the large-scale evolutionary origins, distribution, and diversity remain relatively underexplored. For example, there is no data for the wild ferns within the Caribbean on the GBIF database. Additionally, there is still no checklist for freshwater macrovegetation for the Caribbean.

The frequency of major hurricanes (+3 category storms) in the Caribbean increased between 2010 and 2020. Several taxa show dips in data entry during this period due to both a decrease in biodiversity and in infrastructure to document findings. The global halt caused by the COVID-19 pandemic from 2019 to 2021 also resulted in a decline in the number of species reported, as shown in the graphs. Apart from limited outdoor activities for collecting, several laboratories were closed regionally at this time; therefore, there were no genetic or taxonomic investigations into biodiversity. It is expected that an increase in data entry for the Caribbean in 2022 and the years following is likely. The use of smartphones and artificial intelligence technologies will make it increasingly easier to upload photographs that have been georeferenced, given a taxonomic review, uploaded in seconds, and transmitted around the world.

Culture and Folklore - the Social Side of Biodiversity

Culture, as defined by the Cambridge Dictionary, "is the way of life, especially the general customs and beliefs, of a particular group of people at a particular time." Additionally, "it is also the attitudes, behavior, and opinions of a particular group of people within society." Folklore is the "lore (stories, customs, beliefs) of a group of people" that is passed down through generations, and is primarily learned through oral stories, performance, or craft. It is used to pass on and preserve cultural customs and beliefs of a group of people.

Within the Caribbean, there are several historical influences from Europe as well as from days of African slavery, East Indian indentureship, and Chinese immigration during and after their colonial past. Coupled with the various Indigenous tribes of the Caribbean, namely Kalinago or Caribs, the Arawaks, and the Warao. The perspectives of these groups are now pooled culturally and are influenced by local biodiversity, which can affect their perception of it. For example, serpents have a negative stigma rooted in Christianity and, to some extent, in Islam as well, while being revered in Hindu texts. This plethora of groups undoubtedly influences Caribbean folklore and culture.

Tales of folklore legends include Mama D'lo, a mythical character one might hear about in Trinidad and Dominica. Her name comes from Mama D'leau, loosely translating to "mother of water" in French. She is described as a beautiful woman from the waist up that owns a golden comb, which she uses to comb her long hair. From the waist down, she has the body of a green anaconda and lives in rivers deep within forests, hiding this part of her underwater. While Trinidad is the only Caribbean island with a native population of green anaconda, there are large snakes, such as boas, in Dominica. Both islands have an intricate network of natural drainages. Another folklore character tied to ecosystems is Papa Bois. Stories of him can be heard in Trinidad and St. Lucia. His name loosely translates to "father of the forest" in French. He is one of the oldest characters of Caribbean lore, with some historians saying that he was known as far back as the first inhabitants of the Caribbean islands. Papa Bois is the protector of the plants and animals of the forests (Besson 2001). Half animal and half human, the lower portion of his body is that of a goat while the upper part (his head, chest, and arms) is that of a man, except for the two horns coming out of his forehead. Together, they protect the animals and ecosystems. Mama D'lo protects them from humans who poach, pollute the water, and needlessly kill animals. Unlike her husband, she protects the animals under her care by luring hunters with her beautiful face and her singing, then capturing and sometimes killing them with the strength of her anaconda tail. Papa Bois is said to metamorphose, but he always has a horn either on his belt or on a necklace around his neck. He uses this horn to warn the animals that humans are nearby, defending his forest by changing into other characters to scare or lure away humans who are damaging it. Whilst Papa Bois's origins might be linked to the Indigenous groups of the Caribbean, Mama D'lo has origins in Africa and Europe as we see similarities between her portrayal and that of the Greek Gorgon Medusa.

Other characters have remained consistent throughout time through both oral and written stories such as the Anansi, whose name translates literally to spider. He is an Akan folktale character who is often depicted as his name suggests – associated with stories, wisdom, knowledge, and trickery. Taking the role of a trickster, he is also one of the most important characters of West African, African American, and West Indian folklore. Anansi stories originate in Ghana, and the tales were transmitted to the Caribbean by way of the transatlantic slave trade. Anansi is best known for his ability to outsmart and triumph over more powerful opponents through his use of cunning, creativity, and wit. Despite taking on a trickster role, Anansi often takes center stage in stories and is commonly portrayed as both the protagonist and antagonist.

Culturally, within the Caribbean, there is some degree of fear towards herpetofauna though. Snakes have traditionally been seen as evil or providers of bad omens. On the other hand, the consumption of some large lizards, such as tegus and iguanas, is socially acceptable in the southern Caribbean islands. Marine turtle consumption has a wide range of acceptance. St. Kitts has a season for turtle hunting, but it is illegal to be in possession of any part of a turtle in Trinidad and Tobago. Additionally, Simpson (1962) documented several folklore medicines in Trinidad which utilized frogs and tortoise among other animals as ingredients!

The consumption of sharks is seen as a major street food in Trinidad and Tobago but as unclean on other islands. The Lesser Antillean islands also accept whale hunting, and it is not uncommon to see pilot whale dishes at restaurants being sold as 'black fish.' Therefore, folklore and culture can influence the management of biodiversity, but also biodiversity influences folklore and regional stories.

Caribbean's Threat to Biodiversity 1950 to Today

There are several threats to biodiversity in the Caribbean. Natural threats, such as volcanic activity on Montserrat and St. Vincent within the last decade, has led to changes in species composition of chordates such as birds, mammals, and herpetofauna. These eruptions also affect neighboring islands with their plumes of ash smothering the landscape. Additionally, the above-normal 2023 Atlantic hurricane season was characterized by record-warm Atlantic Sea surface temperatures and a strong El Niño (NOAA 2023). The Atlantic basin saw twenty named storms in 2023, which ranked fourth for the most named storms in a year since 1950 (2020 having thirty named systems) (Colorado State University 2023).

The primary threat to the Caribbean's biodiversity, however, is humanity. Some anthropogenic repercussions are immediate, while others are the result of a century of poor global decisions. Climate change and development are both linked to biodiversity loss. Domestic, industrial, and commercial infrastructure development contributes to climate change, and vice versa.

Climate change poses a threat to many aspects of existence; the Caribbean is not immune. With hundreds of islands composing the Caribbean archipelago, aside from the growing concern of rising sea levels affecting coastal communities, the loss of brackish and freshwater habitats is also worrying. While the biodiversity of these ecosystems will be negatively affected by this impact, the major effects will only be evident fifty years from now. The more imminent threats are the changes in our weather patterns. During the previous five decades, the severity and frequency of named tropical cyclones have steadily increased. These systems accelerate the loss of habitat for coastal ecosystems such as coral reefs and seagrass beds as well as terrestrial habitats, ridding tropical forests of foliage and canopy. Conversely, increases in drought conditions have led to islandic desertification (NOAA 2023).

While it is true that Caribbean flora and fauna are highly adaptive and that there are multiple biomes within the region that maintain this plethora of unique biodiversity, the rate of change in ecosystem composition cannot be supported by populations. Anthropogenic impacts exacerbate the situation.

The main anthropogenic stressor is habitat loss for infrastructure development. While it is important for society to develop to provide better conditions for island residents, we must remain cognizant that this development must be managed and sustainable so that it does not pose a threat or loss of ecosystems now or in the future. That is the major challenge. Because islands have limited land availability, continued expansion would result in fewer natural ecosystems. This, in turn, can lead to problems such as urban heat islands, which elevate temperatures even higher. Additionally, with urbanization comes waste production. Natural habitats on tropical islands are also being destroyed by landfills. These landfills not only degrade natural habitat, but they also emit greenhouse gases like methane during anaerobic decomposition. This, in turn, contributes to issues of climate change and long-term ocean level rise. In both Trinidad and Tobago and St. Lucia, for example, there was double the amount of municipal waste being sent to landfills between 2000 and 2004 (Phillips and Thorne 2004).

Forest fires are another major threat to biodiversity. Dry conditions might be related to lack of rainfall and changes to regional weather patterns and climate change. However, the Caribbean forest fires have been linked to intentional burning for unregulated slash-and-burn practices. In addition, sporadic burning due to decomposition of moist organic matter has generated enough heat to dry surface organic matter, thereby providing kindling for these same fires. In Trinidad and Tobago, the peak fire season typically begins in early January and lasts around four weeks. This coincides with the dry season for the country. There were nine fire alerts reported up to March 2024, when only considering high confidence alerts. This is high compared to the total for previous years going back to 2012. 2016 recorded the most fires in a year, with 28. From 2001 to 2022, Trinidad and Tobago lost 696 ha of tree cover from fires and 22.8 ha from all other drivers of habitat loss. The year with the most tree cover loss due to fires during this period was 2010 with 201 ha lost to fires – 5.9 percent of all tree cover loss for that year. Between March 8, 2021 and March 4, 2024, Trinidad and Tobago experienced a total of 2,692 fire alerts (Global Forest Watch 2024).

There are also transboundary oceanic issues such as the spread of *Sargassum*. Historically, the majority of *Sargassum* was in the Sargasso Sea in the western North Atlantic. In 2011, the geographic range of *Sargassum* expanded, driven by shifting wind patterns. The pelagic macroalgae is now thriving in the open ocean in a region referred to as the "Great Atlantic Sargassum Belt." Massive amounts of *Sargassum* from this area are transported west into the Caribbean Sea, Gulf of Mexico, and tropical South Atlantic via ocean currents. *Sargassum* inundation events occur annually when rafts of this algae are carried to shore by winds and currents. These events are a type of harmful algal bloom that can adversely impact coastal ecosystems, tourism, and public health. Massive amounts of *Sargassum* can form brown tides nearshore, smothering fauna and flora – including coral reefs. *Sargassum* mats may also clog water intake pipes used in critical infrastructure (for example, in desalination plants that produce drinking water). *Sargassum* also contains high levels of arsenic and other heavy metals, organic contaminants, and marine debris. *Sargassum* decomposing on the beach produces hydrogen sulfide, a gas that smells like rotten eggs, which can cause respiratory irritation. Cleanup options are limited and costly (NOAA 2024). Several Caribbean Islands, such as Trinidad and Tobago, have developed Sargassum Management Plans; however, their implementation seems to be restrictive as budget issue arises.

Another transboundary problem would be the ongoing threat of oceanic petrochemical spills. The region's largest oil rig spill within the past decades occurred in the Gulf of Mexico. The Deepwater Horizon oil spill occurred on April 20, 2010, approximately 66 km off the coast of Louisiana – and its subsequent sinking on April 22. The largest oil tanker spill occurred in the Caribbean on July 19, 1979. Two oil tankers, the SS Atlantic Empress and the Aegean Captain, crossed paths and collided resulting in the fifth largest spill 28km off of Tobago. The Atlantic Empress sank, having spilled 287,000 metric tons of crude oil into the Caribbean Sea. By comparison, the 2010 Deepwater Horizon oil spill dispersed approximately 585,000 tons (5 million barrels) of oil, a natural disaster with impacts still being seen today (Loop News 2019). Most recently, an oil spill was spotted by the Trinidad and Tobago Coast Guard on February 7, 2024. They traced it to a barge that had become lodged on a reef about 150m off Tobago's southern coast. The contents of the leaking barge drifted as far as Bonaire.

Both *Sargassum* and petrochemical leaks seem to be issues needing regional securities and legislation. One can only hope the regional body CARICOM (Caribbean Community), which has the Caribbean heads of state as its country representatives, actively implements measures to address future transboundary issues.

Illegal immigration is yet another issue that can address biodiversity (Mohammed and van Oosterhout 2020). Besides climate change and unsustainable exploitation of the environment, socioeconomic inequality and political unrest may also contribute to infectious disease outbreaks and changes in biodiversity in the Caribbean archipelago. Migration among rural coastal communities can reduce the effectiveness of disease monitoring and hinder the isolation of people in infected communities – both strategies underpinning integrated control of emerging infectious disease (EID).

Caribbean islands experience high rates of unregulated immigration from several South American countries. The worsening economic and political situation in Venezuela in 2018 coincided with a sudden marked rise in malaria, with a reported 51 percent prevalence. This, in combination with civil unrest, may result in more frequent Caribbean malaria outbreaks in the future.

Since the early 2000s, the Caribbean has been considered completely malaria-free. Caribbean small island developing states have maintained this status through an integrated control approach, including continued and intensive monitoring, isolation of individuals within infected communities, the control of mosquito breeding sites by draining stagnant water bodies, community fumigation, and other environmental management schemes.

Anopheles is the mosquito vector of *Plasmodium*; understanding this vector underpins effective malaria control strategies. This mosquito tolerates brackish water habitats, and recent global environmental changes and unsustainable environmental exploitation have increased the size of this habitat. For example, approximately 10 percent of Trinidad's coastline is fringed by mangrove ecosystems, which buffer inland saltwater intrusion. However, the loss of coastal mangroves caused by increased sea level and coastal erosion, coupled with coastal infrastructural development, has resulted in saltwater intrusion of watersheds and inland colonization by mangroves. This habitat provides fertile new breeding grounds for vectors such as brackish water-tolerant mosquitoes. In addition, the increased frequency of tropical storms across the Atlantic and flooding creates more stagnant water habitats for mosquito reproduction. These changes undermine the treatment of stagnant water habitats that a successful approach to controlling emerging infectious diseases relies on.

Control of EIDs such as arboviruses and malaria requires increased resources from governments, particularly for disease monitoring in rural, coastal communities. However, more needs to be done. The United Nations has declared 2021 to 2031 as the Decade of Ocean Science for Sustainable Development. The aim is to reverse declining oceanic health caused by climate change. Control of EIDs, however, is equally crucial, and this initiative has potentially much wider implications, as the One Health approach suggests. Marine spatial planning, a strategy for capitalizing on the blue economy, directly addresses habitat use and loss. Particularly in the Caribbean, this strategy should focus on halting the erosion of coastal mangroves.

Like the rest of the world, the small island developing states of the Caribbean face a multitude of challenges related to the mass movement of human populations, elevated ambient air temperatures, changes in weather and rainfall patterns, coastal erosion, human-induced habitat change, and the spread of infectious disease vectors. These changes put additional pressure on the control of EIDs, with the consequence that Caribbean states may soon no longer be considered completely malaria-free. Indeed, the status of EIDs is in constant need of reevaluation, demanding increased investment with the vision that the health and well-being of the people depend on the health and well-being of their environment. For example, the Mayaro arborvirus, which has its origins in South and Central America, is predicted to become a major epidemic in the future, following in the steps of the recent pandemics caused by Chikungunya and Zika viruses. The vector mosquito *Haeamogus sp* was typically found in tropical inland forests, but now, as coastal temperatures rise consistently, it is also found within mangrove ecosystems, as well.

Additionally, illegal immigrants settle in areas where infrastructure to support communities might not exist, creating areas for disease pools. They also exploit wildlife in the newly settled areas as a means of sustenance. This constitutes poaching as it occurs without consideration of laws and regulations. The illegal movement into countries also allows for an illegal wildlife trade. This has the additional issues of introducing zoonotic disease and vector-borne diseases, as well as transmitting alien invasive species. Legal immigrants have their own practices, too, which may seem hygienic and acceptable in their own countries but have negative impacts on their health. One such example lies with Chinese immigrants who see it as acceptable to slaughter domestic cats and dogs. Another example was noted with both the Chinese and Venezuelan communities decimating some freshwater fish and crustacean communities in rivers in Trinidad. While this is not intended to promote xenophobia, the lack of food resources has led to biodiversity exploitation. On the other hand, there was also the case of Nigerian immigrants housing Giant

African Land snails, *Achatina fulica*. In 2008, this alien invasive species escaped and first appeared in wild populations in Trinidad. It has since spread to different parts of the country. This is one of the world's most destructive land snails, making it a quarantine importance.

Prior to the 1960s, several islands relied on agriculture to sustain their economies. More infrastructure, however, was required as economies diversified towards tourism and commerce. Apart from an upsurge in the mining industries to export and import aggregate and damming for water supply, habitat loss was caused by the construction sector.

The Caribbean was thought to be a biodiversity hotspot, particularly in the previous two decades of more consistent documenting of discoveries, as noted in the GBIF dataset. As the rate of climate change shows no signs of slowing, one should expect soon a plateau in biodiversity richness recordings followed by a general fall. Unsustainable development will not only continue but will also be sponsored and fueled by commerce from First World countries. The Caribbean will be in dire need of biodiversity protection if there is no direct legislative policy in place.

International Treaties, Agreements, and Biodiversity Programs within the Caribbean

The Caribbean archipelago represents a biodiversity hot spot (Fig. 2). This has afforded a few insular states to become members of several international bodies and treaties or qualify to access international funding for the purposes of biodiversity conservation. However, not all island states have come on board these platforms. For example, there are currently no IUCN substantive government members belonging to the insular Caribbean. Ironically, there are no GBIF participants within the insular Caribbean, even though most of the biodiversity data for the Caribbean is stored in GBIF and IUCN international databases. GBIF also offers grants for the development of local databases that can be linked to their international servers. Other conventions, treaties, and protocols have had some limited successes in obtaining and ratifying signatories though. These international agreements address issues such as chemical use and movement as well as access to information, which all have a direct influence on the management of biodiversity within the insular Caribbean. This is of particular importance considering the transboundary problems highlighted above.

The Regional Agreement on Access to Information, Public Participation, and Justice in Environmental Matters in Latin America and the Caribbean, known as the Escazú Agreement, was the first international treaty in the region concerning the environment and the first in the world to include provisions on the rights of environmental defenders. This agreement strengthens the links between human rights and environmental protection by imposing requirements upon member states concerning the rights of environmental defenders. This also aims to provide full public access to environmental information, environmental decision-making, and legal protection and recourse concerning environmental matters. It also recognizes the right of current and future generations to a healthy environment and sustainable development (United Nations 2018). However, less than 20 percent Caribbean island state signatories have ratified it. Another under-subscribed protocol is the Nagoya Protocol. This international agreement is aimed at sharing the benefits arising from the utilization of genetic resources in a fair and equitable manner. Still, only Antigua and Barbuda, Cuba, the Dominican Republic, Guyana, and St. Kitts and Nevis have ratified this agreement.

The Convention for the Protection and Development of the Marine Environment of the Wider Caribbean Area (known as the Cartagena Convention) was adopted in Cartagena, Colombia in 1983 and entered into force in 1986. At the time, it was the only legally binding environmental treaty in the Wider Caribbean. The Cartagena Protocol on Biosafety to the Convention on Biological Diversity (CBD) is an international agreement that aims to ensure the safe handling, transport, and use of living modified organisms (LMOs) resulting from modern biotechnology that may have adverse effects on biological diversity, taking also into account risks to human health. The Cartagena Convention presents a legal structure under which members are required to act with the goal of preventing, controlling, and reducing pollution of the Convention area from sources such as pollution from ships, dumping, land-based sources, sea-bed exploration, or exploitation and atmospheric discharges under party jurisdiction. The Cartagena Convention also requires that all parties take measures to protect and preserve rare or fragile ecosystems and the habits of endangered species within the convention zone. Additionally, the Land-Based Sources (LBS) Protocol was a response to the insights gained from this assessment and other evidence identifying the main point sources of marine pollution in the Convention Area. The protocol was adopted to the Cartagena Convention in 1999 and entered into force in 2010. However, only eight Caribbean Island states are ratified members of the LBS Protocol. There are, however, eleven Contracting Parties to the Cartagena Convention and the Oil Spills Protocol within the Caribbean. Another avenue of the Cartegena Convention is the Protocol Concerning Specially Protected Areas and Wildlife to the Convention for the Protection and Development of the Marine Environment of the Wider Caribbean Region ("SPAW Protocol"). This entered into force on June 18, 2000, and currently has only five contracted members within the insular Caribbean.

The Basel Convention on the Control of Transboundary Movements of Hazardous Wastes and Their Disposal is an international treaty that was designed to reduce the movements of hazardous waste between nations and specifically to prevent the transfer of hazardous waste from developed to less developed countries. Here again, only 20 percent of the insular states are signatories. In addition to this, the Rotterdam Convention specifies and highlights trade issues with hazardous chemicals. It is aimed at promoting and sharing responsibilities in relation to the importation of these products. The convention promotes the open exchange of information and calls on exporters of hazardous chemicals to use proper labeling, include directions on safe handling, and inform purchasers of any known restrictions or bans. Signatory nations can decide whether to allow or ban the importation of chemicals listed in the treaty, and exporting countries are obliged to make sure that producers within their jurisdiction comply. Roughly one-third of all insular territories have become signatories.

The GEF ISLANDS project is currently seeking to address the issue of waste management though. This recognizes Small Island Developing States (SIDS) experience unique challenges with managing chemicals and waste due to their limited land mass, high population densities, limited resources, unique biodiversity, high risk of exposure to natural hazards and disasters, vulnerability to the effects of climate change, remoteness from global markets, and small economies of scale. Further, large quantities of waste are generated by the tourism sector, which, although being a major economic activity in many SIDS and contributing to their Gross National Income, places additional stress on already strained waste management systems. This gave rise to the Implementing Sustainable Low and Non-Chemical Development in Small Island Developing States (ISLANDS) funded by the Global Environment Forum (GEF) and implemented by the Basel Convention Regional Centre for Training and Technology Transfer for the Caribbean (BCRC).

The Paris Agreement addresses issues of climate change. It is a legally binding international treaty and was adopted by 196 Parties at the U.N. Climate Change Conference (COP21) in Paris, France, on December 12, 2015, coming into force on November 4, 2016. Its overarching goal is to hold "the increase in the global average temperature to well below 2°C above pre-industrial levels" and pursue efforts "to limit the temperature increase to 1.5°C above pre-industrial levels" (United Nations 2015). All Caribbean territories are signatories to this.

Other initiatives have had limited success within the Caribbean such as achieving the Aichi Target 11 of the Global Biodiversity Strategy, which stated that by 2020, at least 17 percent of terrestrial and inland water and 10 percent of coastal and marine areas, especially areas of particular importance for biodiversity and ecosystem services should be conserved through effectively and equitably managed, ecologically representative and well-connected systems of protected areas and other effective area-based conservation measures. These systems were also to be integrated into the wider landscapes and seascapes.

Several recent regional projects and programs have attempted to address this target. One such project, Critical Ecosystem Partnership Fund (CEPF), was a joint initiative of *l'Agence Française de Développement*, Conservation International, the EU, the Global Environment Facility, the Government of Japan, the MacArthur Foundation, and the World Bank. This project provided approximately 6 million (U.S.) dollars in funding for biodiversity management in the Caribbean Biodiversity Hotspot. Activities included the provision of grants to civil society to manage biodiversity hotspots and the development of several participatory protected area management plans. Under the first phase of CEPF, procedures for private and municipal protected areas in the Dominican Republic and for municipal protected areas in Haiti were established.

Another initiative BIOPAMA (Biodiversity and Protected Areas Management) led by IUCN is aimed to "make the best available science and knowledge available for building capacity to improve policies and better decision making on biodiversity conservation" (Caribbean Natural Resources Institute 2018). Other relevant protected areas programs include the Socioeconomic Monitoring for Coastal Management (SocMon), a global initiative of the IUCN World Commission on Protected Areas (WCPA-Marine) and the Global Coral Reef Monitoring Network. Additional networks addressing biodiversity and protected areas management include CaMPAM (Caribbean Marine Protected Area Management) and Nature Caribé. CaMPAM is a network and partnership focused on capacity building of MPAs (Marine Protected Areas). CaMPAM also facilitates a small grant program and a regional marine protected area MPA database. CaMPAM via funding from UNEP (United Nations Environment Program) supported the strengthening of marine protected areas under the Climate Resilient Eastern Caribbean Marine Managed Areas Network (ECMMAN). Overall, ECMMAN focused on strengthening marine management areas and supporting related sustainable livelihoods. Other ECMMAN components encompassed updating relevant decision support systems and advancing sustainable financing for marine management areas.

Protected areas management was a key focus point on the SPAW work program. This included training and capacity building through the CaMPAM network. The SPAW protocol spoke to the creation of a list of protected areas, a regional network of these areas, and relevant cooperation programs. The SPAW list focused on areas that were a priority for protection in the wider Caribbean. Programs and activities under the World Heritage Convention and RAMSAR convention have also shaped the designation and management of protected areas and biodiversity conservation in the Caribbean. The Caribbean Challenge Initiative (CCI) supports protected areas management, as well. Under the CCI, participating countries were committed to conserving at least 20 percent of their marine and coastal environments by 2020 (the 20-by-20 goal) but several states have only achieved less than 10 percent.

Under the GEF-funded "Improving Forest and Protected Area Management in Trinidad and Tobago" (IFPAMTT) project, biodiversity hotspots requiring protection were identified. The intention was to update the legal designation and boundaries of existing protected areas and to declare new areas as needed. The GEF-funded project on "Conserving Biodiversity and Reducing Habitat Degradation in Protected Areas and their Areas of Influence" in St. Kitts and Nevis focused on strengthening protected areas management. That project also emphasized the inclusion of representative ecosystems within the Protected Area System. Collaboration with NGOs, CSOs, and private sector partners was a focus, as well. Resulting from this, the UNESCO North East Tobago Man and Biosphere Reserve (NETMABR) was established. This encompassed the Main Ridge Forest Reserve, the oldest forest reserve in the western hemisphere. Additionally, the Main Ridge was listed as an asset on the National Trust of Trinidad and Tobago' inventory list. Currently, the fringing reefs and islets of Northeast Tobago are being considered for listing as all three regions have high densities of unique biodiversity. Currently, management plans are being drafted for NETMABR. Additionally, the IUCN is also drafting a State of Protected Areas Report. Grenada has, however, recently launched its National Ecosystem Assessment (Agard et al. 2023). This document highlighted ecosystem system services, biomes, and threats to the islands' natural resources, as well as their sustainability use.

Conclusion and Recommendation

While some countries have diversified their energy dependence away from only fossil fuels, such as oil and gas, others, such as Trinidad and Tobago, have made very small progress. Wind, solar, and thermal energy production are all present in pockets across various Caribbean islands, which is a positive step towards biodiversity preservation. Barbados, for example, has designed several tourist attractions to be powered by solar energy. The Commonwealth of Dominica, Grenada, Montserrat, Saint Kitts and Nevis, Saint Lucia, and Saint Vincent and the Grenadines, all members of the Organisation of Eastern Caribbean States (OECS), are investing in and exploring geothermal energy as a viable alternative to fossil fuel. Additionally, wind power is used for water pumping in Aruba, Bonaire, Cuba, Curacao, Dominican Republic, and Jamaica.

Ridge to Reef management and policies that support their conservation are required. Most Caribbean islands have small land masses, while some states are made up of several islands within a larger archipelago. The water-to-land ratio is higher in most states, which would imply that a major amount of these island republics' natural resources is derived from the water. The term Small Island Developing State (SIDS) was used to refer to all island governments with small land masses around the world. However, there are Big Ocean Island States (BOIS) in the Caribbean. Whether through fishing or tourism, some Caribbean island governments have become more reliant on their marine resources in the previous fifty years. We must be aware that whatever we do on land has an impact on the sea via rivers, which serve as our conduits. Because water sheds and catchments might be quite short, Caribbean island states must guarantee that effective land management techniques are in place to conserve not only terrestrial and freshwater biodiversity, but also the marine environment. Some global species rely on both rivers and oceans, such as the American Eels (*Anguilla rostrata*), which completes its life cycle in Caribbean rivers. River degradation can have an impact on the future population of regional species.

This ties directly into the colors of Sustainable Development Goals (SDG) outlined by United Nations. These are linked with the seventeen SDGs (REF). From the 1950s to the 1980s, the majority of the Caribbean was focused on some element of the Green Economy that was not detrimental to the environment. Trinidad and Tobago's economy hybridized an Energy and Agricultural Economy (Brown and Green respectively) during the 1970s oil boom. However, because the country's GDP was more reliant on the Brown Economy well into the present, the environment is still suffering as a result. Tobago (the twin island state's sister island) is attempting to transition to a Blue Green Economy. In 2020, UNESCO conferred the title Man and Biosphere Reserve for Northeast Tobago on the country, highlighting the island's continued potential for sustainable development. However, in certain countries, such as Haiti, decades of political conflict have resulted in the collapse of environmental and biodiversity protection. Barbados, conversely, is leading the charge, putting focus on the Blue Economy within the last decade. The Caribbean is geographically and economically positioned to implement not just the Blue Green Economy, but also the Gold Economy, which will enable the utilization of renewable energy sources such as wind, solar, and geothermal. This would not only seek the protection of biodiversity but also sustainable development and regional food sovereignty.

There is a need for synergy and collaboration among current regional initiatives which address protected areas management. Outputs, case studies, and guidelines from past projects should be used to inform current project actions. Obtaining financing for protected areas is still challenging, especially considering their user fees do not adequately reflect the natural capital they contain. Private and local protected areas can be used to complement national protected areas, but relevant legal mechanisms may need to be developed. Climate change issues need to be reflected in protected area management plans including species range shifts or an increased abundance of invasive species. Creating ecologically interconnected protected area systems still needs attention as does the availability of Caribbean-specific data on a finer scale.

Although extinction is relatively infrequent under natural conditions, changes in island environments because of human activities have exterminated many populations and others – especially old, endemic species – remain vulnerable. Conservation efforts are strengthened by recognition of aesthetic, cultural, and scientific values of the unique flora and fauna of the West Indies.

The IPBES nature futures framework presents three value perspectives of nature: nature for nature, nature as culture, and nature for society. In the "nature for nature" perspective, people view nature as having intrinsic value, and worth is placed on the diversity of species, habitats, ecosystems and processes that form the natural world and on nature's ability to function autonomously. The "nature as culture" (a one with nature perspective) primarily highlights relational values, where societies, cultures, traditions, and faiths are intertwined with nature in shaping diverse bio-cultural landscapes. Finally, the "nature for society" perspective highlights the utilitarian benefits and instrumental values that nature provides to people and societies (Pereira et al. 2020). As most places on the planet, within the Caribbean, there will be efforts to strive to Eutopia where there is an optimal balance of all three value perspectives.

Unfortunately, the global issue is larger than biodiversity in the Caribbean. Even if every Caribbean state strives to adopt Blue Green Gold economies and fulfill every one of the UN's seventeen SDGs, it is still improbable that all Caribbean island states would survive the next century. Increased storm activity and rising sea levels will be enough to wipe out certain countries, taking their biodiversity with them. Furthermore, global trade without effective waste management, notably for eWaste (electronic garbage), could result in contaminated waterways, threatening numerous ecosystems. While the Caribbean BOIS will continue to work to improve the protections required for the sanctity of biodiversity, the planet's external stressors could bring an end to the Caribbean as we know it. This is further compounded by several threats to biodiversity such as poaching of cetaceans and marine sea turtles under the guise of local cultural practices. For too long, culture has been used as an excuse for the promotion of bad ecological practices. We should be developing a new culture to promote a sustainable Caribbean, incorporating sustainable practices from traditional Indigenous knowledge while still developing and implementing policies based on reliable scientific data. We need to preserve the oceans while keeping and conserving Caribbean heritage above water.

References

Agard, John, Aria St. Louis, and Natalie Boodram, ed. 2023. *Grenada National Ecosystem Assessment 2023*. St. Georges/Barataria: Government of Grenada/Caribbean Natural Resources Institute.

Boakes, Elizabeth H., Philip J. K. McGowan, Richard A. Fuller, et al. 2010. "Distorted Views of Biodiversity: Spatial and Temporal Bias in Species Occurrence Data." *PLOS Biology* 8: 1–11.

Besson, Gérard A. 2001. *Folklore and Legends of Trinidad and Tobago*. Port of Spain: Paria Publishing Company Limited.

Cambridge Dictionary. n. d. "Culture." https://dictionary.cambridge.org/dictionary/english/culture.

———. n. d. "Folklore." https://dictionary.cambridge.org/dictionary/english/folklo re.

Caribbean Challenge Initiative. n.d. "About CCI." https://caribbeanchallengeinitiati ve.com/index.php/about-cci/.

Caribbean Natural Resources Institute. 2018. *Caribbean Community (CARICOM) strategy for the implementation of the biodiversity cluster of Multilateral Environmental Agreements (MEAS)*. Barataria: CARICOM Secretariat.

Colorado State University. 2023. "Named storms 1951 to 2023." https://tropical.atm os.colostate.edu/Realtime/index.php?arch&loc=northatlantic.

Chase Jr., Fenner A., and Horton H. Hobbs. 1969. *The freshwater and terrestrial decapod crustaceans of the West Indies with special reference to Dominica*. Washington, D.C.: Smithsonian Institution Press.

Fanovich, Lanya, Neil D. Cook, Ryan S. Mohammed, and Aljoscha Wothke. 2017. "Citizen-based observations on shark and mobulid species in Tobago, West Indies." *Living World*: 26–37.

Global Biodiversity Information Facility [GBIF]. n.d. http://www.GBIF.org.

Global Forest Watch. 2024. "Trinidad y Tobago." https://www.globalforestwatch.or g/dashboards/country/TTO/?category=fires.

Goreau, Thomas F. 1959. "The ecology of Jamaican coral reefs. Species composition and zonation." *Ecology* 40, no. 1: 67–90.

Guggenheim, David E. 2022. *The Remarkable Reefs of Cuba, Hopeful Stories from the Ocean Doctor*. Lanham: Rowman & Littlefield.

Loop News. 2019. "In history: Tobago, site of the world's largest oil tanker spill." *Loop*, July 19. https://tt.loopnews.com/content/history-files-tobago-site-worlds-larg est-oil-tanker-spill.

McNeill, John Robert, and Peter Engelke. 2016. *The great acceleration: An environmental history of the Anthropocene since 1945*. Cambridge: Harvard University Press.

MacNeil, M. Aaron, Demian D. Chapman, et al. 2020. "Global status and conservation potential of reef sharks." *Nature* 583: 801–806.

Mohammed, Ryan S., and Cock van Oosterhout. 2020. "Malaria, mangroves, and migration: challenges for small island developing states in the Caribbean." *British Medical Journal*, November 13. https://blogs.bmj.com/bmj/2020/11/13/mal aria-mangroves-and-migration-challenges-for-small-island-developing-state s-in-the-caribbean/.

Murphy, John C. 1997. *Amphibians and Reptiles of Trinidad and Tobago*. Malabar: Krieger Publishing.

Murphy, John C., Roger J. Downie, Joanna McLellan Smith, et al. 2018. *A field guide to the amphibians & reptiles of Trinidad and Tobago*. Port of Spain: Trinidad and Tobagos Naturalist's club.

NOAA. 2023. "Coast water temperature guide." https://www.ncei.noaa.gov/produc ts/coastal-water-temperature-guide.

———. 2024. "Sargassum: From Sea to Shore." https://oceanservice.noaa.gov/new
s/sargassum/#:~:text=A%20newly%20established%20population%2C%20drive
n,South%20Atlantic%20via%20ocean%20currents.

Phillips, Williard, and Elizabeth Thorne. 2004. *Municipal solid waste management in the Caribbean A benefit-cost analysis.* New York: United Nations.

Pawan, Joseph Lennox. 1936. "Transmission of the Paralytic Rabies in Trinidad of the Vampire Bat (*Desmodus rotundus murinus* Wagner, 1840)." *Annual Tropical Medicine and Parasitol* 30, no. 1: 137–156.

Pereira, Laura M., Kathryn K. Davies, Eefje den Belder, et al. 2020. "Developing multiscale and integrative nature–people scenarios using the Nature Futures Framework." *People and Nature* 2, no. 4: 1172–1195.

Rivas, Jesús A., Paola De La Quintana, Marco Mancuso, et al. 2024. "Disentangling the Anacondas: Revealing a New Green Species and Rethinking Yellows." *Diversity* 16, no. 2: 1–29.

Sherratt, Emma, María del Rosario Castañeda, et al. 2015. "Amber fossils demonstrate deep-time stability of Caribbean lizard communities." *PNAS* 112, no. 32: 9961–9966.

Simpfendorfer, Colin A., Michael R. Heithaus, Michelle R. Heupel, et al. 2023. "Widespread diversity deficits of coral reef sharks and rays." *Science* 380, no. 6650: 1155–1160.

Simpson, George E. 1962. "Folk Medicine in Trinidad." *The Journal of American Folklore* 75, no. 298: 326–340.

Sullivan, Brian L., Jocelyn L. Aycrigg, Jessie H. Barry, et al. 2014. "The eBird enterprise: An integrated approach to development and application of citizen science." *Biological Conservation* 169: 31–40.

Torres-Cristiani, Leopoldo, Salima Machkour-M'Rabet, Sophie Calmé, et al. 2020. "Assessment of the American Flamingo distribution, trends, and important breeding areas." *PloS One* 15: 1–16.

United Nations. 2015. "Paris Agreement." December 15.

———. 2018. "The Escazú Agreement." March 4.

Appendix

Biographical Notes

Antoine Acker is an Environmental Historian and Professor at University of Geneva, with a particular interest in Latin America's international connections and role in the history of the Anthropocene. He holds a PhD from the European University Institute (EUI, Florence) and has taught at the universities of Bielefeld, Paris 3 – Sorbonne Nouvelle, La Rochelle, Maastricht, and Zurich, as well as the Geneva Graduate Institute, where he was an Assistant Professor. He completed his postdoctorate at the University of Turin and was an invited researcher at the Universities of Bern, Munich (LMU), and Shanghai (SHU), and a visiting professor at the Colegio de México. He is the director of the *AnthropoSouth: Latin American Oil Revolutions in the Development Century* project (Swiss National Science Foundation) and co-director of *Resilient Forest Cities*, a collaborative project funded by the Gerda Henkel Foundation. He is an affiliated researcher at the Maria Sibylla Merian Center for Advanced Latin American Studies (CALAS), the Rachel Carson Center (RCC, Munich), the Max Planck Institute of Geoanthropology in Jena, and an editorial board member of the global history journal *Monde(s). Histoire, Espaces, Relations*.

Miriam Adelman holds an M.Phil. in Sociology from NYU (1992) and a Doctorate (2004) from the Interdisciplinary Program in Social Sciences/UFSC, Brazil. She taught Sociology at the Federal University of Paraná, Brazil for twenty-seven years. To her earlier focus and numerous publications in the fields of Contemporary Sociology, Feminist Theory, and Gender Studies, she has added a more recent interest in Human-Animal Studies. Her current work studies equestrian cultures and ways of life in Brazilian rural communities within contemporary contexts of social, cultural, economic, political, and environmental change (research funded by a grant from Brazil's National Research Council [CNPq]). She is also a translator and poet, working with creative and academic texts in Spanish, English, and Portuguese, as well as a member of the faculty of the Graduate Program in Literary Studies (PGLet) at the Federal University of Paraná (UFPR).

414   Appendix

León Enrique Ávila Romero is Professor and Researcher in Sustainable Development at the Intercultural University of Chiapas (UNICH), where he teaches Postgraduate courses in Social Economy and Solidarity and coordinates the Bachelor's program in Agroecology. He is the leader of the consolidated academic group "Heritage, territory, and, development in the southern border of Mexico," a member of the SNI-CONACyT Level I, and an honorary member of the SEI Cocytech. He is an Agroecology Engineer from the University of Chapingo, an intern in History from the UNAM, a Master of Science in Natural Resources and Rural Development from the *Colegio de la Frontera Sur*, and a Doctor of Agricultural Sciences from the Department of Rural Sociology of the UACH. He was a visiting professor at the University of California at Berkeley (USA), the Catholic University of Bolivia, the University of the Republic of Uruguay, the University of Girona (Spain), and Bielefeld University (Germany). His recent publications include the co-authored book *Los herederos de Quintín Lame y del zapatismo: comunicación, paz-conflicto e incidencias políticas* (2022), the co-authored paper "Disputas hídricas y despojo: El caso de los humedales de Montaña en San Cristóbal de Las Casas, Chiapas, México" (*Argumentos*, 2021), and the book *Alternativas al colapso socioambiental desde América Latina* (2021).

Alberto Betancourt Posada is a PhD in History and Professor at the Faculty of Philosophy and Letters, UNAM, where he coordinates the Permanent Seminar Globalization, Science and Biocultural Diversity. He is a member of the Academic Technical Council of the Thematic Network on Biocultural Heritage of CONACYT. He has served on the UNESCO panel of experts on tropical forest conservation. For more than ten years, he has been part of an intercultural research team made up of Tojol-ab'ales, Tseltales, Tsotsiles, Q'anjob'ales, and Caxlanes (mestizos) professors and students dedicated to documenting and promoting comunitarian biocultural conservation experiences in the Lacandona Jungle and Los Altos of Chiapas. From this collective work, among others, he has co-coordinated the books, *Del monólogo a la polifonía: Proyectos supranacionales y saberes indígenas en la gestión de áreas naturales protegidas (1990–2010)* and *Del saber indígena al saber trasnacional. La explotación de conocimientos indígenas sobre ecología*, as well as authoring the book: *La sabiduría ambiental de América profunda*. He has been a postgraduate professor in Agroecology at the *Universidad Mayor de San Simón*, Bolivia and a visiting professor at the University of the Aegean Sea, Greece.

Rodrigo C. Bulamah is a Postdoctoral Researcher at the Social Sciences Graduate Program, Federal University of São Paulo, working at the interface between history and anthropology. He has a PhD in Social Anthropology from a dual-degree program between *École des Hautes Études en Sciences Sociales* (EHESS) and the State University of Campinas (Unicamp). His main field is the Caribbean, dealing with themes such as colonialism, plantation legacies, religious formations, kinship, historicity, and political ecology. He has written the book *Ruínas circulares: vida e história no norte do Haiti* (Rio de Janiero: Papéis Sevagens Editora, Forthcoming), co-authored the paper "Indigenous Peoples and local communities report ongoing and widespread climate change impacts on local social-ecological systems" (*Communications, Earth & Environment*, 2024), and the book chapter "From Marrons to Kreyòl: Human-Animal Relations in Early Caribbean" in *Global Plantations in the Modern World: Sovereignties, Ecologies, Afterlives* (2023).

Ana Lucia Camphora holds a Bachelor's in Psychology (UFRJ, 1988), a Master's in Psycho-sociology of Communities and Social Ecology (EICOS/UFRJ, 2003), and a PhD in Social Sciences (CPDA/UFRRJ, 2008). In her previous work as an environmental consultant in economic sustainability of protected areas, environmental policy instruments and ecotourism, she developed projects in partnership with the Brazilian Environmental Ministry, UNESCO, and NGOs such as The Nature Conservancy and the Conservation International, among others. Since 2013, she has been an independent scholar, moving to the field of inter-species studies and teaching postgraduate courses in Environmental Law and Animals in Law (2015 to 2018). She published the book *Animals and Society in Brazil from the Sixteenth to the Nineteenth Century* (2021) based on the outcomes of her research. The Brazilian edition had institutional support from the Brazilian Academy of Veterinary Medicine. Her current research is focused on the modern and contemporary history of equines used in medicine.

Regina Horta Duarte has a degree in History from the *Universidade Federal de Minas Gerais* (1985), with a Master's and PhD in History from the *Universidade Estadual de Campinas* (1988 and 1993, respectively). She has been full Professor at the Federal University of Minas Gerais since 1988, with experience in the history of Brazil, history and nature, the history of biology, and the history of animals. She was a board member of the *Associação Nacional de História* (2007- 2009, national ANPUH), where she served as editor-in-chief of the *Revista Brasileira de História*. She participated in the founding of the Latin American and Caribbean Society for Environmental History (SOLCHA) and was elected to the first Board of Directors, 2006–2010, where she is an official member. She remained on the Board of Directors of this entity as Editor-in-Chief of the journal *Historia Ambiental Latinoamericana y Caribeña* (HALAC), between 2011 and 2014. She is a member of the Editorial Board of the Hispanic American Historical Review and coordinates the Center for Animal Studies (CEA) at UFMG.

Lanya Fanovich is Marine Ecologist at the Institute of Marine Affairs, Trinidad and Tobago where she is the Project Manager for the Marine Resilience Initiative (MARIN) Tobago project. In 2011, she earned her Master's degree in Science and

Management of Tropical Biodiversity from The University of the West Indies. She was previously Senior Ecologist at the Environmental Research Institute Charlotteville (ERIC) in Tobago for the past decade, where she developed and implemented citizen-science initiatives. She also worked on natural resource management policy development, conducted research and monitoring on coral restoration and elasmobranch populations, and capacity building and outreach to community groups in rural coastal areas of North East Tobago. She has worked on coral restoration projects and collaborated with the Global FinPrint program to collect data on elasmobranch abundance and distribution in Tobago, contributing to the global assessment of reef sharks and rays. She was also the Reef Check Coordinator for Trinidad and Tobago. Her most recent paper is "Widespread diversity deficits of coral reef sharks and rays" (*Science*, 2023).

Martha Few is Liberal Arts Professor of Latin American History and Gender, Women's, and Sexuality Studies at Pennsylvania State University. Her research concentrates on the history of colonialism, gender and sexuality, medicine, and environmental history in the Mesoamerican areas of North America. Her recent books include the co-authored *Centering Animals in Latin American History* (2013), *For All of Humanity: Mesoamerican and Colonial Medicine in Enlightenment Guatemala* (2015), and the co-authored *Baptism Through Incision: The Postmortem Cesarean Operation in the Spanish Empire* (2020). Few was Senior Editor of the *Hispanic American Historical Review* from 2017–2022.

Reinaldo Funes Monzote is Professor of History at the University of Havana and Coordinator of the Geo Historical Research Program at the Antonio Nunez Jimenez Foundation in Cuba. He is a member of the Academy of History of Cuba and President of the Cuban Society for the History of Science and Technology. He is the author of *From Rainforest to Cane Field. A Cuban Environmental History since 1492*, 2008, awarded with the Elinor Melville prize by the Conference on Latin American History. This is the English version of the original Spanish book titled *De bosque a sabana. Azúcar, deforestación y medioambiente en Cuba: 1492–1926*, winner of the Caribbean Thought Award in 2003 and published by Siglo XXI de México Editores in 2004. In Cuba, it was printed in a new Spanish version, receiving the Catauro Award and the Critics Award in 2009. In 2019, his book *Nuestro viaje a la Luna. La idea de la transformación de la naturaleza en Cuba durante la Guerra Fría* received the Casa de las Américas Award, Cuba, within the category of Socio-historical essay. He is co-author of *Reconstructing the Landscapes of Slavery. A Visual History of the Plantation in the Nineteenth Century Atlantic World* (2021) and coeditor of *Usos agrarios, mensura y representación en Cuba, siglo XIX* (2023).

Biographical Notes 417

Olaf Kaltmeier is Professor of Ibero-American History at Bielefeld University and director of the Maria Sibylla Merian Center for Advanced Latin American Studies in the Social Sciences and Humanities (CALAS). At Bielefeld University he was founder of the Center for InterAmerican Studies (CIAS). Since 2023 he is also director of the collaborative international VW-reseach project "Turning Land into Capital: Historical Conjunctures of (Re-)Production of Wealth in Latin America from the 19th to the 21st Century." His lines of research are indigeneity, social movements, space and landscape, environmental history, state formation, inter-American studies. He has conducted research and teaching in Chile, Bolivia, Ecuador, Argentina, Mexico, Peru, and the United States. He has published more than 200 international and national articles, books, and book chapters. His latest monographies include *Resistencia Mapuche. Reflexiones en torno al poder siglos XVI a XXI* (2022), *Refeudalización. Social, economic and cultural political inequality in Latin America in the early 21st century* (2018), and *National Parks from North to South. An Entangled History of Conservation and Colonization in Argentina* (2021).

Lorelai Kury is Professor of History of Science at the Postgraduate Program in History of Science and Health in Oswaldo Cruz Foundation (Fiocruz) and Professor at the State University of Rio de Janeiro (UERJ). She holds a PhD in History from the *École des Hautes Études en Sciences Sociales* (1995). Her research is supported by a grant from the Brazilian National Research Council (CNPq). She has taught as a visiting professor in France and Portugal and conducted research at the King's College London. Her research interests cover the history of biological sciences in the eighteenth and nineteenth centuries. Her publications have focused especially on the history of scientific expeditions and the construction of knowledge by naturalists. Her main works include: the co-authored paper "O naturalista Veloso" (*Revista de História*), "Global Affinities: The Natural Method and Anomalous Plants in the Nineteenth Century" (*Journal of History of Science and Technology*), and the book chapter "Auguste de Saint-Hilaire's Writings between European and Brazilian Audiences, 1816–1850" (2023).

Aliocha Maldavsky is Professor of Early Modern and Ibero-American History at the University of Paris-Nanterre and directed the French Institute of Andean Studies from 2020–2023. She studied the Jesuit missions in the Iberian world and lay investment in religious institutions during Spanish domination. Her research focuses on the restitution of property to the Indigenous people by the conquistadors in the Andes in the sixteenth century, as well as on the imposition of European animals in the Americas and the environmental and economic history of the colonial Andes. Among her publications are *Vocaciones inciertas. Misión y misioneros en la provincia jesuita del Perú en los siglos XVI y XVII* (2012) and the co-authored *Invertir en lo sagrado: salvación y dominación territorial en América y Europa (siglos XVI-XX)* (2018). She has also published

"Teología moral, restitución y sociedad colonial en los Andes en el siglo XVI" (*Revista portuguesa de filosofía*, 2019) and "Finances missionnaires et salut des laïcs. La donation de Juan Clemente de Fuentes, marchand des Andes, à la Compagnie de Jésus au milieu du XVIIe siècle" (*Archives des sciences sociales des religions*, 2020).

Yolanda Cristina Massieu Trigo has a PhD in Economics from the National Autonomous University of Mexico, a Master's in Rural Sociology from the *Universidad Autónoma Chapingo-Texcoco*, and a Bachelor's in Veterary Medicine and Zootechny from the *Universidad Autónoma Metropolitana-Xochimilco*, where she teaches in the college of Sociology, the Rural Development postgraduate school, and Master's program in Sustainable Societies. Her research topics are: socioeconomic, environmental, political and cultural impacs of agricultural biotechnology; agriculture technological innovation and labor; biodiversity, the commons, political ecology and intelectual property; peasantry and food sovereignty; agrofuels and energy crises; and socioenvironmental, socioeconomic, technological and political problems of contemporary society. She does collaborative work with social and academic associations related to her research topics and is also member of the National Researchers System (Level II). She has many published works (articles and book chapters) – among them three books – and has presented more than 100 papers in academic events and advised forty-five college and postgraduate theses related to her specialty.

Eduardo Relly has been Lecturer at the *Friedrich-Schiller-Universität Jena* and has worked in the collaborative project "SFB294 Structural Changes of Property" (DFG) since 2021, co-leading the subproject "JRT03 Property over genetic resources." Prior to this, he completed his Postdoctorate at the University of Vale do Rio dos Sinos (2019–2020), a PhD in History at the Free University of Berlin (2015–2019), and a Master's in Environmental Sciences from the University of Vale do Taquari, Brazil. Eduardo has carried out research stays at the Bielefeld University (2014) and the Rachel Carson Center of the Ludwig-Maximilian-Universität-München (2021). His expertise concerns the areas of history of science (biotechnology), environmental history, global history, settler colonialism in Latin America, commons theory, biodiversity, and Indigenous knowledges/sciences, as well as analyzing the debates on biopiracy, digitization, and intellectual property of genetic resources within the framework of the Convention on Biological Diversity. He is the author of *Sob a sombra dos Commons* (2022) and was co-editor of the *Revista de História da Unisinos* (2019–2021). He participates in numerous research networks and projects both in Germany and Brazil and has published texts in Europe, the Americas, and Oceania.

Tyanif Rico Rodríguez is Postdoctoral Researcher at the Maria Sibylla Merian Center for Advanced Latin American Studies (CALAS) at Bielefeld University and an invited researcher in the project "Turning Land into Capital (2023–2027)." She is a sociologist (2012) and holds a Master's in Agrarian Social Studies from FLACSO (2014) and a Master's in Social Sciences from *El Colegio de Michoacán* (2016). In 2021, she received an honorable mention for her Doctorate in Geography from UNAM. Her areas of expertise are framed by environmental humanities and feminist perspectives on complex modern approaches to the relationship between society and nature. She is particularly interested in community-based strategies for territorial care and currently investigates the role of affects in strategies of collective and territorial care in a peasant context. Her recent publications include: "Estrategias de Cuidado Territorial y Multiespecie" (Forthcoming), "Cuidado del Territorio y reconocimiento del campesinado como sujeto de derechos" (*Leisa*, 2023), "Usos y Definiciones del Territorio en Contextos de Explotación Minera" (*FIAR*, 2022), and is co-editor of *Territorializing Space in Latin America* (2021). She has researched and taught in Mexico, Colombia, and Germany, as well as participated in numerous international conferences and organized international academic events.

Ryan S. Mohammed is an Aquatic Biologist Postdoctoral Research Fellow at Auburn University in Alabama (USA), an Honorary Research Fellow, Cardiff University, Wales (UK), Council member of Council of Presidents for the Environment (COPE) as the Aquaculture Association of Trinidad and Tobago representative, and a Council member of the National Trust of Trinidad and Tobago, where he serves on the Landmarks sub-committee, which focuses on natural heritage. He is currently investigating co-evolution in predator-prey relationships in the streams of Trinidad, using guppies and killifish as his model species. He was the former Acting Curator of the University of the West Indies Zoology Museum. He completed his PhD at The University of the West Indies, in Aquatic Biology in 2019 investigating parasites in wild guppy populations. He has co-authored more than fifty scientific articles in both international and local journals, documenting potentially invasive and exotic species as well as their ecology. He has additional training in fossil identification from the La Brea Tar Pit and Museum, Los Angeles and Museology and museum management from the National Heritage Museum Institute, New Delhi. He has more than two decades of experience in conducting and management of biodiversity baseline surveys and has worked with FAO and UNESCO on policy and implementation matters of Aquaculture and Blue Economy. He was also a lecturer at the UWI's MSc program in Biodiversity and Sustainable Development in the Caribbean and now serves on the IPBES task force on capacity-building.

Dominichi Miranda de Sá is Professor and Researcher at the Oswaldo Cruz Foundation in Brazil (Fiocruz). She earned her PhD in History from UFRJ in 2003, with doctoral studies at the *École des Hautes Études* (2001–2002, EHESS, Paris). She served as a Visiting Researcher at the *Universidade Nova de Lisboa* in Portugal (2023–2024) and the

Museu Paraense Emílio Goeldi in Brazil (2024). Currently, she is actively involved in the international research project "The Amazon as a microcosm of the Anthropocene: the history of transnational research in Amazonian ecology and the environmental impacts of the Great Acceleration" (2022–2025, CNPq). Her areas of expertise encompass the history of science, environmental history, ecology history, and the twentieth-century history of the Brazilian Amazon. She has co-authored articles such as "Science and the Green Revolution in the Brazilian Amazon" (*Halac*, 2022) and "The Brazilian Amazon: the World's Breadbasket" (*Revista de História USP*, 2019), and has co-edited collections including *Diário da Pandemia* (2020) and *As Ciências na História das Relações Brasil-EUA* (2020), among other articles, chapters, and books in Brazil and internationally.

Magali Romero Sá is Senior Researcher at the Oswaldo Cruz Foundation (Fiocruz), Deputy Director of Research and Education at the Casa de Oswaldo Cruz/Fiocruz since 2017, and a full professor in the Graduate Program in the History of Sciences and Health, COC/Fiocruz. A Research Productivity Fellow at the Brazilian National Council for Scientific and Technological Development (CNPq), she is also a member of the Editorial Board of ISIS (Journal of the History of Science Society) and a member of the Editorial Board of Medical History. Her research interests include the history of tropical medicine; international scientific relations between Brazil, Germany, and the United States; expeditions and scientific collections; environmental history; and health. Currently, she is investigating the scientific relationship between Brazil and the United States in the Brazilian Amazonia in the second half of the twentieth century. She has published several articles in national and international scientific journals, books, and book chapters. She is co-editor *of João Barbosa Rodrigues: Lore and Practices* (2022), *As Ciências na História das Relações Brasil-EUA* (2020), *A cooperação científica Brasil-Estados Unidos na Segunda Guerra Mundial* (2018), *Rondon, Inventários do Brasil* (1900–1930) (2017).

Neil Safier is Associate Professor of History at Brown University and Director of the Center for Latin American and Caribbean Studies. He served from 2013 to 2021 as Beatrice and Julio Mario Santo Domingo Director and Librarian of the John Carter Brown Library. He received his PhD from John Hopkins University in 2004 and has held teaching and research appointments at the University of Michigan, the University of Pennsylvania, and the University of British Columbia, Vancouver. He is the author of *Measuring the New World: Enlightenment Science and South America* (2008) and a range of articles on the history of natural history, environmental studies, and the trans-imperial history of the tropical world, especially South America. He is currently working on a book that connects Brazilian natural history with plantation cultures of the eighteenth-century Caribbean, including sugar, indigo, coffee, and cotton. His recent publications include the co-edited book *Cosmopolitanism and the*

Enlightenment where he published the chapter "Geographies of Cosmopolitanism: Cartography, Natural History, and the Spaces of Knowledge in the Long Eighteenth Century" (2023), as well as the co-authored chapter "Science and Independence in Iberian America" in the *Cambridge Companion to Latin American Independence* (2023).

John Soluri is Professor of History in the Department of History, Carnegie Mellon University (Pittsburgh, Pennsylvania, USA). His teaching and research focus on transboundary approaches to commodities, capitalism, and biocultural histories of Latin America (Central America and Patagonia). He is currently directing "Coffee Break," a collaborative project supported by Carnegie Mellon's Center for Arts in Society. He is author of *Creatures of Fashion. Animals, Global Markets, and the Transformation of Patagonia* (2024) and an updated edition of *Banana Cultures: Agriculture, Consumption, and Environmental Change in Honduras and the United States* (2021).

Christopher Valesey is Assistant Teaching Professor of History at Ball State University (USA). He was a Postdoctoral Teaching Fellow at Penn State University from 2019 to 2020, where he completed his PhD in Colonial Latin American History. He has an MA in History from the State University of New York at Albany. His research interests include ethnohistory, human-animal studies, colonialism, and global history. His dissertation focused on Nahuas' relations with European livestock as key to their connection to the early Spanish colonial state and a primary channel of socio-cultural exchange. He previously served as an editorial assistant for the *Hispanic American Historical Review* and briefly worked as a paleographer and translator for PBS's show *Finding Your Roots*. His latest publications include "Perseverance of the Eagle-Jaguar Military Ethos in Sixteenth-Century New Spain" (*Sixteenth Century Journal*, 2021) and "Animal Auguries and Evangelization in Sixteenth-Century New Spain" (*Viator*, 2021).

Felipe Vander Velden holds a Master's degree (2004) and a PhD (2010) in Social Anthropology from the *Universidade Estadual de Campinas*, Brazil and a postdoctoral degree from Aarhus University (Denmark, 2017) and Leiden University (Netherlands, 2018). He is an Associate Professor at the Department of Social Sciences and the Graduate Program in Social Anthropology at the *Universidade Federal de São Carlos* (Brazil). He has been carrying out research among the Karitiana and Puruborá peoples in the Amazon since 2002. His focuses since 2005 have been on the relationships between human beings and other-than-human beings (especially animals) and, more recently, he has been researching the introduction of cattle ranching among the Indigenous peoples of Lowland South America. He is the author of the books *Inquietas companhias: sobre os animais de criação entre os Karitiana* (2010) and *Joias da floresta: antropologia do tráfico de animais* (2018), as well as of several chapters and articles in various anthropological journals in Brazil and elsewhere.

Kenneth R. Young is Emeritus Professor of the University of Texas at Austin. Currently, he is a visiting professor in the faculty of biological sciences of San Marcos University in Lima, Peru. His doctoral degree is from the Department of Geography of the University of Colorado Boulder (1990) and his M.S. is in Botany from the University of Florida (1984). His research interests include biodiversity conservation and biogeography, in addition to landscape ecology and global change. He has done fieldwork in Mexico, Guatemala, Costa Rica, Ecuador, and Peru. He has published more than 100 articles in ecological, geographical, and conservation journals. He co-edited the *Physical Geography of South America* (2007). Together with Julio C. Postigo, he edited *Naturaleza y Sociedad: Perspectivas Socio-Ecológicas sobre Cambios Globales en América Latina* (2016). His current projects include assessments of conservation needs and social-environmental change in Mexico and Peru.

Marina Zuloaga Rada is a Peruvian Historian and Professor at San Marcos University, Lima. She holds a degree in Latin American History from the *Universidad de Sevilla* and a doctorate from the *Colegio de México*. She published *La conquista negociada: guarangas, autoridades locales e imperio en Huaylas, Perú (1532–1610)* (IFEA-IEP) in 2012, followed by various articles on Indian society in the colonial period in journals and books published in Mexico, Chile, Japan, and Peru. On broader matters, she authored the book *Las luchas por la independencia* (2021) and co-authored *Historia Mínima del Perú* (2014) and (2015). Between 2010 and 2020, she participated in a collective research project on "indigenous reductions" in South America, directed by Dr. Akira Saito (National Museum of Ethnology, Osaka), funded by the Japan Society for the Promotion of Science (JSPS). Currently, she is coordinating a Franco-Peruvian project with Aliocha Maldavski titled "AnimAndes: introducción, recepción e impacto de los animales europeos en los Andes (siglos XVI-XIX). Una contribución al estudio del Antropoceno en América." (San Marcos University, Lima, and *Universidad de París Nanterre*), financed by Prociencia (Peru) and the Ministry of Higher Education and Research (France).

www.ingramcontent.com/pod-product-compliance
Lightning Source LLC
Jackson TN
JSHW011013010225
78206JS00004B/41